The Communist Road to Power in Vietnam

Also of Interest

Vietnamese Communism in Comparative Perspective, edited by William S. Turley

The Third Indochina Conflict, edited by David W. P. Elliott

War of Ideas: The U.S. Propaganda Campaign in Vietnam, Robert W. Chandler

Communist Indochina and U.S. Foreign Policy: Postwar Realities, Joseph J. Zasloff and MacAlister Brown

† *China: A Political History, 1917–1980*, Richard C. Thornton

China at the Crossroads: Nationalists and Communists, 1927–1949, F. Gilbert Chan

† *The Chinese Communist Party in Power, 1949–1976*, Jacques Guillermaz

Communism and Political Systems in Western Europe, edited by David E. Albright

† *The Soviet Union in the Third World: Successes and Failures*, Robert H. Donaldson

† Available in hardcover and paperback.

Westview Special Studies on South and Southeast Asia

The Communist Road to Power
in Vietnam
William J. Duiker

This first comprehensive history of the Communists' rise to power in Vietnam addresses the following key questions: How did Communist revolutionary strategy evolve in Vietnam? What were the role and significance of Ho Chi Minh as revolutionary leader? What was the relative importance of political, military, and diplomatic forms of struggle in Vietnamese doctrine? What were the major factors in the Communist success? How does the Vietnamese revolution compare with other revolutions of modern times?

Beginning with an analysis of political and social conditions in colonial Vietnam, Professor Duiker traces the birth of the Vietnamese Communist Party and its struggle to survive in the difficult years prior to World War II. He then analyzes the gradual development of the strategy of "people's war" from its origins during the period of Japanese occupation to the sophisticated and flexible doctrine that evolved during the war against the United States to the final drama in Saigon in 1975. In his concluding chapter, Professor Duiker attempts to isolate the major factors responsible for the Communist victory in Vietnam and for the failure of the U.S. effort to create a viable South Vietnam.

William J. Duiker is professor of East Asian history at Pennsylvania State University. He was formerly a foreign service officer with the Department of State in both Vietnam and Taiwan.

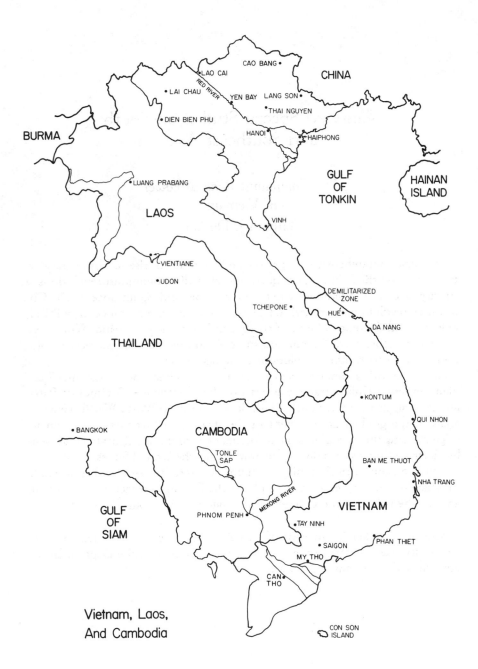

CHINA

CAO BANG

LAO CAI

LAI CHAU

RED RIVER

YEN BAY

LANG SON

THAI NGUYEN

DIEN BIEN PHU

HANOI

HAIPHONG

BURMA

LUANG PRABANG

GULF
OF
TONKIN

HAINAN
ISLAND

LAOS

VINH

VIENTIANE

UDON

DEMILITARIZED
ZONE

TCHEPONE

HUE

DA NANG

THAILAND

KONTUM

QUI NHON

BANGKOK

CAMBODIA

TONLE
SAP

BAN ME THUOT

NHA TRANG

MEKONG RIVER

VIETNAM

GULF
OF
SIAM

PHNOM PENH

TAY NINH

SAIGON

PHAN THIET

MY THO

CAN
THO

Vietnam, Laos,
And Cambodia

CON SON
ISLAND

The Communist Road to Power in Vietnam

William J. Duiker

Westview Press / Boulder, Colorado

Westview Special Studies on South and Southeast Asia

Published in 1981 in the United States of America by
  Westview Press, Inc.
  5500 Central Avenue
  Boulder, Colorado 80301
  Frederick A. Praeger, Publisher

Second printing, 1982

Library of Congress Cataloging in Publication Data
Duiker, William J. 1932-
  The Communist road to power in Vietnam.
  (Westview special studies on South and Southeast Asia)
  Bibliography: p.
  Includes index.
  1. Vietnam—History—20th century. 2. Communism—Vietnam—History. I. Title.
DS556.8.D83   959.704   80-22098
ISBN 0-89158-794-2

Printed and bound in the United States of America

To Yvonne, Now and Always

Contents

Acknowledgments xiii
List of Abbreviations xv

1. Introduction 1

2. The Rise of the Revolutionary Movement (1900–1930) 7

    Vietnamese Nationalism 7
    Ho Chi Minh and the Origins of Vietnamese Marxism 14
    The Formation of the Revolutionary Youth League 17
    The Road to Revolution 19
    The League and Vietnamese Nationalism 24
    The Breakup of the League 29
    The Nghe Tinh Soviets 33
    Nghe Tinh in Retrospect 41

3. The Stalinist Years (1930–1941) 45

    Vietnamese Communist Policy and the Comintern 45
    Clouds of War 50

4. Prelude to Revolt (1941–1945) 57

    War in Europe 58
    The Bac Son Rebellion 61
    The Cochin China Uprising 62
    The Formation of the Vietminh 64
    Toward the General Uprising 72
    March to the South 75
    The Japanese Coup d'État 82
    Creating the Liberated Zone 86
    The Tan Trao Conference 87

5. The Days of August (August–September 1945) 91

    The August Revolution 94

The Lessons of August 100

6. The Uneasy Peace (September 1945–December 1946). 107

   The Vietminh in Power 107
   The Collapse of Communist Power in Cochin China 113
   Negotiations with the French 117

7. The Franco-Vietminh War (1947–1954) 127

   The Chinese Model. 128
   Withdrawal 131
   Equilibrium 134
   The Bao Dai Solution 137
   The Communist Victory in China 139
   The 1950 Border Offensive. 144
   Toward the General Offensive 145
   The Other War 152
   The Navarre Plan 154
   The Battle of Dien Bien Phu 160
   The Road to Geneva. 162
   Conclusions 165

8. Peace and Division (1954–1961) 169

   Communist Strategy in the South, 1954–1957 172
   The International Situation 182
   The Darkest Hour 183
   The Year of Decision, 1959 186
   The Period of Spontaneous Uprisings, 1959–1960 190
   The Third Party Congress, 1960 193
   The National Liberation Front 195

9. The Dialectics of Escalation (1961–1965) 201

   Countering the "Special War" 204
   Building up the PLAF 212
   Fish on the Chopping Block 214
   The Fall of the Diem Regime 219
   The Ninth Plenum of December 1963. 221
   Confrontation with Moscow 223
   The Battlefield Solution 227
   Crisis in Saigon 229
   The Fall of Khrushchev 231
   Conclusion. 233

10. War of Attrition (1965–1968) 235

    Westmoreland's Strategy 237
    Hanoi's Response 240
    The Strategy of Attrition: Washington 246
    The Strategy of Attrition: Hanoi 248
    On the Diplomatic Front 254
    Shoot-out at the DMZ 256
    The Strains of Escalation 261
    Toward the Decisive Hour 263
    The Tet Offensive 265
    The Results of Tet 269

11. Fighting and Negotiating (1968–1973) 273

    The Battle of Khe Sanh 274
    Maintaining the Offensive 276
    Prelude to Negotiations 280
    The Invasion of Cambodia 283
    Bit by Bit 288
    The Easter Offensive 291
    Peace Is at Hand 295
    Conclusions 297

12. The Final Drama (1973–1975) 301

    Testing the Wind 306
    Attack in the North 311
    The Ho Chi Minh Campaign 314
    The Divine Hammer 317
    Dénouement 318

13. At the Crossroads 321

    Factors in Communist Success 322
    Vietnam as Model 329
    Looking Forward 331
    Foreign Policy 336

Notes 343
Selected Bibliography 373
Index 379

Acknowledgments

Until a little over a decade ago, there were few basic studies in Western languages of the origins and development of the Vietnamese Communist movement. In retrospect, it is clear that this lamentable ignorance was in no small measure responsible for the tragic involvement of the United States in the civil struggle in that country. The recent war spawned a new generation of Vietnam specialists, and it is through their labors that we now have a clearer picture of the Communist movement and the reasons for its extraordinary success. But there is still much to learn, and until the Party leadership in Hanoi indicates a willingness to open its archives, our knowledge of the dynamics of the Communist role in the Vietnamese revolution will remain incomplete. For that reason no study of the recent war—including this one—can be more than an imperfect effort to illuminate a murky and highly complex topic. I am grateful for the efforts of all those who have preceded me in this task.

One of the biggest problems involved in undertaking a study of this nature is to amass the scattered and diverse research materials relating to the rise of Vietnamese communism. Over the past few years I have become indebted to a number of individuals who have been of assistance to me in obtaining such materials. I am grateful to King C. Chen, Daniel Hemery, Chau T. Phan, Douglas Pike, Ronald Spector, John Tashjean, Carlyle Thayer, and Joseph Zasloff for furnishing me with useful documents and articles that I had been unable to obtain elsewhere. I would particularly like to thank King Chen for sending me copies of the recent Black Paper and White Paper issued by the governments in Phnom Penh and Hanoi respectively. I would also like to thank the staffs at the Library of Congress in Washington, D.C., the Wason Library at Cornell University, and the National Archives of France, Section Outremer, for their help in utilizing the resource materials at these institutions.

A number of people have offered useful suggestions on various parts of this manuscript. Ed Moise made a number of useful comments on Communist land reform policy during the height of the Franco-Vietminh war. Carlyle Thayer cleared up a number of ambiguities relating to Communist strategy in South Vietnam in the late 1950s. Bill Turley has been helpful in sharing with me his views on the evolution of Communist strategy since the early years of the

Party. Mark Pratt provided comradeship and a *pied à terre* during several short visits to Paris. Ken Post made a number of valuable comments and suggestions on the manuscript. I am particularly indebted to the late William Gaussmann for his suggestions and his encouragement in carrying out this project. His advice and his friendship are sorely missed.

I would like to thank Trinh Thi Ngoc Diep for her help in translating difficult passages from handwritten Vietnamese and Deborah Shade for typing assistance. The National Endowment for the Humanities, the Institute for the Arts and Humanistic Studies, and the College Fund for Research of the College of Liberal Arts at Pennsylvania State University all provided financial assistance in support of this study, for which I would like here to express my appreciation. I am grateful to Kathleen Siljegovic of the Information and Privacy Staff of the Department of State for locating materials in Central Foreign Policy Records and arranging to have them made available to me. As always, and for so many reasons, my deepest gratitude goes to my wife, Yvonne. With this book now completed she will, at least for a while, have a full-time husband again.

W.J.D.

Abbreviations

ACP	Annam Communist Party
ANDPF	Alliance of National Democratic and Peace Forces
ARVN	Army of the Republic of Vietnam
ASEAN	Association for the Southeast Asian Nations
CCP	Chinese Communist Party
CIA	Central Intelligence Agency
CIDG	Civilian Irregular Defense Groups
CINCPAC	Commander in Chief, Pacific
CMEA	Council for Mutual Economic Assistance
CORDS	Civil Operations and Rural Development Support
COSVN	Central Office for South Vietnam
CPSU	Communist Party of the Soviet Union
CRA	Committee of Resistance and Administration
DIA	Defense Intelligence Agency
DMZ	Demilitarized Zone
D.R.V.	Democratic Republic of Vietnam
FCP	French Communist Party
FEF	French Expeditionary Forces
FUNK	National United Front of Kampuchea
GRUNK	Royal National United Government of Kampuchea

GVN	Government of Vietnam
ICP	Indochinese Communist Party
KCP	Khmer Communist Party
KNUFNS	Kampuchean National United Front for National Salvation
MACV	Military Assistance Command, Vietnam
NCRC	National Council of Reconciliation and Concord
NEA	New Economic Areas
NLF	National Front for the Liberation of South Vietnam
OSS	Office of Strategic Services
PAVN	People's Army of Vietnam
PLA	People's Liberation Army
PLAF	People's Liberation Armed Forces
P.R.C.	People's Republic of China
PRG	Provisional Revolutionary Government
PRP	People's Revolutionary Party
SAM	Surface-to-air missile
SEATO	Southeast Asian Treaty Organization
S.R.V.	Socialist Republic of Vietnam
VCP	Vietnamese Communist Party
VNA	Vietnam News Agency
VNQDD	Viet Nam Quoc Dan Dang
VWP	Vietnamese Workers' Party

1
Introduction

On several occasions during the recent war, Communist leaders in Hanoi referred to the conflict in South Vietnam as a "sacred war" to unite the two regions of Vietnam for the first time in over a century. Whether or not such a description of the struggle taking place in the South was appropriate is, of course, a matter of personal opinion. What cannot be denied is that the victory of communism in Vietnam was a spectacular achievement and one of the most significant political events since the end of World War II. It was not simply that their seizure of Saigon in 1975, combined with nearly simultaneous victories in Laos and Cambodia, put the Communists in control of all of the old French possession of Indochina, an event that policymakers in Washington had frequently warned would lead inevitably to the ultimate fall of all of Southeast Asia to communism. It was that this victory had been achieved in the face of determined U.S. resistance. The results tended to throw into question the structure of the U.S. policy of containment of communism in Asia and throughout the Third World.

The nature and shape of this victory has attracted considerable attention from scholars, journalists, and government officials, and in recent years a number of studies on the subject have appeared in Western languages.[1] What has been lacking is an analysis of the Communist rise to power, from the Party's origins in the colonial period to the final triumph in Saigon in the spring of 1975, in an historical context. What follows here is an effort to fill that gap.

This book is the outgrowth of a process that began well over a decade ago. As a foreign service officer serving with the U.S. Embassy in Saigon in the mid-1960s, I was struck by the extraordinary tenacity and impressive organizational capacities of the Viet Cong in the war that was then just under way. The contrast with the performance of the Saigon regime was noteworthy. After leaving government service for an academic career, I decided to study the topic. In a study published by Cornell University Press in 1976, I investigated the emergence of the Communist Party as a major factor in the Vietnamese nationalist movement prior to World War II. Some of the salient factors in the Communists' success and the corresponding weaknesses of their nationalist rivals began to emerge in that earlier study, but it was clear that what the Party had achieved by the start of the Japanese occupation of Indochina in 1940 was no more than a promising beginning. By no means did it satisfactorily explain the success achieved in the struggles that followed. Thus gradually emerged my decision to continue my investigation of Vietnamese communism through the conflict with the French after the Pacific War down to its triumph in the recent war.

Important obstacles impede any serious study of this nature. First and perhaps foremost, it is a topic of considerable magnitude. In an effort to avoid superficiality I have restricted my concern to one of the central issues raised by the conflict – the nature of the Party's revolutionary strategy toward the seizure of power. This book is not a comprehensive history of the war or of the Communist movement *per se*. Nor does it deal with domestic policies in the Democratic Republic of Vietnam (D.R.V.) except where such policies affected war strategy. Finally, it does not pretend to treat in detail French or American efforts to counter Communist activities in Vietnam, except where such efforts obviously relate to the evolution of Communist strategy. Although such issues are vital to an overall understanding of the war, they must be left for future analysis.

A second obstacle has plagued many scholars engaged in research on the war and its antecedents. Although materials exist in abundance, access to official documents on both sides has been severely limited. For the purposes of this study, the major problem is the relative paucity of reliable materials published in the D.R.V. A few studies have appeared on various aspects of the war and its origins, and some official Party or government documents have been published.[2] On the whole, however, much remains obscure, not only about the nature of the decision-making process but about the decisions themselves and the assumptions behind them. For years, it has been surmised that there were disputes within the Politburo over revolutionary strategy. On occasion the Party press has confirmed the existence of such disagreements. Yet, to this day, the views of individual members of the Politburo remain, for the most part, a matter of conjecture. The researcher is therefore reduced to foraging for material – in statements of the official press, in books or articles by leading Party officials in Hanoi, or in official documents, diaries, and training-session reports captured during the war. Such materials can only partially compensate for the lack of official documents on the subject; but until more is available, they must suffice.

Hanoi, of course, is not alone in restricting scholarly access to official materials. Neither the French nor the U.S. government has seen fit to publish all important documents relating to its role in the war. France has released archives dealing with the period leading up to World War II, but those dealing with the postwar period are still not available. Let us hope that a rich harvest will appear within the next few years. The situation is somewhat different in the United States. The fortuitous publication of the Pentagon Papers in 1971 provided scholars with crucial insights into the early years of U.S. involvement in Vietnam. More recently, the Freedom of Information Act has permitted access to individual documents upon request. I have used such materials sparingly in this study, as most relate to the nature of the war as seen from Washington and Saigon. They are nonetheless a rich source of information on the war and deserve intensive analysis.

A third problem is that of credibility. Most of the materials available on the war, official as well as unofficial, are colored by partisanship. Official documents issued in Hanoi, Paris, and Washington often reflected the government line. Books and articles by academics and journalists were frequently colored by the bias of the writer. Because of the sharp emotions involved, dispassionate judgments were difficult to come by. The key issue for this study, of course, is the reliability of materials published by the D.R.V. Obviously, much of this information is propagandistic. Some documents and official statements were deliberately designed to be misleading. For years, Hanoi denied that its troops were involved in the war in the South and described that conflict as an effort undertaken by the National Liberation Front (NLF) of South Vietnam. More recently, the Party has dropped this pretense and asserts with pride that the full resources of North Vietnam were brought to bear in order to bring the conflict to a successful conclusion. (Washington and Paris, of course, were sometimes guilty of similar practices, although perhaps not on a systematic basis.) Under such circumstances, how can official statements or documents issued in the D.R.V. be considered trustworthy? There is no easy solution to this problem, but I believe that most official materials contain at least an element of truth and that a trained researcher can overcome this obstacle and (with an occasional exception) determine the reliability of the materials available. In my research, I have chosen to rely on the veracity of such materials unless there appeared to be persuasive reasons not to do so.[3] As more information emerges from Hanoi, we will have ample opportunity to judge the accuracy of what is currently available.

Given such limitations, it is inadvisable to claim that a definitive analysis of the Vietnamese revolution as seen through the eyes of the Party leadership is now possible. There will undoubtedly be errors of fact and interpretation in this analysis, and all conclusions reached here should be treated with a healthy degree of skepticism. Some will say that the historian should not step in until a more definitive judgment is possible. I disagree. The talents of the historian can and should be put to good use, even in cases in which many of the relevant documents are lacking or are of dubious veracity. Too often, writing by Western social scientists on the war has tended to be of the problem-solving variety. Stimulated by a sense of immediate crisis, it has frequently lacked historical perspective and a sense of proportion.

The effects of this historical myopia were unfortunate. Analysis and policymaking during the war were often undertaken in almost total ignorance

of the long-range cultural and historical factors involved. Scholars and journalists speculated about the possibility of Ho Chi Minh becoming an "Asian
Tito" but had only a limited understanding of his relationship with the Soviet
Union. Or they drew conclusions about the independence of the NLF from
Hanoi's control but had only sketchy notions of the Party's traditional use of
the united front to disguise its role in the national liberation movement. High
civilian and military officials innocently predicted that the war would end in
two or three years in apparent ignorance of the Party's open reliance on the
strategy of protracted war. Or they viewed the Vietnam conflict, and the entire
policy of containment of communism in Asia, through the distorted image of
the Munich Conference of 1938 and the appeasement of Hitler immediately
prior to World War II, as if conditions in postwar Asia mirrored those in
prewar Europe.

Such ignorance of the historical and cultural factors involved in the war has
continued to plague American attitudes in the years since the fall of Saigon.
The Vietnam War and its aftermath have had a traumatic effect on U.S.
foreign policy and now color the attitudes of a generation of Americans toward
the U.S. role in world affairs. In recent years Americans have frequently suc-
cumbed to the temptation to view all international crises (or at least those in
the Third World) through the prism of the Vietnam experience, much as an
earlier generation looked at the Cold War from the perspective of the appeasement of Hitler at Munich. Each new crisis is labeled another potential Vietnam, either for the United States or for its rival, the Soviet Union.

Such concern is understandable. The United States does not need, indeed
cannot afford, another Vietnam. And there are, of course, lessons to be
learned from Vietnam, among which is the proposition that the United States
should not rush blindly into international involvements with little understanding of the factors involved. On the other hand, Americans also do not need a
"Vietnam syndrome" to replace the earlier "Munich syndrome" that guided
U.S. foreign policy for nearly three decades. One of the primary lessons of Vietnam should be that each international crisis must be judged on its own merits,
and not on spurious comparisons with past experience. Although the Vietnam
War does suggest certain serious risks in U.S. military intervention in the Third
World, it does not demonstrate that such intervention will necessarily result in
a repeat of the Vietnam experience.

I do not wish to imply that useful historical lessons cannot be drawn from international crises. Munich certainly illustrated the danger of appeasing an aggressive nation. Vietnam convincingly demonstrated that U.S. firepower had
limited effectiveness when applied with some restraint against a determined
and well-organized national liberation movement. Comparisons across time
and space should not be made without due attention to the local historical and
cultural factors involved.

There are persuasive reasons, then, for extensive historical research into the background of the Vietnam conflict, even though such analysis may be flawed by imperfect knowledge. Several questions relating to the war still cry out for answers. What were the underlying causes of the Communist victory in Vietnam? Were there cultural factors involved that, a priori, doomed the attempt to impose a "Western solution" to failure? Was Saigon's defeat the result of a faulty strategy or, as some maintain, of a lack of U.S. determination? Can the Vietnamese revolutionary model be effectively applied elsewhere, or is it a unique expression of the Vietnamese revolutionary art? Does the result of the Vietnam conflict suggest the futility of U.S. efforts at "nation-building," or might a similar effort be successful in a more propitious environment? These questions are of more than academic importance; they go the heart of postwar U.S. foreign policy toward the Third World.

This study cannot hope to provide definitive answers to such questions. Its objectives are more limited—to search into some of the factors that led to the Communist victory in Vietnam and, specifically, to explore the role played by revolutionary strategy in that process. It is hoped that the insights produced by studies such as this one will assist in obtaining answers to some of the larger questions alluded to above. To the degree that such insights are forthcoming, the historical ignorance that led the United States into Vietnam will not lead it into future crises of similar, or greater, magnitude.

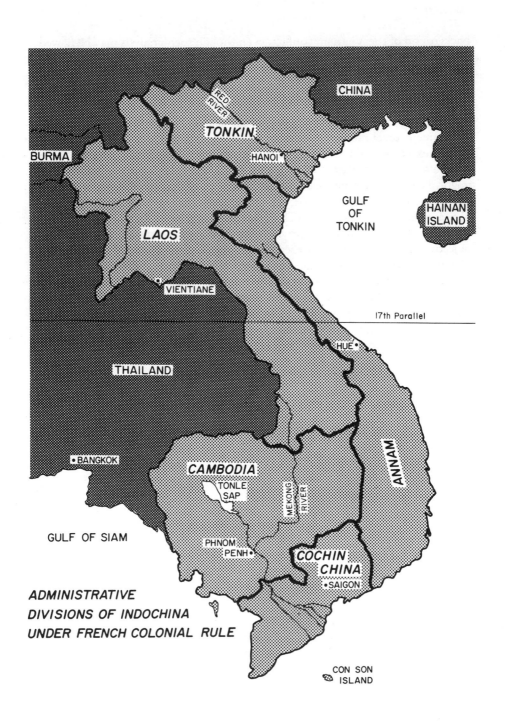

ADMINISTRATIVE
DIVISIONS OF INDOCHINA
UNDER FRENCH COLONIAL RULE

The Rise of the Revolutionary Movement
(1900–1930)

Ho Chi Minh once remarked that, for him, the road to communism went through nationalism. Put in concrete terms, the most significant event in Ho Chi Minh's intellectual life took place in 1920 when, as a young patriot living in Paris, he obtained a copy of Lenin's famous "Theses on the National and Colonial Questions," presented at the Second Congress of the Comintern in Moscow. At that moment, Ho came a Leninist, primarily because Lenin's elucidation of Communist strategy in colonial areas seemed to provide the best means of liberating Vietnam from French colonialism.[1]

The incident is of more than symbolic importance, for in Vietnam, the roots of the Communist movement are deeply intertwined with those of the anticolonial movement. And while Vietnamese communism and nationalism have frequently appeared to go their separate ways, the Communist movement throughout most of its existence has been able to project itself before the mass of the population as a legitimate force representing Vietnamese national aspirations. This symbiotic relationship between nationalism and communism in Vietnam is in no small measure responsible for the triumph of the party over the Saigon regime in the spring of 1975.

Vietnamese Nationalism

It is therefore appropriate to begin this study with a brief examination of the dynamics of Vietnamese nationalism. When Marxist doctrine first appeared in Vietnam shortly after World War I, Vietnamese nationalism was in a state of transition.[2] Early resistance to the French conquest, led by patriotic elements from among the traditional Confucianist ruling elite, had been irrevocably broken in the mid-1880s when the guerrilla bands led by the rebel leader Phan Dinh Phung were defeated in the hills of Central Vietnam. As for the imperial court at Hué, it had by then become a mere instrument of French rule, an effete relic of past glories. Vietnamese territory was divided at the whim of Paris. Cochin China, in the South, became a French colony. Tonkin, the old heartland of Vietnamese civilization surrounding the Red River valley, was legally a protectorate; but in practice French authority was virtually total. Only in Annam, comprising the coastal provinces in the center, was the court permitted to retain the tattered remnants of its former authority.

The decline of the political force of traditional society was quickly reflected in society at large. By the turn of the century, the authority of Confucian ideology and social institutions and of the scholar-gentry class that played the major role as defender of the social order and propagator of official doctrine was beginning to erode. Here French colonial policies exerted a strongly corrosive effect. Influenced by the popular conviction that France had a humanitarian purpose—a *mission civilisatrice* to bring Western culture to its new Asian possession—colonial officials tended to espouse policies that would undermine the influence of traditional Confucian institutions and customs in Vietnamese society. The teaching of the Chinese written language, the traditional means of transmitting Confucian doctrine in Vietnam, was discouraged, and the use of a transliteration based on the Latin alphabet—called *quoc ngu* or the national language—was actively promoted. The civil service examination system, the vehicle for recruitment of young Vietnamese into the official bureaucracy, was abolished, and a new educational system that, while retaining a few elements of the traditional Confucian system, placed primary emphasis on Western culture and values was gradually put into effect.[3]

The inevitable effect of such reforms was to undermine the role of the Confucian scholar-gentry class as the protector of the political, social, and ethical values of Vietnamese society. While for a time the influence of the traditional elite remained relatively unimpaired at the village level (particularly in Annam, where the power of the mandarin continued to reign supreme), its status in the cities and provincial towns rapidly declined. The effects of this decline were soon to be injected into the bloodstream of the embryonic Vietnamese nationalist movement. After 1900, a new generation took up the cause of Vietnamese independence. Themselves the offspring of elite families, they were aware of the larger changes taking place elsewhere in Asia, particularly in China and Japan, and tended to reject a return to the past, preferring instead a comprehensive reform of Vietnamese society along Western lines. Most famous was Phan Boi Chau, the holder of an advanced degree in the traditional educational system, who refused a career in the imperial bureaucracy and founded a revolutionary movement to overthrow French rule and set up a constitutional monarchy in imitation of the Meiji Restoration in Japan. An admirer of Sun Yat-sen, after the 1911 revolution in China Chau became a republican.

Characteristically, the first stage of Westernization in Asian societies has been ambivalent in theory and ineffective in practice. Such was the case in Vietnam. The generation of "scholar-patriots" received their knowledge of the West not from personal experience but indirectly, from the writings of reformist Chinese intellectuals like K'ang Yu-wei and Liang Ch'i-ch'ao. Because of this second-hand knowledge, their grasp of the new world beyond Vietnamese frontiers was superficial and their understanding of mass politics limited. Although their courage and patriotism were well established, their strategy and tactics were primitive; and after Chau was arrested in South China in 1914, the movement lost its dynamism and its influence in Vietnam rapidly declined.[4]

The disintegration of the scholar-patriot movement coincided with the emergence of new social forces that were destined to play a major role in the next stage of Vietnamese nationalism. French commercial activity was rapidly transforming the economic character of Vietnamese society and, by the end of World War I, had given rise to two new social classes of growing importance—an urban middle class and a proletariat. The new Vietnamese middle class was by no means homogeneous. At the upper end of the spectrum was an increasingly affluent commercial and professional bourgeoisie, composed for the most part of bankers, land speculators, absentee landlords (many with substantial landholdings in the Mekong delta), engineers, agronomists, doctors, and merchants. This group benefited substantially from French economic policies. In many cases its wealth was an immediate consequence of the French presence. A few of the more prominent members came from traditional elite families, but most appear to have been self-made men. This new urban bourgeoisie thus had few links with the past, and as its wealth and social prominence increased, bourgeois families increasingly took on a Western cultural veneer—sending their children to French schools, drinking wines and dining on French cuisine, and living in colonial villas in the tree-lined suburbs of Saigon. Indeed, it was Saigon, Vietnam's "frontier city," that became the nucleus of this new class. Located relatively close to the rubber plantations along the Cambodian border and to the newly opened rice lands in the lower Mekong delta, Saigon was the one city where fortunes could be made quickly, even by enterprising Vietnamese.[5]

Below this urban upper crust of the middle class was the noncommercial urban intelligentsia, composed of teachers, journalists, clerks, minor functionaries, and students. To a substantial degree this class came from families with a scholar-gentry background in which emphasis had traditionally been placed on community service and education rather than on the accumulation of wealth. In that sense, this class can be viewed as the first generation of scholar-gentry elite to grow up under French colonial rule. Though some of its members obtained advantages from the French presence and thus at least tolerated the colonial regime, the scattered information available suggests that many came from families that had refused to collaborate with the conquerors and had thus inherited a legacy of stubborn hostility to the colonial regime.[6] This new petty bourgeois intelligentsia formed a potential primary source of discontent against French colonial rule in Vietnam.

The final new element was the proletariat. Totaling about 100,000 in 1918, as a rule this working class was employed in enterprises linked to the colonial regime: in factories in Saigon, Vinh, and Hanoi; in the coal mines of upper

Tonkin; on the rubber plantations of Cochin China; and at dockside in Saigon and Haiphong. Though a few had become skilled workers, the majority still had one foot in the surrounding countryside and often worked in farming villages at harvest time.[7] For the most part, working conditions were abysmal, workdays were long, and pay was low. But although there were signs of discontent, there was as yet little political awareness in working-class districts. Not until the early 1920s did the first clandestine unions begin to appear, the immediate consequence of the return from France of the radical labor organizer Ton Duc Thang.[8]

French rule had begun to transform the cities, and the political and social consequences would begin to be felt in the first postwar decade. But most Vietnamese still lived in the thousands of hamlets and villages scattered along the coastal flatlands or in the vast deltas of the Mekong and Red rivers. Here, except for the "new lands" developed as a result of French irrigation efforts in the swamps and saline marshes of the lower Mekong, the colonial presence was less directly felt; and a superficial view would suggest that the old ways often continued with little interference. In actuality, colonial policies affected the world of the peasant in myriad ways, although the nature of that influence has been a matter of controversy. Defenders of French colonial policy frequently have pointed to the beneficial effects of Western technology—the draining of the marshes in the Mekong delta and the building of new irrigation systems to put thousands of acres of new rice land under cultivation. Following such innovations, rice production in Vietnam soared in the first decades of French rule, and the export of rice became the major source of foreign currency.

Yet other commentators point to a dark side of French agricultural policy. With the commercialization of agriculture came the concentration of land holdings and the seizure of village communal land by the wealthy and a consequent rise in tenancy and rural poverty. In Cochin China, where the most rapid development had occurred, less than 5 percent of the population owned more than half the arable land. At the same time, an inequitable tax system and the hated government monopolies on salt, opium, and alcohol represented a serious drain on the peasants' financial resources and there is some evidence that, while grain production under the French rose to new heights, per capita consumption was declining.[9]

In the early decades of the twentieth century, the rural village for the most part was politically quiescent. This is not surprising since traditionally the anger of the peasant is slow to arouse. With a world view circumscribed by the horizon of village life and activities conditioned by the inexorable harvest cycle, the peasant is normally a passive and conservative force in society. Marx's contemptuous dismissal of the European peasant as a potential enemy of the revolutionary classes, although hardly fair, was not wide of the mark from a political point of view. In Asia peasants were no more involved in the world of politics than their European counterparts; but, as Lenin would come to recognize, they were at least potentially a far more explosive force. Most Asian peasants lived on the knife-edge of survival. Landholdings were small, taxes and other exactions were high, and a capricious climate frequently threatened widespread famine. In Vietnam, as in other agrarian societies in East and Southeast Asia, peasant rebellions against starvation and government misrule were not infrequent.

In colonial Vietnam, the first sign of such conditions appeared in the spring of 1908, when a peasant revolt erupted in several coastal provinces in Central Vietnam. The immediate causes apparently were high taxes, the monopolies, seizures of commune land by the wealthy, and forced labor. Corvée requirements imposed by local authorities on peasants in the area were stiff and were frequently distributed on an unequal basis. The heart of the unrest was in Quang Nam Province, just south of the port city of Tourane (later called Da Nang), but the riots soon spread to adjacent areas. Crowds of peasants gathered before government installations to protest, and when local administrators responded with force, they stormed the government buildings and pillaged and burned the houses of the rich. For the most part, the uprising lacked a political focus and was more a series of skirmishes and demonstrations than an organized revolt, although a few activist scholar-patriots took part, circulating through the area and encouraging the peasants to protest. By May the jacquerie had been quelled, and a few of the ringleaders were executed or sentenced to long terms in prison. But for the government the riots were an ominous portent that the countryside could be a disturbing factor in any future protest against colonial rule.

The 1908 riots were provoked primarily by economic and social conditions; although an element of anti-French sentiment may have been a latent factor, it would be an exaggeration to view the disturbances as an indication that the peasants in Central Vietnam had been infected with patriotic fervor. Predictably, it was in the big cities that the seeds of a new stage of Vietnamese nationalism began to take root. The first shoots ironically appeared in the social class most closely tied to the colonial regime—the affluent commercial bourgeoisie of Cochin China. Near the end of World War I, a small but vocal group of French-educated Saigon intellectuals, centered around the wealthy newspaper publisher Bui Quang Chieu, formed the first open political organization in Vietnam, the Constitutionalist Party. As their future behavior amply demonstrated, the Constitutionalists had limited political goals. Their original objective was to persuade the colonial government to provide greater opportunities for Vietnamese to compete against French and Overseas Chinese in manufacturing and commerce. Later they demanded political reforms, equal pay for equal work, and greater Vietnamese participation in the political process. But they were careful to avoid any demand for national independence and appeared content to strive for a gradual increase in Vietnamese autonomy within the broad framework of continued French rule.[10]

It was among the petty bourgeois intelligentsia, however, that the strongest challenge to French colonial authority was about to appear. In the mid-1920s, a number of anti-French nationalist organizations began to form in all three regions of Vietnam. In Tonkin, a handful of teachers and petty functionaries formed the Viet Nam Quoc Dan Dang (VNQDD or Nationalist Party). The VNQDD was relatively unconcerned with theory and appeared satisfied to adopt a pallid imitation of the ideological principles of Sun Yat-sen's Kuomintang in China. The VNQDD's most characteristic features were an uncompromising hostility to French rule and a commitment to revolution as the only road to power.

The closest equivalent to the VNQDD in Annam was the so-called Tan Viet or New Revolutionary Party. Composed of a mixture of older veterans of previous scholar-gentry-based organizations (some of whom had formed the party while in prison) and younger radicals mostly recruited from schools in Central Vietnam, the party was fundamentally anti-French; but its leadership was divided over whether independence could be achieved through violent or nonviolent means. It had mildly Marxist leanings, but no direct tie with the Comintern in Moscow.

Cochin China, and in particular the burgeoning metropolis of Saigon, appeared to possess the greatest potential for nationalist activity in Vietnam. It was there that the French presence had made its greatest impact and that the bonds of traditional authority had most thoroughly eroded. Because Saigon was the most dynamic commercial and manufacturing center in Vietnam, it possessed a large and increasingly restless petty bourgeoisie, to complement a growing working class. Finally, in Saigon the French were most tolerant of open political activity, by French and Vietnamese subjects alike.

The activities of the Constitutionalists stirred up a sense of political awareness throughout urban society, and in 1925 a number of small but vociferous nationalist organizations were formed to express a generalized discontent with political and economic conditions in Cochin China. The best known and undoubtedly the most popular was Nguyen An Ninh's "Hope of Youth" (Thanh Nien Cao Vong) Party. A journalist descended from a patriotic scholar-gentry family in the Mekong delta, Ninh was a dynamic speaker and by far the most charismatic figure in nationalist circles. He refrained from voicing a direct challenge to French rule and preferred to tell his listeners that the awakening of the Vietnamese nation would have to come from within. But his obvious and frequently voiced disapproval of French policies brought him to the attention of colonial authorities and increased his popularity among the radical youth of Saigon and neighboring rural villages in the northern delta provinces. Indeed, Ninh was almost the only Saigon intellectual to seek out support for his cause in peasant villages in the provinces adjacent to the metropolis. In his appeal to the peasants and in his popularity among the young, Ninh's role in the Vietnamese revolution resembles that of Li Ta-chao—journalist and one of the founders of the Chinese Communist Party—in the Chinese Revolution.[11] Li, however, eventually turned from propaganda to party politics, while Ninh, curiously, had no desire to form a disciplined political organization. Although his criticisms of colonial realities stirred fervent support in radical and progressive circles, the protest movement subsided when he was arrested and sentenced to a short term in jail. Had he persisted in motivating his enthusiastic following in the direction of organized political protest or along the lines of Mahatma Gandhi's movement in India, the Vietnamese nationalist movement might have taken a different course.

Though ineffectual in achieving its objective of national independence, this new generation of urban nationalists nevertheless marked a major step forward in political sophistication. More conscious than their predecessors of the nature of the West, the urban nationalists were more specific in phrasing their political and social demands and clearly represented the first major step in the formation of a modern nationalist movement in Vietnam. Yet at the same time they possessed a number of weaknesses, some of them unique to Vietnam, others common to urban nationalist movements in Asia. Most obvious was an absence of inner unity. The organizations that appeared in the mid-1920s were factions more than parties, centered around an individual or based on regional or ethnic identities rather than on mutual devotion to common political principles. Part of the problem appeared to be that the erosion of the traditional bonds of Confucianism had cut many of the emotional ties linking urban intellectuals with the mass of the rural population. Unlike many other colonial societies in South and Southeast Asia, where activist intellectuals were able to call on the common bond of a great traditional religion—Hinduism, Buddhism, or Islam—and to knit together an anticolonial alliance throughout urban and rural areas of colonial society, this first generation of urban nationalists in Vietnam was unable to come up with a common ideology, a shared set of ideas to bind together Vietnamese of all social classes and all regions. The political scientist David Apter has observed that ideology can provide a sense of solidarity and common identity and thus give needed cohesion to nationalist movements in developing areas. In Vietnam, such an ideology did not yet exist. The ideological symbols of Confucianism had been discredited by the collapse of the traditional institutions and the collaborationist attitude of the imperial court. Little now remained except the concept of Vietnamese nationhood. In the mid-1920s, this was not enough. Regional loyalties still divided intellectuals in the cities, and the life of the peasant was still bounded by family, clan, and village.[12]

The mid-1920s set the pattern for succeeding generations of Vietnamese nationalists, and the movement became characterized by a multitude of parties, endless bickering, mutual jealousies, and sterile debates. It has been suggested that Vietnamese nationalists picked up their bad habits from the French. This is unfair to the latter, for it is hardly necessary to reach to Paris for an explanation. The nature of Vietnamese political parties in the twentieth century was inherited above all from the bureaucratic interest groups and secret societies that had traditionally proliferated in Vietnamese society.

A second feature of this early stage of Vietnamese nationalism was its predominantly urban and socially restrictive character. This was more unintentional than deliberate, but none the less harmful for that. The ideology of petty bourgeois nationalism tended to be democratic in content and expressed in the language of mass politics, but it was primarily urban and elitist in practice. Most nationalist parties were formed among students, teachers, clerks, or other members of the urban petty bourgeoisie and with a few exceptions made little effort to strike roots in rural or working class districts. This was amply reflected in their propaganda. While voicing general support for economic and social reforms, their programs lacked specifics on issues of primary concern to the poor and concentrated on general but amorphous ideas of national independence. Ironically, many young urban nationalists still had family roots in rural villages and some appeared to possess a deep emotional attachment to village Vietnam. But their needs and their identities had been increasingly shaped by their urban environment, a fact that inevitably affected their political attitudes. Not surprisingly, the rural population, its own potential source of patriotic fervor as yet substantially untapped, was unaware of the nationalist movement or simply found it irrelevant to its own immediate needs. That the rural village could be aroused was suggested by the brief but meteoric popularity of Nguyen An Ninh in the provinces around Saigon, but Ninh's initial successes were not followed up.

One explanation for the failure of urban nationalists was their impatience and lack of political sophistication. Few saw themselves as professional revolutionaries. Those who did, like the leadership of the VNQDD, tended to have relatively naive and putschist ideas about the means to be used in overthrowing French rule. The VNQDD undoubtedly represented the most serious threat to the colonial regime, but its leaders viewed the struggle for national liberation as a primarily military affair and stressed recruitment activities among the Vietnamese enlisted ranks in the French army. The French security service—the famous Sûreté—had little difficulty keeping abreast of the party's plans due to an extensive network of informers and when a planned rebellion broke out at Yen Bay and other military posts in the upper Red River valley in February 1930, the authorities were able to quell it in a day or two.[13]

Ho Chi Minh and the Origins of Vietnamese Marxism

In such conditions, Marxism first made its appearance in Vietnam. It seems fitting to begin an examination of the origins of Vietnamese communism with a brief reference to the early career of Ho Chi Minh. For not only was he the founder of the Vietnamese Communist movement and its recognized leader throughout virtually all his mature life, but his own "path of Leninism" provides a useful case study of the sources of the appeal of Marxist ideology in colonial Vietnam.[14]

Ho Chi Minh (born Nguyen Tat Thanh; Ho Chi Minh was a pseudonym adopted later in life) was born in 1890 in Nghe An Province, in the heart of the coastal plains region of Central Vietnam. His father, Nguyen Sinh Sac, came from an educated but impoverished family. After receiving a traditional Confucian education, thanks to the generosity of a neighbor, Sac became an official in the imperial bureaucracy during the early years of French rule. Like many members of the traditional educated elite in the coastal provinces, however, Sac had little liking for the French or for the effete imperial court that now slavishily served them, and he eventually resigned his official position to become an itinerant scholar. From the sketchy materials provided by Ho Chi Minh's official biographers in Hanoi, it seems likely that the father's attitude was passed on to the son. Sac refused to give the young Ho Chi Minh a formal education in the Confucian classics and limited himself to tutoring the boy on the inner ethical content of Confucian philosophy. For Ho's early reading he provided patriotic stories and books on the heroes of Vietnamese history.

For Ho Chi Minh, such ingredients would ultimately harden into a mature world view. By adolescence, he had already developed a strong sense of ethics combined with a fierce patriotism. He also probably had a consciousness of personal destiny. Although his childhood years were spent in relative poverty in a village not far from the provincial capital of Vinh, his father had earned high esteem in neighboring villages, not only for his education and career, but also for his kindness, his courage, and his patriotism in abandoning the bureaucracy in protest against French policies. The young Ho Chi Minh undoubtedly basked in the reflected glory of his father's achievements and was probably stimulated to emulate them. But he was curiously discriminating. During his adolescence, the famous Vietnamese patriot Phan Boi Chau, an old classmate of his father, stopped by to persuade Ho Chi Minh to follow him to Japan. Ho refused, commenting (according to legend) that he preferred to travel to Europe to see Western civilization at its source.

During his adolescence, Ho studied briefly at the prestigious Imperial Academy (Quoc Hoc) in Hué. There are suggestions that, with his simple dress and rustic manners, Ho Chi Minh may have felt out of place among the wealthy sons of officials. While at the academy he apparently took part in student demonstrations in support of the 1908 peasant revolt.[15] Beyond such tantalizing vignettes, his political views and activities are obscure. But he abandoned his studies before graduation in order to accept employment as a language teacher in a modern school in Phan Thiet, a coastal seaport north of Saigon. Within a year he had decided to go abroad and went to Saigon, where he obtained employment as a cook on a French merchant ship. Several years at sea, during which he visited a number of port cities in Africa and Asia, apparently strengthened his anticolonial proclivities. He spent the war years in London, and at war's end he went to Paris, where he immediately became involved in political activities within the Vietnamese community in France.

Up to this point, little distinguished his career and aspirations from those of countless contemporaries. Apart from a poorly documented involvement in a Marxist labor group in London, he was apparently a political novice. Slight and unprepossessing in appearance, he was not at first glance an impressive figure. Only his eyes, which contemporaries described as unnaturally bright and penetrating (one is inevitably reminded of Lenin), gave him a presence and set him apart physically from those around him.

Yet in Paris his career blossomed. In 1919 he achieved instant fame by presenting a demand for colonial self-determination to the assembled representatives of the great powers at the Versailles Peace Conference. And though the wealthy and powerful of the world did not respond to his appeal, the name Nguyen Ai Quoc (Nguyen the Patriot), Ho Chi Minh's pseudonym for the next quarter century, now assumed a degree of notoriety within the Vietnamese community in France. Primarily identified with the cause of Vietnamese independence, he also became increasingly active in the French socialist movement and was a frequent speaker at radical clubs in working-class districts of Paris. Then, in the summer of 1920, he read Lenin's "Theses on the National and Colonial Questions" and decided to join with other radicals in forming the French Communist Party (FCP), which broke away from moderate socialists at a party conference at Tours.

The key to Ho Chi Minh's attraction to Leninism was clearly the Bolshevik Lenin's uncompromising hostility to world imperialism. By contrast, the cautious views of moderate socialists seemed pallid and insincere. Ho immediately became a spokesman for the oppressed colonial peoples and the founder and leader of an organization of radicals from French colonies in France—the Intercolonial Union. Here his outstanding organizational and propagandistic talents first began to be displayed. Under his direction the union held regular meetings, put out a journal (*Le Paria* [The pariah]), and provided a mouthpiece for colonial issues in the Party. In due course, Ho attracted the attention of the Comintern leadership in Moscow as an Asian revolutionary of unusual promise. In the summer of 1923 he was summoned to Moscow to work at Comintern headquarters and attend classes at the new Stalin School for the Toilers of the East, a training institute for revolutionaries of the Third World. He also was a founding member of the short-lived Peasant International (Krestintern) and attended the Fifth Congress of the Comintern in the summer of 1924, where he chided his French comrades for their failure to give adequate attention to the colonial issue. Ho's biting comments must have hit their mark, for at the close of the congress the Comintern leadership directed the FCP to increase its efforts to promote revolutionary activities in the French colonies. Comintern propaganda to French Indochina increased, and the first concrete moves to encourage the formation of a Marxist revolutionary movement in Vietnam were now taken. Ho Chi Minh was selected to be the catalyst. In the fall of 1924 he was assigned by the Comintern to serve as a translator with the mission of Comintern agent Michael Borodin to the revolutionary government of Sun Yat-sen in Canton, China.

Ho's instructions have never been made public by Moscow, but the essentials can be pieced together from available evidence on the nature of Comintern strategy in Asia. This strategy was based on decisions taken at the organization's Second Congress in the summer of 1920. At that meeting the world Communist movement had approved Lenin's strategy for promoting socialist revolution in the precapitalist East. Because of the weakness of the bourgeoisie in most Asian societies, the revolution against feudalism and imperialism could be successfully carried out only through an alliance of several progressive classes, including the peasantry, the proletariat, the petty bourgeoisie, and the national bourgeoisie. This gave an opening to the formation of Communist parties. Although the proletariat in most Asian societies was considered too weak and immature to lead a socialist revolution, it could aid other progressive classes in a united front against the reactionary forces of feudalism and imperialism. Once this first stage of the revolution had succeeded, the Communists, with the support of the most revolutionary elements from the peasantry and the petty bourgeoisie, would break with moderate nationalists and attempt to seize power. The Asian revolution was thus viewed as a two-stage process—a first bourgeois democratic stage and a second proletarian socialist one.[16]

The Formation of the Revolutionary Youth League

If, as seems likely, Ho Chi Minh's instructions were to undertake the formation of a Marxist revolutionary organization in Vietnam, these instructions were deceptive in their simplicity. Not only would it be difficult to circumvent the efforts of the Sûreté to repress all political dissent in colonial Indochina; an even greater obstacle lay in the political innocence of the Vietnamese people. In the mid-1920s few Vietnamese had more than a passing knowledge of Marxist ideology. Of the leaders of the various political organizations active in Vietnam, only a few in the New Revolutionary Party had any knowledge of the ideas of Karl Marx. Awareness of communism was even more limited among the population. French censorship prevented the legal importation of reading materials on Marxism. Newspapers were forbidden to write about the Bolshevik Revolution or about conditions in Soviet Russia in any but critical terms. The only source of knowledge about Marxism—and it was an unreliable one—was books and pamphlets smuggled into Vietnam by Vietnamese living abroad.

On his own, while living in Paris and Moscow, Ho Chi Minh had recognized the lack of political sophistication of his compatriots. In 1922, he had commented in an article that only a few intellectuals in colonies such as Vietnam were aware of the meaning of communism. And most of those who were, he sadly added, preferred "to bear the mark of the collar and to have their piece of bone." As for the masses, they were "thoroughly rebellious, but completely ignorant. They want to free themselves, but do not know how to go about doing so."[17]

The implications were clear: The Vietnamese people needed time to realize that social revolution was the answer to their problems. In the meantime, a political party could be formed to represent in embryonic form the ideas of Marx and Lenin and to appeal to the population on the basis of the one issue that could elicit the most favorable response—national liberation.

The vehicle that Ho Chi Minh used for carrying out these instructions was a new organization formed in 1925 under his guidance, the Vietnamese Revolutionary Youth League (Viet Nam Thanh Nien Cach Mang Dong Chi Hoi). Immediately after his arrival in China, Ho began to contact various patriotic Vietnamese groups in the area and recruited the most radical members for his organization. By mid-year the league had begun to take shape. In keeping with the requirements of the situation, Ho Chi Minh operated on two levels. The league was designed as a mass nationalist party capable of enlisting support from all progressive classes in Vietnam. Its dedication to the eventual realization of a Communist society was not disguised, but neither was it given maximum publicity. Presumably Ho viewed it as the Vietnamese equivalent of the Leninist four-class alliance discussed above. Within the league, Ho set up a secret inner core of six or seven members dedicated to Marxist-Leninist principles. He viewed this inner core as the nucleus of a future Communist party.[18]

By the end of the year, members of the league had begun to return secretly to Vietnam in order to recruit followers. Through Ho's efforts, and with the aid of a small but regular subsidy from the Comintern, the nucleus was gradually enriched by a steady stream of patriotic young Vietnamese. Not surprisingly, most were members of the most radical element in Vietnamese society, the petty bourgeois intelligentsia. Brought to Canton by clandestine means, they received training and indoctrination at a special school with the impressive title of "Special Political Training Course for the Vietnamese Revolution." The training program, usually three months long, was closely patterned after similar institutions in the Soviet Union, with classes on such subjects as the rise of capitalism, the ideology of Marxism-Leninism, the world situation, and the organization of the Revolutionary Youth League. After completing the course, a few graduates found employment in the Chinese police or armed forces; some were sent to the Soviet Union for further study. Most, however, returned to Vietnam with instructions to spread revolutionary doctrine among their friends and colleagues.

The most noteworthy feature of the new organization was its deliberate attempt to appeal to Vietnamese nationalism and to the intellectual class that provided it with its motive force. This was reflected in the patriotic content of the league's monthly publication, *Thanh Nien* [Youth], which began publishing in June 1925. It was also reflected in the symbolic gesture that concluded each training class in Canton. On graduation, the students would be taken to the grave of Pham Hong Thai, a young Vietnamese patriot who had died in 1924 in an unsuccessful effort to assassinate the French governor-general, Martial Merlin, while the latter was on a state visit to Canton. At the grave, the new graduates would make a solemn and moving oath to bring about the deceased patriot's dream of a united free Vietnam.

The Road to Revolution

From a Marxist-Leninist point of view, the predominantly patriotic orientation of the League posed dangers. Too much emphasis on nationalism at the expense of ideology could dilute the quality of league membership and set back Ho Chi Minh's goal of eventually transforming it into a Communist party. There are indications that this indeed became a problem. One graduate of the training program in Canton later reminisced that few of his fellow students had more than a rudimentary understanding of Marxism and that most continued to be motivated primarily by nationalist concerns.

Perhaps as a consequence of Ho Chi Minh's awareness of this problem, in 1926 he wrote a textbook on Marxist revolutionary doctrine, the first to be published in Vietnamese. Entitled *Duong Cach Menh* (hereafter *The Road to Revolution*), this pamphlet was designed to provide league members with a fundamental understanding of Marxist-Leninist theory and how to relate it to the future revolution in Vietnam.[19] The primer is bound to disappoint the student interested in serious exposure to Ho's revolutionary ideas, for it was in essence a highly simplified explanation of Lenin's application of the Marxist revolutionary process to Asian society. The two-stage concept was presented in broad terms, with a first stage leading to national independence in each individual colony, and a second stage resulting in the final destruction of world capitalism and the establishment of a Communist utopia throughout the globe.

Ho Chi Minh's explanation of Marxist class struggle was even more primitive. The core element in the world revolutionary movement, he explained, would be an alliance between the workers and the peasants who, as the world's most oppressed classes, would unite to overthrow their oppressors. About the middle classes he was equivocal. Petty bourgeois elements like students and small merchants were natural allies of the proletariat, but the national bourgeoisie in Vietnam was a reactionary force.

The bulk of the book dealt with the future revolution in Vietnam. The author had little to say about how the revolution might come about and concentrated on the problem of preparation. Victory would not come easily, he warned, for a thousand-year-old society could not readily be transformed. Organization, through the formation of a revolutionary party that would establish links with similar groups throughout the world, was imperative. And, he added, the revolutionaries would need a plan. A handful of rebels (an oblique swipe at the failures of past patriots) could achieve little by simply assassinating a few government officials. Such actions only led to more repression. Above all, a revolutionary ideology that could be understood and followed by all party members was essential. A party without ideology was like a man without intelligence or a boat without a compass. Such comments suggest some of the sources for Ho Chi Minh's fascination with Lenin's message while he was still in Paris. Leninism offered precisely what the Vietnamese liberation movement had heretofore lacked—organization, cohesion, external support, and a plan.

The Road to Revolution was Ho Chi Minh's first serious effort to apply the Marxist view of history to the situation in Vietnam. Although to those familiar with the complexity of Marxist doctrine, his arguments were simplistic, even misleading, they probably possessed a deep inner logic for many frustrated intellectuals. The harsh indictment of Western imperialism voiced the unspoken anger of millions of Vietnamese at the political and economic domination of their country by the French. The plea for unity, organization, and the adoption of revolutionary ideology was attractive to patriots increasingly frustrated by the weaknesses and divisions of the existing resistance movement. And Ho Chi Minh's persuasive argument that the Vietnamese revolution was an integral part of the world revolution must have been soothing to those who feared that Vietnam was too small and powerless to achieve liberation on its own. While Ho's brief treatise can hardly stand as a classic interpretation of Marxism applied to an Asian society (a fact that is freely admitted by Communist historians in Hanoi today), it probably served its purpose well.

From a theoretical standpoint, the most striking aspect about *The Road to Revolution* was its failure to emphasize the leading role of the proletariat in the revolutionary alliance, an omission that raises the question of Ho Chi Minh's understanding of and commitment to a fundamental element in Marxist-Leninist doctrine. The concept of the worker-peasant alliance is pure Lenin, of course, but the Bolshevik leader had been careful to differentiate between the proletariat as the "leading force" and the peasantry as merely the "basic force" of the revolution in Asia. Put bluntly, the proletariat (through the vanguard role of the Communist Party) would direct the struggle, while the villages would provide the foot soldiers. Ho Chi Minh's reference to the worker-peasant alliance totally failed to distinguish between the vanguard status of the proletariat and the subordinate role of the peasant in the revolutionary struggle and seemed to imply a joint venture.

Did Ho Chi Minh intend to suggest that in Vietnam the peasantry would play a major part in the coming struggle for power? This was not the first time that he had alluded to the issue. In his first major speech before an international Communist gathering, his address to the Moscow congress of the Peasant International (Krestintern) in October 1923, he had described the hardships of the rural classes in colonial Asia and had contended that they were the worst victims of colonial exploitation.[20] He made no reference to the implications of the revolutionary struggle for power; this deficiency was rectified a few months later. At the Fifth Congress of the Comintern in July 1924, he was more specific about the consequences of colonial oppression in rural areas of Asia, concluding with an impassioned appeal for Comintern assistance in the liberation movements there:

> In all the French colonies, famine is on the increase and so is the people's hatred. The native peasants are ripe for insurrection. In many colonies, they have risen many times but their uprisings have all been drowned in blood. If at present the peasants still have a passive attitude, the reason is that they still lack organization and leaders. The Communist International must help them to revolution and liberation.[21]

Placed in conjunction with his later comments in *The Road to Revolution*, these speeches reveal Ho Chi Minh's sensitivity to the plight of the Asian peasantry and suggest his awareness of its potential importance in the coming revolutionary upsurge. According to an acquaintance, Ho had been a staunch advocate of the importance of the peasantry while working on colonial and peasant questions in the Agitprop Division of the Comintern in 1924. At that time, the idea that peasants could play an active role in revolution was frequently ridiculed in Moscow, and Ho had laughingly referred to himself as "a voice crying in the wilderness." Three years later, he returned to the subject in an article dealing with the role of the peasant in the revolutionary process in rural and semirural countries.

Technically speaking, Ho Chi Minh did not depart from Leninist orthodoxy. Selecting examples from rural disturbances in China and the Balkans, he demonstrated that without proletarian leadership, peasant rebellion tends to be spontaneous and uncoordinated. Under such conditions,

> the aim of the proletarian party with respect to the peasants is clear. It must win leadership of the movement, organize it, mobilize the peasant masses around certain class slogans which accord with the character of the revolution, and in short must lead the entire movement toward realizing these slogans. The party of the proletariat must coordinate the peasant movement with the revolutionary aims and operations of the proletariat in the industrial centres.

But if the peasant movement cannot succeed without the assistance of the proletariat, the opposite is also true, and here Ho Chi Minh departed from the accepted wisdom in the Comintern. The essence of his views is set forth in the opening sentence of the article:

> Victory of the proletarian revolution is *impossible* in rural and semi-rural countries if the *revolutionary proletariat is not actively supported* by the mass of the peasant population. . . . In China, in India, in Latin America, in many European countries (Balkan countries, Rumania, Poland, Italy, France, Spain, etc.) the decisive ally of the proletariat in the revolution will be the peasant population. Only if the revolutionary wave sets in motion the rural masses under the leadership of the proletariat, will the revolution be able to triumph. Hence the exceptional importance of Party agitation in the countryside.[22]

Ho was thus not arguing for a simple "peasant communism" that will triumph without proletarian leadership. But he was pleading that Communist parties take seriously Lenin's admonitions that the peasant masses must be a "basic force" in the revolutionary process in many societies around the world. The Party must therefore work with radical elements in the village, organize them, and prepare coordinated actions in the towns and the countryside. Ho was particularly critical of Chinese Communist strategy in the Northern Expedition of 1926, when the Party supported the Kuomintang against peasant rebellion in Hunan Province. This, he said, "was the biggest error of the communist leadership at that time."

Ho Chi Minh's convictions about the role of the peasantry in Asian revolutions had serious implications for the nature of the final insurrection to seize power. As mentioned above, he appeared to view the final revolutionary upsurge as a combined action (taken, if possible, spontaneously) in the cities and the rural areas. The details of each revolution would depend in good part on the idiosyncrasies of each society, but he contended that, in general, the Party should concentrate on one or more key provinces with a substantial rural population and a number of major industrial centers. This would facilitate the joint actions of peasants and workers. At the appropriate moment, when revolutionary conditions in that region had matured, armed guerrilla detachments should be formed at the local level among the peasants. He was careful to stress that armed detachments should not be formed "at any given moment" but only in classical revolutionary circumstances, "when the yoke of the ruling classes has become intolerable, and the village masses are in a state of revolutionary ferment and ready to fight actively against the established order." Such spontaneous peasant actions, he said, are symptoms that the country is entering an immediate revolutionary situation.

In the early stages, such guerrilla detachments might be armed only with primitive weapons. Later, as the movement spread and gained proletarian support, weapons could be captured from the enemy and guerrilla actions could multiply. Eventually, as the revolutionary upsurge increased throughout the country, the detachments would become mobile and move on to large-scale operations in other parts of the country. Ho Chi Minh hastened to add that the guerrilla movement was only an "auxiliary factor" in the revolution and that it must ultimately be placed under proletarian leadership. But he insisted that "good leadership of the guerrilla movement by the party of the proletariat is only possible if the latter possesses influence over the peasants, and if the peasants accept its slogans and struggle to realize them."

Ho Chi Minh's brief comments on the nature of the revolutionary process in Asian societies are one of the few references to the subject during the life of the league. His conviction that revolution in Asia would be a prolonged process is suggested by his comment that

> in countries like China, which present an infinite diversity of geographical, economic and political conditions, the revolution (the seizure of power by the proletariat, in alliance with the peasants and urban poor) cannot be accomplished as a single act (i.e., in the space of a few weeks or months), but must necessarily fill an entire more or less prolonged period of revolutionary movements in the various provinces or industrial and political centres.[23]

Ho's comments here serve to clarify his ambiguous references to the subject in *The Road to Revolution* and make clear that his vague statements in the pamphlet did not result from an inadequate grasp of Marxist-Leninist theory. The pamphlet was written primarily as an introductory primer for unsophisticated young patriots, and Ho may have felt that any effort to emphasize the leading role of the working class would have seemed ludicrous to his readers at that stage of their ideological development. Too much should not be made of the doctrinal significance of this early pamphlet.[24] What is clear is that Ho Chi Minh took more seriously than most Lenin's strictures on the need for a close proletarian-peasant alliance in backward countries and viewed the final process as a joint effort of the two oppressed classes.

Were these views reflected in the early activities of the Revolutionary Youth League? Did the league, as one observer has contended, concentrate more on the peasantry than on the proletariat in its organizational activities?[25] Unfortunately, a definitive answer would require more evidence on the organization's recruiting efforts. For the moment, it appears that Ho Chi Minh devoted his earliest efforts to building up a nucleus of radical intellectuals to serve as a source of future Party leaders. Once that leadership had been created, the league would seek to expand the movement in both working class areas and rural villages. Unfortunately, before such plans could be put into effect, Ho Chi Minh was forced to leave South China for Moscow, and leadership of the movement passed briefly to others.

The League and Vietnamese Nationalism

Within a year, the league had become an active political force in Vietnam and a formidable rival for other patriotic organizations throughout Vietnam. In its relations with the latter, the league attempted to be both ally and competitor. In Leninist strategy, the problem was a delicate one: Asian nationalism was viewed as an ally in the struggle against world capitalism, and Communist movements were supposed to seek such allies. But Moscow was skeptical of the sincerity of the progressive attitudes of such groups and concluded that they should be supported only when they were genuinely revolutionary and did not hinder Communist efforts to educate and organize the working masses. All Communist parties were to maintain their independence and to keep in mind that such alliances were temporary, to be discarded once the first stage of the revolution had been achieved.

In Vietnam, Ho Chi Minh's formidable task was complicated by the divisions within the nationalist movement. Before his departure from Moscow, he had asked Dmitri Manuilsky, the Comintern's foremost colonial expert, what Asian Communist parties should do where no mass nationalist party existed. It is doubtful that Manuilsky, a Ukrainian with little experience in Asian affairs, had ever thought about the question. Forced to improvise, he limited himself to an impromptu suggestion: Where no mass nationalist movement existed, the local Communist party should take the initiative to form one under its own leadership.[26]

Whether or not Ho Chi Minh took Manuilsky's offhand comment to heart, the league's relationship with nationalist groups was destined to be stormy and suggested that Ho Chi Minh and his disciples were more interested in domination than collaboration. The Constitutionalists, labeled as false patriots and toadies of the French, were simply scorned. Toward the radical parties, the league was somewhat more conciliatory and sent representatives to negotiate with leaders of the VNQDD and the Tan Viet on a possible alliance. But the league's negotiating position was consistently hard-line: Its rivals were apparently offered not a merger of equals but merely an opportunity to enter the league as individuals. Like Sun Yat-sen's Kuomintang, which decided not to allow the Chinese Communist Party (CCP) to form a "bloc within" it, the league had every intention of remaining the parent organization in any alliance between the forces of nationalism and social revolution.

The effectiveness of such tactics depends on the point of view. While negotiations were underway, the league actively attempted to lure the delegates of rival parties into its organization, and when members of rival groups were invited to Canton to study at the league's training school, they were instructed not to resume contact with their erstwhile comrades on their return to Vietnam.[27] Such behavior attracted a number of members into the new organization, and many of the leaders of the Communist Party were originally members of rival groups. On the other hand, many nationalist leaders were understandably alienated by such tactics and spurned alliance on the terms offered. By 1929, four years after the formation of the league, no major alliance had been achieved.

Still, the league had made considerable progress during these years and soon developed into the most active of the anti-French political organizations in Vietnam. By the end of the decade, membership had reached about 1,000, with a nucleus of 200 graduates from the training program in Canton. Significantly, the league had sunk roots in all three regions of Vietnam and was making serious inroads into the following of its competitors. One indication of progress was that by 1929 the French intelligence services in Indochina were beginning to devote more attention to the league than to all of its rivals put together.[28]

As one might expect, the league's appeal was strongest among the most radical and anti-French elements of Vietnamese society. According to the recent estimate of a prominent Communist historian in Hanoi, 90 percent of league members came from the urban petty bourgeoisie.[29] It is difficult to corroborate such evidence, for reliable statistics are scarce, but a high percentage of the leadership came, like Ho Chi Minh, from families with a strong Confucian tradition. On a geographic basis, the majority came from provinces in the Center or the North, where the strength of the cultural heritage had disintegrated more slowly than it had in the Westernized and commercial South. The comparison with China is irresistible and persuasive: The early leaders of the CCP were most likely to be intellectuals descended from rural scholar-gentry families, while those of the rival Kuomintang tended to come from commercial families lacking a traditional Confucian background. Communists frequently came from areas relatively little exposed to Western influence, such as the Central Yangtze provinces or Szechwan; Sun Yat-sen's followers (like Sun) were more likely to be from the more Westernized coastal areas.[30]

The similarity with China cannot be mere coincidence and merits further examination. What was the source of the league's appeal among the urban Confucian intelligentsia? One major factor was the nature of its message. At first glance, it may seem paradoxical that Vietnamese intellectuals proved so receptive to the Marxist vision, since in so many respects Confucianism and Marxism are antithetical. Where Confucianism is built on a relatively static conception of human society, Marxism is dynamic and unabashedly progress-oriented; where Confucianism tends to deprecate material wealth as an obstacle to high ethical standards, Marxism glorifies the productive process and views man as a natural creator; where Confucianism is fundamentally hierarchical and accepts the existence of enduring differences in human status and capacity, Marxism is consciously egalitarian and attempts to abolish or minimize such differences.

Yet, on further reflection, many of these apparent contradictions lose their force. In the first place, Marxism was entering the bloodstream of Vietnamese society at a time when Confucianism had substantially lost its appeal to patriotic intellectuals. Often precisely those aspects of Confucian philosophy and practice that ran counter to Marxism—its sense of hierarchy, its bucolic air and its ritualism, its inherent conservatism and resistance to change—were most strongly rejected by the younger generation. In that sense, the new ideology appealed because it was viewed as a corrective for the fatal weaknesses of its predecessor. It has been observed of the cultural revolution in China that the clash between Confucian traditional and modern Western ideas became so bitter (a question too complex to be discussed here) that young intellectuals were driven to reject the past rather than to attempt a synthesis of native and foreign ideas.

The hypothesis seems relevant in Vietnam. The failure of the Confucian system to stem the French advance in Vietnam and the willingness of the court and much of the bureaucracy to accept a role as instruments of the colonial regime left a legacy of bitterness and disgust among patriots. For the modern intellectual, Marxism might be attractive because it seemed to be the most modern, the most scientific, and the most anti-Confucian of all contemporary ideologies. To be a Marxist represented a grand gesture of contempt for the corrupt past as well as the humiliating present.

Yet ironically Marxism was hardly a wholehearted rejection of Confucianism, whatever it may have appeared to would-be modernizers. There are a number of underlying similarities between the two doctrines: the belief in one truth, embodied in quasi-sacred texts; the concept of an anointed elite, trained in an all-embracing doctrine and responsible for leading the broad masses and indoctrinating them in proper thought and behavior; the stress on personal ethics and selfless service to society; the subordination of the individual to the community; the belief that material wealth is not the ultimate end product of human endeavor but should be firmly subordinated to more spiritual goals; and the conviction that human nature is malleable and can be improved through corrective action. In a world of rapid change, where the moorings of traditional beliefs had been severely shaken, Marxist-Leninist doctrine represented a comforting and persuasive antidote. It was plausible; it was (or at least claimed to be) scientific; it was practical and up-to-date; and it had a satisfying air of intellectual solidity, probably an important factor in a Confucian society. And, of course, it offered an explanation of the problem, a reasonable alternative, and a path for action.

Without realizing it, then, the radical intellectual might find Marxism congenial because it possessed certain comfortable similarities to the belief system inherited from the past. Many of these similarities would be unspoken assumptions about the nature of man and the universe, about the correct relationship between the individual and society, about human responsibility and perfectibility. In that sense, it is tempting to view Vietnamese Marxism as a type of reformed Confucianism, as Confucianism adapted to modern conditions, a dynamic new ideology dedicated broadly to ideals that had animated the philosophy of the old Master, but more scientific and suitably revised to meet the challenges and possibilities of the modern era. By definition, of course, Marxism is not a synthetic ideology; it is iconoclastic, antitraditional, and universalist and cannot easily coexist with other belief systems. Still, in many ways it is an easier step from Confucianism to Marxism than to capitalism, to a community-oriented socialist society than to one constructed on a libertarian, individualist basis.[31]

This point can be further elaborated by an analysis of the role of Ho Chi Minh in the growth of the movement. In human affairs, the medium is often as important as the message, and Vietnamese communism is no exception. For it is hard to avoid the conclusion that the character of Ho Chi Minh was as important as Marxism-Leninism in the early success of the league. Almost without exception, Vietnamese recruited to join the organization and participate in its training program in Canton commented on his extraordinary personality. Although Ho restricted himself to a somewhat avuncular role as teacher and spiritual adviser, he was clearly the guiding force behind the movement, at least until his departure for the Soviet Union in the spring of 1927. In this role, he was strikingly effective, according to memoirs dating from the period. As a teacher, he was well informed on contemporary affairs and persuasive; as an adviser, he was fatherly and kind; as a patriot and a revolutionary, he set a sterling example by his simplicity and high standards of ethical behavior. Whether or not this image is an accurate one (and the portrait is too much in keeping with comments made by foreign, non-Communist acquaintances to be dismissed as pure propaganda), Ho Chi Minh undoubtedly exerted a formidable influence on the movement as a role model for young revolutionary intellectuals. Like Erik Erikson's Martin Luther and Mahatma Gandhi, Ho Chi Minh was able to embody in his own experience the struggles and goals of a generation undergoing great change. The potential force of such a link between leader and masses is well documented and needs no elaboration here.[32]

What is particularly significant about this is not simply that Ho was viewed by his followers in near ideal terms (although that in itself is no mean feat), but the degree to which he personified the heroic figure of the Confucian "superior man" (the *chün tzu* or, in Vietnamese, *quân tu*).[33] Ho Chi Minh projected all the desirable qualities in Confucian ethics: rectitude, probity, sincerity, modesty, courage, and self-sacrifice. To impressionable young Vietnamese intellectuals disgusted with the hypocrisy, corruption, cowardice, and greed of so many prominent figures in colonial society, Ho Chi Minh was the rare exception, the "superior man" in the broadest sense.

In his writings, too, Ho frequently resorted to the use of Confucian motifs in an effort to reinforce the appeal of his ideas among young intellectuals. A good example can be found in *The Road to Revolution*, in which he devoted one entire

section to the behavior of the revolutionary. Ho's list of desirable characteristics has a strong Confucian flavor: The revolutionary must be thrifty,
impartial, prudent, greedy for learning, generous, steadfast, willing to sacrifice.
He must place national interests above his own, be little desirous of material
things, be ready to give guidance, be courageous, and ready to obey the Party.[34]
This description stands in marked contrast to the famous nineteenth century
"catechism of a revolutionary" by the Russian terrorist Nechaev, which was
much admired by Lenin and became the bible of his Bolshevik Party. To
Nechaev, the revolutionary was the blind instrument of the revolutionary
cause. He must be ruthless in pursuit of his goal, show absolute obedience to his
party, and be willing to abandon all human ties with friends and family. He
must be prepared to sacrifice all recognized standards of morality, to lie, to
cheat, and to steal in the interests of the revolution.

Presumably nothing in Ho Chi Minh's list would contradict Lenin's convictions of the duties of a Party member. But what is left out is significant. For
where Nechaev assumed that contemporary standards of morality had little
relevance to the revolutionary code of conduct, Ho Chi Minh assumed that a
revolutionary code need not do violence to traditional Confucian morality. Indeed, except for those few references to the Party, Ho's commandments could
easily be accepted in any devout Confucian home.

Was Ho Chi Minh's pose deliberate? Was he consciously dressing Marxist
concepts in Confucian clothing to attract recruits from the scholar-gentry class?
The answer cannot be stated with certainty, but it is probably yes. Ho Chi
Minh was a master at manipulating personal relationships for his own advantage, and it is doubtful that he often acted spontaneously without calculating
the consequences. Yet there is more here than mere expediency, for Ho's ethical
standards have continued to serve, even after his death, as a crucial element in
his legacy to the Party and to his countrymen. It is perhaps easiest to conclude
that for Ho Chi Minh, the image of the "superior man" was taken seriously and
that the simple ethical principles expounded to him by his father had taken
root in his consciousness and flourished in his mature life.

Although the assumption is difficult to confirm, it is possible that, for many
of the young intellectuals recruited into the league, such political and moral factors may have been more important than economic ones. This is certainly not
to deny that economic factors were present. As John T. McAlister has pointed
out in his provocative study, *Viet-Nam: The Origins of Revolution*, the frustrated
career ambitions of urban intellectuals may have been a key factor in the
growth of revolutionary sentiment prior to the August Revolution in 1945.[35]
This argument appears to have only limited relevance to the situation under
discussion here. Many league members seem to have been recruited directly
from school before they completed their education. There is no evidence that
they would have acted otherwise had lucrative professional careers beckoned.
On the contrary, the vast majority seem to have been motivated by a fierce and

somewhat selfless sense of patriotism. In this case, the moral imperative of serving the Vietnamese nation in its hour of crisis appears to have been the crucial factor.

The Breakup of the League

One of the strengths of the league was its success in presenting a public face of single-minded devotion to the common cause. Of the various nationalist groups in Vietnam, it appeared alone in avoiding factionalism and building a base in all three regions of the country. This image was somewhat misleading, however, for under the surface problems were brewing. The basic dilemma was that the league had been constructed on the basis of an inner contradiction. The public face was dedicated primarily to a national revolution, and thus directed at moderates as well as radicals, but the inner core was committed to the objective of building a Communist society. For three years, the inner tension between ideology and nationalism had been contained. During this period Ho Chi Minh and his colleagues had tended to stress the national image over the revolutionary one. But as the decade neared an end, the contradiction between nationalism and social revolution broke out into the open. There were apparently several reasons for this. The conflict in 1927 between the Kuomintang and the CCP forced Ho to flee China for Moscow. His successors lacked his sense of finesse in handling political issues. They were harassed by Chinese authorities and forced to move the league's headquarters on several occasions. Some were arrested and served short terms in prison.

As such troubles disrupted the Party's apparatus at the top, unrest within the ranks began to surface. Sometime in early 1929, radical members in the Tonkin Regional Committee began to express dissatisfaction with what they considered the ideological flabbiness of the policies adopted by the league headquarters in South China. A major source of their concern was the composition of the membership. The organization had not been making a major effort to recruit among the small but growing industrial proletariat but, as we have seen above, had relied primarily on the ability of returning students to spread support for the movement among their friends and relatives. Relatively few had extended their recruiting activities into poorer communities. Only in Saigon, where the labor organizer Ton Duc Thang had built up a vigorous movement among factory workers, was there a substantial proletarian component in the league apparatus. The organization had been somewhat more active in rural areas—particularly in Nghe An, home province of much of the leadership—but nonetheless the vast majority of the members came from the urban bourgeoisie. A second source of discontent among radicals was the dilatory attitude of the leadership toward the establishment of a formal Communist party—a decision that they felt was absolutely necessary to shore up the ideological underpinnings of the Vietnamese revolutionary movement.

Such radical discontents had probably existed before the convening of the Sixth Comintern Congress in Moscow in the summer of 1928. But the decisions taken at that congress—first to be held since the 1924 meeting—undoubtedly added impetus to the radicals' complaints, for the Sixth Congress signaled a major shift in direction for world Communist strategy. Disappointed by recent events in the Dutch East Indies and in China, where the alliance between the Kuomintang and the Communists had ended in disaster, and impelled by domestic political considerations to take a more leftist line in internal affairs, Stalin (now the dominant figure in the Comintern, as in the Soviet Union) compelled congress delegates to abandon the broad united front strategy initiated at the Second Congress eight years earlier. Communist parties in colonial areas were now instructed to reject alliances with bourgeois nationalist parties, on the grounds that the indigenous bourgeoisie had turned away from revolution and could no longer be trusted as an ally of the proletariat. Furthermore, Communist parties must be purged of their petty bourgeois elements and "bolshevized." Practically speaking, this meant that working class representation in Communist organizations should be increased and internal party rectification movements should be initiated to cleanse them of impure elements. Party members of middle class origin should be required to undergo a process of "proletarianization"—literally to put on overalls and attempt to find work in factories to increase their awareness of the proletarian outlook.[36]

Finally, the Sixth Congress, under Stalin's prodding, saw a new revolutionary wave on the horizon. Communist and proto-Communist organizations throughout the world were instructed to increase their capacity to respond to the rising discontent in their own societies and to heighten revolutionary awareness by initiating strikes and mass demonstrations among the workers and the poorer peasantry and by setting up cells in factories, schools, and villages in preparation for the revolutionary upsurge to come.

The reports of the Sixth Congress, once they became available in Vietnam, undoubtedly intensified the militancy of the Tonkin radicals. Leader in the agitation for a more radical outlook was Tran Van Cung, first secretary of the North Vietnamese Regional Committee. A native of Nghe An and an ex-member of the Tan Viet Party in Annam, Cung had become convinced after working in factories that urban workers could not be mobilized to support the league by vague patriotic slogans. The organization must emphasize issues of importance to workers—higher salaries, better working conditions, reduced working hours—in order to win labor support. This could not be done, he felt, without the transformation of the league into a full-fledged Communist party.

The league had attempted to respond to the new directives from Moscow late in 1928. League members were directed to move into factories, and a few labor unions were formed. This was not enough for Tran Van Cung, however. He persuaded other members of the Tonkin Regional Committee to form a Communist cell composed of the most radical members of the group and obtained approval from the constituency to propose the formation of a Communist party at the First Congress of the league, scheduled for the spring of 1929.

At the congress, the Tonkin delegates made a formal proposal to disband the league and establish a Communist party in its stead. For a variety of reasons, however, the majority of delegates at the congress opposed the proposal, and it was rebuffed. In a burst of anger, Cung and all but one of the Tonkin delegates left the congress, simultaneously announcing their determination to form a Communist party among their followers on their return to Vietnam. Soon after their arrival in Hanoi, they established a new organization, entitled the Indochinese Communist Party (ICP or, in Vietnamese, Dang Cong San Dong Duong), and began to compete with the league for recruits, claiming that the league was composed of "false revolutionaries . . . who have never carried their efforts to the proletarian masses."

The situation soon degenerated from drama into absurdity. The congress carried on its business without the Tonkinese delegates and adjourned. The leadership soon realized, however, that it had made a serious tactical error, since the new ICP formed in North Vietnam was rapidly luring members away from the league. By midsummer the league had decided to transform itself into a Communist party—the Annam Communist Party (ACP, or Annam Cong San Dang). To add to the confusion, radical members of the Tan Viet Party, in a desperate effort to preserve their own following, renamed their organization the Indochinese Communist League (Dong Duong Cong San Lien Doan). As is so often the case, radicalism fed on itself. By the beginning of the new decade, there were three competing Communist parties in French Indochina.[37]

The reaction from Moscow to the bewildering events in Vietnam was rapid and predictable. In October a blistering letter was dispatched to the league, criticizing the leadership for its failure to prevent the disintegration of the revolutionary forces in Vietnam into three rival factions. The lack of a united party at this time of high promise was a serious danger to the development of communism and was "entirely mistaken." The Comintern, still persuaded of the imminence of revolution in Asia, openly supported Tran Van Cung's faction in Hanoi and asserted that the objective conditions for a capitalist revolution were already present in Vietnam. "The absence of a Communist party in the midst of the development of the workers' and peoples' movement," it warned, "is becoming very dangerous for the immediate future of the revolution in Indochina."[38] The league was criticized for showing "indecisiveness and indifference" and for not making greater efforts to recruit among Vietnamese workers. Finally, Moscow concluded that "the most urgent and important task of all the Communists in Indochina is the formation of a revolutionary party possessing the class characteristics of the proletariat, that is a popular Communist party in Indochina," and suggested that a unity conference be convened, chaired by a representative of the Comintern who would be sent as a mediator.

Throughout the remainder of 1929 the three factions competed for followers, exchanged insults (the most common was "menshevik"), and engaged in brief and abortive negotiations. Then, in the fall of 1929, the Comintern sent Tran Phu, a promising young Vietnamese student at the Stalin School, to visit Ho Chi Minh (who was then in Siam) to convey Moscow's instructions that he should intervene to restore unity in the movement. Ho arrived in Hong Kong early in January 1930 and immediately instructed each faction to appoint a delegation to meet with him to iron out the outstanding differences. By the end of the month, two representatives from the ACP and one from the ICP had arrived in the British colony; the unity conference was convened on February 3 in a small house in a working class district in Kowloon, on the Chinese mainland across from the city of Hong Kong.[39]

Agreement was surprisingly easy to achieve. Ho Chi Minh gently lectured the delegates for having permitted the break to take place and warned them against engaging in mutual recriminations. The only issue, he insisted, was how to restore unity. It soon became evident that the major differences between the two parties were based more on personal pique and regional suspicion than on ideology. To end the split he suggested the dissolution of both parties and the formation of a new organization, to be entitled the Vietnamese Communist Party (VCP), into which all who approved the aims and met the standards could be accepted as members. There was a quick and probably relieved acceptance of the proposal by all the delegates.[40]

With the thorniest problems resolved, the remaining issues were dealt with without difficulty. Further meetings, held "in an atmosphere of unity and love," drafted a temporary program and new Party statutes and made plans to set up mass associations and an antiimperialist front. Ho agreed to draft an appeal for support, and representatives were chosen to return to Vietnam to form a new Party apparatus. For the most part, the Party would be composed of remnants of the ICP and the ACP. Members of the Communist League (which had not been represented at the unity conference) could be accepted into the Party as individuals. A provisional Central Committee composed of nine members was selected to run the Party until formal elections could be held. Tran Phu was named secretary general.

The appeal showed that the influence of Moscow had had its effect. While calling for the support of the major exploited classes in Vietnam (workers, peasants, soldiers, youth, and students), it deleted the middle class from consideration and talked of the construction of a "worker-peasant and soldier government." Confiscation of the property of imperialists and of the "reactionary capitalist class" was called for and, in place of Ho Chi Minh's earlier concept of a dual worker-peasant vanguard, the appeal stated that the Party "is the party of the working class."[41] There was no longer any doubt that the movement led by Ho Chi Minh was dedicated to social revolution.

The Nghe Tinh Soviets

Within weeks, the prospects for that social revolution appeared suddenly to brighten. The unrest that so often appeared to lie just beneath the surface of Vietnamese society erupted in 1930 in open rebellion, the first major challenge to colonial authority since the turn of the century. The mere fact of the uprising was disquieting to the French. What was more significant, and from the government point of view, ominous, was that for the first time the unrest was focused on two classes that until now had taken little active part in the resistance movement—the workers and the peasants.

The origins of the 1930 revolt have attracted considerable attention from scholars in recent years. Some have contended that the uprising was essentially spontaneous and reflected, above all, the anger of poor peasants and workers at deteriorating economic and social conditions. Others are convinced that the agitational activity of local Communist cadres was a major and perhaps decisive factor in the uprising. Such scholarly ambivalence is not particularly surprising, for contemporary observers were similarly divided over whether the rebellion should be ascribed to Communist activists or to deeper long-term causes.[42]

Chronic economic and social problems in Vietnam were sufficient, in themselves, to provide a potential source of unrest. Working conditions for the urban proletariat, as well as for laborers in the coal mines and rubber plantations, were atrocious, as a number of visiting French writers and journalists had reported. During the late 1920s the league and some of its competitors had attempted to take advantage of such conditions and had begun to set up secret organizations in factories and plantations. The combination of internal discontent and outside organization was explosive, and by the final years of the decade the number of workers' strikes had increased significantly, with workers demanding higher wages, shorter working hours, and fairer treatment.

Conditions were no better in the countryside. High taxes and high rents, land concentration (especially in the South), mandarin venality (a particular problem in Central Vietnam, where the imperial bureaucracy still retained considerable authority), confiscation of communal lands by the wealthy, and resentment against the state monopolies on alcohol, salt, and opium all contributed to a high degree of peasant resentment. The effects of such factors on village livelihood is somewhat controversial, and was more severe in some areas than in others, but French policies contributed to considerable hardship in rural areas. Characteristically, however, the anger of peasants had been slow to arouse, and although there had been some unrest—notably in Cochin China during World War I—the last major expression of peasant unhappiness had occurred more than two decades earlier, at the time of the "revolt of the short hairs" in Central Vietnam in 1908.[43]

The Depression exacerbated the general economic malaise of the poorer classes in colonial Vietnam. By the end of the decade, the impact of the world economic crisis began to affect Vietnam. Foreign capital began to leave the country and unemployment rose. In some enterprises half the workers were laid off. Some took to the streets; others were compelled to return to the over-crowded villages whence they had come. But the villages were no haven of security; as the price of rice fell, farm income plummeted and peasants found it more difficult to pay their taxes and meet their other financial obligations. With land values dropping, countless acres of arable land were abandoned by their peasant owners.

Whether such conditions were sufficient to account for the ferocity of the uprising is a matter of dispute. The relationship between economic conditions and revolt in colonial Vietnam has inspired considerable scholarly interest in recent years. Were the peasants in Cochin China—where the effects of the capitalist market system and land concentration were more severe—more likely to rebel against intolerable conditions than those in the coastal plains of the Center, where economic conditions were poor but the peasants were allegedly protected by the survival of the traditional "corporate village," which could equalize hardship and pain? Although the subject is one of considerable interest, I do not propose to enter this debate, since it is not directly germane to the main theme of this study. It might be worth noting, however, that the 1930 revolt in Vietnam does not provide convincing support for either hypothesis, since there was significant unrest in both Cochin China and Central Vietnam. Only in the Red River delta did the peasant villages remain quiet. Moreover, extraneous factors helped to account for the high degree of unrest in the Center—disastrous weather conditions, the proximity of urban discontent in the provincial capital at Vinh, and a higher degree of agitational efforts by the new Communist Party. Under such conditions, it is difficult to isolate single causes.[44]

Was the rising discontent in Vietnam a harbinger of a major revolt against French colonial rule? The Comintern thought so and interpreted signs of unrest as another indication of an impending revolutionary upsurge throughout Asia. According to French intelligence reports, the Comintern representative who came to Hong Kong at the end of 1929 to inspect the league's performance brought with him a message from Moscow to be conveyed to the Vietnamese comrades: that a bourgeois democratic revolution would quite possibly break out in the near future, and that the Party should be ready to transform it into a social revolution to seize power for the working class.[45]

It was not, of course, quite that simple. As the new decade dawned, Comintern strategy for promoting and waging revolution in Asian societies represented an amalgam of inherited precepts from the Bolshevik Revolution in

1917, Vladimir Lenin's *Theses on the National and Colonial Questions* presented at the Second Comintern Congress in 1920, and the experience derived from the abortive Chinese revolution of 1926 and 1927. The key issue was the relative importance of peasant rebellion in the Asian revolutionary process. The Chinese experience encouraged those who claimed that the force of spontaneous rural unrest could play a significant role in the Asian revolution. But it also confirmed others' doubts that such spontaneous unrest by itself could lead to a revolutionary upsurge that would topple the government. Comintern strategy reflected an uneasy compromise between such views. It called for local Communist parties to intensify their efforts in rural areas in preparation for a possible peasant rebellion. If unrest broke out, party activists were encouraged to organize it and to form guerrilla detachments in rural villages. But Moscow cautioned against an overemphasis on the role of the peasantry in the revolutionary process. The leadership of the revolution in Asia rested with the proletariat alone, not with an alliance of peasants and workers. Rural revolt could provide a catalytic force behind the final surge to victory, but it could succeed only if it spread rapidly to the cities, where party activists were to set off an urban insurrection to seize total power.[46]

Presumably the new Vietnamese Party was instructed in the implementation of the new strategy by Tran Phu, the young Communist who had recently returned to South China after attending training sessions at the Stalin School in Moscow. During the early months of 1930, as the new Party attempted to organize an apparatus within Vietnam, it began to intensify its efforts to organize restless workers and peasants in the towns and villages. Secret party cells were set up in factories and commercial enterprises in some of the major industrial centers and in the rubber plantations of Cochin China. Similar activities took place in rural villages in the Mekong delta and in the densely populated provinces of Central Vietnam. Accurate statistics on the extent of such efforts are scarce, but French intelligence reports confirm that in the key central provinces of Nghe An and Ha Tinh local notables began to complain to higher authorities about "strangers" arriving from outside the province to agitate among the local residents. By late spring the situation in some districts had become alarming, with such agitators holding nocturnal meetings and openly attempting to stir up the embers of discontent. According to French figures, by midsummer there were about 300 Communist activists in the two provinces. A few months later, the figure had risen to 1,800.[47]

Did such activities raise the level of discontent in Vietnamese cities and villages? The answer is uncertain, for it is possible that, as in 1908, revolt would have broken out in any case. Nevertheless, Communist efforts helped mobilize angry workers and peasants to voice their demands. This was certainly the case at the Phu Rieng rubber plantation in Cochin China, often cited in Communist histories as the kickoff of a year of rebellion. The riots there in March had their origins in economic discontent, but there is clear evidence in both

Communist and French sources that local Communist organizers provoked the workers into voicing their grievances.[48] More than a thousand laborers, stimulated to a high pitch by dismal working conditions and notoriously brutal treatment by Vietnamese foremen, took part in organized demonstrations and were subdued only with difficulty.

The pattern was soon to be repeated elsewhere. Within weeks, workers at a cotton factory in Nam Dinh and at a match factory near Vinh struck for redress of grievances. Here again, the demands were primarily economic but clandestine Communist organizers (who had apparently set up secret labor unions in both enterprises) played a part in stimulating the unrest. By the end of April, it had become clear to the French that the agitation was part of a broader pattern. Evidence accumulated that the new Communist Party had made plans to hold massive rallies throughout the country on May 1 to raise the level of discontent and to demonstrate Vietnamese solidarity with the international workers' movement. Forewarned, local French authorities prohibited gatherings and May Day was relatively quiet, with only a few minor scuffles. Significantly, however, where incidents did occur, leaflets and red banners made it clear that the Communists were behind the agitation.

By mid-spring, the stirrings of discontent began to penetrate the countryside. There were a few peasant riots in scattered areas of Cochin China—most sparked by local complaints over high taxes. But the eye of the growing storm was located in the province of Nghe An, with its capital city of Vinh. Traditionally one of the most rebellious provinces of Vietnam, Nghe An had produced a disproportionately high percentage of radical leaders in the anti-French resistance movement. The land was poor and overcrowded, and there was substantial tenancy, particularly in the districts of Nghi Loc, Thanh Chuong, and Nam Dan. Where private landownership existed, farmers frequently possessed miniscule plots.[49] Then, early in 1930, much of the area was devastated by disastrous floods. By midsummer, the region was threatened by drought. According to government estimates, in some districts nearly 90 percent of the population was dying of hunger. With no rice or maize available, peasants were forced to survive on their traditional last resort—sweet potatoes.

A unique factor undoubtedly contributed to the inflammatory situation. Poverty and density of population led many peasants to abandon their villages and, seeking a way out of grinding poverty, take employment in the factories of Vinh and its industrial suburb of Ben Thuy. Many of them retained ties with their home village and returned there to help with the harvest. The likelihood of urban-rural cooperation was thus higher than in other regions and more explosive in its revolutionary potential. Ho Chi Minh could hardly have picked a more appropriate province to test his hypothesis that revolution in a rural Asian society should begin in a highly populated province adjacent to a major industrial or commercial center.

When the discontent broke out in the factories of Vinh and Ben Thuy, then, it quickly spread to the surrounding countryside. Angry peasants from the upriver districts of Thanh Chuong, Nam Dan, and Nghi Loc, bolstered by their urban cousins, began to protest against worsening rural conditions. Rioting peasants demanded a moratorium on payment of the personal tax and the return of village communal lands confiscated by wealthy landowners. When their demands were ignored, the demonstrations escalated into riots, and manor houses, pagodas, market places, and local government installations were pillaged and burned. Tax rolls were destroyed. Suicide troops ran from village to village to fan revolutionary sentiment and stir up trouble in surrounding areas, and the agitation soon began to spill over into Ha Tinh Province, directly to the south.

For a time, the local authorities seemed paralyzed. Village notables, through fear or sympathy, often refused to suppress the disorders and sometimes joined in.[50] Local mandarins, who had earlier ignored storm warnings, now were terrorized and fled to the provincial capital. Throughout the central provinces, government authority was rapidly disintegrating. In the rebellious districts local Communist organizers encouraged angry peasants to take the law into their hands and to form local village associations (called soviets, after Bolshevik practice) to replace the now-disintegrating governmental apparatus in the area. By early September, revolution was running rampant throughout the central provinces of Nghe An and Ha Tinh. Peasant village soviets (usually formed by calling for a meeting of village residents in the local village *dinh,* or temple, and electing a directing committee to replace the existing village council of elders) sprang up like mushrooms in the districts of Nam Dan and Thanh Chuong and called for the seizure of communal land confiscated earlier by wealthy families, the annulment of local taxes, the lowering of rents, and the distribution of excess rice to the needy. Village militias, usually armed with sticks and spears or knives, were formed for self-defense purposes (in Party histories, these so-called *doi tu ve* are now considered the direct ancestor of the modern Vietnamese People's Liberation Army). In a burst of zeal, some party cadres attempted to reform peasant habits and superstitions; "useless" ceremonies such as funeral and wedding banquets were simplified or eliminated, and stiff penalties were imposed for gambling and stealing. Classes to teach *quoc ngu* were instituted.

Most of the new soviets were dominated by the poorer peasants in the village, and there was considerable pressure, not only for a reduction of rents and taxes, but also for a redistribution of land. In this case, however, the local Party leadership (with a few exceptions) attempted to enforce a relatively moderate policy. Provincial Party directives called for the seizure of previously communal lands, but not for the confiscation of all landlord land. In general, this policy was observed, although in some areas of famine peasants seized the lands of wealthy landowners on their own initiative.[51] In a few cases, peasants set up cooperatives, but they were soon abandoned.

Unavoidably, bloodshed resulted. Landlords and rich peasants who did not flee the village were often mistreated. Village notables were evicted and their homes and property were destroyed; in some cases they were forbidden to leave their villages. In some areas, the rich and the powerful were executed, although accurate figures on the numbers killed are lacking. There is evidence that at the beginning, some moderate elements sympathized with and participated in the movement at the village level, but most were soon turned off by its radicalism and violence.

For the newly formed Regional Committee in the Center, the riots represented an opportunity that was apparently eagerly grasped. For the Central Committee in Hong Kong, however, the revolt raised a number of excruciating questions. Although the Party leadership presumably had accepted Moscow's prediction that revolution was on the horizon and had carried out Comintern instructions to stimulate discontent in Indochina, it is likely that the suddenness of the crisis came as a surprise. Could this potentially explosive situation be transformed into a social revolution to end half a century of French rule in Indochina, as the Comintern seemed to imply in its letter of the preceding October? Was the party ready for an open confrontation with the colonial regime? If revolt in the Center gained momentum, would the rest of the country follow? Most important, could the hostility and discontent among workers and farmers in Central Vietnam be injected into the cities and spark an urban insurrection? Would the restless but volatile urban bourgeoisie join the fray or, as the Comintern feared, would it simply watch in silence while the French restored order in rebellious areas?

In the late summer of 1930 there were no easy answers to such questions, and the Comintern had little advice to offer. Moscow had made it clear that the Party's relative youth and inexperience could not serve as an excuse for inaction. In its letter of October 1929, it had stated pointedly that the lack of an organized Communist party should not prevent revolutionaries from giving their active support to a spontaneous uprising led by workers and peasants. Above all, it reasoned, the Party should not fall behind the masses in its revolutionary activism.

As for the Party's need to ascertain whether the objective situation favored the revolutionary forces, there also the Comintern could provide little assistance beyond suggesting that the final decision on such questions could be reached only by the Party leadership on the spot. In Moscow's view, what was important was that the Vietnamese Marxists get ready for the new revolutionary upsurge that Stalin insisted was at hand.

In September, the new Central Committee began to gather in Hong Kong in preparation for its first formal session since the unity meeting in February. It had a number of matters to attend to (including the renaming of the Party, at Comintern request, the Indochinese Communist Party, or ICP). But it is certain that the nationwide strikes and the unrest in the Center became the focus of considerable attention. By now it was increasingly apparent that the outbreak in the Center was not likely to result in a nationwide rebellion against French rule. The tax riots in Cochin China, which were apparently not specifically directed by Communist activists, were beginning to subside. Elsewhere, the rural areas were quiet, particularly in the populous Red River delta, where the local Party leaders were openly critical of people's inertia. Even in the Center, calm was beginning to return in some areas, as French retaliatory efforts began to take hold. In the cities, there were a few worker strikes in Saigon and Hanoi in response to the plight of compatriots in the Center, but no united or organized action to relieve the pressure by preventing the government from concentrating its military forces on the central provinces. As for the urban bourgeoisie, it had for the most part been frightened by the dark image of violence and class war that increasingly emanated from the soviet movement (an image undoubtedly encouraged by the French); it watched the events in the Center in fascination or in horror, but it did not rise. (The VNQDD, the only other major radical party in the country, had launched its own revolt in February and had suffered a disastrous defeat.) In this respect, the Comintern had been proven correct. The Vietnamese bourgeoisie, for several years a progressive element, was now vacillating and could no longer be counted upon as a staunch ally of the revolutionary forces.

On the other hand, the Party could hardly disown a rebellion that it had helped to stimulate and that had been predicted and encouraged by Moscow. It was a delicate situation. A premature revolt might be branded as adventuristic, but an even greater error (in the eyes of the Comintern) would be to fall behind the masses in their struggle for liberation. Under the circumstances, the Party leadership settled for caution. In September, according to documentary evidence available in Hanoi, the Central Committee had sent a directive to the Regional Committee in Annam criticizing the turn to violence and suggesting that an uprising would be premature and risky. On the other hand, it was obviously too late to disavow the events in the Center:

> In Thanh Chuong and Nam Dinh at this time, the Executive Committee [of the Central Vietnamese regional committee] is already advocating violence (setting up soviets, dividing land, etc.). Such measures are not appropriate at this time, because the preparation of the Party and the masses is insufficient, and there is little armed violence. Isolated violence in various regions at this time is premature and adventuristic. But with things as they are, we must behave in such a way as to preserve Party and soviet influence so that even if they are defeated the meaning of the soviets will penetrate deeply into the minds of the masses and the influence of the Party and the peasant associations will be maintained.[52]

In October, a second directive from the Party center to all levels explained more clearly the views of the Party leadership on the soviets:

> If the masses are at the point of spontaneous action, then the Party has no alter-
> native but to lead them immediately. But in this case the Executive Committee is
> actually *promoting* [the unrest]. This is very mistaken, because (1) although the
> situation in some areas is revolutionary, in general the level of consciousness and
> struggle of the workers and peasants is not high, and (2) although there is a high
> level of consciousness and enthusiasm in some areas, this is not generally the case.
> Therefore to carry out sporadic isolated violence is adventurism and an erroneous
> policy.[53]

This attitude apparently set the framework in which the October meeting
had to operate. Party units were directed to give propaganda support but not to
rise. In an effort to monitor the situation more effectively (lack of communication with events in the Center was one of the major problems for the Party
leadership, as for Ho Chi Minh, now serving as liaison officer for the Far
Eastern Bureau of the Comintern in Hong Kong), the plenum decided to send
a member of the committee, Nguyen Phong Sac, to advise the Regional Committee in central Vietnam, and to establish a permanent bureau (Trung Uong
Thuong Vu) of three members in Saigon to direct Party affairs within
Vietnam.[54]

The French response, when it came, was fierce and inexorable. The French
military forces located permanently in the area were considered to be inadequate (there were only a handful of Vietnamese troops under the command of
a French noncommissioned officer at Vinh). When the seriousness of the situation became apparent in September, legionnaires were dispatched and they
pacified the rebellious districts with brutal thoroughness. Local French
authorities were convinced that only severe measures would have the desired
effect, and on the worst day—September 9—French airplanes bombed a column of thousands of peasants marching toward the provincial capital, with
devastating effect. Security measures were put into effect in the troubled areas,
and the local police rounded up all those suspected of being Communists or of
involvement in the uprising. Gradually, the regime's efforts began to take hold.
By early 1931, the insurgents had suffered severe losses in a series of pitched
battles with government forces. Bad planning, strategic errors, and a lack of
weapons began to undermine the momentum of the revolutionary forces, and
dissension arose in the ranks. At the end, the movement's mass support began
to drain away, in the inevitable pattern of peasant jacqueries from time im-
memorial, and villages surrendered their Communist leadership to the
authorities.[55] By late spring, the last of the soviets had been forced to surrender. Sullen but exhausted, the rebellious districts once again fell under the
boot of their colonial masters.

For the newborn Indochinese Communist Party, the price of failure was severe. In a few weeks, Ho Chi Minh's painstaking efforts to build up the nucleus of a loyal and disciplined Party were swept away in the fury of French repression. In the immediate aftermath of the revolt, more than one thousand suspected Communists were seized and charged with involvement in the events. Eighty were executed, including several from within the top leadership of the Party, and nearly 400 were sentenced to long terms in prison. Virtually the entire Central Committee was seized during a plenary meeting in Saigon, including Party Secretary General Tran Phu, who died in prison the following September. According to Communist estimates, total losses to the Party were 2,000 dead and 51,000 militants were arrested. Up to 90 percent of the Party leadership ended up in prison or before the firing squad. The purge extended beyond the border. Police in Hong Kong, alerted by the seizure of a Comintern agent in Singapore, rounded up several Party members serving abroad, including Ho Chi Minh.

Nghe Tinh in Retrospect

The Nghe Tinh revolt raises a number of interesting questions, not only about the extent of Comintern responsibility, but also about the causes and character of peasant rebellion in Asia. The first is perhaps easier to answer than the second. There appears to be no doubt that the Comintern's insistence on the imminence of revolution in Asia played a role in instigating the revolt. Local Communist Party organizers were acting in direct response to the instructions of the Comintern when they provoked the agitation in factories, on rubber plantations, and in the villages.

Moscow's advice to the young Communist movement was based on two related assumptions: (1) that a revolutionary upsurge in Vietnam was imminent, and (2) that this upsurge had a reasonable chance of developing from a bourgeois revolt into a second stage led by the proletariat, even in the absence of a mature and disciplined Communist Party. In the first assumption, Moscow was at least partly right. In the Center, a revolutionary situation of almost classical proportions had arisen. Here, several factors converged to create an explosive situation: a long tradition of rebellious behavior; a corrupt and unpopular imperial government with an image (largely deserved) of weakness and incompetence; the presence of an organized revolutionary movement native to the region and well entrenched at the local level; and the fortuitous combination of urban-rural ties in the vicinity of the provincial capital, the lack of adequate government forces in the area, a chronically high degree of poverty, overcrowding, and landlessness; all compounded by the sudden climatic disaster.

Unfortunately for the revolutionary cause, the high level of discontent in Annam was not duplicated elsewhere. Although pockets of unrest existed in several areas, the discontent in the North and the South was not as generalized or as deep as it was in the Center. In actuality, most rural areas were apathetic, and in the cities the earlier wave of nationalism was at a temporary standstill. In that sense, the Party's agitational efforts in the rubber plantations and the Mekong delta had been misleading for, by suggesting that discontent was widespread and explosive, they may have led to an unwarranted optimism among Party members.

Under such circumstances, Moscow's second assumption, that a rural uprising in one area of the country could take hold and spread to other rural areas and into the cities, was a dangerous misreading of conditions in Vietnam. More specifically, the Comintern had underestimated the complexities involved in instigating a successful rebellion in a colonial society in Southeast Asia and had miscalculated the means to carry it out. In the conditions then pertaining, a Communist revolt waged against colonial power in Southeast Asia had little chance of success. Peasant rebellions and nationalist revolts, such as the VNQDD uprising at Yen Bay, were of course real signs of local unrest and undoubtedly encouraged strategists in Moscow to believe that a revolutionary upsurge was on the horizon in Vietnam. But, as the Comintern had correctly foreseen, peasant revolts were unlikely to succeed unless they could spread to urban areas. In 1930, however, revolutionary elements lacked the capacity to pose a serious challenge to the government authority in the cities. Not only were the radicals too few in number, poorly organized, and lacking in weapons, but they were operating in an environment favorable to the enemy. The cities represented the heart of colonial power and, unlike the tottering traditionalist monarchies that had fallen under the onslaught of revolutionary forces in Europe, the colonial regimes in Southeast Asia did not lack the will or the capacity to defend their interests. Urban discontent, such as had occurred in Saigon a few years earlier, could provide a momentary irritant but was unlikely seriously to challenge the stability of the colonial regime.

The French were more vulnerable, of course, to attack in the countryside. Even there, however, the assumption that a peasant revolt could assume nationwide proportions was a misreading of Asian conditions. For a variety of factors—geographic and climatic differences, variations in landownership or in the nature of governmental administration, as well as the notorious volatility of peasant discontent—made it difficult to establish a rural insurgency movement on a nationwide basis and to sustain it long enough and with enough intensity to shake the colonial regime. This was one of the primary lessons of the Nghe Tinh uprising. To transform a rural rebellion into a serious threat to colonial rule would require an experienced revolutionary Party, disciplined, sure-handed, and able to tread the thin line between excessive caution and adventurism. It would require organization and painstaking preparation in order to build a broad base of support throughout the countryside. And it would require a firm base among anticolonial elements in the cities. In a word, it would require a full understanding of the protracted character of revolt in Asia.

Here Comintern revolutionary doctrine had been seriously deficient. For, in advising the infant Communist Party that a revolution could succeed in the absence of a mature and experienced revolutionary organization, it had placed a premium on revolutionary spontaneity and had dangerously underestimated the difficulties of staging a successful insurrection. It is true that the overall thrust of Comintern influence was on the need to form a highly professional and disciplined revolutionary organization. And Lenin had first seen the importance of linking social revolution to the forces of peasant discontent and nationalism in Asia. This tradition had been transmitted to the Vietnamese revolutionary movement through Comintern directives and the training provided at the Stalin School. Without it, there would have been little to distinguish the Communists from their rivals.

But, by 1930, the Comintern—mesmerized by the vision of a revolutionary outbreak throughout Asia—had forgotten the implications of its own prescriptions for revolution in the area and its influence seriously misled the young Communist Party and contributed in no small measure to its tragic defeat. Ho Chi Minh had come somewhat closer to reality in his 1927 article on armed insurrection. He had sensed the importance of the force of rural revolt, had pleaded for greater attention to the role of the peasant in the revolutionary process in rural societies, and had correctly foreseen that Asian revolutions would necessarily be protracted. Still, he too had overestimated the capacity of the Communist leadership to transform a spontaneous revolt into a nationwide uprising and had underestimated the ability of the colonial regime to quell any challenge to its authority. It was a lesson that he would not forget.[56]

To return briefly to the issue raised earlier: Was the 1930 revolt spontaneous or the work of Communist activists? It is still too early for a conclusive answer. Obviously both objective and subjective factors played a role in the final result. But the evidence currently available suggests that the active participation of local Party cadres was a major factor in stimulating the revolt. At a minimum, the intervention of local Party operatives transformed a disorganized jacquerie into a relatively disciplined uprising. Eventually, peasant anger escaped the confines of Party control and the revolt deteriorated into sporadic terror and violence. Party inexperience and the ambivalence of the leadership undoubtedly contributed to the tragic results. But to the perceptive, there were useful lessons to be learned from the catastrophe. It demonstrated the explosive power of peasant discontent in rural villages and indicated that if city and country could be effectively linked, a revolutionary alliance would be created that, like wind and rain, would sweep everything before it and wash away the debris of centuries.

3
The Stalinist Years
(1930–1941)

In later years, Communist Party historians in Hanoi would occasionally claim that the Nghe Tinh revolt had set the Vietnamese revolution on a new course that would inexorably lead to victory nearly half a century later. By that reasoning, the rebellion could be portrayed as the first step in the emergence of an independent revolutionary doctrine based on an alliance between radical urban intellectuals and a revolutionary peasantry, a combination frequently set forth as the prerequisite for successful revolution in Asia. Unfortunately, the record is not quite so clear-cut. In fact, in the early 1930s more than ever, ICP strategy was made in Moscow. And Moscow was not yet ready to trim its ideological sails to adjust to Asian realities.

Vietnamese Communist Policy and the Comintern

One of the major sources of Soviet domination over the fledgling Vietnamese Communist movement was its continuing influence over the Party leadership through the famous Stalin School, the Communist University of the Toilers of the East. Whether Ho Chi Minh formally graduated from this institution has not been disclosed, but it is probable that he first absorbed there the intricacies of Marxist-Leninist doctrine. During the early years of the movement, many of the Revolutionary Youth League's leading members had no Moscow experience, a fact that (at least to Moscow) may have explained the organization's erratic behavior. By the late 1920s, the Comintern was actively attempting to remedy that defect and the most promising young members of the league were being sent to Moscow for ideological training. In 1931, according to estimates of the French Sûreté, there were approximately forty Vietnamese studying in the various programs offered at the Stalin School. Each received an intensive introduction into the history of the Communist Party of the Soviet Union and a strong foundation in the Stalinist interpretation of Marxist-Leninist doctrine.

The injection of this new "Stalinist" core into the bloodstream of the Vietnamese Communist movement had already begun when the Nghe Tinh revolt broke out in 1930, and at least two members of the new Central Committee, including secretary General Tran Phu, were returnees from Moscow. But the French seizure of the ICP leadership in the spring of 1931 accelerated the process and facilitated the replacement of league veterans by Moscow-trained people. As soon as the news of the arrest of the old Central Committee reached Moscow, the Comintern decided to send several students at the Stalin School back to Vietnam by circuitous routes to form the nucleus of a new leadership.

Because of the harsh French repression, Comintern plans for the revival of the ICP were extremely cautious. For the moment, the Central Committee was not reestablished. In its place, a temporary External Direction Bureau (Ban Chi Huy Hai Ngoai) was set up in Kwangsi Province in South China under the leadership of Moscow returnee Le Hong Phong. Within Vietnam, the regional apparatus was in disarray and it was decided to rebuild the Party from the ground up. Each returned student was instructed to create a cell that would absorb any Party remnants still operating in his immediate vicinity.

The policy was not immediately successful. The French (whose agents were scattered throughout the revolutionary movement), were well informed as to the movements of the students when they left the Soviet Union, and most were arrested soon after their arrival in Vietnam. According to French sources, by late 1932, out of thirty-five Vietnamese who were registered at the Stalin School in the early 1930s, seventeen had been arrested, two had surrendered, ten were still in Moscow, and only six were active in Vietnam.[1]

Prison, however, was not always the end of the road. The French jails in Indochina were full of radicals during the early 1930s and were so well organized and controlled by their Communist inmates that they were labeled "schools of Bolshevism." Indoctrination was achieved by the memorization of texts printed on toilet paper; a Party journal, *Lao tu tap chi* (The prison review), was secretly published and distributed; and clandestine Party meetings were held, complete with the singing of songs to keep up spirits. Many Communists died in prison and others betrayed the Party, but the ICP was able to recoup its losses by luring new recruits from rival organizations. Then there were periodic amnesties ordered from Paris, which enraged the local French intelligence services in Vietnam. In the year 1933 alone, more than six thousand prisoners were released by decree from Paris. Sometimes the large number of ex-prisoners in the Party caused problems. Veteran Communists suspected that many had been transformed into French agents while in prison, and one ICP source contended that only one ex-prisoner in a hundred could be trusted after his release.[2]

It is a measure of the tenacity of the Party that, despite such problems, it began to revive. By 1933, regional committees had been secretly reestablished. The healthiest was in Cochin China, where Stalin School graduate Tran Van Giau was able to build a dynamic organization despite French harassment and frequent brief stays in prison. The government's concern soon began to be reflected in French intelligence reports, which increasingly complained that the

Sûreté was powerless to counteract the resurgence of revolutionary forces in Indochina.

Because most new Party leaders were veterans of training in Moscow, it is not surprising that more than ever before or after ICP policy reflected the policies of the Comintern and of Stalin. The defeat of revolutionary forces in China and Indochina had not diminished the conviction in Moscow that a new revolutionary wave leading to the disintegration of the capitalist system was in the offing. Indeed, although the Nghe Tinh revolt had gone down to defeat, Soviet commentaries continued to insist that the revolutionary situation in Vietnam was excellent. Nor had the example of Nghe Tinh diminished Moscow's stubborn conviction that revolution in Asia must be built on the small Asian proletariat. Comintern directives emphasized the necessity for proletarian leadership of local Communist parties, while moderate forces were viewed with suspicion. The Vietnamese Party leadership was criticized for its failure to recruit aggressively among the Vietnamese proletariat and at one point was instructed to send more candidates of worker origin to the Stalin School in Moscow. The party did its best to comply. Intellectuals were required to meet more stringent requirements for admission into the Party than were workers. The slogan of the period was "to the enterprises," as the Party stressed the organization of cells in factories and enterprises in preparation for an eventual seizure of power by a Bolshevik-style insurrection in the cities of Asia.[3]

The Party could hardly totally ignore the peasants, of course. In some areas, particularly in Cochin China, where economic conditions had begun to decline since the onset of the Depression, local activists recruited in rural villages, forming seemingly harmless farmers' benevolent associations. Sporadic efforts were undertaken to organize the peasants in Annam and Tonkin as well but these met with little success, as cadres reported that the farmers were apathetic and frequently hostile.[4] Significantly, what little success the Party did have in rural areas was often a cause for concern to higher echelons, whose urban-oriented members feared that too much effort in the countryside would dilute the proletarian leadership within the Party. This concern appears to have been particularly strong with reference to developments in Cochin China. An article in the December 30, 1933, issue of *Tap chi Cong san* (hereafter referred to as *Communist Review*) stressed the necessity for worker leadership and commented with obvious regret that

> the workers' movement is less developed in Cochin China than the peasant movement. In the cities, members of our Party are fewer than in the countryside. This is because revolutionary work is more difficult among workers than among peasants. In particular, it is very hard to penetrate enterprises at a time when the number employed is diminishing. Second, revolutionary propaganda among workers demands time.[5]

Similar problems apparently existed elsewhere. Said the review *Bolshevik*, the official organ of the External Direction Bureau:

> There are still some comrades in Tonkin who believe that the peasants constitute the principal force of the Indochinese revolutionary movement and not the proletarians, on the pretext that the rural masses constitute nine-tenths of the population. We recognize that the peasants are numerous, but quantity should not be confused with command. In effect, if we consider the peasants as the leading force, one must believe that the directing role of the revolutionary movement should be in their hands and not in that of the workers. Such a judgment is mistaken, because the peasantry is a heterogeneous class anxious to retain its land, very amorphous and slow from an ideological and practical point of view, and very disunited—and thus very poorly qualified to assume the direction of a revolutionary movement.[6]

The new leadership also followed Moscow in its limited view of the united front. Not only were moderate reformists such as the Constitutionalists considered unsuitable for alliance, but even radical nationalist parties like the VNQDD were thought unreliable. In fact, the concept of nationalism itself was viewed as "a vestige of the petty bourgeois ideology of the intellectuals and dreamers of the Revolutionary Youth League and the Tan Viet parties." *Communist Review* was critical of "the tendency toward national and patriotic ideology" in the Party press and of patriotic slogans that suggested that it was necessary to have a national revolution before the world revolution.[7]

There is little doubt that such ideas were at variance with the strategy that Ho Chi Minh had advocated a few years earlier and that had been put into practice by the league leadership up to its dissolution in 1930. Indeed, there is some evidence that the new party leadership considered Ho Chi Minh ideologically unreliable and did not hesitate to criticize him for his errors. A chief source of dissatisfaction lay in his reliance on the forces of nationalism and in his willingness to consider the Vietnamese bourgeoisie and small landholders as potential allies in the resistance movement. Both errors had been included in the Party's temporary political program of February 1930, evidently drafted by Ho Chi Minh, and they were transcended by the new program drafted the following October by Party Secretary General Tran Phu.

We are in debt to Nguyen Ai Quoc, said an article in *Communist Review*,

> but our comrades should not forget the nationalist legacy of Nguyen Ai Quoc and his erroneous instructions on the fundamental questions of the bourgeois democratic revolutionary movement in Indochina, and his opportunist theories which are still rooted in the spirit of the adherents of the League and the *Tan Viet*. . . . Nguyen Ai Quoc did not understand the directives of the Communist International; he did not fuse the three Communist organizations of Indochina from top to bottom and did not put into prior discussion the tactics that the Communist

International had to apply to extirpate the opportunist elements of these sections. The brochure entitled "political principles" and the statutes of the unified Party did not exactly follow the instructions of the Communist International. Nguyen Ai Quoc also advocated such erroneous and collaborationist tactics as "neutrality with regard to the bourgeoisie and the rich peasants," "alliance with the middle and small landowners," and so forth. It is because of such errors from January to October 1930 that the ICP followed a policy which in many respects was in opposition to the instructions of the Communist International even though it had energetically led the masses in revolutionary struggle, and it is equally because of this that the policy followed by the soviets of Nghe An was not consistent with the Party line.[8]

Given such attitudes, it is clear that the Moscow-trained Party leadership had not embarked on a direct path toward the broad national struggle against foreign imperialism in the postwar period. On the contrary, ICP strategy in the early 1930s adhered strictly to the current line in Moscow. And the current line in Moscow still reflected a broad belief in the universal applicability of the Bolshevik model.

To some students of Party history, it is puzzling that the ICP did not, at this critical juncture, express a greater interest in the experiment being undertaken at Juichin in South China. By this time, the Maoist faction within the CCP had already begun to fashion its strategy for a seizure of power—a strategy based on control of the rural areas and the active support of the peasant masses.

In fact, during the early and mid-1930s the ICP had tenuous ties with its fraternal party in China. In the previous decade, the league had relied on the CCP to a degree for training, for ideological direction and for the maintenance of secure and reliable communications with Moscow. But such practical links had been rendered more difficult by Chiang Kai-shek's harassment of Communist activities in South China after the breakup of the Kuomintang-CCP alliance. Moreover, Vietnamese revolutionaries apparently felt that the CCP was preoccupied with its own problems and tended to view sister parties in Southeast Asia with condescension. By the late 1920s, Comintern officials had grown increasingly concerned over the situation and temporarily deprived the CCP of some of its directing authority over Communist activities in Southeast Asia. Then, too, for the Vietnamese, doctrinal verities and the guiding hand of experience were to be found in Moscow. From Ho Chi Minh on down, ties with the Soviet Union were considered more important than the informal ones with the CCP.

The situation did not change when Mao began to practice his heretical doctrine in the hilly borderlands of Kiangsi Province. By all accounts, the Vietnamese were barely aware of his presence and had no contacts there in the early 1930s. Even communications with CCP headquarters in Shanghai were sporadic. In 1932, soon after his release from prison in Hong Kong, Ho Chi Minh was reduced to making contact with the CCP through a letter-box drop at the home of Sun Yat-sen's widow, Soong Ch'ing-ling. By contrast, communications with the Comintern continued, although with increasing difficulty, and most ICP leaders shared the old-school-tie link with the Stalin School. It is not surprising that, for the ICP in the 1930s, all roads led to Moscow.

Clouds of War

In 1933, a moderate shift took place in the attitude of the Comintern toward the concept of the united front. The rise of Hitler—once it became evident that Nazism was not just a passing phenomenon but a real threat to the Soviet Union—stimulated interest in the bourgeoisie as a progressive force against fascism. There was still to be no alliance with bourgeois parties as a whole, but Communist parties were instructed to attempt to win over the progressive urban middle class. This policy shift may have confused the ICP leadership, which continued to follow a rigidly narrow policy toward other classes, and someone in the Party asked the Comintern for clarification. This inspired the famous "Entretien avec les camarades indochinois," an article published in late 1933 by the Ukrainian leader Dmitri Manuilsky under the pseudonym of Orgwald. The article attempted to discourage the Vietnamese Communists from taking an excessively narrow view of the united front. There were few urban workers in Vietnam, it reminded them, and in the course of its struggle the Party must attempt to win over the peasantry and even some of the bourgeoisie. The most effective means of winning such support, it said, was that of antiimperialism. In response to a question about the attitude to be taken toward the nationalist parties in Vietnam, the author hedged. That depends, he said, on the objective situation: What classes do they represent? Do they oppose imperialism? If so, the Communist can struggle alongside them, while unmasking their inconsistencies and making demands that go further than theirs. Communists and their allies should march separately, he said, but struggle together. It was also important to remember, he added, that the revolutionary wave had not declined. The Nghe Tinh debacle of 1931 was not a defeat, just a momentary ebb in the revolutionary tide.[9]

Moscow's stubborn conviction that revolution was on the horizon reflected a serious misreading of reality in Vietnam, as in the world. In Vietnam, the turbulent events at the end of the preceding decade had been succeeded by a period of lethargy. If the radicals had been soundly reproved, the middle classes had been frightened by the specter of communism in Central Vietnam and became increasingly hesitant to support radical causes openly. The French, shaken by the revolt, encouraged the trend by offering a few modest reforms designed to win moderate support.

The rise of Hitler in Germany demonstrated that the trend in the West was as much toward the right as toward the left. In Asia, Japan's expansionist policies led Tokyo to try to revise the balance of power in the Pacific. Convinced that protection of the Soviet Union from world fascism must take precedence over all other claims, Stalin unveiled a new policy at the Seventh Comintern Congress, held in Moscow in the summer of 1935. Member parties were instructed to join in popular fronts with non-Communist parties in defense of the world progressive forces headed by the Soviet Union.[10] Once again, the perceived needs of the Soviet Union were translated into a new revolutionary strategy for the world Communist movement.

The new policy took the ICP leadership by surprise. Only four months earlier, in March, the Party had held its First National Congress in the Portuguese colony of Macao. The decisions taken there had represented a reaffirmation of existing strategy, as determined by the directives of the Thirteenth Plenum of the Comintern's Executive Committee of December 1933. The political resolution issued at the end of the meeting had stressed the vision of two opposing camps, imperialist and socialist, and emphasized a narrow concept of the united front.

Le Hong Phong, chief ICP delegate at the Moscow congress, transmitted the new policy to the ICP. Realizing the incompatibility between the policies enunciated at the Macao conference and the new popular front strategy, he called a plenary meeting of the new elected Central Committee in July 1936 to bring ICP policies into line with those of Moscow. The resolution of that plenum is apparently not extant, but the nature of the decisions taken can be ascertained from a confidential letter explaining the new policy that the Central Committee sent to the lower echelons of the Party. The letter informed the Party membership that the basic ICP task at this time was to follow the new Comintern line and to create an antiimperialist popular front. Revolutionary action, it said, does not consist only of violence and preparations for the general insurrection. The general uprising leading to revolutionary victory would only come when the objective and subjective conditions are present in Vietnam and when the world situation is appropriate. The Nghe Tinh uprising and the Yen Bay revolt were some of "the most glorious pages in the history of our people," but they went down to defeat because "they were launched hastily, before the realization of indispensable conditions."[11] The Party could not hasten this process.

For the moment, the letter continued, the Party's policy must coincide with the actual conditions in Vietnam and throughout the world. Because the main danger to the worlds' peoples is fascism, the Communists must join with other progressive forces in Indochina in a common struggle against this menace. All nationalist parties must be considered as potential ICP allies. Parties like the VNQDD should not be scorned but should be encouraged to combat at the Party's side. The Party's attitude toward the moderates must also be changed. Up to now, the ICP "has tried to alienate them from us by treating them without distinction and their members as antirevolutionaries and as running dogs of imperialism." Such policies are mistaken, a product of the Party's failure to realize that the situation has changed. In times of prosperity, the national bourgeoisie tends to follow the imperialists, but they have suffered badly during the recent economic crisis and at least some of them can now be counted in the progressive camp. To enlist their support, the Party must encourage the formation of a broad front that is based not on narrow class struggle but on demands for peace, food, and national liberation. This collaboration should not be permitted to undermine the Party's independence of organization or the sanctity of its ultimate goals and program. But it should be aimed at broadening the base of the movement and at increasing the level of legal activity while maintaining the Party's secret apparatus for future contingencies.

It was one thing to announce a new popular front strategy and quite another to put it into effect. During the 1930s, hostility between the ICP and rival nationalist organizations ran high, as Party cadres actively attempted to undermine their competitors. It would take a major effort to undo this animosity. Moreover, the Party's move into the open would also depend on the willingness of the colonial government to permit the Communists to operate in the political arena, something they had heretofore not allowed.

The latter problem was at least partially resolved in the spring of 1936 when a new Popular Front government came to power in France under the leadership of the Socialist Léon Blum. Although the FCP was not formally a part of the governing coalition, it did offer its support in parliament. The new government in Paris promised to order the formation of a colonial commission to study conditions in the colonies. The fresh political climate in Paris soon began to influence conditions in Indochina, as the government adopted a more open attitude toward Vietnamese political activities, particularly in Cochin China.

In an effort to take advantage of the new situation, the Party leadership elaborated demands for reform and sent out a public letter to all nationalist parties asking for cooperation in drawing up a list of demands conforming to the interests of the majority of the population for eventual submission to the colonial government. It also proposed that an "Indochinese congress" be formed to solicit the views of the people and to transmit these views to the Colonial Commission when it visited Indochina.

To implement these plans, the Party began actively to seek out cooperation from other nationalist groups and progressive political factions throughout Vietnam. In the Center and North, local Party groups attempted to coordinate efforts with other parties in electing candidates to the regional legislative assemblies established by the French in the immediate postwar period. A representative was sent to South China to talk with squabbling VNQDD factions about possible alliance.[12] In Cochin China, where political activity was more openly permitted, the Party cooperated with moderates and progressives in appointing an Executive Committee to stimulate the movement to form an Indochinese congress.

Party-building efforts were not neglected. Recruitment was stepped up in working-class areas and, significantly, in rural villages. Because of the more relaxed policies followed by the government in Saigon, such activities were most successful in Cochin China. The keystone of the ICP's strategy in this area was the formation of so-called action committees, small organizations created by Communist cadres at the local level—in villages, factories, schools, and commercial enterprises—to formulate the masses' demands for reforms on the part of the French administration. This technique, though tacitly permitted by the authorities, was highly effective in entrenching the Party apparatus at the local level and in enhancing its appeal as a voice for popular discontent. Much of the Party's support in working class areas in Saigon and Cholon and in villages in the Mekong delta in later years can be traced to this early effort.[13]

The new strategy was not uniformly welcomed by Party regulars. Many endorsed the new approach only with reluctance. Veterans of the long years of clandestine operation distrusted the "politicos" who operated in the open, publishing journals and taking part in legislative assemblies. Others felt an instinctive inability to cooperate with moderate nationalists. Even the ICP press, now tacitly permitted to publish under certain restrictions, reflected this attitude, and the leadership was forced to criticize the editorial staffs for their inadequate attempts to appeal to middle-class interests and concerns. In working-class areas, union organizers were reluctant to transform their hard-won secret organizations into quasi-legal "mutual assistance associations," which would be more easily subject to crackdowns by the authorities. By 1937, the grumbling and discontent had reached the point where an enlarged Central Committee plenum met in August and September and issued a directive that was highly critical of sectarianism and the failure of some Party members to follow the new strategy.[14]

Ironically the Party's closest collaborator during the early 1930s was the one organization that Moscow now specifically ruled out for alliance. Trotskyism had made its appearance in the Vietnamese radical movement in the late 1920s, when a number of Vietnamese studying in Paris had been attracted to this offshoot of Marxism-Leninism. During the early 1930s the Trotskyites were granted permission to publish in Cochin China and had set up their own newspaper, *La Lutte*. For several years, members of the ICP had collaborated with the Trotskyites on the editorial board and in putting up candidates for election to the Saigon Municipal Council. Although Moscow did not formally permit such cooperation, for a while it appeared to tolerate it.

As the popular front developed, however, cooperation became more difficult. Trotskyites opposed the Comintern strategy of alliance with bourgeois parties against the common danger of fascism and accused the ICP of collusion with the class enemy against the interests of the proletariat. For a short time, collaboration continued in the midst of growing friction. A message from the External Direction Bureau (probably written in the summer of 1936) said that "if the Trotskyites sincerely enter the popular front, we will voluntarily accept them, but we will always be careful, because we must judge people by their acts, not by their words."[15] By 1937 however, rivalry had increased and it broke into the pages of *La Lutte*, as Trotskyites and Stalinists on the editorial board traded jibes and bitter charges on the front page of their newspaper. The final decision to break off relations was apparently made in Moscow. In May 1937, Secretary General Gitton of the FCP—probably speaking for Moscow—sent a letter to the ICP in which he said that French comrades considered that any further collaboration with the Trotskyites in Vietnam would be considered "impossible."[16] Even then, the ICP may not have responded with sufficient alacrity, for in midsummer a high-ranking member of the FCP paid an official visit to Indochina, presumably to convey to the Party leadership in Vietnam the seriousness with which Moscow viewed any further cooperation with Trotskyites in Saigon. After this visit, collaboration ceased entirely and in succeeding years the two factions competed for support among workers and intellectuals in Saigon—not always to the ICP's advantage.

How effective was the popular front from the Communist point of view? Did it serve the interests of the ICP as well as those of Moscow? Certainly on a short-term basis the strategy was not particularly effective. The movement to establish an Indochinese congress was viewed by the French government (probably with reason) as laden with potentially anti-French overtones, and it used a variety of techniques to divide the movement and prevent it from gaining momentum. The action committees were disbanded by government decree, and a number of Communists were arrested. Even the planned visit of the Colonial Commission to Indochina was eventually cancelled at the request of the colonial authorities. By mid-1937, the congress movement was over.

Nor did the Party's effort to create a vast democratic front with substantial ICP participation achieve gratifying results. Although a few minor parties cooperated with the ICP on short-term issues, the Vietnamese middle class was politically inert during the 1930s and still fundamentally suspicious of the Communist motives. From the VNQDD to the moderate Constitutionalists, reaction to the ICP's front policy was cautious. When the momentum began to decline in 1937, the Party had not broadened its alliance to any substantial degree.

Yet the policy had succeeded in other ways. For the first time, the Party had moved into the open, particularly in Cochin China, and in the process it had managed to expand its influence in several areas—among urban workers in the industrial sectors of Saigon-Cholon, many of whom increasingly came to view the Communists as the staunchest defenders of their economic interests; among the rural population in Cochin China, where economic conditions were deteriorating and peasants were favorably impressed by the ICP's campaign to abolish the unpopular capitation tax; and among urban intellectuals, many of whom gradually came to view the Party as a fundamentally nationalist force, indeed the only political force capable of mounting effective resistance to the French colonial regime. Less success was achieved in Annam and Tonkin.

Stringent French policies are a partial explanation, but Party historians admit that incompetent leadership also played a role. Outside of Cochin China, the drive to form action committees had only modest success and in some areas was totally prohibited by government authorities. Strictly speaking, the congress movement was a striking success only in the South, where more than six hundred committees were formed and thousands participated in gathering "*cahiers des voeux.*" Even if the Party had built a substantial basis of support in Cochin China, its future in the Center and the North was still in doubt.

The Party also took advantage of the respite from government oppression to build its membership. According to French figures, the size of the Party increased markedly during the period of the popular front and by early 1939 it had more than two thousand members and forty thousand followers.[17] When compared to the records of its rivals, its performance was even more impressive. The VNQDD, with its leadership in South China, was relatively inactive in Vietnam during this period. The Constitutionalists, riven by personality conflicts, were in a state of near disintegration. A few minor moderate political parties had been formed among urban intellectuals but were too intimidated by official harassment to pose a serious threat to the government. By the late 1930s, the ICP was virtually alone in carrying the banner of Vietnamese nationalism.

In sum, the popular front period opened a new era in the history of the Communist Party in Vietnam. For the ICP had returned to the strategy of the league and once again began to seek support from peasants and urban moderates in pursuit of a common goal. The change had been somewhat hesitant and the results were ambivalent, but at least a precedent had been set. Taking advantage of the respite from the crushing oppression of the colonial security apparatus, the ICP began to operate, under certain obvious constraints, within the public domain. Three years of semilegal activity served to domesticate the Party, to expose it to public view as "communism with a human face," and to show that the Communists were not wild-eyed fanatics but patriotic Vietnamese struggling to build a better Vietnam. The period of the Popular Front brought the ICP into the mainstream of Vietnamese politics—a position from which it would not henceforth retreat without a struggle.

Prelude to Revolt
(1941–1945)

The main justification for the popular front, in Moscow's eyes, had been to unite all political forces against the danger of world fascism. Until 1938, fascism seemed to pose relatively little danger to the population of French Indochina. Germany was distant. Japan, although aggressive and unpredictable, was bogged down in China and appeared to be more interested in Manchuria and Soviet Siberia than in the lands to the south.

By 1938, however, Japanese attacks in South China had raised the specter of war over Indochina. Despite reassurances from French military sources that the Indochinese Union was "perfectly capable" of defending itself against any aggressive force, there was a widespread public impression that French forces were inadequate to protect France's colonial possessions in Southeast Asia. Japan's invasion of South China (including the occupation of Hainan Island across the Gulf of Tonkin from Haiphong harbor) and its growing interest in forming a Tokyo-Bangkok axis showed that the Japanese government had designs on Southeast Asia.

The authorities in Hanoi were now concerned and attempted to take remedial action. The budget was increased and taxes were raised to permit larger expenditures for defense. Plans were drawn up to double the size of military schools in the French army, as a means of encouraging volunteers for armed service. In attempting to strengthen Indochina against a possible external attack, however, the government faced a painful dilemma. Not only was it expected to provide for the defense of Indochina, but it was also requested to help meet the defense needs of metropolitan France against possible German attack. Paris was desperate for Indochinese recruits for military service and factory labor. There was no question where the priorities lay. When General Catroux replaced Jules Brevie as governor-general of Indochina in the summer of 1939, Minister of Colonies Mandel informed him bluntly that the foremost need was to protect France in its hour of crisis. The needs of Indochina would have to wait.

The ICP, still guided by Moscow's determination to pursue the strategy of the popular front, found itself supporting the government, at least on the issue of national defense, although characteristically it combined its support with sharp criticism of the way defense policy was being carried out. An editorial in the Party's official journal *Dan chung* [The people] said that the Party

> approves the defense of Indochina against fascist aggression. We assert that the measures taken by the government are totally insufficient, that we must increase the ability of the masses to help in a spiritual as well as a material sense. If it wants this, the government must proclaim democratic freedoms and improvements in living conditions so that the people can increase their strength to resist. At the same time, it must organize the masses in national defense units [*hoi quoc phong*], so that when the war comes, the masses will be armed. Only then will we have defensive strength.[1]

The Party's decision to support the government, obviously inspired by the Comintern, was not an easy one and led to embarrassing attacks from the Trotskyites, who refused to support the popular front and labeled ICP behavior as treasonous to the working class of Indochina. To some degree, the criticism stuck. In the Saigon municipal elections in 1939, a Trotskyite slate easily defeated the Stalinist entry.

War in Europe

The news of the signing of the Nazi-Soviet pact in late August 1939 and the German attack on Poland in September had immediate repercussions in Vietnam. Governor-general Catroux, who arrived to take over his post on the day of the Nazi invasion of Poland, declared general mobilization in Indochina. Moderates leaped to the support of France as it declared war on Germany. Le Quang Liem, a member of the Constitutionalist Party and an editor of the moderate French-language newspaper *Tribune Indochinoise*, declared that "to serve France in war is the first duty of the Indochinese peoples toward the protecting nation" and called on all his countrymen to respond to the order for general mobilization.

The Communists did not share in the atmosphere of unity that followed the outbreak of war in Europe. Indeed, the signing of the Nazi-Soviet pact in August was a clear indication that Stalin had abandoned his attempt to form an alliance with the Western democracies against Hitler's Germany and Japan. In France, the FCP was quickly driven to cover. In Indochina, Catroux followed suit and immediately took action against the ICP. In late September, he closed down its newspapers and declared the Party illegal. In the short run, the government's action was a serious blow to Communist fortunes in Vietnam. The Party had made rapid strides in increasing its membership during the summer of 1939, and its position as a major force had never been so well established. In the days following the outlawing of the Party, 2,000 suspected Communists were arrested throughout Vietnam, 600 of them in Cochin China alone.[2] Among those seized were several Party leaders. Ironically, however, the French crackdown ultimately proved to be a vital tonic to the Party's fortunes. Compelled to abandon its emphasis on urban areas, the Party retreated to the countryside and began to entrench itself in preparation for a long period of illegal work. This involuntary shift in its center of gravity had momentous consequences for the future.

For the time being, the unexpected events of August and September forced the Party to reassess its political strategy and to devise a replacement for the now-defunct popular front approach that had dominated its thinking for three years. In early September, immediately after learning of the French declaration of war on Germany, the ICP's new secretary general, Nguyen Van Cu, convened an expanded meeting of the North Vietnamese Regional Committee to consider the means of adjusting the Party's strategy to deal with the new situation.[3] The conference discussed the possibility that the colonial authorities would take immediate action against the ICP and ways by which the Party could protect its cadres and revolutionary bases and make an orderly shift to secret operations.[4] There was apparently some consideration of a proposal to use the opportunity presented by France's preoccupation with war in Europe to stimulate an uprising aimed at national liberation. After all, Moscow had often commented that world war was normally the best time for revolution. Ultimately, the regional conference decided to postpone any major decisions until the convening of a Central Committee plenum. In the meantime, it decided to take preliminary measures to protect the Party's cadres and to begin to build strong revolutionary bases in mountain and forest regions. At the close of the conference, Nguyen Van Cu left for Saigon to convene a meeting of the full Central Committee.

The Sixth Plenum of the Party Central Committee took place November 6–8, in the village of Hoc Mon in Gia Dinh Province, twelve miles (twenty kilometers) from Saigon.[5] Although documents from the plenum are not widely available to Western scholars, it is possible to piece together from various sources the new line promulgated by the Party leadership. Most important, perhaps, the plenum recognized that the existing definition of the united front, calling for cooperation with all progressive groups to defend Indochina against Nazism and fascism, had to be revised. Now viewing the European conflict as a capitalist war between two reactionary forces—fascist capitalism and democratic capitalism—the conference announced the formation of a new Antiimperialist National United Front to struggle for national independence. Evoking the spirit of such Vietnamese heroes as the sisters Trung, Tran Hung Dao, Le Loi, and Phan Dinh Phung, the declaration called for an alliance of all Indochinese peoples against imperialist war. Not surprisingly, the class components of the new front differed in some respects from those of its predecessor. Where the popular front had called for alliance with all progressive and reformist parties, the new front would not ally with national reformists (such as the

Constitutionalists), but only with the most anticolonial elements in Vietnamese society.

What was most significant about the Sixth Plenum, however, was not the makeup of the new united front, but its view of revolutionary strategy. Since the formation of the popular front in 1936, the Party's strategy had called for legal or semilegal activities to defend Indochina against the danger of world fascism. Armed struggle against the class enemy and preparation for the final general uprising to achieve power were rejected. Now, once again, the struggle against colonialism and for national independence was to receive high priority. The Party was to prepare the conditions for an uprising leading to national liberation. In the words of one Party historian, this was the first time the ICP had pointed to "national liberation" as the number one task.[6]

In preparation for the violent struggle to come, the plenum called for the formation on a nationwide basis of mass associations among the proletariat and peasantry. The new narrower focus of the front did not mean a return to emphasis on class struggle, however. As had been the case since 1936, class interests were to be subordinated, first, to the defense of world socialism and, now, to the interests of national independence. The main strength of the Party, as always, was to lie in the proletarian-peasant alliance. But alliance with patriotic elements among the middle class and even the feudal landlord class was necessary. If class struggle was "too tense," said one commentator, alliance with bourgeois and feudalist elements would be difficult to realize.[7] The result was an uneasy balance between national and class interests.

While the ICP was attempting to put its affairs in order so as to respond to the new situation, the government in Hanoi was seeking to put Indochina on a war footing to prepare for the increasingly probable war with Japan. Catroux's approach was to win support for his policies by combining the carrot with the stick. On September 21, he declared a general amnesty. Yet he was ruthless in his determination to root out communism in Indochina. In a speech in late September he indicated his intention to undertake "a total and rapid" attack on the ICP. All direct and indirect activities of the Party were to be prohibited, all of its organizations were to be disbanded, and any of its members seized by the authorities were to receive heavy prison sentences.

The year 1940 confirmed Japanese plans for expansion into Southeast Asia. Frustrated at its inability to force the Chinese government of Chiang Kai-shek into submission, Japan in early summer demanded that the French close the Hanoi-Kunming railway to shipments of war-related goods to China. Catroux sought support abroad, but he was unsuccessful, and in June he bowed to *force majeure* and agreed to close the border. For the latter, he was dismissed by the new Vichy government in France and replaced by the commander of French naval forces in the Pacific, Admiral Jean Decoux.

At the end of August, Vichy reached an agreement with Tokyo, by which the Japanese formally recognized French sovereignty in Indochina in return for military facilities and transit rights through Indochina and the right to station occupation troops in Tonkin. To work out the details, Decoux was instructed to negotiate with General Nishihara, chief of the new Japanese mission in Hanoi. Final agreement was reached on September 23. Shortly afterward, Japanese troops began to disembark at Haiphong harbor before the eyes of an anxious populace.

The Bac Son Rebellion

On the night of September 22, as the negotiations in Hanoi were closing, Japanese troops crossed the border in force and attacked French troops at the frontier town of Lang Son. Accompanying the Japanese were troops of a pro-Japanese nationalist force loyal to Prince Cuong De, the figurehead member of the Nguyen royal house who had been selected by Phan Boi Chau as titular head for his revolutionary organization forty years before. In recent years, Cuong De had lived in Japan, and he put his trust in Tokyo's promises to restore Vietnamese independence. As the nationalist troops advanced, they appealed to local Vietnamese troops under French command to support the Japanese invasion and to attack their erstwhile colonial masters, who were retreating southward toward Thai Nguyen. In Hanoi, the French protested and the incident was quickly resolved. Nishihara sent a subordinate to the border area and a cease-fire was arranged. French military forces and administrative personnel were permitted to return to their posts, and the Japanese abandoned their Vietnamese allies, who were then easily put down by the French.

When local Communists in the border area became aware of the temporary vacuum created by the Japanese attack at Lang Son, they saw an opportunity to respond to the Sixth Plenum's call for uprisings against the French colonial regime. The border zone around Lang Son, inhabited primarily by minority peoples, had been a fruitful area for Communist activities since the early 1930s, when the first ICP cells were created. By the end of the decade, the Party organization was stronger there than in the densely populated Red River delta to the south. Planning for the revolt was apparently undertaken by a group of Communists who had recently escaped from Lang Son prison during the Japanese invasion. Seeing the chaos left by departing French forces and the unrest of the surrounding population, they held a secret meeting on September 27 and made plans for a military uprising designed to establish revolutionary power throughout the area.

The first major attacks took place at Mo Nhai and Binh Gia, in mountainous Bac Son District a few miles west of Lang Son. Local Communist cadres set up self-defense units, executed class enemies, and established a revolutionary administration.[8] The French soon retook both areas, but the revolutionaries counterattacked and struck elsewhere. For a while, guerrilla activities spread throughout the border area as the Communists prepared to launch an attack on the fort at Lang Son. But the rebels' lack of organization and experience eventually told the story, and by late October the Communist forces, defeated in several engagements, had been forced to retreat to inaccessible mountain areas, there to await order from higher echelons.

The Cochin China Uprising

There was little immediate response elsewhere in Indochina to the unrest in the border area. To a degree, this reflected the watchful attitude of the local population. The French surrender in Europe in June 1940 had been totally unexpected in Indochina, where French military prowess and invincibility had appeared to be a permanent fact of life. In the case of the Communists, the quiet confirmed the weakness of the Party in the face of several months of suppression. In much of the country, especially in the cities, the Party was simply unable to respond.

In Cochin China, however, local Communists were preparing to respond in their own way. Popular discontent was on the rise in the South and provided, at least momentarily, an opportunity for the ICP to release its frustration at the events since the previous September. At the root of the unrest in the South was economics. High taxes, a fall in the price of rice, and an increase in unemployment all served to cut the standard of living for the average Vietnamese. Throughout the spring and summer of 1940, peasant riots took place in several delta provinces. Resentment in rural villages was rising against French conscription for military service along the Cambodian-Thai border, where the threat of war was high. Peasant protests against conscription took place in several towns and villages throughout the delta.

As the wave of discontent in the South rose, the Party's Regional Committee for Cochin China attempted to ride the crest, concentrating its propaganda on peasants and newly-drafted Vietnamese troops. By autumn, half the indigenous troops in Cochin China were allegedly sympathetic to the Communists, with the ICP estimating that up to 30 percent of the entire population of the colony was on its side.[9]

Since the beginning of the year, the regional Party Committee in the South had been discussing the problem of how to implement the Sixth Plenum resolution calling for preparations for an armed revolt against French power.[10] After the French surrender in June, it hastily convened an expanded Party conference in My Tho, which agreed to undertake preparations for an uprising. On October 8, committee member Phan Dang Luu was dispatched to Tonkin to participate in the upcoming Seventh Plenum of the Central Committee and to request its permission to launch an uprising.

The plenum convened on November 6 in a suburb of Hanoi.[11] The meeting took place in the immediate aftermath of the abortive revolt in Bac Son, and its decisions reflected an understandable ambivalence about the possibilities of armed uprising. The session reaffirmed the decision of the Sixth Plenum to call for preparations for a future armed uprising against French power, and it affirmed the contention that, if conditions were favorable, a local uprising could be launched in one area of the country even if Vietnamese society as a whole was not in a revolutionary situation. But it condemned what it considered the mistakes committed at Bac Son. The local leadership at Bac Son, it claimed, did not know how to establish revolutionary power, did not know how to conduct propaganda activities and develop revolutionary strength, and, when the battle was over, did not know how to retreat.[12] The decision to abandon the cities for the countryside was termed an error that weakened the Party's urban base. Then, it said, the Party had lost an opportunity to launch a general uprising after France surrendered in June 1940. Finally, it criticized the new united front as vaguely defined and not sufficiently focused on the worker-peasant alliance. Looking to the future, the plenum concluded that Vietnam was not yet in a directly revolutionary situation, but that the revolution could break out in the form of local uprisings where conditions were appropriate, leading the way toward a general uprising that would result in a seizure of power in the country as a whole. In preparation for that moment, the Central Committee called for the conservation of the remnants of the Bac Son forces, which were to be reorganized as guerrilla units, and for a revolutionary base in the Viet Bac (the Vietnamese term for the northern mountain areas of Tonkin) to wait for the appropriate moment to launch an uprising.

Given the judgments above, it is not surprising that the plenum suspected that conditions for an armed uprising were lacking in the South. Local forces were too small, and units in the Center and the North were in no position to give adequate support. So Phan Dang Luu was informed that an uprising in Cochin China should be postponed until the Central Committee could send a representative to check on the national situation and provide proper leadership. If the uprising should fail in spite of such preparations, the rebels must be prepared to make an orderly retreat and transform the defeated forces into guerrilla units.

Phan Dang Luu returned to Cochin China in mid-November to give his colleagues the bad news. But on the 22nd, he was seized en route, together with several members of the Saigon Party Committee: Le Hong Phong, Nguyen Van Cu, and Phong's wife Nguyen Thi Minh Khai, secretary of the South Vietnamese Party Committee.[13] The French, advised of the upcoming revolt, declared martial law and disarmed all indigenous troops in the area.

In the delta, the Regional Committee was growing increasingly restive. Since the restoration of the Party apparatus in Cochin China in the early 1930s, under the direction of Stalin School returnee Tran Van Giau, the regional Party organization had possessed a unique degree of autonomy and under Giau's autocratic leadership was somewhat inclined toward making decisions independent of the national Party leadership. Now, with 15,000 in the uprising organization and the rebellious troops increasingly impatient for action, the Regional Committee decided that it could wait no longer for the return of Phan Dang Luu and decided to schedule the outbreak for the night of November 22–23. The uprising was concentrated on several district and provincial capitals throughout the Mekong delta. French military posts were to be attacked, communications links cut, and revolutionary power established at the village level. Attacks took place as scheduled in such delta towns as Soc Trang, Bac Lieu, Tan An, Vinh Long, and Can Tho, as well as in rural areas along the edge of the Plain of Reeds. In some areas, the masses seized power, formed revolutionary tribunals to punish class enemies, and raised flags in the name of the National United Front. There were plans for an attack on Saigon as well, but the French prevented disturbances by confiscating weapons and blocking entrances to the city.

The French response was swift. In Saigon an attempted uprising was quelled in a day; in the delta, unrest dragged on and was finally put down in early December. Unlike their counterparts in the Viet Bac, the rebels were unable to preserve their forces by retreating to isolated areas and their defeat signalled the temporary collapse of the Party in Cochin China.[14]

The Formation of the Vietminh

In the spring of 1940, Ho Chi Minh returned to South China, after an absence from the area of more than seven years. Since his release from prison in Hong Kong he had spent most of his time in the Soviet Union as an instructor at the Institute for the Study of National and Colonial Questions. There has been speculation that he was relatively inactive because he was temporarily in disfavor with Stalin. Unfortunately, there is little evidence to prove or disprove this contention. It is clear that he had been ill and had been forced to spend several months in a sanatorium in the Caucasus. By 1938 he had recovered and left the Soviet Union to join Chinese Communist forces in North China.

Since Ho's departure from Asia in 1933, the situation in China had changed radically. In the first place, the Chinese Communists had begun to revive after their disastrous defeat at the hands of Chiang Kai-shek in 1927. After several years of bare survival in the hills of Kiangsi Province, the headquarters of the movement had been transferred to the relatively secure area at Yenan, in the bleak highlands of Shansi Province. Here the Communists gradually began to regain their strength. Here, too, Mao Tse-tung began to extend his domination of the movement and to impose his ideas on the Party.

Ho Chi Minh arrived in Yenan sometime in the fall of 1938, after an arduous trip. At one point, travelling under the name Ho Quang as a member of the Communist Eighth Route Army, he went on foot, pushing a cart for several days from Sian to the Communist headquarters at Yenan, several hundred miles to the north. Ho remained in the Communist wartime capital only a few weeks. There is no record of what he did there or whether he met Mao Tse-tung. From Yenan, he travelled with a delegation led by General Yeh Chien-ying (he later became secretary of defense and chairman of the Standing Committee of the National People's Congress in Peking) to the city of Hanyang. He did not remain there long, perhaps because the city was soon evacuated to avoid Japanese forces advancing up the Yangtze River. When the Kuomintang government moved its wartime capial to Chungking, in mountain-rimmed Szechwan Province, Ho Chi Minh went south with General Yeh's group to Kweiyang, where he allegedly taught the techniques of guerrilla warfare to Nationalist troops. Later he travelled further south to the city of Kweilin, where he served as a radio operator and as manager of the liaison office of the Eighth Route Army in northern Kwangsi Province.

It is unfortunate that we know so little about Ho Chi Minh's activities in wartime China, for it is likely that the experience was quite valuable in providing him with the opportunity to flesh out his still relatively amorphous ideas on a strategy for seizing power in Vietnam. Throughout his years as a revolutionary leader, he had kept abreast of events in China, but there is no indication that he had ever established direct contact with the Maoist faction within the CCP. Yet Mao's ideas on Asian revolution paralleled those of Ho Chi Minh in several respects, and it seems logical that Ho would have found it useful to study Chinese experience at first hand. While still living in Canton in 1927, he had been highly critical of the CCP decision to support the Kuomintang against the forces of peasant unrest during the Northern Expedition (a view also held by Mao Tse-tung in his famous "Report on the Hunan Peasant Uprising") and presumably approved, from a distance, the strategy formulated by Mao Tse-tung in the hills of Kiangsi Province at the end of the decade.

During the 1930s, Ho Chi Minh made no apparent reference to such views while living in Moscow, prudently avoiding the possible wrath of Joseph Stalin. By 1940, however, the situation had begun to change. Soviet preoccupation with the crisis in Europe provided more latitude for Asian Communist leaders to draw up strategies for the liberation of their own societies. Clearly, Ho Chi Minh was not about to let such an opportunity pass.

On his arrival in Kweilin in 1939, he attempted to get in touch with the ICP Central Committee in Vietnam, using the aid of the local Kwangsi office of the CCP as intermediary. The Central Committe, in turn, was equally anxious to make contact with him. A few of the top leaders of the Party were aware that Nguyen Ai Quoc had not died in Hong Kong, as had been widely reported in the press, but had gone on to Moscow. When they heard that he had arrived in South China, they sent an envoy to Lungchow, in Kwangsi Province, to meet him. The delegate ran out of money, however, and was forced to leave before Ho Chi Minh's arrival.[15]

The next April, Ho went on to Kunming, capital of Yunnan Province. Yunnan, like Kwangsi, had become a popular residence-in-exile for Vietnamese nationalist groups. Not only the VNQDD and the ICP, but the pro-Japanese Phuc Quoc as well as remnants of Phan Boi Chau's nearly defunct organization had been active in the area for several years, particularly among Vietnamese workers employed on the Hanoi-Kunming railroad, which had been built by the French at the end of the previous century. With the area now in a highly fluid state as a result of the Japanese invasion along the southern Chinese coast, the southern provinces of Yunnan and Kwangsi presented a relatively secure haven for Vietnamese nationalists and a potential base for political activities in Vietnam.

On his arrival in Yunnan, Ho Chi Minh got in touch with local Communist operatives and resumed his effort to establish contact with the Central Committee in Saigon. For its part, the committee had earlier that spring sent two young and dedicated Party members—Vo Nguyen Giap and Pham Van Dong—to China to find him. In later years, of course, Giap and Dong were destined to become Ho's close comrades-in-arms and coleaders of the Party in the postwar era. Pham Van Dong, offspring of a well-known scholar-gentry family in Annam, had gone to Canton in his twenties to join the Revolutionary Youth League and had studied at the Whampoa Academy. After returning to Vietnam, he was arrested by the French and spent several years in jail. He was released during one of the periodic amnesties granted by the government in Paris and played a role during the popular front as a journalist in Hanoi. Giap, also from Central Vietnam, was originally a member of the New Revolutionary Party and joined the ICP in the early 1930s. With a degree in history from the University of Hanoi, he also became a journalist in Hué during the popular front and in 1940 was teaching at a private high school near Hanoi.[16]

Sometime in the late spring, Giap and Dong arrived in South China and joined Ho Chi Minh and other young Communist Party members in the area, including Phung Chi Kien, a graduate of Whampoa Academy and a member of the CCP since 1927, and Vu Anh, a Communist of worker origin who had been employed on the French-run Yunnan railway. The small group now attempted to prepare the Party to take advantage of the coming crisis. In the process, some of Ho Chi Minh's ideas for future ICP strategy began to emerge. To solidify links with the CCP and to strengthen his colleagues' understanding of the Maoist concept of people's war, he sent Giap and Dong to Yenan to attend a Chinese Communist Party school.[17] Then he turned his attention to the problem of building up an alliance with nationalist factions in South China. Until now, all efforts to establish a united front with nationalists had been abortive, partly because the Party had seemed reluctant to cooperate on a basis of equality. But in 1939, while in China, Ho Chi Minh had written a report to the Comintern recommending that the ICP cooperate sincerely with non-Communist nationalist parties in a broad national democratic front that would include moderate middle-class nationalists as well as progressive Frenchmen. In contrast with his earlier attitudes, his present position was that the ICP should not "demand that the front recognize its leadership."[18] Now he attempted to put his new approach into practice.

In the early months of 1941, at Chingsi near the Vietnamese border, he set up a new united front called the Vietnamese Liberation League (Viet Nam Giai Phong Dong Minh Hoi) to attract support from all nationalist groups in the area. A non-Communist, Ho Ngoc Lam, was named chairman. To protect the organization from Chinese harassment and to secure the sponsorship of local Kuomintang military authorities, Communist involvement was clandestine. The commander of the southwest military area, General Chang Fa-k'uei, was relatively apolitical in his views and anxious to organize the Vietnamese political forces in South China for participation in a possible Chinese invasion of Indochina. For several months, the Communists obtained considerable profit from their arrangements along the border and scores of young Vietnamese fled to South China willing and eager to enlist in the patriotic cause. With Chang Fa-k'uei's cooperation, a military training program was set up for Vietnamese exiles at Chingsi. Members of the ICP took part covertly and soon began to lure many of the trainees into their organization.

With events moving so fast, Ho Chi Minh sensed that the potential for revolution in Vietnam was suddenly vastly improved and his headquarters in South China now became the focus of Communist policymaking efforts. Giap and Dong were recalled from their trip to Yenan (they had apparently only gotten as far as Kweiyang before receiving a telegram from Ho canceling their instructions), and several additional members of the ICP Central Committee arrived from Vietnam to take part in the planning. Included were Hoang Quoc Viet, a veteran of the movement and a onetime labor organizer in the coal mines of northern Tonkin; Hoang Van Thu, a promising member of Tho nationality; and Truong Chinh (real name Dang Xuan Khu), who was descended from a mandarin family in Nam Dinh and had been a member of the movement since the late 1920s.[19] It was decided to convene a plenary meeting of the Central Committee somewhere in the border area in the spring of 1941. The primary aims of the conference would be to ratify the creation of a new Communist-dominated united front and to confirm the formation of a new strategy for the liberation of Vietnam from foreign rule.

For symbolic reasons, Ho Chi Minh felt that the meeting should be held on native soil, so he sent Vu Anh to Vietnam to find a secure spot somewhere in the mountainous region near the Chinese border. The border area was still infested with the remnants of the abortive Bac Son uprising, and in February he dispatched Phung Chi Kien to form the nucleus of a new guerrilla force in the area (to be named the first platoon of the National Salvation Army, or Cuu Quoc Quan) and to transform the area into a base for the revolutionary forces operating in the Viet Bac.[20]

Eventually, the conference was held in the small mountain village of Pac Bo, just a few miles south of the border. The area was mountainous and virtually secure from attack from the outside. At the same time it was close to the frontier and retreat to China, if necessary, would not be difficult. In February, Ho Chi Minh entered Vietnam with a small retinue and set up his headquarters in a cave at Pac Bo. Even prior to the conference, he directed his followers to agitate among the local population, most of whom were of the minority Nung tribe, to set up mass organizations.

The Eighth Plenum of the ICP convened at Pac Bo in early May 1941. In attendance were a number of the top leaders of the Party—including Hoang Van Thu, Vu Anh, Truong Chinh, Phung Chi Kien, Hoang Quoc Viet, and Ho Chi Minh himself, attending officially as a delegate of the Comintern.[21] The meeting took place in a small hut, with a bamboo conference table and blocks of wood serving as chairs. As Party historians note, it was the first time since the founding session of the Party in February 1930 that Ho Chi Minh had taken an active part in a meeting of the internal Party leadership.

In the history of the Vietnamese Communist movement, the Eighth Plenum is traditionally regarded as the moment when nationalism and a rural strategy of people's war became identified as the two pillars of Vietnamese revolutionary doctrine. Strictly speaking, neither concept originated at Pac Bo. The concept of the national united front had been used by the Party since its infancy with varying degrees of success. The strategy of guerrilla war had first been utilized, as a matter of necessity, by Communist units during the Nghe Tinh revolt of 1930–1931 and, more recently, by the Bac Son rebels after their defeat by main force French units in the fall of 1940.

Nevertheless, the plenum at Pac Bo, under the direction of Ho Chi Minh, clearly set forth these concepts as the guiding strategy of the Party in its continuing struggle for power in Vietnam. At the heart of the new approach was the plenum's assertion that the demands of ideology and class war must be subordinated to those of the antiimperialist struggle for national independence. To provide a vehicle for this new strategy, a new front organization was established, the famous League for the Independence of Vietnam (Viet Nam Doc Lap Dong Minh, or Vietminh for short). Oddly enough, the name of the new front caused the most concern, according to the recollections of Vo Nguyen Giap. At a meeting in Chingsi earlier in the year, Ho Chi Minh had brought up several possible names for the front but had made it clear that he felt many were inappropriate, either because they were too harsh or because they had been sullied by previous use. His favorite, not surprisingly, was the one that was eventually adopted. The Communist movement would be known as the Vietminh for the next decade.

The deliberate shift of emphasis from ideology to nationalism, a transformation that had been underway since the Seventh Comintern Congress in 1935, had obvious implications for the composition of the new organization. All patriotic elements in Vietnam, regardless of class, were welcomed into the front against the common adversary. Not only the bourgeoisie and rich peasants, but wealthy landlords, Overseas Chinese merchants, and patriotic Frenchmen were considered potential allies.[22] To protect the Party against the dangers posed by the admission of such diverse groups, Ho turned to the Maoist model, which called for Party dominance over the front organization. Unlike Mao, however, Ho made a great effort to disguise the Party's role in order to maximize its appeal to moderates.

The decision to appeal for the support of patriotic but socially conservative elements was justified by a return to the reasoning that had marked Lenin's first attempt to draw up a strategy for Asian Communist movements in 1920. According to the resolution issued at the close of the plenum, not only the proletariat but also the petty bourgeoisie, rich peasants, landlords, and officials were groaning under dual French and Japanese oppression. As a result,

> the landlords, rich peasants, and native bourgeois class have greatly changed their attitude. Before they had an antipathy to revolution and wanted to destroy it or were indifferent. Now it is different, and with the exception of a few running dogs who flatter and fawn on the Japanese enemy, the majority have sympathy for the revolution or are neutral. . . . If before the landlords and native bourgeoisie were the reserve army of the antirevolutionary imperialists, they have now become the reserve of the revolution.[23]

An additional aspect of the new political strategy was the decision to establish a series of mass associations (called "national salvation associations" or *cuu quoc hoi*) representing the various interest groups in society—workers, peasants, students, women, artists and writers, even Buddhist bonzes. Such associations, under surreptitious Party control, would be used to enlist popular support for the revolutionary cause and to funnel Party and front directives down to the mass of the population.[24]

At first glance, the new strategy had considerable potential. In contrast to previous occasions, when Communist policies had often been made in Moscow and had reflected the ideological proclivities of the Comintern leadership, the new approach was tailored to the situation in Vietnam. One of the weaknesses of the made-in-Moscow strategy had been its failure to give adequate attention to the two major political and social forces in colonial Vietnamese society—nationalism and the land revolution. The new front was clearly designed to remedy that deficiency and to knit together an alliance of urban nationalists and rural poor in a common effort to achieve independence and social reform.

But there was a price to pay for the Party's effort to extend its appeal to moderate nationalists. The decision to place patriotic concerns before those of revolution meant that the social goals of the Vietminh would have to be muted in order to avoid alienating moderates. Specifically, the slogan of land seizures was to be abandoned and replaced by a more limited appeal for a reduction in land rents and the confiscation of the property of French imperialists and Vietnamese traitors. As the Party resolution made clear, the adjustment was tactical only:

> This does not mean that our Party is ignoring the problem of class struggle in the Indochinese revolution. No, the problem of class struggle will continue to exist. But in the present stage, the nation has prime importance, and all demands which are of benefit to a specific class but which are harmful to the national interest must be subordinated to the survival of the nation and the race. At this moment, if we do not resolve the problem of national liberation, and do not demand independence and freedom for the entire people, then not only will the entire people of our nation continue to live the life of beasts, but also the particular interests of individual social classes will not be achieved for thousands of years.[25]

In effect the plenum had revived the concept of a two-stage revolution that Ho Chi Minh had advocated more than a decade before, with the first stage directed at resolving the pressing problem of national liberation. Only after the defeat of the Japanese and French imperialists and the realization of full independence would the Party begin to move toward the second stage of social revolution. The Communists would take a short step now in order to take a longer step later.

There were substantive changes in ICP military strategy as well. Like the two previous plenums of 1939 and 1940, the conference at Pac Bo emphasized that victory in the Vietnamese revolution would come by means of an armed uprising. For the first time, however, the Party leadership specifically recognized the importance of a rural strategy based on the force of peasant discontent. Where previously the Party had viewed the guerrilla approach as a concession to necessity—a recognition of the military weakness of the Party and its inability to operate effectively in urban areas—it now considered it as the most effective means of seizing power in Vietnam. For example, the Seventh Plenum had instructed the regional Party leadership in Cochin China to resort to guerrilla warfare *only if* the primary goal of waging frontal attacks on French-controlled areas did not succeed. Such, too, had been the pattern of events at Bac Son.

With the 1941 plenum at Pac Bo, the ICP turned guerrilla warfare into an integral element of its revolutionary strategy. The Bac Son guerrillas were to be preserved and turned into an effective unit to operate in the mountainous provinces of the Viet Bac. Local self-defense and combat self-defense militia were to be established in all villages under Vietminh control, and an armed force possessing political as well as military functions was to be created in all provinces where Party elements were active. Eventually, a liberated zone would be created in preparation for the launching of the final insurrection to seize power throughout the country. Clearly, the Party planned this uprising for the end of the Pacific War. According to the resolution:

> We must prepare a force to be ready for a favorable opportunity to defeat the

enemy, i.e., when the Pacific War and the resistance in China turn in our favor; then with the force that we then possess, we can lead an uprising in a single region, and seize victory and open the way to a general uprising.[26]

The new program clearly represented a major shift in the Party's strategy and marked the final abandonment of the lingering reliance on the Bolshevik model. The key to success would be the Party's ability to link the forces of urban nationalism and peasant rebellion in a single coordinated effort to achieve independence and to destroy the power of feudalism and imperialism in colonial Indochina. Here the Party was venturing into relatively uncharted territory. What were the ultimate causes of peasant revolt in Asia? Could the Party harness the primitive and unpredictable force of angry peasants and channel it to meet its own needs? Could moderate elements in urban and rural areas be brought to give their enthusiastic support to a movement that possessed potential revolutionary overtones?

There was, of course, a precedent for the new Vietminh program. To the north, Mao Tse-tung and his colleagues had been grappling with such problems since the formation of the national united front with Chiang Kai-shek's government in Nanking in 1937. Clearly, one major source of inspiration for the Vietnamese strategy was Chinese. Although the documents issued at the plenum make no specific reference to this debt, the similarities with the Maoist model are readily apparent: (1) the formation of a broad united front including all patriotic elements in the population and directed primarily at the goal of national liberation, (2) the open recognition of the dual importance of political and military struggle, (3) the reliance on protracted guerrilla war in preparation for the final stage of general uprising, (4) the establishment of a military force under the direction of the Party, and (5) the carving out, by this force, of a secure revolutionary base in rural areas.

Some Western observers have speculated that the major advocate of the new strategy was Vo Nguyen Giap (who was later to put its military aspects into practice) or, alternatively, the new Party secretary general, Truong Chinh (who in later years was frequently identified as the leading member of a pro-Chinese faction within the Vietnamese Party leadership).[27] In his written recollections of the period, Giap refers briefly to his own growing interest in guerrilla tactics, even before his first meeting with Ho Chi Minh in South China in 1940 (in this account, Giap first heard about guerrilla war in conversations with the Tho leader Hoang Van Thu). Truong Chinh later wrote a well-known treatise on Vietnamese revolutionary strategy that borrowed liberally from Mao's writings.

The bulk of the evidence, however, suggests that the major source for the new strategy was Ho Chi Minh. In the first place, despite his long absence from the scene, Ho was still the unquestioned leader of the Party. His international reputation, his personal ties with Soviet leaders in Moscow, and his formidable experience within the movement all gave him a position within the Party that could not be matched by any of his younger colleagues. It is extremely doubtful that either Giap or Truong Chinh—neither of whom had studied in Moscow or had substantial acquaintance with international communism—possessed the experience or the status in the Party to bring about so momentous a change.

Even more persuasive, perhaps, is the fact that in a number of respects the new strategy seemed to reflect Ho Chi Minh's evolving views on the course of the Vietnamese revolution. The importance of the key forces of nationalism and land revolution date back to his ideas during the life of the Revolutionary Youth League. The emphasis on guerrilla tactics had been expressed in his 1927 article, which was written in Moscow. Admittedly, at that time he had not seen the importance of seizing a liberated base zone secure from attack by government forces. The lessons of Nghe Tinh and the Maoist experience in China undoubtedly had changed his mind on this score. Finally, the dual emphasis on an urban and a rural strategy—the implications of which would only become clear four years later during the August Revolution of 1945—was a direct product of Ho's thinking in the 1920s and not a reflection of Maoist concepts. Indeed, from this time forward, Vietnamese Communist strategy would place far greater importance than its Chinese counterpart on the role of the cities.

In summary, the new Vietminh strategy appears to have been essentially an elaboration of ideas developed by Ho Chi Minh over several years and fleshed out with the practical experiences of the Chinese revolution. That Ho considered the latter of importance is verified by the fact that, after his return to the border area, he translated several Chinese and Russian works on guerrilla war into Vietnamese and wrote a brief history of the Chinese experience.[28]

Toward the General Uprising

With the main lines of its new approach established, the Party could turn to the arduous task of putting the plan into reality. The ultimate objective was a general uprising to overthrow colonial power. Ho Chi Minh shared Lenin's conviction that political struggle alone would be insufficient to defeat the class enemy. But he was also a cautious man and convinced that a premature uprising could do great harm to the Party's prospects. The revolt would require careful planning and would have to take into account the conditions in the nation as a whole. In general the Party and the front apparatus, as well as the new mass associations, would have to be extended to all provinces and among the national minorities as well as among ethnic Vietnamese. A revolt based solely on local conditions, like those of 1940, simply squandered revolutionary strength. Such local rebellions should be permitted only in specific instances, when local conditions suggested that the enemy would be unable to strike back. At the very least, the planners should be prepared for the possibility of defeat, so that an orderly retreat could minimize losses and preserve the movement intact. The Bac Son revolt had met this last condition and thus made it possible to use the area in the future as a base for the buildup of revolutionary forces. But the Cochin China outbreak had not, with the result that its rebellious forces were decimated and the Party's local apparatus was almost totally destroyed.[29]

A second prerequisite for success was the existence of favorable objective conditions within Vietnam. In practice, this meant that the ruling authorities should be in a state of military, political, and economic disintegration. This might come about as a result of military defeat or of social revolutions in France or Japan that incapacitated the local ruling clique. Combined with this was the classic Soviet formulation that the local population must be unwilling to tolerate continued colonial or fascist rule and be willing to sacrifice all for the revolutionary cause.

A final prerequisite for revolt was a favorable international situation. Where Mao and the CCP, operating in a vast society only indirectly affected by imperialism, could afford to view the revolutionary process in relative isolation from the external situation, Vietnam, a small nation under direct colonial control, could not. That unfortunate reality would color Ho Chi Minh's revolutionary thought throughout his life. Like it or not, the general uprising would have to await the ripening of conditions within Vietnam and in the international situation as well. In this case, the most favorable conditions would occur when the democratic forces were victorious in the Pacific War and Allied troops were preparing to enter Indochina.[30]

In 1941, the general insurrection still lay far in the future. There were pressing problems following the Pac Bo plenum. The first, in order of priority, was to prepare the political ground by building up the Vietminh apparatus throughout the country. The second was to create a revolutionary base area in the border zone and to transform the scattered guerrilla units into a powerful military force. Shortly after the conference, Ho Chi Minh drafted an open letter to the populace, announcing the formation of the new united front and appealing for support. Conscious of the need to win widespread support from traditionalists as well as progressive elements, he wrote the letter in demotic characters and opened with an appeal to "elders, prominent personalities and intellectuals," as well as to workers, peasants, tradesmen, and soldiers. The letter was blatantly patriotic, recounting the history of Vietnam from the ancient Hong Bang dynasty and citing the great patriotic heroes of the past. It called for unity in the interests of national salvation, reminiscent of the glorious period when Vietnam had repulsed a Mongol invasion seven centuries before, and stressed that at present the issue of national liberation was of paramount importance and should have priority over all other concerns. He who has money, it said, should give money; he who has strength should contribute his strength; and he who has talent should donate his talent.[31]

If the political issue had national implications, the military problem, at least in the beginning, was primarily regional in scope. The immediate need was to organize the remnants of the abortive Bac Son uprising into the nucleus of the National Salvation Army and to carve out a revolutionary base area in the mountainous regions of the Viet Bac. According to Ho Chi Minh's plan, once the revolutionary forces had secured control over the remote border area, they could gradually expand southward to the provinces of Bac Can and Thai Nguyen, on the fringe of the Red River delta. From there, not only could they communicate with the Central Committee, which, under Truong Chinh, was now secretly located in the suburbs of Hanoi, but they could also extend the movement into the densely populated provinces of the delta.

In charge of the effort to build the first units of the National Salvation Army were Phung Chi Kien, Luong Van Chi, and the Nung guerrilla leader Chu Van Tan. The remaining guerrilla units from the Bac Son uprising were to be reorganized as guerrilla forces and instructed to carry out political and military activities around Bac Son and Vu Nhai, directly to the west of the border town of Lang Son. New recruits were to be selected from the mountain villages in the area and sent across the Chinese border to attend the training classes run by the Kuomintang at Chingsi; they were then to be sent back to Vietnam for placement in Communist units. When this program proved to be too time-consuming, shorter training classes, only a few days in length, were set up at mobile training bases in the border regions.

The selection of the border region was probably dictated by several considerations. First and foremost, it was one of the few areas that were relatively secure against attack and occupation by government forces. The rugged and frequently tortuous terrain of the Viet Bac had often served as a base for rebels opposed to the central authorities in Hanoi. At the turn of the century, pirates with no political leanings and a few fervent nationalists, like the famous Hoang Hoa Tham, had stubbornly resisted French efforts to bring the area under control. It had taken the latter several years to pacify the region and end resistance. Now, once again, the mountainous provinces would serve as a refuge for rebels.

A second and equally important factor was the accessibility of the area to the Chinese border. Not only could the ICP leadership retreat beyond the frontier in case of need, but the southern Chinese provinces could be used as a training base for thousands of young Vietnamese patriots. With the political situation in the area volatile as a result of the war with Japan, the Communists had a unique opportunity to turn the situation to their advantage and put to the test Mao's dictum that a liberated base area should ideally be located near a frontier.

None of this would be useful, of course, without support from the local population—the sea in which the guerrilla fish must swim. Since the early 1930s, the people of the area had shown a high degree of sympathy with the revolutionary cause. The bulk of the local population was composed of minority nationalities, but the Party had been sensitive to the issue and as early as October 1930 its Political Program had promised self-determination for all nationalities in a future Vietnam. Such tactics were successful, and Party activities in the Viet Bac had thrived in the 1930s. A number of non-Vietnamese natives of the area—including Hoang Van Thu, Le Quang Ba, and the notorious Hoang Dinh Giong, the "Stalin of Cao Bang," had moved into the higher echelons of the Party apparatus. By the end of the decade the northern border provinces had become, in the estimation of the Party leadership, significantly more promising than those of the populous but politically inert Red River delta.

As the Party's tiny military forces in the border zones began to take shape, the political influence of the Vietminh gradually began to penetrate the area. Throughout, the movement carried the stamp of Ho Chi Minh, who flooded it with a stream of sage advice. It is necessary to respect local customs scrupulously, he said. Dress like the native population in your area and learn the local language. Be patient and thorough in your organizational work. The Vietminh appeal was translated into verse in the local languages. Gradually, in response to his patient prodding, the Vietminh tide began to flood the villages of the North. Mass salvation associations for youth, women, and peasants were formed, first at the village and district levels and ultimately at the provincial level. In the villages, self-defense units began to appear and soon almost all villages in Vietminh-controlled areas had at least one unit. Vietminh administative committees began to be formed at the local level. Where a prerevolutionary local administration continued in existence the local notables, either through fear or conviction, often would not take action without asking the advice of local Vietminh committee members.[32]

The Party's organizational efforts did not go unobserved. Although the year 1941 had seen the gradual extension of Japanese influence in Indochina, the Vichy government still preserved military and administrative control over Indochina. By fall, the French were increasingly concerned about the deterioration of their authority in the border region and dispatched military units to attack the Vietminh forces near Bac Son. Chu Van Tan's units managed to evade capture, but those under Phung Chi Kien and Luong Van Chi were engaged and forced to retreat to the Na Ri area, where they were ambushed. Phung Chi Kien was killed in the battle; Luong Van Chi was captured and died in prison. Chu Van Tan's forces, breaking up into small units, managed to survive, and after several months of arduous fighting in late 1941 and early 1942 finally achieved their first victories.

March to the South

As 1941 came to an end, the movement was clearly on the way up. French attacks harassed the revolutionaries severely, but they were by now deeply rooted in the border provinces and could not be evicted. In December, the international situation took a favorable turn. Following the Japanese attacks on U.S.

bases at Pearl Harbor and the Philippines, the United States entered the war. For the Vietminh, it meant the promise of another ally. On December 21, 1941, the Central Committee published a communiqué, "The Pacific War and the Urgent Tasks of the Party," which gave the broad outlines of its strategy and related it to the Allied war effort: (1) cooperation with the Kuomintang and (2) cooperation with the United States and Great Britain and the promise to grant them economic advantages, so long as they provided assistance to the Vietnamese revolution. If the Allies gave support to the French in reestablishing colonial control in Indochina, the Vietminh would protest energetically and continue its struggle for independence. There was a hint of controversy within the Party apparatus over current policy; "leftists" called for a general uprising as soon as Kuomintang troops entered Indochina.[33]

The changes in the international situation seemed also a harbinger of better things in the Viet Bac. With the new year, successes began to outnumber failures and in May a meeting of local leaders was held to stabilize the growing liberation zone in the Bac Son-Vu Nhai area and to extend the military base throughout the entire northern frontier area. Military units in Cao Bang Province decided to extend their activities southward toward the delta. Throughout the year, both groups made gradual progress and in February 1943 the Central Committee met in Vong La in Bac Ninh Province and decided that the situation was sufficiently promising to begin preparations for the general uprising.[34] The Cao Bang forces reached Lang Coc, not far north of the provincial capital of Thai Nguyen, where, in the heart of the jungle, they linked up for the first time with elements of Chu Van Tan's National Salvation Army expanding from the east at Bac Son. The conditions for the creation of a liberated zone over the entire area of the Viet Bac had been created. Permanent military units were now in operation at the district level, and political cadres were circulating among the local population. In recognition of the spread of the movement, the ICP Interprovincial Committee for the entire border area now moved to the south of Cao Bang and was reestablished in a small cabin in a mountain forest between the villages of Nguyen Binh and Hoa An. It was not luxury, but it was an improvement over the primitive conditions at Pac Bo.

Beyond the Viet Bac, the Party was encountering difficulties. The expansion of Japanese power in Indochina had not led to a decline in French control. More accurately, it had supplemented the existing administration with Japanese military occupation forces. Still, it must have seemed to Party leaders that the new situation offered fertile soil for propaganda activities. The war had brought increasing hardship to the population. Unemployment was high in working-class areas in the big northern cities. Commerce was badly hurt, and taxes and war requisitions were almost punitive. By 1943, the government seizure of paddy rice had begun to create serious unrest in farming areas.

Despite such grounds for discontent, however, Vietnam seemed, for the moment, more lethargic than revolutionary. Political parties had been disbanded at the time of the French declaration of war on Germany in 1939. The coming of the Japanese did not ease matters and, to many nationalists, the only sensible choice seemed to be to withhold judgment and await the course of events. Public opinion in urban areas was timid and reserved. Even pro-French elements seemed willing to adapt to the new circumstances. Other groups, like the Cao Dai sect in the Mekong delta, became vociferously pro-Japanese, presumably in the hope that their new overlords would grant the independence or autonomy that they had so long awaited.

Perhaps this is one reason why the Vietminh Front had relatively little success at first in attracting support among urban bourgeois intellectuals. Part of the problem, too, can be ascribed to the almost constant harassment Party members faced from the French authorities. After the Bac Son revolt, virtually all the Party's cadres in Hanoi were arrested. Hoang Van Thu, perhaps the most promising young leader to have emerged during the early war years, attempted to set up paramilitary units in the Hanoi suburbs but was seized during a French raid in August 1943 and was eventually executed.[35]

The Party did not have much greater success among workers. Despite the high rate of unemployment (figures on miners, for example, showed a decline from 49,000 in 1940 to only 25,000 in 1944), the workers' movement was relatively inactive, perhaps because many had fled to the villages after being laid off. The only real bright spot was in the countryside. By the spring of 1943, rice requisitions by authorities, in addition to forced labor and military conscription, had led to serious unrest in many rural areas. The degree of Party involvement at the village level is not well documented and needs more study. But there were indications that an explosion that could rival the famous revolt at Nghe Tinh might be brewing.

In 1942 an event took place that could have been disastrous for the Party. While travelling incognito to confer with CCP officials in South China, Ho Chi Minh was arrested and placed in prison. His absence was soon felt in the movement. At Chingsi, the non-Communist leadership of the Vietnamese Liberation League expelled its ICP members. The immediate cause for the breakup was the arrival at Chingsi of Nguyen Hai Than, an old émigré who had once been a follower of Phan Boi Chau. Than was apparently aware of the Communist persuasion of several members of the organization and reported that fact to the local Kuomintang authorities. In January 1942 Pham Van Dong and Vo Nguyen Giap were forced to flee from Chingsi and return to Vietnam. The break may have been inevitable, for the local nationalists had grown increasingly critical of the tendency of the ICP members of the league to seduce young arrivals and entice them into their own Vietminh organization.

By mid-1943 the league (now without its Communist members) had virtually disintegrated. Its major VNQDD members had left for Yunnan Province, and the VNQDD had split into squabbling factions. This was hardly helpful to Chang Fa-k'uei, who had just received orders from Chungking to begin preparations for an eventual Chinese invasion of Indochina. Badly in need of intelligence on the situation across the border, Chang was anxious to turn the local Vietnamese nationalist factions into a useful political organization, and at a conference at Liuchow in August 1942 he had persuaded the Vietnamese to set up a new nationalist front—the Vietnamese Revolutionary League (Viet Nam Cach Menh Dong Minh Hoi, or Dong Minh Hoi for short). Like its predecessor, it was sponsored by the Chinese, but it specifically excluded the ICP. Most of its members were members of the VNQDD or of the Phuc Quoc.[36]

Chang soon discovered, however, that the new League was ill-suited for his purposes. Its leadership was weak and incompetent; worse, it appeared to have no interest in carrying on activities in Vietnam—activities that it was virtually incapable of carrying out in any case, since none of the top members had contacts in Vietnam. Internal factionalism compounded the problem.

At about this point, Ho Chi Minh was released from prison. Whether or not his release was the result of an arrangement with Chang Fa-k'uei, who wanted the canny revolutionary to lead the faltering Vietnamese national alliance, has never been established.[37] Whatever the case, for a period of time he remained in Liuchow under administrative surveillance and devoted his efforts to restoring Communist participation in the nationalist alliance in the area. To allay the suspicions of non-Communists he used his new pseudonym of Ho Chi Minh.

The following March, Chang Fa-k'uei convened a new congress of the Dong Minh Hoi at Liuchow. Virtually all Vietnamese political groups were represented, with Pham Van Dong and Ho Chi Minh representing the Vietminh. During the meeting, much of the bitterness felt by other nationalist groups about Vietminh activities surfaced in acrimonious charges. Ho Chi Minh, reassuring and affable, took the position that the future—and the unification of all nationalist groups in a single effective front organization—was all that mattered. The conference eventually agreed to form a new organization directed at the liberation of Vietnam from foreign control. The veteran nationalist Truong Boi Cong was selected as chairman of the ruling committee; Ho became an alternate. The VNQDD dominated the organization, but the Communists were adequately represented.[38]

The revitalization of the Dong Minh Hoi did not result in any fundamental changes in the political balance in South China. Rivalry between the Communists and the VNQDD continued, in Yunnan as in Kwangsi, and the ICP continued to be the more effective organization. As for Ho Chi Minh, he was now anxious to return to Vietnam. He continued to work on Chang Fa-k'uei, conceding that he was a Communist but asserting that his main desire was for Vietnamese independence and assuring the Chinese leader that communism would not work in Vietnam for another fifty years. At one point, according to one scholar, he submitted to Chang an outline of his proposed activities after entering Vietnam. Promising to lead a group of trained men into Vietnam to carry out guerrilla activities against the Japanese, he said that he would do his utmost to unite all parties and groups in Vietnam behind the Chinese-sponsored Dong Minh Hoi (including the VNQDD and the Constitutionalist Party as well as the ICP and a handful of Communist front organizations). The ultimate goal was independence, which would be achieved with the cooperation of the Chinese government.[39] The crux of the project, from Ho's point of view, was the proposal to set up two guerrilla bases near the Chinese border, for in connection with these units he requested financial assistance and weapons from the Chinese. Specifically, he asked for 1,000 guns, including 6 machine guns, 4,000 grenades, and a subsidy of $50,000 in Chinese dollars. He did not receive the weapons, but he did get the money.

In August 1944 with a retinue of eighteen men trained and armed by the Chinese, Ho Chi Minh returned to Vietnam. Arriving at Pac Bo in September, he found that preparations for the coming general uprising had progressed during his absence. The year 1944 had seen considerable improvement in the Party's fortunes in North Vietnam. Vietminh control had spread throughout the entire area north of the Red River delta. The revolutionary armed forces were growing, and morale was high. Such portents had led the Party leadership in the Viet Bac, at a meeting of the Interprovincial Committee in July, to declare that preparations for the uprising were 90 percent completed. With the situation favorable and the masses ready, a general uprising could be launched in the Viet Bac within two months. A final meeting was to take place after the return of Ho Chi Minh to obtain his approval and set the exact date of the insurrection.[40]

To their dismay, Ho rejected the plan. When Vo Nguyen Giap went to Pac Bo to obtain his approval, Ho observed that the necessary conditions for victory were not in evidence. Although the situation in the North was improving, revolutionary conditions did not exist elsewhere, and if an uprising broke out in the Viet Bac, the Party apparatus in the rest of the country would be unable to launch armed struggles in response. If that were the case, the enemy would be able to concentrate his forces on the rebellion in the North and defeat it.[41] Ho conceded that the time for purely political work had passed but insisted that it was still too early to give priority to the military aspects of the struggle:

> Now the time for peaceful development of the revolution is past, but the time for a full uprising has not yet arrived. If we only act in political form then we will meet disaster. The struggle should be moved from the political toward the military. But at this moment, the political work is still more important than military actions.[42]

As a consolation to his disappointed colleagues, Ho Chi Minh did agree to set up the first units of the new revolutionary armed forces as a token of his recognition that a new stage in the Vietnamese revolution was about to begin.

These so-called armed propaganda detachments (*tuyen truyen giai phong quan*) were designed as a transitional organization with the capacity to perform both military and political tasks. The first units, to be formed and commanded by Vo Nguyen Giap, were to be set up in forested areas of Cao Bang Province and would have primarily political duties—to build a mass base in the frontier zone as a staging area for the coming general uprising. In the long run, however, they were destined to play a major role in the Communists' struggle for power and to be the forerunner of the future People's Liberation Army of Vietnam. As Ho Chi Minh commented to Giap at the time:

> The propaganda brigade of the Vietnamese liberation army is summoned to become the eldest of a numerous family. I hope that still other brigades will see the day in the near future. Although modest at its beginnings, it will see opening before it the most brilliant perspectives. It is the embryo of our future liberation army, and it will have for its field of battle all the territory of Vietnam, from North to South.[43]

The first unit, formed on December 22, 1944, consisted of 34 men. In the beginning, its duties were essentially limited to propaganda and mobilization of the local population in the Viet Bac. Right from the start, however, it possessed a military component. In keeping with Ho's directive to "win the first battle" in order to impress the population with the strength of the revolutionary forces, the armed propaganda detachment attacked French camps at Phai Kat and Na Ngan only two days after its formation. The enemy camps were destroyed, and a number of weapons were captured. The unit then moved north to consolidate the border area and await the eventual order to move south.

By early 1945, it was apparent that the war was nearing its end. Under the hammer blows of U.S. military power, the Japanese forces were being driven from their entrenched positions in the South Pacific. For Ho Chi Minh, it was essential not only that the Vietminh be in a strong military and political position within Vietnam, but that it secure a solid position as a recognized member of the victorious alliance headed by the United States. Only thus would the Communists have a reasonable chance of securing power in Vietnam from the colonialists without inspiring the intervention of outside powers. During the fall of 1944, Ho kept in touch with General Hsiao Wen, Chang Fa-k'uei's political commissar and a man who had shown a willingness to cooperate with the Vietminh leader. Ho's letters to the Chinese military leader had been warm and informative, demonstrating the continuing willingness of the Vietminh leader to offer assistance to the Chinese in their projected invasion of Indochina.

Meanwhile, there were two new elements in the power equation in South China. A French military mission, dominated by Free French units loyal to General Charles de Gaulle, had been established at Kunming and was showing interest in maintaining a French presence in postwar Indochina. At the same time, American units were increasingly active in the area, including an Office of Strategic Services (OSS) mission attempting to obtain military information on Japanese troop movements in Indochina and to establish an effective network of agents there to provide information and assistance for the rescue of downed American fliers.

In January 1945 Ho Chi Minh decided to return to South China to strengthen the Vietminh's links with other Allied units in the area. He went first to Kunming and then to Paise, the new headquarters of the Dong Minh Hoi and Chang Fa-k'uei since the fall of Liuchow to the Japanese. There he found that, in his absence, the Dong Minh Hoi had virtually ceased to exist and its non-Communist leaders had left Kwangsi for Yunnan or Kweichow. Competition between the Communists and the various nationalist groups in South China continued to be intense, particularly in Yunnan, where Communist activities had seriously undermined the VNQDD party organization.

Although the Dong Minh Hoi was now moribund, Ho Chi Minh apparently still hoped to use it for his own purposes, so as to monopolize Chinese and other Allied aid to Vietnamese resistance groups in the area. With little cooperation from non-Communist groups, he set up a so-called Action Committee of the Dong Minh Hoi on April 12. At first the new committee was clearly dominated by the Vietminh, but when other nationlist groups complained at the Communist complexion of the new directing body, Ho Chi Minh agreed to add several new non-Communist members.

During the next several months, Ho Chi Minh struggled with some success to persuade the Americans to provide him with arms and other material support. With the French, the problem was more complicated. In December 1943 representatives of de Gaulle's Free French organization had issued a statement promising a new political status for the French colonies after the war. But it had also indicated their intention to maintain a French political presence in Indochina. In a declaration dated June 4, 1944, the Vietminh protested against any French decision to reject Vietnamese independence in the postwar period. A month later, Ho Chi Minh got in touch with the local French military mission and passed on a brief memo indicating Vietminh demands. Conscious of the need to avoid a confrontation with France or its allies at a delicate stage in the war, he kept his demands moderate—political autonomy in return for economic concessions, with full independence in ten years.[44]

The response of Jean Sainteny, head of the French mission, was polite but noncommittal, as he lacked directives from Paris. But it seemed likely that Ho's demands would be unacceptable to the French. On March 24, 1945, the French government had talked of autonomy for the five states of Indochina in a French Union, but with no suggestion of full independence. Ho Chi Minh wished to keep the channel of communications open, however, and through American intermediaries suggested talks with Sainteny on the postwar situation. Sainteny agreed, but heavy rains and the fast pace of events intervened, and when the war concluded the French and the Vietminh had been unable to hold direct negotiations.

The Japanese Coup d'État

On March 9, 1945, the Japanese, sensing the growth of Gaullist feeling among the French community in Indochina, staged a coup and abolished the French colonial administration. French civilian and military authorities were imprisoned, and two days later the Japanese permitted Emperor Bao Dai to revoke the Treaty of 1884 that had established the French protectorate over Vietnam and declare the independence of Vietnam under Japanese tutelage. Shortly afterward, Bao Dai formed a government under the Vietnamese educator and historian Tran Trong Kim.

On the surface it appeared that the Japanese action, by providing an outlet for moderate nationalist feelings, might cut the ground from under the ICP. But it soon became clear that the grant of independence was spurious. Japanese authority was maintained, and the ex-French colony of Cochin China was not even included in the bargain—its status was left ambiguous, and Japanese control there remained total. Then, too, the composition of the new Vietnamese government was not appealing to progressive Vietnamese. Prime Minister Kim's cabinet was moderate to conservative in orientation and included a number of figures who had been known in earlier years for their Francophile predilections. The new situation was hardly one to make fervent nationalists rejoice.

Moreover, the timing of the coup was particularly fortunate for the Communists. The French authorities in Hanoi had been planning to attack Vietminh positions near Thai Nguyen, at the northwest corner of the Red River delta, where Ho Chi Minh's forces had maintained their headquarters since the autumn of 1944. The campaign had been scheduled to begin on March 12, three days after the coup. Then, too, the Japanese decision to abolish French colonial rule served to undermine the legitimacy of the French presence in Indochina and to make any return to the area by Gaullist forces more difficult. At the end of the war, a political vacuum would exist and the Communists would be in a good position to fill it.

More important, perhaps, general conditions in Vietnam were beginning to appear more auspicious for the revolutionary cause. Government repression had kept the cities quiet and the local Party apparatus there was relatively inactive, but conditions in the countryside were more promising. In rural areas in the Center and the North, the threat of famine hovered over the land. Agricultural production, buffeted by bad weather, was down from a yearly average of more than 1 million tons in the immediate prewar period to less than 850,000 tons in 1944, and a considerable proportion of that had been confiscated by the government. In Cochin China, the harvest attained normal levels, but rice exports to other areas of Indochina were prohibited. Early indications were that the 1945 harvest, because of flooding and lack of manpower, might be even lower. In the winter of 1944–1945, famine struck and there were estimates of up to 2 million dead, with corpses lying along the roadside. By one estimate, nearly one Vietnamese in ten was suffering from hunger.[45]

Ho Chi Minh saw the new developments as a great opportunity, providing the potential for a giant leap forward for the revolutionary cause. Nothing had shaken the colonial regime more than the peasant riots of 1908 and 1930, both the consequence of previous agricultural crises. Moreover, the Japanese coup simplified the situation for the ICP, because Japanese forces as a rule occupied only the major urban centers and made little effort to establish their authority in the countryside, where the French local administration still operated without legal or political direction from Hanoi. As for the Bao Dai regime in Hué, it could be viewed as mere bits of flotsam and jetsam that could easily be washed away in the revolutionary tide. A circular dated December 1944, of which Ho Chi Minh was the probable author, had already predicted the course of events:

> The armed insurrection of our people will be unleashed at the last stage of the world war, when England, America, and China come to seize Indochina, when Gaullists and French fascists collide in Indochina, when French and Japanese enter into combat and the French and Japanese fascists enter into conflict with the democracies.
>
> Hour H is near. . . . Germany is practically defeated and her defeat will provoke that of Japan, which will not be able to resist the general offensive. Then the Americans and the Chinese will penetrate into Indochina, while the Gaullists rise against the Japanese. The latter will be overthrown by the French fascists and replaced by a military government.
>
> All the puppet, incompetent, and weak governments will fall. Indochina will slip into anarchy. We will have no need then to seize power, because there will be no more power. We will form a government which will reign everywhere where our enemies, the French and the Japanese, are absent, incapable of maintaining their prestige because of their military weakness.[46]

Whether or not the circular was written by Ho Chi Minh, it clearly bears the stamp of his political genius. For now, with the destruction of the French colonial administration and the accelerating weakness of the Japanese occupation regime, his contention that the most propitious time for a general uprising would be at the close of the war seemed amply vindicated by events. As the concluding paragraph of the circular declared:

> Our future uprising will thus be undertaken in very favorable conditions, unique in the history of the struggle of our country. The moment being propitious and

the factors favorable, it would be unpardonable not to take advantage of it. It would be a crime against the history of our country.

It now remained to take advantage of the political vacuum created by the weakness of the Japanese. At the news of the coup, Truong Chinh called a meeting of the Standing Committee in Bac Ninh Province, ten miles (sixteen kilometers) from Hanoi, to consider the implications of the latest events for Communist strategy. After three days of intense discussion, the committee issued a directive entitled "The Franco-Japanese Conflict and Our Actions."[47] According to the new instructions, the period of the general uprising was fast approaching and Vietnam had now entered a "preinsurrectionary period" when political and military priorities were of equal importance. The enemy was in a growing state of crisis. The French had lost control and the ranks of the Japanese were in confusion. There were growing food problems and massive unemployment in the cities.

Under the new circumstances, the main adversary for the moment was clearly Japan. With the French regime of Jean Decoux removed from power, French resistance groups could now be considered as potential allies in the revolutionary struggle against Japanese fascism. The united front must be broadened at all costs to encompass patriotic Frenchmen and the moderate Vietnamese bourgeoisie in the cities. In the countryside, revolutionary forces could seize local power wherever conditions warranted—up to the district and even in some cases to the provincial levels. In those areas where a revolutionary takeover could be achieved, people's committees should be formed to replace existing authority. Elsewhere, secret militia units and a skeleton administrative structure should be set up to prepare for action when the order for the general uprising was given. Even in enemy-controlled urban areas, the revolutionary forces must be readied—liberation committees should be formed in factories, mines, in suburban villages, and city streets.

In practical terms, the ICP strategy called for a two-stage uprising, starting with a Maoist-style seizure of power in the rural areas, where revolutionary strength was more firmly established than in the cities. Village-based forces would then move to the outskirts of the major cities to assist urban revolutionaries in the revolutionary takeover in the heart of the enemy camp. Communist military forces prepared to respond to the new situation. Vo Nguyen Giap's armed propaganda detachments in Cao Bang divided into separate groups and began to move south into Thai Nguyen Province, the jumping-off point for the delta. Further to the east, Chu Van Tan's National Salvation Army, now over 3,000 strong, began to liberate the eastern districts of the Viet Bac and to form revolutionary administrations at the district level in the provinces of Tuyen Quang and Lang Son. In April, the two linked up at the new mountain headquarters in the tiny village of Tan Trao, not far from Thai Nguyen City.[48]

On April 15, a military conference attended by revolutionary leaders throughout the Viet Bac convened at Hiep Hoa in Bac Giang Province. At this first major military conference in the history of the Party, it was concluded that military issues now had priority. The conference called for the establishment of a base area consisting of the seven existing combat zones in the Viet Bac. The headquarters of the new People's Liberation Army would be established in the liberated zone, and small and secure bases should be set up in other areas in case of the necessity of retreat. The existing military forces, now united at Tan Trao, were to be fused into the new People's Liberation Army (PLA). Guerrilla war was to be expanded in all areas, and local paramilitary units were to be established wherever feasible. The command structure was to be headed by the Military Revolutionary Committee for North Vietnam under the overall command of Vo Nguyen Giap, head of the new PLA.

Shortly after the conference, Ho Chi Minh instructed Giap to visit him to discuss the situation. Ho agreed that the general situation was good, but he cautioned his visitor that three conditions had to be fulfilled before the Party launched its general insurrection: (1) the enemy must be in an untenable position, (2) the people must be clearly conscious of being oppressed, and (3) the revolutionary forces must have carefully prepared the ground for the struggle ahead. The two then agreed on the choice of Tan Trao as revolutionary headquarters for the coming struggle.

While the Party's military leaders were preparing the Viet Bac for the coming uprising, the apparatus in the cities was busy setting the stage for the urban general uprising. In Hanoi the situation was promising. Labor unrest was on the increase, and in the suburbs alone over 2,000 had joined workers' salvation associations. Communist propaganda among Vietnamese troops in the capital area was having growing success. In the rural areas of Tonkin, the peasant movement was rising fast as famine increased the menace of disorder, and in some villages Vietminh elements were able to initiate seizures of government granaries. The ICP leadership instructed local cadres to emphasize the issue of hunger and the government's inadequate response to it. By mid-spring all provinces in the North had a Vietminh organization. In the Center, too, unrest was on the rise, particularly in Quang Ngai Province, where there had already been an uprising in the district of Ba To, with over 100,000 peasants enlisted in salvation associations by mid-summer. Ironically, the quietest provinces in Annam were Nghe An and Ha Tinh, site of the revolt fifteen years earlier. According to Communist historians, the local Party organization there had not yet fully recovered from French repression after the 1930 uprising.

By contrast, in Cochin China the movement seemed momentarily weaker in rural areas than in the metropolitan center of Saigon and its Chinese sister city of Cholon. In the Mekong delta, the Party's organizational efforts were increasingly hindered by two growing Buddhist sects, the Cao Dai and the Hoa Hao, which had flourished in the less traditional and "open village" atmosphere characteristic of the delta provinces. The rise of the two syncretic sects, described by one observer as "archaic social units," appeared to reflect a series of factors in the villages of the Mekong delta: the breakdown of the security of the peasants on their land as the result of commercialization and the movement of local landlord elites into the big cities, and the failure of nationalist parties in Saigon to devote adequate attention to the rural population.[49] ICP efforts to penetrate nonsect areas had some success in the late 1930s, but in 1940 its organizational base was destroyed. Five years later it had still not fully recovered.

The Communists were stronger in Saigon. There party organization had been in a perilous state during the early years of the war because of the seizure of the regional ICP leadership during the 1940 uprising. By 1945, however, it was again on the march. At the root of its recovery was its growing appeal among workers and intellectuals. According to ICP figures, by the beginning of 1945 it had managed to establish secret labor organizations in seventy enterprises with more than 3,000 members. In the absence of reliable communications with the Central Committee in the North, the southern leadership was forced to improvise, and it reacted to the March directive by setting up its own youth organization in Saigon, the Vanguard Youth (Thanh Nien Tien Phong). Led by the clandestine Communist Pham Ngoc Thach, the Vanguard Youth operated as a Vietnamese-style boy scout organization, with uniforms, songs, and a strongly nationalist orientation. Despite competition from a Japanese-sponsored rival, it had enlisted more than 200,000 followers in the Saigon metropolitan area by mid-summer. Beginning in urban schools and factories, it spread gradually to rural areas surrounding the city and soon had over one million members in virtually every province in Cochin China. In the absence of a liberated zone, the Vanguard Youth served as the nucleus for the Communist effort in Cochin China.[50]

Creating the Liberated Zone

Throughout the spring and early summer of 1945, the Communists relentlessly built up their power in the mountains north and northwest of Hanoi. By May, their trained forces in the Viet Bac had reached 5,000, although many lacked weapons. Where Vietminh control had been established, people's revolutionary committees were formed; elsewhere, secret liberation committees were set up in villages and hamlets sympathetic to the revolutionary cause. Until June no revolutionary authority existed above the district level. In that month a Vietminh conference of cadres from all six provinces of the Viet Bac (Cao Bang, Lang Son, Ha Giang, Bac Can, Tuyen Quang, and Thai Nguyen) decided to set up a liberated zone throughout virtually all the districts in these provinces, except for the provincial capitals. In this zone, people's revolutionary committees were set up at all local levels. Communal lands, as well as property of the colonialists and their Vietnamese "running dogs," were distributed to the poor. Universal suffrage and democratic freedoms were declared and the corvée was abolished. Classes to teach *quoc ngu* were set up and local self-defense militia units were formed in all villages. At the top, a provisional directing committee for the Cao-Bac-Lang liberated area was established under Ho Chi Minh to rule over a population of more than 1 million. Even along the fringes of the delta the Vietminh forces began to operate with little resistance, since the Japanese guarded only the towns and the communication routes. To lay the groundwork for the complex period ahead, secret contacts were established with Tran Trong Kim, prime minister of the Japan-supported Bao Dai government, and with Phan Ke Toai, the imperial delegate in Tonkin. Toai agreed secretly to protect the revolutionaries from government harassment.

The Tan Trao Conference

By late July Japanese surrender appeared imminent. The Party leadership began preparations to form a provisional republican government under Vietminh direction. The link with the Allies and the paper alliance with the nationalist groups represented under the umbrella of the Dong Minh Hoi provided a degree of legitimacy to the Vietminh cause. What was needed was a provisional political authority under Communist control that could assert its power in Vietnam in the name of the victorious Allies as the war came to an end. This government could then negotiate with the Allied occupation forces, which, according to the decision of the Potsdam Conference convening at the end of July, would consist of the Nationalist Chinese in the north, the British in the south.

To Ho Chi Minh, always fearful of the possibility of foreign intervention, the legitimacy of the revolutionary forces in the eyes of the Allies and the Vietnamese population was the key to retaining power. To this end he strongly recommended the convening of a national congress of Vietminh delegates before the close of the war. According to Communist sources, some Party leaders doubted the need for such a congress and contended that the Party should simply seize power and allow the revolution to establish its own legitimacy. Ho Chi Minh continued to press for a congress, however, not only to provide the new government with a firm legal basis, but also to isolate the Dong Minh Hoi, which was still formally in existence in South China. Ho had his way, and in early August sixty delegates, representing Party members, sympathizers, and representatives of the national minorities, began to converge on the jungle base at Tan Trao.[51]

To prepare the agenda of the congress and to coordinate ICP policy, the Party's Central Committee held its own Ninth Plenum at Tan Trao on August 13, in the immediate aftermath of the atomic blasts at Hiroshima and Nagasaki and the entry of the Soviet Union into the Pacific War. Apparently the issue of the Party's future strategy excited considerable disagreement. Some continued to hold that the Party was strong enough to seize power on its own and contended that this would provide the revolutionaries with a strong basis on which to conduct negotiations with the French. Others feared the weakness of the revolutionary forces and felt that it would be difficult to prevent the return of the French. The best strategy would be to build up the strength of the revolutionary forces gradually without actually attempting to seize power, while carrying on negotiations with the French colonial authorities.

Ho Chi Minh had been seriously ill and was unable to take an active part in all of the debates. He did attend most of the meetings, however, and through his suggestions was able to exert an influence. As always, he played the role of conciliator. Agreeing with the optimistic view that the Party was in a position to seize power, he was nevertheless cautious in his assessment of the situation. Since the reaction of the occupation forces to a general uprising could not be predicted, the revolution should be launched in such a way as to leave open an avenue of retreat. The first moves should thus take place in areas where the Party was already in a strong position, such as the Viet Bac. If the situation developed in a promising way, the uprising could be gradually extended from the base areas to rural areas throughout the country. Then, once urban elements were adequately prepared, revolutionary forces would gather in the suburbs of the major cities and enter at the proper moment to help the urban Party apparatus to seize power in the major cities.[52]

In the end, the plenum accepted Ho's plan. Declaring that the international situation was excellent and agreeing that the period of preparation was over and that the period of direct and general uprising had begun, the conference drafted an appeal to the entire people to rise. A national insurrection committee headed by Secretary General Truong Chinh was vested with the responsibility of directing the uprising. It only remained for the National Congress to formalize the decision to rise.

The National Congress of the Vietminh League opened on August 16 in a three-room thatch hut on the banks of a small stream. In a series of brief sessions, the congress ratified the decision to launch a general uprising, elected the National Liberation Committee (Uy Ban Dan Toc Giai Phong) chaired by Ho Chi Minh that would serve as a provisional government until elections could be held, and issued a ten-point program. On the morning of the seventeenth, the National Liberation Committee publicly affirmed its sacred duty to the fatherland in a ceremony in front of the communal temple. It was undoubtedly an emotional moment. Ho Chi Minh spoke briefly in the name of the committee and, turning toward the new flag of the movement— a gold star on a red background—read an appeal to the Vietnamese people to rise in revolution:

The Vietminh Front is at present the foundation of the struggle and solidarity of our people. Join the Vietminh Front, support it, make it greater and stronger!

At present, the National Liberation Committee is, so to speak, in itself our provisional government. Unite around it and see to it that its policies and instructions are carried out throughout the country!

In this way, our fatherland will certainly win independence and our people will certainly soon win freedom.

The decisive hour in the destiny of our people has struck. Let us stand up with all our strength to liberate ourselves!

Many oppressed peoples the world over are vying with one another in the march to win back their independence. We cannot allow ourselves to lag behind.

Forward! Forward! Under the banner of the Vietminh Front, move forward courageously![53]

Symbolically, the appeal was signed, for the last time, Nguyen Ai Quoc.

5

The Days of August
(August–September 1945)

There is an element of chance in all classical revolutions. Lenin was doing more than merely paying homage to the role of the unknown when he observed that revolution is infinitely more complex in reality than in theory. The August uprising bears out the truth of this aphorism. For in spite of all the careful planning that had taken place as a result of the March directive of the Standing Committee, there was a distinct aura of spontaneity and improvisation about the insurrection that occurred on the heels of the Japanese surrender to the Allied forces in Asia. When the tocsin announcing the onset of the revolution was sounded on the steps of the village *dinh* (temple) at Tan Trao, many of the local committees of the Vietminh scattered throughout the country were isolated from direct contact with the Party leadership and had not been immediately apprised of developments at the National Congress. In ignorance of the decisions reached at Tan Trao, they were compelled to take measures into their own hands as they reacted to the confusing events that followed the end of the war. It is useful to keep this fact in mind in evaluating the major events surrounding the August Revolution, lest we assume that the Party was able to orchestrate the uprising from its headquarters outside of Hanoi. In actuality, in many areas local Vietminh organizations jumped the gun. Beginning on August 14, uprisings took place in rural districts all over North Vietnam. In some cases, the attacks were launched by local Vietminh units. In others (at least, so claim Party historians), the local population seems to have risen spontaneously. Where units of Vo Nguyen Giap's PLA were operating, they often assisted local forces in taking power. According to Truong Chinh, the main form of struggle was the "armed demonstration," a combination of political and military action that would later be described as a unique aspect of the Vietnamese revolution.[1] Where power was seized, people's liberation committees were established and class enemies were punished. In the meantime, PLA units began to move in force toward Hanoi and attacked several cities and towns on the fringes of the Red River delta. In a few cases, as in the provincial capitals of Thai Nguyen and Tuyen Quang, the local authorities offered resistance but, in the absence of directions from the government in Hanoi, such opposition was half-hearted at best. By the end of the week, most of the district and provincial capitals north and northwest of Hanoi had fallen to the revolutionary forces.

The situation was more complicated in Hanoi, where the Japanese were present in force. There were also several companies of Vietnamese troops and military police under the command of the government of Tran Trong Kim. All summer, the Vietminh Municipal Committee had been attempting to infiltrate the ranks of the local military units and the police, but although a few had joined the revolution, most still obeyed their superiors.[2] To take the city, the Communists would be compelled to rely on the disarray or disintegration of the government. In midsummer of 1945, the chances of that were very good. By early August, there were signs of Japanese defeat, and the Vietnamese government reflected the growing weakness of its patron. On the 13th, Prime Minister Kim resigned and transferred power to a committee that played the role of a provisional government. The new committee immediately convened a meeting of local political groups to discuss the rapidly evolving political situation and, in an effort to defuse the power of the radicals, invited the Vietminh to attend. The local Vietminh committee agreed to send a delegation to the meeting, but it refused the government's plea to abstain from the use of force and imposed its own counterdemand that the provisional government resign.

On the fifteenth, news of the Japanese surrender reached Hanoi. The local Japanese military command immediately turned over its remaining functions to Vietnamese authorities. That evening, the ICP Regional Committee for Tonkin convened a meeting at the village of Van Phuc in Ha Dong Province. It had not yet received from the Central Committee any word of a formal decision to rise, but, in view of the situation in the capital, the committee members agreed that they could wait no longer to take advantage of the momentous opportunity, created by the end of the war, to change decisively the history of the Vietnamese nation. The situation had developed as Ho Chi Minh had predicted: The Japanese were in confusion, the local Vietnamese authorities seemed indecisive, the middle class was restive and seemed receptive to the Vietminh, and a sense of desperation was growing in the villages.

The Standing Committee's March directive had clearly underscored the need to act rapidly at the moment of decisive opportunity and had encouraged all Vietminh units to act on their own initiative to take advantage of local conditions. Using that as justification, the Regional Committee decided to call for partial uprisings in the ten provinces of the Red River delta, in order to occupy provincial capitals and seize weapons in preparation for the second stage, an outbreak in the city of Hanoi, on the following day. To direct operations, a five-man military insurrectional committee was set up under the command of local Party chief Nguyen Khang. For the moment, the committee would operate in the Hanoi suburbs. On the decisive day, it would move into the center of the city.[3]

The Hanoi Party apparatus had been attempting to prepare for this day for several months. It had been assiduously promoting its cause in working-class areas and among students and low-level government officials, and had set up national salvation associations (*cuu quoc hoi*) and secretly organized self-defense militia. As early as the end of 1944, the most enthusiastic members of the *cuu quoc hoi* were encouraged to enroll in selected companies of assault militia and so-called honorary units—terrorist organizations designed to assassinate members of the pro-Japanese regime and other enemies of the revolution.[4] In the suburbs, armed propaganda detachments were formed among local villagers in preparation for the decisive moment when they would be instructed to move into the city to mobilize the urban masses for the coming general uprising. During the insurrection these units would be used as shock troops to supplement urban elements, who were considered to be inadequate in numbers and weaponry to topple government authority on their own initiative.

On the morning of the seventeenth, Vietminh units in the Hanoi suburbs went into action. The local administration was deposed, and government seals, the symbols of political authority, were seized or, in some cases, turned over voluntarily to newly established people's revolutionary committees. Self-defense units were set up and armed with sticks, sabers, or guns. By nightfall virtually all the communes surrounding the city were in rebel hands and the waves of revolution were lapping at the gates of the capital.[5]

Inside Hanoi, unrest was increasing. On the afternoon of the seventeenth, a large crowd gathered at the National Theater in the main square to attend a meeting of political parties and factions loyal to the provisional government of Tran Trong Kim. As the meeting started in the main auditorium, pro-Vietminh elements filed into the balconies and began to chant, demanding independence and power to the people. To complete the disruption, agitators descended from the balconies and erupted onto the floor of the hall, ripped down the flag of the imperial regime, and raised the red and gold standard of the Vietminh. Armed propaganda units seized the rostrum, announced the surrender of Japan, and appealed to the audience to support the Vietminh. The meeting climaxed in a march, with the massive crowds gathered on the square in front of the theater pouring into the surrounding streets and, despite a heavy summer downpour, forming a column that, chanting "support the Vietminh," marched to the palace of the imperial delegate.

That evening, Hanoi Party chief Nguyen Khang called a meeting of the Municipal Committee. With the suburbs rapidly falling into the hands of the Vietminh and the population within the city rising to a peak of radical fervor, Hanoi appeared ripe for revolution. The committee decided to devote the eighteenth to smuggling weapons into the city and dispersing armed propaganda units to strategic points in order to agitate the masses. On the following morning, the general uprising would be launched in the very heart of the enemy's lair. To supplement the Party's estimated 100,000 sympathizers within the city, reinforcements would be transported from the industrial and agricultural suburbs, where militia units were ready and waiting. Appeals were printed in Japanese calling on occupation troops to refrain from interfering in the proceedings. On the night of the eighteenth, the military insurrectionary committee moved into the city from the suburbs.

The August Revolution

On the morning of the 19th, a crowd estimated at 200,000 gathered in Ba Dinh square in front of the National Theater. Since dawn, thousands of peasants had been drifting in from the neighboring villages of Thanh Thi, Thuan Tin, and Phu Xuyen and they now congregated with workers, students, petty merchants, and government officials in anticipation of the coming events. Shortly before noon, a member of the Vietminh Municipal Committee came out on the upper balcony of the theater and proclaimed that the general uprising had begun. A few minutes later, the crowd began to branch into several columns and to march in separate groups to several key points in the city—the city hall, the central police headquarters, and the palace of the imperial delegate to North Vietnam. In a few instances, they met with momentary resistance. At the palace, units of the local civil guard were deployed in front of the building and the officer in charge seemed determined to resist. But when Vietminh assault units gathered for an attack and engaged in a short skirmish, he surrendered.[6] In most sectors of the city, opposition to the revolution simply melted away.

There was virtually no reaction from the Japanese. During the day Vietminh authorities negotiated with representatives of the occupation forces and an agreement was reached that the Japanese troops would not intervene. As for the local Vietnamese government, it, too, was a weak reed and disbanded before the tangible evidence of Vietminh power. By late afternoon, the capital was in the hands of the revolution.

Leon Trotsky once observed that, outside of Petrograd and Moscow, the Bolshevik insurrection had been a "revolution by telegraph." Following the consolidation of revolutionary power in the major cities, the new authorities simply sent messages to the provincial Party apparatus in outlying districts, informing them that a new government was in power and instructing them to take command in local areas. To this extent, the Vietnamese revolution followed its Russian counterpart. On the completion of the uprising in Hanoi, the Vietminh leadership dispatched telegrams to localities throughout the North where revolutionary power was not already installed, announced the Vietminh victory in the capital, and instructed their followers: "If possible act as in Hanoi. But where the Japanese resist, attack resolutely. It is necessary at all costs to seize power." In localities throughout Tonkin not already in Vietminh hands, the success in Hanoi was repeated. In the provinces of Ha Dong, Phuc Yen, and Vinh Yen, in the panhandle as well as the upper Red River delta, Vietminh forces swept aside the half-hearted resistance of local authorities and the Japanese, and by the twenty-second the red wave had submerged the North.

Outside Tonkin, the revolution developed more slowly. Ho and his colleagues counted on the efforts of revolutionary victories in the North to provide a catalyst for insurgency forces elsewhere, but Vietminh units in the Center and the South did not possess the advantages of a liberated base area and a red army and were often poorly informed about events taking place elsewhere in Vietnam. Under the circumstances, they did surprisingly well. In the Center, the main theater of action was in the imperial capital of Hué, where local Communists had begun to organize for the coming uprising soon after receiving the March directive from the Standing Committee. In contrast to the situation in Hanoi, however, there were several well-organized political factions loyal to the Japanese or the French in the area. These groups were bolstered by the presence of almost 5,000 Japanese troops. Nor was the general population mix as favorable to the revolution as it was in Hanoi or in Saigon: There was relatively little industry in the area and thus little worker organization. Some support for the Vietminh came from students and petty government officials, but the nucleus of radical sentiment in the central coastal provinces came from the rural population, where the Vietminh had built a strong organization in poor villages.

On hearing the news of the uprising in Tonkin, local Party leaders in the central provinces lacked direction and seemed momentarily confused. Only when the artist To Huu, an envoy from the central Party leadership, arrived in Hué did the local Provincial Committee meet and declare the onset of a general uprising. As in Hanoi, preparations began outside the city, with a revolutionary takeover in neighboring rural communes and the organization of peasant self-defense militia. Then, on the twenty-third, the revolutionaries, in the form of an enthusiastic crowd of 150,000, many of them militia units from outside the city, took power. As in Hanoi, the Japanese and local Vietnamese forces stood by and permitted the insurgents to have their way.

Elsewhere in the Center, the main area of revolutionary activity centered around the district of Ba To in Quang Ngai Province. The area had been restive since the failure of a Communist-led revolt early in the year, but the remnants of the revolutionary forces had been able to withdraw into the hinterland. After regrouping, they had attempted to return to the offensive and in midsummer had formed a national salvation committee representing more than 100,000 members throughout Quang Ngai Province. During the week of August 13–20, they seized power in villages throughout the district of Ba To and a week later formed a provisional people's revolutionary committee at the province level. The victory was temporary, for the French soon counterattacked and restored their authority, but the Vietminh tenaciously dug in and kept its apparatus alive.[7]

Cochin China was undoubtedly the knottiest problem for the Communists. Although the Party was reasonably well represented in the area, particularly in Saigon where the Vanguard Youth had considerable support among workers and youth, it faced a number of potential rivals who were better organized than the scattered non-Communist groupings in the Center and the North. In Saigon there were a number of middle-class nationalist parties, some with a pro-Japanese orientation, as well as the small but pesky Trotskyite organization under the brilliant French-trained journalist Ta Thu Thau. In the countryside, conditions were less conducive to revolution than in the North. There had been no famine in Cochin China, and the spread of Vietminh support in rural villages was hindered by the Cao Dai and the Hoa Hao, whose populist and quasi-mystical faith had earned the emotional support of up to 2 million peasants in the areas south and west of Saigon. A final impediment was the presence of three Japanese army divisions, supplemented by more than 5,000 Vietnamese police.

As in Hué, the Party leadership in Saigon had no reliable link with the Central Committee in the North, and as the end of the war approached it tended to follow its own instincts in preparing for the general uprising.[8] With Communist strength concentrated in the Saigon metropolitan area and a weaker Party organization in the countryside (except for the famous "red belt" of pro-Communist villages in the Saigon suburbs), the Municipal Committee decided on the Saigon-Cholon metropolitan area as the natural focus for the uprising. In early August, radical elements within the Vanguard Youth in the factories and neighboring villages were secretly organized into 350 separate paramilitary units totaling more than 100,000 members. One problem was how to deal with the non-Communist nationalist groups operating in the area, now gathered into the loosely organized National United Front. But the major issue was whether to stage an uprising whenever local conditions were ripe or to await a directive from the central Party leadership in the North.

On the first question, the Party leadership decided to make an effort to bring the nationalists over to its side. On the fourteenth, Tran Van Giau, top Communist in the Saigon area since the early 1930s, met with representatives of the front and persuaded them not to attempt to obstruct the Vietminh from seizing power.[9] They were apparently convinced by Giau's argument that his organization had official recognition from the victorious Allies. On the second question, indecision was reflected in Party councils as late as the seventeenth, when a meeting of the local leadership was convened to discuss future plans. Some, convinced that the Party was too weak to seize power on its own inititative, advocated a legal effort to compete for influence after the return of the French. The majority supported a proposal for a general insurrection but could not agree on a date. As a compromise, it was decided to launch an uprising on the twenty-first in the town of Tan An, a district in the lower delta region south of Saigon where the local Party organization was already well organized, in order to test the reaction of the Japanese. In the meantime, the Vietminh in Saigon would surface and begin to mobilize the masses.

On August 20 news of the uprising in Hanoi reached Saigon. That same evening, the Vietminh leadership held a massive meeting at a downtown cinema and announced a program of action. Nguyen Van Tao, a top Party member long active in Saigon journalism circles and once a member of the FCP Central Committee, announced that the Vietminh would now begin to operate in the open, and he freely conceded that the Vanguard Youth was one of its components. Vietminh flags and leaflets appeared throughout the city, and a massive nationalist demonstration sponsored by the National United Front took place in downtown Saigon. According to some estimates, the crowd was nearly half a million and included 100,000 peasants loyal to the religious sects and parading behind a monarchist flag.

The following day, news of the success of the uprising in Tan An arrived in Saigon. Flushed with the news of victory and confident of Japanese intentions to stand aside, local Party leaders decided to prepare for an immediate uprising. Tran Van Giau called a meeting of the National United Front and persuaded the members of the other parties represented to disband the front and join the Vietminh.

On the twenty-fourth the Regional Party Committee set up an uprising committee and agreed to schedule the uprising in Saigon for the following day, to be followed by insurrections in all provinces of Cochin China. Meetings were held at Vanguard Youth headquarters with representatives of all parties, and most agreed to follow Vietminh leadership. That night, assault troops seized all major enterprises in the Saigon area and raised the Vietminh banner, while thousands of villagers organized in paramilitary units prepared to enter the city from the neighboring suburbs at dawn. The next morning, public offices in dowtown Saigon were occupied. There were a few scattered clashes, but local Japanese forces were induced to surrender, and in two hours the city was in revolutionary hands. To direct the city, the multi-party Committee of the South was set up. Six of its nine members were Vietminh members, and Tran Van Giau was selected as president. When Hoang Quoc Viet, envoy from the Central Committee, arrived in Saigon the following day, victory seemed reasonably secure.

Outside the city, the revolution lagged behind. Most of the provinces south and west of Saigon were in the hands of the surging Hoa Hao movement, now over a million strong. Although the Hoa Hao, like the Cao Dai, were anti-French and at least protonationalist in inspiration, they were, if anything, more concerned to achieve regional autonomy than to subordinate their interests in the broader goal of national independence. From the start, the sects' inherent regionalism and religious orientation clashed with the universalist pretensions of the Vietminh in the South, and by early autumn hostility between the groups had become commonplace. In September, a particularly bloody clash between Hoa Hao and Vietminh units took place at Can Tho, in the heart of the delta, and left dozens dead. Distaste for the French led the Hoa Hao leadership to continue efforts to cooperate with the Vietminh, but the relationship was an uneasy one.

In some nonsect areas, there was briefly a whiff of social revolution in the countryside. In some cases, poor peasants (whether or not instigated by local Communist activists is not clear) seized land and caused property damage, prompting fears by local Party leaders that excessive radicalism could undermine the still fragile structure of cooperation with the nationalists. Nguyen Van Tao espressed such views in a directive to local Party officials: "All those who have instigated the peasants to seize the land owners' property will be severely and pitilessly punished. We have not yet made the Communist revolution which will solve the agrarian problem. This government is only a democratic government. That is why such a task does not devolve upon it.[10]

In a week, the revolution had swept to power in much of Vietnam, from the Chinese border to the Gulf of Siam. When Ho Chi Minh was informed of the success of the uprising in Hanoi, he left Tan Trao and went in secret to a small house owned by a friend on the outskirts of the city, where he remained for several days, receiving reports of the stirring events throughout the country. The news of victory undoubtedly had an exhilarating effect on the revolutionary leadership. Many of Ho's colleagues were ready to follow Lenin's example in Petrograd and to claim total power in the name of the Vietminh. Ho Chi Minh was more conscious of the strength of the forces opposing the revolution, however, and at a meeting of the Liberation Committee he argued strongly for the formation of a provisional government that would include members of other parties and factions, in order to broaden the base of support for the new order. The other members of the committee were carried along by Ho's reasoning and several non-Communists were included in the provisional government of the new Democratic Republic of Vietnam (D.R.V.), which was announced on August 28. The key members, however, were members of the Vietminh. Vo Nguyen Giap and Pham Van Dong, not yet generally known as members of the ICP, were selected as ministers of the interior and of finance. Ho Chi Minh, identified only as "a national patriot who had devoted his whole life to achieving his country's independence," was named president and minister of foreign affairs.

Ho Chi Minh was probably also responsible for the decision to offer to Emperor Bao Dai the position of supreme political adviser to the new regime. Highly conscious of his own weak position as puppet of the fading power of Japan, Bao Dai had decided before war's end to request the Vietminh to form a cabinet to replace that of Tran Trong Kim. But in the frenetic last days of

August, the emperor's authority was ignored. On the twentieth, a mass meeting of leftist intellectuals in Hanoi had demanded the emperor's abdication and the formation of a new Vietminh government. The emperor had responded two days later by calling on the Vietminh to form a new government. By then, however, it was too late, and when a telegram from Hanoi arrived at the imperial palace demanding his abdication, Bao Dai gave in. A three-man delegation led by veteran Communist (and later minister of propaganda) Tran Huy Lieu went to Hué and accepted his resignation.[11] Ho Chi Minh evidently approved of the decision to depose the last ruler of the Nguyen dynasty but characteristically attempted to make use of Bao Dai's lingering authority over the Vietnamese people by inviting him to take a position in the new government.

A few days after the liberation of Hanoi, Ho Chi Minh moved into the capital and quietly took up residence with other top members of the Party in the house of a Party member on Hang Ngang street. For several days he lived quietly, working over the draft of the Declaration of Independence for the new Vietnamese republic. After he had finished it, he discussed it with many of his top lieutenants. Vo Nguyen Giap later recalled that Ho Chi Minh once remarked that it was the happiest period of his life.

The morning of September 2 dawned bright and sunny. Beginning in the early hours, thousands of peasants began to stream in from the suburbs and to mingle with other thousands of workers, students, merchants and government officials congregating in Ba Dinh Square. The provisional government had declared a national holiday, and the city was festooned with streamers and banners carrying slogans in several languages: "Vietnam for the Vietnamese," "Down with French Colonialism," "Support the Provisional Government," "Support President Ho Chi Minh," and "Welcome to the Allied Mission." Chinese occupation troops had begun to arrive from the north and mingled freely and amicably with the hundreds of thousands of Vietnamese in the downtown area. The crowd was orderly and friendly, and a French observer noted that there were no signs of hostility to the few Europeans in the crowd.

At noon, the independence ceremony began at Ba Dinh Square. President Ho Chi Minh appeared on the balcony of the National Theater, wearing a faded khaki suit and white rubber sandals—the uniform that he would thenceforth wear for all state occasions.[12] His speech was short and to the point. He simply read the new Vietnamese Declaration of Independence on which he had been working during the past few days. The declaration opened with a passage borrowed from the American Declaration of Independence: "All men are created equal. They are endowed by their Creator with certain unalienable [sic] Rights; among these are Life, Liberty, and the pursuit of Happiness." Ho then added that "all the peoples on the earth are equal from birth, all the peoples have a right to live and to be happy and free," and he quoted from the Declaration of the Rights of Man and the Citizen drawn up in 1791 in the midst of the French Revolution. This was followed by a harsh indictment of the brutal and undemocratic character of the French colonial regime in Vietnam. He concluded with a ringing declaration of Vietnam's right to be free: "Viet Nam has the right to enjoy freedom and independence and in fact has become a free and independent country. The entire Vietnamese people are determined to mobilize all their physical and mental strength, to sacrifice their lives and property in order to safeguard their freedom and independence."[13]

Having concluded his reading of the declaration, Ho Chi Minh gazed out at the crowd and asked quietly, "My fellow countrymen, have you understood?" According to the account of Vo Nguyen Giap, who was standing next to him at the rostrum, one million voices cried out in unison their ringing affirmation.

The Lessons of August

The August Revolution was so obviously an extraordinary achievement that it is important to keep in mind that a number of fortuitous circumstances contributed in no small measure to the Communist victory. The rapid disintegration of government authority in both urban and rural areas, coupled with the delayed arrival of Allied occupation forces after the surrender of Japan, created a political vacuum at the levers of power. The appearance of famine in the countryside—a factor so familiar to students of the revolutionary process—provided the sense of desperation that gave the Communists access to the villages and fueled the rural insurgency. In the cities, all authority had crumbled and the urban population was watchful, anticipating the arrival of a new force capable of mastering the situation. In the perceptive view of the noted French Vietnamologist Paul Mus, French colonialism had lost title to the Confucian Heavenly Mandate by its failure to protect the Vietnamese from the Japanese. Political legitimacy would be granted to whatever force could effectively claim power and reestablish order. In the classic sense, Vietnam in August 1945 was ripe for rebellion.[14]

Yet objective conditions alone do not make a revolution, and it is to the credit of the Communists that they were able to grasp the opportunity so enticingly offered at the end of the Pacific War. In other colonial societies, the vacuum might have been filled by non-Communist nationalism. But in Vietnam, the nationalists were unable to rise to the challenge. Plagued since the early 1920s by factional and regional divisions, an inability (or an unwillingness) to build a mass base in the countryside, and an absence of any overall sense of the Vietnamese revolution, the urban bourgeois parties, variously moderate and radical, pro-Japanese, pro-Chinese, or pro-French, were collectively almost inconsequential in the political situation that followed the fall of Japan.[15] Only the ICP possessed the sense of timing and the understanding of the strategic nuances of the situation to rise to the occasion. The final point is crucial. For the August Revolution, above all, was a triumph of understanding. As Vo Nguyen Giap explained, it

> was a new development of revolutionary struggle: combining political and armed violence, and carried out simultaneously in the countryside and the cities, the principal means being the political strength of the masses; this strength, organized into a broad united front based on the alliance of the working class with the peasantry, was mobilized, organized and led by the party of the working class. Thus, we can clearly see that the practice of the August 1945 general insurrection had a highly creative content. In a former colonial and semi-feudal country like ours, the revolution of national liberation does not necessarily take the form of a protracted struggle, or that of an armed uprising in the cities, but it is quite possible for it to combine in a creative manner these two forms of struggle.[16]

In this passage, Giap has clearly staked out Hanoi's claim to a share in advancing the revolutionary art. The August Revolution was neither a carbon copy of the Bolshevik uprising, nor of the Chinese Civil War, but a sophisticated combination of the two. Recent scholarship in Hanoi has elaborated on the argument and contends that the unique character of the August uprising lies in its adroit coordination of political and armed struggle. Is such a contention justified? On the face of it, the argument is open to serious question, for all great modern revolutions had both a political and a military character. This is particularly true in the case of those revolutions inspired by the thought of Karl Marx, though one form of struggle may predominate in each individual case.

The Bolshevik Revolution is a case in point. The major thrust of the October insurrection was political: the disintegration of government authority, the gradual Bolshevik takeover of the Petrograd Soviet, the virtually bloodless coup on the night of October 25, and the "revolution by telegraph" (to repeat Trotsky's felicitous phrase) in the provinces. Yet the military factor was not negligible. Unable to build a revolutionary armed force while operating in Petrograd under the watchful eyes of the Provisional Government, the Bolsheviks relied on the subversion of key army units in the capital area. At the moment of insurrection, the transfer of loyalty by such units played a major role in the success of the uprising.

By contrast, the Communist rise to power in China, on the surface, was primarily a military affair. In the course of a protracted struggle, the CCP had forged its liberation army into a powerful force of more than a million men and, at the moment of truth, Communist military power was decisive in the victory over the Kuomintang. Still, the Party's political strategy had been instrumental in putting it into position to challenge Chiang Kai-shek after the Pacific War. If military power was decisive at the climax of the Civil War, it was the political success of the CCP that had brought the Nanking government to the brink of disintegration and achieved a major "transfer of allegiance" of the Chinese population to the Communists.

The significance of the August Revolution, then, must be found not in the simple fact that the ICP used both political and military struggle, but in the degree to which these factors were carefully interwoven in the fabric of the Party's revolutionary strategy. To put the issue another way, the contribution of the August Revolution was less theoretical than practical—the sophisticated and flexible manner in which the Party applied political and military struggle to the concrete situation in Vietnam. Astute manipulation of the two forms of struggle at the opportune moment was the key to victory.

Here, perhaps, Vo Nguyen Giap has a point. For in the complex situation at the end of the war, a strategy placing sole reliance on either political or military struggle would have been insufficient and possibly disastrous. The Party lacked the necessary military strength to impose its will. Moreover, the challenge of the August Revolution was primarily political—to fill the political void left by the Japanese defeat and to make a convincing case (to the Allies as well as to the local population) that the Vietminh Front effectively represented the interests of the Vietnamese people. Political struggle alone, however, was clearly insufficient, for the filling of the power vacuum left by the defeat of Japan would require the rapid action and demonstration of armed might that only military force could provide. The decisive importance of military strength was clearly illustrated in the South, where the weakness of the Party's military apparatus facilitated the pacification effort undertaken by the British occupation troops. Where the Party possessed armed forces, they were adroitly used to supplement the armed strength of the masses and to fill the power vacuum. A carefully orchestrated balance of political and military struggle was thus the most effective means by which the Party could take advantage of the weakness of the enemy and overcome its own disadvantages.

Giap's second claim is that a key to the Party's success lay in its capacity to operate in both the cities and the countryside. Where the Bolshevik insurrection had been predominantly urban, and the Chinese revolution primarily rural, he claimed that the August Revolution combined the two approaches in a single integrated strategy. Ho Chi Minh had noted the importance of this factor in his 1927 article, but the Party had been burdened in the 1920s and 1930s by a lack of organization in both areas and by the urban bias of the Comintern leadership. Not until the 1940s did a joint urban-rural strategy become a major component of Vietnamese revolutionary doctrine, thus justifying Giap's contention. As the uprising unfolded, the Vietminh Front was reasonably successful in making its appeal in both areas. Peasants in the impoverished villages of the North viewed the front as an engine of radical social reform. Bourgeois nationalists in the major cities saw it as a patriotic movement fiercely dedicated to national independence, but moderate in its political and social outlook. In the climactic phase of the uprising, the Communist-led front achieved considerable success in linking town and country in the final surge for power.

Famine, more than anything else, made the strategy possible. Ho Chi Minh had carefully crafted the Vietminh Front to appeal to all patriotic groups, regardless of social class. In 1941, this had implied an essentially moderate rural program, and the Eighth Plenum had advocated a land reform program that could win the allegiance of the poor without alienating patriotic landlords. As the CCP found out, however, straddling the agrarian question can be an awkward posture and costly in its consequences. Famine permitted the ICP to escape this dilemma. As early as 1943 the Party had become sharply conscious of the importance of the issue and began to make it a major element in propaganda directed at the densely populated Red River delta, criticizing Japanese confiscation of grain, conscription, and high taxes. In regions controlled by the Party, rents were reduced, taxes were lowered and, in some cases, the land of the wealthy was seized and distributed to the poor. As the food crisis deepened, local operatives took the lead in instigating peasant demonstrations to protest the government's refusal to release rice held in granaries for local consumption.

Whether or not the issue of famine was a decisive factor in the Revolution, the Party leadership apparently thought that it was. In his 1947 study of the August uprising, Truong Chinh quoted Stalin on the need to find one focal issue that could become the central question of the revolution. In Vietnam, said Chinh, that question was famine and he added that Communist-led armed demonstrations in front of government granaries were the key to the development of the movement in rural areas throughout the North.[17]

The significance of the famine issue for the August Revolution is suggested by the history of rural revolt in North Vietnam. Throughout the preceding decade the Red River delta, to the despair of Party activists, had remained relatively impervious to the shockwaves of rural unrest elsewhere. In fact, there had been no rural unrest of serious proportions in the Red River delta since the French conquest. Now, desperation transformed the North into a tinderbox of revolt. While the proximity of PLA units was undoubtedly a factor in stimulating the active participation of Tonkinese peasants in the uprising, the rapidity with which provinces throughout the delta fell to Vietminh control suggests the force of hunger as an issue in the Revolution. For the most part, peasant radicalism was apparently spontaneous and in some cases even went beyond the wishes of Party activists.

The famine issue permitted the Party to ride the crest of rural unrest without being forced to draw up a radical program that might have alienated moderate nationalist elements in the cities. And, as Ho Chi Minh had realized nearly two decades earlier, the cities would have to play a crucial role in lifting the revolutionary forces to victory in Vietnam. In China, the CCP counted on the power of the People's Liberation Army to overwhelm the forces of Chiang Kai-shek in the countryside and then to seize the cities. The Vietnamese Communists with their miniscule armed forces could not hope for the same achievement. Lacking the offensive power of its Chinese comrades, the ICP would be forced to count on the support of its followers in the cities. Previously, the Party had lacked the strength to challenge the French in urban areas. In August 1945, however, it had an unprecedented opportunity to fill the vacuum left by the end of the war.

The trouble was that, even under such favorable conditions, the Party apparatus in several of the major cities, weakened by years of colonial oppression, was in no position to make a major contribution to the August uprising. To compensate, the Party was forced to supplement its urban forces with additional militia units brought in from neighboring rural villages. The stratagem would become familiar in the years ahead.

The relative weakness of the Party's urban base raises serious doubts about the urban-rural balance that Hanoi claims underlay the August Revolution. Were the cities an integral element in the insurrection? Did the urban populace as a whole support the revolution? Unfortunately, the evidence is too scanty at present to justify a definitive conclusion. Accounts of the uprisings in the major cities suggest that factory workers and students were fairly active in the revolutionary cause, and it seems clear that such groups made up the bulk of the Party's paramilitary forces. There are fewer indications of active involvement on the part of functionaries or merchants despite the founding (with Vietminh support) of a Vietnamese Democratic Party representing the interests of bureaucrats and intellectuals. This has led one observer to comment that, on the whole, the middle class did not support the revolution.[18] For the moment, it is perhaps advisable to reserve judgment on this issue. Although there is little evidence of active middle-class involvement in the urban uprisings, there was equally little active individual hostility to the Vietminh on the part of bourgeois elements, even in Saigon. For the most part, the Vietnamese urban middle class appeared to stand warily on the sidelines. It accepted the Vietminh Front's carefully cultivated image of moderate nationalism but did not take to the barricades to resist the return of colonial power.

The ICP's ability to project an image of moderation was undoubtedly a major factor in its success during the August Revolution, a fact of which Ho Chi Minh was obviously aware. The pose could not last indefinitely, of course, and was only possible because of a series of fortuitous conditions: the disorganization of its nationalist rivals, the fluidity of the external situation, and the absence of legal political bodies like the Petrograd Soviet or the city Duma that would have compelled the Party to show its colors. It is a tribute to the Party's sensitivity to the situation, however, that it was able to manipulate these conditions to its advantage.

To sum up, the flexible combination of political and military, urban and rural struggle was a major factor in the victory of the August Revolution. While the victory was primarily political and rural, the urban and military components were by no means of negligible importance and may have been crucial to success. And although the Party's claim to revolutionary uniqueness may be somewhat overstated, the leadership should receive high marks for (as Giap put it) the creative way in which it applied theory to the concrete situation. For the first but by no means the last time, the Vietnamese Communists had demonstrated that although they had relatively little to offer in the way of theoretical innovations of doctrinal importance, they were masters at the art of applying simple revolutionary concepts in an effective manner.

The Uneasy Peace
(September 1945–December 1946)

During two frenetic weeks in August the Communists, behind the mantle of the Vietminh Front, had seized political power in much of Vietnam. To keep it, however, would be quite another matter, for their victory was more a consequence of the chaos at the end of the war and the temporary disorientation of their rivals than it was a testimony to their power and influence in Vietnam. With the prospective arrival of the Chinese and British occupation forces in Indochina, and the probable return of the French as a consequence, the ICP would have new realities to face.

The Vietminh in Power

Furthermore, the new government's authority in Vietnam was shaky at best. Although the struggle that had led to the revolutionary takeover had been engineered by the Communists, they had seized power in the name of a broad nationalist alliance linked to the Allies' victory elsewhere in Asia. The Party itself was small and still inexperienced. Unlike the CCP, it had not had the luxury of two decades of de facto rule in a liberated area. The mass base of the Vietminh Front was broad—embracing peasants, workers, students, and some merchants and intellectuals in the major cities—but shallow, for the Communist coloration of the leadership was not as yet directly evident to the vast majority of supporters. As a result, although the Vietminh had been generally welcomed by the populace as an indigenous political force leading the struggle of the Vietnamese people for social justice and political independence, such generalized approval would not easily be translated into firm political support in the event of a serious internal conflict among indigenous forces. Indeed, even as the month of August came to a close, rival political parties in all three regions of Vietnam were beginning to gear up to express their opposition to Communist rule over the new provisional government. Neither the VNQDD and the Dong Minh Hoi in the North nor the moderate and pro-Japanese parties in Cochin China were likely to stand idly by while the Communists consolidated their power.

For the Communists, then, the month of September inaugurated a period of intense political activity of almost unprecedented complexity. From the Party's point of view, the struggle would have to be carried on at two levels—against the returning French, the Allied expeditionary forces, and the Japanese occupation troops on the one hand, and against their Vietnamese rivals within the nationalist camp on the other. In a strategic sense, the problem was clear: The ICP could not hope to face both sets of adversaries at the same time. Militarily as well as politically, the Party was too weak to neutralize the French and the Allied occupation forces while competing against their internal nationalist opponents. It could clearly not afford the luxury that had permitted Lenin after the success of the Bolshevik Revolution to dispense with moderate leftist support in his attempt to stay in power. On the contrary, it would be essential to employ a strategy that could take advantage of the internal contradictions among ICP adversaries and to mobilize a maximum amount of support against one enemy at a time. And this policy of flexibility and conciliation would have to be carried out without diluting the Party's authority by losing control over the instruments of power, and without losing the support of the more radical elements within the movement and the nationalist camp as a whole.

In short, the situation posed a serious challenge to the technique of the united front that the ICP had used with varying degrees of success since the founding of the Party fifteen years before. It would require a policy of infinite flexibility and sensitivity to the nuances of international politics and a heightened comprehension of the power relationships that were likely to emerge in the immediate postwar period. It would require a leadership with the international experience and the delicate sense of timing that, within the Vietnamese Communist movement, only Ho Chi Minh could provide.

As if these problems were not enough, the new provisional government also faced the serious social and economic problems that had beset Vietnamese society during the final years of the war. The single overriding issue was hunger. Famine, which had struck with such ferocity during the previous winter, was an even more serious threat in the months ahead, as the 1945 harvest was well below average. By one estimate, it would reach only half the normal tonnage. The greatest crisis was being felt in Tonkin, where widespread flooding had led peasants to abandon more than 400,000 hectares of rice land. Later, drought limited the fall harvest and government experts predicted that food would run out by February. With war beginning in the South, there was little prospect for exports to the North from the rice surplus areas in the Mekong delta.[1]

Another serious problem, which might be exacerbated by the end of the Pacific War, was the high level of unemployment in urban areas during the war years, which had now become virtually chronic. Far-reaching measures would be called for to alleviate the industrial depression that had lasted since the great crisis of the early 1930s. Here again, the Communists would be walking a tightrope. Given the severity of the crisis and the nature of their basic support, radical measures seemed to be called for; yet government policies would have to be sufficiently moderate to avoid alienating the moderate elements within the broad alliance that the Party hoped to put together against the returning French colonialists.

The first measures taken by the new government indicated the care with which the Party attempted to construct its antiimperialist front. The new Party strategy had first been outlined in the ten-point program promulgated by Ho Chi Minh at the Tan Trao congress in mid-August. The program made no reference to the Party's long-term Marxist goals but was limited to such relatively noncontroversial proposals as tax reduction, seizure of the land of French colonialists and their Vietnamese collaborators, distribution of this land and village commune lands to needy peasants, an eight-hour day and increased rights for workers, the guarantee of basic freedoms to all Vietnamese, and the establishment of an independent democratic republic over the entire territory of Vietnam.[2]

The first acts of the new government in Hanoi were clearly designed to fulfill the promises incorporated in this program. In September preliminary steps were taken to establish democratically elected people's councils at all levels of government and elections for the new National Assembly were scheduled for the end of the year.[3] Within the new state, democratic rights were guaranteed, including equality for all citizens regardless of age, sex, religion, or ethnic background. A decree of September 8 ordered free instruction in the national language with the aim of making all Vietnamese over the age of eight literate within one year. Students were organized to lead a mass education movement throughout the country.

In the economic field, famine was the most serious immediate problem. To alleviate the crisis, the government tried a variety of measures. The long-term solution, in the view of the Party leadership, was collectivization of all arable land, but such harsh measures would destroy the united front in the immediate postwar period. So a variety of more moderate steps were taken, including moral exhortations to the population to conserve grain, encouragement of alternative crops, such as manioc and sweet potatoes, subsidies for farmers expanding the amount of land under cultivation, the establishment of the Farm Credit Bureau to provide loans to the poor, reduction of rents, and distribution of communal land to needy families at the village level. Finally, the capitation tax was lowered by 20 percent, and the hated monopolies on alcohol, salt, and opium were abolished.[4]

Characteristically, Ho Chi Minh put his own personal stamp on the program. Government officials, from the top down, were exhorted to fast one out of every ten days and to donate the food conserved to the needy. As always, the president himself lived frugally, rising at five and performing his daily physical exercises before arriving at his office, often before his subordinates.[5] Periodically he issued appeals to the officials of the new government, cautioning them against arrogance, bureaucratism, and isolation from the people. The Communists were especially careful to espouse moderate policies within the urban economy. Public utilities and a few major industries were nationalized, but in general trade and manufacturing were left in private hands, and the government issued circulars granting assurances that private property would be respected.

Such measures represented a serious effort to win the acquiescence of moderate elements while retaining the support of radicals within the movement. The balancing act was not always successful. Some radicals wanted harsher land policies. In northern Annam and in the province of Quang Ngai, poor peasants agitated for an immediate redistribution of land. In many rural areas, the Party's moderate policies were widely ignored and Party zealots confiscated property, divided land, and even suppressed traditional peasant rituals indiscriminately. In November, the Central Committee was compelled to issue a directive warning Party members that the Indochinese revolution was still in the national liberation stage. Class struggle must be subordinated to such slogans as "full independence" and "power to the people" and, as in 1941, the antifeudal revolution must be subordinated to the needs of the antiimperialist revolution.[6]

In a broad sense, however, the policies of the new government were moderately successful and as summer passed into fall it began to win the support or at least the toleration of Vietnamese of a wide variety of political and religious persuasions. Even the Roman Catholic hierarchy noted its open approval of the new government in a pastoral letter to the 2 million Vietnamese Catholics, and many Vietnamese Catholics joined the new Vietminh-sponsored Catholic National Salvation Association. At one point, the French bishop of Saigon was brought to exclaim in frustration: "On nous a changé nos Annamites!"[7] On September 23 the Vietnamese Catholic hierarchy requested the Pope in Rome to pray for Vietnamese independence.

Nothing that the Communists could do, however, could assuage the suspicion of many of their nationalist rivals, to whom any true reconciliation and cooperation with the ICP seemed extremely difficult, if not impossible. The loose alliance formed in South China with several of the nationalist parties operating in Tonkin had been plagued by mutual suspicion and began to disintegrate during the last months of the war, despite Communist attempts to revitalize it. The Vietminh seizure of power at the end of the war seemed even more concrete proof of Communist perfidy and solidified the hostility of many nationalists toward the new government and President Ho Chi Minh.

The trump card of the nationalists lay with the Chinese expeditionary forces, who were scheduled to arrive in North Vietnam shortly after the war. These troops, some 180,000 strong, began to arrive in early September. In the perhaps biased view of Vo Nguyen Giap, they were a tattered lot, with none of the panache and discipline of his own People's Liberation Army, but they represented a serious threat to the Communists. No only had their com-manders the power to suppress the provisional government; they also had developed a friendly relationship with the ICP's rivals, the Dong Minh Hoi and the VNQDD, which could serve to provide the latter with very real advantages in the coming struggle for dominance in Vietnam.

The nationalist leaders entered Vietnam in the wake of the Chinese troops and with the latter's assistance soon began to seize control of areas earlier taken by the Vietminh in the mountainous areas north of the capital. Certain of Chinese backing, they were also persuaded to take a hard line in negotiations with the Vietminh once they had settled in Hanoi. The VNQDD set up an op-position newspaper, and a loudspeaker at its downtown headquarters began to denounce the "red terror."

In the beginning, the ICP played a cautious game with its major rivals in the nationalist movement. Its basic policy was to neutralize them through concilia-tion or intimidation and gradually to isolate them from the mainstream of Vietnamese politics. One Hanoi Party publication commented that the Party should attempt

> to isolate them before the masses of the people, utilize the force of the masses as a means of pressure to enable the government to repress the counter-revolutionaries, and in case tangible proofs could be adduced against them, to pro-ceed to wipe out their forces step by step. In case they receive the support of their masters, it was necessary to neutralize them gradually; compromise might also be reached while safeguarding the revolutionary power.[8]

As the final sentence suggested, one matter of high priority was to neutralize the effects of the Chinese occupation forces. It became President Ho Chi Minh's major duty during the last months of 1945 to conciliate Generals Lu Han and Hsiao Wen, the commanders of the Chinese troops, in order to pre-vent them from taking action against the Vietminh in favor of its nationalist rivals. Ho's efforts have been exhaustively discussed in earlier studies and need not be detailed here. Suffice it to say that he felt that every effort must be made to avoid clashes with the Chinese, at the same time not letting the government be humiliated. As a Communist publication commented:

> With regard to the Chiang Kai-shek troops, it was necessary to avoid clashes, underline their mission which was to disarm the Japanese troops, prevent their acts of aggression, check their acts of intervention in the internal policy of the country; in case they attacked the national sovereignty, it was necessary to stand ready to launch an unarmed opposition, to mobilize the masses to demonstrate, in a word, to "oppose a political struggle to them."[9]

Despite Ho Chi Minh's efforts, a few clashes took place between Chinese and Vietnamese forces. On the whole, however, the policy was successful. Much of the credit undoubtedly must go to Ho Chi Minh himself, who emphasized on several occasions his desire to follow Chinese orders. On one occasion he even offered his life as a guarantee that there would be no further anti-Chinese acts, and he consistently stressed the determination of his government to follow the famous precepts of Sun Yat-sen. To reduce Chinese suspicion, he changed the name of the Vietnamese People's Liberation Army to "national defense guard," and instructed the government's forces to avoid provoking the Chinese at all costs. There was evidently some resistance within the Party to the policy of conciliation, and a few incidents with the occupation troops appear to have been deliberately instigated. But on the whole, the Party was able to avoid a confrontation and, throughout their stay, the Chinese took a fairly neutral stand in the political situation.[10]

The Chinese did insist, however, that Ho Chi Minh's government negotiate with the other Vietnamese parties in order to obtain their participation in the government and attempted to restructure the old united front to prevent Viet-minh domination. By early November, the nationalists had set up a nationalist bloc dominated by members of the VNQDD and the Dong Minh Hoi and began to demand the immediate formation of a government of national union, with participation by all major political groups. Threatened by a widespread boycott of the scheduled elections for the new National Assembly, Ho Chi Minh agreed to begin negotiations with the other parties in an effort to reach a common front against the French. Before serious negotiations began in mid-November, the Party leadership took the drastic step of formally dissolving the ICP and replacing it with a Marxist study group. In secret, as Party histories later conceded, the Party apparatus continued to exist. Observers have speculated over the years as to the motive for the decision. The reason given by the Party, though perhaps not complete, is persuasive. By apparently abolishing the Party, the leadership hoped to allay nationalist suspicions of the new provisional government.

Serious negotiations between the government and the two major nationalist parties, the VNQDD and the Dong Minh Hoi, began in mid-November. Sensing themselves in a strong position, the nationalists at first took a hard line and demanded that the provisional government resign. Then they demanded several cabinet seats and the presidency. This, however, was too much even for Ho Chi Minh, who offered the nationalists three cabinet seats and the forma-tion of a supreme advisory council under Nguyen Hai Than. This was rejected. After several weeks of skirmishing, agreement was finally reached in mid-December. A provisional coalition government with Ho as president and Nguyen Hai Than as vice president was to be set up on January 1, 1946. General elections to choose members of the National Assembly and a new government would be held five days later. Regardless of the results of the balloting, 70 out of a total of 350 seats in the new legislative body would be reserved for the two major non-Communist parties, 50 for the VNQDD and 20 for the Dong Minh Hoi.[11]

The Collapse of Communist Power in Cochin China

The situation was even more complicated in the South. Communist strength was measurably weaker in Cochin China than in Tonkin. Although the Party had recovered well enough from the crisis of 1940 to play a dominant role in Saigon during the August uprising, its potential influence was diluted by the presence of a number of well-organized rivals—the economically influential moderate parties in Saigon and the religious sects in the countryside. In the South, too, the influence of French colonial elements was more vociferous and firmly established than elsewhere in Vietnam.

Under the circumstances, it is hardly surprising that the Communists soon found themselves on the defensive in Cochin China. During the confusing period after the Japanese surrender, the Vietminh, aided by the persuasiveness of their claim to the support of the victorious Allies, had obtained a controlling voice in the Committee of the South, the organization set up by nationalist groups to serve as a provisional political force and to greet the British forces on their arrival in Saigon. It was not long, however, before the Vietminh leaders found themselves outmatched. Once it became evident that the Vietminh Front had strong Communist overtones and did not represent the will of the great powers, moderate nationalist elements began to oppose its domination of the committee.

Beyond the confines of the ruling group, the situation was even more volatile. On September 2, the Vietminh called for mass demonstrations by all nationalist groups in downtown Saigon. Thousands of Vietnamese turned out. Some were members of the Vietminh or its puppet organization, the Vanguard Youth; others represented rival nationalist groups or the religious sects. Emotions were running high, and predictably the situation got out of hand. When local security forces opened fire on unruly mobs, the crowd turned nasty and began to attack any foreigner unfortunate enough to be on the streets. Before the trouble had subsided, five Frenchmen had been killed and scores wounded. Although it is highly unlikely that the Vietminh had instigated the disorder, it put the local leadership in a delicate spot and suggested that the local Vietnamese administration was incapable of maintaining law and order. On the other hand, any attempt by the Vietminh to rein in the passions of the moment would undoubtedly have been harshly attacked by extreme nationalist and Trotskyite elements in the city.[12] For once, the Party found itself uncomfortably in the middle. Convinced that more was to be lost by radicalism than by moderation, Duong Bach Mai, the Communist security chief in Saigon, attempted to exercise a calming influence. By the next day, the momentary fever had passed but the Communists were being exposed to harsh criticism from radical nationalist sources.

Within a few days the British expeditionary forces began to arrive. Their commander, General Douglas Gracey, had little sympathy with Vietnamese nationalist aspirations and immediately demanded that the Vietnamese political groups lay down their arms. Tran Van Giau was realistic enough to realize that the revolutionaries were not yet strong enough in Cochin China to seize power on their own and attempted to conciliate the British, despite resistance from non-Communist elements in the Committee of the South. Criticized for his moderation, Giau was forced to resign the presidency of the committee, which was now expanded to thirteen members, only four of whom represented the Vietminh. At one stroke, the Vietminh ceased to be *primus inter pares* and became simply one of several parties claiming to represent the interests of Vietnamese nationalism in the South.

During the next few days, the position of the Vietminh continued to deteriorate. Gracey, egged on by French *colons* who resented the arrogant pretensions of the "natives," began to crack down on Vietnamese activities. On September 21 martial law was declared and French troops, newly released from Japanese prisons, were rearmed and began to manhandle local citizens on the streets. When clashes resulted, the French seized the local administration and the Committee of the South was forced to flee the city. By now, the Communists were growing desperate. A joint meeting of the Party's Regional Committee, supplemented by members of the Saigon Municipal Committee and two representatives from the Central Committee, convened to formulate a strategy to deal with the rapidly changing situation. The conciliatory approach was discarded and a new policy, calling for the launching of a movement of resistance against resurgent colonialism, was adopted. The first stage was to be nonviolent in character: An appeal for a general strike was issued, and Party activists attempted to shut off communications into the city and to cut off the supply of food from rural areas. In the meantime, cadres were dispatched to neighboring villages to prepare the countryside for battle. For the next few days, Saigon became a city under siege.

On September 24, serious clashes between Vietnamese and French troops took place in Saigon, resulting in a bloody massacre when enraged mobs of Vietnamese penetrated into French residential areas of the city and killed more than 150 Europeans, some in particularly hideous circumstances. Gracey did not hesitate to strike back. He instructed French troops to occupy and shut down all Vietnamese enterprises and announced that all crimes against the public order would be punishable by death. During the next few days, rebellious elements were tracked down or compelled to flee the city for the surrounding suburbs. For a brief period, there were attempts to reach a negotiated settlement. In early October, Jean Cédile, the chief French civilian representative in Cochin China, reached a tentative compromise with the Committee of the South calling for a truce. But the Vietminh was now becoming increasingly intransigent and demanded independence and a return to the status quo of August 23. On October 10 the negotiations broke down.[13]

During the remainder of October and the first weeks of November, British forces drove Vietminh units from the suburbs while French troops, bolstered by the arrival of a full division of regulars on October 25, broke the siege of Saigon and began to strike into the countryside. The key Mekong delta towns of My Tho, Can Tho, Vinh Long, and Go Cong were occupied, and communications links were gradually opened up with the lower delta provinces. At the same time, several provincial and district capitals in the Central Plateau fell into French hands. Lacking an organized military force of the quality of the PLA, the Committee of the South, again dominated by the Communists, ordered a general mobilization in an effort to recruit new elements—often members of the old French militia and even a few Japanese deserters—to increase the size of their forces, now some 20,000 strong. These initial efforts had only limited success, and as French forces advanced, the insurgency leadership was forced to withdraw deep into the delta and set up its headquarters on Ben Tre Island.

For the moment, the Communists were in a perilous position in the South. The events of the past few weeks had not only cost the Party its dominant position in Saigon, but had also resulted in a significant narrowing of the movement, with many of the urban nationalist factions withdrawing from the alliance with the Vietminh. At that point, the Communists appeared to write off their nationalist rivals. During the following weeks, a number of well-known moderate political figures, including Pham Quynh, Nguyen Van Sam, Bui Quang Chieu, and several top figures of the Trotskyite faction were assassinated, apparently on Tran Van Giau's orders.[14] Relations with the sects also continued to deteriorate, and their armed forces clashed repeatedly with units of the Vietminh, even while the French turned to the "oil spot" technique that had worked successfully against bandits in the Viet Bac at the end of the nineteenth century. (In this technique government forces, after pacifying individual districts, would attempt to extend security to neighboring areas.) Increasingly isolated, the insurgents retreated to the most inaccessible regions of Cochin China—the Plain of Reeds, the Tay Ninh rubber plantations (where sympathy with the revolutionary cause was strong among plantation workers), and the dense U Minh forest in the heart of the Ca Mau peninsula. Hindered by inexperience, lack of weapons, and a high desertion rate (according to one French observer, 10,000 deserted in January alone), the revolutionary forces were inexorably driven onto the defensive.[15] Like it or not, the Communists, whose strength had been based in the Saigon area since the failure of the 1940 uprising, were going to have to learn to live off the land.

In Hanoi, Ho Chi Minh was acutely conscious of the vulnerability of the revolutionary forces and throughout the final months of 1945 attempted to pre-

vent the outbreak of full-scale hostilities with the French regime. Even the international situation was no longer as favorable as it had appeared earlier in the
year. The United States, despite appeals from Ho Chi Minh, was disinclined to
become involved. Even Moscow seemed reluctant to come to the aid of its
client. Preoccupied with European problems and sensitive to any incident that
would complicate its relations with Paris and disturb the possibility of Communist participation in a new French government, the Soviet Union apparently viewed the conflict in Vietnam as a potential embarrassment and, during
the autumn months, advised the ICP to avoid hostilities if at all possible. In
September, the American reporter Harold Isaacs was shown a document from
the FCP that advised the Vietnamese to make certain that their actions met
"the requirements of Soviet policy" and warned that "premature adventurism"
might not be in line with Soviet perspectives.[16] The message suggested that the
Vietnamese should have patience until new French elections, which might
bring the Communists to power, were held in October. According to Isaacs,
the Vietnamese were hurt and bitter and felt isolated by Moscow's attitude.

The troubles in the South thus put Hanoi in an uncomfortable position. As
in 1930, the Party was challenged to provide assistance to its beleaguered comrades without exposing the movement as a whole to serious risks. As early as
the end of August, the Central Committee had issued a directive calling on the
population of Cochin China to resist the return of French troops and to
launch a struggle for complete independence.[17] But as the situation
deteriorated into open conflict in October, the problem suddenly became more
complicated. Within the Party leadership, unanimity was elusive. Some allegedly argued for an open confrontation, others for a more cautious approach.
Vo Nguyen Giap spoke for the majority in advocating scorched earth tactics
(*nha khong dong vang*, literally dead city), an economic blockade of cities, and
protracted guerrilla warfare in the countryside.

Within these restrictions, the government in Hanoi could provide assistance
on a limited basis. Throughout the fall, enthusiastic young cadres, dressed in
padded jackets and leather boots and wearing gold stars on their new caps,
went south. In their footsteps went Party veterans like Hoang Quoc Viet and
Le Duan. The equivalent of several regiments was eventually dispatched,
mostly drawn from the border provinces of Nghe An, Quang Tri, Quang Nam,
and Quang Ngai. In some cases, according to a Party source, whole villages
volunteered. From Hanoi, President Ho Chi Minh issued an appeal for international sympathy for the revolutionary cause. The French, he said,

> have sabotaged the peace that China, the United States, Britain, and Russia won
> at the cost of scores of millions of lives. They have run counter to the promises
> concerning democracy and liberty that the allied powers have proclaimed. They
> have of their own accord sabotaged their fathers' principles of liberty and equality.
> In consequence, it is for a just cause, for justice in the world, and for Viet-Nam's

land and people that our compatriots throughout the country have risen to struggle, and are firmly determined to maintain their independence. We do not hate
the French people and France. We are energetically fighting slavery, and the
ruthless policy of the French colonialists. . . . We are not invading another's country. We only safeguard our own against the French invaders. Hence we are not
alone. The countries which love peace and democracy, and the weaker nations all
over the world, all sympathize with us. With the unity of the whole people within
the country, and having many sympathizers abroad, we are sure of victory.[18]

Hanoi's efforts to stem the tide of French advance, at least in the short run,
had little effect, and early in the new year Giap went secretly to Nha Trang on
the southern coast to appraise the situation. Unfortunately we have little information on the results of his evaluation but there are indications that the local
leadership was seen as part of the problem. Tran Van Giau, one of the few
Stalin School graduates still active at the upper levels of the Party, had had a
reputation as a hardliner since his return to Saigon in the early 1930s. Now,
under his leadership, the insurgency movement had become increasingly identified with a policy of brutality and terrorism and it became clear that, without
a change, an effective alliance with non-Communist elements in the South
would be difficult to realize. Early in 1946, he was replaced by Nguyen Binh, an
ex-member of the VNQDD who had been recruited to the Vietminh before the
war. Apparently Giap viewed the problem as one of personal leadership rather
than overall strategy, because Binh was instructed to continue the scorched
earth tactics that had been followed by his predecessor.[19]

Negotiations with the French

On the surface, the weak position of the Communists in Cochin China was
in stark contrast to the situation in the North. The elections of January 6 had
resulted in a resounding electoral victory for the Vietminh Front. With 97 percent of the electorate voting, the Communists and their political allies won 300
seats and the Front became the dominant political force in the new National
Assembly. Although there were a few complaints of coercion to vote for Vietminh candidates, most observers felt that the elections were relatively fair and
the results reasonably representative of attitudes among the population. The
vote was a striking testimony to the organizational abilities of the Communists
and to the success of their effort to portray the Front as the central force in the
struggle for independence and political and social progress in Vietnam.[20]

The electoral victory strengthened the Party's position in Tonkin, but serious
problems remained. The rival nationalist parties promised to become ever more
vocal as the Vietminh-dominated government attempted to cope with the
broader problem of reaching a settlement with the French. Talks had been pro-
ceeding between Ho Chi Minh and the French representative, Jean Sainteny,
since the previous October, often to accusations of treason by nationalist

elements. The urgency of the issue was underlined in mid-February by the conclusion of an agreement calling for the evacuation of the Chinese and their replacement by French forces. The threat of the imminent arrival of colonial troops in early March placed increasing pressure on President Ho Chi Minh to reach an agreement with Paris before a confrontation became inevitable.[21]

Even for the nimble mind of Ho Chi Minh, it was a situation of extraordinary delicacy. The government's military weakness made a negotiated accord with the French imperative. But the intensity of patriotic feeling in Vietnam and the shallowness of popular support for the Vietminh made compromise a political gamble. To the nationalists, there was poetic justice in the situation. Ho Chi Minh and the ICP were paying the price for their decision not to share real power the preceding autumn. During the final days of February, the president seemed almost desperate for a solution. At one point, he approached Bao Dai, still supreme political advisor to the young republic, and appealed to him to take over the government in order to allay the distrust of the great powers and win nationalist support for a settlement. Bao Dai was acutely aware of the pitfalls in the situation, however, and stalled. By nightfall Ho Chi Minh, for reasons as yet unclear, had changed his mind and withdrew the offer.[22] A few days later he tried to broaden his base of support through a reorganization of the cabinet. Aided by the Chinese, who were pressuring the nationalist parties to accept an accord, on March 2 he was able to win agreement on the formation of the new Government of Resistance and National Reconstruction. Ho retained the presidency, but four of the ten cabinet ministers were nationalists and two were neutralists, leaving only four members of the Vietminh or allied parties.

Thus armed, at least temporarily, with the backing of a multiparty coalition, Ho resumed his talks with Sainteny. There were two major issues in the negotiations. First, under what conditions should the French be permitted to return to North Vietnam? The Hanoi government was willing to permit France to retain cultural rights and to maintain a temporary and modest military presence in the North, and to associate Vietnam with the French Union. But Ho Chi Minh adamantly insisted on a maximum of political autonomy for Vietnam.[23] Secondly, what should be done about the French colony of Cochin China? The French insisted that the colony had a right to determine its own future; Ho Chi Minh was unwilling to concede even the theoretical possibility of a division of the territory of Vietnam.

The situation was not an easy one. But despite the conflicting emotions that a compromise settlement would undoubtedly arouse, the Party leadership decided that it had little choice. As a directive of the Standing Committee issued on March 3 phrased it, the political situation was considerably more complex than it had been during the August Revolution. In the summer of 1945, the Party had been able to manipulate the international situation to its own advantage. Now, the contradictions among the imperialist powers had been at least temporarily harmonized (*hoa hoan*). The progressive forces throughout the world, led by the Soviet Union, were unable to come directly to the aid of the Vietnamese revolution. Under such conditions, a "fight to the end" would leave the Party weakened and isolated. The question is not "whether or not we wish to fight," the committee pointed out. "The problem is to know ourselves and to know others, to realize all conditions which are favorable and unfavorable in the country and abroad and to advocate correctly."[24]

The decision to compromise was confirmed in a policy directive issued on the fifth after a meeting of the Standing Committee in Ha Dong Province. Arguing that a policy of moderation was necessary in order to avoid a disadvantageous situation, the committee contended that compromise with the French would give the Party time to preserve and strengthen its forces and to prepare for a new opportunity to advance the revolution. For the present, emphasis would be shifted to the political, economic, and cultural aspects of the struggle.[25]

It is highly unlikely that the decision was unanimous. Party documents admit that many Party members were perplexed by the decision and some felt that it was unnecessary. The directive warned against the dangers of both rightism and leftism, but, from the context, it seems likely that most opposition came from those who wanted to face the issue directly. In the end, it may have been only the insistence of Ho Chi Minh that made the decision stick.

Armed with the concurrence of the Party leadership, Ho Chi Minh attempted to resolve the major issues with Sainteny. It is not necessary here to discuss in detail the tortuous negotiations that led to the final signing of the preliminary Ho-Sainteny Agreement on March 6. Suffice it to say that the agreement represented a compromise on both major points. France agreed to recognize the Democratic Republic of Vietnam (D.R.V.) as a free state, with its own army, parliament, and finances. The D.R.V. accepted a modest French military presence in North Vietnam and membership in the French Union. A plebiscite was to be held in Cochin China to allow the people there to determine their future. Details would be ironed out in future negotiations.

The compromise was considerably less than the total independence for all of Vietnam that many Party members felt should have been a minimum basis for settlement. It was, indeed, little more than Ho Chi Minh had proposed in 1944, before the August Revolution. Ho was not particularly pleased, as he admitted to Sainteny, and it is probable that he signed with considerable trepidation. The formal signing of the agreement took place on the afternoon of the sixth. It was initialled by VNQDD leader Vu Hong Khanh as well as by Ho Chi Minh and Sainteny and was witnessed by representatives of the United States and Great Britain.

Could Ho Chi Minh make the agreement stick? The immediate signs were not particularly auspicious. Reaction from the Vietnamese population was cautious, and even Jean Sainteny observed that the population reacted to the news of the pact with indifference or hostility.[26] The Central Committee felt it advisable to send prominent Party figures to the provinces to explain the reasons for the decision. Vo Nguyen Giap, who admitted the agreement "came rather as a surprise to our compatriots," travelled to Haiphong to explain the agreement at a mass rally. Reaction in nationalist circles was predictably hostile, despite Vu Hong Khanh's presence at the ceremony. Even Bao Dai was angry and left for Hong Kong, pursued by a conciliatory letter from Ho Chi Minh. Whether or not they realized the complexity of the situation, many nationalists relished the discomfort of the government and were not averse to taking advantage of it for political purposes.

Ho Chi Minh's efforts to assuage the doubts of his countrymen were almost frantic. In a ceremony held at the central square in Hanoi, he defended the agreement and pleaded for the people's understanding. "I would rather die," he cried, "than betray my country." He was followed on the balcony of the National Theater by Giap who, comparing the preliminary agreement with the Treaty of Brest-Litovsk, concluded by the Soviet government with Germany in March 1918, called it a necessary step to preserve the revolution. There were, he said, only three choices—long-term resistance, short-term resistance, or negotiations. Because the general situation was not favorable, a negotiated settlement was the only sensible policy.[27]

In pleading for the agreement, Ho had said that it would be worth it if the French kept their word. But in the days that followed, the signs were not auspicious. The arrival of 15,000 French troops in Tonkin soon led to incidents and to controversy over the terms of the accord. Vacillation on the meaning of the term "free state" soon surfaced in Paris, and hostility to the plebiscite in Cochin China was particularly strong among French circles in Saigon. The new high commissioner, Admiral Thierry d'Argenlieu, appeared determined to set up a separate Cochin Chinese republic with direct ties to Paris and publicly labeled the preliminary agreement a "Munich." He refused categorically to meet with Ho Chi Minh in either Hanoi or Saigon and threatened to sabotage further negotiations. Ultimately a meeting was held, under frigid circumstances, on a French cruiser in Along Bay on March 24, but it did not ease the crisis. Attempts to resolve the problem through a meeting between Vo Nguyen Giap and d'Argenlieu at Dalat in the Central Highlands concluded in "cordial disagreement." The admiral's attitude at Dalat, conceded one French observer, "did not put Ho precisely in good humor."[28]

Formal talks to implement the preliminary agreement began at Fontainebleau, outside Paris, in late spring. The negotiating team from Hanoi was led by Pham Van Dong, but Ho Chi Minh soon decided to watch over the conference from Paris and left for France on May 31. On his arrival, he discovered that the French government's attitude had stiffened and that even the FCP appeared unsympathetic. Negotiations lasted throughout the summer, but the major differences could not be overcome. A plea to his old friend, now minister of Overseas France, Marius Moutet not to leave him empty-handed had little effect, and in mid-September, after the departure of the rest of the Vietnamese delegation, he reluctantly agreed to a temporary modus vivendi. "I have just signed my death warrant," he remarked to a French acquaintance on leaving the scene of the negotiations. Traveling directly from Fontainebleau to the Mediterranean port of Toulon, he left by sea for Vietnam and arrived at the port of Haiphong on October 20.[29]

In his absence, the policy of the Vietnamese government had appeared to harden. During the early months of 1946, the Vietminh Front had become increasingly identified in the public mind with the Communists and, just before his departure, Ho Chi Minh had been instrumental in setting up a new front organization, the National United Front of Vietnam (Hoi lien hiep quoc dan Viet Nam, or Lien Viet for short). The aim of the new front was to enlist the support of moderate, non-Communist elements in Vietnam who were unwilling to join the Vietminh Front. During the summer months, however, relations with several of the nationalist groups deteriorated. In the South, the Vietminh alliance with the dissident religious sects, painstakingly reestablished in the spring, collapsed once again during the summer months and both Cao Dai and Hoa Hao units left the front. In the North, nationalist leaders were unreconciled to the government's policy of negotiations with Paris and continued to attack the Ho-Sainteny Agreement. On a local level, they refused Vietminh proposals to strengthen cooperative efforts and to merge local organizations in a common front. Exasperated, the government launched attacks on nationalist-held areas throughout North Vietnam in late June and July. The VNQDD headquarters in Hanoi and its newspaper were closed down, the party's militia was forced to disband, and many of its most prominent leaders fled to exile in China. With this step, the government virtually broke the back of its opposition in the North. The move was costly, however, for it revealed the hollowness of the government's carefully preserved claim to represent the views of all patriotic political forces in Vietnam.[30] The creation of a puppet pro-Vietminh VNQDD party was persuasive only to the naive, and, despite periodic efforts to solicit moderate support, government rule grew noticeably harsher during late summer and early fall.

The tense political atmosphere and the lack of progress in the negotiations in France were persuasive evidence to the Party that a renewal of hostilities was probable, and during the summer the Hanoi government intensified its efforts to improve the quality and strength of its armed forces. The defense budget was increased, and French-owned factories were transformed into arms manufacturing plants. New military schools were opened to train military officers in guerrilla tactics. The regular forces were augmented (by June there were more than 31,000 north of the 16th parallel), and two new base areas for such units were established—one in northern Tuyen Quang Province and the other in the Chi Né forest, west of the Day River in Hoa Binh Province. Other areas were to be defended by militia and guerrilla force units, now numbering nearly one million.[31] Party control of the army was strengthened by placing political officers in every military unit at the platoon level and above.

A heightened level of activity was also observable in the South. Although the new leadership in the region did not immediately reverse Vietminh fortunes, the insurgent forces managed to survive the French autumn offensive and throughout the succeeding spring and summer increased the effectiveness of their guerrilla operations. The departure of French regular units for the North reduced the military pressure, and, by late spring, the insurgents began to seize the initiative. In June, Nguyen Binh launched an offensive northwest of Saigon, near the towns of Bien Hoa, Ben Cat, and Thu Dau Mot, and during the summer months began to set up guerrilla bases in several provinces, notably in the Plain of Reeds, the U Minh forest, and along the Cambodian border. The desertion of Hoa Hao and Cao Dai units in midsummer had undoubtedly been a setback, but the insurgency continued to grow in nonsect areas. During the summer, units of regimental strength were being formed, as well as armed propaganda detachments of the type used during the August Revolution. According to Vo Nguyen Giap, most of the new recruits were peasants (as they were in North Vietnam), but some were workers from the rubber plantations and many of the officers were workers from Saigon.[32] In rural villages controlled by the movement, committees of resistance (uy ban khang chien) were formed and, in some areas, several villages would link up to form small resistance bases. Terror squads were established to punish traitors. According to a perceptive French observer, the Vietminh was able to recoup most of the ground lost during the previous autumn and by November controlled nearly three-quarters of the total area of Cochin China.[33] In a burst of optimism, the ICP Central Committee decreed the formation of a Provisional Resistance Committee and claimed that it was the only legal administrative authority in the South.[34]

To what degree the heightened tension in North Vietnam was a consequence of Ho Chi Minh's extended absence cannot be stated with certainty. Although he was certainly capable of brutality toward those he considered to be enemies of the Vietnamese Revolution, Ho was normally sensitive to the danger of isolating the Party from moderate elements in Vietnamese society and had been careful to pursue every opportunity to avoid, or at least postpone, an open confrontation with the French. Upon his return, then, it was in character for him to resume his efforts to win the Party over to a policy of moderation. Given the mood prevailing in Hanoi, such efforts could not have been popular, and some observers have suggested that the Party leadership, angry at his decision to sign the modus vivendi in Paris, may have briefly attempted to reduce his influence. Party histories, of course, make no reference to major dissatisfaction with his policies. It is not unlikely that such opposition did exist, for since the end of the August Revolution there had been an undercurrent of discontent with his strategy of pursuing a negotiated settlement. But there is no evidence that Ho Chi Minh was in serious danger of losing his prominent position in the Party or the government. Within two weeks of his return, he was able to win a vote of confidence in the National Assembly for the policies of his government—and for the modus vivendi. In early November, a new cabinet was formed, which suggested that his dominant position within the revolutionary movement remained secure. He retained the presidency and, after having given it up to a non-Party figure the previous January, again took over the Ministry of Foreign Affairs. Giap became minister of defense, and Communists occupied several other key positions. With the departure of many non-Communist nationalists during the summer, the new cabinet was markedly more leftist in composition, as was the National Assembly itself, in which less than half of the seventy nationalist seats guaranteed in January were still occupied.

In resuming his dominant position within the Party, Ho may have been able to rely not only on his own persuasive capacities, but on support from Moscow. Although the Soviet Union made few public references to the situation in Vietnam during the final months of 1946, a commentary in the Soviet press in December by Madame Vasilyeva, a long-time instructor of Vietnamese Communists at the Stalin School, warned that the ICP should avoid hostilities and rely on the "new France."[35]

Though the new cabinet suggested a harder line in Hanoi, Ho Chi Minh continued to pursue his efforts to delay hostilities. On October 30, in accordance with the terms of the modus vivendi, both sides accepted a cease-fire in Cochin China. It was not particularly effective (some sources claim that Nguyen Binh refused to allow his troops to be regrouped and disarmed), but tension did decrease in the South in the final weeks of the year. In Tonkin, however, incidents between Vietnamese and French units occurred with increasing frequency. French authorities in Indochina, anticipating hostilities in the near future, initiated moves to strengthen their military position in major centers in the Red River delta. When in early November the French decided to open a customs house in Haiphong, Ho Chi Minh protested and warned that the French action could have "grave consequences" in the delicate situation. A few days later, a major clash between French and Vietnamese forces occurred at Haiphong. The conflict was patched up on the spot, but the French military command in Saigon became convinced that only a hard-line policy would bring the Vietnamese to heel. During the next few days, French troops were involved in a number of ugly incidents with Vietnamese forces in Tonkin and a French naval and air bombardment of Haiphong harbor on the twenty-third took a heavy toll in civilian casualties. Although the French government in Paris still seemed anxious to achieve a peaceful settlement, its representatives in Vietnam were taking matters into their own hands.

The Haiphong incident may have convinced the Party leadership that war was inevitable. Until now Ho Chi Minh, despite pressure from militant elements in the Party leadership, had labored to prevent or at least delay a military confrontation. By late November, however, he seemed increasingly resigned to the possibility and discussed with Giap the need to make preparations for a resumption of hostilities. According to Giap, Ho asked him how long revolutionary forces could defend Hanoi. He replied that the capital could be defended only for a month, but that the countryside could be held indefinitely. Then, concluded Ho Chi Minh, they should return to Tan Trao.[36]

In early December, the situation worsened. During the first two weeks of the month, the frequency of incidents between French and local Vietnamese forces increased sharply as each side, seeing war as virtually inevitable, attempted to strengthen its positions for the coming storm. Local French authorities were naturally concerned to protect the life and property of European residents in Tonkin and built up their forces and secured communications routes throughout the lower delta. In the first weeks of December, more than one thousand French legionnaires landed at ports in Central and North Vietnam.

The French decision to augment its forces and strengthen its military position in North Vietnam may have persuaded the Party leadership that war was unavoidable. On the seventh, Vo Nguyen Giap dispatched a circular instructing all military units to be prepared to launch an attack on French installations by the twelfth. The following day, a proclamation of the Hanoi Vietminh Front Municipal Committee appeared in the local press: "The moment of peril has arrived. The Committee appeals to all compatriots to remain calm, to preserve unity and to hold themselves ready to rise as soon as the government issues the order."[37]

In the capital, preparations for war intensified. The D.R.V. had decided that, although the major cities could not be held indefinitely, local militia units in the city could maintain positions long enough to delay the enemy and permit an orderly withdrawal to prepared positions in the countryside. Intensive efforts were undertaken to prepare Hanoi for the coming struggle. Tunnels and trenches were constructed to permit communication from one sector to another without the use of main arteries. Factories vital to national defense were dismantled and removed to rural areas. Government ministries and nonessential citizens were ordered to evacuate the city. Militia units in the capital region were beefed up; by mid-month they numbered nearly 20,000.

During the early days of December, talks continued between Sainteny and Vietnamese representatives. But although they continued to be cordial, no progress was reported. According to one source, the views of the two sides on a settlement were "diametrically opposed." Up until the last moment, however, Ho Chi Minh continued to hesitate. At one point, he remarked to a member of the Democratic Party that war was too important to be taken lightly and that, although it was virtually inevitable, it was best to delay it, even if for only a few days.

On December 15, Ho Chi Minh made one last bid for a peaceful settlement. A new government under the moderate socialist Léon Blum came to power in Paris in early December. The ICP did not view Blum or his party as particularly friendly to the Vietnamese cause, but he had declared that a solution in Indochina must be based on the wishes of the local population. Ho addressed a last-minute appeal to the new prime minister. He offered to cease preparations for war if the French would remove their reinforcements from Tourane, return to positions held before November 20, and cease attempting to expand the territory under their control in the Center and the South. But the message (probably by the design of French authorities in Saigon) did not arrive in Paris until December 26. By then it was too late.

Tension had already reached unprecedented levels in Hanoi. Incidents took place involving casualties on both sides, and French paratroopers roamed the downtown area tossing grenades into Vietnamese houses and harassing passersby. The government began to erect barricades on the major thoroughfares. The French authorities demanded that all fortifications be removed and warned that, in case of noncompliance, French military units would occupy all key installations in the city. When the D.R.V. did not reply, French patrols destroyed Vietnamese barricades near the citadel, where the bulk of French troops were located, and sent a second ultimatum demanding that Vietnamese self-defense forces in the capital area be disarmed and that responsibility for local law and order be handed over to the French army.

For the Party leadership, hesitation was replaced by determination. On the eighteenth, the Central Committee met in Ha Dong Province to assess the situation and prepare for hostilities. Vo Nguyen Giap now had three divisions totalling 30,000 stationed around the city—at Ha Dong, near the race course, and beside the Fleuve du Grand Lac. It was decided, however, to restrict military activities in the area to local self-defense forces, in order to preserve main force units for future combat. According to the plan, Vietminh forces opened their attack on the electrical factory during the evening of the eighteenth, in order to cut power throughout the city and then attack French installations and the European residential section. Similar attacks took place on French positions in cities throughout the delta and along the northern coast, while other units cut communications routes between major urban centers.

The Vietminh had counted on the element of surprise, but the French had been forewarned of the attacks by an agent during the afternoon of the nineteenth and had placed their forces in the Hanoi region on the alert. During the night, French units began to methodically clear the French quarter of the city and by midmorning had assaulted the presidential palace and seized Gia Lam airfield, north of the river. By nightfall they had taken control of the central sector of Hanoi, while Vietminh militia units clung tenaciously to the Vietnamese sector of the city and Ho Chi Minh set up his government temporarily at Ha Dong, six miles southwest of Hanoi.

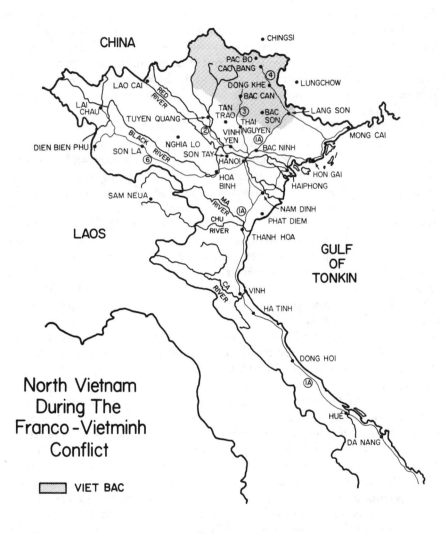

CHINA

• CHINGSI

PAC BO
CAO BANG
DONG KHE ④
• LUNGCHOW

LAO CAI

RED RIVER

BAC CAN

LAI CHAU

TAN TRAO ③
THAI SON

LANG SON

TUYEN QUANG

② NGUYEN
VINH YEN ⓐ
BAC NINH

MONG CAI

DIEN BIEN PHU

BLACK RIVER

NGHIA LO
SON LA ⑥
SON TAY

HANOI

HON GAI

HOA BINH

HAIPHONG

SAM NEUA

MA RIVER

ⓐ NAM DINH

CHU RIVER

PHAT DIEM

THANH HOA

LAOS

GULF
OF
TONKIN

CA RIVER

• VINH

• HA TINH

• DONG HOI

ⓐ

North Vietnam
During The
Franco-Vietminh
Conflict

HUÉ

DA NANG

▭ VIET BAC

The Franco-Vietminh War
(1947–1954)

For over a year, Ho Chi Minh had maneuvered brilliantly to avoid, or at least to postpone, the resumption of military conflict. Contemporary French accounts characterized the Vietminh attacks of December 19 as blatant aggression, but it seems more accurate to say that while some firebrands in the Party had been advocating a return to violent struggle since the failure of the Fontainebleau negotiations during the summer, Ho had only acquiesced when it became clear that further delay might seriously prejudice the Party's position.

Ho Chi Minh's reluctance to resort to violence was probably based less on moral than on practical considerations. Although the military forces at the disposal of the D.R.V. had increased significantly since the previous summer—by December the Hanoi government had over 50,000 men under arms, including the regional guerrillas—and now outnumbered French main force units stationed in Vietnam, they were poorly armed and often had had only the most rudimentary training.[1] They could not hope to stand up to the challenge of a serious French effort to restore colonial rule in Indochina.

Nor was the international situation, always a factor in the back of Ho Chi Minh's mind, particularly favorable for a resumption of hostilities in Vietnam. As the political situation in France began to stabilize, French attitudes toward the crisis in Indochina had hardened. The FCP, still hopeful of playing a major role in postwar French politics, was carefully assuming a patriotic stance toward the colonies and would be of little immediate assistance to the Vietnamese in promoting public disenchantment with colonial policies in France. The United States, considered a potential source of diplomatic support during the August Revolution, was now reassessing its foreign policy in Asia and appeared less likely to look with sympathy on the Vietnamese cause. Even the Soviet Union, the ICP's major ally for a generation, was now primarily concerned with the political situation in Europe and had shown little enthusiasm for a new upsurge of the Vietnamese revolution. If the Vietminh chose to fight, it would fight alone.

Vietminh weakness seemed clearly reflected in the first exchange of diplomatic feelers between the two sides, for the D.R.V. clearly appeared more anxious to end the conflict. Less than two weeks after the reopening of hostilities, Ho Chi Minh proposed a cease-fire and the convening of a peace conference in Paris on the basis of the Ho-Sainteny Agreement. The implications of this proposal were clarified in April by a message from D.R.V. Foreign Minister Hoang Minh Giam, which accepted a French cultural and economic presence in Vietnam and affiliation with the French Union as an associated state in return for Vietnamese control over its army, finances, and foreign affairs and the unity of the three regions. As a negotiating position, Giam's proposal was decidedly moderate.

Paris, however, was in no hurry. Still angered by what it considered Ho Chi Minh's perfidy in launching the attacks in December (a feeling exacerbated by reports of Vietminh atrocities against French civilians in Hanoi) and evidently confident that military force could succeed where diplomacy had failed, the French government expressed little interest in negotiations. Prime Minister Blum publicly expressed his belief that negotiations could only take place when order had been restored. This relatively uncompromising attitude was reflected in the first official contacts between the two sides after the December attacks, the mission to Vietminh headquarters by French academician Paul Mus. The selection of Mus, born in Indochina and long a sympathizer with Vietnamese national aspirations, appeared to be a conciliatory gesture. But his message contained conditions that Mus himself, as well as the government in Paris, must have known the D.R.V. could only reject. The French demanded the virtual surrender of Vietminh forces before the establishment of a cease-fire. Ho's reply was conciliatory but adamant: In the French Union, he said, there was no place for cowards, and if he accepted the French conditions, he would be one.[2]

The Chinese Model

Whether or not the Party leadership seriously believed that a negotiated settlement of the conflict was possible, for the time being it was obviously placing its primary reliance on the strategy of protracted war. In 1941 the ICP had first turned to the Chinese experience, with the formation of the Vietminh Front. At that time, the Party's indebtedness to the Maoist doctrine of people's war was not explicitly stated, and the borrowing process was selective rather than doctrinaire, practical rather than theoretical. Although several cardinal elements of Vietnamese Communist strategy appeared to be lifted from Maoist teachings, the centerpiece of Maoist doctrine—the three-stage process of withdrawal, equilibrium, and general offensive—was not formally adopted. Rather, Ho Chi Minh had provided his colleagues with a simple three-stage process of his own—political struggle, a balance of political and military struggle, and a final phase of predominantly military struggle.

With the resumption of military conflict and the military option at least temporarily paramount, the Party turned once again to the Maoist model for inspiration. Indeed, there were soon indications that the Party's reliance on the Chinese approach would be even more explicit than during the August Revolution. On December 22, only three days after the opening of hostilities, the Vietnamese government issued a declaration announcing that there would be three stages in the coming struggle against French colonialism: (1) a defensive phase, during which the Vietnamese might reluctantly be compelled to abandon the major cities to the French; (2) a phase of equilibrium, when the strength of the revolutionary forces would be growing and those of the enemy in decline; and (3) a final phase of general offensive.[3]

Early in 1947, signs that the Vietnamese were going to rely on the Maoist model were confirmed with the publication of Truong Chinh's famous treatise, *The Resistance Will Win*.[4] By now Chinh had begun to emerge as the foremost spokesman for the Party on ideological matters; the appearance of his short book, the first major exposition of Vietnamese revolutionary strategy since the formation of the Vietminh Front, led many observers to conclude that he had now become the ICP's major military strategist as well. Chinh's analysis confirmed that the Party viewed the upcoming conflict as a protracted war, based on Mao's three stages. In the first defensive stage (*phong ngu*), the revolutionary forces would resort to both positional and mobile warfare to harass the enemy, simultaneously retreating from heavily populated areas to previously prepared defensive positions in the countryside. The second stage of equilibrium (*cam cu*), which Chinh described as the "key stage" of the conflict, would be reached when the strength of the French had reached its maximum and the enemy was preoccupied with pacifying the rural areas and mopping up resistance forces. At this point, he warned, the revolutionary forces would be subject to occasional bouts of pessimism and the temptation to compromise. Yet this would be the moment when they would be called upon to intensify their activities and to wage guerrilla operations in enemy-controlled areas in order to expand the territory under their own control. The final stage was that of general counteroffensive (*phan khoi nghia*), consisting of large-scale attacks on enemy forces and involving both mobile and conventional forms of combat. Chinh cautioned that the transition from one stage to another could not be rigidly predicted and would be dependent upon a variety of factors, including the strength of the revolutionary armed forces, the level of popular support for the insurgency, and the degree of demoralization of enemy troops.

On the surface, Chinh's analysis was pure Maoism, an almost mechanical application of Chinese techniques to the Vietnamese revolutionary struggle. Yet, in certain key areas he demonstrated a willingness to depart from Chinese teachings. First, he disagreed with Mao Tse-tung's interpretation of the role of terrain in revolutionary strategy. Mao had contended that certain key factors unique to the situation in China permitted the successful application of people's war: (1) its semicolonial status, which limited imperialist rule to the cities and left the rural areas substantially untouched by enemy control, and (2) its vast territory, which allowed revolutionary forces to wage extensive guerrilla operations in areas far removed from the heartland of enemy authority. Predictably, Chinh took issue with such assumptions. Conceding that terrain was an important factor in protracted war, he claimed that active popular support and a disciplined people's army led by the Communist Party could overcome the disadvantages of geography and colonial status. Even a country like Vietnam was not too small for the establishment of revolutionary base areas.[5]

Chinh also departed from Mao in his view of the preponderant importance of the world situation. From the beginning, he contended, external factors would play a major role in promoting the Vietnamese revolutionary cause. In particular, the impact of the war on public opinion would have a vital bearing on French policy. The longer the war lasted, the more the Vietnamese revolutionary movement would earn the sympathy of democratic forces in France. Ultimately, declining morale and increasing public resistance to the war would seriously weaken the French military effort. At the same time, it was possible that a shift in the world balance of power (here Chinh clearly meant the growing political and military power of the Soviet Union) might further undermine the imperialist order.

In such conditions, Chinh declared that absolute military superiority was not a precondition for the launching of the final stage of general offensive to achieve total victory and a revolutionary seizure of power. Superiority might be relative, a combination of military power with political and diplomatic factors. Similarly, he was somewhat ambiguous on the possible conclusion of the war. Although the bulk of his comments implied a military end to the conflict, at one point he conceded that the democratic parties in France might negotiate seriously and thus permit a diplomatic settlement of the conflict. But he also implied that the Party might use diplomacy for its own purposes, stating that "false negotiations" might be held to weaken the enemy's resolve while the revolutionary forces prepared for their final military offensive.[6]

Despite some departures from Maoism, Truong Chinh's analysis was a reasonably straightforward application of Maoist doctrine to the revolutionary struggle in Vietnam. Much of the book draws liberally on Mao's writings, particularly *On Protracted War*, written at Yenan in 1938. This has led some observers to speculate that the secretary general had become the leading figure in a pro-Chinese faction within the Party leadership, in contrast to the traditionally pro-Soviet orientation that had existed since the formation of the Vietnamese Revolutionary Youth League twenty years earlier. Such assumptions should be treated with caution. Though it is true that on several later occasions, Truong Chinh's positions on various aspects of Communist policy coincided with the views of the CCP leadership in Peking, his brief 1947 treatise should probably not be taken as an indication that he was instrumental in obtaining his colleagues' approval of the policy. Available evidence suggests that the adoption of the Maoist approach had broad approval within the Party leadership. It was logical that Chinh, as secretary general with a flair for doctrine, be designated the Party's spokesman to explain the strategy to be used in the war against the French.

Withdrawal

The December 22 directive, which suggested that during the first stage of struggle Vietnamese forces might be compelled to abandon the major cities, turned out to be an accurate forecast. During the early weeks of 1947 French forces gradually seized most of the major provincial capitals in North and Central Vietnam and reopened the major transportation routes in the delta and down the coast. The imperial capital of Hué was attacked by French units marching north from Da Nang and after a siege of six weeks fell to the French in early February. Wherever possible, Vietminh forces avoided combat in order to preserve their small main force units and most of the fighting, including the rearguard skirmishing in urban areas, was undertaken by guerrillas or local paramilitary forces.

The Vietminh did attempt to hold Hanoi for a longer period. After the attacks launched on December 19, the French seized the airfield and the area surrounding it north of the river and then began methodically to retake the city. But Vietminh local units and a small conventional force struggled to maintain a toehold in the Vietnamese sector in order to permit the main force units to achieve an orderly withdrawal to their major base areas in Tuyen Quang and Bac Can provinces. They finally abandoned the area and melted into the surrounding villages in February, on the eve of a projected French offensive.[7] Beyond the cities, the Vietminh remained in control of much of the Tonkinese countryside. In early April, a central Party cadre conference issued a resolution confirming the earlier directive calling for a protracted war and decided on an immediate shift to guerrilla techniques in order to regain the initiative and establish a tactical advantage during the defensive phase. To achieve this end, a number of main force regiments were to be broken down into smaller guerrilla units in order to harass and deplete French forces. Each village under Vietminh control was instructed to establish a self-defense militia unit, and training programs on guerrilla warfare, taught by deserters from the French foreign legion and the Japanese army, were established in liberated areas.

For the Vietminh, it was a race against time—to build up its strength before the French could break the back of the resistance. During the spring and summer, the French appeared content to consolidate their control over highly populated areas in the Red River delta and the central coast. In the fall, however, hoping to end the war quickly, they launched an offensive with the objective of destroying the bulk of Communist forces and seizing the Vietminh headquarters in the heart of the Viet Bac. In the first phase, a force consisting of twelve infantry batallions and three armored squadrons advanced northward from Hanoi to the junction of the Red and Clear rivers and seized the provincial capital of Tuyen Quang. The second stage involved a march up Route 4 from Lang Son to Cao Bang, combined with a paratroop drop on Vietminh headquarters near Bac Can in the hope of taking Ho Chi Minh and his principal subordinates by surprise. In the latter objective, the French were disappointed; Ho Chi Minh and his aides avoided capture by less than an hour. But in other respects, the offensive achieved its aims. French forces were able to inflict heavy casualties on Vietminh units and then advanced northward to garrison Route 4 and close the Chinese border. According to one French observer, total Vietminh losses were over 10,000. Moreover, it was compelled to abandon major segments of the liberated zone in the Viet Bac. French casualties were listed as 1,000 killed in action and 3,000 wounded.[8] Additional defeats took place in the Northwest, where inexperienced Vietminh units fighting in set positions absorbed heavy losses and were forced to disperse and flee into the mountains. The French then formed an alliance with the local T'ai leader Deo Van Long and set up an autonomous minority region, defended by 8,000 local minority troops. For the moment, the situation in upper Tonkin was not auspicious for the insurgency.

As always, the situation in the South followed its own momentum. Nguyen Binh had broken the October cease-fire by launching a series of localized attacks on December 21, two days after the opening of hostilities in Hanoi. But Binh's major immediate problem was more political than military in nature: to knit together the disparate forces opposed to French rule in Cochin China. He had little more success in this effort than his predecessor Tran Van Giau. Hostility between the Vietminh and the sects escalated during the winter months and climaxed in the spring of 1947 when the Vietminh seized Huynh Phu So, the mystical leader of the Hoa Hao sect, and executed him on a charge of treason. The death of the "mad bonze" ripped asunder all remaining Communist hopes for an alliance with the sect forces in the delta and led surviving Hoa Hao leaders to form an alliance with the French in return for a promise of administrative autonomy. The Cao Dai had followed a similar path, signing a convention with the French in return for the release from prison of the movement's religious leader, Pham Cong Tac.

Binh's failure to apply the Communist front policy effectively in Cochin China came at a crucial point in the Franco-Vietminh conflict. The hard-line policies followed by the Hanoi regime during the last half of 1946 had alienated moderate opinion throughout the country. The opening of conflict in December offered the Party a new opportunity to stitch together a loose alliance with anti-French elements throughout the country, for in the early months of 1947 a number of nationalist elements seemed tentatively inclined to cooperate with the Vietminh in a common struggle against colonialism. Throughout the year, the Vietminh attempted to respond to the new political situation. The D.R.V. cabinet was once again modified to project a more moderate image. Vo Nguyen Giap and Pham Van Dong, both widely perceived as Communist hard-liners, were replaced in the cabinet by non-Communists. Phan Ke Toai, imperial viceroy in Tonkin at the end of the war, replaced the veteran ICP labor organizer Ton Duc Thang as interior minister, while the moderate Hoang Minh Giam remained as minister of foreign affairs. In the new twenty-seven-man cabinet, there were now only three overt Marxists (instead of six in the previous one), four Democrats, four Socialists, two nationalists, two Catholics, one Buddhist, eight independents, and two ex-mandarins. Despite his open maneuverings with the French, Bao Dai was retained as supreme political adviser.[9]

At first, the French seemed oblivious to the political implications of the conflict, but the Vietminh diplomatic offensive may have changed their minds, and the fall 1947 border attacks coincided with a political effort designed to isolate the Vietminh by establishing links with an indigenous political force with whom the French could cooperate against the Communists. The centerpiece of the strategy, called the "Bao Dai formula," was an effort to persuade Bao Dai to return from Hong Kong as chief of state to provide a focus for moderate nationalist sentiment. The new approach abandoned the earlier attempt led by Admiral Thierry d'Argenlieu to separate Cochin China from the remainder of the country in favor of an effort to create a new Vietnamese state out of all three zones that would cooperate with the French against the danger of a Communist Vietnam.

From the Vietminh point of view, the French political offensive was potentially more dangerous than its military counterpart in the Viet Bac, for if the various non-Communist factions could be unified into a cohesive force it could, for the first time, offer a serious alternative to the Vietminh Front for the loyalty of the Vietnamese people. Previously, the divisions within the nationalist movement had been a major advantage to the Communists in their efforts to dominate Vietnamese nationalism. Even under the pressure of Communist successes during and after the August Revolution, the moderates in Cochin China had established few links with the extreme nationalists in the North. For this reason, at the outset the Vietminh appeared to have the edge in obtaining the cooperation of radical nationalists in Tonkin. Many of the latter, like Nguyen Tuong Tam and Nguyen Hai Than, harbored a visceral dislike for the French and, although increasingly suspicious of the Vietminh, appeared to view the front as a lesser evil. When, in March, a Vietminh representative contacted nationalists in South China, several expressed a cautious interest in reviving the anti-French alliance that had broken down the previous summer. But they were soon dissuaded and in March a conference of nationalist groups held in Canton resulted in the formation of a new National United Front, which would appeal to Bao Dai, now in Hong Kong, to form a government against the "red terror" of the Communists.

For a brief period, the new front showed promise, as both Bao Dai and the religious sects in the South indicated their interest. But in the end, the familiar disease of Vietnamese factionalism reasserted itself. Personal conflicts, exacerbated by inherent differences between moderates and radicals over tactics and goals, led to growing tensions within the movement and ultimately proved fatal. The French contributed to the problem by their intransigence on the issue of Vietnamese independence, and the front eventually collapsed. But the willingness of ardent nationalists to consider cooperation with the Saigon moderates against the Vietminh was evidence of one of the Communists' major weaknesses—their inability to broaden their political base in urban areas beyond the radical fringe traditionally sympathetic to the Party and to its ideology. The dilemma was a crucial one. Without the support or at least the sympathy of such groups, the Leninist multiclass nationalist alliance, the centerpiece of Communist political strategy in Vietnam, would be forever unattainable. And without an effective united front, the Party's most effective political weapon would be useless.

The Vietminh performance in the first year of the war had been mixed. It had been able to survive the first onslaught of French military attacks, but at the cost of severe losses in weapons, in territory, and in personnel. On the political front, the effort to knit together an alliance with non-Communist elements had run aground on their traditional suspicions of the Communists and on the seductive attractions of the Bao Dai formula. For the moment, the French had seized the initiative both in politics and on the battlefield.

Equilibrium

Actually, the Communists' fortunes were about to improve. By the end of 1947, the Party leadership had apparently concluded that the process of withdrawal had been substantially completed. Through painstaking efforts and the recruitment of new forces in villages under Vietminh control, the losses from the first French military offensive had been gradually recouped and the size of the revolutionary forces began to increase. Although the French had successfully occupied most of the Red River delta and had dislodged the Vietminh from substantial parts of the Viet Bac, the Party sensed that they had reached maximum strength and would now begin pacification and mopping-up activities, on the assumption that the capture of the Vietminh leadership was no longer necessary. A meeting of the Party's Standing Committee in January 1948 formally decreed the end of the first stage of withdrawal and the beginning of the second stage of equilibrium.[10] Generally speaking, the inauguration of the second stage of people's war meant that the Vietminh would now attempt to seize the initiative on the battlefield. The main objective would not simply be to survive, but to wear down enemy forces and to expand the territory under Vietminh control, thus permitting an increase in recruitment and a growth in the financial and material resources available to the revolutionary forces. According to Vo Nguyen Giap, the primary form of struggle in the new stage would be guerrilla operations, which would be expanded throughout enemy areas in Vietnam. But Giap conceded that guerrilla war by itself would be inadequate to achieve the major objectives of the new stage. At least a few large and well-equipped regular units, capable of mobile operations over a relatively wide area, would be required.[11] During the final months of 1947, a few select mobile battalions were formed, and by early 1948 the first battalion-sized attacks were launched on French forces.

Size alone, of course, was virtually meaningless. Without modern weapons, the new mobile forces of the Vietminh would be at a serious disadvantage in direct combat with the French. The D.R.V. had managed to obtain a few weapons from the Japanese occupation forces and had established a number of small weapons factories in areas controlled by the liberation forces.[12] But if the conflict were ever to escalate to the final stage of general offensive, foreign sources of supply would clearly be required. Although this was probably one of the Party's primary reasons for concern, there was some cause for optimism, for in 1948 the international picture began to brighten. The Soviet attitude toward struggles of national liberation in developing areas was in transition. The change was first signaled by the famous "two camp" speech by Stalin's presumed successor Andrei Zhdanov. Soon, favorable references to armed struggle began to appear with increasing frequency in the Soviet media. By 1948 Moscow was giving open verbal support to armed insurgency movements directed by Communist parties throughout Southeast Asia.[13]

Direct military aid from Moscow, however, still seemed unlikely. For this reason Party leaders were probably even more elated at the changing situation in China. Under the hammer-blows of the PLA the military forces of the government of Chiang Kai-shek were gradually disintegrating, increasing the likelihood of total Communist control over the China mainland. Such a prospect opened up an immense vista of future assistance to the Vietnamese revolution and undoubtedly bolstered the Party as it attempted to map out its future strategy.

During 1948 the military buildup continued at a rapid pace. From an estimated 50,000 troops, including regional guerrillas, at the beginning of the war, the Vietminh forces increased to more than 250,000 men two years later. They had attained near numerical parity with the French, although they were still markedly inferior in firepower. Paralleling the growth of the revolutionary armed forces was an increase in the size of the party's political apparatus, from 50,000 in 1947 to more than 150,000 a year later.[14]

With the expansion of guerrilla activities in 1948, the amount of territory under Vietminh control increased significantly. By the end of the year the Vietminh had reoccupied most of the Viet Bac, as well as sections along the central coast. In the South, Vietminh control was gradually extended from the core areas in the U Minh forest, the Plain of Reeds, and Tay Ninh province and expanded northward toward Thu Dau Mot and into the forested areas northwest of Saigon, where a number of small liberated base areas sprang up. One experienced Western observer estimated that the Vietminh now exercised control over 55 percent of all villages throughout the country, with a total of over 12 million people, more than half the entire population of Vietnam.[15] In areas where Vietminh rule held sway, a revolutionary administration began to appear. For convenience, all administrative, united front, and military functions were combined into a single Committee of Resistance and Administration (CRA).[16]

The ability of the Vietminh to expand its rule at the village level was undoubtedly a testimony to the general effectiveness of its rural program, as well as to its strategic and organizational abilities. But Communist publications show that the effort to maximize support in rural areas by integrating the themes of national liberation and social revolution had not been an unqualified success. Since the late 1930s the Party had attempted to win vital support in the countryside by emphasizing issues of crucial importance to the peasant masses: reducing taxes, abolishing the hated monopolies, and distributing grain during the famine at the end of World War II. But it had consistently held back from adopting a radical land policy for fear of alienating patriotic elements among the wealthier classes at the village level. This moderate policy continued during the early years of the Franco-Vietminh conflict as the Party set forth a program calling for interest rate and rent reductions, while downplaying land redistribution. Only the land of the French and that of Vietnamese collaborators was to be confiscated and distributed to the poor. Evidently the results were disappointing. According to a later account by Truong Chinh, the Party miscalculated its interests by failing to mobilize the rural poor and overestimated the value of support from the patriotic landed gentry. Landlord elements, coddled by the Party's moderate program, were able to dominate the united front organizations set up at the village level, thus undermining efforts to enforce regulations calling for rent reductions and limited land seizures. Poorer peasants consequently dragged their feet and refused to put their hearts into the war. In 1948, only 820,000 were enrolled in the Vietminh's peasant associations.[17]

In 1948 and 1949, the Party attempted to correct the situation. A number of cautious revisions were introduced into the program, calling for an enforcement of regulations and expanded efforts to improve the rural standard of living. At least half the members of village administrative committees were now to be poor or middle peasants. Yet these changes were diluted by continued local reluctance to enforce regulations against landed elements and by the exemption of families of soldiers and cadres from "excessive" confiscation. Although statistics indicate that the proportion of poor peasants in village CRAs increased to more than 50 percent by the end of the decade, the proportion was markedly lower at higher levels.[18]

The Bao Dai Solution

In the face of the Communist challenge, the French attempted to put together a Vietnamese government under Bao Dai that could attract nationalist support while accepting a continued French presence in the area. Bao Dai was reluctant to accept a settlement promising less than complete statehood, but he was increasingly hostile to the Vietminh, and the French astutely played on his fears that they would deal with Ho Chi Minh if he refused to cooperate. In 1949, the ex-emperor was persuaded to sign an agreement providing for "associated statehood" for all of Vietnam within the French Union. It was considerably less than full independence, but it was an advance over the status quo, and Paris hoped that it would provide a credible counterforce to the Vietminh. Equally important, the agreement was aimed at satisfying the United States, which had refused to support the French effort without evidence that Paris was moving toward meeting Vietnamese nationalist aspirations. Before the end of the year, Washington had set up a military assistance program to support France and the Bao Dai government in the struggle against the forces of international communism in Vietnam.

The new government was greeted more critically in Vietnam than in Washington. The continuing colonial presence made French claims of "independence" appear a travesty. Within the nationalist community, relatively few rallied to the new regime, except for the affluent Saigon bourgeoisie and some anti-Communist groups such as Catholics and the Cao Dai and Hoa Hao official hierarchy. In an effort to broaden the popular base of the new regime, the new prime minister, Nguyen Phan Long, an ex-Constitutionalist with a reputation for opportunism, released some political prisoners, reduced the role of the police and the secret service, and appealed to the Vietminh to cooperate in the common struggle for independence.

Nguyen Binh saw the new situation as an opportunity and attempted to turn it to his advantage. But he spurned Nguyen Phan Long's offer of conciliation. Through the Vietminh-controlled "Voice of Nam Bo" Binh responded harshly to Long's offer and described the new Bao Dai solution as a betrayal of Vietnamese aspirations for independence. He also began to step up Vietminh revolutionary activity in urban areas in an effort to take advantage of the gradual transfer of authority in Saigon to the new Vietnamese government. Vietminh agents infiltrated the Saigon police and civil administration and (according to a French journalist in Saigon at the time) a special assassination unit was formed under a young Communist activist by the name of Tran Van Tra. During the winter of 1949-1950 Binh initiated a civil disobedience campaign in Saigon in protest against the return of Bao Dai and the rising U.S. military presence. From Vietminh headquarters in the heart of the Mekong delta came threats of war and a food blockade against the crowded urban centers.

It was apparently at this moment that Binh prepared to launch his bid for power. This period is poorly documented in Communist histories of the revolution, and in the *Outline History* it is entirely passed over. Without further evidence to the contrary, it is difficult to avoid the conclusion that, by accident or design, the insurgency was operating almost independently of the Party in the North. In the Mekong delta, Binh launched a series of local offensives against the provincial capitals of Tra Vinh, Soc Trang, and Can Tho and attempted to cut major transportation routes. In Saigon, youth assault troops, called "Vietminh fighters," held protest meetings in schools and demonstrated behind red flags in the downtown streets. The Vietminh political and military offensive did not bring the French to their knees, but it did discredit Nguyen Phan Long's conciliatory approach and lead to his replacement by the bluff and brutal Nguyen Van Tam, whose tough policies against subversives quickly pacified Saigon and virtually wiped out the Party's urban apparatus. It also frightened the French, who suddenly realized the potential perils in the situation, and during the summer French military units struck hard at Vietminh forces in the delta. Badly bruised in a series of pitched battles with French regulars, the remaining Vietminh fled to the Plain of Reeds.

Binh paid a heavy price for his failure. Whether or not he had flagrantly disregarded Party strategy with his rambunctious attacks in Cochin China has not been officially confirmed. But there seems little doubt that there was disapproval of his policies in high quarters. Binh and several of his followers were purged from the leadership in the South, and in 1951 he was killed in an ambush on his way north. That same year, in an apparent move to eliminate the persistent problem of Southern regionalism, the Committee for the South was abolished in favor of a new Central Office for South Vietnam (Trung Uong Cuc Mien Nam or COSVN for short), staffed by loyal members of the Central Committee and directly subordinated to the Party leadership in Hanoi. The secretary of the six-man committee was Le Duan.[19]

The Party's apparent ability to unleash social agitation in Saigon in 1950 is somewhat misleading, for, in general, its organizational efforts in urban areas had only indifferent success. In later Party histories the agitation in Saigon is described as the high point of the Vietminh effort in the cities. Part of the problem can be ascribed to the security efforts of the police. Part, too, may stem from the fact that active support for the Vietminh from moderate urban elements had begun to decline, particularly after Nguyen Binh's "red days" in Saigon, which undoubtedly frightened many. Finally, there is also evidence that the Party was somewhat uncertain how to utilize its support in urban areas most effectively.

Were its traditional supporters—students, workers, and petty bourgeois intellectuals—more valuable when recruited to serve in guerrilla units in the countryside or as clandestine organizers in the enemy-controlled cities? Vacillation on this issue led to inconsistency and confusion. For example, many Vietminh sympathizers had left Saigon in the fall of 1945 to join guerrilla units in rural areas. During the next several months, many returned to serve as union organizers in the factories of Saigon and Cholon; they formed 200 separate labor organizations with a total membership of more than 20,000. Then, in 1947, a D.R.V. government decree called for a new policy of noncooperation with the authorities in French-controlled areas and appealed to its supporters to leave the city to join resistance units in the countryside. At least 6,000 Vietnamese heeded the appeal and left for war areas, but this in turn caused problems as many labor organizations were weakened by the loss of their most effective and loyal cadres.[20]

The Communist Victory in China

By the end of the decade, the conflict in Vietnam was beginning to show signs of a stalemate. The Vietminh had managed to fend off the first French efforts to cripple the insurgency effort, and by 1948 their growing guerrilla forces had begun to pose a security problem for government authorities throughout the country. The events in Cochin China in early 1950 demonstrated that they were capable of mounting a major military effort in selected areas. But there were as yet few signs of a conclusive shift in the political or military balance of forces in favor of the revolution. Decisive action by government authorities had checked Nguyen Binh's offensive in Cochin China and driven the insurgency back to its base areas in the Plain of Reeds and the forests of the Ca Mau peninsula. The political situation in Saigon returned to normal and the Bao Dai government, although hardly popular, managed to govern with the help of pacification operations by French military forces in the Mekong delta and around Saigon. In the North, similar vigorous French operations in the summer of 1950 disrupted Vietminh control of rice-rich districts in the heart of the Red River delta and posed a severe threat to the food supply of the insurgency movement.

The Communist victory in China and the arrival of Communist military units in the Vietnamese border areas in late 1949 added a new and potentially crucial element to the situation. Until then, the Vietnamese Party's links with the CCP had been fairly tenuous. With CCP military units concentrated far to the north and preoccupied with completing the overthrow of the Chiang Kaishek government, Chinese aid had been essentially limited to the establishment of a few training units in the border area. An attempt by Vo Nguyen Giap in the fall of 1947 to travel to Communist-controlled areas in North China had proved abortive.

The establishment of the People's Republic of China (P.R.C.) in the fall of 1949 improved the situation markedly. In January 1950, the D.R.V. sent Vo Nguyen Giap to Nanning to meet with Communist officials and to request military assistance and diplomatic recognition from the new China. Two weeks later, an agreement was reached calling for Chinese military aid, the establish-

ment of training camps, and the building of roads in the border area.[21] At the
same time, China became the first nation to grant formal diplomatic recognition to the D.R.V., a helpful counterstroke to Washington's recognition of the
Associated State of Vietnam a few days earlier.

On the whole, however, the new relationship remained limited in scope and
relatively unpublicized. According to one Vietminh official, there was no provision for active Chinese intervention in the Vietnamese conflict unless the survival of the Vietminh appeared threatened. That arrangement may well have
been mutually agreeable: The Chinese were probably reluctant to become
closely involved in Vietnam at a time when consolidation of their own regime
on the mainland was essential. For their part, the Vietnamese may have believed that excessive dependence on the Chinese could have disadvantageous
consequences. Both sides presumably recognized that active Chinese involvement in the Indochina conflict could trigger a military response from the
United States. The limited agreement formally signed by Ho Chi Minh in
March of 1950 was clearly designed to provide assistance to the Vietminh
without unduly increasing the risks of foreign involvement.[22]

Although the new relationship was clearly limited in scope, however, it was
to have momentous consequences for the struggle in Indochina and to change
the character of that conflict in several respects. On the one hand, it led to a
more open reliance by the Vietminh leadership on the Chinese model of people's war. In the months following the establishment of full diplomatic relations
with Peking, a spate of references appeared in the Vietnamese press on the
significance of the Chinese model for the Vietnamese revolution. At one point,
Ho Chi Minh appeared anxious to give the impression that Chinese aid had
been a decisive factor in changing the Vietminh approach to the seizure of
power. In an interview with the American journalist Andrew Roth in August,
he remarked that the Vietminh movement had "changed its tactics" and was
now following the Chinese model. Shortly thereafter, a campaign was inaugurated in Vietminh-controlled areas to study the Chinese experience. CCP
documents and training materials were translated into Vietnamese and
distributed widely among the troops and political cadres, and study sessions
were held in military and civilian organizations to master the new doctrine.[23]

There may well have been an element of artificiality in the sudden outpour-
ing of praise for the Maoist model in the Vietnamese press. Clearly, the Party
had already decided to adopt key elements of the Chinese approach at the
beginning of the conflict in 1946. The famous "three treasures" (*san pao*) of
Maoist doctrine—Party, united front, and armed struggle—had become integral
components of Communist revolutionary strategy in Vietnam as early as 1941.
One can only conclude that this unctuous praise of the Maoist model was
undertaken mainly to flatter the Chinese Communist leadership and encourage its continued assistance to the Vietnamese struggle for national liberation (the resemblance to Ho Chi Minh's famous decision to include a brief

quotation from the American Declaration of Independence in the D.R.V. constitution is almost too obvious to mention). That the Chinese expected imitation can hardly be doubted. At an international conference of trade union representatives held in Peking in late 1949, Mao's heir-apparent Liu Shao-ch'i had publicly praised the Maoist strategy of people's war and recommended its application to insurgency movements elsewhere in Asia—an implicit hint to the Vietnamese.

Although stroking the egos of Chinese leaders may have been a major reason for the new public deference to China, it is nonetheless true that the new relationship with Peking led the Vietminh to make a number of significant adjustments in its strategy. On the international scene, it now openly moved further into the socialist camp. For several years, the Vietminh had minimized its Communist affiliations to both foreign and domestic audiences. As late as the previous October, Ho Chi Minh had suggested to an American reporter the possibility of a "neutral" Vietnam. Now, with the Peking affiliation in hand, as well as the formal recognition from Moscow that had followed shortly after, the D.R.V. openly advertised its new "lean to one side" policy toward its socialist allies.[24] As an additional confirmation of the significance of the shift, a cabinet shuffle that increased the visibility and influence of Communist hard-liners within the government was announced.

In a second move that further underlined the shift to the left, the Communist Party, allegedly dissolved in the fall of 1945, was formally reestablished in early 1951. The reappearance of the Party as an overt organization, now to be renamed the Vietnamese Workers' Party (VWP or Dang Lao Dong Viet Nam), took place at the Second National Congress of the Party (the Macao congress was termed the first), held in Tuyen Quang Province in February 1951. The meeting was attended by slightly more than 200 delegates, representing approximately 500,000 Party members throughout the country. The congress did not make any major changes in the leadership of the Party. Ho Chi Minh was elected as Party chairman and Truong Chinh remained secretary general. The new Central Committee of twenty-nine members consisted for the most part of veterans who had been active in Party struggles since before World War II, and a Politburo of seven members and one alternate was chosen.[25]

Truong Chinh's keynote speech at the congress confirmed the assumption that henceforth the Communist Party would play an open and leading role in the Vietnamese revolution. For the first time since the formation of the Vietminh League in 1941, the Vietnamese revolution was placed in a Marxist-Leninist framework: The immediate objective was the waging of a people's national democratic revolution led by the Party. In this revolution, the anti-imperialist task had clear priority over the antifeudal task. Chinh affirmed, however, that once the task of overthrowing imperialism in Vietnam had been achieved, a people's democratic regime would be set up under proletarian (i.e., Communist Party) leadership that would "grow over into a socialist revolution."[26] In other words, there would be no extended period of transition between the achievement of the two stages—bourgeois democratic and socialist—of the Vietnamese revolution.

Was the decision to revive the Party as an overt organization taken as the result of Chinese advice? There have been suggestions that Chinese Communist leaders urged a stronger emphasis on the role of a Marxist-Leninist organization in the struggle for national liberation in Vietnam. Whether or not this is the case (and it is worth noting that Ho Chi Minh was always careful to conciliate potential great power benefactors), there was a logical internal reason for reviving the Party's open apparatus. With the establishment of the Bao Dai government, the D.R.V.'s new links with Peking, and increasing U.S. involvement in the conflict on the side of the French, the primary reasons for attempting to disguise Communist leadership of the revolutionary movement appeared to have little remaining validity. Not only would an open declaration of Communist leadership over the Vietnamese national liberation struggle appeal to both Stalin and Mao Tse-tung, but it would stimulate the forces of social revolution in the final rush for power in Vietnam.

As always, however, the Party leadership was careful to protect its flanks. By avoiding the open title of Communist, the new Party hoped to avoid unnecessarily alienating moderates. According to an inner-Party memorandum, the term "worker" was preferable to that of "Communist" because it would facilitate the Party's efforts to win support from gentry elements and the religious sects. The name "Communist" could be restored when conditions were favorable.

There was also significance in the change in nomenclature from "Indochina" to "Vietnam." According to the Party document cited above, the decision to form three separate parties for Vietnam, Laos, and Cambodia was based on the need to observe national susceptibilities (suggesting that Party members of Lao and Khmer extraction were growing restive under direct Vietnamese control). There was also a doctrinal justification for the split of the ICP into three separate national organizations. The name "Indochinese Communist Party" had originally been adopted by Vietnamese leaders in October 1930 at the behest of the Comintern on the grounds that as a result of French colonial rule, the revolutionary paths of Vietnam, Laos, and Cambodia were fundamentally related, but in actuality there had been little support for the ICP in Laos and Cambodia except among Vietnamese nationals. Now it was formally recognized that the revolutions in the three countries would move at different speeds. While Vietnam was heading toward a national democratic revolution and then directly on to socialism, Laos and Cambodia were moving toward "popular democracy." The socialist revolution presumably would be delayed for several years.[27]

The Vietnamese decision in 1951 to separate the old ICP into three parties did not mean that the Party had lost interest in the rest of Indochina.

Although separate revolutionary movements were now to be set up in Laos and Cambodia, a joint alliance of the three organizations was established in March. According to the memorandum cited in the paragraph above, the Vietnamese had no intention of relinquishing control: "The Vietnamese Party reserves the right to supervise the activities of its brother parties in Cambodia and Laos," it asserted. And although in recent years Hanoi has claimed that the old concept of the Indochinese Federation, first broached at the Central Committee meeting held in October 1930, was "formally abandoned" at the 1951 conference, the document cited above noted that, although there were henceforth to be three separate parties, "later, if conditions permit, the three revolutionary Parties of Vietnam, Cambodia, and Laos will be able to unite to form a single Party: the Party of the Vietnam-Khmer-Laotian Federation."

One final move deserves brief mention here. In order to adjust the Party's front policy to the new reality, the Vietminh Front, now clearly identified with communism, was abandoned in favor of the broader Lien Viet Front in the hope of attracting wider support from moderates and progressives for the national liberation struggle.

Perhaps the most significant consequence of the new relationship with China was that it permitted the Party to reevaluate its strategic options. Specifically, Chinese aid created potential conditions for a significant strengthening of the revolutionary forces and the launching of the third phase of people's war, the general counteroffensive. This was undoubtedly the subject of intense discussion at the Third Plenum of the Central Committee held in February 1950, shortly after the initialing of the new aid pact with China. The results of that discussion were contained in a lengthy analysis of revolutionary strategy by General Vo Nguyen Giap. In a pamphlet entitled "The Military Task in Preparing for the General Counter Offensive" and published sometime in 1950, Giap discussed at some length the implications of the new situation.[28] According to the author, the conditions for a switch to the third stage of people's war were now present. In this final stage, the revolutionary forces would move gradually onto the offensive, to destroy enemy forces and positions in large chunks and eventually to attack the cities and win complete victory. Giap listed four conditions that would characterize the transition to the final phase: (1) the absolute moral superiority of the revolutionary forces and the corresponding disintegration of the will of the enemy to resist; (2) the continuing national superiority of the enemy in purely military terms, which would pose difficult but not insuperable problems for the Vietminh; (3) the increasing importance of international factors (a reference to growing Chinese assistance to the Vietminh); and (4) the superior strategic leadership of the revolutionary forces.

In what battlefield conditions would the new stage appear? Here Giap insisted on the need for flexibility in thought and action. While conceding the possibility that the third stage might be launched by a major battle (the 1947 campaign in the Viet Bac) or a quick victory (as in the August Revolution), he thought it more likely that it would emerge gradually through a series of battles of increasing size and intensity in several areas of the country, leading to a gradual shift in the balance of forces on the battlefield. Whether the final stage would be brief or protracted would depend on the capability and astute leadership of the revolutionary forces, and on the rapidity of the disintegration of the enemy's will to resist.

The major thrust of Giap's argument was the need to advance cautiously but confidently toward a final military confrontation with the enemy, moving from limited attacks on smaller positions to large-unit attacks on major positions and finally to assaults on enemy-held cities. His primary concern was the unpredictability of the international situation—in the possibility of growing U.S. or British involvement in the conflict, or that in the face of a crumbling position in the North, the French would attempt to consolidate their hold on the South.

The 1950 Border Offensive

In his pamphlet, Giap had pointed out that one of the major consequences of rising Chinese aid levels and the projected transition to the third stage would be to increase the strategic importance of Tonkin and the northern border area in the Vietnamese revolution. By contrast, the significance of Cochin China, already somewhat of a sideline to the main show in Tonkin, would now be further diminished. While remarking that the French must not be permitted to consolidate their defensive position in South Vietnam, Giap emphasized that the Party's strategy would be to concentrate its forces for a final confrontation in the North.

For the immediate future, the highest priority was to seize control of the areas adjacent to the northern frontier in order to facilitate the movement of goods and personnel from China. Since the fall offensive of 1947, the French had maintained a limited military presence on the northern border. While guerrilla units roamed the nearby mountains at will, the French occupied a string of border posts from Mong Cai near the coast to Lang Son, Dong Khe, Cao Bang, and Lao Cai in the interior. In order that communications between these posts could be maintained, frequent military convoys were sent up Route 4 as far as Cao Bang, despite the tortuous terrain, heavy jungle growth, and a rising level of guerrilla activity along the road. It soon became evident that Party military leaders had selected the border area to test the capacity of the revolutionary forces to advance to a higher level of conflict. In the summer of 1950 Vietminh units, now with substantially increased firepower, launched a series of aggressive attacks on enemy convoys, making it increasingly difficult for the French to maintain security along the border route, particularly at its Western extremity. Some French military officers advocated a continuing effort to control the border area, but Paris ultimately decided to evacuate the western posts along Route 4 and hinge the French defense of the frontier zone at Lang Son, farther to the east. To camouflage the move, a convoy was dispatched westward along Route 4 from Lang Son. At a prearranged moment, the French garrison at Cao Bang was instructed to depart and meet the convoy halfway, whence it would be escorted back to Lang Son.

The French effort was both too little and too late. The Vietminh now had about thirty well-armed battalions operating in the area, and the first known unit at full division strength, the 308th, had recently attacked and overrun a French military post at Pho Lu, twenty miles east of Lao Cai. Unwittingly, the French strategy played directly into Vietminh hands. The party leadership had come to see control of the Viet Bac and the reconstruction there of a vast liberated zone as the key to placing pressure on the rich grain-growing areas of the Red River delta and to assuring easy access to China, and in a series of bitter attacks launched amidst the dense jungle growth and limestone cliffs near Dong Khe, Vietminh forces virtually wiped out both French columns in the most disastrous engagement of the war for the French.[29] French survivors trickling back to Lang Son reported an ominous development: For the first time the Vietminh had not resorted to ruse but had launched direct attacks, complete with bazookas, mortars, and recoilless rifles and pushed their attack to the limit. In the border area, at least, the insurgents had reached parity.

In retrospect, the autumn border offensive seems to have marked a decisive shift in the course of the war. Badly mauled by the enemy, the French decided to evacuate the entire inland section of the border zone and retreat to a single redoubt at Mong Cai on the coast. In the process, they left behind 11,000 tons of ammunition and abandoned virtually all of Vietnam north of the Red River delta. The decision had no little military significance. The Vietminh were now in a position to raid the delta at will and to retreat to their liberated zone in the Viet Bac with little fear of a French response. It also offered them unrestricted access to China and thus to the promise of military assistance from the entire socialist camp. In a word, it put them in a position, for the first time, to seize the initiative in the war.

Toward the General Offensive

In Paris, the Vietminh border offensive had made the French dilemma depressingly clear. No longer could the government delude itself and the public that the conflict in Vietnam was just another nasty but manageable colonial war. Victory could not be achieved without a vastly increased commitment on the part of the entire French nation. In the words of Pierre Mendès-France, then an ambitious young parliamentarian, France had to make a choice: Either it must choose to fight, in which case it had to increase substantially its troops and financial support, or it must seek a compromise political settlement. Mendès-France left little doubt that he preferred the latter solution.

For the French government, neither solution was politically attractive but the second was unthinkable. In a pattern that would be repeated countless times before the end of the conflict, it attempted to evade the dilemma by giving the appearance of renewed determination to end the insurgency, while in actuality avoiding the hard and unpopular choice of increasing the French commitment to the war. In 1950, one means of achieving this end was to call on the United States for military assistance. Here the French were reasonably successful. Convinced, in the words of one top official in the Truman administration, that "the choice confronting the United States is to support the legal government in Indochina or to face the extension of Communism over the remainder of the continental area of Southeast Asia," the United States swallowed its distaste for French colonial policies and agreed to funnel increased amounts of military assistance to French forces fighting in Indochina.[30]

The second strategy was to create a Vietnamese national army that could supplement the French Expeditionary Forces (FEF) in Indochina by carrying out pacification and garrison duties, thus freeing the FEF for combat operations against Vietminh main force units. In 1950, French forces in Indochina had surpassed 200,000 men. But with the corresponding growth of the revolutionary forces, the French found it increasingly difficult to fill troop needs in Vietnam through existing recruitment levels in France. According to General Henri Navarre, later commander-in-chief of French forces in Indochina, the situation was particularly serious in Tonkin, where only the Northwest and the major cities of the delta were securely in French hands. With Vietminh regular forces rapidly increasing (three main force divisions had been formed and two more were in the process of creation), the Red River delta was now open to Vietminh penetration.[31] There was considerable reluctance in French political and military circles to build a Vietnamese national army, but opposition to a higher draft call-up in France and rising troop demands in Indochina forced the issue. The use of Vietnamese to replace Frenchmen was too tempting to ignore. In 1950, under substantial pressure from the United States, which promised assistance, the new Army of the Republic of Vietnam (ARVN) began to take shape.

None of this changed the fundamental fact that, by 1949, French strategy was gradually shifting to the defensive. The process was disguised by the appointment in the fall of 1950 of the aggressive and talented General de Lattre de Tassigny as high commissioner and commander-in-chief of French forces in Indochina. De Lattre had an instinct for the offensive and was deeply opposed to the forces of international communism. On his arrival in December, he immediately attempted to instill a new sense of determination in the French effort in Vietnam. On the battlefield he combined aggressive tactics with a fundamentally defensive strategy. Viewing the Red River delta as the key to the security of Vietnam and also to victory in the war, de Lattre attempted to strengthen the French position in the area by building a series of concrete blockhouses along the fringes – the famous de Lattre line – to prevent infiltration by Vietminh units. But de Lattre faced the same challenge that had plagued his predecessor, General Carpentier – insufficient forces to accomplish both the offensive and defensive tasks that would be required to control, if not to defeat, the insurgency. Prior to his departure from Paris, he had received the promise of reinforcements but the political unpopularity of raising draft calls or calling up the reserves took precedence, and in the end de Lattre received considerably less than he had requested.

None of this escaped the attention of the Vietminh military leadership. The success of the autumn border offensive, the rising level of aid from China, and the growing unpopularity of the war in France seem to have created the impression that the military balance was now shifting decisively in favor of the revolution. According to Communist sources, discussion increasingly took place within high Party councils on how and when to move to the third and final stage of people's war. In early 1950, there were already signs of preparation for a major escalation of military activity. The government had called for general mobilization and put forth the slogan "prepare strongly for the general counteroffensive." But when, where, and in what conditions should it occur? There was general agreement that the autumn offensive, although highly gratifying and a major step forward for the revolution, should not itself be considered the kickoff for the third stage but should be viewed, in the words of one high Party officials, as a "partial offensive" that signalled the gradual shift to the general offensive.[32]

There was some confusion, and perhaps disagreement, over the conditions required for a shift to the third stage. Was a "preponderance of forces" required over all of Vietnam or just in one area? Or could the offensive be launched at a time when the revolutionary forces had seized the initiative but did not possess a superior balance of forces on the battlefield? According to the Party's official history, there was some sentiment within the Central Committee that, because the Vietminh did not yet possess a preponderance of forces in North Vietnam, a proposal to launch a general offensive would be premature. Others favored such a proposal in the conviction that, unless the revolutionary forces could expand their control in the Red River delta, the shortage of rice in liberated areas would soon become desperate. Already the government had called on the population to severely reduce its consumption of rice in order to provide sufficient supplies for the armed forces.

In his pamphlet cited above, Vo Nguyen Giap had declared that the revolutionary forces could move into the third stage before they possessed an absolute material superiority over the French on the battlefield. What was required, in his view, was a clear superiority over the enemy at the local level.[33] Giap was thus probably one of those most vociferously in favor of a fairly early shift to the third stage. There seems little doubt that he was one of the major proponents of the need for a final phase of general counteroffensive to achieve total victory for the revolutionary forces. In *People's War, People's Army*, written after the close of the war, he remarked that the Vietnamese revolution "had to move" to a third stage and that the three-stage concept was a "general law of a revolutionary war such as Vietnam."[34] He did not overlook the importance of guerrilla warfare, however, and in his 1950 pamphlet had stressed the importance of guerrilla operations, not only when the insurgency forces were weaker than their adversary, but also during the third stage, to harass enemy communications and coordinate with main force units. But a revolutionary war could be victorious, he claimed, only when it could liberate land and annihilate a substantial proportion of the enemy's military forces. For that reason, mobile warfare or large-scale positional warfare would be the major forms of combat in the final phase of the conflict. According to Giap, mobile warfare would play the primary role, not only because of the need to establish local superiority in attacks on enemy positions in widely scattered regions of the country, but also because mobile war allegedly could most effectively utilize the spiritual advantages of the revolutionary forces. For the most part, positional warfare should be avoided, as it tended to magnify the enemy's material superiority on the battlefield. It could be used in specific instances as the strength of the revolutionary forces increased and that of the French declined.[35]

Evidently the majority of the Party leadership accepted Giap's analysis of the situation. In an article published in the July 1950 issue of the Party's theoretical journal *Tap chi Cong san (Communist Review)*, Secretary General Truong Chinh declared that the Third Plenum of the Central Committee had viewed the forthcoming general counteroffensive as probably taking place on one battlefield, while revolutionary forces held back the enemy through guerrilla operations and smaller attacks in other regions of the country. Chinh conceded that in some cases offensives might be launched on two or three battlefields at once, but he thought that primary emphasis was likely to be in a single region. By implication, the revolutionary forces would require a preponderance of military power in only one area of the country.

Chinh admitted that not all agreed with the view that conditions were ripe for a gradual shift to the third stage. Optimists called for an immediate launching of a major offensive, on the grounds that the French will to resist was rapidly disintegrating. Others were more pessimistic, doubting that the revolutionary forces possessed the capacity to engage in an open confrontation with the French. Chinh opposed both extreme views and took the position that the Party should prepare carefully for an eventual transition to the third stage. Elaborating on Giap's analysis, he asserted that the general counteroffensive was not likely to result in a quick victory, but would be a complex process involving a series of violent battles over a protracted period. Assistance from the United States or Great Britain, he cautioned, might serve to prolong French resistance or to bring a more reactionary government to power in Paris. Conversely, he warned that rising Chinese aid to the Vietminh did not guarantee success for the revolution, which must still rely primarily on its own efforts to achieve victory.[36]

Clearly, the decision to advance to the third stage was not an easy one. At the Second Party Congress in February 1951, Ho Chi Minh admitted that the issue was still controversial and that "some comrades" thought that the offensive had been set forth too early, while others had wanted it to be launched in 1950. The party's official history concedes that there were "erroneous views" among cadres and party members about the shift to the third stage, but it is noticeably ambiguous about the details.[37]

What were apparently the opening stages of the long-expected offensive were launched in January 1951. The plan was to strike at several places on the fringes of the Red River delta in a series of conventional military attacks and then, in a second phase, to move directly against the major cities of Hanoi and Haiphong. At that time, the Vietminh had more than eighty well-armed battalions within twenty-five miles of Hanoi. The French suspected, correctly, that the first thrust would take place at the western end of the delta, where the Vietminh had the equivalent of more than a division of main force regulars. On January 13 twenty-one battalions of the 308th Division attacked the provincial capital of Vinh Yen at the point where the Tam Dao Mountains jut onto the edge of the plains of the Red River. The initial Vietminh thrusts were deadly. Only with a liberal expenditure of artillery and air support were the six thousand French defenders able to prevent a major breakthrough. On the following day, de Lattre ordered an emergency airlift of reserve battalions from Cochin China to hold the city. During the next two days, heavy fighting continued with Vietminh regulars streaming down from the southern spur of the Tam Dao massif in a series of human wave attacks. They were finally driven back on the seventeenth after suffering heavy losses—some estimated up to six thousand killed in action—from French air attacks.[38] At Vinh Yen, at least, French superiority in firepower had made the difference.

The failure to take Vinh Yen may have represented a severe setback for Vietminh strategists, but it did not change their plans. Shifting units of several divisions to the east, in late March, they ordered an attack at Mao Khe on the northeastern edge of the delta north of Haiphong. Once again the attackers were able to break through the first French line of defense, but after a series of vicious battles they were stopped in the heart of the town. They finally abandoned the attack, on the twenty-eighth, after suffering losses of more than 1,000 dead. The final attack, combining Vietminh main force units and local forces earlier infiltrated into the area, took place in May in the area of Phu Ly and Ninh Binh on the Day River directly south of Hanoi. Here the apparent objective was to wipe out French posts in the area and reoccupy the coastal province of Phat Diem. Once again, the Vietminh were initially able to penetrate French positions but were forced to withdraw in early June after suffering heavy casualties.

The series of military offensives, although undoubtedly worrisome to the French, did not achieve the expected breakthrough, and, as the reverses multiplied, evidence of dissatisfaction with the new strategy began to surface in the media. In May, one broadcast observed that military attacks should take place only when victory was assured. Others obliquely criticized the offensives by praising Maoist strategy and the use of guerrilla techniques. Such comments were echoed in the Chinese press, which stressed the need for caution.[39] After the third series of attacks on the Day River in May and June, the message apparently got through, and the strategy was abandoned.

Perhaps understandably, Communist historians have devoted relatively little attention to the 1951 offensives. The official party history, which seems primarily concerned to determine whether or not the series of attacks represented the opening of the third stage of general offensive, barely mentions the offensives. Presumably they would have been regarded as the opening steps of the general offensive if they had been successful and had led, as expected, to major Vietminh victories in the Tonkin delta. As it was, the Party attitude toward the entire question of the third stage during the Franco-Vietminh conflict remains ambiguous.[40]

The retrospective controversy over the precise stages of people's war is primarily of concern to academics, of course. But there is no denying the effects in terms of Vietminh strategy. From a military point of view, the failure of the offensive of early 1951 showed the continuing weakness of the revolutionary forces in conducting regular war, particularly in terms of problems of logistics and combat support. It also demonstrated that the French, as Chinh had warned, had not yet wearied of the fight. There are hints that Vo Nguyen Giap, the presumed architect of the policy, was chastised and directed to undergo a period of self-criticism before resuming direction of Vietminh military strategy.[41]

The fact remains, however, that the failure of the 1951 Vietminh offensive did not essentially alter the emerging military situation in Vietnam. Paris was still unwilling to provide adequate support to its military commanders in Indochina and, in consequence, French military policy continued to be caught between an offensive and a defensive posture. During the remaining months of his tenure, de Lattre attempted to achieve maximum results with his limited resources. In the spring and summer of 1951 he concentrated on pacification operations in the Red River delta and on strengthening the de Lattre line by placing his most effective troops along the perimeter. Then, in August, in an effort to cut off Vietminh forces in the mountains of the Viet Bac from the coastal areas of Central Vietnam, he occupied the city of Hoa Binh, which sits astride a major communications route from Tonkin into Annam. To handle the problem of dispersal of forces, he set up mobile units the size of a U.S. regimental combat team, called Groupes Mobiles, which could provide rapid movement for both defensive and offensive operations.

Vo Nguyen Giap and his fellow Party strategists were well aware of the insoluble nature of the dilemma in Paris, and with total military victory apparently out of reach for the foreseeable future, predicated their strategy on taking maximum advantage of French weakness. By now, the French could ill afford to match losses with the Vietminh on a one-to-one basis. Moreover, a continued high level of combat in Indochina would keep the conflict before the attention of the French public and further erode French support for the war effort. What the Vietminh obviously required was a low-cost, high-return strategy that could grind down French strength and morale and keep the French off balance, but at a cost the revolutionary forces could afford. While the concept of the general offensive was apparently not entirely abandoned, it was recognized that it would not be a major rushing offensive combining all forces, but "an offensive during a strategical stage according to plan to make the enemy lose."[42]

During the next two years the Vietminh launched several major battles in strategic areas, primarily in Tonkin, in Annam, and in the Northwest. There was relatively little military activity in South or South Central Vietnam, where French pacification efforts had taken hold and destroyed much of the Vietminh apparatus. According to one estimate, only 20 percent of all Vietminh military forces were in the South. Many peasants had fled the liberated zones, and the manpower potential of the insurgency had declined by as much as one-half.[43]

The primary tactic of the revolutionary forces during this period was to concentrate their efforts in areas of French weakness, with the aim of wearing down French military power and forcing a dispersal of French military units. In places of its own choosing the Vietminh would emerge from the mountains and engage enemy forces in open combat. Such was the case at Hoa Binh. Accepting de Lattre's challenge to contest this key communications link in southern Tonkin, the Vietminh launched heavy attacks on French positions in the city and Hoa Binh became the Verdun of Indochina. After several months of intense combat—in a battle that the late Bernard Fall labelled "the meatgrinder"—the French abandoned the city in February 1952 and returned to the de Lattre line. De Lattre meanwhile had returned to France, dying of cancer barely a month before this loss.

For the Communists, the battle at Hoa Binh had the additional virtue of distracting the French from the continued infiltration of the Red River delta. For the de Lattre line had been in some respects no more effective than its equivalent in France, the Maginot Line. Vietminh forces simply bypassed the French blockhouses or attacked and overran them one by one. In either case, by the end of the year revolutionary organizations had been reestablished in as many as half the villages of the delta. And, with the victory at Hoa Binh, there was a growing sense within the movement that victory was on the horizon.[44]

In the fall of 1952, the Vietminh opened a new front in the far Northwest. The French, with the help of anti-Communist minority tribesmen, had held this extensive region of forbidding mountains and narrow valleys since 1947. Now, in mid-October, three Vietminh divisions crossed the Black River, attacked Nghia Lo, and cut through the French forces stationed in the area. The French retreated to Na San and Lai Chau. Ignoring the French huddled at Lai Chau, the advancing Vietminh units concentrated their efforts at Na San. Here they attacked and did not disengage until early December, after a four-day battle in which they suffered several thousand casualties. The failure to seize Na San was only a temporary setback. Early the following spring they regrouped to seize Sam Neua and threaten Luang Prabang, the capital of the Laotian Protectorate. Having accomplished their purpose and forced the diversion of several French units into the area, they stopped and then returned to the Red River delta.

The Other War

In their writings on the advance to the third stage, Party leaders like Vo Nguyen Giap and Truong Chinh had emphasized that political work in enemy-held areas was a crucial factor in the struggle for victory. The continuing problems encountered by the French in putting together an effective government coalition to oppose the Vietminh movement was persuasive evidence that there was opportunity in political struggle. In fact, however, the Party was encountering difficulties of its own in the political arena. In the cities, the effort to put together a dynamic alliance of workers, students, and the bourgeoisie in a common effort against French imperialism had run into the brick wall of French repression and Vietnamese indifference. After the climactic events of early 1950 in Saigon, the movement there had declined rapidly. Effective police action had weakened the municipal party apparatus, and the mass of the population, in the words of a later Communist historian in Hanoi, became increasingly weary and bored with the Vietminh-led antiwar movement.[45] The urban movement was even weaker in the North. Hanoi had lacked an effective municipal Party organization since the abandonment of the city in early 1947. Within a year the population had begun to return to the city, but the local Party apparatus was unable to recover its former effectiveness and was characterized by the Central Committee as insufficiently aggressive. Without a high degree of political activism among progressive classes in Vietnam's two major urban centers, the chances of unleashing a major popular uprising to accompany the third stage of general counteroffensive seemed slim. By 1952, the Party leadership had apparently accepted the fundamental reality that the contribution of the cities to the Vietnamese revolution would be limited to low-level political struggle.[46]

The failure of urban areas to fulfill the early expectations of Party planners obviously placed a heavier burden on the countryside. The Chinese Civil War provided a precedent for the belief that a protracted people's war could be victorious without a general uprising in the cities. But if the Party hoped to make good use of its support in rural areas, it would have to resolve the continuing problem of dealing with the united front at the village level. The measures taken in the late 1940s to reduce land rents and interest rates and increase productivity in the countryside had apparently achieved only limited results. In general, private property continued to be respected in liberated areas as the Party attempted to win the support of patriotic landlords and rich peasants in the revolutionary struggle. From the Party's point of view, the consequences were sometimes unfortunate. Wealthy villagers continued to dominate many local front organizations, and government regulations on rent reduction and interest rates were frequently ignored.[47]

By the time of the Second Congress the problem had become serious enough to require action and the Central Committee had taken some minor corrective measures. But decisive action was impeded by the overall political strategy: In his political report at the congress, Truong Chinh had declared that the primary task of the Vietnamese revolution at that stage was to defeat imperialism and achieve national independence. Although the antifeudal mission was a crucial one and "must be carried out at the same time as the antiimperialist mission," it must take place, he warned, "according to plan and step by step in order to simultaneously develop the people's revolutionary forces and firmly maintain the great unity of all the people to wage the resistance war and defeat the imperialist aggressors."[48] As a result, the Party's land program still held back from the general confiscation and redistribution of land. While conceding that the landlord class was in general the enemy of the revolution in rural areas, Chinh contended that some patriotic elements of the old landed gentry could be persuaded to serve the Vietminh temporarily.

Within a year, however, the Party had decided that only more radical measures could win the allegiance of the rural poor and effectively mobilize them in the revolutionary cause. Landlords were now classified in three categories, and the land of the most reactionary was confiscated and distributed to the poor. Land rents were widely reduced and in a few areas labor exchange teams, the first step in the socialization of the countryside, were formed. As Truong Chinh remarked later, it was the first time since the Sixth Plenum in 1939 that the Party had attacked the entire feudal class.[49]

In January of 1953, the Central Committee announced a comprehensive program to accelerate the antifeudal revolution throughout liberated areas. Relying heavily on Chinese experience at the height of the Civil War, the plan called for a further drastic reduction in land rents and the seizure of the land of landlords not cooperating in the war effort. Land reform tribunals composed of six to ten members, usually poor peasants, were established to undertake surveys of village landholdings, and "speak bitterness" sessions were held in which the poor were encouraged to criticize the malpractices of wealthy elements. Although comprehensive figures are not available, scattered Communist statistics suggest that the program had some effect. In liberated areas in the North, 15 percent of the land was distributed to 20 percent of the peasants. In Cochin China, 307,000 peasants received a total of 410,000 *mau* (one-sixth of an acre) of agricultural land. If Party sources are to be believed, such measures raised the commitment of poor and middle peasants to the revolutionary cause and facilitated their mobilization for the war effort during the remainder of the war. The land revolution had by no means been entirely completed, however. The rural proletariat (*co nong*) still comprised 14 percent of the population in North Vietnam, down from 20 percent before land reform.[50]

In the fall of 1953, the Party prepared to push ahead once again. At a national conference held in November, Truong Chinh proposed a harsher policy on landlords and submitted a draft land reform law calling for the confiscation of the land and property of virtually the entire landlord class. On December 1, Ho Chi Minh announced the new agricultural policy in the National Assembly. All landlord land was to be seized and distributed to the landless, the poor and middle peasants. Landlords classified as progressive in their political views would be compensated for their losses by government bonds but would be compelled to give up all land beyond the amount needed for their personal livelihood. Rich peasants, who were described by one Party source as "exploited, but tied to the feudal regime," were to be left alone.[51] Because of the advent of negotiations and the termination of the conflict in the summer of 1954, the effects of this "final solution" were not to be felt until peace had been restored. What clearly emerges from the Communists' struggle to come to terms with the land reform issue is that the dilemma between nationalism and social revolution in the countryside was never totally resolved. As the events of the following year demonstrated, however, the Party's military strategy was not significantly undermined by the continuing problems in the political realm.

The Navarre Plan

In the spring of 1953, General Henri Navarre was appointed as the new commander of French forces in Indochina. On the surface, the move appeared to signal a more aggressive French military strategy, for Navarre reputedly brought with him a new determination to bring the conflict to a successful conclusion. The task before the new commander was considerable. For nearly two years French policy, in his words, had been carried on "empirically, from day to day." In the meantime, the forces of the insurgency and the territory under their control had continued to expand. In particular, penetration of the Red River delta by revolutionary forces continued apace and parts of six Vietminh divisions were located within easy striking distance of Hanoi. Virtually all of the Viet Bac and the Northwest, with the exception of a few provincial and district capitals, was in the hands of the revolutionaries. The strength of the Vietminh in Central Vietnam, a prime source of rice and recruits, also grew steadily. Moreover, the Vietminh forces had significantly increased since the abortive 1951 offensive. According to General Navarre, the insurgents now possessed a total force of more than 350,000 armed troops organized in eight mobile infantry divisions and one artillery division. More were coming from training schools across the Chinese frontier.[52]

French force levels in the spring of 1953 were clearly inadequate to counter this rising challenge. Out of a total of 500,000 in the FEF, 350,000 were tied down in static defense assignments. In terms of combat troops, Navarre had at his disposal only three divisions, seven Groupes Mobiles, and eight paratroop battalions. The new Vietnamese army had been expected to supplement French units, but footdragging in Paris had hampered the growth of the program and in 1953 ARVN forces had reached only about 100,000. And the quality of these new indigenous troops was, according to Navarre, seriously open to question.

On assuming command in May, General Navarre requested twelve additional infantry battalions and various support units to provide the FEF with the equivalent of seven mobile divisions, a force adequate to take the offensive against the Vietminh regulars. The ARVN was to be expanded with U.S. assistance. He also drafted a military strategy to seize the initiative on the battlefield. But Navarre was soon to experience the frustration that had plagued his predecessors and to discover that political considerations in Paris took priority over military requirements in Indochina. As public support for the conflict declined, the will of the French government to carry on the war was seriously eroded and many politicians were speaking openly of seeking a compromise solution. Some recommended that French forces withdraw to enclaves in the highly populated areas, others that the North be entirely evacuated and that a defense line be established at the 18th parallel. Such proposals were not necessarily received with sympathy in the government, but they undeniably had an effect on its war strategy. Navarre was told that his own military plans must reflect the determination of the government to terminate the war by the spring of 1956, when national elections were scheduled. By implication, he would have to gear his strategy to the likelihood of a compromise political resolution of the conflict.[53]

If Navarre was hampered by such limitations, he was nonetheless a good soldier and he attempted to devise an approach that could simultaneously seize the initiative on the battlefield and make possible a political settlement in the foreseeable future. Rejecting the enclave strategy, which he claimed would simply permit the Vietminh to expand its forces for a major offensive against the French-held coastal provinces, he drew up a plan based on three basic phases. During the first phase, to be carried out in the fall and winter of 1953-1954, French forces would concentrate their efforts on securing the vital Red River delta. Lacking the strength to inflict serious defeats on Vietminh main force units, French combat forces would be limited to a few selective offensive operations in order to throw the enemy off balance and prevent it from launching major attacks.

Then, in early 1954, when the rainy season made Vietminh movement difficult, French mobile units would launch a major attack on Vietminh-held coastal areas in Central Vietnam, south of Da Nang, the famous "Interzone V." Here, according to French intelligence sources, Vietminh forces were relatively weak—the equivalent of a little more than a division of regulars. Yet this liberated area, populated by nearly 2 million people, was a major source of provisions and recruits for the revolutionary armed forces. A successful operation here would permit French occupation and pacification of an area that for years had effectively served the Vietminh cause. Finally, in the fall of 1954 when French units had reestablished superiority, Navarre would turn back to the north to launch a general offensive in order to pursue and destroy the Vietminh main force units.

The success of Navarre's plan was predicated on several factors: the government's willingness to provide him with adequate troop strength to carry out his plan, his ability to seek out and engage Vietminh main force units, and the assumption that there would be no massive increase in Chinese aid to the revolutionary forces. With regard to the first condition, the signs were ambiguous. Navarre's strategy and his requests for the necessary military increases to carry it out were discussed at a meeting of the National Defense Committee in Paris. Although the committee did not explicitly approve his plan, it apparently gave him tacit assurances to that effect, and Navarre proceeded on that belief.[54] Navarre's other assumptions, it would later become clear, were unwarranted.

The first step in Navarre's plan was to reassert French control over the strategically important Red River delta. According to his estimate, on his arrival the Vietminh was in control of about half the villages in the delta; one-third were contested; and the remainder were controlled by the French. Only the major cities and the communications routes between them, Phat Diem and Son Tay Provinces, and most of Ha Dong Province were under secure government control. The heart of Vietminh strength was located in Thai Binh, Hung Yen, Ninh Giang, and much of Nam Dinh, Hai Duong, and Bui Chow.[55] During the fall of 1953, Navarre concentrated half of his effective main force strength in the delta to attack key areas occupied by the Vietminh. But Giap refused to commit his elite forces against the French units and melted into the hills. Whether, as Navarre claimed, the French attacks had forestalled a major Vietminh offensive planned for autumn (just before the rainy season in the delta) has not been determined. In September and October, French Groupes Mobiles were able to attack and occupy the bulk of Thai Binh and Ninh Binh Provinces. Then, on October 20, the French assaulted units of the 320th Vietminh Division located on the southwest face of the delta near Phu No Quan just as it was about to attack, causing 3,000 casualties and, again according to Navarre, forcing the enemy to abandon a planned offensive in the area.[56]

While General Navarre mapped out his own strategy to reverse the balance of forces and strengthen the French military position in Indochina, Party leaders had drawn up their plans for the 1953 campaign at the Fourth Plenum held in late January. According to the published documents from the conference, revolutionary forces were to be instructed to continue to avoid open confrontation with French regular units while concentrating on searching out the weak points in the enemy's overall position, forcing him to further disperse his forces.[57] Although occasional efforts would be made to seize territory through guerrilla war and attacks in the Red River delta, the main field of activity would be in the Northwest, in Laos, and in Cambodia, where superiority of forces at the local level and the element of surprise would benefit the revolutionary cause. During the spring and summer, the Vietminh avoided contacts with French forces in the delta while other units launched their own campaign in the mountainous provinces of Northern Laos, thus further isolating the scattered French positions in the Northwest.

In September the Party Politburo met to assess the military situation and formulate preliminary plans for the winter-spring campaign of 1954. At that time, some consideration was apparently given to a shift in approach that would attempt to counter Navarre's moves in the delta. In the end, however, the conference agreed to continue the existing strategy of pressing the Vietminh advantage in the Northwest and the Upper Mekong valley in Laos. This would encourage the further scattering of French troops throughout the Indochina theater, thus opening up opportunities for Vietminh attacks on isolated outposts under advantageous conditions. The details of this plan were worked out at a meeting of the Central Military Party Committee in November.

The defense of Laos and the Northwest presented a problem to the government in Paris. Since the previous Vietminh offensive a year earlier, the French had abandoned most of the area and now occupied only one major base at Lai Chau, the capital of the now defunct T'ai Federation, and a few minor guerrilla outposts throughout the region. Like the border region with China, Upper Laos and the Northwest were geographically isolated, thinly populated, and peripheral to the primary French concerns in the populous coastal areas. That Paris attached little intrinsic importance to their retention was suggested by a government directive in April 1953, which instructed the French commander in Indochina to abandon territory to the Vietminh rather than endanger the security of the French Expeditionary Forces.

Surprisingly, Navarre was apparently not informed of this decision, and when he told the National Defense Committee that he considered Laos vital for both strategic and political reasons, he was not corrected.[58] Navarre felt that control of the upper Mekong would allow the Vietminh to launch attacks in the central coastal region in coordination with units located in Interzone V. Navarre therefore felt that it was necessary to compel the Vietminh to halt its offensive before it reached the royal capital of Luang Prabang. Lacking the strength to strike directly into the heart of the Viet Bac in order to cut the Vietminh communications link with China, he decided that the most feasible way to counter the Vietminh thrust was to seize and hold a strategic point in the Northwest on the road into Laos. For several reasons, he considered Lai Chau inappropriate and thought that it should be abandoned. Dien Bien Phu offered several advantages. Although it was now occupied by the Vietminh, it was centrally located, and Navarre was convinced that, because of the impenetrable mountains in the area, the Vietminh could not pass into Laos without controlling the town. Also, because the town was located in a fairly broad valley, French armored vehicles could assist in its defense. Moreover, the crests of the surrounding mountains were located a minimum of six to seven miles (ten to twelve kilometers) from the local airfield, and French intelligence estimated that enemy artillery, to be effective, would have to be placed on the interior slopes of the mountains, where it would be vulnerable to French counterfire. Finally, the weather at Dien Bien Phu was superior to that of Lai Chau, where landings at the town airfield, located at the end of a deep and narrow gorge, were frequently hazardous.[59]

Navarre decided to gamble that control of Dien Bien Phu would force the Vietminh to abandon its offensive, and in mid-November French paratroop battalions occupied the town, which was soon reinforced by units transferred from Lai Chau. The Vietminh did not immediately react and for the remainder of the fall and early winter continued their advance into Upper Laos, occupying the provincial town of Sam Neua and entering the Plain of Jars. But the Vietminh leadership was undoubtedly conscious of the strategic location of the new French base and felt that, even if Navarre had underestimated his adversary's ability to bypass the town, French occupation represented a potentially serious threat to the long and tenuous Vietminh transport link with China, which came down through the Viet Bac. At the same time, Giap saw clearly that a Vietminh victory at Dien Bien Phu could have a damaging impact on French morale and provide a spectacular background for any negotiations during the next year.

The Vietminh advance into Laos had forced Navarre to respond, but it had not diverted him from his intention to inaugurate the second phase of his strategy at the opening of the new year. In January, French forces launched the first attacks in a six-month campaign, labeled "Opération Atlante," designed to clear out Vietminh units in the Central Vietnam provinces of Phu Yen, Binh Dinh, Quang Ngai, and Quang Nam and to permit the definitive pacification of this key area. By this move, Navarre hoped to disrupt expected Vietminh plans to launch an offensive in the region later in the year, possibly in coordination with similar attcks in Laos.

Navarre's plan presented difficult problems to the Vietminh leadership. The area was of vital importance to the revolutionary cause and its loss could do incalculable harm, in terms of morale as well as its military and political consequences. Yet stubborn defense of the area would play into Navarre's hands and expose precious main force units to concentrated attacks by French regulars and airpower in the open plains of the coastal zone. The leadership decided to leave defense of the area to regional forces and to send regular units westward, into the northern sector of the Central Highlands, in a major offensive against French positions there. This move had already been planned at the September strategy conference as a means of preventing the enemy from consolidating its position in the South. It was now reaffirmed in the belief that vigorous attacks in the highlands would force the French to divert forces from coastal operations and permit the revolutionary forces to retain the initiative. In the meantime, local forces in the lowlands, supplemented by the mobilization of the civil population, would resist French units attempting to pacify the area.

The Vietminh strategy was effective. French units were able to advance virtually unmolested, except for local harassing actions, in coastal areas of Phu Yen and southern Binh Dinh provinces, but they found it difficult to make contact with the enemy. In the meantime, Vietminh attacks in Kontum Province forced the French commander to send reinforcements to the area and then to abandon the provincial capital in order to concentrate his forces at Pleiku. Other Vietminh units advanced into Laos and briefly occupied the Mekong River town of Thakhek before retreating into the Bolovens Plateau.

In March, Navarre resumed the offensive with a three-pronged assault on Qui Nhon and southern Binh Dinh Province from the south and west and from the sea. But fierce Vietminh attacks pinned down French units along the coast, while forces in the highlands attacked Pleiku and cut Route 19, the vital link to the sea. In the process one French Groupe Mobile was virtually wiped out by an ambush on Route 19 east of Pleiku, thus cutting all links between French forces at Pleiku and the coast.[60]

While French and Vietnamese military units sparred bitterly for advantage in the mountains and rice fields of Indochina, diplomats from the two countries moved hesitantly toward a confrontation at the conference table. For several years after the abortive trip of Paul Mus to the Viet Bac in 1947, neither side had expressed much interest in a negotiated settlement. Ho Chi Minh had attempted to keep the channels of communication open, pledging that the war would stop as soon as the French accepted Vietnamese independence. He was even careful not to renounce membership in the French Union and promised that foreign capital and a French cultural presence would be welcome in the new Vietnam. Whether or not these diplomatic gestures were meant seriously, in the late 1940s the French were clearly not interested in a compromise settlement, and they pursued the chimera of the Bao Dai solution. When Emile Bollaert arrived as the new high commissioner in the spring of 1947, he took a moderate position on negotiations at first but eventually, on orders from Paris, toughened his stance: Vietnam was offered freedom within the French Union, but that freedom was severely limited, for the French would reserve to themselves control of defense, foreign affairs, and finances. The Vietnamese would be permitted to run their own internal affairs and to decide for themselves on the role of Cochin China. In some respects, this was less than had been tentatively agreed upon in the Ho-Sainteny agreement of March 1946. Vietminh interest in negotiations cooled, and after the Communist victory in China offered the promise of substantial military assistance, it may have declined even further.

In 1953, signs of movement began to appear. According to King Chen, the opening gambit came in March when the new Soviet leadership decided to lessen the tensions in the Cold War and hinted at a political solution to the conflict. By autumn, possibly influenced by vague threats from John Foster Dulles of "grave consequences" if China entered the war, Peking had fallen in line. By now, too, Paris was beginning to speak openly of its interest in a compromise settlement. In October, Prime Minister Joseph Laniel announced that France would be willing to accept a diplomatic solution to the conflict. Ho's reply came in November. In an interview with a Swedish journalist he remarked that if Paris was interested in a settlement, the D.R.V. was ready to examine French proposals.[61] Finally, at a meeting of the foreign ministers of the great powers in February, it was announced that a peace conference to settle the Indochina conflict would be held in May in Geneva.

The Battle of Dien Bien Phu

Two days after the announcement, French sources in Indochina learned that Vietminh units in Upper Laos were streaming east toward Dien Bien Phu. Clearly, the Party leadership had decided that an attack on the isolated French outpost, carefully timed to coincide with the opening of the peace conference, could exert maximum impact on the outcome of the negotiations. In his recollections of the battle, Giap remarked that the French occupation of Dien Bien Phu incited lively discussion in high Party councils. Here, the Vietminh could bring to bear two of their primary advantages—control of the surrounding terrain and a capacity to move rapidly and transport goods from China. Yet an attack on the French post would be substantially different from past tactics. Previously the Vietminh had tied the French down in camps of this size and then attacked elsewhere. But now Party strategists decided to attack a fortified camp for the first time with a force of more than one or two companies. Why? According to Giap, it was the key to the Navarre plan and must be wiped out if the French were to be defeated. Could the Vietminh win? That, of course, was the crucial question. The Vietminh had the geographical advantage and strong forces in the area. Supplying the base by air would be difficult for the French, whereas Vietminh logistical problems, although complex, were not insurmountable. To take Dien Bien Phu would be difficult, but not impossible.[62]

The nature of the proposed attack also excited disagreement. Some advocated a lightning assault, to take advantage of the element of surprise. Giap rejected that idea, however, because of inexperience and the lack of a guarantee of success. A better approach would be to wear down the enemy gradually, to use Vietminh artillery to destroy the airstrip and cut off the French source of supplies and gradually neutralize French firepower, and to seize their strong points one by one.

By early March, captured documents had revealed to the French that a major offensive was projected and would be synchronized with the upcoming negotiations in Geneva. Chinese military assistance was on the rise, and there were indications that Moscow and Peking had promised to help the Vietminh present a favorable military situation by the time of the conference in early May. The major effort would take place at Dien Bien Phu, but attacks would be launched elsewhere, in Cochin China, the Central Highlands, and Laos, and along the Hanoi-Haiphong route, to hinder the French from dispatching reserve units to the besieged mountain base in the Northwest.

The siege of Dien Bien Phu began on March 13. The Vietminh had managed to concentrate in the area thirty-three battalions of main force regulars, a total of 49,500 combatants, in addition to more than 55,000 support troops and nearly 100,000 transport workers. The French garrison totaled approximately 16,000 men.[63] The French would have to be supplied by air, the attackers by long lines of coolies recruited from the coastal provinces, each carrying an average of thirty pounds of provisions ten miles each night over rough mountain trails. Much of the aid came from China; the level of Chinese aid had risen from 10 to 20 tons a month in 1951 to 1,500 tons a month in the spring of 1954.[64] Although the bulk of it consisted of petroleum and ammunition, there were also large artillery pieces from the Soviet Union, carried piece by piece from the Chinese border at Lang Son, a distance of more than 200 miles.

Detailed descriptions of the attack need not detain us here. But two aspects of Vietminh tactics are worthy of brief mention: the construction of a network of several hundred miles of shallow trenches to permit the attacking forces to advance toward the outlying French defense works without severe exposure to French firepower, and the brilliant use of artillery. A series of tunnels was dug in the slopes of the mountains facing the besieged fortress. Artillery pieces could be moved rapidly within the tunnels to new firing locations, thus preventing French gunners from zeroing in on their Vietminh counterparts.

By March 27, the airfield was unusable. Soon the outer defense works began to fall to human wave attacks, and the guns turned on the inner redoubt. The final stage took place on May 7 when, in Giap's somewhat laconic description, "Our troops launched an offensive from all directions, occupied the enemy's headquarters and captured the whole enemy staff."[65] The French defeat had been total. More than 1,500 of the defenders had died, 4,000 were wounded, and the remainder were taken prisoner or were listed as missing. About seventy escaped and made their way back to the French lines. Vietminh losses, according to a French source, were more than 25,000, with nearly 10,000 killed in action.[66]

For years, the reasons for the French defeat at Dien Bien Phu have been controversial. Navarre has been faulted for having selected the site in the first place. The size of the valley, which he had viewed as an advantage, was too large for the few troops available to him, and they were unable to occupy the high ground. Monsoon rains slowed down the supply of equipment and provisions. There were also errors in intelligence. A crucial miscalculation was underestimation of the ability of the Vietminh to transport heavy artillery pieces and bring them to bear on the defending positions. Not all the blame should be placed on Navarre, however. A French military commission that was directed to undertake a postmortem in 1955, although it did not totally absolve Navarre from responsibility for failure, pointed out that the commander's plan was sabotaged above all by the refusal of the government to supply him with the promised reinforcements until it was too late.[67] The commission argued that he should have considered evacuation when a siege appeared likely, but Navarre was not alone in his conviction that Dien Bien Phu could be defended. During the weeks prior to the siege, several military experts from France and the United States visited the camp, and many pronounced it invulnerable.

The Road to Geneva

On May 7, the day after the French garrison at Dien Bien Phu, its forces badly depleted by the constant pounding of Vietminh forces, had surrendered, the conference on Indochina opened. It was attended by France, the Indochinese states, and their respective allies, the Soviet Union, the P.R.C., Great Britain, and the United States. The details of the conference and the terms of settlement need not delay us here. Suffice it to say that after setting forth conditions for a cease-fire that the French obviously would not accept—French recognition of the sovereignty and independence of all of Vietnam, Cambodia, and Laos under their respective Communist-led insurgency movements, withdrawal of all foreign troops, and then general elections in Vietnam, in return for which the Vietnamese agreed to examine the issue of membership in the French

Union and a French cultural and economic presence in Vietnam—D.R.V. negotiators eventually adopted a more conciliatory attitude, and the final agreement, reached in July, represented a compromise.

France agreed to grant total independence to all of Vietnam. For the purposes of arranging a cease-fire, two regroupment zones were established, divided by a demilitarized zone at the 17th parallel, with the Vietminh to the north, the French and supporters of the Bao Dai regime to the south. As neither Vietnamese government would accept the permanent partition of Vietnamese territory, a political protocol was drafted that called for consultations between representatives of the two zones within one year of the close of the conference. These consultations were to lead to national elections and a single unified government in 1956. In Laos, the royal government supported by the French was recognized as the sole legal authority in the country, but the Communist-led insurgency movement set up in 1951 by the Vietminh—popularly called the Pathet Lao—was granted a regroupment zone in two Upper Laotian provinces, on the understanding that the two sides would negotiate a political solution. In Cambodia the royal government of King Sihanouk was recognized as the legal representative of the Cambodian people. The tiny Khmer Rouge (Red Khmer) movement received no recognition.

As with most conflicts that end on a note of compromise, there is an ambiguous quality about the Franco-Vietminh War and its somewhat anticlimactic conclusion. Among the major unresolved questions was the attitude of Party leaders toward the settlement. Were they reasonably satisfied with the results of the conference, or had they been compelled to bow to the wishes of Moscow and Peking? There has been speculation that party leaders were reluctant to abandon the promise of a military solution and were only brought to accept a compromise agreement by means of pressure from their allies. Bitter comments by Vietminh representatives at Geneva are frequently cited as evidence to this effect. More recently, sources in Hanoi have claimed specifically that pressure imposed by the P.R.C. compelled the Vietnamese to accept a negotiated settlement when, in purely military terms, they might have been able to achieve total victory.[68]

It is not unlikely that there was some unhappiness within the Party, even at the top level, over the decision to accept a compromise, despite the laconic statement in the official Party history that the Sixth Plenum in July had "unanimously approved" the Politburo's decision to negotiate. It would indeed be strange if there had not been resistance to the decision, as since the August Revolution militant elements within the Central Committee had been opposed to any compromise with the French. Ho Chi Minh admitted as much in his statement to the Central Committee on July 15, 1954, when he remarked that some wanted to fight on and failed to see the United States behind the French.[69] From the standpoint of top Party strategists, negotiations would not be appropriate until the French position had disintegrated or a highly favorable situation on the battlefield had been established, conditions that had not been clearly established in the spring of 1954. Although both Peking and Moscow had agreed to increase military assistance to the revolutionary forces in the final months before Geneva, it is not improbable that such aid had been contingent upon Vietnamese willingness to come to the conference table. If such is the case, top Party figures may have harbored no little resentment at their allies for pressing them into a compromise settlement.

Too much, however, should not be made of such signs of resentment for, as the more astute members of the Party leadership undoubtedly realized, more was at stake then just the situation on the battlefield. The key must be seen in Ho Chi Minh's allusion to the possible intervention of the United States. The ever-practical Ho must have been aware that U.S. troops might be introduced into Indochina if a reasonable solution was not reached at Geneva. This would have complicated Communist strategy in Vietnam immensely. On the other hand, if France could be induced to withdraw from Vietnam, the Communists' only rival for power would be the Bao Dai government in Saigon. While Party militants may have been restive, it is probable that Ho Chi Minh's incisive and dispassionate evaluation of the situation was persuasive. Reluctantly or otherwise, the Party leadership probably approved the accords on its own initiative.

Concern at the possible intervention of the United States was further demonstrated by the Party's decision to accept partition rather than a cease-fire based on enclaves. According to one Party document, the leadership seriously debated the relative advantages of each solution and finally decided on the former. The reasons were that under an enclave solution, the Vietminh would be restricted mostly to small and rural areas, communication would be difficult, and the Party would be unable to consolidate and develop its forces. This in turn would encourage the United States to provoke incidents as an excuse to intervene and resume the war.[70]

Could the Vietminh have achieved a military victory in the absence of a political settlement? This question aroused considerable controversy in the years following the Geneva Agreement. Some sources sympathetic to the French maintain that after Dien Bien Phu the Vietminh were too exhausted to pursue their advantage. Navarre pointed out that, after the siege, Vietminh pressure slackened on all fronts. He predicted that no new major attacks were likely before autumn.

Others have contended that Vietminh units had begun to return to the delta in early summer and, in the unstable conditions in that area, would have been in a position to push straight to Hanoi.[71] There is no doubt that the situation in much of the delta appeared precarious during the summer months. The troop ratio was increasingly favorable to the Vietminh, and Navarre requested three additional divisions to forestall the possibility of defeat. He received directives from Paris instructing him to protect the French Expeditionary Forces at all costs and suggesting the possibility of a concentration of forces within the

Hanoi-Haiphong axis, or even a withdrawal south of the 18th parallel.

There are probably too many imponderables to permit a categorical answer to the question. The disarray of the French military forces in the delta seems well established, but the Party's ability at that moment to launch a concerted attack on French positions in the heart of the Red River delta appears open to serious question. Would the French government have provided additional reinforcements? Would China have provided a high level of assistance to the Vietminh had the war continued? Would the United States have activated contingency plans drawn up by the Joint Chiefs of Staff to inject U.S. combat units into Tonkin? Lacking answers to such questions, one can only speculate.

Conclusions

Retrospective explanations for the Communist victory have focused on a wide variety of factors. Some have pointed to the mistakes made by the French – the failure to grant sufficient autonomy to moderate political forces, to comprehend the dynamics of political and social change in a traditional society in transition, and to grant adequate support to the French military commander in the field. Others have cited the role of Chinese military assistance, emphasizing that until the Communists had risen to power in China, the Vietminh lacked the firepower to pose a serious threat to French rule in Indochina. Finally, still others attribute Vietminh success primarily to the theoretical and organizational abilities of its leadership and to its ability to tap the loyalties of the mass of the Vietnamese population.

Revolution is too complex a phenomenon to be ascribed to single causes. In analyzing the reasons for the Bolshevik victory in the Russian Revolution, for example, it would be ludicrous not to mention several factors: the effects of the European war, the incompetence of the tsar's government, the weaknesses of the moderate provisional government set up after the February uprising, and the astute leadership of Lenin, Trotsky, and other Bolshevik leaders. The Chinese Revolution, too, was clearly the product of a variety of objective and subjective factors.

Such was the case in Vietnam. Certainly French failures played a role in the outcome. The intransigence in Paris over indigenous participation in the political process, at a time when most other colonial societies in Southeast Asia had already reached independence, undoubtedly undercut the power of moderate nationalists and left a vacuum that the Communists were eager to fill. The stubborn determination of the French to retain a presence in Indochina did not by any means drive all Vietnamese nationalists into the arms of the Vietminh, but it did discredit the French-sponsored Bao Dai regime and lead many patriotic intellectuals to withhold their support from it. Although the Vietminh did not win in the cities, it could console itself that the French attitude prevented many urban moderates from siding with the enemy.

Then, too, a number of underlying economic and social problems in colonial Vietnam undoubtedly contributed to popular support for the revolutionary cause. High taxes, high interest rates, and the colonial monopolies all drained the farmers' meager savings. Official corruption and the government's indifference to the poverty and suffering of the mass of the population in urban and rural areas alike built up a reservoir of latent hostility that was frequently channeled into active resistance by Vietminh propaganda and organizational efforts. In the words of the French scholar Paul Mus, Vietnam in the postwar era was a nation "off balance." The inevitable effect of colonial policies had been to undermine and ultimately destroy traditional institutions and the Sino-Vietnamese world view that underlay them. The passing of traditional society was not, as Mus conceded, altogether a bad thing. It was the "historic function" of colonialism to pave the way for the emergence of a new and more viable society, capable of meeting the challenges of the modern world. But the effects of French colonial policy were primarily destructive, not constructive: The traditional patron-client relationship, although hardly ideal, had at least provided a measure of protection for the tenant in difficult times. Under the French, tenants were thrown onto the mercies of the marketplace and lost what little protection they had against economic crises or climatic disasters. Vietnamese society under French direction gradually developed a commercial and manufacturing sector but colonial policies, rooted in the requirements of French economic interests in Indochina and the metropole, did not encourage the emergence of a vigorous and independent commercial and manufacturing Vietnamese bourgeoisie. In the perceptive view of Clifford Geertz describing a somewhat similar situation in the Dutch East Indies, Vietnam was a nation caught in a state of permanent transition, the old society destroyed, the new one powerless to be born.[72] The potential for widespread discontent in such circumstances needs no elucidation.

A second factor frequently cited to explain Vietminh success is the role of Chinese assistance. There is undoubtedly some truth in this contention. Until 1950, the Vietminh were virtually incapable of posing a severe military challenge to French forces and were generally restricted to waging guerrilla warfare and ambushes against government outposts in isolated areas. Later, with the aid of a steady stream of weapons and equipment from the north, they were able to mount several offensives and by 1954 had reached near parity with the enemy. But it is really misleading to imply, as some do, that the Vietminh could not have won without outside help. The French were equally dependent upon outside assistance after 1949, when U.S. military aid became a major factor in the French effort. And, of course, the French themselves could be classified as outsiders. In the absence of any foreign involvement, the Vietminh would have won easily. Chinese aid simply permitted the Vietminh to match the military escalation already taking place on the French side. It did not win the war for them.

Neither Chinese assistance nor the objective conditions in Vietnam could have been decisive in the absence of an effective revolutionary organization able to take advantage of them. The reasons for this effectiveness can be more appropriately dealt with in the concluding chapter of this book. Suffice it to say at this point that there were a number of factors crucial to the success of the Communists: organization, dedication, revolutionary strategy, and the extraordinary leadership of Ho Chi Minh. This is not to say that the Party's efforts were uniformly successful, or that its strategy was carved in stone. On the contrary, it ran into considerable difficulties in attempting to counter French military escalation and was compelled to make a number of refinements in its original approach. The shift in strategy that took place in 1950 is a case in point. With the decision to "play the China card" following the Communist rise to power in Peking, a number of significant adjustments were introduced. Specifically, the new strategy called for increasing reliance on military struggle, on a rural approach at the expense of the cities, and on the force of social revolution over that of nationalism.

It is probably not advisable, however, to overstress the long-term significance of this shift in emphasis. The final years of the war were dominated by the military confrontation in rural areas, but the Party continued its effort to win support in the cities, although at a reduced level of priority. It does not appear that the overall balance between urban and rural support was fundamentally disturbed, although comprehensive statistics are difficult to come by.[73] The bulk of the rank and file in the armed forces were probably peasants, but the urban component was not insignificant, particularly at the upper levels of the Party. And although the Communist complexion of the Vietminh Front presumably turned away many of its former supporters, the front managed to regain the image of a nationalist force among the Vietnamese population as a whole.

Practically speaking, of course, the Party's decision to reach for the military option was simply a recognition that a primarily political strategy could not be victorious against a well-armed and determined adversary. In a sense, the decision to match the enemy's military escalation represented a considerable risk because, by downgrading the importance of political struggle, it reduced the major advantage possessed by the Communists in the war. The Party would now be put in the position of matching its own primary area of weakness—military power—against the major strength of its adversary.

The military consequences were predictable. After more than three years of a relatively high level of conflict, the war threatened to settle into a stalemate. But in the process the Party leadership discovered a new area of political weakness in the enemy's armor—the psychological effects of the war in France. To what degree Vietminh strategy after 1951 was predicated on its possible impact on French public opinion cannot be determined with certainty at the time of this writing. The first reference to the use of this factor as an aspect of the

Party's revolutionary strategy had come in 1947 when Truong Chinh had suggested that "false negotiations" might be used as a means of obtaining a psychological advantage over the enemy. There was little further reference to this technique until 1953, perhaps because the French had previously shown little interest in a diplomatic settlement. But as declining public support for the war undermined the French government's capacity to carry on the war effort, the dynamic potential of this weapon must have become clear to Party leaders. The seeds of what would later be termed a "psychomilitary strategy"—destroying the enemy's will to fight through adroit military, political, and diplomatic maneuvers—had been planted.[74]

How the struggle would have concluded had great power interests not intervened will never be known. By 1954, the Vietnamese revolution had become a hostage to the Cold War—to the rising determination of the United States to counter the expansive force of communism in Asia and the decision of Moscow and Peking to moderate their own support for revolution in order to avoid a confrontation with Washington. The revolution had been caught in the vortex of events beyond the control of the Party. Whether or not it would be able to transform these events to its own advantage in the future remained to be seen.

8
Peace and Division
(1954–1961)

For the second time in less than a decade, a tenuous peace had come to Vietnam. And, as in September 1945, with the signing of the Geneva accords the focus of the Vietnamese revolution shifted temporarily from the military to the political. Although the Party leadership, now back in Hanoi after eight years in the wilderness, had reason to be disappointed at the elusiveness of total victory, the new situation did not justify unalloyed pessimism. For, while policymakers in Washington might persuade themselves that moderate Vietnamese nationalism would now be able to rise above its historic weakness and develop a political maturity sufficient to guarantee the survival of a non-Communist state in the South, the Communists had a different perspective.

To the D.R.V., the historical record spoke for itself. Trained to view social change through the prism of Marxist-Leninist class analysis, the Communists saw the bourgeois nationalists in the South as isolated from the masses, afflicted with inveterate factionalism, and tarred with the brush of collaboration with the imperialists. If they had posed little threat to the French colonial regime, they would be equally inept in providing an alternative force to the Communists in an extended struggle for power in South Vietnam.

True, there were a few sources of moderate concern. For one, Ngo Dinh Diem, the prime minister of the new government, was a puzzle to the Communists, as to many of his other fellow-countrymen. Diem indeed was something of an enigma. Descended from a family with connections at the imperial court in Hué, Diem was easily identified in Communist eyes with the reactionary feudal interests that had long ago been discredited in the fight for Vietnamese independence. On the other hand, Diem's credentials as a patriot were fairly impressive. In the early 1930s, he had resigned from Bao Dai's cabinet in Central Vietnam, allegedly in protest against the emperor's failure to win autonomy from the French. During the succeeding years, he had rigidly opposed all contacts with the French and, while reserving his primary hostility for the ICP, refused to grant his approval to Bao Dai's Associated State of Vietnam. Diem was one of the few prominent non-Communist nationalists in South Vietnam who could not be accused of collaborationist tendencies.

Moreover, Diem, unlike most non-Communist figures in Vietnam, had a potential constituency that extended well beyond Saigon intellectual circles. A devout Roman Catholic, he had close ties with the church hierarchy in Vietnam and a bishop for a brother. In the aftermath of the Geneva Agreement, several hundred thousand Catholic refugees had fled the North for the South. As a rule, they were better educated and more politically sophisticated than their Buddhist compatriots. Organized and directed by Diem, they would provide a counterforce of considerable strength to the Communists in South Vietnam.

A second source of disquiet for the Communists lay in the international situation. The Eisenhower administration had been openly dissatisfied with the negotiations at Geneva and had publicly disassociated itself from the political accords, which called for the holding of unification elections in both zones of Vietnam. At a press conference held not long after the shape of the settlement had begun to emerge, Secretary of State John Foster Dulles had warned bluntly that Washington would now turn its efforts to building up the non-Communist states in South Vietnam, Laos, and Cambodia. By late summer, the United States was showing increasing signs of desiring to fill the gap that would be left by the imminent departure of the French from South Vietnam. In September, the Southeast Asian Treaty Organization (SEATO) was formed. Although South Vietnam was not formally included as a signatory (the Geneva Agreement had called for the neutralization of the new states in Indochina), it was covered by an "umbrella clause" attached to the treaty, which left the door open for U.S. military intervention in case of renewed violence anywhere in Indochina. It was too early to say with assurance how durable Washington's support for the new South Vietnamese government would be, but it was clear that Washington viewed South Vietnam as a potential bulwark against the further spread of communism on the Southeast Asian mainland.

In contrast to the increasing militancy in Washington, support for the Vietnamese revolutionary cause in Moscow appeared lukewarm at best. The new Soviet leadership that had assumed power at the death of Stalin in the spring of 1953 appeared anxious to reduce Cold War tensions. For its own reasons, China was following the same path and at the Bandung Conference held in 1955 had committed itself to a policy of peaceful relations and noninterference in the internal affairs of the neutral states in the Third World. While Peking was dubious about the prospects for the holding of reunification elections, it did not feel that the time was ripe for the resumption of revolutionary war.[1]

Yet, although neither Moscow nor Peking appeared to view a resumption of the war in Vietnam as in its national interest, the general outlook in Hanoi must have appeared reasonably bright. The political agreement reached at Geneva (agreed to by most of the conferees, but not by the Bao Dai government or the United States) had called for national elections in 1956. Whether or not these elections ever took place, Diem's chances of stabilizing the situation in the South must have seemed dubious in Hanoi. Few objective observers gave the new regime in Saigon much chance for long-term survival. Reports sent back to Washington by U.S. intelligence sources in Vietnam in late 1954, for example, expressed pessimism as to whether Diem could do the job. Such views had little effect in Washington, however, for the decision by the Eisenhower administration to support the new government of Vietnam (GVN) was based less on logic than on the emotional imperative to counter the further expansion of communism in Asia. In September, President Eisenhower sent a letter to Ngo Dinh Diem promising U.S. support in building up a viable non-Communist society in South Vietnam. Although the offer of support was carefully qualified, it was nevertheless a clear indication of Washington's growing commitment to the survival of an independent and non-Communist South Vietnam.

Diem wasted no time in demonstrating that if he erred, it would not be on the side of inaction. Sensing that unity of command was crucial for the success of his government, he immediately took steps to gather power in his hands and put an end to the traditional fragmentation of South Vietnamese society. He had indeed a number of potential rivals: pro-French politicians clustered around Chief of State Bao Dai; the Binh Xuyen of Le Van Vien, the so-called river pirates who controlled crime and vice in Saigon and its sister city Cholon; and, of course, in the lower Mekong delta, the sects. During the winter, Diem moved rapidly and forcefully against these elements, and although official Washington had momentary misgivings and seriously considered withdrawing its support, Diem's gamble paid off. By early 1955, he was firmly in control. In October, after a hasty referendum, he replaced Bao Dai as chief of state in the new Republic of Vietnam. Diem's powerplay had been costly, however, for the sects, which had reluctantly cooperated with the Bao Dai regime against the Vietminh, were now alienated from Saigon. In his feisty effort to assert control over sect-held areas in the delta, Diem risked driving these crucial elements once again into the arms of the Communists.

For the moment, the success of Diem's efforts soothed nervous souls in Washington and the bleak outlook of the fall and winter of 1954-1955 was gradually replaced by a mood of cautious optimism. With American advice, Diem established a political system based loosely on the U.S. model and was elected the first president of the Republic of Vietnam. He also appeared willing to attack one of the most important issues left over by the French colonial regime—the inequitable distribution of land in rural areas. In Ngo Dinh Diem, it seemed, the Eisenhower administration had discovered a charismatic leader who could subdue the inveterate factionalism that had for so long undermined the force of Vietnamese nationalism and create a cohesive force that could rival the tempered strength of Ho Chi Minh and his Communist Party.

Communist Strategy in the South, 1954–1957

For the Party leadership in Hanoi, Diem's performance in the South was probably disconcerting, but not necessarily cause for alarm. Given the realities of the situation, an early resumption of revolutionary struggle in the South was out of the question. Above and beyond the reluctance of the Soviet Union and China to support a renewal of hostilities in Vietnam, there were persuasive domestic reasons to avoid a resumption of the conflict. The D.R.V. would need time to consolidate its authority north of the 17th parallel. With the Party fully in control, the North would soon begin the arduous task of advancing toward socialism. As the Party leadership conceded, this would be a complex and difficult task in an underdeveloped society like North Vietnam. For the foreseeable future, precious natural and human resources would have to be transferred from revolutionary war to nation-building. After a decade of struggle, there was undoubtedly a tangible and natural desire, in the South as in the North, to taste the fruits of peace.[2]

Under the circumstances, it is understandable that for the moment the Party leadership preferred to count on the implementation of the procedures set up at Geneva and to hope that unification elections could be held in order to avoid a costly and bitter struggle. Communist leaders in Hanoi appeared willing, at least for the time being, to pursue a peaceful course. At its Sixth Plenum, held in July 1954, the Central Committee declared its support for a political settlement, but warned that if such means failed it would not hesitate to resort to force once more.[3] Party leaders may have reminded themselves in private (as they did occasionally in public) of the Marxist-Leninist teaching that revolutionary waves come in cycles, that a high tide must be followed by a trough, and that a period of regroupment is necessary before the next revolutionary outbreak.

The immediate hope, of course, was for the holding of national elections as scheduled. There has been much speculation over whether the Hanoi Party leadership expected the elections to take place. In public, high D.R.V. officials expressed confidence on several occasions that the elections would be held and in 1955 and for several years thereafter suggested consultations and the normalization of relations with the GVN in the South. In private, however, there may have been considerable skepticism. Prime Minister Pham Van Dong was quoted as remarking to one foreign observer: "You know as well as I do that there won't be elections." Once Ngo Dinh Diem had made known his refusal to hold consultations (the formal statement to that effect was issued in August 1955), the prospects for such elections obviously declined. Officially, however, the D.R.V. attempted to maintain a positive posture on the issue, primarily to prevent lower-level cadres and sympathizers from becoming disillusioned and questioning the validity of Party strategy.[4]

In the immediate post-Geneva period it was indeed difficult to predict whether or not the elections would ever be held. Even the Eisenhower administration, which had reason to fear the results, seemed prepared for the possibility that they would take place and hoped to set up stringent conditions that the Communists would find it impossible to accept. Under the circumstances, the Party leadership could only hope that the national elections would occur, for the outcome was likely to be a coalition government with Communist participation, a promising stepping-stone for a transition to a Communist-dominated government. At the same time, Party leaders were prepared to accept other eventualities, including a resumption of revolutionary war. Whatever their private hopes and fears, they had long since learned the necessity of maintaining flexibility in matters relating to the revolution. A Party directive issued sometime in the late summer or autumn of 1954, for example, observed that "we must be firm, long-suffering, and flexible. . . . We will gain nothing by being impatient or overbold."[5]

For the moment, then, the Party attempted to prepare for either contingency. According to various estimates, between 50,000 and 90,000 Vietminh sympathizers went to the North after the accords while approximately 10,000 to 15,000 remained in the South. Of the latter, some abandoned political activity, while others were directed to reorganize the Party and the front apparatus on a peacetime basis. Local leaders were instructed to avoid violence and to restrict their activities to peaceful and legal ones, such as the promotion of national elections. On the other hand, the Party leaders in the South should act to protect the remaining revolutionary forces in the area and to maintain the security of the clandestine apparatus. Activities should be conducted on both the legal and semilegal level. Illegal methods were to be used only on a selective basis.[6]

In public, Party activists behaved as though elections would be held on schedule. The various national salvation associations (the *cuu quoc hoi*), which had been affiliated with the Vietminh since the August Revolution, were disbanded and replaced by apparently innocuous functional organizations representing the various interest groups in society. The major political effort to promote the implementation of the Geneva accords took place in Saigon, where a movement among leftist intellectuals had operated with limited effectiveness during the War of Resistance. Less than two weeks after the signing of the agreement, a Saigon-Cholon Peace Movement (Phong Trao Hoa Binh Saigon-Cholon) was formed by several Saigon figures long active in Vietminh circles, including the lawyer Nguyen Huu Tho. The movement was designed specifically to attract non-Party intellectuals with patriotic inclinations who were considered potentially hostile to the Diem regime. Similar groups were set up on a small scale in rural villages sympathetic to the Communists.[7]

The Party's clandestine organization was not totally dismantled, but it was reduced in size. The Central Office for South Vietnam (COSVN), the southern branch of the VWP Central Committee that had been set up in 1951 to provide localized direction for the war in Cochin China, was abolished and replaced by a Regional Committee for the South (Xu uy Nam Bo). Below this committee were three interzone committees, responsible for five to seven provinces each. Le Duan, who had been the principal Party leader in the area during the last years of the war, remained in charge, with another southerner, Pham Hung, as his duputy.[8] As before, headquarters for the secret Party leadership was deep in the Plain of Reeds.

The Party's effort to avoid confrontation with the Saigon government was not particularly successful. Diem refused to play by Hanoi's rules and, far from permitting the old Vietminh apparatus to function on a legal basis, moved vigorously to dig it out root and branch. By the fall of 1954, government security forces had begun to harass the peace movement in Saigon. Several of its leaders were arrested and eventually the headquarters was closed down. In rural areas, Diem launched a "Denounce the Communists" (*To Cong*) campaign, with an emphasis on those areas where the Vietminh organization had traditionally been strong. Communist sources claim that 25,000 suspected Communist sympathizers were arrested, more than 1,000 were killed, and 4,231 were injured.[9] Diem also declared ideological war on communism. Aided by his younger brother and political counselor Ngo Dinh Nhu, he set up several government-sponsored political organizations that were designed to compete with the Communists. Nhu made liberal use of Leninist organizational techniques. To provide an ideological alternative to communism, he attempted to popularize the philosophy of Personalism, a somewhat unwieldy combination of Catholic and Marxist concepts that stressed an amalgamation of Asian communalism and Western libertarianism as the foundation of the new society.

Diem's determined efforts weakened the Communist apparatus in South Vietnam, and his somewhat unorthodox behavior presented the Party leadership with problems. Comments about Diem in a secret Party history of the period are revealing:

> Before Diem unveiled his treacherous face, the people only had a vague idea about him and his administration. Basically, they realized he was just another puppet and they thought he would be in power only for two years. But they did not know that he was dangerously crafty and different from the previous puppets. Some people in the upper strata and many Catholic refugees mistakenly regarded him as a revolutionary scholar. That is why when the U.S.-Diem versus France–Bao Dai clash took place, the people who resented the French and their lackeys were rather pleased to see them defeated by the U.S.-Diem; and a number of people even supported Diem.

Diem paid a high price for his success, however, for his efforts to repress Communist-sponsored activities alienated many non-Communist Vietnamese. Heavy-handed censorship and arbitrary arrests of opposition figures angered Saigon's vociferous corps of intellectuals. In the rural areas corrupt and arrogant officials used their powers indiscriminately and sometimes with brutality. The law was utilized to carry out private vendettas, and the innocent were frequently compelled to pay bribes to avoid arrest.[10]

Such insensitive behavior was undoubtedly a promising sign to Hanoi that the Saigon regime was on the road to self-destruction. In the short run, however, it placed the D.R.V. in an awkward position at a time when Diem's adamant refusal to hold consultations obviously threw Hanoi's political strategy into question. In fact, the Party's immediate options were limited. In August 1955, the Central Committee convened its Eighth Plenum to consider a response and apparently decided that, for the time being, Diem's action should have no effect on the party's strategy toward the South. Primary emphasis would remain on political struggle, and armed activities were to be authorized only in exceptional circumstances. A communiqué issued after the meeting reiterated the Party's preference for unification by "peaceful means" and declared that priority would continue to be assigned to the program of building a socialist society in the North. As if to underline its preference for a peaceful solution, the plenum called for the formation of a broad new Fatherland Front (Mat Tran To Quoc) in the two zones to pressure the United States and the Diem administration to permit reunification elections.[11]

But Diem's declaration of war placed heavy pressure on the revolutionary faithful in the South, who had to bear the full force of the government's repressive activities. Several Communist sources allude to the growing sentiment among the Party rank and file to adopt a more aggressive policy to protect and promote the revolution. Evidently, however, this sentiment was not immediately shared by the new Regional Committee which, in line with official policy in Hanoi, continued to believe that the policy of peaceful political struggle was "the only and correct strategy of struggle." When, in late summer, the committee held its first conference to consider the decisions of the Eighth Plenum in Hanoi, it apparently voiced its approval of existing policy, although it recommended that pressure be placed on the Diem regime to liberalize its policies and hold national elections.[12] The effects of this strategy were apparently beginning to damage the effectiveness of the revolutionary movement in the South. According to the official Party history a number of cadres abandoned their belief in the revolutionary principles of Marxism-Leninism and turned to peaceful reformism. Those who attempted to resist the Diem regime were harassed by government security forces, and their organizations were broken up.

Diem's repressive policies did have a salutary impact on one aspect of Party strategy. One source of active resistance to the Saigon regime was the sect areas. Diem had aroused hostility among the sects by his campaign to bring them under his rule, and in late 1955 an alliance called the Vietnamese National Liberation Front (Mat Tran Quoc Gia Giai Phong Viet Nam), which included Hoa Hao and Cao Dai elements as well as a number of Binh Xuyen under Vo Van Mong who had fled from Saigon to the countryside in order to escape Diem's persecution, was set up under the nominal command of the Hoa Hao military commander Ba Cut. Under constant harassment by government security forces, military units under Ba Cut's command were soon reduced to a sheer struggle for survival.

The sects' relations with the Communists had been strained since shortly after the end of World War II, but now a shared hostility toward the Saigon regime reduced old resentments, and in late 1955 remnants of Ba Cut's forces met with Communist military commanders at a resistance base in the Plain of Reeds and agreed on a plan to coordinate their activities. For the most part, such forces avoided open confrontation with government units and restricted their activities to remote areas, such as the Ca Mau Peninsula, the Plain of Reeds, and the Parrot's Beak. Many of the units under Party control, in fact, were stationed across the border in Cambodia's eastern provinces. According to Party histories, it was through such primitive military organizations that the first units of the future People's Liberation Armed Forces (PLAF) in the South began to take shape.[13]

The first signs of a possible change in the Party's strategy in the South began to appear in the winter of 1955–1956. According to one captured document, several delegations arrived from the North in the fall to help southern operatives reorganize their political and military apparatus. One military delegation was led by Van Tien Dung, later to become commander of all revolutionary forces in South Vietnam. Reportedly, the primary objectives of Dung's delegation were to set up new base areas and to consider the possible need for the further dispatch of reinforcements from the North. The results of that visit are not known; but further developments were in the offing. The following March, Le Duan, chairman of the Regional Committee for the South, allegedly expressed the conviction at a meeting of the committee that the Party must begin preparations for a possible resumption of armed struggle. On the basis of Le Duan's statement, the committee reportedly approved a limited increase in the Party's local military forces, including the formation of twenty main force battalions and the mobilization of guerrilla squads in villages sympathetic to the revolution. Duan's views were presumably passed on to the Central Committee in Hanoi, which was preparing to convene its Ninth Plenum in mid-April.[14]

If Le Duan's recommendation for a change in policy arrived in Hanoi in time for consideration by the Central Committee, the timing was not particularly opportune, for the plenum was apparently being held to consider major decisions on global Communist strategy reached at the Twentieth Congress of the

Communist Party of the Soviet Union (CPSU) held in January. The Moscow congress, the first to be held under the leadership of new CPSU party chief Nikita Khrushchev, had inaugurated a policy of peaceful coexistence with the West and approved a statement regarding the heightened possibilities of a peaceful transition to socialism. Such attitudes had presumably already been conveyed to VWP leaders in early April, when Anastas Mikoyan, on a visit to Hanoi, called for strict observance of the Geneva accords and stressed the special importance of reunifying the two zones of Vietnam through nationwide elections.

At the Ninth Plenum Truong Chinh, who had attended the CPSU congress along with Le Duc Tho, reported on the decisions reached in Moscow. Quoting the congress resolution on the importance of peaceful coexistence with the West, he criticized unnamed Party members who disagreed with the policy of reunification by peaceful means:

> There are some people who do not yet believe in the correctness of this political program and in the policy of peaceful reunification of the country, holding that these are illusory and reformist. The view of the CPSU 20th Congress on the form of transition to Socialism in different countries, and of the possibility of preventing war in the present era, has provided us with new reasons to be confident in the correctness of the policy of the Vietnamese Workers' Party and Fatherland Front in the struggle for national Reunification.[15]

If there was opposition to the existing policy within the Party leadership, it did not prevail. At the close of the conference, the Central Committee approved a continuation of the policy of placing priority on political struggle. But there were signs that the Party was prepared to consider alternatives. The resolution issued at the close of the conference warned that:

> Reactionary forces still exist in the other half of our country, and are still plotting to instigate war. Therefore, we must constantly enhance our vigilance and exert efforts to consolidate National Defense in order to meet all eventualities.[16]

That the confusion over policy at the highest levels of the Party was shared by other Party members and the population at large was reflected in a lengthy article printed in *Nhan dan* in mid-July. According to the writer, there was considerable disagreement and uncertainty over strategy among the Party faithful during the War of Resistance against the French. Some were overly optimistic and impatient for a quick victory. Others were pessimistic and doubted that the revolutionary forces would eventually triumph. Similar "complex ideas and illusions" were prevalent among many people and Party members today. People who are "simple in their thoughts" were sure in their minds that national elections would certainly be held and they became disappointed and pessimistic when the elections did not take place. Others are "reluctant to carry on a long and hard struggle" and search for a quick unification by abandoning peaceful methods. They fail to realize that the best means of achieving quick unification of the country is "to positively build up the North, positively to unite and struggle with perseverence and patience in the South, and not to be afraid of difficulties and hardship."[17]

The continuing controversy within the Party leadership over the issue of reunification was reflected in the Tenth Plenum of the Central Committee, held in October of 1956. The Plenum was apparently convened in part to assess policy in the South in light of the international situation and the Diem regime's refusal to hold consultations with the D.R.V. on national elections. But the Central Committee was unable to reach a conclusion on a policy recommendation and asked the Politburo to research the problem for further consideration. According to Vo Nguyen Giap, a report presented by the Politburo at the conference had noted deficiencies in the public understanding of the problem and pointed out that the struggle for reunification was fundamentally a revolutionary task that would require an extended period of time.[18]

It was at this point that Le Duan, head of the Party's Nam Bo Regional Committee, wrote a document that is now described by Hanoi sources as of pivotal importance for the future course of the revolution in South Vietnam. Duan's *The Path of Revolution in the South* [Duong loi cach mang mien Nam] was apparently presented as a proposal to the Eleventh Plenum, held in December.[19] On the surface, Duan's viewpoint appeared to coincide with that of the advocates of a peaceful policy within the Central Committee. He conceded that at its present stage the Vietnamese revolution had two major tasks, building socialism in the North and liberating the South. He further agreed that the existing policy of peaceful political struggle in the South conformed to existing realities (i.e., the current weakness of the Party apparatus in South Vietnam). And the policy of peaceful reunification, he admitted, was in line with the conclusions recently reached at the Twentieth Congress of the CPSU earlier in the year and with the general situation in Vietnam and throughout the world.

Yet Duan's apparent approval of the current line in Hanoi was somewhat deceptive, for in actuality the central thrust of his argument implied the need for a more vigorous approach to the revolution in the South. Although not formally deviating from the existing policy of peaceful struggle, he suggested that there was a difference between reformism, based on "legal and constitutional struggle," and the political struggle of a revolutionary movement which "takes the revolutionary political forces of the masses as its foundation." Clearly, Duan desired a more aggressive and activist approach to political struggle than the one that was currently being followed.

Moreover, Duan contended that the Party, as the vanguard of the revolutionary process, must be ready to lead the masses to seize power. Otherwise, a favorable opportunity to overthrow the reactionary regime in Saigon might be wasted. Such an occasion had arisen in 1945, he pointed out, when the Soviet Union and its allies had defeated the fascist armies of imperial Japan. At that time the Vietnamese revolutionary forces were able to seize power with relative ease, as they had been preparing the ground since 1936. If the party had not readied its strength beforehand, the favorable conditions might have changed and the August Revolution would not have occurred. Today, Duan warned, many cadres responsible for guiding the revolutionary movement regrettably "had not yet firmly understood the strength of the revolutionary masses" and thus failed to lead them in a political struggle against the reactionary regime.

To sum up, Le Duan's pamphlet, although not recommending (as is sometimes asserted) a major shift toward a more military approach in the South, did appeal for an increased effort to promote reunification and, if necessary, to prepare for a possible revolutionary upsurge to come. The vision was more Leninist than Maoist, of an uprising on the model of 1917 or 1945 rather than of a people's war along the lines of the Chinese Civil War or the recent War of Resistance against the French. But it did leave open the possibility that the struggle to complete the unification of the two zones might require the resumption of revolutionary war.

Duan's short treatise was taken up at the Eleventh Plenum of the Central Committee held in December, and it undoubtedly provoked lively discussion. In view of the high regard in which the pamphlet is currently held in Hanoi—it is frequently described as a document of "pivotal importance" in the history of the Vietnamese revolutionary movement—it seems probable that his proposal, which in any event seemed to coincide with the inclination of the Politburo at the October conference, served as the basis for a new consensus within the Party leadership on the need for a more aggressive policy in the South. The plenum apparently did not approve a major shift in the Party line. An article published in *Hoc tap* and reprinted in *Nhan dan* a few days after the conference said that the consolidation of the North was still the primary task. "We must not allow the winning over of the South," it said, "to detract from the requirements of consolidating the North."[20] But the plenum did approve a new policy of punishing selected enemies of the revolution in South Vietnam. According to a Communist defector, the purpose of the new approach was to protect the Party's southern apparatus by throwing fear into the ranks of the enemy and creating confidence among the masses that the revolutionary movement was able to take care of its own.

The decisions reached at the Eleventh Plenum were transmitted to the Committee for the South. Although the chairman of that committee, Le Duan, was an advocate of a new and more militant approach, there is evidence from a number of internal Party documents that some members of the committee, perhaps even a majority, favored a continuation of the post-Geneva strategy of peaceful struggle. According to one secret Party history, many members of the southern leadership were reluctant to abandon their conviction of the validity of the line of peaceful struggle and the possibility of reunification elections and "did not clearly set forth the essential role of the armed struggle in respect to the revolutionary line." In consequence, they had undertaken inadequate efforts to train and arm the masses and to build up the revolutionary armed forces in preparation for a resumption of armed struggle. Only in late 1956, "through central's guidance" (perhaps a reference to directives of the Eleventh Plenum), did the Committee correctly reassess the situation and recognize clearly "that revolution was the only correct way to lead the South Vietnamese people toward taking over the administration."[21]

If this interpretation is correct, Le Duan's criticisms of cadres who had failed to understand the strength of the revolutionary masses may have been directed at fellow members of the southern leadership, and his decision to present his case to the Central Committee may have been a means of appealing over the heads of the Committee to the Party leadership in Hanoi. Fortunately for Duan, as we have seen, key Party leaders were themselves coming to similar conclusions.

The results of the new policy in the South began to appear early in 1957, when observers noted a significant increase in terrorist activities directed at government officials or other key personnel in rural areas of South Vietnam. Hanoi sources claimed that those targeted for punishment were normally corrupt officials, "cruel tyrants," "wicked landlords," and "traitors." Critics charged that many of those eliminated were people considered more dangerous to the movement: honest village officials and popular teachers who might lead the masses astray. Corrupt elements, considered by the Party as their best (if unwitting) allies, were frequently left alone. Whether or not that was official policy is not easy to say. Internal Party documents frequently criticized arbitrary terrorism while recognizing the value of a carefully planned policy of "elimination of traitors" as a means of promoting the growth of the movement.[22]

Hanoi's growing preoccupation with the possibility of a return to armed struggle was underscored in March 1957 when the Twelfth Plenum approved a program to modernize the armed forces.[23] The work of consolidating national defense and building the people's army, announced the official communiqué, "is one of the main tasks of the whole party and people." In what may have been a gesture to the peace faction, it also appealed to the two cochairmen of the Geneva Conference to call once again on Diem to hold consultations and agree to a normalization of relations between the two zones. The D.R.V., it said, would be willing if necessary to delay unification by ten to fifteen years.[24]

Active consideration of a change of strategy in Hanoi highlighted the need for much organizational work in the South before a resumption of revolutionary war could be seriously considered. First and foremost, the Party had to rebuild its apparatus in the countryside. Diem's repressive efforts had seriously depleted the movement, particularly in provinces in the Mekong delta and along the central coast that had traditionally been sympathetic to the revolution. Now conditions in rural areas had to be surveyed, and provinces pinpointed where the presence of the government was weak or particularly resented. In villages sympathetic to the revolution, local cadres had to initiate the painstaking process of organization and recruitment in preparation for a possible revolutionary upsurge.

Thanks to Diem, in many areas they had a receptive audience. In those villages where the Vietminh had been active in the war against the French, land had been distributed among the poor and the landlords driven off. By 1952, 400,000 acres had already been divided among more than 250,000 peasants in Cochin China alone. After 1954, the landlords had returned and with government assistance had reclaimed their property. Some attempted to collect back rents from their tenants or raised the current level to exorbitant rates, sometimes to more than 50 percent of the annual harvest. Corruption, official arrogance, and abuse in the application of the "Denounce the Communists" campaign added fuel to peasant resentment.

The GVN was not totally inactive in attempting to fill the vacuum at the local level. In order to strengthen Saigon's influence in the villages, Diem replaced elected administrative councils (first established by the Bao Dai regime in 1953) with appointed village heads. To provide evidence that the government was interested in providing services to the people, the GVN set up the Civic Action Program to send idealistic young cadres to the rural villages to encourage local development and self-help projects. Finally, in October 1956, the government passed a land reform program to establish a more equitable distribution of land in rural areas.

None of these programs had the desired results. The imposition of government-appointed village heads was resented as an effort to reduce village autonomy. The Civic Action Program was plagued from the start by corruption, inefficiency, and a lack of adequate financial support. Although the land reform program arguably represented a step forward, it suffered by comparison with the reforms previously instituted by the Vietminh. Under the latter poor peasants had received land without charge; under the government program they were compelled to compensate the previous owner. Moreover, the amount of land ticketed for possible transfer was simply inadequate: Landowners were allowed to retain up to 250 acres of cultivated land for their own use. Two years after the program had been put in operation, less than 10 percent of the eligible peasants in South Vietnam had received land.

Although the Communists had little reason to fear that the new government regulations would rally the rural population to the side of the GVN, they did face a dilemma with their own program. The return of the landlord class to liberated areas after 1954 had led to rent increases and the seizure of land previously distributed by the Vietminh to the poor. The Party wished to defend the interests of the poor villagers but, as had been the case during the struggle against the French, they hoped to avoid alienating patriotic elements among the landed gentry or frightening urban moderates. They therefore approached the issue with caution. The Party's new rural program was directed not at reducing rents, but at maintaining them at existing levels. As for the land seizures, cadres were instructed to inform the peasants that although land transfers completed during the pre-Geneva period were valid, this was not equivalent to granting permanent title to the new landholder, and peasants who had received such land were encouraged to make private arrangements for purchases from the previous owner.[25] Party documents acknowledged that it might be difficult to explain the new policy to poor villagers. As during the previous conflict, the Party was having problems in setting up a program that could win support from both the patriotic gentry and the poorer peasants in the countryside.

The International Situation

Apparently the attitude of the Soviet Union was one major reason for Hanoi's hesitation in embarking on a more active path in the South. For despite Le Duan's optimism about the favorable international situation, Moscow's new global strategy still presented a serious dilemma to the party leadership. Without Soviet military aid and diplomatic support Hanoi could hardly hope to achieve its major objectives, in the South or in the North. To guarantee the stability of the Moscow connection, the D.R.V. had publicly adhered to a policy of close alliance with the USSR. Yet the Soviet leadership appeared firmly opposed to any exacerbation of the situation in Vietnam that could heighten world tensions and disturb the current emphasis on peaceful coexistence. In January, the Soviet Union had made a surprise announcement, proposing the admission of both Vietnamese states into the United Nations. Hanoi had apparently not been consulted. This may have been the reason for visits by several high-ranking Party figures to Moscow during 1957. Le Duan (who had been recalled to Hanoi sometime in early 1957 to become acting secretary general of the Party) visited Moscow shortly after the proposal was made, and it was subsequently dropped. In July, Ho Chi Minh himself embarked on an extended state visit to the USSR and other Eastern European countries. On his return at the end of the August, he claimed that he had achieved "unity of views" with fraternal countries in the socialist camp. Then, in October, he departed again in the company of Le Duan for Moscow to attend the fortieth anniversary of the Bolshevik revolution and the Conference of Communist and Workers' Parties in Socialist Countries. According to one Communist source, the visit was "one of the pivotal events" in the modern history of Vietnam.[26]

Hanoi's basic objective was evidently to win bloc support for a possible renewal of revolutionary war in the South and to obtain the promise of increased aid for that purpose from Moscow. In the first instance, the Party was at least partly successful, for the conference communiqué, while emphasizing the possibility of a peaceful transition to socialism, added: "In conditions in which the exploiting classes resort to violence against the people, it is necessary to bear in mind another possibility—the non-peaceful transition to socialism. Leninism teaches and history confirms that the ruling classes never relinquish power voluntarily."[27]

The statement may have been drafted and inserted into the communiqué at the behest of Ho Chi Minh, since it closely resembled a declaration he had made at the Ninth Plenum of the VWP in April.[28] It suggests strongly that a majority in the Party leadership had now come around to the belief that a policy of military violence might ultimately be necessary to achieve victory in the revolution in the South. The rise of Le Duan to acting secretary general of the Party, replacing the recently demoted Truong Chinh, adds evidence to the supposition.

How effective Vietnamese representations were in persuading the Soviet leadership to accede to their views is difficult to say. After 1957, Soviet aid levels rose. On the other hand, the later course of Soviet-Vietnamese relations indicates that Moscow continued to withhold any formal endorsement of a strategy of armed struggle in South Vietnam.

The Darkest Hour

The historian, searching for the roots of what would later be called the "Second Indochina War," could make a persuasive case that the first two steps in the escalation of the conflict occurred in 1955, when Diem launched his "Denounce the Communists" campaign, and in 1956, when Hanoi responded by permitting its followers in the South to take limited measures in self-defense. From this limited "challenge and response" the more dangerous armed confrontation gradually emerged. Before the end of 1957, several hundred GVN officials had been assassinated by revolutionary activists. The Saigon regime was quick to react, and during 1957 it intensified its campaign against the Communists and other groups hostile to the Diem regime. More than 2,000 suspected Communists had been killed and another 65,000 arrested before the end of the year. For the first time, ARVN military units attacked Communist base areas in the Plain of Reeds, on the Ca Mau peninsula, and in Zone D, one of the Party's major base areas, north of Saigon, causing severe losses to the revolutionary infrastructure. In contested villages, carefully constructed self-defense units were broken up and the sect armies were reduced to a mere token force. Party membership in the South, which had stood at about 5,000 in mid-1957, had fallen to one-third that level by the end of the year. Party histories concede the difficulties faced during this period, admitting that GVN efforts reduced the prestige as well as the real strength of the revolutionary movement and "significantly weakened its ability to carry on the struggle." It was, in the words of one historian in Hanoi, "the darkest period" for the revolution in the South.[29]

In desperation, local leaders in many areas began to act on their own initiative. Organized armed units were formed, even though this violated the Party line. Such was the case in Quang Ngai Province, long a stronghold of revolutionary sentiment and a frequent target of ARVN military sweeps. At the other end of the country, several units at company strength began to operate in the U Minh forest in response to Saigon's attacks. By mid-1958 a battalion had been established in Zone D. And by the end of the year, a "command of the People's Armed Forces in Western Nam Bo" was set up to coordinate activities with the General Staff of the remaining sect armed forces who, with two battalions of their own, were still operating in several provinces of the Mekong delta. Tran Van Giau later described this period as the "embryonic stage" of revolutionary war, characterized by unarmed, partially armed, or armed self-defense actions in overt legal struggle of the masses.[30] The primary focus of revolutionary activity was north of Saigon, in the Communist redoubt of Zone D. This area had several advantages for an insurgency movement. It was heavily forested and therefore difficult for the government to penetrate; it was close to the Cambodian border, a classical advantage in Maoist people's war; and it was relatively accessible to the two major potential focal regions of Communist activity, the lower delta provinces and the Central Highlands. Hereafter it would become a key base area for the revolution.

For the most part, the fledgling revolutionary armed forces, soon to become known to the world as the Viet Cong (a derogatory term used by the Saigon government and translated as "Vietnamese Communists"), at first limited their operations to defensive activities. But occasionally they took offensive actions in selected areas, using guerrilla techniques to launch ambushes on ARVN units and on remote GVN-controlled villages or military outposts. Much of this activity took place in the Central Highlands, a region that until now had been relatively uninvolved in the Vietnamese revolution. Communist units had been active in the area since the mid-1930s, when revolts by the local minority tribesmen had led to the formation of a few resistance bases in the northern provinces. And in 1945, rebel tribesmen in the western half of Quang Ngai Province had actively supported the uprising in Ba To District near the coast.

But the Vietminh did not attempt to exploit the area systematically until 1953, when Communist military leaders in the coastal provinces south of Da Nang (the famous Interzone V) were ordered to coordinate their activities with the main battlefield in the North. In the Central Highlands, the Party made some effort to integrate the disparate tribal groups into the National Union Front and set up a series of small liberated bases along the ridge of the Annamite Mountains, which cut through the heart of the area. But the minority peoples of the region, racially more distinct from the lowland Vietnamese than their counterparts in the North, were harder to organize and the area remained a backwater of the revolution during the war against the French.

The end of the war brought change to the peoples of the highlands. The Diem regime settled many Catholic refugees from the North in so-called rural development centers in relatively unpopulated areas in the highland provinces. In many cases these centers transgressed upon the traditional land rights of minority peoples, who were frequently compelled by the low fertility of the land to move their fields. Arrogant attitudes of the government's civil and military representatives exacerbated the natural suspicions between the minorities in the area and the Vietnamese government in Saigon, which made little effort to respond to minority susceptibilities. By 1958, the situation had deteriorated so badly that some minority groups revolted and demanded autonomy from the central government.

By contrast, Communist strategy was carefully crafted to avoid arousing the suspicion of local minorities. Since the 1930s, ICP policies had stressed a cautious approach that emphasized respect for local customs, equality of treatment, and political autonomy, and avoided any references to communism. After Geneva, more than 1,000 minority cadres were sent north for training at the Central Minority School in Hanoi. Soon they began to be infiltrated back into the Central Highlands where, with the aid of local tribesmen, they set up several small revolutionary bases in remote mountain areas.[31] One Communist report claims that during the late 1950s more than 100 villages in the highlands came under revolutionary administration.

At first the Party's forces in the area avoided armed struggle, in accordance with instructions from Hanoi. Revolutionary elements were forced to operate in secret in order to avoid government repression and to retain their revolutionary bases in the mountainous western sectors of the region. Self-defense units were formed in villages sympathetic to the cause, but, in order to avoid arousing suspicion by the authorities, their mission was described as protection against bandits.

By the summer of 1956, however, the area once again began to stir with unrest. In lowland districts in Quang Ngai Province, demonstrations organized by Party agitators broke out against the GVN presidential elections. In the turmoil, a few government officials were assassinated. When Saigon struck back and tried to destroy the revolutionary bases, the local revolutionary forces attempted to retaliate and then retreated into the mountains, where they began to make plans to expand their activities.

With the receipt of a copy of Le Duan's *The Path of Revolution in the South*, which suggested that a more vigorous approach would be required to overthrow the reactionary Diem regime, Vo Chi Cong, one of the top Party leaders in the area, sent two cadres to the higher echelons to report the situation in Quang Ngai Province and request directives. According to Communist accounts, Tran Nam Trung, head of the Central Vietnamese Regional Committee and himself a veteran of the Ba To uprising in 1945, approved on his own initiative Cong's request to make preparations for armed struggle in the area "pending the establishment of a new line."[32] But he cautioned the Quang Ngai leadership to act with discretion in order to avoid government reprisals and to obtain approval from higher echelons before launching an actual revolt. In July 1958, a meeting of representatives of various ethnic groups in the area was convened under Party leadership in upland Tra Bong District to draw up tentative plans for an armed uprising. In the meantime, three large base areas were to be set up in both lowland and upland districts of the province so that resistance elements in the lowland areas could retreat to the mountains when necessary. Radical youths were to be recruited and sent to Tra Bong to train and to help form combat villages and armed units in upland areas. In March 1959, a forty-five-man provincial platoon composed of minority tribesmen was set up, the first in the area since 1954. There was a strong temptation to launch armed attacks on local villages, but orders from higher levels were to await the promulgation of a new military line.[33]

The Year of Decision, 1959

Up to now, the Party leadership in Hanoi had resisted a decision to escalate the conflict to a higher level of violence, despite appeals from some quarters in the South. A directive entitled "Situation and Tasks for '59," presumably drawn up by Party strategists in Hanoi for transmission to the southern leadership, conceded the difficulties faced by the revolutionary movement in South Vietnam, but did not approve a change in policy. From the context it seems clear that Hanoi continued to question the revolutionary consciousness of the masses and the ability and readiness of the Party's organization in the South to lead them. According to the directive, the struggle movement against the Diem administration was beginning to develop strongly, but it was still scattered and lacked a strong sense of political awareness. Unrest was widespread, but it was often spontaneous and rarely under Party leadership. Moreover, many members of the Party organization in the South still lacked a clear sense of the current Party line. Although that situation had improved since 1956, when the Eleventh Plenum had approved the new more activist line, many cadres were still too pessimistic in their evaluation of the situation and leaned toward a "reformist" policy rather than one of leading the masses in the political struggle. Others (from the context it appears that this was considered to be a lesser problem) were guilty of a "leftist deviation," that is, of emphasizing the need for armed struggle.[34]

Sometime in late 1958, Le Duan made a secret inspection trip to South Vietnam, presumably to evaluate the situation there in preparation for a major policy review by the Central Committee in Hanoi. Duan's report on his return to the D.R.V. was presented at the Fifteenth Plenum of the Central Committee in January; it had fateful consequences.[35]

There are few published references to this conference in Party histories, and no major documents issued by the meeting have appeared in the Party press. The *Outline History* comments laconically,

> In January 1959, at an important conference, South Vietnam's revolutionary leaders pointed out that South Vietnamese society was a neocolonial and semifeudal one. The Ngo Dinh Diem administration was a reactionary, cruel, war-like one which had betrayed the national interests. It was obviously a U.S. tool for aggression and enslavement. The direction and task of South Vietnamese revolution could not diverge from the general revolutionary law of using revolutionary violence to oppose counter-revolutionary violence, rising up to seize political power for the people. It was time to resort to armed struggle combined with political struggle to push the movement forward.[36]

The failure to identify the "important conference" with the Fifteenth Plenum in Hanoi was probably tied to the decision by VWP leaders to conceal D.R.V. involvement in the rising struggle in the South—a device that would imply that the struggle was indigenous to South Vietnam and, it was hoped, would discourage any increased U.S. involvement. But there is little doubt that the decision was made at the Hanoi plenum. This has been conceded in a history of the Party published in the newspaper *Nhan dan* in early 1980. According to this source the Fifteenth Plenum stressed that the proper course for the Vietnamese revolution at the time was to use "the political force of the masses" in coordination with armed force to topple the Diem regime and lead the revolution to a successful conclusion.[37]

Why was the decision made at this time? Hanoi sources imply that there were two main reasons. On the one hand, popular resentment against the Diem regime had reached significant proportions, creating a potential revolutionary situation. According to the *Outline History*:

> The US imperialists' policy of enslavement and war-provocation, the Ngo Dinh Diem clique's acts or [sic] terrorism and national treachery had caused utter suffering and tensions in the people's life in the South. As 1959 began, the people's life was seriously in danger. The people from various walks of life were seething with anger. Workers and peasants were especially excited and eager to struggle. They felt they could no longer live under the US-Diem regime but should rise up in a life and death struggle with the enemy.[38]

On the other hand, party leaders apparently feared that the GVN's policy of terrorizing the opposition had seriously weakened the revolutionary organization in the South and given a spurious sense of stability to South Vietnamese society. This external impression of stability, Hanoi insisted, only disguised the real weakness within:

> We say that in 1959, the South Vietnamese administration was relatively stable due to the fact that it controlled the administrative machinery at all levels, controlled the army and was able to implement its major policies, etc. However, to attain this temporary stability, it was forced to oppress the masses with extreme cruelty, with police and military terrorism as the essential means. So, stability was acquired at a very high price—*that of complete political failure*.[39]

Under such conditions, the very factors responsible for the regime's stability would lead to its weakening and ultimate disintegration.

The evidence suggests that the Party leadership had come around to the view that the Saigon regime was rapidly deteriorating, creating favorable conditions for a seizure of revolutionary power. On the other hand, it was increasingly clear that Diem could not be overthrown without a commitment to revolutionary violence. The size of Diem's forces and the ferocity of his hostility to the Communists destroyed the possibility that the regime could be transformed or overthrown by peaceful political struggle. But unless the party could protect and expand its forces in the South, it would be very difficult to defeat Ngo Dinh Diem before he succeeded in eliminating all opposition. Hanoi must act, even at the risk of incurring Moscow's displeasure.

The Party was now ready to gamble that a new revolutionary upsurge was in the offing in South Vietnam. But the Fifteenth Plenum was only a first step in formulating a strategy to overthrow the Saigon regime. What forms of violent struggle should be used? How should military and political struggle be combined in the most efficacious way? Was the Maoist three-stage process used during the Franco-Vietminh conflict relevant in the new situation? Unfortunately, Party historians have given us little to go on and we are reduced to speculation. There is some evidence that at the time the basic decision was taken, the Party leadership was uncertain and perhaps divided about the precise forms of struggle to be used. According to one captured document, at the time of the plenum there were "many opinions and hesitancies" about strategy, as "details of the South Vietnamese movement and the revolutionary experience were insufficient to formulate a precise program."[40] Only two years later, it continued, was a specific program drawn up that was based on the revolutionary situation in Laos and Vietnam at that time.

At the least, there seems to have been a minimum consensus in Hanoi that although Diem's growing political weakness was still a major factor—indeed, it was the trump card of the insurgency—a purely political effort would be insufficient to overthrow the Saigon regime. The appointment of Le Duan as secretary general and Hanoi's efforts to persuade the Soviet Union to consider Vietnam as a possible exception to the worldwide application of "peaceful roads to power" suggest that the majority of the Central Committee had by now come to that conclusion. If that was the case, the primarily political armed propaganda units that had characterized the Party's military effort during the August Revolution and that were once again the predominant form of insurgency organization in the South would be unable to counter ARVN forces, which were being armed and trained for conventional combat by the United States. More would be required. How much more would become a matter of debate.

For the moment, then, it is probable that Party strategists in Hanoi were compelled to improvise a response to the needs of their compatriots in the South. In a broad sense, their answer to the problem was the strategy called simply "revolutionary war." This form of conflict was described by one Communist document in general terms as consisting of a protracted war, based on a combination of political and military struggle. In general, the war would gradually progress from small- to large-scale combat and from the rural areas to a final overthrow of the enemy in the cities. But, at least in available documents, there was no specific reference to the classic Maoist three stages of people's war, which may have been somewhat discredited because of its misapplication during the War of Resistance against the French. And there was more than a hint that the Party leadership hoped to use various forms of political struggle more effectively than had been the case at the close of the war against the French. The specific form that this should take was described as "the political force of the masses," which appeared to consist of the use of armed demonstrations by civilians in coordination with armed attacks by military units.

It is also likely that the Party leadership had a different scenario in mind for the final leap to victory than had been applied during the previous conflict. There was apparently considerable optimism that victory could be achieved without resort to a final stage of large-scale military offensive. The underlying weakness of the Diem regime was becoming more apparent day by day. This weakness was the Communists' strength. If the various opportunities for legal and illegal struggle could be effectively utilized, the "political force of the masses" could be mobilized and, in conjunction with the armed strength of revolutionary forces in the South, bring the Saigon regime to its knees through a general uprising launched both in the cities and in the countryside. Alternatively, a progressive disintegration of the Diem regime could lead to negotiations and the formation of a coalition goverment with active participation by the Communists.

The apparent effort to avoid an open militarization of the struggle in the South was not simply a reflection of Hanoi's desire to limit the costs of the conflict or to accede to Moscow's desire to prevent the Vietnamese revolution from becoming a major issue in East-West relations. More importantly, it probably reflected a desire to dissuade the United States from becoming more openly involved, an occurrence that would change the character of the conflict and possibly lead to a repetition of the high-level military confrontation that had taken place in the struggle against the French.[41] At a minimum, the Fifteenth Plenum had recognized that the existing U.S. presence in the South made a protracted struggle probable. If the civil struggle in the South could be kept from escalating into a major military conflict, the likelihood of increased U.S. involvement could be minimized.

The Period of Spontaneous Uprisings, 1959–1960

By May, the Politburo had drawn up operational directives based on the decisions taken at the January plenum and communicated them to the Party leadership in the South. During the remainder of the year, preparations were undertaken to move to the new stage. To assist in the process, regroupees began returning from the North to provide the southern insurgency with a nucleus of experienced and loyal cadres. Of the approximately 90,000 who had gone North in 1954, some of the most dedicated had received training at the Xuan Mai Training School near Hanoi in preparation for a possible resumption of revolution in the South. Now they were infiltrated back into South Vietnam in groups of forty to fifty or more, normally travelling by truck to Laos and then continuing on foot into South Vietnam. On their arrival, they were placed in leading positions within the insurgency apparatus.[42]

Throughout 1959 the level of conflict in South Vietnam intensified. According to Communist statistics, during the first six months of the year, there were 2,134 "struggles" in South Vietnam, with more than 500,000 participants. A few involved raids by combat units on ARVN posts, mostly north and northwest of Saigon, but most consisted simply of mass demonstrations instigated and led by Party cadres. A Communist historian claims that by the end of the year the insurgents had inflicted 4,000 casualties on the enemy while capturing 2,000 weapons.[43]

The rise in revolutionary activity elicited a quick response from Saigon. Under a new law entitled 10-59, the government launched a new effort to round up Communists and break the back of the insurgency. The new regulations increased the penalties for subversive activity and allowed anyone convicted of acts of sabotage or infringement of national security to be tried and sentenced to death by special roving military tribunals. ARVN forces also struck hard against Communist base areas in the Plain of Reeds and the *terre rouge* areas northwest of Saigon. Finally, in an effort to achieve better control over the rural areas and to isolate villages from revolutionary influence, Diem ordered the establishment of so-called rural community development centers, or "agrovilles," at strategic locations throughout the country. In theory, the new organizations, consisting of some 300 to 500 rural families each, would provide both the benefits of urban civilization (such as education, health, and sanitation) and security from outside attack. In actuality, the agrovilles fell victim to the general incompetence of the Saigon regime. They were widely disliked by peasants, who were compelled to leave their ancestral villages and were herded, often by force, into a sterile new environment where they were compelled to use their own labor without compensation to build the new agrovilles.[44] By 1960, rural protests against the new organizations had reached a crescendo and construction slowed to a virtual halt.

Communist historians date the beginning of the new stage (described by some as the first stage of revolutionary war, since no main force units were used) as late 1959 and early 1960, when a series of "partial and spontaneous uprisings" broke out in selected areas in the lower Mekong delta and the Central Highlands. As described in Party journals, the primary characteristic of these uprisings was the attempt to make use of the "political forces of the masses" in the revolutionary struggle. The uprisings were launched in one or more villages within a contested district, with the objectives of dispersing governmental authority and establishing revolutionary power at the local level. As a rule, the attacking forces were composed of two elements: unarmed or partially armed civilians, organized and directed by the Party, and organized guerrilla units operating in the vicinity. Once power had been seized in a given hamlet or village, the guerrillas would move on to another to spread the movement. In the meantime, additional paramilitary units would be formed among radical youths in the newly liberated areas to help defend the revolutionary conquests.

The two "partial and spontaneous uprisings" most often cited in the Party literature took place in areas long sympathetic to the revolution—in Ben Tre Province (renamed Kien Hoa by the Diem regime) in the heart of the lower Mekong delta, and in Tra Bong District in Quang Ngai Province, where Party leaders had been preparing for an uprising for several months. The uprising in Ben Tre began on January 17, 1960, with attacks on isolated government outposts in several districts in the province. Ben Tre had a long tradition of rebellion against central government authority. In the nineteenth century, it had been one of the few areas in the South to resist the establishment of French control. In 1930, it had again erupted briefly as local peasants demonstrated in support of their compatriots in Nghe An and Ha Tinh. During the Franco-Vietminh conflict, it had come briefly under the control of revolutionary forces, at which time the area underwent land redistribution, but after Geneva the landlords returned and repossessed their property. According to one Communist source, reprisals were exacted and many landlords, with official support, attempted to collect retroactive rents for the period prior to their return.[45] Peasant hostility occasionally broke out against landlord exactions in the mid-1950s but was suppressed with some loss of life. The government retaliated by attempting to root out the revolutionary infrastructure. According to one Communist estimate, by 1959 more than 2,000 Communists or sympathizers had been killed in the province, and 85 percent of the local revolutionary apparatus had been destroyed.[46]

Hanoi's decision to switch to a policy of limited armed struggle reached the area in mid-1959, and the remnants of the provincial leadership immediately began to prepare for a local seizure of power. In early January 1960, under the chairmanship of a prominent female revolutionary, Nguyen Thi Dinh (later to become vice-minister of defense of the Provisional Revolutionary Government), local cadres met in conference and decided to launch an uprising. Lacking weapons, they decided to use the classical model of the August Revolution. Civilian demonstrators were armed with bamboo sticks or fake weapons and trained to use subterfuge to seize government outposts.

The opening attack on January 17 was launched on Cu Lao Minh island, but the main focus of the uprising was located in Mo Cay District. Local youths disguised as main force troops attacked government posts in several hamlets. The defenders fled in panic, and within a few days the insurgents had managed to seize more than a hundred military posts and watchtowers and had liberated more than 72 of the 100 villages in the district.[47] With revolutionary power established throughout the area, revolutionary tribunals were formed and began to execute traitors, while landlord property was confiscated and once again distributed to poor peasants supporting the revolution.

The period of revolutionary triumph was short-lived. On the twenty-fourth, ARVN forces arrived in strength and gradually subdued the rebels, who were forced to flee into the mangrove swamps along the coast or into the Plain of Reeds to the northwest. But the agitation did not subside immediately. Demonstrators (often predominantly women) from local villages marched to the district capital of Mo Cay to protest government atrocities and demand compensation for damages caused by government troops.

The uprising in Quang Ngai Province broke out on August 28, 1959, in response to a provincial Party directive. It began in sixteen villages in mountainous Tra Bong District and was sparked by protests against GVN parliamentary elections. As in Ben Tre, the Party made a maximum effort to use the political force of the masses. Civilian demonstrators marched to the district headquarters and complained about the scheduled GVN elections. Soon the riots escalated into violence, and villages and hamlets in upland areas were seized by local military units. When government troops responded, the insurgents set up guerrilla forces to protect their territorial base. In contrast to the uprising in Ben Tre, the insurgents in Quang Ngai were able to hold their positions and by the end of the year had set up a liberated zone consisting of nearly fifty villages and a total population of several thousand people.[48] Headquarters of the zone was in northern Tra Bong and Son Tay districts, where links were established with existing base areas in Kontum and Quang Nam provinces. Another smaller base area was established in the lowland districts of Ba To and Minh Long consisting of eighteen villages. During the year these areas were gradually consolidated and expanded, and a revolutionary administrative apparatus was set up at the provincial level.

There was more to the Party's new strategy than just an attempt to escalate armed struggle in an effort to seize power in selected local areas. Indeed, there are signs that the southern leadership, ever cautious, desired to dampen the enthusiasm of local activists who attempted to seize power in areas abandoned by the enemy, on the grounds that such action was premature and could provoke a brutal response. It was also critical of the tendency of some cadres to resort to terrorism and excessive violence against local citizens, thus frightening moderates and damaging the policy of seeking broad support among the masses. Primary emphasis, insisted the Committee for the South, should be on organization, propaganda, and the development of political struggle in preparation for the future general uprising.[49]

By March 1960, the situation in South Vietnam had grown sufficiently serious to come to the attention of the U.S. Embassy. In a report to Secretary of State Christian Herter, Ambassador Eldridge Durbrow noted the rising incidence of Viet Cong activities in various provinces around the country and a marked rise in the size and aggressiveness of insurgency forces. Part of the problem, Durbrow noted, resulted from the behavior of government officials and the short-sighted policies of the Diem regime.[50]

The Third Party Congress, 1960

In September 1960, the Third National Congress of the VWP, the first to be held since the Resistance Congress of 1951, met in Hanoi. The meeting, attended by 576 delegates representing more than 500,000 Party members throughout the country, was apparently called to ratify the crucial decisions made by the Central Committee during the preceding year. In the political report to the congress, Le Duan, the Party's new secretary general, avoided specifics on the Party's strategy in the South. It would be, he said, "a long and arduous struggle, not simple but complex, combining many forms of struggle."[51] It would require flexibility and a move from lower to higher forms and from legal to illegal forms of struggle. The starting point would be the stimulation and development of the revolutionary power of the masses. There was no mention of active involvement on the part of the D.R.V. That the Party leadership did not expect that it would be required, at least for the immediate future, was suggested by the fact that the congress was asked to approve a five-year plan for socialist industrialization in the North.

There were signs that disagreements over the strategy to be followed in the South persisted. In his own address to the delegates, Minister of Defense Vo Nguyen Giap commented: "A number of our comrades are not fully aware of the plots of . . . United States imperialism and their lackeys. They do not understand that while our policy is to preserve peace and to achieve peaceful reunification, we should always be prepared to cope with any maneuver of the enemy."[52]

Whether Giap was referring to the advocates of a peaceful policy within the southern leadership is not clear. In any event, the fact that the Third Congress had approved an ambitious program of industrial development in the North suggested that within the Party leadership, domestic concerns continued to hold a high priority. It seems clear that the decision to renew the struggle in South Vietnam did not represent an abrupt reversal of priorities in the Vietnamese revolution, but an attempt to establish an even balance between them. The resolution issued at the close of the conference clearly reflected this strategy, stating that the Vietnamese revolution now had two major strategic tasks: to complete the socialist revolution in the North and to liberate the South and complete the reunification of the country. Obviously, the goal of national reunification had now reached parity and the two tasks were viewed as interrelated and reinforcing. As a further indication of the growing importance of the Southern revolution, there were now four South Vietnamese in the new Politburo: Le Duan, Pham Hung, Le Duc Tho, and a military figure of rising prominence in the party, Nguyen Chi Thanh.

The shift to a more activist policy in the South formally announced at the Third Party Congress coincided with the Conference of Communist and Workers' Parties held in Moscow in November. With the split between Moscow and Peking threatening to break into the open, the question of support for national wars of liberation was a major issue at the conference, and the Vietnamese representatives undoubtedly lobbied to win the support of the socialist camp for their new strategy. The Soviet leadership, pressed from the left by the radical views of the P.R.C., was driven to give more vocal support to revolutionary struggles in the Third World, and this was reflected in the conference statement issued at the close of the meeting. While stressing the need to preserve peace, the statement also pointed out that in order to win freedom and independence the oppressed peoples would be forced "to rise up to wage a revolutionary struggle against colonialism, to strive to build and develop their own revolutionary forces, and to use appropriate forms of struggle, armed and non-military struggle, according to the concrete conditions in each country."[53]

In early January Nikita Khrushchev underlined this point in a militant speech in which he said that although world wars could be prevented, popular wars of national liberation would continue as long as imperialism existed. Such wars—and here he referred specifically to the conflict in South Vietnam—"are not only admissible but inevitable," and the Communists would "support just wars of this kind whole-heartedly and without reservation."[54]

There is little doubt that Khrushchev's speech and the conference statement in Moscow that had preceded it were inspired by events in Vietnam and by the personal persuasiveness of Ho Chi Minh, who had led the D.R.V. delegation at the conference. On the return of the delegation to Hanoi, the Third Plenum of the new Central Committee convened in early January and unanimously endorsed the new statement. There is also evidence that this plenum ironed out some lingering confusion over strategy in the South. One Party document commented that there had been at the time of the original decision in 1959 "an initial hesitation" in the Party which caused "a short period of time" to be lost, but that the problem had been resolved in January 1961 when the Party leadership set forth a clear statement of the requirements of the situation. Unfortunately, the resolution published at the close of the meeting was brief and relatively unenlightening, making only a passing reference to the Moscow statement and its allusion to the need for oppressed people to wage a revolutionary struggle against the forces of colonialism. A recent Party history has been a little more forthcoming about the situation. According to this source the Politburo met in January 1961 to evaluate the situation in the South following the spontaneous uprisings of 1959 and 1960 and to establish guidelines for the future direction of the revolution. Predicting that the short period of stability in the South was now at an end, the Party leadership called for an intensification of both armed and political struggle to bring about a general uprising which, in the view of the Politburo, could occur at any time. The Party's military forces were to be strengthened and liberated base areas expanded so that armed violence could play a role equal in size and importance to that of political struggle. The Central Military Party Committee in Hanoi was assigned the task of helping the Central Committee develop guidelines for this expansion of military activity in South Vietnam. There was one note of caution, as the Politburo predicted that the United States might decide to send troops to stem the rising tide of revolution in South Vietnam.[55]

The National Liberation Front

The escalation of struggle in the South made a reinvigoration of the revolutionary apparatus and the formation of a new united front doubly important. In the months following the Third Congress, the Party decided to return to the operational arrangements used in the war against France. COSVN, the old southern branch of the Central Committee that had been abolished in 1954, was reconstituted with General Nguyen Chi Thanh as chairman, and Pham Hung as his deputy. Beneath COSVN were placed five regional Party committees and a sixth for the Saigon metropolitan area. Below the regions, provincial and district committees were created to supervise Party chapters in hamlets and villages. Military units were merged with the aim of forming a revolutionary armed force. At a conference held in Zone D in February under the direction of Tran Nam Trung, military units in the delta and the Western Highlands were merged into the new People's Liberation Armed Forces (PLAF) under unified command, which, in the minds of Party leaders, were probably expected to bear the brunt of the coming struggle against the Saigon regime. Before the end of the month new units, sometimes in coordination with sect forces, had begun to make contact with the enemy.[56]

The revitalization of the mass movement in the South was a more complicated but equally important operation. If indeed the Party hoped to achieve victory by a fairly low level of military activity combined with the active involvement of the revolutionary masses, then the reconstitution of the national front was a crucial element in the process. What was needed above all was a new and dynamic front that could, in the Party's words, "rally all patriotic classes and sections of the people" in the South against the Diem regime. Since 1954, the Party had lacked a front organization in the South with such qualifications. The Saigon-Cholon Peace Movement formed in 1954 had been restricted to urban intellectuals and limited its activities to the promotion of national elections. The Fatherland Front, set up in Hanoi in 1955, was too closely identified with the North and therefore with the Communists. The new alliance should not appear simply as an urban nationalist phenomenon or as a mere appendage of mass organizations in the D.R.V., but as a dynamic organization indigenous to the South that could serve as a magnet for all dissident elements, urban and rural, opposed to the Diem regime.

The character of this projected front was described to the Third Party Congress by Party elder statesman Ton Duc Thang: It would be based on the Leninist concept of the four-class alliance, but in deference to the complexity of South Vietnamese society would also encompass the various religious and ethnic minorities, as well as all patriotic parties and individuals in South Vietnam.[57] The aims of the organization, he pointed out, should be kept correspondingly general in order to appeal to the widest possible range of the population. It would emphasize nationalist and social reformist themes and have as its final objective the creation of a peaceful, unified, democratic, and prosperous Vietnam, beginning with the formation of a national democratic coalition government that would discuss peaceful unification with the North. There would obviously be no mention of communism.

The absence of such a front was remedied on December 20, 1960, with the formation of the National Front for the Liberation of South Vietnam (NLF, or Mat Tran Dan Toc Giai Phong Mien Nam Viet Nam). As described in the *Outline History*, the new organization was founded at a secret conference of representatives of various classes, parties, religious groups, and nationalities "somewhere in the liberated area of South Vietnam." Included in its Central Committee were members of virtually every major segment and class in southern society—the religious sects, Buddhist and Catholic organizations, women's groups, and two puppet political parties created by the Communists, the Radical Socialist Party (Dang Xa Hoi Cap Tien) and the South Vietnam Democratic party (Dang Dan Chu Mien Nam), both counterparts of existing parties in the North.[58] Like its famous predecessor, the Vietminh Front, the NLF was set up administratively at various levels up to its central Presidium but functioned primarily at the village level, where it operated through the familiar mass organizations.

The aims of the new front were set forth in a ten-point program issued at the conference and reflected the objectives previously emphasized by Ton Duc Thang at the Party congress in Hanoi. Repeating the contention of the Third Congress that there were two major enemy forces in South Vietnam, imperialism and feudalism, it asserted that at the moment the sharpest contradiction in the South was between the mass of the population and the U.S. imperialists and their henchmen in Saigon. The operational implication of this belief was that the major emphasis of the new front was to be nationalist rather than revolutionary, aimed at the national democratic rather than the social revolution. To avoid alienating patriotic elements, the front's land policy in liberated areas would be restricted to rent reduction and the confiscation of the land of traitors and cruel landlords. There was, of course, no suggestion that the front was controlled by the Party, or that it had any intimate connections with organizations in the D.R.V. The executive leadership of the front was composed of individuals who were not, for the most part, publicly identified as Communists although some, like Chairman Nguyen Huu Tho, had been closely linked to the Vietminh cause in the South since the 1940s. Most of the top officials were professionals, although there were several representatives of various social or minority groups, such as Nguyen Thi Dinh, heroine of the Ben Tre uprising, and Y Bih Aleo, chairman of the Communist-sponsored Western Highlands Autonomy Movement. To limit identification of the front with the Party, the number of open Party members in leading positions at all levels was strictly limited.[59]

The Party's success in establishing a new united front with no obvious links with the regime in Hanoi had momentous effects on the worldwide image of the insurgency movement. Although most sophisticated foreign observers had little doubt that there were close ties between the leadership of the new front and the Party in the D.R.V., there was a pervasive impression that the NLF possessed at least a modicum of autonomy and thus represented a legitimate alternative to the GVN in expressing the aspirations of the population of South Vietnam. This impression lent substance to the widely held view that the insurgency movement in the South had its roots in the indigenous population and was not simply a creature of the Party leadership in Hanoi. So long as this view prevailed, Washington's insistence that the rising struggle in South Vietnam was an armed attack from the North would appear of dubious validity.

How valid was this impression? As in the case of so many aspects of the Vietnam conflict, the answer all too often depended on the political preference of the individual observer. Today it is possible to obtain a somewhat clearer view. Unquestionably, hostility to the Diem regime among wide strata of the local population was a significant factor in the rising level of insurgency in South Vietnam. The revolutionary movement could hardly have grown and prospered without a solid base of support in both the cities and the countryside. It is also true that the vast majority of cadres sent south in the months following the Fifteenth Plenum were regroupees native to the South. On the other hand, it is also apparent that from the beginning the movement was organized and directed from the North. Although discontent was widespread throughout the South, it is highly unlikely that the unrest would have achieved enough coherence and dynamic force to challenge the power of the Saigon regime without the organizational genius provided by the Party leadership in Hanoi. In that sense, the insurgency was a genuine revolt based in the South, but it was organized and directed from the North.

Did Hanoi, as some claim, deliberately set out to destroy the Saigon regime by force? The evidence here suggests that this was not the case. Party strategy had originally hoped that reunification could take place by peaceful, or at least quasi-peaceful means. Only with reluctance was Hanoi compelled to reassess the situation as a result of the repressive policies put into effect by the Diem government, policies that prevented the revolutionary leaders in South Vietnam from organizing and carrying out a political struggle to achieve the overthrow of the existing government. To say that, of course, is not to deny that Hanoi had every intention of securing control of the South eventually, by whatever means proved necessary. To many outside observers, convinced that the South Vietnamese people deserved the opportunity to control their own destiny, Hanoi's attitude was tantamount to naked aggression. To Party leaders, South Vietnam would not fulfill its national destiny until the reactionary regime in Saigon had been overthrown and a new unified Vietnam established in both zones. Between these two contrasting views, a common understanding of the political and moral realities of the Vietnamese revolution would be virtually impossible to attain.

By the beginning of 1961, the southern insurgents, stimulated from the

North, were on the march. Several provinces, including a number in the delta and along the central coast, had come under the partial control of the revolutionary forces. In Hanoi, the initial confusion over policy had been at least temporarily resolved and the foundations of a coherent revolutionary strategy were beginning to emerge. In the world at large, the insurgents now appeared to possess the vocal support of the socialist countries and the sympathy of many others. A new stage of the Vietnamese revolution was about to begin.

DEMILITARIZED ZONE
QUANG TRI
KHE SANH
HUÉ
A SHAU
VALLEY
DA NANG
HOI AN
⑭
TRÀ
BONG
①
CHU LAI
QUANG NGAI
DAK TO
①
KONTUM
⑭
AN KHE
PLEIKU
⑲
QUI NHON
IA
DRANG
VALLEY
㉑
TUY HOA
①
BAN ME THUOT
NHA TRANG
⑭
DA LAT
CAM RANH BAY
㉒
⑪
PHAN RANG
TONLE
SAP
CAMBODIA
THAILAND
LAOS
MEKONG
RIVER
AN
LOC
①
PHAN THIET
TAY
NINH
ZONE C
PHNOM PENH
③
ZONE D
PARROT'S
BEAK
BIEN HOA
①
CHAU DOC
SAIGON
SIHANOUKVILLE
PLAIN
OF
REEDS
AP BAC
BINH GIA
④
MY
THO
VUNG TAU
PHU
QUOC
ISLAND
HA
TIEN
RACH
GIA
BEN TRE
CAN
THO
U MINH
FOREST
④
CA MAU
PENIN-
SULA
BAC LIEU

South Vietnam
At War

▓▓▓ CENTRAL HIGHLANDS

The Dialectics of Escalation
(1961–1965)

The new administration of John F. Kennedy came into office just as the rising level of violence in South Vietnam was beginning to attract the attention of worried policymakers in Washington. Until late in 1960, the major area of crisis had been in Laos, where the hard-line anti-Communist position of the Eisenhower administration had resulted in the fall of the neutralist Prime Minister Souvanna Phouma and the defeat of his efforts to establish a coalition government with the Communist Pathet Lao. With the rise to power of the U.S.-supported General Phoumi Nosavan—of whom trouble-shooting diplomat Averell Harriman was to remark, "If he's our strongman, we're in trouble"—the smoldering crisis in Laos threatened to erupt into full-scale war.

By contrast, until the final days of the Eisenhower administration, Washington had viewed the situation in South Vietnam as generally under control. For several years Ngo Dinh Diem had been able to draw upon a reservoir of U.S. goodwill stemming from his surprising success in consolidating his rule in Saigon during the months following the Geneva Agreement. As Diem's weaknesses became more apparent in the final years of the decade, Washington did not immediately take note and continued to slumber in the illusion that all was reasonably well in Saigon. By mid-1960, with the rapid escalation of violence in the countryside, such illusions could no longer be held, and Vietnam was among the major problems that President Eisenhower bequeathed to his successor.

Southeast Asia was not the only area of the world where U.S. foreign policy appeared to be unraveling. Before the new leadership in Washington had had adequate time to prepare its foreign policy initiatives, it was faced with the Bay of Pigs disaster in Cuba and an unsatisfactory meeting between President Kennedy and Soviet Party leader Khrushchev in Vienna, where the Soviet leader confirmed the suspicions aroused by his speech in January that Moscow was about to give more open support to national liberation struggles in the Third World. Khrushchev's challenge, coming on the heels of the Bay of Pigs fiasco, could be viewed as an indication that Moscow sensed a lack of toughness on the part of the new president. When, later in the year, the administration decided to pursue a compromise settlement in Laos, a decision to take a stand in South Vietnam was almost inevitable.

Caught in the rhetoric so lyrically expressed in his inaugural address, Kennedy seemed driven to demonstrate U.S. willingness to defend governments under pressure from Communist-inspired rebellions. Molded in the activist tradition of recent Democratic administrations and convinced that one of the greatest weaknesses of Eisenhower's foreign policy had been the failure to take the initiative in the struggle against international communism, the new president approached the Vietnam crisis with the conviction that a positive and resourceful attitude could turn the tide.

The situation in South Vietnam when Kennedy took office was hardly promising. Throughout 1960 signs of the continuing growth of the insurgency forces aroused concern in U.S. intelligence circles that the GVN military forces would be unable to cope with the situation. In April 1961, a task force on the Vietnam situation formed at the request of the White House reported that the situation was "critical but not hopeless" and recommended a significant increase in U.S. military aid to the Diem regime.[1]

By now, the broad shape of Communist strategy in South Vietnam was beginning to emerge. In its last year in office, the Eisenhower administration had grudgingly begun to revise its assumptions that the primary threat to peace in Vietnam would come in the form of a conventional military attack across the demilitarized zone and had developed plans to counter the insurgents' guerrilla strategy. But it was left to the new administration to draw up a comprehensive approach to the problem. The essence of the Kennedy strategy consisted of the recognition that the problem was as much political as military. To destroy the insurgency movement, it would be necessary to break Communist control at its source—in the rural village. And the war at the village level had both political and military components: to "win the hearts and minds" of the South Vietnamese peasants by providing them with persuasive economic and social reasons to support the Saigon government and to provide them with security from attack by insurgency forces outside the village. If the Communists could be isolated from the village—if, to use the lively metaphor popularized by Mao Tse-tung, the fish could be removed from the sea—then their access to recruits and provisions would be severely restricted and the rebellion would wither and die.

The political side of the new strategy called for increased efforts to persuade and assist the Diem regime to improve economic conditions in the countryside, to provide increased access to land, education, and upward social mobility. The military problem was to transform the GVN's army from one primarily concerned with the threat of external attack to one designed to counter internal subversion. This would entail the breakdown of many of the ARVN's larger conventional units into smaller ones and the development of security forces capable of rapid deployment and effective counterinsurgency activities at the local level.

The centerpiece of the new counterinsurgency strategy in the countryside would be the new organization called the strategic hamlet (*ap chien luoc*). Smaller than the agrovilles set up earlier by the Diem regime, the strategic hamlets were to be built, where possible, on existing social administrative organizations in the countryside. A total of 14,000 hamlets and villages in South Vietnam was to be consolidated into more than 11,000 strategic hamlets. The new hamlets would have their own houses, schools, wells, and watchtowers and were to provide for their own security. A major advocate of the new program, R. K. Thompson, a former British defense secretary and the official who had designed the antiterrorist campaign in Malaya, was brought in by the Diem regime as an adviser.

The new strategy was undoubtedly a step forward from the rigidities of the former approach, but, in the last analysis, it could be no stronger than the performance of the government in Saigon. Unless the Diem regime could successfully reverse the political and social decline that had begun to accelerate during the late 1950s, the innovations suggested by Washington would be no more than castles in the sand. Awareness in the White House of the crucial nature of Saigon's performance led to several fact-finding visits to South Vietnam by high-level U.S. officials in 1961 and 1962 and a new and tougher stance by the Kennedy administration toward the GVN. Beyond such pressure, of course, lay the ultimate and heretofore unanswered question: What if the Diem regime was unable to improve itself?

Bureaucracies do not easily tolerate innovation, and it is not surprising that the new strategy led to intense debate and controversy in Washington. Military planners in the Pentagon did not necessarily oppose the Strategic Hamlet Program, but some feared that tying down a large proportion of Saigon's military forces in static defensive positions would diminish the ARVN's ability to launch aggressive operations against revolutionary combat units. Diplomats grumbled over the presidential order that all foreign service officers must attend a course on guerrilla warfare prior to departing on an overseas assignment. In some cases the issues were indeed crucial. Should U.S. combat troops be injected into South Vietnam to provide military support for the ARVN and a morale boost for the population? General Maxwell Taylor visited Saigon in October 1961 and returned with the recommendation that a token force of U.S. combat troops be dispatched to South Vietnam. The president, however, nervous that such an action would open the door to further involvement, rejected the proposal. He did agree to a compromise, approving an increase in U.S. advisers and the introduction of a small number of combat support troops.

Countering the "Special War"

The decision by the Kennedy administration to increase U.S. involvement in South Vietnam may not have been a complete surprise to Hanoi, but it was undoubtedly unwelcome news, for it added a new dimension to the already complicated situation in the South. Since the Fifteenth Plenum had decided to escalate the struggle, the consensus within the Party leadership had apparently been that victory could be achieved without a massive military effort along the lines of the final years of the Franco-Vietminh conflict. The Central Committee resolution of January 1961—according to Party sources the guiding document for revolutionary strategy in the South—had stressed that political struggle would be the basic factor, apparently in the belief that the key to victory was the political weakness of the Ngo Dinh Diem government.[2]

It was clear that political struggle, by itself, would be insufficient to overthrow the Saigon regime and would have to be supplemented by armed violence. But what combination of armed and political struggle would be required? Would the southern revolution take the form of a popular uprising in rural areas and the cities, supported by modest military operations, along the lines of the August Revolution of 1945? Or would it culminate in a general offensive similar to that launched during the War of Resistance against the French? At this juncture, the Party leadership appeared to be uncertain, and left both possibilities open.

Within the Party leadership in the South, emphasis on the importance of political struggle was particularly strong. Several documents captured by ARVN units in South Vietnam during the early 1960s reflected this conviction. One, written sometime in early 1960, stressed that armed struggle should be used primarily to support the political struggle and should not take the form of guerrilla warfare or a resistance war. Asserting that the chances of realizing victory through a primarily political effort were excellent, it warned that a miscalculation by Party leaders could lead to increased involvement by the United States and a long and costly armed conflict. A second, entitled "Situation and Tasks" and written sometime in 1961, took the same position, claiming that the combination of political and military struggle was working effectively in the South and would force the Saigon government into a passive position and ultimately lead to a general uprising. Because the primary weakness of the Diem regime was in the realm of politics, the "political force of the masses," rather than high-level military struggle, was more likely to succeed in the long run. By this reasoning, a gradual intensification of the political struggle against the Saigon regime, supplemented by selective armed violence, and using the full revolutionary power of the oppressed masses, would inevitably culminate at some future date in an uprising in urban and rural areas that would topple the Saigon regime. Armed struggle would be used to accelerate the decline of the enemy, but the primary focus would be on political struggle.[3]

The decision by the Kennedy administration to intensify its efforts to stem the political and military decline of the Diem regime in mid-1961 complicated the situation for Hanoi and may have thrown into question the optimistic assumptions held earlier in the year. According to scattered evidence, a COSVN conference held in October issued a resolution that placed more emphasis on the military aspects of the struggle and even raised the possibility of a major military effort similar to the one at the end of the war against the French.[4] Asserting that the revolutionary situation in the South was entering a period of "high tide," the resolution called for an increase in armed attacks and partial uprisings. Because of the savage repression by the Diem regime, it said, armed violence and not just political struggle would now be necessary.

This analysis was clearly controversial within the insurgency leadership in the South. One captured document written sometime in 1962 was critical of the October resolution and claimed that it showed a lack of understanding of the situation in South Vietnam and in the world at large. It conceded that increased U.S. involvement suggested the need for more military preparations and eventually a higher level of armed struggle, but it vigorously rejected excessive militarization of the conflict, such as it claimed had occurred prior to 1954. The Party should not change the course of its struggle, "i.e., shift to an all-out war to achieve our revolutionary task," just because the United States was waging war against it. Such a change, the document stated,

> would not be advantageous to us because we would not be able to make full use of our people's strength and capacity for struggle. . . . Thus, underestimating the importance of political struggle would be very dangerous; it would mean giving up a very efficient weapon and an extremely important force. Political struggle will have long-lasting effects; as the result of the strength of the revolution, the role of the political struggle will be transcendent (for instance, in case of negotiations, a cease-fire etc.). Even in the event the U.S. sent troops in large numbers to the South, it would not mean that we would no longer be able to carry out political struggle, but political struggle alone would not be enough to decide our victory and the enemy's defeat.[5]

This document was equally critical of the October resolution for its reference to a revolutionary "high tide" and its apparent conviction that victory in the South could be achieved in a relatively short time. This, it claimed, seriously underestimated the difficulties faced by the revolution. The Party's military and political strength was still inadequate, and its liberated areas too small, to cope with the power of the Saigon regime backed by the United States. In particular, it requested guidance on how to deal with the new strategic hamlets, which it described as a "vicious" attempt by the United States and its client in Saigon to isolate the revolutionary forces from the mass of the population in the countryside.

Other documents tended to confirm this estimate, commenting that although the Diem regime possessed a number of fundamental weaknesses, so did the insurgency movement—hesitations within the Party leadership before 1959, the people's fear of the power of Saigon, the weakness of the revolutionary armed forces and base areas, errors committed in coordinating political and military struggle, and (probably the most important factor of all) the absence of a revolutionary high tide among the mass of the population. One cadre's notebook observed that the revolutionary surge in South Vietnam was "not yet strong and steady" and that the people still "lacked the spirit" to oppose the forces of the Saigon regime and the U.S. imperialists. In a word, a mature revolutionary situation did not yet exist in South Vietnam.[6]

According to the COSVN document cited above, the proper strategy was to concentrate on a gradual strengthening of the Party's guerrilla forces and bases and of its political apparatus and a gradual intensification of both political and military struggle in the context of a protracted and step-by-step approach to victory. Particular emphasis should be placed on building up the guerrilla forces and bases for a possible increase in military conflict, but the role of political struggle should not be ignored; it should remain as an essential factor in the revolutionary effort: *"Our course of action at this time will still consist in intensifying the armed struggle as well as the political struggle, in combining these two forms of struggle to repulse the enemy step by step and develop such conditions as will enable us to defeat the enemy completely."*[7]

What effect such appeals had on the Party leadership in Hanoi cannot be ascertained with certainty. One source favorable to the use of violence as a means of achieving victory in the South commented later that there had been a brief period of hesitation and confusion within the southern leadership when the United States had established a military command in Saigon under General Paul Harkins in 1961, but that it had been quickly overcome. Whatever the case, events outside Vietnam appeared to take a hand in influencing Hanoi's view of the future course of the revolution in the South and at least temporarily reduced the divergence of views between advocates of a political strategy and those favoring a greater use of force. The willingness of the Kennedy administration to accept a negotiated solution to the civil war in Laos—eventually concluded at Geneva in July 1962—gave rise to brief optimism in Hanoi that Washington might be ready to accept a compromise settlement in South Vietnam as well. By this reasoning, the rising tide of revolutionary sentiment in Asia, Africa, and Latin America, combined with a crisis in Berlin, had served to weaken U.S. resolve to resist the momentous changes taking place in the world. A gradualist policy of weakening and isolating the United States in South Vietnam might result in a new willingness in Washington to reach a compromise agreement along the lines of the projected settlement on Laos.

Party leaders appeared to recognize that the Kennedy administration viewed the Saigon regime as the last bastion against a wave of Communist expansion in Southeast Asia and would be reluctant to accept a negotiated solution to the conflict in South Vietnam. Therefore a period of fierce struggle would be necessary to wear down the resistance of the Diem government and persuade the United States that defeat was inevitable. The key to success would be the ability of the Party's forces in the South to bring Saigon to the point of collapse without at the same time provoking Washington to increase the level of U.S. involvement in South Vietnam, or even to take the war to the North. For this purpose a combination of political struggle with low-level guerrilla warfare was considered most appropriate. The objective would be not to inflict a total defeat on the enemy, but to create a "no win" situation and lead Washington to accept a political settlement and the formation of a coalition government including the NLF in Saigon. Instructions to this effect were apparently transmitted in early 1962 to the Party leadership in the South and resulted in a COSVN conference in April and the issuance of a revised plan of action that abandoned the allusion to an all-out military offensive and a prediction that victory could be achieved through a combination of political and military struggle.[8]

While the Party's forces in the South were directed to lead the United States and its client state in Saigon into a cul-de-sac, Hanoi began to put out diplomatic feelers on a possible negotiated settlement of the conflict. As a token of its serious attitude, it replaced its previous demand for the abolition of the Diem regime with a simple call for a coalition government including "all political parties, cliques, groups, all political tendencies, social strata, members of all religions," a phrase that implicitly included members of the Diem regime itself. Simultaneously, D.R.V. representatives in Paris sounded out neutralist Vietnamese politicians living in exile on their interest in joining a future coalition government with the NLF.[9]

How the Party viewed the nature of this possible coalition government was disclosed in the secret instructions to COSVN noted above. According to this directive, Party sources would approach prominent Vietnamese personalities who were considered acceptable by the United States but were secretly in sympathy with Hanoi's aims in South Vietnam. Once a coalition government had been established, these figures could be added to the government with Washington's concurrence, along with others openly identified with the NLF. This government, now operating under de facto Party control, could then hold talks with the D.R.V. about a reunification of the entire country by peaceful means.[10]

For a brief period, Hanoi's interest in a negotiated settlement was paralleled in Washington. According to Allan Goodman, whose 1978 study, *The Lost Peace*, is one of the more perceptive studies on the Vietnam negotiations, President Kennedy authorized Averell Harriman to approach D.R.V. delegates at the Geneva conference with an offer of secret talks and to suggest that the Laotian settlement could be a model for Vietnamese neutrality. Washington, however, was approaching the problem from a different perspective than

Hanoi. In the summer of 1962 the Kennedy administration was momentarily optimistic about the general situation in Vietnam and gave serious consideration to establishing a limit on U.S. involvement in South Vietnam. The secretary of defense was directed to draw up plans for a phased withdrawal of U.S. aid and advisers.[11]

Hanoi's response came on July 20, 1962, when the NLF issued a four-point manifesto, which indicated that the only basis for peace was the immediate withdrawal of U.S. troops and the formation of a coalition government. It suggested that until such conditions were fulfilled, there was nothing to negotiate about. When the United States declined to accept these conditions, the D.R.V. implied that a cease-fire could be separated from the demand for the withdrawal of U.S. troops. But when Washington did not respond, Hanoi returned to the four points.

There is considerable confusion over the meaning of this flurry of diplomatic exchanges. Allan Goodman suggested that Hanoi rebuffed U.S. overtures for a compromise settlement in the conviction that the United States would not stand firm in South Vietnam and the Diem regime would soon collapse of its own accord. Gareth Porter, in his study of the negotiations, contended that Hanoi was truly interested in a settlement along Laotian lines and implied as much in a *Nhan dan* editorial welcoming the agreement on Laos in July.[12] Perhaps the most that can be said on the basis of present evidence is that Hanoi was interested in pursuing the possibility of a negotiated settlement leading to a coalition government, but only on strongly favorable terms. When it became clear that Washington did not seem to be negotiating out of a sense of weakness, Hanoi lost interest.

The failure to make progress toward a political settlement, the adoption by Saigon of the Strategic Hamlet Program, and the growing U.S. presence in South Vietnam in 1962 and early 1963 probably strengthened the conviction among top Party strategists that a substantial role for armed struggle would be required. One clear expression of this view came from the well-known CRIMP document, written sometime in the winter or early spring of 1963. According to the author, who was probably a high-ranking and knowledgeable spokesman for the Party leadership in the South, the revolutionary war in South Vietnam would inevitably have to be resolved by force, and would have to move from a small-scale confrontation to a high-level military conflict. Specifically, the document took issue with the assumption that political struggle alone was the trump card of the revolution: "While we were only engaged in a simple political struggle the weakness of the enemy becomes [sic] his strengths and created severe difficulties for us, but when we launched the revolutionary force to oppose the enemy, the enemy's shortcomings were revealed."[13]

The author was careful not to disparage the importance of political factors. Indeed, he described the political struggle as "the origin, as the base" for the revolution as a whole. In the war against the French, he said, political struggle had been limited "to utilizing propaganda in order to uphold the righteousness of our cause" and to mobilize support for the revolutionary struggle from all segments of society. Politics would play a larger role in the present stage of the revolution. It would become an active supplement to the armed struggle, not simply in the early stages of the conflict, but down to the final victory itself, with the "political force of the masses" joining with the Party's armed units in "attacking the enemy at the front lines."

Nor did he advocate a repeat of the openly military approach taken during the previous war against the French. While taking to task "the rightist and hesitant thoughts of people who did not dare to push the armed struggle because they had incorrectly appraised the enemy," he also opposed the "dogmatic" view that the Party must "follow the style used during the period of the Resistance." That approach, he conceded, was not appropriate in the existing situation. Moreover, in an obvious reference to previous statements about the current situation in the South, he admitted that force could be applied only in a revolutionary situation, when the internal contradictions within society had developed to a decisive degree. In the immediate aftermath of Geneva the masses had wanted peace, and the revolutionary apparatus in the South was too weak to compete with the Diem regime.

Now, however, the revolutionary tide in the South had reached a high wave, and the question of the moment was not whether force should be used, but when and how it should be applied. Here the author indicated that although a blatant imitation of past strategy was inadvisable, previous experience would be useful in devising an approach to the new situation. Specifically, it would necessarily follow the basic principles of people's warfare in backward and colonial countries. It would take the form of a protracted conflict, involving the use of the familiar three types of forces, and would move from guerrilla war to higher forms of war. The culminating phase would represent a synthesis of the August Revolution with the Maoist model of people's war—a general offensive by the revolutionary forces in rural areas combined with a popular uprising led by the oppressed masses in the cities. His description of the final phase of general offensive and uprising is particularly striking:

When the South Vietnam cities, particularly Saigon-Cholon, are able to rise up in coordination with the rural areas the South Vietnam revolution will have the capability of overthrowing the enemy through the means of a general uprising. At this time we are unable to affirm how the general uprising will evolve. But it is certain that it will be an uprising of the rural masses moving into the cities, composed of armed forces which have been organized and have been in combat for many years and of political forces of the rural and city masses which will at that time rise up in armed revolt with every type of weapon at their disposal; it will not explode at the same time at every place but will encompass many periods; perhaps it will begin after several large battles have changed the ratio of the enemy military forces in comparison to ours, encouraging the masses everywhere, particularly in the cities, and causing disorder in the ranks of the enemy after which the masses could immediately rise up everywhere and the liberation army could move in (particularly into the enemy military strongholds, the larger cities, and Saigon-Cholon) to continue the mass revolt.

From the analysis above, it is clear that one of the major issues facing Party strategists was how to use the geographical features of South Vietnam most effectively. While the experience gained in the war against the French would obviously continue to have relevance, the unique features of the South would require serious consideration. This issue was dealt with in some detail in the CRIMP document, which probably draws on previous directives from high Party councils in Hanoi.[14] In the new situation, the South was to be divided into three major strategic areas, the mountains, the lowland plains, and the cities. Each area was viewed as possessing its own particular importance to the success of the revolution. As was the case during the war against the French, the rural areas were considered the key to victory, as they were relatively independent of Saigon's rule. For the purposes of the present conflict, the rural areas in South Vietnam were divided into two separate strategic areas, the mountains and the lowland plains. The mountains consisted primarily of the Central Highlands, which formed the backbone of the country from an area fifty miles north of Saigon up to the Demilitarized Zone (DMZ). The importance of mountainous terrain as an ideal liberated base area had been established early in the history of the Party when the Viet Bac became the first major liberated zone for the Vietminh and the jumping-off point for most of its later operations in North Vietnam during the war against the French. In South Vietnam, the Central Highlands were now called upon to play the same role in the struggle against the Diem regime and the Americans. The highlands had many of the attractive features that had made the Viet Bac crucial during the earlier stage of the revolution: proximity to border regions; inaccessibility to enemy operations and obvious advantages for guerrilla operations; a minority population hostile to central government authority; and proximity to vital populated areas along the coast. Because of the weakness of the GVN apparatus there and the small population, the area was viewed primarily as a military problem, even though the revolutionary forces were themselves quite small at the time. Here the revolutionaries would construct stable and firm base areas and build up the large-scale military units that would later advance to the heartland areas held by the enemy.

If, according to the author of the CRIMP document, the Central Highlands were seen as the logical starting point and defensive bastion for the revolutionary forces, the densely populated lowland plains were the real key to success. Here the revolution must find its recruits and obtain its provisions. Unless the rich rice-growing provinces could be wrested from government control, the prospects for victory would be dim. For whoever controlled the delta and the coastal lowlands controlled the vast majority of the population of the country and therefore the human and food resources so vital to the war effort. The lowlands were thus the major contested area between the GVN and the insurgency. At the moment, neither the Saigon regime nor the revolutionaries were dominant. Support for the revolution was strong in the coastal region stretching from Nha Trang up to the port city of Da Nang and in a few provinces in the Mekong delta. But much of the delta, particularly where the sects were strong, tended to resist the Communists or favor the GVN.

But if the importance of the lowlands was generally conceded, there was some disagreement over the suitability of the area for military operations. Except for key base areas like the U Minh forest, the Plain of Reeds, and the wooded areas north of Saigon, insurgency forces would be relatively exposed and at the mercy of the larger and better armed government troops. In the light of such difficulties, some Party figures felt that revolutionary activities in the lowlands should be restricted to political techniques and paramilitary operations, with military units similar to the armed propaganda units formed in the months prior to the August Revolution. As a whole, however, the Party leadership was convinced that this key area could be seized by military force and recommended efforts to mobilize the masses in the area to support armed struggle against the ruling authorities. Although large and stable liberated zones such as had existed during the war against the French were perhaps not feasible, smaller base areas located near strategic communications routes and towns could be established to harass the enemy and permit the insurgent forces to operate effectively in the area until a major military effort was possible.

The cities presented the knottiest problem for the Communists. This was the realm of the enemy, the one area in South Vietnam that the revolution, despite efforts for more than a generation, had been unable to crack. It was not that the urban social classes were necessarily unsympathetic to the revolution. According to one Communist document, there was "a relatively high degree of awareness" among the urban population, not only among the workers but also among petty bourgeois intellectuals and even among some of the national bourgeoisie. But as Party sources conceded, the urban classes were often vacillating and their attitudes had been affected by decades of direct exposure to French and U.S. influence. Moreover, it was in the cities where the power of Western imperialism was most firmly established and provided a vital bulwark for the delicate stability of the Diem regime. Only if that power could be shaken or withdrawn could the revolution achieve its final triumph.

Under the circumstances, it would not be easy to transform the urban masses into a major component of the antigovernment united front. That Party strategists were determined to make the attempt despite the obstacles before them is a measure of the importance they attached to the role of the cities in the general uprising to come. The Party's urban work would take place at two levels: in secret, among the radical proletariat and the progressive elements of the petty bourgeoisie, to build up an effective revolutionary apparatus that could undertake clandestine operations and then surface at the moment of uprising; and quasi-openly, through the united front, to drain away popular support for the Saigon regime from the politically volatile middle class. Through its secret organizations, political and military, the radical hard core would be responsible for setting off the general uprising. But it would succeed only if the middle classes, at the crucial moment, swung their support to the revolution.

Building up the PLAF

While Party leaders groped for a strategy to deal with the growing U.S. presence in South Vietnam, civilian and military cadres at the local level struggled to prepare the forces of the revolution for the challenge. Although Party directives called for intensive efforts to improve capabilities in both military and political fields, it was clear that the immediate objective must be to increase the size and effectiveness of the revolutionary armed forces in order to cope with GVN repression and, in the words of one Communist historian, to move from the stage of "uniform uprisings to seize power at the local level" to a higher stage of "expanded guerrilla war against enemy sweeps."[15]

By 1961, this process was already well under way. The size of the PLAF exceeded 15,000, well above the total of less than 3,000 two years earlier.[16] Most were in guerrilla units under the direction of the regional Party committees. There were few organized main force units or self-defense units at the village level (the failure to organize at the village level was one of the major criticisms leveled by Party leaders in secret documents). The goal was to set up the PLAF on the familiar three-tiered basis. Fully armed regular units capable of combat operations against ARVN conventional forces and commanded by COSVN or the regional headquarters would form the backbone of the revolutionary army. Below that level would be the full-time guerrillas, usually operating at company size under provincial or district command. The guerrillas would normally restrict their combat activities to operations against the enemy's local units, but when necessary could coordinate their activities with main force units in the area. At the lowest level was the village militia, divided into an armed combat militia (du kich chien dau) and the regular village militia (du kich xa). The former was composed of vigorous youth in the village and could take part in military operations; the latter usually had older men and was to be used only for defense. The local militia could be used to supplement higher-level units operating in the area and was often a recruiting pool for higher-level units.[17]

During the early years of the insurgency, the vast majority of PLAF recruits were indigenous South Vietnamese. Yet, from the beginning, regroupees trained in North Vietnam provided a nucleus for the movement. According to U.S.

government sources, infiltration rose from approximately 2,000 annually in 1959 and 1960 to a minimum of 3,700 in 1961 and more than 5,000 in 1962.[18] The return of the regroupees did not substantially affect the size of the local forces; by one estimate they made up less than 20 percent of the entire PLAF. But their numbers were no reflection of their importance, for they often served as political cadres or officers, providing an element of experience and ideological steadiness to the young and frequently untrained recruits from the rural areas.

It is likely that one of Hanoi's major concerns as it attempted to revitalize the movement in the South was to guarantee that leadership remained firmly in the hands of Party leaders in the North. Since the 1930s the Party's apparatus in Cochin China had faced unique problems and had tended to operate somewhat independently from the Central Committee, which was usually located in Tonkin. The isolation and autonomy of the southern leadership had created problems, particularly when it was under the control of the ambitious Tran Van Giau, and irritation on the part of top Party figures at Giau's independent policies may have been one of the reasons for his dismissal from the leadership of the movement in the South in the late 1940s. Then, too, traditional cultural and historical differences had long generated a degree of mutual antagonism and distrust between North and South, and from the time of the Franco-Vietminh War communism was frequently identified in the minds of southerners as a Northern phenomenon.

In the new conditions of struggle, when the southern leadership would inevitably be operating somewhat independently of Hanoi, the threat of a restoration of southern regionalism undoubtedly concerned Party leaders in Hanoi. The danger would be exacerbated by the fact that the NLF, the overall parent organization of the movement, would consist of thousands, perhaps millions, of Vietnamese who were not members of the Party. For obvious reasons, the NLF leadership itself would be composed primarily of non-Party southerners. To reduce the temptations of autonomy, a number of mechanisms were established to provide guidance from the North. The top COSVN leaders were all Party veterans with a history of loyalty to the organization. At the end of each year a leading COSVN member attended a Politburo meeting in Hanoi to consult with Party leaders and receive directions for future strategy in the South. Party figures also played key roles in the administrative structure of the NLF. Finally, in early 1962 Hanoi decided to set up a southern branch of the VWP, the People's Revolutionary Party, or PRP (Dang Nhan Dan Cach Mang Viet Nam). The PRP was initially described as an independent party with no formal connections with the VWP in the North; this was a fiction designed to avoid identification of the southern movement with the Party leadership in the North. In reality the PRP was directly subordinate to the parent organization in the D.R.V. through COSVN. There was no attempt to disguise the Marxist-Leninist orientation of the organization. It was described as "a revolutionary party of the working class in South Vietnam," which would be guided by the principles of Marxism-Leninism.

Fish on the Chopping Block

One of the major concerns of Party strategists in the South was the Strategic Hamlet Program, initiated by the Diem regime in the early spring of 1962. In defiance of the advice of Robert Thompson and U.S. civilian advisers, Diem was anxious to build the strategic hamlets quickly and hoped to complete the program (which was to include almost the entire rural population of 10 million) by the end of the year. The first "preparatory" stage would normally consist of sweep operations by ARVN units to clear out insurgency forces and establish a stable government presence in the area. According to one Communist source, during the height of the program there were anywhere from 80 to 3,000 sweeps a month involving 10,000 to 15,000 ARVN troops. After this military stage, ARVN forces would remain in the area for several months in order to carry out pacification operations and assist villagers in the construction of the hamlets. When this phase was completed, local self-defense forces would become responsible for security and government agencies would institute the needed political and economic reforms. U.S. advisers had suggested that the program be launched in relatively secure, if vital, areas in the key provinces near Saigon and in the Central Highlands province of Kontum. Later the program could expand southward into the populous delta and to other provinces in the highlands. Diem, however, decided to initiate the program in troubled Binh Duong Province, near the Communist base areas of zones C and D, where GVN pacification operations were already under way. Other programs were soon initiated on the Ca Mau peninsula and in the coastal provinces of Phu Yen, Binh Dinh, and Quang Ngai, all areas of substantial revolutionary activity.[19]

There is evidence that the new GVN program was viewed with considerable concern in Hanoi. Even a partial success would deprive the Party of its vital link with the rural villages in the South and make the guerrillas—in the colorful phrase of one Communist writer—"fish on the chopping block." In response, the Party set up training programs to advise local units on how to destroy the new organizations. Where possible, the hamlets were to be seized by direct attack; where that was impossible, they were to be infiltrated and destroyed from the inside.[20]

The campaign against the strategic hamlets did not have immediate effect. In the early stages, many peasants welcomed the new hamlets as a means of improving their security and livelihood. Many foreign observers were optimistic and claimed to see a visible improvement in the general situation in the countryside during the spring and summer of 1962. The improved situation carried over into the military struggle, where Communist casualties rose and ARVN troops, apparently bolstered by higher morale and new U.S. helicopters, launched more offensive operations. The Kennedy administration was so elated that it briefly considered setting up a schedule to remove the U.S. military advisers. By midsummer, however, Communist operations against the hamlets had intensified. Some were repeatedly attacked and destroyed.

The program also began to suffer from internal weaknesses. Because the hamlets were built so quickly, administrative mix-ups resulted and promised facilities were often not provided. In some cases the "strategic hamlet" was no more than an existing hamlet with a fence. Training for the new self-defense forces was inadequate, and assistance from ARVN units was often lacking. Finally, as with the agrovilles, peasants resented often having to work without compensation, and the inevitable corruption and favoritism that accompanied all GVN efforts further reduced support for the program. Although as late as the spring of 1963, Robert Thompson was able to claim that the program was a qualified success, it was having problems. According to Bernard Fall, only 1,500 of the 8,500 strategic hamlets were viable.[21]

Emboldened, the insurgents more and more went on the attack. Having improved their capacity to operate against helicopters, they began to strike at battalion force level. Party histories cite the battle of Ap Bac, a village in the lower delta near My Tho, as a symbol of the new stage. In December, a PLAF battalion attacked this village and drove off the local government forces. When ARVN reinforcements arrived, the attackers, though outnumbered four to one, struck again and inflicted heavy casualties.[22] To Hanoi, it was a significant victory—the first concentrated attack by PLAF regular forces in South Vietnam. To the GVN it was a humiliating defeat and an ominous sign for the future.

While trying to destroy the government's administrative apparatus, the insurgents also attempted to build up their own. At the public level, the major effort was to expand and strengthen the NLF. By 1962, the front had 300,000 members and a passive following of more than a million. It had committees in thirty-eight of forty-one provinces and in all regions of South Vietnam and held its First National Congress early the same year.[23]

At the same time, the amount of territory under NLF control gradually increased. In such liberated areas the most crucial problem for the Party, as internal documents confirmed, would be to win the support of the peasants. The key issue was land reform, and the program began to be implemented in liberated areas in the early 1960s. In general, it closely resembled the one that had been promulgated during the war against the French, leading only in gradual stages to full land reform. The first phase, which usually began soon after liberation, was deliberately moderate to avoid unnecessarily alienating anti-Diem elements in the countryside. Only uncultivated or commune land, the land of absentee landlords, or land that had been confiscated during the earlier conflict was distributed. Even there, the Party attempted to avoid compulsion, and advised peasants to make private arrangements wherever possible to compensate the previous owners. Landlords were classified in two types, progressive and evil, and only the latter were punished. Those receiving land included middle peasants as well as the poor and landless. According to one Rand Corporation Study, the amount of land received depended on the individual situation but averaged about one-half hectare (1.2 acres) per family.[24]

The original program was completed in liberated areas in 1964. According to Communist statistics, a total of 1,546,275 hectares (3.8 million acres) of land had been distributed to needy peasants. Virtually all peasants now had at least some land, and most were now classified as middle peasants.[25] There was no hint of collectivization, but nearly 3 million peasants had been enlisted in "rotating chore teams," the first stage in the socialization process in the countryside. The program was not without problems. In some cases, the military situation made it difficult to carry out. In others, there was too little cultivable land available or there were complaints of favoritism. But according to another RAND study, the majority of the peasants in liberated areas approved of the program and such satisfaction was presumably a major factor in the ability of the movement to enlist recruits in the countryside. The Party was careful to present an image of local initiative and voluntary participation. The first stage used the Chinese "three with" system, in which trained cadres lived with poor peasants and encouraged them to carry out the program with the support of the movement. In the beginning, taxes were "voluntary contributions" and only gradually did they become compulsory.[26]

In minority areas, the Party was less concerned with economic issues than with cultural and political autonomy. Because of the Saigon government's insensitivity to minority attitudes, a serious rebellion against central authority was brewing in the Central Highlands. The Communists moved deliberately into the vacuum. On May 19, 1961, at a congress chaired by NLF member Ibih Aleo and attended by representatives of thirty different nationalities, the Central Highlands Autonomous Movement (Uy Ban Dan Toc Tu Tri Tay Nguyen) was founded. Although one American expert described it as a paper organization, by 1962 the NLF had assisted sympathetic tribesmen in setting up an autonomous zone in the mountainous area. Communist propaganda, following a practice dating back to 1930, was careful to stress the right of self-determination and the right of all peoples to retain their culture and customs.

Perhaps the most challenging task was to develop and expand the movement in the cities. Not only were the urban areas under the direct rule of the Saigon government and thus much easier to control, but the cities also felt the strongest effects of American cultural and economic influence. The expansion of commerce and manufacturing had undoubtedly created strains in Vietnamese society. Cultural dislocation and resentment of social and economic inequalities and of perceived foreign economic domination are familiar phenomena in most Third World societies today. But Western influence also brought a measure of affluence and artificial well-being to important sectors of the urban population and the growth of what the Communists would call the "poisonous weeds" of decadent bourgeois culture. In brief, the expansion of Western influence was both an opportunity and a threat to the revolution. The escalation of the U.S. presence would exacerbate many of the cultural problems in a transitional society, but it also tied many urban Vietnamese to the American economic machine.

As stated, the Party's task in the cities would be two-fold: (1) to build up a secret apparatus among radical elements to serve as the nucleus for a future general uprising and the seizure of power, and (2) to mobilize broad support from moderate elements through the framework of the front. In the first instance, the most crucial class would be the proletariat. From its early days, the Party had taken pride in the strength and ideological awareness of the Vietnamese proletariat and its active role in the revolution. In particular, the working class in Saigon-Cholon had a tradition of revolutionary activism under the French colonial regime. Although the South as a whole had fallen behind the rest of the country in revolutionary ferment, the movement in Saigon had far surpassed that of Hanoi and other provincial capitals around the country. Thus, the Party had grounds for optimism about the possibility of building a strong urban base among the growing proletariat in the South, particularly in Saigon-Cholon, where nearly half the South's workers were employed.[27]

During the first few years following the Geneva Agreement, the Party's urban activities were rather limited. In part, this may have reflected the prevailing policy of promoting peaceful legal struggle. But it was also a product of the competition provided by the progovernment union organized by Tran Quoc Buu, as well as of Diem's vigorous efforts to suppress subversive activities throughout South Vietnam. In any case, until 1960 the urban movement in the South was quiescent, with few strikes and workers' struggles and little indication of Party influence among workers. Although unemployment, low salaries, and poor working conditions were fairly common, there was little political activism. Where labor strikes did occur, most were primarily concerned with economic issues.[28]

Serious attempts to organize the labor union movement began with the formation of the NLF and the establishment of its affiliate labor organization, the Workers' Liberation Association of Vietnam (*Hoi Lao Dong Giai Phong Mien Nam*), in May 1961. The first efforts were concentrated on setting up labor organizations at the basic level, in the individual factory or enterprise.[29] As activism among workers grew, the Party began to form secret self-defense organizations in preparation for the future revolutionary uprising. Communist sources claim that in 1961 nearly 300,000 workers participated in the struggle movement, a number that more than doubled within a year.

Work among the urban middle class was scarcely less important to the revolutionary cause. Here again, the Party continued to be reasonably optimistic. Although it regarded South Vietnamese intellectuals as lazy, mentally undisciplined, and prone to coffeehouse theorizing (classic Marxist criticisms of petty bourgeois intellectuals) and saw some as tainted by collaboration, the Party apparently was convinced that most could be won over, at least temporarily, to the revolutionary cause. According to one captured document, for example, GVN officials and ARVN officers, unlike their counterparts under the Bao Dai regime, were not to be classified automatically as lackeys of imperialism, but as misguided patriots.[30] For the most part, the Party relied on the appeal of nationalism to approach urban moderates and went to considerable lengths to identify Ngo Dinh Diem as a puppet of the United States (thus, of course, the constant use of the epithet "My-Diem," or American-Diem, as a label for the Saigon regime), a technique facilitated by the growing U.S. presence after 1961.

There are numerous indications, however, that the Party had limited success in its efforts to rally support from moderates. One of the major problems was its ambiguous attitude toward the leading elements of existing social, political, and cultural organizations in South Vietnam. Many of these groups were strongly anti-Diemist in their inclinations and would seemingly have made good candidates for cooperation with the Communists in a common cause. On the surface, the Party leadership was conscious of this opportunity and instructed its urban apparatus in the South to maintain good relations with the leadership of such groups. The Party had never been comfortable in dealings with those over whom it had no control, however, and captured documents show that this tendency continued to bedevil its urban strategy. While paying lip service to the need to cultivate the leadership, party leaders often indicated that the prime duty was to extend the movement among the rank and file.[31]

A good example of this ambivalence can be seen in Communist relations with the Buddhist movement. Out of 14 million South Vietnamese, at least 10 million were Buddhists. Only about 6 million, however, actively practiced the religion. Traditionally, Buddhism had been loosely organized in Vietnam and under the French regime it had played little role in politics. Since independence, however, Buddhist monks had formed quasi-political Buddhist associations to protect and expand activities among the general population. Most famous was the An Quang Buddhist Association under Thich Tri Quang in Hué. How much support such associations had among the faithful is a matter of dispute. But in the early 1960s Tri Quang and a number of other Buddhist monks took the lead in building up opposition to the Diem government, which they perceived to be pro-Catholic, and briefly led an active movement among students, intellectuals, and townspeople throughout South Vietnam. Curiously, the Communists had little success in manipulating the movement and internal documents demonstrate that the Party viewed the association leadership as composed of petty bourgeois intellectuals preoccupied with Western liberal democratic attitudes and not particularly susceptible to Communist leadership. The party preferred to operate through the NLF-sponsored

Committee for the Safeguarding of Buddhism, which, though safely under the thumb of the movement, did not have the appeal of Tri Quang's organization.[32]

The Fall of the Diem Regime

For the moment, however, objective conditions were moving more quickly than the Party leadership, for Diem was his own worst enemy. By 1961 his dictatorial tendencies, his intolerance of opposition, and his persecution of those considered to be a danger to his rule created a political crisis in the cities. In the capital, the atmosphere became sullen and moderate politicians warned Diem that he must liberalize or face the prospect of open revolt. As is so often the case with an unpopular government, resentment focused on a key figure close to the pinnacle of authority who symbolized the reactionary and evil character of the regime. In Diem's case, that role was played by his brother and political counselor, Ngo Dinh Nhu. Saturnine in appearance and ruthless in behavior, Nhu became the Rasputin of the Saigon regime, the *éminence grise* who established a number of proto-Leninist political movements and mass organizations to mobilize popular support for the Diem government and provide a rival force to the local power of the Communists. Nhu's actions to stifle all opposition to the regime and his identification as the source of the government's brutal repression of rural discontent had earned him the hatred of thousands—perhaps millions—of Vietnamese. These feelings affected attitudes toward the president himself.

When such pent-up hostility and frustration break out into open opposition, they often do so with an explosive force that astonishes the world. And the catalytic force—what is often called the "accelerator" of a revolution—frequently originates with a minor incident that electrifies the soul of a society. Often it is an example of unnecessary brutality by the armed forces against the unarmed populace—a Bloody Sunday in Moscow in 1905 or the Kent State massacre in May 1970.

In the history of the Diem regime, that event was the harassment of the Buddhist demonstrators by ARVN forces in Hué in May 1963. The incident was relatively petty. From the beginning, Diem government policies had appeared to discriminate against the Buddhists while favoring the nation's 2 million Catholics, many of whom were staunchly anti-Communist refugees from the North. By early 1963, the Buddhist Association in Hué had become increasingly vociferous in its criticism of the regime and its policies. In response, government officials refused Buddhists the right to carry their flag in a march on a Buddhist holy day. Thousands demonstrated in protest and were put down by ARVN troops, with several casualties. When the news spread, protest riots broke out in Saigon. Diem refused to make a conciliatory gesture, and, when the protests began to take on a clearly antigovernment character, ARVN military forces raided the major pagodas in Saigon and arrested several bonzes in a display of brutality. Public opinion was outraged, and, when a Buddhist monk protested by setting himself afire on a public street in downtown Saigon, the reaction against the regime's actions reached worldwide proportions.[33]

In Washington, the crisis in South Vietnam posed an awkward dilemma for the Kennedy administration. There had been some qualified optimism that the situation in South Vietnam was improving. Now it was apparent that the crux of the problem was in Saigon, and during the summer Washington made clear its disapproval of the recent policies of the Diem regime.[34] In response Diem threatened to open negotiations with the NLF and to send the U.S. advisers home. In midsummer, the crisis escalated. As Buddhist discontent rose to a fever pitch, unrest began to surface in the ranks of the army. Several top Saigon military figures began to discuss a possible coup to overthrow the Ngos and bring a military government to power. The Kennedy administration, apprised of the situation, at first hesitated, but, as the political situation continued to deteriorate in early fall, it finally flashed its approval: If Diem were to be overthrown, Washington would offer its support to a new military government.

Diem was deposed in an almost bloodless coup on the night of November 3. Refusing an offer of protection by the United States, he took refuge in a church in Cholon. Early the following morning he was arrested and with his brother Ngo Dinh Nhu assassinated by his captors en route from Cholon to Saigon. In place of the now universally detested Diem regime, a new Military Revolutionary Council, chaired by the charismatic but politically indecisive general Duong Van Minh, took power.[35]

The overthrow of Ngo Dinh Diem must have been greeted in Hanoi with mixed feelings. To a certain extent, it was a bonus for the revolution. Whatever his weaknesses, Diem had been a staunch anti-Communist and a symbol of South Vietnam's fierce determination to resist a Communist victory. His overthrow validated Hanoi's long-standing claim that the Diem government was rotten to the core and lacked popular support. It also confirmed the existence of a continuing high degree of political factionalism and instability in Saigon.

Yet Diem's overthrow also presented problems for the insurgency. For the time being at least, the new military government basked in the warmth of national popularity. Ngo Dinh Diem had been a symbol of much that was wrong in South Vietnamese society, and now that he had fallen, those who had caused his overthrow were welcomed as heroes. As for Duong Van Minh, he was a southerner, and although many suspected that his taciturn and relaxed demeanor disguised mediocre talents, he was, at least momentarily, the most popular figure in the South.

At first, Hanoi appeared uncertain how to treat the new government. In the first few days following the coup, it attempted to test the government's will to resist the revolutionary forces, perhaps in the hope that a revolutionary uprising might succeed during the chaos following the coup in Saigon. Around the country, Communist-inspired incidents rose by 50 percent compared to the period prior to the coup and Western intelligence sources remarked on a rise in the rate of infiltration from the North. At first, the new government seemed to lack the will and the resources to respond, leading U.S. Secretary of Defense Robert McNamara, in a brief stab of pessimism, to warn that if current trends were not reversed in two to three months, the Communists might be able to seize power in Saigon.[36] By December, however, ARVN forces had begun to respond more vigorously and the pressure slackened. Hanoi now began to send out peace feelers to the new government. But with the promise of continued U.S. support, Minh and his colleagues were determined to continue the fight, and when they turned down Hanoi's offers the NLF formally announced that the struggle would go on.

The Ninth Plenum of December 1963

In December of 1963, the Ninth Plenum of the VWP Central Committee convened in Hanoi. By all indications, it was a stormy meeting. According to Le Duan, it took several days of debates before the committee approved the resolution drafted earlier by the Party Politburo. The events in the South had created the need for a new perspective on the war. Diem's failures and the massive hostility that he had incurred at home and abroad had been the prime source of Saigon's weakness and the greatest source of optimism in Hanoi that victory could be achieved without a massive military effort. With his fall and a new government riding the crest of a wave of popularity, the vision of a general uprising to bring the revolutionary forces to power inevitably began to fade. Worse yet, the conviction in Hanoi that the United States would accept the logic of defeat and withdraw from South Vietnam now appeared to be a miscalculation. Indeed, U.S. support for the new government had been immediately affirmed, and when President Kennedy was assassinated in November, his successor Lyndon Johnson seemed to show even less interest in U.S. disengagement from the conflict.

Such factors did not fail to influence the revolutionary movement in South Vietnam. Disillusionment and pessimism began to infect the rank and file, and U.S. sources reported a significant rise in the rate of desertions from revolutionary units.[37] Support for the NLF and its related organizations also showed a decline. With the Ngos removed from power, much of the revolutionary ferment that had been gradually building up in Vietnam began rapidly to dissipate.

It was now increasingly clear to Party leaders in Hanoi that victory in the South would not come without a long and probably costly effort. The early optimism that a high level of military confrontation would not be required had now been replaced by the grim conviction that only armed struggle involving the mobilized force of the D.R.V. in the North would lead to success. The decision was momentous: The Ninth Plenum decided to respond to the challenge and escalate the level of armed violence in the South. According to the resolution approved at the close of the conference, the immediate task was to strengthen the PLAF in order to effect a basic change in the balance of forces in the South. The resolution talked in general terms of the need to improve the coordination of military and political forms of struggle, but it was the need for an expansion of the armed might of the revolution that emerged most clearly:

> Now [that] we are stronger than the enemy politically, we must continue to strengthen our political forces. However, we are still weaker than the enemy militarily. Therefore *the key point at the present time is to make outstanding efforts to rapidly strengthen our military forces in order to create a basic change in the balance of forces between the enemy and us in South Vietnam.*

The reasoning had been expressed earlier by Vo Nguyen Giap in his own military writings and now was repeated in the resolution:

> If we do not defeat the enemy's military forces, we cannot overthrow his domination and bring the revolution to victory. To destroy the enemy's military forces, we should use armed struggle. *For this reason, armed struggle plays a direct and decisive role.*[38]

Only with armed struggle, said the resolution, could the prestige and position of the masses be brought fully into play.

The committee was quick to state that the decision to escalate the level of violence in the South did not mean that it was discarding existing tactics and strategy in their entirety. The war would continue to be protracted in character, with victory to be achieved "step by step." Base areas, the three types of military forces, and the concept of the three key regions continued to have immediate relevance to the revolution. But there was an increasing conviction that the revolution in the South, like its predecessor, would gradually escalate into a military confrontation involving large-scale units. This belief necessitated a revision in the Party's view of the culminating stage of the revolution. Instead of a Maoist general offensive, or a general uprising in the tradition of the August Revolution, the committee now accepted the view expressed by the author of the CRIMP document that the war "would inevitably evolve into a general offensive and uprising to achieve the complete victory." There was no specific reference to the three stages of Maoist people's war, which may indicate that the concept was then considered somewhat too rigid to reflect the complexities of the Vietnamese revolution, but the new approach nevertheless coincided in some respects with the strategy used in the past. Although the new strategy was more flexible than the Maoist model it replaced, it still called for a gradual movement from low-level warfare to the use of large mobile forces, a clear reflection of Giap's view that only mobile or positional warfare could annihilate the main forces of the enemy. The final stage similarly represented a resurrection of Ho Chi Minh's strategy during the August Revolution—a military offensive in rural areas combined with a popular uprising in the cities, leading to the final seizure of power. There was only one break in the litany of militancy in the resolution: "There is the possibility that the South Vietnam Revolution must go through a transitional period which entails complex forms and methods of struggling before it attains the final victory," an obvious allusion to the possibility of a negotiated settlement.

Anticipating comparisons with the strategy used during the war against the French, the resolution was at pains to point out that the new situation was different in a number of respects. Then, it said, early successes had come only from the insurgents' "burgeoning capabilities." Only after 1949 did the Vietminh have a strong rear and favorable international conditions. Now, on the contrary, there were several factors assuring success: a strong base in the North, a favorable world situation, and a weak GVN. The Saigon government, it pointed out, was not a strong government born of a successful national liberation movement (presumably a reference to such Asian governments as Sukarno's in Indonesia, U Nu's in Burma, or that of the Congress Party in India), but a reactionary government supported only by feudal and comprador bourgeois elements and reliant on U.S. support.

Confrontation with Moscow

Behind all of the Party's assumptions about the past and future course of the revolution in the South lay one crucial and unanswered question: How would the United States respond? Would it react to the challenge by raising the level of its own involvement or, as the Party had hoped before the fall of the Diem regime, would it accept a compromise settlement and withdraw its advisers? Hanoi was certainly not unaware of the importance of the question and in the resolution referred to two possibilities: Either U.S. involvement in the conflict could be contained within the framework of the "special war" (Hanoi's term for the Kennedy administration's counterinsurgency strategy) or Washington could decide to change the terms of the conflict and send U.S. and possibly third-country troops, thus raising the level of conflict to a limited war. The Party obviously hoped for the former and cautiously suggested the possibility that the United States would accept defeat, as it had in China, or a compromise settlement, as it had in Korea and, most recently, in Laos. But Hanoi conceded that Washington might decide to intervene in strength if it was convinced that escalation would increase the likelihood of a successful outcome, or if it was persuaded that the D.R.V. would be unable to react. The resolution dismissed this alternative as only a "remote possibility," on the grounds that the

United States would be unable to evaluate the consequences of such a decision. As Hanoi had only a limited capacity to influence U.S. foreign policy, it affected a fatalistic attitude: "Let us strive to deal with the first eventuality and prepare for the second." If the United States should decide to intervene, the revolution would have another obstacle to surmount, but it would still be victorious.

The issue was of double importance because it inevitably involved Hanoi's relations with Moscow. In recent years these relations had noticeably cooled as a result of Vietnamese disapproval of Soviet foreign policy decisions and Soviet concern over the possibility that the revolution in South Vietnam could escalate into a world crisis. The D.R.V. had opposed several of Khrushchev's decisions, including his backdown in the Cuban missile crisis, his decision to support India in the border war with China, and the signing of the Nuclear Test Ban Treaty with Washington. On issues of relevance to the socialist camp, the Vietnamese increasingly supported the Chinese position. Not surprisingly, Soviet aid levels began to drop and Chinese military assistance, although still limited in both quality and quantity, began to rise.[39]

The major issue, clearly, was Moscow's lack of support for the Vietnamese revolutionary cause in the South. For years Hanoi had carefully tailored its strategy to Soviet susceptibilities. Now, however, it was clearly growing restive. In the early summer of 1963, in an article in *Hoc tap*, General Nguyen Chi Thanh had referred pointedly to the issue:

> We do not have any illusions about the United States. We do not underestimate our opponent—the strong and cunning U.S. imperialism. But we are not afraid of the United States. . . . If, on the contrary, one is afraid of the United States and thinks that to offend it would court failure, and that firm opposition to United States imperialism would touch off a nuclear war, then the only course left would be to compromise with and surrender to United States imperialism.[40]

An anonymous article in the September issue of the same journal quoted Lenin on the unlikelihood of a peaceful accession to power and contended that nuclear weapons did not diminish the importance of wars of national liberation, citing China, Cuba, and Vietnam as examples of successful revolutionary struggles since the advent of the nuclear age.

The decision at the Ninth Plenum to escalate the struggle obviously raised the possibility of further antagonizing the Soviet Union. With Moscow's backing so crucial to the success of the Vietnamese effort in the South, it is probable that moderate elements within the leadership urged their colleagues to avoid a serious rupture with the Party's longest and closest ally and supporter. The care with which the Party reassured Soviet leaders emerges clearly from the resolution. The basic goal of the Vietnamese revolution was "to restrict the war within the framework of South Vietnam and to defeat the enemy on the main battlefield." Even if Washington decided to intervene in the struggle, it said,

"The possibility that a limited war in South Vietnam would turn into a world war is almost non-existent because the purpose and significance of this war cannot generate conditions leading to a world war," an obvious reference to the fact that Vietnam was peripheral to U.S. (or Soviet) security interests.

Yet Hanoi was clearly conscious that Moscow would find it difficult to agree, and probably for this reason it published a treatise entitled "The World Situation and Our Party's International Mission," which provided a detailed defense of Hanoi's strategy in the South in terms of its effect on the international environment.[41] The statement, which was probably distributed to all world Communist parties, attempted to assuage Soviet fears that the Vietnamese revolution could lead to a wider war and pleaded for heightened support by socialist countries for wars of national liberation in the Third World. Claiming that the concept of peaceful coexistence is something that exists between different systems, not between oppressors and the oppressed within a given society, the statement asserted that peaceful coexistence and revolutionary struggle were interdependent, not contradictory. Experience proves, it said, that it is an illusion to believe that power can be seized by peaceful means. It asserted that "the national liberation movement alone—the content of which is the people's national democratic revolution—can help the nations achieve complete independence."

In January Le Duan, accompanied by Le Duc Tho and the poet To Huu, made a brief visit to the USSR to present Hanoi's views on the escalating war in the South. Apparently the talks did not change opinions in Moscow. The communiqué issued after the close of the talks was vague and suggested continued disagreement. Although the Soviet Union promised "resolute support" for the Vietnamese struggle, the talks were described merely as a "frank and useful exchange of views."[42] Nor did the Vietnamese show signs of backing down. An article in the January issue of *Hoc tap* reiterated points made in the December statement and called on socialist countries to take the offensive against world imperialism.

The rift with Moscow, and the magnitude of the decision at the December plenum, undoubtedly exacerbated existing tensions within the Party leadership over strategy in the South. In a speech presented at the plenum and reprinted in *Hoc tap* the following February, Le Duan conceded that "a few of our Party members, the majority of whom are intellectuals" were doubtful of the ability of their leaders to understand complex problems of Marxism-Leninism and international affairs. Presumably this statement referred to those who were reluctant to ignore Soviet advice on the global situation. Duan defended the Party leadership vigorously on this point and pointedly remarked that "it is the CCP headed by Comrade Mao Tse-tung which has carried out most satisfactorily the instructions of the great Lenin," an unmistakable reference to the fact that Peking, not Moscow, had expressed full support for the struggle for national liberation in Vietnam. Duan also criticized unnamed "honest Marxists" who disparaged Maoist concepts and ridiculed them as populist.[43]

For the time being, then, Hanoi had shifted perceptibly toward China. As later events would show, however, the decision was taken for the tactical purposes of maximizing support for the Vietnamese revolution and was not the result of a victory of pro-Chinese elements within the Party leadership. In fact, if recent disclosures on the course of Sino-Vietnamese relations can be believed, those (such as Le Duan and presumably Vo Nguyen Giap) who engineered the shift had harbored deep suspicions of Chinese motives since the CCP's rise to power in 1949. According to the 1979 White Paper, Party leaders had long suspected that Peking's long-term objective in assisting the Vietnamese liberation movement was to keep Vietnam weak and divided in order to restore China's paramount influence in Indochina. Hanoi's motives in publishing such claims may be open to question (they are clearly related to the tensions that emerged from the 1979 Sino-Vietnamese conflict), but the White Paper clearly suggests that ideological affinity had not substantially reduced Vietnam's historic distrust of Chinese policy in Southeast Asia. Peking, in turn, did little to allay such fears. While granting substantial assistance to Hanoi, it persistently tied its Vietnam policy to the course of the Sino-Soviet dispute. In the summer of 1964, Teng Hsiao-p'ing offered a massive aid program to Hanoi on the condition that the latter reject future assistance from Moscow. Hanoi refused. A year later, when the Soviet Union proposed a cooperative effort to assist the D.R.V., Peking rebuffed the proposal.[44]

To many observers, Hanoi's decision to escalate was somewhat of a puzzle. Given the risks of U.S. intervention and the progressive disintegration of the GVN, why did the Party feel compelled to take the gamble? One reason appears to be Hanoi's reading of the American mood and intentions. Recent history suggested that the best way to persuade Washington to disengage would be to create a further deterioration in the situation in the South. After all, the United States had withdrawn from China in the late 1940s under similar circumstances and later had accepted negotiated settlements in Korea and Laos. If Washington could be brought to realize that the situation in Saigon was beyond repair, it might be willing to accept a political settlement or a simple withdrawal of the U.S. presence. But this must be achieved quickly and forcefully. If the Vietnam crisis were allowed to drift without a decisive resolution, the danger of U.S. escalation would increase. Consequently, a determined effort to overturn or at least seriously weaken the Saigon regime in a relatively short period was vital.

A second possible factor leading to the decision was the inherited experience of the Party in leading the Vietnamese revolutionary movement. Since the colonial period, the Party had learned by bitter experience the truth of Mao Tse-tung's famous dictum that power grows out of the barrel of a gun. It was the massed power of the armed forces, combined with the political violence of the aroused masses, more than peaceful struggle, compromise, and negotiations, that had led to the inexorable advance of the revolution. Although there had undoubtedly been a period after the Geneva Conference when the Party had hoped for a political solution to the crisis, there may well have been an underlying conviction among a number of veteran leaders of the Party, such as Le Duan, Vo Nguyen Giap, Le Duc Tho, and perhaps Ho Chi Minh himself, that armed struggle would ultimately be the key to victory. Giap, for one, had expressed this view in *People's War, People's Army* when he had asserted that the escalation of a guerrilla war into a mobile war was a "general law" of revolutionary wars, as only when the military forces of the enemy had been annihilated could complete victory be achieved. Now, in 1964, he returned to the issue. In an article entitled "The South Vietnamese People Will Win," he commented:

> At the price of their hard-won experiences, our compatriots in the South realized that the fundamental trend of imperialism and its lackeys is violence and war; that is why *the most correct path to be followed by the peoples to liberate themselves is revolutionary violence and revolutionary war.* . . . Only by revolutionary violence can the masses defeat aggressive imperialism and its lackeys and overthrow the reactionary administration to take power.[45]

This sentiment was echoed in an article in the July 1964 issue of *Hoc tap*, which said that the path of negotiations and concessions was not the path to consolidate power. Revolution can and should be settled "only by the use of revolutionary acts and the force of the masses to defeat the enemy forces."[46] Such militant views might be passed off as mere revolutionary rhetoric by an advocate of revolutionary violence or as a rationalization of the failure to achieve rapid victory through political means, but it is nonetheless likely that the Party viewed a military victory as more clear-cut and thus less subject to complexity than a triumph achieved by political means.

The Battlefield Solution

Throughout the next several months, the Party's apparatus in the South attempted to carry out the objectives established by the Central Committee in Hanoi. According to a resolution issued by COSVN early in 1964, the revolutionary forces were to intensify their efforts to change the balance of forces in South Vietnam and prepare for a general offensive and uprising to lead to a complete victory. Control over the strategic Central Highlands was to be consolidated, and PLAF attacks were to be extended gradually into the crucial lowland areas in order to tighten the noose around the neck of the Saigon regime. Main force units should be strengthened so that they would be capable of launching attacks at company and battalion level to disperse and wear down the enemy. In general, Hanoi's decision to escalate was a glittering success. During 1964 the areas under the control of revolutionary forces expanded significantly. A stable liberated zone, extending from the plateau regions of the Central Highlands to the fringes of the Mekong delta, gradually began to emerge. According to virtually all observers, by the end of the year the Communists controlled half the population and more than half the total land area of South Vietnam. The only reasonably secure areas for the GVN—and even that was being brought into question—were in and around the major cities.[47]

As the liberated areas expanded, the size of the PLAF also increased rapidly. It was now spearheaded by an estimated thirty to forty-five main force battalions, supplemented by 35,000 guerrillas and 80,000 irregulars. Part of this expansion came from a rise in the rate of infiltration. Although the precise figure is controversial, there was a clear rise in the movement of D.R.V. units into South Vietnam during the year, facilitated by the completion of the so-called Ho Chi Minh trail through southern Laos. Regular units of the People's Army of Vietnam (PAVN) began preparing to move to the South as early as April, and according to U.S. intelligence sources the first complete tactical unit left the North in October and arrived in the South two months later.[48] While southerners were recruited into the PLAF in increasingly large numbers, the percentage of infiltrators within the movement was on the rise, a sign of the increasing commitment of the North to the struggle in South Vietnam. As before, the disciplined and indoctrinated northerners frequently held leading positions in the PLAF and the NLF, raising the potential of regional tensions within the movement.

As the level of combat rose, ARVN losses increased from 1,000 a month at the beginning of the year to more than 3,000 in December. Signs of the disintegration of government authority were everywhere in the countryside. In the Central Highlands, despite a U.S. effort to solidify minority support for the GVN, discontent rose to fever pitch in the early autumn. The United States had set up special forces camps in the area to train minority tribesmen and enroll them in self-defense units called Civilian Irregular Defense Groups (CIDG). But when during the summer responsibility for the groups was turned over to the ARVN at Saigon's insistence, Vietnamese arrogance led immediately to problems, and in September a serious revolt broke out among Rhadé tribesmen in Ban Me Thuot. Only with the aid of U.S. advisers was the crisis defused.

In the lowland provinces, there were equally ominous developments. With the GVN weakening, the momentum of the Strategic Hamlet Program ground to a halt. Attacks on government-controlled villages increased, and the coastal provinces south of Da Nang once again became contested areas. There were signs in Saigon of an impending offensive on the capital area. According to William Colby, then chief of the Far Eastern Section of the Central Intelligence Agency, the Communists now held the initiative throughout South Vietnam. GVN morale was down, and little progress against the insurgents was being achieved.[49]

General William Westmoreland, the new commander of the U.S. Military Assistance Command in South Vietnam (MACV), attempted to strengthen GVN security by assisting ARVN forces in mounting a coordinated offensive to relieve the pressure on the capital. Labeled Operation Hop Tac (Cooperation), it involved a concerted military offensive by units of the ARVN Fifth Division against Communist-held areas in provinces surrounding Saigon. Once an area had been cleared, pacification operations would begin, with U.S. civilian advisers helping to provide schools, dispensaries, and other services to the area.[50]

Crisis in Saigon

Sensing impending victory, the Communist leadership began to plan for heightened operations in the cities, particularly in Saigon. The Ninth Plenum had called for increased efforts by the Party apparatus in urban areas to prepare for a future general uprising to accompany the final surge to victory. One French scholar cited information that the Party now attempted to infiltrate numerous cadres from rural areas into Saigon to prepare for a "battle of the cities," which would involve "new and complex tactics." A major aspect of activity would be to strengthen the Party's secret apparatus and to train assassination and sabotage squads to commit acts of individual terrorism against Americans and American installations in the city. According to one captured document, Party strategists assumed that such attacks could seriously undermine American morale and speed departure of the United States from South Vietnam.[51]

Adding to the security problems caused by Viet Cong activities was the growing political crisis in Saigon. After the brief surge of popular enthusiasm brought about by the fall of Diem, the new government lapsed rapidly into incompetence and the Military Revolutionary Council soon fell apart. Throughout 1964 and into 1965, a series of coups led by diverse military and civilian figures impeded U.S. efforts to restore orderly civilian government. Feeding on the instability at the top, a situation of near-anarchy emerged in Saigon. A sense of malaise sparked by growing disenchantment with the war infected all classes of urban society. Bitter riots broke out between Catholics and Buddhists in downtown areas of the city. To Hanoi, it must have appeared as if the long-awaited opportunity for the general uprising was at hand.

In an effort to take advantage of the situation, Party leaders called for an increased effort to expand the political base of the movement through alliances with anti-American and anti-GVN political forces and with democratic and patriotic personalities not normally inclined to cooperate with the NLF. Clearly a major target of this effort would be the Buddhist movement led by Tri Quang, even though his movement was viewed as politically reactionary and as infiltrated by enemy agents.[52] As before, however, the Party's Saigon apparatus appeared unable to put theory into practice. A captured document entitled "Problems of Party Leadership and Party Slogans in Urban Centers" provides some insight into this problem. According to the author, by late 1964 the objective conditions for a revolution had appeared in Saigon, but the Party's municipal leadership was accused of having "fuzzy concepts" with regard to the urban struggle. The failure to deal effectively with the Buddhist movement was specifically cited. Claiming that it should be possible to rally the Buddhist leadership to the side of the revolution, the author complained that, "generally speaking, we have not been positive in leading the movement." Whether knowingly or not, he pointed to the source of the problem, conceding that the Buddhist elites were bourgeois in their inclinations, compromising by nature, lacked a mass base, and were ambivalent about the revolution. The local leadership, he admitted, faced a difficult problem in reconciling the divergent revolutionary goals of rallying moderates and mobilizing the popular masses.[53] To Hanoi's consternation, major political forces in Saigon continued to elude the Party's control.

Throughout 1964 the Johnson administration attempted to deal with the rising crisis in South Vietnam without fundamentally changing the terms of the conflict. Soon after his accession to the presidency, Johnson had made it clear that he was not interested in disengagement or in a "Laotian solution" to the war. According to one source, Johnson insisted that he was determined to avoid a repetition of the China episode of the 1940s.[54] On the other hand, the administration was reluctant to raise its military commitment to its client state in Saigon. With 1964 a presidential election year, it was a dangerous time for foreign policy initiatives.

Johnson did try to take a tough line while avoiding a major escalation of the conflict. In August, the Tonkin Gulf crisis erupted when Communist naval craft fired on U.S. warships off the North Vietnamese coast. In retaliation, Johnson approved air strikes on naval bases in the D.R.V., a move the Joint Chiefs of Staff had been urging for several weeks. He also obtained congressional support for a Tonkin Gulf Resolution, which gave the president the power "to take all necessary measures to repel any armed attack against the forces of the United States and to prevent further aggression."

There was only a glimmer of light beyond the threatening clouds of war. During the summer, Hanoi approved a Soviet proposal to reconvene the Geneva Conference. In October, UN Secretary General U Thant suggested secret talks between Hanoi and Washington and reported that the D.R.V. leadership had indicated to him its willingness to meet U.S. representatives in Rangoon. For nearly six months, there was no response from Washington. Administration spokesmen later claimed that there were indications from other sources that Hanoi was not seriously interested in negotiations. The Canadian representative of the International Control Commission had visited Hanoi in late summer and was told by Prime Minister Pham Van Dong that unless the United

States withdrew from Vietnam and ended all support to the GVN, there would be nothing to negotiate about.[55] On that basis, U.S. officials had assumed that the peace initiative was nothing but a propaganda gesture and did not bother to explore it further.

It is doubtful, in any case, that Hanoi was serious. Given the political and military situation in South Vietnam, it was obviously preferable to await probable further deterioration of the GVN, which could lead, at most, to an outright victory through a general offensive and uprising or, at the least, to a negotiated settlement highly advantageous to the D.R.V. It is likely that Hanoi had responded to the Soviet proposal only to avoid provoking its ally. The previously cited article in the midsummer issue of *Hoc tap* had taken a militant stance on negotiations, and, when Moscow invited the D.R.V. to send a representative to present its case to the Security Council, the offer was rejected by Hanoi.

The Fall of Khrushchev

U.S. reprisals against North Vietnam in August and the threat of a wider war in the South had made the question of Hanoi's relations with the Soviet Union more crucial than ever. The increase in aid from the P.R.C. was welcome, but China could not provide the sophisticated weaponry that would be needed if Washington decided to launch sustained air attacks on D.R.V. territory. Soon after the Tonkin attacks, Hanoi approached Moscow for increased aid and Le Duan made a brief visit to Moscow in August, presumably for that purpose. Moscow, however, was still nervous about the potential for great power confrontation in South Vietnam and, contending that the insurgency forces were in a strong position in the South, suggested negotiations. It was probably in an effort to obtain Moscow's commitment to heightened military aid that Hanoi accepted the Soviet proposal to join a reconvened Geneva conference.

In late October, Hanoi's dilemma was resolved with Nikita Khrushchev's fall from power in Moscow. Whether the removal of the Soviet Party chief was related to the Vietnam crisis is uncertain. What does seem clear is that the power shift in the USSR led to a change in Soviet policy toward the conflict in Vietnam. In late October, three weeks after the accession to power of the new joint leadership of Leonid Brezhnev and Alexander Kosygin, Pham Van Dong went to Moscow, ostensibly to attend the forty-seventh anniversary of the Bolshevik Revolution. The new Soviet leadership, apparently less fearful of offending the United States and anxious to prevent a closer Vietnamese relationship with Peking, promised to increase its military assistance to Hanoi and pledged to support the D.R.V. if it were attacked by the United States. One source notes that Moscow agreed to support a general offensive in the South if the United States continued to refuse meaningful negotiations. For its part,

Hanoi apparently agreed to stop its criticism of Soviet foreign policy and to make every effort to keep the war from spreading beyond South Vietnam. In the words of one captured document, Hanoi promised Moscow that it would "harmonize" the interests of the Vietnamese revolution "with those of the international proletariat."[56] The NLF set up a permanent mission in Moscow, and plans were made for a formal visit by Prime Minister Kosygin to Hanoi early in 1965. At least for the moment, the Party had won firm support of its policies in South Vietnam from the most powerful country in the socialist camp.

By the end of 1964, the crisis in South Vietnam was rapidly approaching what the Party frequently called "a mature revolutionary situation." In the capital, political anarchy marked the virtual demise of the GVN. In rural areas, the strength of insurgency forces was reflected in the change in the nature of combat with government units. In the final days of the year, a Viet Cong main force unit at regimental strength, armed with Soviet AK-47 automatic rifles, assaulted an ARVN ranger battalion in sustained combat near Binh Gia, a Catholic village about forty miles east of Saigon. In a week-long battle, the attackers inflicted heavy casualties on the government troops. Similar attacks took place near the Cambodian border and in the Central Highlands. The disintegration of ARVN forces appeared to accelerate, and there were reports that local commanders were making "live and let live" agreements with Viet Cong forces in the vicinity. To the Party leadership in Hanoi, the "battle of Binh Gia" was conclusive proof that the U.S. "special war" had gone down to ignominious defeat; it also symbolized the rising strength of the revolutionary forces. Operation Hop Tac, designed to clear out insurgency forces in the capital area, had been a severe disappointment and failed to stem the rising tide of revolutionary activities in the villages around Saigon. In a postmortem, General Westmoreland offered a variety of explanations: The government units lacked troops and aggressive leadership, local forces were too weak, and funding was lacking for pacification improvements.[57]

For the Communists, the situation in the South was evolving so rapidly that the Party was clearly having difficulty making the necessary adjustments. A year-end assessment issued by COSVN military headquarters, although generally optimistic about the situation, noted that the PLAF was not sufficiently prepared and did not possess adequate military strength to impose a direct defeat on the enemy. This cautious estimate was confirmed a year later in a letter written by a top Party official in early 1966 and later captured. This letter stated categorically that the Saigon regime had reached near-collapse so quickly that the southern movement "had not yet acquired adequate conditions to cope with the rapid development of the situation, and to make the puppet army disintegrate in a basic and irretrievable manner."[58] For once, despite its efforts, the Party had been unable to rise to the challenge. In a later moment of reflection, Le Duan confessed that the war had developed even more rapidly than Hanoi had anticipated.

Conclusion

By the end of 1964, for the second time in less than twenty years, the Communists approached the portals of victory. The Johnson administration, in an effort to justify its decision to escalate U.S. involvement, would contend that South Vietnam was the victim of armed aggression from the North. Clearly the revolution in the South was directed from Hanoi, and by the mid-1960s D.R.V. participation had become a major factor in the conflict. But Washington's claim of outside intervention, however justified by the course of future events, could not disguise the fact that the primary source of the revolutionary ferment in the South lay in the political weakness of the Saigon regime and the popularity of the revolutionary cause in the South. The decision of the Kennedy administration to increase its involvement complicated the problem for Hanoi and compelled it to resort to a higher level of revolutionary war, but it did not substantially resolve the underlying political problems in the GVN or arrest the seemingly inexorable slide of the South toward communism.

War of Attrition
(1965–1968)

Until early in 1965, a succession of U.S. presidents had maneuvered successfully to avoid being faced with the ultimate question in U.S. Vietnam policy: What was to be done if the GVN could not hold? It was Lyndon Johnson's misfortune that under his presidency it became clear that the crisis could no longer be contained without substantially increased U.S. involvement. With near-chaos in Saigon and the specter of military collapse in the countryside, Maxwell Taylor, the new U.S. ambassador in Saigon, reported that unless Washington took some action, South Vietnam would meet defeat "in the fairly near future."[1]

The Party leadership had hoped that when the severity of the crisis in South Vietnam had reached this point Washington would withdraw or opt for negotiations and a compromise settlement. But as Hanoi would now discover, such hopes were seriously misplaced. Unlike his predecessor, Lyndon Johnson was not plagued by doubts about the wisdom of U.S. involvement in Vietnam. Haunted by memories of the Chinese Civil War, Johnson was determined that there be no repetition of that defeat under his presidency. To prevent the further decay of the security of the free world in Southeast Asia, the United States must act to defeat the insurgency in South Vietnam.

Lyndon Johnson's tough attitude was shared by many of the advisers he inherited from the Kennedy administration, including Secretary of State Dean Rusk, who was convinced that the United States should respond tit-for-tat to any Communist challenge in Southeast Asia. Although there were still figures within the administration who harbored doubts about the advisability of committing U.S. prestige irrevocably to the survival of the Saigon regime, Johnson was not tolerant of dissenting views among his foreign policy advisers, and after 1965 their voices were rarely heard at the top levels of power.[2]

It was easier to agree on the need to respond than on how to respond. There was, in fact, no clear consensus within the administration over how to deal with the rapidly deteriorating situation in Southeast Asia. Some, concerned with the adverse trends in force levels between the GVN and the NLF, felt that

increased U.S. involvement should take the form of the introduction of combat troops. Although statistics were lacking, it was firmly believed in
Washington that infiltration from the North was rapidly rising and that for the
first time fully armed units of the PAVN were included in the number. ARVN
forces were still superior in numbers, but the recruitment of additional troops
would be increasingly difficult because of the high level of draft evasion and the
twenty-year-old age limitation. Moreover, the vast majority of ARVN forces
were tied down in static defense positions connected with the pacification program. Some counterinsurgency experts maintained that it would require a ratio
of ten to one in favor of the government forces to control the insurgency, and the
GVN simply did not possess the manpower to establish such a superiority.[3]
The addition of U.S. troops would both stiffen the backbone of the Saigon
regime and release the ARVN for more effective pacification operations in the
countryside. Among those in Washington who advocated such a course was
the president himself. Others, including Ambassador Taylor and MACV commander Westmoreland in Saigon, were initially reluctant to introduce U.S.
fighting units into South Vietnam in the belief that such a move might
stimulate antiforeign sentiment and a tendency to let the United States "carry
the ball."[4]

One alternative to the injection of U.S. combat forces into South Vietnam
was a policy of sustained air strikes against military and industrial targets in the
D.R.V. According to advocates of such a course, there were a variety of possible benefits: It would reduce the infiltration of men and supplies into the
South; it would raise morale in Saigon; it would punish Hanoi and
demonstrate that the North could not hope to support the insurgency effort in
the South cost-free.[5] Another possibility raised was the creation of an international force to be stationed along the Demilitarized Zone and westward into
Laos in order to prevent infiltration. The subject was raised by the president in
December 1964, but because it would take considerable time to implement, it
was not followed up.

Early in February 1965 a U.S. military installation at Pleiku in the Central
Highlands was attacked by Viet Cong artillery, killing 8 Americans and
wounding 100 others. The incident took place while National Security Adviser
McGeorge Bundy was on a brief visit to South Vietnam, and he phoned the
White House from Saigon to recommend that the attack be used as a pretext
for a firm reprisal. Johnson approved, and, on the same day, U.S. fighter-
bombers launched an air strike against military barracks at Dong Hoi in the
D.R.V. panhandle. When the Communists retaliated with the bombing of a
U.S. noncommisioned officers' billet at Qui Nhon, killing 23 American ser-
vicemen, additional air strikes followed. On February 13, the president announced Operation Rolling Thunder, described as "a program of measured and
limited air actions" against military targets in the D.R.V. south of the 19th

parallel. Beginning with three or four strikes per week, the operation gradually developed into a series of sustained attacks launched without announcement.

In South Vietnam, ARVN losses continued at a dangerously high level. According to General Westmoreland, South Vietnamese forces were suffering casualties at a rate of almost an infantry battalion a week. Air strikes by U.S. B-52s against enemy areas in Zone D had some effect but were "not sufficient to reverse the course of the war." The situation was particularly bad in northern I Corps and in the Central Highlands, where there were signs of a possible Communist offensive to cut the country in two, reminiscent of the Vietminh attacks against French forces in 1953 and 1954. The situation was nearly as fragile in Saigon, where one government followed another in an almost farcical game of political musical chairs.

At MACV headquarters in Saigon, General Westmoreland was increasingly pessimistic. He had felt that air strikes against the D.R.V. could not resolve the crisis in the South but had acquiesced in the policy for lack of an alternative. By March he concluded that the GVN could not survive the enemy's mounting military and political offensive for more than six months unless the United States increased its military commitment. In a blunt report to Washington, he declared that, if present trends continued, "We are headed for a VC takeover of the country," probably within a year.[6] Westmoreland concluded that there was no alternative to the introduction of U.S. combat units.

Westmoreland's Strategy

Westmoreland's immediate hope was to break the tide of Communist advance and provide a minimum of security to highly populated areas. To do this he had to bolster shaky ARVN defenses in the north and in the Central Highlands and to prevent a possible Communist assault on Saigon. A secondary but ultimately vital concern was to stem the flow of infiltration into South Vietnam from the D.R.V. To meet these objectives, in March he requested two battalions of Marines to protect the airfield at Da Nang, on the central coast. Shortly thereafter he requested that a U.S. army unit be stationed at Bien Hoa, north of Saigon, and that a second at division strength bolster the GVN position in the Central Highlands.

Westmoreland was not content to restrict U.S. efforts to shoring up ARVN defenses. During the spring he devised a three-stage plan to reverse the Communist advance and lead to complete victory in South Vietnam. During the first stage, which was to last through the end of 1965, the objective was to secure populated areas, stifle the enemy's initiative, and halt the downward trend in the war. Then, during the dry season in early 1966, U.S. forces, assisted by ARVN units, would launch major "search and destroy" offensives in high-priority areas to break the hold of the Viet Cong in the countryside. If the enemy persisted after that point, a final stage would be required to destroy the enemy within one or one and one-half years after completion of the second stage.[7] In the early stages, the basic objective would be to cut off enemy sources of food, men, and weapons. Marines would be responsible for offensive operations in the northern provinces (in GVN military parlance, I Corps), while army units would take the lead in the Central Highlands and along the central coast (II Corps) and in the provinces around Saigon (III Corps). No U.S. forces would be stationed in the Mekong delta (IV Corps), partly because enemy operations were limited in that area, and partly because of GVN reluctance to station U.S. forces in heavily populated provinces.

The first detachment of marines, a total of about 3,500 men, landed on the beaches of Central Vietnam north of Da Nang in early March. Although their basic mission was to protect U.S. installations at the airbase in Da Nang, they were gradually drawn into a more active role in the countryside. Shortly afterwards, the First Cavalry (Airmobile) Division arrived at Qui Nhon, where Westmoreland hoped to use it to stop a predicted Communist effort to cut South Vietnam in half. Westmoreland intended to deploy these army units at An Khe, on Route 19 leading to the Central Highlands, but this forward strategy did not receive universal approval from U.S. policymakers. Ambassador Taylor continued to be reluctant to engage U.S. combat units in overt operations against Communist forces and preferred to restrict U.S. activities to the coastal areas. At first, Lyndon Johnson followed Taylor's recommendation, but at a meeting in Honolulu with Secretary of Defense Robert McNamara in April, Westmoreland was able to obtain approval of a strategy that called for the introduction of more than 75,000 U.S. troops to secure base areas, leading to a series of deep probes to disrupt enemy control in the countryside.[8]

By summer, the pace of battle had begun to quicken. The revolutionary forces continued to hold the initiative in confrontations with the ARVN, particularly in southern I Corps, much of II Corps, and in the districts north of Saigon. Several district capitals had been abandoned, and Western sources feared that the entire Central Highlands could fall before the onset of the winter dry season. Throughout the country security was increasingly tenuous as transportation and communication lines were being cut. But by now, Westmoreland was ready to make his move. In June, in response to a series of attacks at Song Be and Dong Xoai in Phuoc Long Province northwest of Saigon, a U.S. airborne brigade, assisted by ARVN and Australian units, launched a short thrust into Zone D to throw the enemy off balance and provide protection for the U.S. air base at Bien Hoa. As Westmoreland noted later, it was the first assault into that Communist base area in several years.

The first open confrontation between U.S. and Viet Cong forces took place south of Da Nang, on the Batagnan peninsula on the central coast. Marine units had established a base at Chu Lai, a few miles to the north, and soon discovered a Viet Cong regiment in the area, protected by a cluster of combat villages. To remove the threat, marine units launched a sweep operation complete with helicopters and an amphibious landing. In a week of heavy fighting, labeled by Hanoi the battle of Van Tuong, U.S. forces destroyed the combat villages and extensive tunnel complexes and killed more than 500 of the enemy. U.S. casualties were listed as 50 dead, with 150 wounded in action.[9]

But Westmoreland's chief area of concern during the summer of 1965 was the Central Highlands, where a major Communist offensive to strike to the coast and isolate the northern provinces from Saigon was anticipated. Westmoreland planned to use units of the First Cavalry Division at An Khe on Route 19 to anticipate the Viet Cong offensive and keep the highway open from the coast to the provincial capital of Pleiku. His plan was criticized by Admiral Grant Sharp at CINCPAC headquarters in Honolulu, who feared a repetition of the defeat of the French in the area in 1954. Westmoreland, however, was determined to prevent a Communist move onto the coastal plains of Binh Dinh and Phu Yen Provinces, where government pacification operations were under way, and was not to be dissuaded.

In October, two PAVN regiments attacked a special forces camp at Plei Me, not far from Pleiku in the northern sector of the Central Highlands, and then ambushed a relief column and put the special forces camp under siege, possibly the first step in a plan to destroy the three CIDG camps in the area and capture Pleiku. Westmoreland dispatched units of the First Cavalry Division to the area. They helped break the siege at Plei Me and then pursued Viet Cong forces into the hills. In November, U.S. units finally located three PAVN regiments in the Ia Drang valley, near the Cambodian border at the base of Chu Pong Mountain. After a week of bloody fighting, U.S. forces reported the killing of more than 1,000 of the enemy, while the Americans lost 300.[10] The battle at Ia Drang valley demonstrated that the revolutionary forces were not yet able to match U.S. firepower and mobility.

By the end of the year, Westmoreland had achieved his basic aim of stabilizing the military situation in South Vietnam. The insurgents had failed to maintain the momentum they had established at the beginning of the year, and their hold over key areas of the country had perceptibly weakened. The U.S. expeditionary force in South Vietnam now numbered nearly 200,000 men. But if security was up, so was infiltration. There was now the equivalent of ten PAVN regiments in the South, and they made up about 30 percent of all combat units in the area. Although the insurgency forces had suffered heavy casualties, the total strength of the PLAF was now estimated at 221,000 men. In Washington questions were already being asked about the value of Westmoreland's strategy of aggressive "search and destroy" actions in comparison to the painstaking but thorough pacification operations preferred by many civilian advisers. Under the circumstances, Senator Mike Mansfield's comment that "defeat has been averted, but victory is nowhere in sight" seemed apt indeed.[11]

Hanoi's Response

Despite the brave front put up by Hanoi, the U.S. decision to escalate the conflict in the South posed a severe challenge to the revolution. In effect, Washington had turned Mao's famous dictum against Hanoi. By raising the importance of the military factor, the United States had pitted its primary strength—technology and firepower—against the major weakness of the Communists. At least for the moment, the importance of politics, the Communists' cardinal advantage, would be severely reduced.

Hanoi was now faced with a series of almost equally unattractive alternatives. Any effort to match the United States in a war of attrition would not only be costly in terms of human casualties and materials; it would also seriously risk a spillover of the war into North Vietnam, with the attendant effects on the program of socialist construction. The Third Party Congress had kept the two goals of the revolution rigidly separate, indicating that elements within the leadership would strongly oppose any measures in the South that might endanger the rate of progress toward a socialist society in the D.R.V. Moreover, further escalation in the South, with the risk of a "wider way," would place Hanoi's delicate relations with the Soviet Union in serious jeopardy.

On the other hand, any decision to back away from a confrontation in the South must have seemed equally unpalatable. To retreat from the challenge would be to accept a postponement, *sine die*, of the victory of the revolution and the reunification of the two zones. And it would have a serious negative effect on the morale of the insurgency forces in the South, who had already struggled for several years at great sacrifice on the assumption that the North would not let them down.[12] Under such circumstances, Hanoi had little choice but to respond in one form or another. It had already made a substantial commitment in arms and lives to the revolution in the South. It had geared up for a major push for a decisive victory. To downgrade the level of insurgency and retreat to the stage of guerrilla warfare would be to lose the initiative on the battlefield and discourage the thousands of insurgents fighting in the jungles and rice paddies in the South. If the United States could force the Communists to retreat with a show of force, it would doom the revolution to failure. Hanoi thus had to respond. It only remained to determine how to respond.

The decision by the Johnson administration to increase the stakes in Vietnam took place just as Soviet Prime Minister Kosygin made his state visit to Hanoi. Whether or not the American bombing of Dong Hoi while Kosygin was in Hanoi had any effect on the talks is not known. In any case, it seems likely that the meeting resulted in a bargain. The Soviet Union promised "all necessary support and assistance" to the Vietnamese and agreed on a military assistance program that ultimately amounted to several hundred million dollars' worth of aid to Hanoi, including surface-to-air missiles (SAM) and antiaircraft equipment. On the other hand, Kosygin probably linked Soviet promises of aid to Hanoi's promise to limit the conflict to the South and to pursue the possibility of a negotiated settlement. Shortly after Kosygin's return to Moscow, the Soviet government proposed a new international conference on the Indochina crisis, and the D.R.V. quickly indicated its willingness to attend. Then there was a brief flurry of diplomatic proposals from Hanoi and the NLF leadership. On April 8, Prime Minister Pham Van Dong issued a four-point proposal for a settlement of the Vietnam crisis, calling for the removal of all foreign troops from Vietnam, observation of the Geneva accords, settlement of South Vietnam's internal affairs in accordance with the NLF program, and the peaceful reunification of the two zones.[13]

In one sense, the proposal represented a softening of earlier Communist demands for the resignation of the Saigon government. It indicated Hanoi's willingness to drop immediate removal of the U.S. presence as a precondition for peace talks and hinted that the four points should not be taken as prior conditions, but just as "working principles." But now Hanoi demanded as a prerequisite for opening negotiations an immediate and unconditional halt to the U.S. bombing of the D.R.V. This became the key sticking point in the diplomatic sparring between the two sides. Washington offered a brief five-day halt to see if Hanoi would cease infiltration, but Hanoi refused a reciprocal gesture, and there the matter rested.[14]

How serious were the peace feelers emanating from Hanoi and Washington in the spring of 1965? On the Vietnamese side, D.R.V. willingness to back away from its earlier insistence on a strict acceptance of the four points was an indication that it was willing to make at least a gesture toward a compromise peace settlement. Beyond the need to conciliate Moscow, the U.S. decision to escalate had undoubtedly been something of a shock to Party leaders, and they may have been willing to consider opening negotiations if that was the price for a bombing halt. But in Washington, there was probably relatively little interest in a diplomatic settlement. Having made the difficult decision to escalate, the Johnson administration felt that negotiations should not be undertaken until the military situation had markedly improved. Based on this view of the situation, Washington tied a bombing halt to the removal of North Vietnamese troops from the South, a demand that Hanoi obviously could not accept. Moreover, there was a feeling in Washington that negotiations in 1965 could be disastrous for morale in the GVN. When in late summer Pham Van Dong repeated Hanoi's hard position—no talks without prior acceptance of the four points—the diplomatic sparring ceased, and both sides turned temporarily to the battlefield.

The flurry of diplomatic activity had not been entirely fruitless as far as Hanoi was concerned. The events of the winter and spring of 1965 had resulted in markedly improved relations with Moscow and a promise of Soviet assistance for the struggle in the South. Moscow had endorsed Hanoi's four-point peace proposal and accepted a permanent mission of the NLF in Moscow. Then in July, the two countries signed an agreement in Moscow calling for substantial Soviet military and economic assistance. In turn, Hanoi's relations with Peking cooled when the P.R.C. rebuffed a Soviet proposal to coordinate military aid to North Vietnam. Although Chinese assistance to Hanoi continued, the D.R.V. had obviously returned to its traditional policy of maintaining an intimate link with Moscow.

With prospects for a satisfactory political settlement dim for the foreseeable future, Hanoi now settled in for a protracted military struggle. The possibility of an outright victory over U.S. military forces with their awesome advantage in firepower was obviously slight. Party strategists were thus compelled to seek to regain the initiative by locating and magnifying the vulnerable areas in the enemy's position. Based on past experience, the enemy's major weaknesses were political: the intrinsic instability of the Saigon regime, and the underlying softness of public support for the Vietnam war in the United States. The introduction of U.S. forces into South Vietnam did not fundamentally change the underlying structural weakness of the GVN. Indeed, Hanoi probably counted on rising U.S. force levels to increase antiforeign sentiment among the South Vietnamese and thus stimulate the peace movement in the South. In the United States, opposition to the war was already beginning to surface on campuses and among intellectuals. If it could be carefully cultivated by appropriate propaganda from Hanoi, it could expand into a major political force that could compel the Johnson administration to bring the conflict to the conference table and to remove U.S. troops.

The key to exploiting the enemy's political weaknesses was to maintain military pressure so that casualties would be high and the war would remain on the front pages. A lowering of the scale of conflict would only reduce the pressure on the enemy and allow the United States and its allies in Saigon to pursue their objective of stabilizing the situation in the South at low cost. Thus a high level of conflict seemed called for. But how could Hanoi cope with the awesome U.S. advantage in weaponry and technology?

The basic decision to respond to the U.S. buildup was taken in December 1965 at the Twelfth Plenum of the Central Committee. The previous meeting, in March, had been held before the scope of the U.S. response had become clear and had set forth two possibilities: Either the United States would remain in the stage of "special war" or Washington would move to a "limited war" and send U.S. combat forces. The resolution issued at the close of the Twelfth Plenum, claiming that the fundamental balance of forces remained unchanged despite the U.S. entry into the war and that the revolutionary armed forces would be able to maintain the initiative on the battlefield, called upon the Party to mobilize its members, the armed forces, and the entire people, to "foil the war of aggression of the US imperialists in any circumstances, so as to defend the North, liberate the South, complete the national people's democratic revolution in the whole country, advancing toward the peaceful reunification of the country."[15]

One of the clearest expositions of the assumptions behind the decision reached at the Twelfth Plenum came in a letter written in March 1966 by a top Party official under the pseudonym "Anh Sau." Anh Sau has sometimes been identified as Le Duan, but it is more likely from the context that the author was the commander of the revolutionary force in the South, General Nguyen Chi Thanh.[16] Thanh, a veteran Communist from Central Vietnam who had joined the Party in the late 1930s and risen rapidly in the military ranks during the war against the French, was a fervent advocate within the Party leadership of an aggressive policy in the South.

In his letter, Anh Sau conceded that although the Ninth Plenum in December 1963 had foreseen the possibility of increased U.S. involvement, Washington's decision to escalate had been somewhat unexpected, adding laconically that "things do not always develop in strict accordance with our subjective judgment and intentions." Since the previous plenum held in March 1965, the United States had introduced 200,000 troops into South Vietnam. The decision of the Twelfth Plenum in December had "emerged from this new situation."

The author declared, however, that it was important not to overestimate the Americans. It was undeniably true that the United States was a major imperialist nation and possessed military power vastly superior in quantity and quality to that of the Vietnamese revolutionary forces, but it had major weaknesses as well. Buffeted by successive defeats in China, Korea, Cuba, and Laos, the United States was being driven gradually onto the defensive and could no longer carry out its will in the global arena. Even within Vietnam U.S. forces, with all their technological superiority, would have only a limited capability to achieve their goals. "Anh Sau" predicted that U.S. military commanders, like the French before them, would attempt to realize several objectives in Vietnam: to engage and destroy revolutionary main force units, to protect their own bases and populated areas, to reduce and if possible eliminate sources of aid from abroad, and to strengthen the ARVN and stabilize the Saigon administration. But even if U.S. troop levels in South Vietnam should rise to double their present size, claimed the author, the imperialists would be unable to achieve their objectives. In the first place, the Saigon regime and its armed forces were on the verge of disintegration, while the military and political strength of the revolution in the South was rising to a crescendo. Under such conditions, U.S. units would be unable to seize the offensive and would be compelled to disperse in order to defend threatened regions of the GVN. Moreover, the United States no longer possessed the military strength to enforce its will anywhere in the world. The Johnson administration could not escalate at will in the South, and even if it expanded the war into Cambodia, Southern Laos, or North Vietnam itself, it would risk facing the united strength of Vietnam's socialist allies.

How, then, should the war develop? According to Anh Sau, the Twelfth Plenum had correctly described the war as a protracted struggle that should be won "bit by bit" within a relatively short time. The revolutionary forces must stand firm everywhere and "take the initiative on the entire battlefield" in order to place maximum pressure on the United States and irreparably weaken the puppet regime in Saigon. In general, revolutionary units must direct their attacks at both U.S. and ARVN troops, but must concentrate their efforts on the latter. The Saigon regime and its armed forces were the primary weak links in U.S. strategy, and if they could be discredited and defeated the United States would have no means of remaining in South Vietnam, as its "neocolonial" strategy depended on its ability to rule through the puppet administration in Saigon. Therefore, although revolutionary strategy must be aimed in part at weakening U.S. forces so that they would be "unable to protect the puppet army and administration," the primary objective would be to *"basically annihilate the puppet army"* in order to hasten the collapse of the Saigon regime and thus frustrate Washington's neocolonial scheme.

But could the liberation armed forces sufficiently handle U.S. units so that the main blows could be directed at the ARVN? Anh Sau's answer was that it was not necessary to defeat the entire "gendarme policy" of the United States throughout the globe, but only within the framework of the conflict in South Vietnam. As the United States did not possess vital interests in Southeast Asia, once Washington was faced with the likelihood of the defeat of its policy in South Vietnam, it would certainly decide to withdraw. The defeat of the United States, then, meant "destroying as much of their potential as possible, checking their military purpose, crushing their aggressive scheme, thus preventing them from enlarging and protracting the war of aggression, and forcing them into submission on specific conditions and finally getting them out of South Vietnam."

Anh Sau's letter was an optimistic and vigorous defense of Hanoi's decision to match U.S. escalation. Between the lines, however, it is possible to read signs that there was dissent over the new policy within the Party leadership. Some unnamed comrades were criticized for believing that "the revolution in the South should be allowed to develop itself." This, said the author, was mistaken. On the contrary, the struggle should be actively promoted so that it could make great strides and achieve victory in the shortest possible period of time. Others may have doubted the Party leadership's ability to understand the United States; the author vigorously countered that argument: "Previously, to understand and evaluate U.S. imperialism, we had to discuss it with the fraternal countries. Today, through our collision with the U.S. imperialists . . . we have been able to evaluate their schemes and capabilities on our territory."

Anh Sau's analysis did not quiet the doubters within the Party leadership.

There were references in the media that "some of our people don't think we can resist." There was also a barrage of criticism from Peking, where concern over the possibility of an escalation of the war ran high. Chinese leaders advised Hanoi to remain in the stage of guerrilla war until the P.R.C. was ready to offer substantial military assistance. Of particular interest was the famous article by Chinese defense minister Lin Piao entitled "Long Live the Victory of People's War." Ostensibly the article was a historical analysis of errors made during the Chinese revolution, but Lin implicitly criticized the Vietnamese for not knowing when to retreat and lectured them on the proper application of people's war.[17]

Such advice was apparently not welcome, and during the winter and early spring of 1966 leading Party figures in Hanoi responded vigorously to Peking's attack. An especially sharp retort came from Le Duan himself. At an army conference in May, he pointed out that:

> Creativity is a very important problem. Without a spirit of creativity, we cannot successfully carry out the revolution. We cannot automatically apply the revolutionary experience of other countries in our country. Our party line is correct, because it was conceived in a creative manner. It has cleverly associated Marxism-Leninism with the revolutionary realities in Vietnam. Our party has paid special attention to studying the experiences of the fraternal parties, but it has not studied them mechanically. We must have the requirements of the Vietnamese revolution in mind while studying these experiences. We must also know how to apply these experiences to the concrete conditions of Vietnam. Creativity is a manifestation of the spirit of independence and autonomy, patriotism, and a high revolutionary spirit. If we are obsessed with an inferiority complex and with a desire to rely on others, we cannot have a spirit of creativity. We are not genuine revolutionaries. We do not understand Marxism-Leninism.
>
> It is not fortuitous that in the history of our country, each time we rose up to oppose foreign aggression, we took the offensive and not the defensive. . . Taking the offensive is a strategy, while taking the defensive is only a stratagem. Since the day the South Vietnamese people rose up, they have continually taken the offensive.[18]

During the months following the Twelfth Plenum, several top Party figures commented favorably on the new strategy. An article by Vo Nguyen Giap published in the January 1966 issue of *Nhan dan* set the tone. Claiming that the intrinsic weaknesses in the U.S. position would inevitably cause its policy of escalation to fail, Giap claimed that the art of people's revolutionary war would ultimately be victorious. A second article by General Nguyen Van Vinh, PAVN deputy chief of staff and head of the Central Committee's Reunification Department, further elaborated on Giap's main point. Vinh admitted that if only economic potential and sophisticated arms and technology were counted, the United States had the advantage. But Vinh contended that even if it introduced half a million troops into the struggle, the United States would be unable to prevail over the people's war of the Vietnamese masses. Key factors that would undermine the U.S. advantage in firepower would be lack of public support for the war in the United States, the weakness of the Saigon regime, and geographical distance.[19]

In effect, by the end of 1965 both Washington and Hanoi had decided to exercise the military option to achieve their objectives in South Vietnam. In the apt phrase of the late Bernard Fall, 1965 became "the year of the hawk." The reasoning of both sides was clear and, ironically, quite similar. Both were convinced that the sands were shifting under the feet of the other and were therefore unwilling, for the moment, to make a fundamental compromise in their ultimate goals. Although neither was struggling for total and unconditional victory, each felt that negotiations could not take place until a favorable situation had been created on the battlefield. It remained to be seen whose prognosis of the total situation was the more accurate.

The Strategy of Attrition: Washington

As the Party leadership in Hanoi made its momentous decision to match the U.S. challenge, General Westmoreland in Saigon made preparations to take the offensive. During the previous summer and fall, the Communists had lost the initiative, and U.S. forces were now deployed in strength in strategic areas in South Vietnam. The marines had secured key areas along the central coast. The First Cavalry Division, which had fought the bloody battle in the Ia Drang valley the previous autumn, had now been shifted to Binh Dinh Province. The First Infantry Division was now located north of Saigon, and the Fourth was in the rubber plantation area adjacent to the Cambodian border.

With his force levels nearing 200,000 Westmoreland hoped that he would be in a position to launch aggressive sweep operations against enemy main forces and guerrilla units in the countryside. Only thus, in his view, could the Communist threat to South Vietnam be contained. Of highest priority, because of its proximity to the capital, was III Corps, the military region adjacent to Saigon. North of the capital, in the forests of Zones C and D, the Viet Cong had constructed a virtually impenetrable base area that had not been invaded since 1962. If Hanoi could link this area with the Central Highlands, it could pose a grave threat to the very survival of the GVN. The keystone was the province of Binh Dinh, populated by nearly a million Vietnamese, many of them sympathetic to the revolution since the War of Resistance against the French. A final crucial region was located just south of the Demilitarized Zone. Here the threat was both military and political. The area was obviously vulnerable to surprise attacks by North Vietnamese forces from across the border in the D.R.V. and was therefore defended by the marines and by ARVN's best unit, the First Division. The political danger came from the traditionally strong sense of regionalism in the area. Resentment of Diem's treatment of the Buddhists had been particularly strong in Hué, and the new I Corps commander, the charismatic and enigmatic Nguyen Chanh Thi, had recently adopted a position of independence from the government in Saigon.

Westmoreland's plan was to use U.S. troops to take the offensive in these key areas during the dry season in early 1966; ARVN units would follow up with pacification operations. To guarantee success he felt that he would need more troops, and in February he presented his case to top U.S. and South Vietnamese civilian and military officials at a Honolulu summit conference held to plan the future course of the war. By now President Johnson was beginning to feel the pressure of war expenditures and public opinion, and he asked the MACV commander how long he anticipated the war would last. Westmoreland, now somewhat more cautious as a result of the heavy fighting the previous year, predicted that the conflict could last several years. With some reluctance, Johnson granted the commander's request for additional forces.[20]

During the spring and summer of 1966, U.S., Australian, and South Korean forces launched several operations designed to throw the enemy on the defensive. For the most part, ARVN troops were used in clear-and-hold operations, in garrison duty, or in combat against Viet Cong guerrilla units. The major area of operations was in the jungles north and northwest of Saigon, where elements of the U.S. First Division launched a series of offensives culminating in September in a major attack, involving over 20,000 U.S. troops, against Zone C. For the most part, the Viet Cong avoided contact with the attackers. There were nonetheless several bitter battles, after which the defenders withdrew across the Cambodian border.[21]

While the First Division attempted to root out Viet Cong strongholds near Saigon, the First Cavalry took the offensive along the central coast. During the early part of the year it had launched assaults into the Bong Son and An Lao valleys, areas in Binh Dinh Province traditionally sympathetic to the revolution. Other operations took place in the district of Tuy Hoa and a few miles south of the provincial capital of Quang Ngai. Although Viet Cong losses were not significant, by autumn the Communist hold on the central provinces had been weakened.

By now, the shape of Westmoreland's strategy was beginning to become clear: big operations, supported by massive use of firepower and capable of grinding down all resistance. But questions were beginning to be raised about Westmoreland's approach. Critics pointed to the lack of surprise, the increasing damages caused by U.S. sweeps to the civilian population, and the relative lack of attention to pacification operations and "the other war." Some indicated a preference for the more cautious and thorough approach taken by the marines in the northern provinces. There U.S. units avoided the big-unit strategy and concentrated on pacification operations through the use of Combined Action Platoons (CAPs). CAP troops lived in the villages and assisted local residents in construction activities.[22] The issue of "the other war" came to a head at the Honolulu conference in February 1966. By this time a military government under generals Nguyen Cao Ky and Nguyen Van Thieu had finally promised the return of stability in Saigon. The Johnson administration now decided to put pressure on the new GVN leadership to move toward a constitutional system and a renewed effort at national development. It is noteworthy that the effort to revitalize the pacification program resulted in bitter controversy between the military and civilian bureaucracies in Washington and within the U.S. mission in South Vietnam. At issue was whether pacification should be considered primarily a political or a military problem, a matter of social development or of national security. Eventually, the military view prevailed. At the strong request of Westmoreland, the new program, named Civil Operations and Rural Development Support (CORDS), was placed under MACV. U.S. advisory teams were stationed in all provinces and most districts, and a revolutionary development program was set up by the GVN at Vung Tau to train fifty-nine-man Vietnamese cadre teams who were to be sent to strategic hamlets, now renamed new life hamlets, in a new effort to "win the hearts and minds" of the rural population. Other programs were set up to encourage desertion (*Chieu Hoi*) and to destroy the Communist infrastructure (the Phoenix program).

The Strategy of Attrition: Hanoi

Despite Anh Sau's brave words, the U.S. buildup posed severe political and military problems for the Communists and threatened to take away the initiative they had possessed since the opening of the conflict in 1959. Unable to match U.S. firepower and mobility, the revolutionary forces were inexorably driven back from the populated provinces into isolated areas in the mountains and along the Cambodian border. Any hopes Party strategists had possessed of launching a major offensive to destroy the heart of Saigon's power, at least for the moment, would have to be postponed.

But as the resolution of the Twelfth Plenum had demonstrated, Hanoi was not yet ready to concede the battlefield to the Americans. That, certainly, was the conviction of the commander of the revolutionary forces in the South, General Nguyen Chi Thanh. Thanh was convinced that the United States had neither the manpower nor the perseverance to accomplish the dual objectives of Westmoreland's strategy—to engage in sweep operations to throw the insurgency off balance and ultimately to destroy it, and to provide military security in populated areas to permit successful pacification. This dilemma had plagued, and ultimately defeated, the French. To Nguyen Chi Thanh, the United States with all its advantage in technology could not avoid the same fate.

Thanh thus insisted on the need for an aggressive military strategy that would not only harass U.S. and ARVN operations, but also occasionally launch full-scale attacks at regimental size in areas of Hanoi's own choosing. Revolutionary units were to stand firm in their positions and even to expand, where possible, into the jungles and the lowlands in an effort to maintain the military initiative on the entire battlefield. This policy of high-level military confrontation would keep the pressure on the United States and maximize wear and tear on ARVN forces. It would also reap a propaganda advantage by keeping the war on the front pages of U.S. newspapers. Only by taking the offensive could the Party's armed forces achieve success in the protracted struggle and advance toward decisive victory.

Whether or not Thanh's analysis of U.S. underlying military and political weaknesses was accurate, the strategy he developed as a result of that assessment was costly. To provide the necessary manpower and equipment for the front lines, the D.R.V. economy would have to be transformed into a strong rear base for the struggle in the South. Peacetime construction efforts would be reduced or abandoned and the entire economy placed on a war footing. To protect defense efforts from intense U.S. bombing, vital industries had to be dismantled and moved to isolated areas in the interior. In the end, virtually the entire population was mobilized: Young men of draft age were conscripted into the armed services while women replaced them in the fields and factories and even served in the self-defense militia or in the antiaircraft artillery units that sprang up around the country to defend the North against U.S. bombing raids.[23]

Even with the D.R.V. mobilized into an "all for the front lines" posture, the liberation forces would face intimidating problems in coping with the enemy's technological superiority on the battlefield. For here, as nowhere else, Hanoi would be in a state of permanent disadvantage. Thanh's answer was to combine two aspects of people's war: conventional-sized units and guerrilla tactics. Main force units operating up to regimental level and armed with light weapons were to use guerrilla techniques of stealth, stratagem, and rapid mobility in launching assaults on enemy units and installations. Where weaponry would not suffice, moral superiority would. In a view reminiscent of the French faith in the power of élan to repulse German armies in the early stages of World War I, Thanh contended that the militant spirit of the revolutionary forces would counter the U.S. advantage in firepower.

Thanh admitted that it would not be an easy task. In an article published in the July 1966 issue of *Hoc tap*, he remarked that, to win, "high courage, a strong will, and great patience" would be required.[24] He praised the southern leadership for sensing the dangers inherent in the U.S. military escalation in 1965 and launching an ideological campaign to eliminate a sense of inferiority, pessimism, and "rightist conservative thought" within the movement.

Throughout 1966 and into early 1967, the PLAF attempted to maintain the initiative on the battlefield. According to an article by one high-ranking field commander in the South, the primary objective was to keep U.S. forces off balance and blunt their efforts to seek out and destroy the insurgency units. A secondary goal was to disrupt and weaken pacification operations and weaken ARVN units.[25] A definitive assessment of the results of that strategy is beyond the scope of this study. What is certain is that it led to heavy casualties while realizing few visible results. Although the body count figures provided by MACV were probably inflated, it seems undeniable that the battlefield losses suffered by the insurgency forces were heavy. To compensate, infiltration from the North was stepped up, and by late 1966 it was running at a total of more than 5,000 a month. Some were used as "fillers" for PLAF Units unable to obtain replacements through local recruiting. Increasingly, however, main force units of the People's Army of Vietnam (PAVN) were brought down the trail system in the Laotian panhandle and began to play a central role in the fighting.

To make the situation worse, military escalation appeared to have exerted relatively little impact on the enemy's will to resist. While Thanh's aggressive strategy had succeeded in keeping the war on the front pages of U.S. newspapers, public hostility to the war in the United States had not measurably affected the administration's determination to stick to its hard-line strategy. As U.S. troop levels increased, the battlefield situation shifted inexorably to the disadvantage of the liberation forces, who were reduced to nipping at the edges of government-held areas in the Central Highlands and along the central coast.

Eventually the high costs and limited achievements of Nguyen Chi Thanh's strategy emboldened critics in Hanoi. One of the most prominent was evidently Vo Nguyen Giap himself. Giap, of course, had long advocated a high level of conflict in the South and had frequently remarked that people's war in Vietnam must necessarily pass through a final stage of general offensive. But Giap was also a firm believer in the art of the possible, as well as in the rational use of resources, and Thanh's profligate use of Hanoi's precious main force units in headlong assaults on enemy positions he considered wasteful. There was a proper time for confrontation with the enemy. But that moment needed planning and preparation, as well as a careful husbanding of resources. In an article published in 1967 and entitled "Big Victory, Great Task," he stressed the protracted character of the people's war in the South and asserted that the revolutionary movement must be willing to wait fifteen to twenty years for victory. Turning to recent history for an example, he pointed out that in the war against the French, Party strategists had concentrated their main force units for use in carefully selected areas where the enemy was vulnerable. Large-scale attacks were launched only in cases where the revolutionary forces possessed clear superiority. Giap, it seems, had not forgotten the lessons learned after the failure of the Tonkin delta offensive of 1951.[26]

Giap's views found a sympathetic response among some members of the southern military command. One apparently high-ranking military leader in the South, writing under the name "Cuu Long" and presenting his views on liberation radio in the fall of 1966, took issue with the current big-unit high-cost strategy. Claiming that large forces do not guarantee victory, he emphasized the need for more flexible tactics in the South. In a second article published in a D.R.V. military newspaper two months later, he praised the role of guerrilla war in the revolution and bluntly complained that it was being underutilized in South Vietnam. Asserting that if successfully coordinated with other forms of war, guerrilla tactics could achieve substantial destruction, even of heavily armed enemy forces, he concluded that "the qualitative aspects of the armed forces must be understood in a more thorough and versatile way."[27]

Thanh did not suffer in silence and struck back harshly at his critics. In the July 1966 *Hoc tap* article cited above, he criticized those who refused to face up to the U.S. challenge and who tended to "overestimate the enemy and underestimate ourselves." He castigated an unnamed opponent for using "empty, illogical arguments" and an addiction to "old customs" that resulted in mechanically copying one's past experiences or those of foreign countries and then applying them to live revolutionary realities. Calling concerns over "what phase of war we are in" or whether the revolutionary forces had the two-to-one superiority necessary in order to take the offensive "a kind of divination," he defended the aggressive strategy currently in use in the South.

Nguyen Chi Thanh undoubtedly had powerful defenders within the Party leadership in Hanoi, and for a time he was able to win continued approval for his politics from the Politburo. But criticism of his approach continued among top military figures in the D.R.V. and eventually had their impact. During the dry season campaign of the winter and spring of 1966-1967, efforts were undertaken to achieve a higher degree of coordination between regular and guerrilla operations and a more cautious expenditure of precious main force units.

Although the strategy that had emerged from the decisions reached at the Twelfth Plenum had resulted in the further militarization of the war, Party strategists had not abandoned the view that political struggle had an important role to play in the Vietnamese revolution. In his own analysis of the situation in the July 1966 issue of *Hoc tap*, Nguyen Chi Thanh had criticized the view of some observers that the growing U.S. involvement had rendered political struggle superfluous. He stressed that it would serve to exacerbate existing contradictions between the local population and the foreigners and provide new opportunities for the NLF to rally political forces behind its banner. Party documents confirm that Hanoi strategists still viewed the urban general uprising as an integral component of revolutionary strategy in the South. The cities of South Vietnam, now swelled by the presence of hundreds of thousands of refugees from rural villages, were a potentially explosive source of discontent against the GVN regime. Most of these refugees were classified as poor peasants or rural proletariat and were considered potentially sympathetic to the revolution. Among the urban population in general, Party strategists were optimistic that not only the laboring masses, but also the majority of the petty bourgeoisie, now totaling nearly 4 million people, were a "mature force" and a sure ally of the proletariat. Although some were influenced by Western decadent culture and some were vacillating towards the revolution, all were being exploited by imperialism, and most could be brought to favor the revolution.

The civil strife that erupted in Da Nang in the spring and summer of 1966 in support of I Corps commander Nguyen Chanh Thi demonstrated the volatile nature of the urban population and its susceptibility to revolutionary ferment. In March Tri Quang, with apparent support from General Thi, had endeavored to set up a "Buddhist force" in opposition to the government in Saigon, now increasingly dominated by Nguyen Van Thieu, a Catholic. In response, Thieu dismissed Nguyen Chanh Thi as commander of I Corps and replaced him with a Thieu supporter. A popular figure in the North, Thi was supported by many Vietnamese in Hué and Da Nang and a general strike broke out that soon developed separatist overtones. In May, ARVN forces were dispatched to the area and helped new I Corps commander Ton That Dinh crush the rebellion with some brutality.

The Party's local leadership was conscious of the potential benefits that might accrue from the Da Nang crisis and tried to take advantage of it by infiltrating the dissident movement in order to stir up unrest among the populace and the local ARVN troops. But although hostility toward the central government attained substantial proportions, the Party's local apparatus was unable to seize a leading position in the movement and take advantage of the crisis. As one high Party official in Hanoi lamented, the Communists had "missed an opportunity to win a bigger victory" and to organize the Party's forces in Da Nang.[28]

But the violence in Da Nang was persuasive evidence that the cities could still play an active and perhaps crucial role in the revolution in South Vietnam. Hanoi's attitude toward the role of urban areas was elucidated in a letter written by a member of the Party leadership (the writer is identified only as "Ba") to the municipal leadership in Saigon sometime in 1966. Ba stressed the importance of urban areas to the struggle in South Vietnam, not only because they were one of the three strategic areas crucial to success, but also because of the need to strengthen proletarian leadership over the revolution as a whole. "We are mistaken," the letter said, "if we only employ the peasants as the main force" of the revolution.

Much of the letter was devoted to an analysis of the situation in urban areas in the South and to the measures that should be taken to prepare for the coming general uprising. The Saigon municipal leadership was instructed to concentrate on the recruitment of youth, "the most fervent elements ready to die to counter the aggressors and traitors," into guerrilla and special action (terrorism and sabotage) units, and of women, who were potentially useful agents to send into market areas to agitate and stimulate the formation of a female "political army" to demonstrate against living conditions and the injustices of the Saigon regime. A third potential source of support, as the uprising in Da Nang had amply demonstrated, might come from the South Vietnamese armed forces, who could often be counted on to rally to the masses in the midst of a popular uprising.

As usual, Ba also called for active efforts to infiltrate and influence moderate political parties and religious organizations, and to "create conditions for alliance between the revolutionary force and the intermediate class, the progressive elements of the [political] factions and religious groups, the dissidents within the enemy's ranks, or [to] neutralize a definite portion of the puppet army and administration and make it easier for the masses to rise at the moment of the general uprising." Where possible, left-wing factions were to be formed in such organizations to win over sympathetic elements and neutralize the others in a crisis. Action slogans were to be aimed at "the most pressing needs of the masses—welfare and democracy—which are apt to attract the large majority of the masses to the struggle." The letter conceded that the political consciousness of the urban population was still weak (a PRP pamphlet printed in 1965 had lamented that the Party "has not been positive in leading the movement" in the cities) but insisted that conditions for a general uprising had appeared and labeled the immediate future as "an important transition period" when preparations for the final uprising should be undertaken. Revolutionary bases should be created in factories, utilities, and communications enterprises so that, at the proper moment, control could be seized by force. Covert organizations should be set up, and Party activists were told to take advantage of any incident to provoke hostility between the masses and the GVN or its U.S. masters—a street accident, a police raid on a market, an American soldier who refused to pay a taxi fare.

How and when would the general uprising take place? The letter showed that Hanoi was determined to maintain a flexible attitude on both questions. In some cases, it said, power could be seized right at the beginning, as in the August Revolution. In others, as in February 1917 in Russia, the revolutionary forces would have initially to share power with the bourgeoisie. The Party was equally flexible on the question of timing. In general, it felt that victory would come at a moment when military victories in rural areas could be combined with an uprising in the major cities. Power could be secured only when the nerve centers and command organs of the enemy had been destroyed and when the masses were "determined to rise up to free themselves from [the] enemy's rule, when the tools of violence in the hands of the rulers, principally the armed forces, are paralyzed or disintegrated due to a conflict with a foreign imperialist country or due to an internal war." On the other hand, the revolution could not succeed so long as the ruling class was in control of a strong military force. Therefore it would be necessary to inflict heavy losses on U.S.

troops and simultaneously destroy an important part of the puppet army, "thereby driving it to an inevitable collapse." How did the Party feel that these two components should be most effectively combined? In general, Ba seemed to feel that the urban uprising should break out in response to successes already achieved in rural areas. But, obviously conscious of the unpredictability of urban unrest, he remarked that although the uprising should not take place *without* a general offensive, it need not wait until the latter had been substantially completed. In effect, an uprising could give a boost to the offensive, as in March 1966 when unrest in Da Nang led to revolts in two ARVN divisions and the temporary paralysis of Saigon's armed forces in the area: "In the coming period, if while our repeated military successes are driving the enemy into a dangerous and confused situation, in a given city, including Saigon-Cholon, the masses, seething with revolutionary zeal, want to rise up to overthrow [the] puppet administration, then I think that this uprising can take place without waiting for the military offensive to win a basic victory." Such uprisings, he postulated, could be "a series of consecutive uprisings similar to those of the February and October revolutions in Russia, one uprising paving the way for the next one."[29]

On the Diplomatic Front

With the military situation still somewhat unclear, the Party leadership in the summer of 1966 could not have been particularly optimistic about the chances for a major leap forward for the revolution in the near future. The presence of large numbers of foreign troops appeared to rule out the possibility of a decisive military victory on the battlefield. Party strategy thus focused on maintaining the initiative until a combined general offensive and uprising could be launched that in turn would lead to negotiations, followed by the withdrawal of the Americans and the formation of a coalition government, including Communist elements, in Saigon. In this perspective, a peace conference to end the war was virtually inevitable at some point. The problem was that negotiations could not be formally undertaken until the situation on the battlefield was sufficiently favorable. In the meantime, the Party's negotiating strategy could be used to serve the needs of the war effort and weaken U.S. public support for the war. For that reason, throughout 1966 and 1967 Hanoi flashed its willingness to open diplomatic talks but insisted on the prior condition of an unconditional cessation of U.S. bombing of the North.

Captured documents appear to confirm this assessment of the situation. A letter by Le Duan to Nguyen Chi Thanh, probably written sometime in 1966, remarked that political and diplomatic struggle would be of prime importance, but that the Party's diplomatic strategy "must be properly used to efficiently serve the political and military aims of our strategy of pitting the weak against the strong."[30] At the moment, he noted, the situation was complicated because of views in other world capitals. The United States wanted to negotiate from a strong position. Meanwhile, some of Hanoi's socialist allies "which sincerely support our struggle, but in view of diplomatic reasons and their domestic administration and misunderstanding of the situation in our country" were attempting to persuade the Vietnamese to take the issue to the conference table. The Party's strategy on negotiations, he concluded, must serve its concrete political aims. How to achieve these aims would be a matter for the Politburo to decide.

General Nguyen Van Vinh elaborated in an April 1966 speech the Party leadership's view as to how negotiations should be coordinated with the course of the war in the South. A Central Committee plenum in April 1966, he said, had decided that "at present the situation is not yet ripe for negotiations." Clearly, the Politburo was convinced that peace talks would not be useful until the situation on the battlefield had become more favorable:

> As long as we have not yet acquired adequate strength, a situation where fighting and negotiations are conducted simultaneously does not exist. Fighting continues until the emergence of a situation where both sides are fighting indecisively. Then a situation where fighting and negotiations are conducted simultaneously may emerge. In fighting while negotiating, the side which fights more strongly will compel the adversary to accept its conditions.[31]

Nguyen Van Vinh thus postulated a new version of the old Maoist three-stage process: a fighting stage, a stage of fighting and negotiating, and a final stage of negotiations and final agreement. Whether or not the war would resume after the conclusion of the agreement depended upon the comparative balance of forces. If the revolutionary forces were capable of dominating the adversary, the war would not resume. How should the decision be taken on when to open serious negotiations? Here General Vinh was somewhat ambiguous. While insisting on the one hand that if the enemy wants to negotiate, it must accept several conditions, such as stopping the bombing of the North, withdrawing its troops, and dismantling its military bases, he added that whether to impose such conditions would depend on "the situation prevailing at the time."

In any event, Vinh claimed that revolutionary forces must fight even more vigorously after negotiations had begun, because "the decisive factor lies in the battlefield." To compel the enemy to accept Hanoi's conditions, the revolutionary forces must achieve military victories. If the fighting were halted during the negotiations, success could not be achieved. On the other hand, "if we conduct negotiations while fighting vigorously, we can also take advantage of the opportunity to step up the political struggle, military proselytizing, and activities in the cities."

General Vinh confirmed Le Duan's reference to the fact that the Party's stand on negotiations was controversial. Some countries, he said, wanted the

Party to enter into any form of negotiations, so that a big war would not break out. Others were dubious that Hanoi could defeat the Americans, while several socialist countries in Eastern Europe were convinced that conditions for successful negotiations already prevailed. China, on the contrary, felt that conditions for peace talks were not yet ripe and attempted to persuade the Vietnamese Party leadership not to negotiate but also not to take the offensive until the Chinese had acquired adequate strength to assist the Vietnamese "to launch a strong, all-out, and rapid offensive, using all types of weapons and heeding no borders." Vinh made it clear that the Vietnamese would decide when to negotiate. Party policy, he concluded, "is to continue fighting until a certain time when we can fight and negotiate at the same time." The time for negotiations would be decided by the Politburo, on the basis of the actual situation in the South and the opinions of friendly countries, whose support was vitally important to the success of the revolution.

Hanoi's determination to go its own way did not cause irreparable problems in its relations with its allies, for both Moscow and Peking—spurred on, no doubt, by competition for Vietnamese support in their ideological dispute—continued to provide a fairly high level of military and diplomatic assistance. But Party leaders continued to be unhappy about the Sino-Soviet split and were convinced that it was harming the revolutionary struggle in the South. For the time being, Hanoi was determined to maintain an independent role and avoid taking sides in the dispute. Party leaders made few public criticisms of either Moscow or Peking, while deploring the lack of unity within the socialist camp. According to General Vinh, Party leaders rejected Chinese claims that the new Soviet leadership was as revisionist as it had been under Khrushchev and were grateful that military assistance from the USSR had increased substantially since 1965. On the other hand, Hanoi periodically praised China for its willingness to help the Vietnamese in their struggle. In private, however, there may have been considerable irritation in Hanoi over Peking's unwillingness to cooperate with Moscow to provide massive assistance to the Vietnamese. There was also unhappiness over Chinese suggestions that the Vietnamese comrades restrict their activities in the South to low-level guerrilla struggle. Such, at any rate, is the claim made by Hanoi in the 1979 White Paper. According to this source, it was China's publicly stated unwillingness to become involved in the Vietnam conflict that persuaded the Johnson administration to instigate the Gulf of Tonkin incident and initiate the bombing of the D.R.V.[32]

Shoot-out at the DMZ

The key to the success of Hanoi's strategy would rest with its ability to attain its military objectives on the ground. In public, Nguyen Chi Thanh was optimistic. In an article published in May 1967, he claimed that U.S. forces were running into increasing problems in pacifying the South. U.S. units were scattered and had a low combat efficiency. They were unable to shield pacification operations undertaken by ARVN troops from Viet Cong attacks. To take advantage of such weaknesses, he wanted to retain the initiative by launching simultaneous attacks in all three strategic areas in Vietnam with the coordinated strength of main force units, regional guerrillas, and political and paramilitary forces at the local level. He did not reiterate his earlier calls for large-scale offensive operations against U.S. units, however; this suggests that criticisms by other Party leaders in Hanoi may have moderated Thanh's aggressive policy. It was the general's last article. He was killed during the summer of 1967, probably as the result of a U.S. bombing raid.

An article by Truong Son (pseudonym) amplified Thanh's views. Noting that the basic U.S. objective was to force the insurgency movement back to the guerrilla stage through a combination of offensive sweeps and pacification efforts, Truong Son predicted that U.S. forces were not adequate to carry out both tactics. He conceded that the U.S. army had greater mobility than the French but claimed that this could not compensate for the accelerating weakness of the GVN and the mounting public protest against the war in the United States. He predicted that during the coming dry season Westmoreland would begin to shift his forces gradually toward a greater emphasis on pacification—a sure sign of declining momentum.[33]

It was out of such conditions that the next major campaign of the war would develop. Beginning in the summer of 1966, U.S. intelligence sources reported a significant buildup of North Vietnamese units in Quang Tri Province, just to the south of the DMZ. Whether this concentration was a feint to divert U.S. forces to the area, the prelude to a serious effort to seize the northern provinces, or both, is still a matter of dispute. Given Hanoi's now well-established strategy of probing for enemy weaknesses and then striking at vulnerable positions, it is probable that the Party's next action would depend on the enemy response. If a substantial number of enemy troops were deployed in the north, it would provide heightened opportunities for the PLAF elsewhere. If not, the northern provinces presented favorable opportunities for a Communist victory. Close to the DMZ and the Laotian border, the north offered the promise of a sanctuary and short supply lines to the D.R.V. Geographically, it was a propitious area for insurgency activities. Except for a narrow strip of coastal plain, Quang Tri Province was relatively mountainous and much of it was covered with forest or thick grass, ideal for troop movements.[34]

In response to reports of enemy troop movements, General Lewis Walt, commander of the Marine Amphibious Task Force in I Corps, dispatched a battalion of marines to occupy a special forces camp at Khe Sanh, a rocky outgrowth overlooking a key mountain route entering the area from the west. At first, the marines found nothing. But by midsummer, patrols began to encounter increasing enemy activity. In Saigon, General Westmoreland was convinced that Hanoi intended to strike in the area south of the DMZ as a prelude to an assault on the entire province. The bombing of the Ho Chi Minh trail through Laos had reduced its effectiveness as an infiltration route into the South, and the best alternative routes went through Khe Sanh and the A Shau valley slightly to the south. At first, Westmoreland suggested that an international force be stationed along the border. When this was rejected in Washington, he decided to strengthen U.S. forces in the area to head off the expected North Vietnamese offensive. In July, several U.S. and ARVN units, supplemented by air and artillery support, launched an operation into the area designed to take the enemy by surprise and throw it off balance. The action began with a helicopter drop near the Rockpile, a prominent high point just south of the DMZ. The assault units encountered a substantial enemy presence, and there was heavy fighting throughout July and August. Marine units were able to seize and hold the Rockpile in the face of heavy attacks by North Vietnamese units, but the Communist buildup in the area continued.[35]

Throughout the remainder of the year, Westmoreland remained convinced that Hanoi was determined to seize the area, comparing it to Vietminh operations in the Northwest during the last years of the war against the French. To counter Hanoi's plans, he ordered the formation of a strongpoint obstacle system based on a series of fire and patrol bases located on high ground just south of the DMZ—at Cam Lo, Dong Ha, Khe Sanh, Camp Carroll, and the Rockpile. The bases would be protected by artillery pieces with a range of twenty miles, capable of reaching targets above the DMZ.

In a sense, Westmoreland's decision to occupy the border zone played into Hanoi's hands, for it turned U.S. attention to the unoccupied border regions and away from the more crucial regions along the coast. Moreover, there was an obvious resemblance to Dien Bien Phu over a decade earlier: The border zone appeared to be an ideal location for the Communists to achieve a spectacular victory that could seriously undermine popular support for the war effort in the United States. But to the confident Westmoreland, it offered an opportunity to interdict major infiltration routes into South Vietnam and to provoke a large-scale confrontation between U.S. units and the elusive North Vietnamese main force divisions.

During the winter months, the North Vietnamese began to initiate artillery attacks on U.S. firebases in the area. Then, in late April, they launched a major ground assault on the base at Khe Sanh. Hidden by heavy jungle growth and elephant grass, the Communist forces were able to occupy the area around Khe Sanh, but in spite of some of the heaviest fighting of the war, resulting in heavy casualties on both sides, they were unable to overrun the fire base itself, and in early May the attacks were finally broken off. The North Vietnamese units remained in the area, however, and kept the base under siege.[36]

What was the purpose of the Communist attack near the DMZ? In an article in *Nhan dan*, Vo Nguyen Giap claimed that the main objective was to draw

U.S. forces away from populated areas and frustrate the pacification effort. Westmoreland considered Giap's article a "planned deception" and labeled the battle of Khe Sanh a "Dien Bien Phu in reverse."[37] In this case, Westmoreland may have had a point. The magnitude of the attacks, undertaken by some of the PAVN's crack divisions, and the high casualties incurred suggest that Hanoi had hoped to achieve a spectacular victory in the area. On the other hand, the attacks did force the redeployment of U.S. troops and have a perceptible effect on world opinion. Westmoreland's comment was certainly an overstatement. Despite heavy casualties, Communist pressure on the Quang Tri Province remained high and nearly 60,000 North Vietnamese troops, the equivalent of four divisions, remained in the area.

Along the Demilitarized Zone U.S. forces were on the defensive; further south, they went on the attack. The Communists were still entrenched in the jungles northwest of Saigon, despite earlier efforts to clear out these crucial base areas. Now, in January 1967, troops from two U.S. divisions, supplemented by an airborne brigade, a cavalry regiment, and ARVN infantry units, launched a major strike—labeled Operation Cedar Falls—into the Iron Triangle, one of the insurgency movement's major base zones. The operation was designed to clear out enemy fortifications and clear several hundred square miles of jungle growth and transform it into a free-fire zone. Civilians inhabiting the area were rounded up and evacuated, Viet Cong tunnels and bunkers were destroyed, and the dense forest was leveled with bulldozers. But in the three-week operation, little contact was made with the enemy. Only 700 Viet Cong were reported killed, while U.S. losses were less than 100. It was one of the biggest operations of the war, but it had been of questionable value. Civilian casualties were high, and the enemy returned in the wake of the allied departure.[38]

The following month, the same units returned to the attack and launched the largest operation of the war, Operation Junction City. A total of 45,000 troops entered Zone C in Tay Ninh Province, site of an attack the previous year. Once again they failed to locate the enemy, but they did manage to destroy Viet Cong fortifications in the area and apparently compelled COSVN to move its headquarters across the border into Cambodia. In conjunction with Operation Fairfax, launched near Saigon, the attacks temporarily reduced the threat to the capital region.

Further to the north, U.S. units were engaged in clearing operations to permit the pacification of crucial areas along the central coast. In Binh Dinh Province, insurgency forces lacked the strength to launch a major offensive to cut the South in two, but they periodically emerged from small base areas in the hills to attack progovernment villages along the coast. And they continued to have considerable local strength in some lowland districts, particularly in the narrow river valleys near the coast north of Qui Nhon. In the early summer of 1967, the First Cavalry Division launched sweeps from Phu My to Bong Son and north to An Lao, areas of consistent support for the revolution. U.S.

sources claimed that the operations were a success and that nearly half the guerrillas in the area had been eliminated. But as always, most of the insurgents had simply melted into the mountains to the west and filtered back into the area once the Americans had left.

Similar operations were underway in southern Quang Ngai Province, in Duc Pho District, just to the east of Ba To on the central coast. This was another region historically sympathetic to the revolution and it was honeycombed with combat villages. During the spring and summer of 1967 U.S. units raided the area, destroying villages and evacuating the population. By the end of the year nearly a quarter of the total population of 700,000 in Quang Ngai Province had been turned into refugees.[39]

Only in IV Corps was there relative quiet. There were an estimated 80,000 Viet Cong in the Mekong delta, but more than half were local or regional forces, and most young recruits for the PLAF were sent to serve in combat units further to the north. Still, less than half of the more than 5,000 villages in the area were firmly under GVN control, and with no U.S. military presence in the delta, Communist units were able to operate with relative impunity. To provide an element of stability, Westmoreland finally decided to place the U.S. Fourth Division in Dinh Tuong Province, with its headquarters on the Dong Tam River near My Tho. The Saigon government raised no objection.

By the summer of 1967, Westmoreland felt that progress had been achieved in the military effort. According to one U.S. estimate, the proportion of the population under revolutionary control had declined to approximately 17 percent or less than 3 million people. Some of that, of course, was a consequence of the rise in the number of refugees, now more than a million, who had fled from rural areas to the cities. Hanoi's loss, however, was not always Saigon's gain. Many of the refugees were forced to live in squalid shantytowns in the suburbs of the major urban centers and thus became a festering source of potential discontent against the government. Nor did the GVN always manage to fill the vacuum left by the forced departure of liberation forces from rural villages. The pacification program continued to be plagued by corruption, official arrogance, and ARVN misbehavior, and U.S. reports indicated that in many areas pacification efforts had lost ground during the last half of 1967.

The enemy's high casualty rate was good news to MACV, of course. But according to Pentagon estimates, several hundred thousand young males reached draft age in the D.R.V. each year. Unless infiltration routes could be effectively plugged, Hanoi would be able to replace its losses in the South for an indefinite period of time.[40] In the meantime, manpower needs of the U.S. command in Saigon continued to mount. Although by mid-1967 U.S. troops levels had reached nearly half a million, Westmoreland contended that he needed 80,500 additional troops to achieve his minimum objectives, bringing the total to 550,000. With a maximum of 670,000, nearly 200,000 more than existing levels, he would be able to drive into Cambodia and Laos and establish an amphibious hook north of the DMZ. In Washington, however, rising public pro-test and the higher costs of the war were beginning to take their toll, even within the administration. Defense Secretary McNamara, one of the first figures within the inner circle to entertain serious doubts over the strategy followed in Vietnam, was reluctant to approve the request, and when he asked the general how long the war was likely to last, Westmoreland replied three to five years. He eventually received somewhat less than his minimum request, giving him a total of 525,000 U.S. troops.[41]

The Strains of Escalation

By the summer of 1967, both sides were beginning to feel the pinch of escala-tion. Although each was able to refer to its own indices of the degree of success or failure, it was perhaps difficult at that moment to sense whether the tide of war was beginning to run strongly in one direction or the other. From one standpoint, the situation was promising for the revolution. Despite U.S.-sponsored efforts to provide an aura of legitimacy to the South Viet-namese government by persuading the generals in Saigon to write a new democratic constitution and hold presidential elections—elections that resulted in the formalization of military authority through the election of Nguyen Van Thieu as president and his colleague and rival, Nguyen Cao Ky, as vice-president—the Saigon regime was little closer to establishing the popular accep-tance and legitimacy that had eluded its predecessors since the Geneva Con-ference. The performance of the ARVN remained dubious. There were now half a million U.S. troops in South Vietnam, but less than 20 percent were in combat units, and they were, in Vo Nguyen Giap's words, stretched "taut as a bowstring" from the delta to the DMZ. In the United States, hostility to the war was growing and would clearly be a major factor in the 1968 presidential elections. Giap predicted openly that the United States "lacked the patience" to wage a protracted war, and signs to that effect were beginning to appear in abundance.[42]

But although such similarities with the early 1950s must have been gratifying to the Party leadership in Hanoi, there were some disquieting trends also, for the sheer weight of the U.S. presence was beginning to place a severe strain on the performance and attitudes of the insurgency forces in the South. The high casualty rate imposed by Thanh's strategy had thinned the ranks of the local forces disastrously and forced the Party to rely increasingly on troops brought down from the North. This, in turn, had gradually transformed the image of the war in the minds of many South Vietnamese from a civil struggle between South Vietnamese of different ideological persuasions into a form of armed at-tack from the north, thus giving increasing credence to American and GVN propaganda. After decades of separate existence, many southerners had developed a sufficient sense of regional identity to resent the threat of domination from the North, whatever its political form. Moreover, the U.S. buildup and the increasing involvement of main force units from the North had perceptibly changed the character of the conflict and, as southern Party leaders had feared, made military needs more important than political ones. Finally, the continuing increase in the size of the U.S. presence and Washington's stubborn refusal to concede defeat raised questions as to the inevitability of a revolutionary victory and led to an increasing sense of pessimism within the movement.

Studies by American social scientists working in South Vietnam demonstrated that the U.S. escalation had posed serious problems for the insurgency movement. The numbers of volunteers for service in the PLAF declined; volunteers now made up less than 50 percent of all new recruits. The Party was compelled to institute a draft for all males between the ages of eighteen and thirty-five years of age. All those not subject to the draft were called upon to perform "people's labor" for up to three months each year. Taxes were increased, and cadres often had to resort to force or terrorism to achieve compliance from villagers unwilling to pay. With the Party's image of success beginning to fray around the edges, peasants became increasingly reluctant to contribute to or participate in the movement. Party regulars, in turn, began to lose touch with the masses or were infected with corruption, favoritism, or arrogance. Poor discipline was observed among the troops; desertion and misbehavior toward villagers became increasingly common.[43]

Verification of such conclusions came from captured documents. One representative report on the situation in Phu Yen Province complained of growing problems caused by U.S. and ARVN pacification efforts. With the growing weakness of the local revolutionary forces and the loss of initiative on the battlefield, coordination of mobile and guerrilla operations declined, and troops and cadres began to develop "corrupt, easy-going, reckless and deceitful" attitudes. The problem apparently had nationwide implications. According to a report issued by the Current Affairs Section of COSVN in 1966, relations between Party members and the masses at the local level had deteriorated, often in a "very alarming way." Cadres were often "passive and pessimistic," and suffered from "friction with the masses." Many no longer lived in the villages or served with local armed units. Chapter meetings of local PRP groups were no longer held with regularity, and the local revolutionary administration in liberated or contested areas was often loose and uncoordinated. The concept of "from the masses, to the masses" was frequently ignored, and indiscriminate terror and favoritism were often reported.[44] References to such problems in internal documents should not be viewed as an indication that the movement's infrastructure was on the verge of collapse, but they do suggest that there were definable limits to the Party's ability to mobilize the population in South Vietnam in support of the revolutionary cause. For the moment, the movement had lost its image of inevitable success. The effects were apparent as heretofore sympathetic Vietnamese began to shift perceptibly toward neutrality in the conflict.

Toward the Decisive Hour

Since the escalation of the conflict in the early 1960s, Hanoi's military strategy had been based on the premise that victory would come as a result of a combined general offensive and uprising. The introduction of U.S. combat troops apparently did not change that assumption. While conceding that a total military victory over combined U.S. and ARVN forces was improbable, the Party leadership was convinced that severe reverses must be imposed on the enemy's military forces before the United States could be compelled to withdraw from South Vietnam. One captured notebook made the interesting observation that "experience in world affairs has shown that Americans are more impressed by force than by reason" and that, as a result, "no agreement can be reached as long as we fail to win on the battlefield."[45] The importance of military struggle in the war against the Americans was expressed in more authoritative fashion by Vo Nguyen Giap in an article printed in the September *Nhan dan*. Because the U.S. imperialists have escalated the level of military struggle in South Vietnam, he said, the revolutionary forces "must therefore resort to revolutionary violence in order to oppose this counter-revolutionary violence and they must use the military struggle to oppose the armed aggression of the enemy."[46]

How to achieve this military victory was something else again. The aggressive strategy pursued since early 1966 had achieved only limited results. Although it would be misleading to label Nguyen Chi Thanh's approach a total failure, it had been a costly one, with few immediate benefits, and was clearly toned down in 1967. The objective of a "decisive victory in a relatively short period of time," confirmed by the Thirteenth Plenum in late 1966, must still have seemed far away in the summer of 1967.[47]

Sometime during the spring or early summer of 1967, the Party leadership decided that a major offensive and uprising should be launched during the following year in order to realize a great leap forward in the revolution and a possible total victory. Precisely when or how the decision was reached has not been determined. According to the testimony of one captured PAVN officer, planning for a major offensive began under the direction of Nguyen Chi Thanh in the spring of 1967. Thanh viewed the projected operation not as a single blow but as a series of "violent surges" combined with a general uprising in major urban areas, to be launched whenever the time was ripe.[48] After Thanh's death in July, planning continued under his successor and ex-deputy, Pham Hung.

Final approval for the plan, apparently given at the Party's Fourteenth Plenum in late 1967, called for a general offensive in rural areas combined with a popular uprising in the major cities. This, of course, had been the foundation of Hanoi's strategic thinking since at least the Ninth Plenum in December of 1963. The general offensive, to be launched in several stages, would be designed to disperse or destroy a substantial proportion of the enemy's armed forces in rural areas. Then a popular revolutionary outbreak would take place in major population centers to undermine the stability of the Saigon regime and, all conditions being met, lead to its ultimate collapse. If the uprising did not succeed in achieving the total overthrow of enemy power, it would be followed by a series of military offensives during succeeding months to wear down the enemy and lead either to victory or to a negotiated settlement.

Did Hanoi expect total victory? This has been a matter of controversy. Some observers have portrayed the Party's decision to launch the offensive as a sign of desperation, a last-ditch gamble to secure the overthrow of the Saigon regime. Others have suggested that from the beginning the attacks were designed primarily for their propaganda and psychological value and not for any expected major military advantage. In actuality, neither view appears justified. In the first place, internal documents indicate that the Party leadership was reasonably optimistic that the situation in South Vietnam had reached the point where a revolutionary "great leap" along the lines of the Bolshevik Revolution and the August Revolution was possible. By this reasoning, the presence of nearly half a million U.S. troops and the corresponding expansion of GVN control in the countryside disguised the political weakness of the Thieu regime. The urban unrest during 1966 was a persuasive sign of this instability and, according to one captured document, might have led to the collapse of the GVN had "the necessary subjective and objective conditions" been present. Presumably the author of the document was referring to the inadequacy of the Party's urban leadership and the absence of military offensives in rural areas. If this view of the situation was correct, the cities in South Vietnam were ripe for revolt, and any kind of incident, or revolutionary "accelerator," combined with an offensive in the countryside, could set off a chain reaction that could topple the Thieu regime.[49]

Directives issued by higher echelons just prior to the offensive confirm this optimistic estimate. Although it is fair to say that some of the Party's references to impending victory were meant as exhortations to encourage the troops, the Party leadership did seem persuaded that the situation in Saigon was "highly revolutionary" and that the progressive social classes were "increasing their sympathy for the revolution." The key to stimulating this spirit would be military success in rural areas: "If we do not use our military force to neutralize the enemy force," said one directive, "the masses will not be able to gain victory through political activity alone. There will be little chance of success and much risk of being exposed to casualties."[50]

What is particularly noteworthy here is the sensitivity of the Party leadership to the unpredictability of the revolutionary process and to the explosive character of popular discontent, especially in urban areas. As the world has had good reason to recognize in recent years, revolutionary outbreaks often seem to occur with little warning, in societies that give the external appearance of political stability. For Hanoi, of course, this issue was of more than academic importance and Party leaders, temporarily frustrated at their inability to obtain a decisive shift in the balance of power in the countryside, appeared to turn their hopes to the volatile situation in urban areas as a means of redressing the situation. Several documents cited the example of the Bolshevik Revolution in 1917 and Lenin's "artful, flexible, and opportune" tactics to turn the rapidly changing situation in Russia to his advantage.

Still, the Party was taking a gamble that the crisis in the cities could be turned to its advantage at a time when it lacked the military potential to do serious damage to the enemy's armed forces. And the very unpredictability of revolution could be a disadvantage as well, for there was no guarantee of success. As one Party document remarked:

> Concerning the process of the revolution in general, as well as the process of the uprising in particular, the leaders cannot anticipate all specific conditions and situations that will develop. There are many conditions and factors we already know. However, there still remain many factors we cannot anticipate or that we do not know. The basic problem is that we must fully comprehend the general evolution of the situation, the strategy of the revolution and the principles relating to the guidance of the uprising. Efforts should be made to create maximum favorable conditions. It is of utmost importance that we are highly determined *in our actions*. In the process of these actions, events will enable us to act better.[51]

Clearly, the Politburo felt that the chance of success justified the risk involved. Whether or not total victory was achieved, some risk had to be undertaken to compel a shift in strategy in Washington, and the existing strategy showed little immediate promise of achieving that result. It was not a mark of desperation, because the Party was careful to make allowance for failure to achieve its maximum objectives. At a minimum, Hanoi was counting on the combined offensive and uprising to weaken the political and military foundations of the Saigon regime and to trigger a shift of policy in the United States, thus increasing the likelihood of a negotiated settlement favorable to the revolutionary cause.

The Tet Offensive

The first stage of the general offensive was launched in October 1967, with a series of "limited uprisings" in relatively isolated or border areas of the South—at Song Be and Loc Ninh near the Cambodian frontier; at Dak To, sitting astride a natural infiltration route into the Central Highlands; and at Con

Thien, a U.S. firebase near the DMZ. No attacks were scheduled in the Mekong delta, where the revolutionary armed forces were relatively weak. Here local Party organizations were instructed to form guerrilla groups and suicide squads (for the purpose of assassinating "local tyrants") in preparation for the climactic stage of general offensive and uprising to come. The probable aim of this first phase was to disperse U.S. and ARVN troops and draw them away from populated regions.

Rumors of the impending offensive had been circulating in Saigon for weeks, and Westmoreland had ordered the reinforcement of a number of special forces camps considered particularly vulnerable to Communist attacks. The assaults, when they came, were strong, and casualties were high on both sides, but the Communists were unable to seize any of their major objectives and were forced to withdraw when further reinforcements arrived.[52] A COSVN resolution described this first stage as a "great and unprecedented success" that had forced the enemy into a defensive position, but admitted that it had not annihilated the enemy forces or "created favorable conditions for motivating the masses to arise in towns and cities."[53] The true vulnerability of the enemy had yet to be clearly established.

By late fall, the U.S. military command in Saigon was convinced that a major Communist offensive was likely to occur early the following year. Information on troop movements showed that the rate of infiltration was now running at more than 20,000 a month and that main force units were beginning to move from the border toward populated areas. Captured documents alluded to a coming military move of considerable magnitude. Westmoreland attempted to prepare for the situation but predicted that the most likely objective of an attack would be near the Demilitarized Zone. In the early weeks of 1968 he ordered the strengthening of U.S. forces at Khe Sanh and other northern border posts. There was little concern over the situation in the capital region and, as a gesture of confidence, responsibility for the military security of the Saigon metropolitan area was transferred from U.S. to ARVN units. Early in the new year, signs pointed to a major Communist offensive during the Tet holidays at the end of January and Westmoreland suggested that the GVN cancel the cease-fire scheduled for the period. Thieu rejected the request but agreed to shorten the cease-fire and maintain ARVN units at half strength for the duration. U.S. forces were kept on alert, but intelligence sources did not take warnings of an attack particularly seriously.

Early in the morning of January 30, a series of small attacks took place in the Central Highlands and along the central coast. The following day the Communists launched a heavy nationwide attack on provincial and district capitals throughout the country. A total of thirty-six of the forty-four provincial capitals, five of the six autonomous cities, and 64 of the 242 district capitals, as well as countless hamlets and villages, were put under assault. For the most part, the attackers were local units of the PLAF. The Communists had been moving North Vietnamese main force units toward populated areas for more than two months, but most were kept on reserve and presumably would be introduced into combat only in the event that a total victory appeared likely.

Approximately 80,000 Communist troops were involved in the offensive.[54] The magnitude of the attacks took Saigon almost completely by surprise. Most ARVN units were not at full strength as a result of the holiday cease-fire. Bolstered by the element of surprise and the strength of the initial attack, Communist forces penetrated into a number of major cities, including Quang Tri and Da Nang in the north, Nha Trang and Qui Nhon along the central coast, Kontum and Ban Me Thuot in the Central Highlands, and sixteen provincial capitals in the Mekong delta.

In most cases, after the initial surprise, the invaders were thrown back after two or three days of heavy fighting. For the most part, the brunt of the counterattack was borne by U.S. firepower rather than ARVN units. As a result, damage to urban areas was extensive, since in many areas heavy bombardment by U.S. planes or artillery had been required to evict the enemy—thus eliciting the well-publicized comment by one U.S. military officer that the delta capital of Ben Tre had to be destroyed in order to save it.[55]

The most effective attack took place at Hué. There had been indications of a Communist plan to attack the old imperial capital since early in the war. North Vietnamese regular units at division strength had been in the mountains since 1966 and had built a logistical base in the A Shau valley on the Laotian border. Because Hué had a special historical meaning to many Vietnamese, an attack on the imperial capital would have a maximum propaganda effect, not only in Vietnam but throughout the world.

On January 30, under cover of a heavy fog, several main force battalions totaling more than 12,000 troops infiltrated the city, seized most of the area south of the Perfume River, which ran through the heart of the metropolitan area, and then crossed to the north bank and captured the bulk of the northern half of the city. By sunrise on the thirty-first, they controlled the city except for the U.S. military compound on the south bank of the river and the ARVN First Division headquarters. Evidently the Party hoped to retain control of the city and win support from anti-American and anti-GVN civilian groups for a popular uprising, for a temporary revolutionary administration was established that proceeded to exact brutal vengeance on GVN officials, foreigners, and prominent local figures considered unsympathetic to the revolution. The scope of the massacre has been the subject of intense controversy, but there seems to be no doubt that it took place. According to Guenter Lewy, whose 1978 book *America in Vietnam* is one of the more balanced studies of the war, a captured document stated that, during the occupation of the city, the Communists "eliminated 1,892 administrative personnel, 38 policemen, 790 tyrants." Most of these killings were apparently planned in advance.[56]

Within a few hours, local government forces had recovered from their surprise and with the support of U.S. Marines began to evict the insurgents from the south bank of the river. But the battle for control of the imperial citadel on the north bank was bitter, for the Communists brought in reinforcements from PAVN units beyond the suburbs and managed to retain a toehold in the city until February 25, when they were finally driven out after a bitter street battle. By U.S. estimate, total enemy casualties were 5,000 killed; allied military losses were put at 500 dead.[57]

If the battle of Hué had maximum psychological impact on world public opinion, the assault on Saigon undoubtedly represented a greater threat to the Thieu regime. It was kicked off with a series of attacks by suicide squads against a number of major installations within the city or its environs—on Independence Palace, on the Saigon radio station and racetrack, the new U.S. Embassy compound in the heart of the city, and on Tan Son Nhut airfield and the nearby headquarters of the Joint General Staff in the outskirts. Captured documents show that the Communists had hoped to seize a number of these key points within the city and to paralyze the GVN administration. The suicide squads, composed of from three to fifteen members each, had infiltrated the city several days before and had been waiting for the uprising in safe houses. If their efforts were successful, assault and propaganda units would surface within the city and begin to incite disorder and a mass uprising against the Thieu regime. Should the government show signs of panic and incipient disintegration, military units stationed outside the city would prepare to make their presence known. Agitation would be concentrated in working-class areas, where sympathy for the revolution was strongest. The Party seemed uncertain of the welcome it would receive in Saigon. Although several sources voiced confidence that the urban population was ripe for revolution, some also conceded that many townspeople "did not understand our policy" and were living in "the false happiness and demagogic culture of the enemy."[58]

In the event, the Communist suicide attacks were driven back, but not before they had inflicted considerable damage and achieved a gratifying propaganda impact. The major propaganda victory was achieved by slightly more than a dozen commandos who managed to penetrate the high outer walls of the U.S. Embassy compound in the heart of the city and invade the ground floor of the Embassy chancery, killing five Americans in the process. They were able to defend their position, under the eye of television cameras, until finally all were killed in counterattacks during the morning.[59]

As the commandos threw Saigon into a turmoil, additional Communist main force troops attacked the city from the suburbs, probably hoping to cut Saigon in half. About a thousand were able to penetrate into the city, mainly in small units. There were several ARVN battalions in the area, but they displayed little cohesion and only by the second day, when they were reinforced by U.S. troops brought in from the outside, did they begin to evict the attackers.

Meanwhile, the Saigon Uprising Committee was established and local agitation squads circulated throughout the city and appealed to the populace to revolt. The formation of a new united front, called the Alliance of National Democratic and Peace Forces (Lien Mien Dan Toc Dan Chu va Hoa Binh o Viet Nam), was announced in Hanoi and a four-point platform was issued, calling for the overthrow of the Thieu regime, the withdrawal of U.S. troops, and negotiations to set up a democratic, independent, peaceful, and neutral South Vietnam. Although not publicly identified with the North or the NLF, the new front was clearly a creature of Hanoi and patently designed to appeal to moderates who had withheld their cooperation from previous organizations of the NLF.

On the second day, the GVN went on the offensive, and ARVN forces and the local police began to root out Communists from the capital and its sister city of Cholon. Westmoreland sent U.S. forces into the city and set up a ring of U.S. units in the suburbs to prevent an orderly Communist retreat. By February 5, resistance had collapsed.

The Results of Tet

The Tet Offensive broke like a clap of thunder on an astonished world. Certainly that was the case in the United States. Lulled by government assurances that progress was being made in South Vietnam, most Americans were not prepared for the realization that the Communists were capable of launching a major attack into the heart of Saigon and other cities in the South. The Johnson administration responded quickly to minimize the damage and, once the immediate threat had been averted, echoed the comments of General Westmoreland in Saigon that the Tet Offensive had been a major defeat for the Communists. From a strictly military standpoint, Westmoreland was correct. The Communists had been unable to hold any major urban center except Hué for more than a few days. The hoped-for general uprising had not materialized, and prisoners captured during the offensive admitted that they had been disappointed at the relative lack of support for the revolution among the urban population. Even in I Corps, where North Vietnamese regulars had taken part in the battle, the Communists were unable to retain control of the two northern provinces. In the process, they had suffered the heaviest casualties of the entire war. According to U.S. sources, they had lost 32,000 killed and 5,800 captured in the course of the attacks. Allied losses were put at a little more than 3,000: 1,000 Americans and 2,028 South Vietnamese.[60] Equally important, the revolutionary infrastructure, built up carefully in cities, towns, and rural villages, had surfaced during the Tet Offensive in an effort to maximize the chances of success and had suffered badly in Saigon's counterattacks. One experienced Australian journalist estimated that 40 percent of the Party's political cadres were killed or otherwise immobilized during the offensive.[61]

In general, the offensive was more successful in rural areas than in the cities. In several provinces, it severely damaged the pacification program and many villages returned to revolutionary control. One Party document claimed that revolutionary administrations had been newly set up in more than 600 liberated villages between the start of the offensive and the end of March. At least for the moment, the Communists once again had access to the vital rural villages. Here, too, however, the gains were in some cases less than anticipated. ARVN units as a whole did not break as anticipated, and villagers in many areas did not welcome the insurgency forces with the expected enthusiasm.[62] On the other hand, informed U.S. sources admitted that the offensive had nearly succeeded in several areas, and in some instances defeat was averted only by the timely intervention of U.S. forces. There was considerable concern as to whether ARVN could stand up to future attacks.

Obviously, however, there was more to the Tet Offensive than its immediate military consequences. From the political point of view, it marked a crucial turning point in the war. By now, the war had become above all a test of wills between Hanoi and Washington. The Johnson administration, caught on the buzz saw of mounting expenditures and rising public discontent with the war, was unwilling to make the commitment necessary to achieve a decisive military victory. It had to gamble that half a million U.S. troops could prevent the Communists from achieving significant military successes and thus provide Saigon with enough breathing room to improve its own capacity to handle the insurgency. Hanoi was convinced that the GVN would be a pushover without U.S. support and that the Americans lacked the patience to win a protracted war. In the phrase so familiar to veteran observers of the war, the United States had to win; Hanoi had only to show that it would not lose.

Here, of course, was the true significance of Tet. For despite the heavy losses suffered by the revolutionary forces, the February offensive showed that the Communists were still capable of shaking the Saigon regime to its very foundations. In brief, it showed Washington that the war was unwinnable on any acceptable terms. The result is history. In March, President Johnson made the fateful decision to pursue a compromise settlement in the Vietnam War. When General Westmoreland requested 200,000 additional U.S. troops for South Vietnam, a presidential commission headed by new Secretary of Defense Clark Clifford concluded that the general's request would only further Americanize the war and recommended that additional troops be sent only upon condition of a better GVN performance. Johnson accepted the report and announced a halt in U.S. bombing raids above the 20th parallel, promising a total cessation if Hanoi demonstrated restraint in its own prosecution of the war. The D.R.V. responded quickly. While denouncing the partial bombing halt, it declared its willingness to open discussions with U.S. representatives on the unconditional cessation of bombing so that other talks could take place.

A balanced view of Tet, then, must view it in highly qualified terms and not simply as a victory or defeat for either side. Hanoi's gamble that South Vietnam was ripe for revolt had been shown to be a miscalculation. The mistake was costly and undoubtedly contributed to Hanoi's new willingness to open the door slightly to negotiations without an unconditional bombing halt and without a decisive shift in the military balance of forces. On the other hand, the Johnson administration had clearly recognized the failure of its strategy of achieving victory through military pressure. The door was open to a period of fighting and negotiating in which Hanoi's major objective would be to maneuver the United States out of the war.

11
Fighting and Negotiating
(1968–1973)

Although the Tet Offensive was frequently described in the Western world as a massive single effort by the Vietnamese Communists to achieve a total military victory in the South, it was viewed by the Party leadership in Hanoi as simply one phase of an extended military and political operation lasting several months. The first stage, begun in the fall of 1967, had been designed to test GVN defenses in key regions in the Central Highlands and along the Cambodian border. If successful, it would wear down the enemy's military strength and divert it from populated coastal regions. The second stage, involving military attacks on major cities throughout the country, was directed at stimulating a revolutionary upsurge by the masses in urban areas. If it achieved optimum results, it would lead to the overthrow of the Saigon regime and the formation of a coalition government with the Communists as a major or even dominant political force. At a minimum, it would further reduce the morale and the military strength of the GVN and lead to a stage of fighting and negotiating.

As described in the previous chapter, the bulk of the military forces sent into attack during the Tet Offensive were local units of the PLAF. Most of the North Vietnamese divisions and many of the main force units of the PLAF were held in reserve. Only in I Corps, where the Communists appeared determined to inflict permanent military damage on the GVN in the northern provinces, were reserve units brought into play in order to supplement operations by local forces. Had the February offensive shown signs of destroying a significant portion of the GVN forces, or had there been indications of a major breakdown in Saigon's ability to govern, those reserve forces might have been moved into urban areas to provide the final surge to victory. But when it became clear that the Tet Offensive would achieve only limited military goals, Hanoi's main force units were not immediately engaged.

The third stage of the 1968 offensive opened in mid-February, with a series of attacks on smaller cities, towns, and villages throughout South Vietnam. In some cases actual military assaults took place. In others, there were simply rocket or mortar attacks on government-occupied cities and towns. The climax

273

came in early March with assaults on about a dozen cities, mostly in the Mekong delta. The delta had not absorbed heavy attacks during the earlier stages of the offensive, but a number of ARVN units had been withdrawn from the area at the height of the fighting during the Tet holidays, thus probably encouraging the Party leadership in the belief that military struggle might achieve beneficial results in the area.

According to captured documents, the aim of the new stage was to keep the military pressure on Saigon and expand liberated areas in the South. A resolution issued by a COSVN conference in March pointed out that the war had entered a new phase, described as "a very fierce, complex phase of strategic offensive attacks aimed at securing final victory." The objective was to create "a seething revolutionary atmosphere with continuous attacks and continuous uprisings." The resolution emphasized that even political struggle should now take on a military character:

> It is necessary to understand clearly that the substance of the present political struggle is not "to stage demonstrations and present petitions" but *to make use of violence to overthrow the enemy state power and build the people's revolutionary state power.*

The party's urban apparatus was instructed to do its part by stimulating the popular movement against the Saigon regime:

> In towns, cities, and district seats where our military forces are strong enough to enable conquest, we must resolutely motivate the masses to arise and seize the state power; in places where our military forces are not strong enough to take control, we must maintain and develop the struggle, quickly strengthen the revolution's real strength and create [favorable] conditions for the conquests of these places.[1]

In rural areas, the insurgency leadership was instructed to defeat enemy sweeps, cut off vital communications lines to isolated towns, expand and connect major liberated base areas, and exert pressure to encircle and destroy enemy towns and cities. Within liberated areas, the revolutionary state power was to be strengthened through the holding of popular elections, the construction of combat villages, and the repression of counterrevolutionary elements.

The Battle of Khe Sanh

In actuality, this post-Tet phase of the general offensive had only limited success. The urban attacks had nuisance value but did not result in any spectacular seizures of power. It now became clear that the main focus of Communist concern had shifted to northern I Corps where, according to one American journalist, at least seven PAVN and five PLAF divisions were concentrated. And the infiltration rate continued high, running at nearly 20,000 per month throughout the spring.[2] Khe Sanh, the isolated U.S. firebase selected by the Party leadership for an effort to achieve a spectacular victory on the eve of the negotiations, was located in the midst of rugged hills just south of the DMZ. The Communists had elements of two PAVN divisions—a total of some 15,000 men—in the immediate vicinity, while the U.S. and ARVN forces at the base numbered only about 6,000. Many observers had remarked on the similarity to Dien Bien Phu and doubted that Khe Sanh could be adequately defended. Like Dien Bien Phu, it was isolated, in the midst of difficult terrain, and surrounded by mountains. Communications with the outside world were tenuous at best. In Saigon, General Westmoreland fully expected a major attack at Khe Sanh before the end of March. But unlike many of his critics, he did not fear comparison with Dien Bien Phu. Although he conceded that there were certain risks, he claimed that Khe Sanh could be held. In contrast to Dien Bien Phu, U.S. forces held the high ground, for the firebase was on a small plateau, not in a wide valley. Although the North Vietnamese had artillery in the area, overall the Americans would have the advantage in firepower. Moreover, the base was closer to populated areas along the coast and would be able to receive much better air support. On the other hand, it was also closer to Communist supply lines leading from North Vietnam than had been its counterpart in 1954.[3]

The battle of Khe Sanh began in January and lasted for nearly three months, during which the isolated base was exposed to almost constant attacks. The attackers hid in the high elephant grass around the base and laid down a heavy artillery and mortar barrage. But the defenders were assisted by almost continual air support—three hundred tactical air sorties a day dropped 35,000 tons of bombs. And although the airstrip came under heavy fire, communications with the outside world were never cut. The biggest Communist success came at Lang Ve, nine miles away, where North Vietnamese troops, with the aid of Russian tanks, overran a special forces camp. Finally, in early April, U.S. units stationed on the coast launched an attack up Route 9, linked up with Khe Sanh, and relieved the siege. Soon thereafter attention shifted to the A Shau valley and the area west of Hué, which was now cleared with the help of the ARVN First Division.

In the meantime, a second phase of Communist attacks took place in May. The most publicized was an abortive attack on Saigon by combat units near Tan Son Nhut airfield and rocket attacks on the city itself. For a brief period, a handful of suicide squads managed to infiltrate Cholon in an operation called by the local American community a "mini-Tet," but they were eliminated within a few days. Communist sources concede that this final stage of the 1968 spring offensive and uprising did not fulfill expectations. With the element of surprise lost, the attacking forces suffered heavy casualties and achieved few successes. Moreover, there were ominous signs of pessimism and unwillingness to sacrifice within the movement, as well as apathy among the masses. A series of further attacks took place in mid-August, but had no better success.

Military operations up through the end of August 1968, including the Tet Offensive at the beginning of the year, had cost the Communists more than 75,000 dead and wounded.[4] The cost could be justified if it influenced American behavior in the opening rounds of the negotiating process then under way in Hanoi and Washington. Throughout the spring and summer of 1968, sparring between the two sides continued over the issue of prerequisites to negotiations. Hanoi had responded to Johnson's offer in late March but had only agreed to talk about a U.S. bombing halt. In early exchanges, it repeated its demand for a total and unconditional cessation of bombing above the Demilitarized Zone and U.S. acceptance of the NLF four points. The United States countered by demanding the mutual withdrawal of all foreign troops from the South and a pledge by Hanoi that it would not attempt to seize South Vietnam by force. For the moment all that had changed was that the two sides were willing to discuss negotiations without prior conditions.

Finally, in October, came a breakthrough. Against his better judgment, President Johnson took the advice of subordinates and announced a total bombing halt of the D.R.V. and called for the opening of formal talks in Paris.[5] Hanoi was informed that Washington's action did not call for a reciprocal gesture from the D.R.V. The speech did not specifically state that the halt was unconditional, however, and Johnson refused a request by Hanoi to put the promise in writing. The D.R.V. at this point dropped its demand for an unconditional bombing halt and tacitly agreed to a U.S. demand not to launch artillery attacks on Saigon. Talks could now begin.

Maintaining the Offensive

The long and costly offensive launched in the early weeks of 1968 had a perceptible effect on the military and political capacities of the revolutionary movement. Most of the fighting had been borne by the local forces, which, along with the political infrastructure, had suffered the bulk of the casualties. In the wake of the attacks, recruitment was down and desertions were on the rise. Hanoi was increasingly compelled to fill the gap with PAVN units infiltrated from the North. This in turn gave rise to unrest among southerners over the domination of the movement by northerners and to occasional complaints that Hanoi was attempting to "break up" the PLAF or place it under tighter Party control. One prominent member of the NLF complained of growing northern dominance of the movement and the excessive militarization of the conflict. According to one estimate, by late 1968, of a total of 125,000 main force troops in the South, 85,000 were North Vietnamese.[6]

The GVN did its best to compound Hanoi's problems. Taking advantage of the temporary weakness of the insurgency forces, the Saigon regime intensified its efforts to uproot the revolutionary infrastructure and improve security in the countryside. One knowledgeable observer estimated that more than 2,000 Viet Cong cadres were being arrested each month in the new CIA-supported Phoenix Program. An "accelerated pacification campaign" was launched to recoup GVN losses at the village level. With the threat from Communist main force troops diminished, ARVN and U.S. divisions were broken up into smaller units in order to promote the pacification effort.[7] In many crucial provinces, there were surface indications of progress. But the rise in the number of refugees was alarming. In Quang Ngai, nearly one-third of the population of the entire province was now living in refugee camps. And, as always, the key question remained: Would the Viet Cong not simply return after the government troops departed?

With its force levels depleted by the losses incurred during the Tet Offensive, Hanoi was in no position to respond effectively to the challenge from Saigon. But a failure to react could have a significant effect on the morale within the movement and lead to a further decline in revolutionary momentum, already damaged by the failure of the offensive to achieve total victory. Internal documents dating from the summer and fall of 1968 clearly reflect the pervasive sense of disillusionment at various levels within the movement. One report conceded that many had expected Tet to lead to total victory and that

> some [of our personnel] have lost confidence in the higher echelon leadership and in the revolutionary capability of the people. They think that our assessment of enemy capabilities is inaccurate, our strategic determination is erroneous, and we have to lower our requirements and prolong the war. They become doubtful of victory, pessimistic, and display a shirking attitude.[8]

Even within the higher echelons, there was evidence of some second-guessing over strategy. Truong Chinh, long considered an advocate of cautious policies in South Vietnam, remarked in a speech printed in September that "we must know when to go on the defensive." Chinh's view was evidently not an isolated one. The American journalist Robert Shaplen reported a purge of pro-Soviet elements in the Party in late 1968, apparently because of Moscow's view that more emphasis should be placed on the political struggle in South Vietnam. And there were signs of discontent with events in Vietnam among Hanoi's major allies, leading Party spokesmen to stress the virtues of self-reliance and to complain with a degree of defensiveness, "we are not beginners at the art of revolution."[9]

Pressure from without often seemed to increase unity within the Party leadership in Hanoi. In any event, although there was probably a general recognition that the general offensive and uprising had not achieved all its objectives, there was, at least for the moment, a conviction that the existing policy of high-level armed struggle must be continued. For years it had been assumed that in order to accelerate the disintegration of the South Vietnamese armed forces and compel the United States to withdraw its troops, the revolutionary forces must fight even harder after the beginning of the stage of simultaneous fighting and negotiating. Without such pressure, Washington would have no incentive to compromise. For the moment, in other words, Hanoi had little choice. There was a growing recognition, however, that it would be a long war. As one captured document stated, "Victory will come to us, not suddenly, but in a complicated and tortuous way. This victory is a limited victory, not a complete and clear-cut victory."[10]

During the spring and summer of 1969, then, Hanoi attempted to maintain the pressure on the battlefield. Maximum results had to be realized at minimum cost. Unlike the previous year, emphasis was placed not on a coordinated surge, but on a series of attacks waged throughout the country "simultaneously, continuously, widespreadedly [sic]," often undertaken by small-scale and paramilitary units. For the most part, North Vietnamese divisions were kept out of combat, as several began to congregate in III Corps in preparation for a possible attack on Saigon.[11]

As it turned out, the 1969 military campaign, after a promising beginning, was a serious disappointment. The PLAF had some limited success in launching attacks on cities and towns in the delta, but it was largely unsuccessful in hindering pacification efforts. Problems of morale, popular apathy and hostility, low combat effectiveness, and confusion on objectives among cadres continued. As a result, as one internal document conceded, "Generally speaking, our campaign was not strong or continuous." Such difficulties did not immediately cause Party leaders in the South to question existing strategy. According to a captured resolution issued at the close of a COSVN conference in July, heavy pressure must be maintained on the enemy through a high level of political and military struggle. Otherwise, warned the document, the United States could not be compelled to seek a negotiated settlement but would attempt to outwait the D.R.V. in a protracted conflict; it might even extend the war into neighboring Laos and Cambodia.[12]

Still, the disappointing results of the 1969 campaign must have put further pressure on the militants in the Politburo. With a new military stalemate developing in the South, there was evidently a rising sentiment for lowering the level of armed struggle and reevaluating priorities. Although the precise terms of the debate within the Party leadership are not clear, it seems likely that the controversy was less over long-term goals than over tactical responses to the current situation. Some members may have argued that with the large U.S. presence still in South Vietnam, it would be advisable for the time being to put greater emphasis on economic reconstruction and prepare for a new wave of attacks in the future. As always, Truong Chinh appeared to be in the forefront of those advocating moderation in the South. There is no indication, however, of any major shake-up in the balance of forces within the party leadership. When Ho Chi Minh died in September, Secretary General Le Duan, long considered among the most militant of Party leaders, appeared to emerge as the most influential figure in the Politburo.[13]

In the end, the debate in Hanoi led to a decision to reduce the level of combat in South Vietnam. The relevant Politburo documents have not been made public, but a captured COSVN resolution issued in October described guerrilla warfare as "of particular importance" at the time and as the best way to cope with a powerful and stubborn enemy. The immediate strategic objective was to combine political and military struggle to wear down the enemy gradually and to frustrate the enemy's pacification effort. Particular emphasis was placed on rebuilding the Party's political infrastructure.

Thus, by late 1969, the thrust of the revolution in the South had at least temporarily abated. A major exposé of the new line came in December with the publication of an article by Vo Nguyen Giap, entitled "The Party's Military Line is the Ever-Victorious Banner of People's War in our Country." More sober than his article of late 1967, it stressed the importance of combined political and military struggle as the basic law governing revolutionary violence in Vietnam and emphasized the gradual defeat of the enemy. It appealed for a spirit of self-reliance and creativity and pointed out that "we cannot copy foreign experiences nor be complacent with the experiences we have acquired."[14]

Some foreign observers viewed the new retrenchment strategy as an indication that the Party had entirely abandoned the concept of a gradual progression to full-scale military confrontation and now hoped to win the war at stage two. Douglas Pike, labeling the new stage one of "neo-revolutionary strategy," remarked that it imposed less strain but could not be victorious, since it imposed no pressure on the United States. It is possible that some in the Politburo felt that a final stage of main force conflict could be avoided. But Giap's article clearly indicates that, in his mind at least, the conservative tactics adopted in late 1969 were meant to be temporary, for he concluded his analysis with a strong reiteration of his frequently voiced belief that revolutionary war in Vietnam must necessarily advance to the stage of regular war. At the beginning, he said, the revolutionary forces are small and can only carry out guerrilla tactics. This, however, is only a temporary expedient:

> To keep the offensive, they must ceaselessly develop guerrilla war and partial insurrection. From regional forces, they must build increasingly strong main force units, and incessantly develop the guerrilla war into a regular war. Only through *regular war* in which the main force troops fight in a concentrated manner and the armed services are combined and fighting in coordination with regional troops, militia guerrillas, and the political forces of all the people, can they annihilate im-

portant forces of the enemy, liberate vast areas of land . . . and create conditions for great strides in the war.[15]

The advance from guerrilla war to regular war was thus "the law for achieving victory in the people's war in our country." The key issue was to know how "to transform guerrilla war into regular war at the correct time and the correct place."

Giap's comments were seconded in an article by Politburo alternate member General Van Tien Dung. Dung stressed the need for flexibility and the avoidance of a dogmatic adherence to the concept of "distinct phases":

> Our enemy, the form of his war of aggression, the social, political, economic, and cultural conditions, the national characteristics, and the space and time factors of our fight have inherent characteristics which are different from those of other countries. These practical conditions require *us to be constantly creative in learning from the experiences acquired by the fraternal countries in fighting the aggressors.* The practical conditions of our fight also constantly change and, therefore, *do not permit us to mechanically utilize our own combat experience which is no longer practical.*[16]

A crucial aspect of this reexamination of revolutionary strategy was the increasing recognition of the importance of advanced technology and weaponry. In the past, most of the Party's military leaders had tended to subordinate the role of firepower in revolutionary war to other factors, such as the combined force of people's war (Vo Nguyen Giap) and human will (Nguyen Chi Thanh). Now, in an implicit recognition that the Americans could not be defeated unless the revolutionary forces could achieve military parity on the battlefield, influential military planners called for a heightened effort to modernize the PAVN.[17] Confirmation of the new strategy appeared at a plenary meeting of the Party's Central Committee in February 1970. Brief published reports from the meeting indicated that, for the moment, economic construction in the D.R.V. would receive equal priority with war needs in the South.[18]

Prelude to Negotiations

Party leaders had contended that negotiations could begin when an indecisive situation had been created on the battlefield. Apparently that minimum condition had been created with the Tet Offensive in 1968. But Hanoi viewed the opening of negotiations as distinct from a situation in which conditions for a diplomatic settlement had been reached. For that, a favorable military situation was a prerequisite. Because that would take time, Hanoi's objective would now be to string out the negotiating process by imposing conditions until the United States had been driven by military defeat and domestic unrest to make fundamental concessions at the conference table. The first condition was a total bombing halt in the North. This became a prerequisite to negotiations for a very practical reason: Hanoi would find it difficult to achieve a favorable military position in the South as long as the bombing lasted. Once this condition had been granted and peace talks had begun, a second condition for a settlement would be imposed—the prior removal of U.S. troops.[19]

Realistically, Hanoi could not expect to obtain total victory at the conference table. The essence of diplomacy is compromise. What could reasonably be expected was an agreement calling for a withdrawal of all U.S. forces and the formation of a coalition government in South Vietnam under conditions that would permit the Communists gradually—and, it was hoped, with a minimum of violence—to move to a position of dominance and unification with the D.R.V. A crucial issue in negotiations would thus be the nature of such a coalition government. Could it include members of the existing Thieu government, or at least political elements in South Vietnam unsympathetic to the Communists? Or should Hanoi demand a dominant position for the NLF and its followers?

The issue was broached in a training document, probably written in late 1967. According to this source, the insurgents would fight until the Americans agreed to withdraw and "recognize a broad national democratic coalition regime to be established in South Vietnam with the South Vietnam NLF as its core." Acceptance of the NLF as a key element in the new government, it said, was a crucial factor, for

> only such a broad, national democratic regime based on these two conditions can have the capacity to become a national, democratic, people's regime for the four revolutionary classes based on the worker-peasant alliance led by the workers, to guarantee independence for the nation, land for the tillers, reunification of our country, and a step forward in the task of building socialism for the whole country.[20]

Whether this statement represented official policy in Hanoi is unknown. Given the Party's desire to prolong the negotiating process it is likely that it represented a position from which Hanoi could retreat at its convenience and by miniscule degrees. In any case, for the credibility of Hanoi's demands for a coalition government to be firmly established, it must have a political entity in South Vietnam that could claim to represent the legitimate interests of the people. For years, sources close to the Party had been hinting at the possibility that a provisional revolutionary government might be formed in South Vietnam. Had the Tet Offensive achieved a greater degree of success, it is likely that it would have been formed at that time. Now, with the opening of negotiations, the creation of a political force with governmental pretensions was clearly in order. In May 1969, representatives of the NLF and the new "third force" Alliance of National Democratic and Peace Forces (ANDPF) met in a liberated area near Saigon to engage in preliminary discussions on the formation of such a government. In early June the Congress of Delegates, comprising eighty-eight representatives and seventy-two guests, formed a new "government of anti-U.S. resistance for national salvation." To provide the new Provisional Revolutionary Government (PRG) with an administrative apparatus at the local level, people's revolutionary councils were formed at the provincial, district, township, and village levels in liberated areas throughout South Vietnam. According to the Liberation Press Agency, by the summer of 1969 such councils had been elected in 1,268 townships, 124 districts, and three cities.[21] By the end of the year, Hanoi claimed that the government had been established in forty-three provinces in the South.

For the Nixon administration, which came into office in January 1969, the Vietnam crisis presented a number of dilemmas. The administration was committed to obtaining "peace with honor," to withdrawing U.S. troops without giving the appearance of turning South Vietnam over to the Communists. The uncomfortable reality, however, was that its predecessor had been forced to increase U.S. involvement precisely because the Saigon regime was unable to survive on its own. Nixon's answer was a combination of diplomacy and Vietnamization. The diplomatic card must be played in such a way as to seek an honorable exit from the war while granting Communist participation in the political process in the South, but without irreparably damaging the Saigon government's chances to survive in head-to-head competition with the NLF. Vietnamization was designed to indicate Washington's commitment to strengthen ARVN forces while gradually withdrawing U.S. troops. It would be a delicate operation. U.S. forces could not be withdrawn so rapidly as to destabilize the military situation in South Vietnam and encourage the Communists to launch a major new offensive. On the other hand, the departure of U.S. troops must be sufficiently rapid to mollify critical opinion in the United States and to convince the American people that President Nixon had found a way out of the war.

The Nixon plan for Vietnam thus did not necessarily call for a negotiated settlement. It accepted the possibility of a diplomatic solution if Hanoi could be persuaded that an outright military victory was unlikely. In the absence of flexibility from Hanoi, the policy of Vietnamization should strengthen Saigon sufficiently so that the insurgency in the South could be contained, if not actually defeated. In the opening exchanges in Paris, the U.S. representative presented stiff conditions for a settlement: withdrawal of all foreign troops (including those of the D.R.V.) from South Vietnam and insistence that the compromise political settlement include the Thieu regime in Saigon. On the first issue, Hanoi stood fast and described the U.S. demand for mutual troop withdrawal as a "cunning plot aimed at confusing the aggressors with their victims." A letter from Ho Chi Minh to Nixon in the summer of 1969 said that the U.S. withdrawal should be unconditional and on the basis of D.R.V. proposals. But Hanoi did indicate that compromise was possible on the second issue. In May the NLF issued a ten-point program in Paris that hinted at the possibility that participation by members of the Thieu government might be acceptable in a future coalition government.[22]

It must have been clear to Hanoi from the nature of Washington's conditions that a favorable settlement was not a likely prospect for the immediate future. Under the circumstances, it made sense to maintain a stiff diplomatic posture and await the further removal of U.S. troops from the South, thus improving prospects for victory on the battlefield. Indeed, the Nixon administration had already set a date for the final removal of all U.S. forces. General Creighton Abrams, Westmoreland's successor at MACV, was informed that the basic objective of the new administration was to end the U.S. military commitment to the GVN by June 1972. The drawdown of U.S. troops would begin slowly to allow Saigon a breathing space and then accelerate after 1970. At some point the declining curve of the U.S. presence would inevitably intersect the rising level of the size of the revolutionary forces in the South.

The Invasion of Cambodia

One of the major military consequences of the rising U.S. presence in South Vietnam in the mid-1960s had been to force the insurgency back from the provinces around Saigon into the border region near Cambodia. In fact, the eastern provinces of Cambodia had been used as a base area by the revolutionary armed forces since the mid-1950s. After the arrival of U.S. combat forces, the area was increasingly used as a sanctuary from enemy sweeps and a secure area for the location of COSVN headquarters. Vietnamese Communist use of the area had received the tacit if reluctant approval of the Cambodian government of Prince Norodom Sihanouk, who hoped thereby to maintain amicable relations with Hanoi. By the late 1960s, the city of Sihanoukville on the Gulf of Siam had become a major port of entry for provisions and equipment destined for the insurgency forces in South Vietnam, particularly after other routes had been closed off by U.S. bombing raids and naval patrols along the South Vietnamese coastline.

The situation was one of considerable delicacy. Relations between the Vietnamese Communists and their Cambodian comrades had become increasingly strained in recent years. In the years immediately following the Geneva Conference, the Cambodian movement (called at that time the Cambodian People's Revolutionary Party, or Pracheachon) was small and dominated by a pro-Hanoi leadership under Son Ngoc Minh. According to claims by the Pol Pot regime in 1979, Hanoi compelled the Cambodian insurgents to reject a policy of armed struggle in order to avoid undermining Cambodia's precarious but useful neutrality. In the mid-1960s, however, leadership of the Party (now renamed the Khmer Communist Party, or KCP) was seized by an extremist faction under the Paris-trained intellectual Pol Pot (real name Saloth Sar). Radical in its social orientation and intensely nationalist, the new KCP leadership adopted a policy of armed struggle against the Phnom Penh regime, despite growing irritation in Hanoi.

The increasing use of Cambodia's eastern provinces by Vietnamese military units (one Hanoi source admits that the Vietnamese were "massively present" in the area, while a so-called Black Book issued by the Pol Pot regime in 1979 claimed the total number reached 300,000, undoubtedly an exaggeration) created problems, not only with Sihanouk's government but with the local Cambodian population. For example, a captured notebook written by a Viet Cong cadre in 1969 remarked that the insurgency leadership had encountered serious difficulties in relations with the prickly Sihanouk, who had grown increasingly irritated at Vietnamese use of the eastern provinces. Suspicion and hostility, a product of centuries of conflict and mutual dislike, characterized relations between the PLAF and the local Cambodian population. The higher echelons had directed that the local population be treated with consideration, but Vietnamese condescension and contempt for the slower and more passive Cambodians was not easily overcome. The captured notebook referred to some of the more common problems encountered: lack of respect for Cambodian territory, lack of courtesy in handling civilians, and—in an interesting complaint that U.S. troops in South Vietnam could share—Vietnamese troops complained that it was difficult to tell the difference between friend and foe.[23]

The Communist presence in the area was of course no secret in Washington. Hanoi's use of Cambodian territory as a sanctuary had been a source of serious concern to the U.S. military command in Saigon for years. By the late 1960s, MACV claimed that there were at least 50,000 insurgency forces in the border area, raiding the South Vietnamese border provinces with impunity and then withdrawing to safety in Cambodia. But the Johnson administration had never approved Westmoreland's requests for permission to launch air and ground attacks into Cambodian territory, in the belief that the political risks outweighed the potential military advantages.

Under the Nixon administration, the policy began to change. MACV commander Creighton Abrams, irritated at heavy Communist activity along the border and evidently fearful of a predicted Communist offensive on Saigon, requested permission to launch selective bombing attacks on the Viet Cong base areas on the Cambodian side of the border. The request was approved, but the raids were kept secret in order to avoid alerting the media and antagonizing public opinion.[24]

In March 1970, Sihanouk was overthrown and replaced by a new government under General Lon Nol. There was considerable speculation at the time about possible direct U.S. involvement in the coup, but evidence to substantiate the charge is lacking and it is likely that the coup was planned and carried out by military and civilian figures disgruntled by Sihanouk's neutralist foreign policy and his tolerance of Vietnamese occupation of the border provinces.

The coup represented a serious threat to the revolutionary movement in South Vietnam. The new government cancelled the trade agreement allowing the D.R.V. to use Sihanoukville and demanded that the Viet Cong leave Cambodian territory within three days. COSVN leaders opened negotiations with Phnom Penh in an effort to resolve differences, but when Lon Nol refused to be dissuaded, Hanoi decided to throw its full support to the Khmer insurgency movement.

During the regime of the charismatic Prince Sihanouk, the KCP had been weak and its strategy ineffective. According to one recent Vietnamese source, in 1970 there were only about a hundred Cambodian guerrillas in the eastern provinces.[25] But with the invasion of Cambodia in 1970, the significance of the insurgency movement there suddenly became more obvious, and Hanoi moved quickly to revitalize it. It seems likely that at this time the Vietnamese agreed to sponsor the KCP's new militant strategy in Cambodia and to provide the necessary assistance to promote its growth. But Hanoi was no doubt also determined to guarantee that the revitalized Party would be receptive to Vietnamese direction. It was probably for this reason, as well as to provide a nucleus of trained pro-Vietnamese activists, that several hundred Khmer Communists who had been living in the D.R.V. since 1954 were now returned to Cambodia to take part in the movement. In succeeding months, with the active assistance of experienced Vietnamese cadres, the KCP began to intensify its organizational efforts at the village level in the eastern provinces under Viet Cong control.

In April, a conference was convened in South China, where representatives of the three Indochinese parties agreed to coordinate their efforts to evict the U.S. imperialists from Indochina and to form an Indochinese confederation after victory. A patriotic alliance (the National United Front of Kampuchea, or FUNK) and a shadow government (the Royal National United Government of Kampuchea, or GRUNK) were formed, allegedly at Hanoi's insistence, under the titular head of Prince Sihanouk, who had sought refuge and support in Peking. Leadership of both, however, was in the hands of the KCP.[26]

In Washington, the White House saw the coup as an opportunity to end Communist occupation of the border provinces, and for the next few weeks there was intensive discussion within the administration on how to take advantage of the crisis to strike at Communist sanctuaries along the border. Some high figures in the Departments of State and Defense were reluctant to take any action at all, but others recommended an invasion of the eastern provinces, either by ARVN forces only or by a joint force of U.S. and South Vietnamese units. President Nixon eventually authorized a plan for a joint operation, in which more than 30,000 troops would strike several miles into Cambodian territory to destroy Communist bases in the area and then withdraw. The attack opened on April 28, beginning with an advance into the Fishhook and the Parrot's Beak, two areas heavily infested with Viet Cong bases, and then, a few days later, into several other base areas along the border. The attack encountered little resistance and advanced essentially unmolested, but it did not locate COSVN headquarters, which, according to later Vietnamese claims, was located at the village of Xa Mat, in deep bunkers at the northern tip of Tay Ninh Province. More important, perhaps, it aroused massive protests in the United States from those who feared that the invasion would simply widen the war into an all-Indochina conflict. The shock waves of protest soon reached Congress, which passed legislation compelling the administration to remove U.S. troops from Cambodia before the end of June.

The invasion of Cambodia remains today one of the most controversial steps taken by the United States during the entire Indochinese war. The Nixon administration claimed that it had lowered U.S. casualties, diminished the military threat to Saigon, and thus accelerated the withdrawal of U.S. troops. Critics took issue with these claims. In a 1979 book on the Cambodian crisis, journalist William Shawcross cites U.S. government studies to the effect that although the invasion may have briefly disrupted Communist logistics and thus reduced the immediate threat to the capital area, it had little effect on U.S. casualties and actually set back the pace of Vietnamization.[27]

At the moment, evidence of Communist intentions is probably too scanty to permit a firm judgment on the issue. On a short-term basis, and from a strictly military point of view, it seems hard to deny that the invasion disrupted Communist operations and delayed Hanoi's plans to launch a new offensive in South Vietnam. If that is the case, the invasion not only provided a measure of increased security for the capital area, but also additional breathing space for the program of Vietnamization to take hold.[28]

A more serious criticism of the Nixon strategy in Cambodia is that it unnecessarily widened the war and initiated the process that led to the fall of Cambodia to the Communists and to the tragic civil war and subsequent death by starvation or execution of perhaps millions of Cambodians. This is the central thesis of the Shawcross study. In his memoirs, Henry Kissinger has vigorously denied that the Nixon administration must bear primary responsibility for the Cambodian tragedy and points out that the takeover of the eastern provinces by the Vietnamese Communists was already well under way before the invasion took place. Hanoi, not Washington, had widened the war into neighboring Cambodia. Kissinger contended that he suggested the neutralization of Cambodia to D.R.V. representative Le Duc Tho, but that Tho had summarily rejected the offer, pointing out that the Communists would eventually take it over anyway.[29]

Kissinger's argument is not without merit. The course of the war in South Vietnam had inexorably eroded the fragile neutrality of Cambodia and by early 1970 only U.S. reluctance to act against Communist base areas in the border provinces had prevented it from becoming openly involved in the conflict. If, as the above chronology suggests, Hanoi had already given the signal to escalate the struggle against the new Lon Nol regime, Kissinger may well be correct in contending that it was too late to reestablish Cambodian neutrality either through Lon Nol, a return of Sihanouk, or some form of bilateral guarantee with Hanoi. The Nixon administration can perhaps be faulted for not making a greater effort to explore the possibility, but it is probably true that the dynamics of the Vietnam War made an erosion of Cambodian neutrality almost inevitable, despite the efforts of both Hanoi and Washington to prevent it.

That does not mean that the Nixon administration was blameless in the affair. Based on the evidence at hand, it appeared to be virtually ignorant of the potential political dangers inherent in the new situation and to view the new circumstances solely from the standpoint of the short-term military advantages involved. Although Kissinger may be justified in pointing out that all of Washington's alternatives were unpalatable, it is nevertheless hard to believe that the invasion was the best option available under the circumstances.

For Hanoi, the Cambodian crisis presented both danger and opportunity. It undoubtedly complicated the Party's plans in South Vietnam and forced military strategists to divert their efforts to the widening conflict in eastern Cambodia, but it also stimulated the growth of the Khmer revolutionary movement and permitted an open Vietnamese involvement in the area. Although all the possibilities were not clear, said one document, "the recent coup d'état appears to have given the Revolution a great leap forward, created a revolutionary government and laid the ground for an anti-American Front of the Indochinese peoples." The new Lon Nol government was viewed as weak, the United States as lacking the capability to wage a long war in Cambodia. Communists who had returned from the D.R.V. began to train local cadres and to set up a Khmer revolutionary organization. A special effort was made to build up a new political and military infrastructure at the village level, including national salvation associations. Most members were poor peasants or workers, but cadres were encouraged to include a few progressive members of the Sihanouk government or Buddhist monks, provided that they were sufficiently anti-American and anti-Lon Nol.

In attempting to direct the course of the Cambodian revolution, Hanoi was clearly running the risk of exacerbating Cambodian resentment of possible Vietnamese domination. Captured documents show that the Party was sensitive to this danger. The impression that revolutionary organizations had been initiated by Vietnamese troops was to be avoided, said one. Cadres were instructed to be tactful and sensitive in dealing with their Cambodian counterparts: "They should absolutely avoid manifesting pride of being from a larger country. They should not be too enterprising and do everything by themselves instead of giving advice and letting the Cambodian revolutionaries do their job. They should not infringe on the Cambodians' customs, disturb their way of living, or violate their property."[30]

Over the next few months the revolutionary movement gradually built up a base area between the border and the Mekong River, with a radius of almost forty miles in every direction. Hanoi's fear of conflict between Vietnamese units and the KCP, however, turned out to be justified. The radical leadership of the KCP under Pol Pot and Khieu Samphan showed the traditional Cambodian suspicion of Vietnamese motives and attempted to isolate the pro-Hanoi cadres within the Party. It also distrusted Sihanouk and resented Vietnamese pressure to accept the prince as the figurehead leader of the new patriotic front. By 1972, the KCP had undertaken a purge of suspected disloyal elements within the Party, and conflicts between Cambodian and Vietnamese at the local level frequently led to bloodshed.

Bit by Bit

Whether or not the Cambodian operation set back Communist military plans in South Vietnam, it did not fundamentally alter the course of the war or the Party leadership's revolutionary strategy in the South. The Politburo apparently was careful to ensure that its activities in Cambodia did not detract from the main battlefield in South Vietnam. One internal document declared that the Party would focus its main effort on the battlefield in South Vietnam while attempting to assist the Cambodian revolutionary movement. Up to that time, it noted, the Cambodian civil war had not caused a serious problem because Communist forces had been "rationally employed" there and therefore had done nothing which "badly hurts" the situation in South Vietnam. Regardless of what happens, the report said, "we will not get ourselves in trouble" in Cambodia.[31]

The Party's determination to persist was clearly reflected in the communiqué issued at the end of the Nineteenth Plenum, held in January 1971. It referred to the need to mobilize the entire "Party, people and army" to make new efforts to wage the revolution in the South and promised that the Vietnamese "will do their utmost to fight shoulder to shoulder with the fraternal Laotian and Cambodian peoples to drive the U.S. aggressors out of the Indochinese peninsula." While referring to the importance of promoting the process of socialist construction in the North, the communiqué left no doubt that the Party leadership continued to believe that only military force would bring the revolution in South Vietnam to a successful conclusion: "The rich experiences gained during our revolutionary struggle tell us that the aggressors will agree to end the war only when they cannot continue to fight and when their hope of victory has definitely been checked. The balance of forces on the battlefield determines the way the war develops." Although the balance of forces in the war was shifting in the Party's favor, it concluded, the enemy would admit defeat only when the ARVN and U.S. forces had suffered "even greater losses." Thus, it admitted, "our people's resistance must continue to progress before we can force the enemy to admit defeat."[32]

Unfortunately, the full resolution of the plenum has not been published, but a captured study guide written at approximately the same time probably reflected Hanoi's view of the situation. Admitting that enemy activities had caused problems for the revolutionary forces, it said that emphasis should be placed on a gradual buildup of the Party's military and political forces and on the need for patient and painstaking efforts to defeat the enemy's pacification plan so as to expand the liberated areas "bit by bit." Attempts to liberate "entire areas at one time" should be avoided, and cadres who were impatient and wanted a "quick victory" were criticized for not seeing the "vicious aspects" of the enemy's efforts to destroy the revolutionary infrastructure. On the other hand, the document warned against pessimism and pointed out that the internal weaknesses within enemy ranks would be certain to lead to victory in the future. It also made clear that the Party leadership had not abandoned its plans to make use of political struggle in the cities. Cautioning against an over-reliance on the role of military struggle, the study guide called for intensified efforts to build up the revolutionary movement in urban areas.[33]

For the immediate future, then, the Vietnam War was transformed into a small-unit war for control of the villages. GVN pacification operations were seriously cutting into the areas controlled by the PRG, and even some hard-core Communist base areas in the Mekong delta had been cleared out by ARVN sweeps. As always, however, the long-term success of GVN efforts was open to question. One of the major techniques used by government forces was to evacuate the local population to refugee camps. Some surveys suggested that areas where forcible evacuation had taken place were often sympathetic to the NLF. One American specialist was quoted as saying that in many cases pacification amounted simply to military occupation.[34]

But the Communists, too, continued to have problems. Recruitment was down, and the desertion rate was on the rise. According to U.S. sources, the strength of the PLAF dropped from 250,000 in 1968 to less than 200,000 three years later. And the strain of the seemingly endless struggle was beginning to affect morale. Some expressed the fear that the situation in the GVN had reverted to what it had been in 1958 and 1959; others complained that things were worse since Ho Chi Minh's death; above all there was a sense of isolation and of irritation at the lack of support from Vietnam's socialist allies.[35]

One of the reasons for the relative success of the GVN was the new "land-to-the-tiller" program established by the Thieu regime in 1970. By the late 1960s, Washington had finally become convinced of the importance of the land issue in the war and began to press the Saigon regime to revive the land reform program, dormant since about 1961. Surveys indicated that half the rural population in the delta had no land, while two-thirds had less than two acres. The average amount of rent charged was 34 percent of the annual harvest (as compared with the legal maximum of 25 percent). Polls showed clearly that the peasants in the Mekong delta wanted more land.

The Thieu regime was understandably somewhat reluctant to pursue land reform vigorously for fear that it would be resented by landlords. But by 1968, under increasing pressure from the U.S. Embassy, it began to take action. Rents were frozen, and 50,000 families received government-owned land. Two years later the Saigon government pushed a "land-to-the-tiller" bill through the Lower House. The new law called for the automatic transfer of land titles to the tenant, with compensation to the original landowner paid by the government. The amount of cultivable land permitted to an individual family was limited to 37 acres. By 1972 tenancy in rural areas of South Vietnam was down from about 60 percent to 34 percent, and almost 400,000 farmers received a total of 1.5 million acres of land under the program.[36]

A second source of concern to Hanoi was the GVN's new effort to create a part-time militia in rural villages. Membership in the new People's Self-Defense Force Program was compulsory for all nondraft-age males between 16 and 50, and by 1971 it was estimated that 4 million were enrolled. The aim was to provide local self-defense at the village level, thus permitting ARVN units to take up the slack in combat efforts left by the departure of U.S. troops. Many foreign observers were critical of the program, noting that the membership figures were inflated and that villagers often resented being compelled to participate. Some contended that it was ineffective. But Communist documents suggest that the Party was nonetheless concerned about the program and anxious to undermine it.

In the long run, the key issue was likely to be how well the ARVN could fight. Once the Americans left, the GVN would be forced to rely primarily on its own military forces, and Hanoi was clearly determined to put them to the test. An indication of the scope of Saigon's problem appeared in early 1971 when 16,000 ARVN troops, with U.S. air support, invaded lower Laos in a campaign designed to cut the Ho Chi Minh trail. After an uneventful advance, the ARVN units were attacked on the trail by several North Vietnamese main force divisions, assisted by Soviet tanks and rockets. The South Vietnamese defended themselves with courage but were clearly outclassed, and after several weeks of heavy fighting were forced to retreat across the border. ARVN casualties totaled almost half the invading force, and eight battalions were put out of commission.[37] The abortive operation did not demonstrate the truth of Hanoi's contention that under pressure ARVN would disintegrate "by large chunks," but it did show that in a direct confrontation with the PAVN, the South Vietnamese would have a difficult time. General Van Tien Dung later claimed that Hanoi had deliberately provoked the confrontation in order to test the strength and resilience of ARVN forces and that only logistical problems had prevented North Vietnamese units from continuing their advance to the Vietnamese coast.[38]

The continuing military stalemate was reflected at the conference table in Paris. In 1970 and early 1971, the Nixon administration offered a variety of proposals designed to interest Hanoi in a compromise settlement. In the fall of 1970, Kissinger suggested a cease-fire in place (the only kind in which the D.R.V. appeared interested) and a total bombing halt. But the North Vietnamese delegate simply restated Hanoi's public insistence on U.S. acceptance of the four points. Then, the following spring, Kissinger added the promise of a unilateral withdrawal of U.S. forces provided that Hanoi ended its own infiltration. At first, Hanoi simply reiterated its insistence on the overthrow of the Thieu regime and on adherence to the four points. But in the early summer it presented a new package calling for a U.S. withdrawal, the formation of a coalition administration in Saigon, and a cease-fire to take place after the formation of the new government. The move did suggest some flexibility in Hanoi, but the proposal continued to require the one condition that Washington would not accept—the removal of Nguyen Van Thieu as president of the South Vietnamese government.[39]

The Easter Offensive

According to Henry Kissinger, Hanoi's decision to launch the 1972 Easter Offensive was probably reached some time the previous October when Le Duc Tho, the Politburo's chief representative at the peace talks in Paris, developed a "diplomatic illness" and departed for Hanoi. Others have speculated that the plans were made during the summer or that the offensive had been planned all along.[40] The timing of the decision, although not without interest, is less important than the motives involved. In a 1974 monograph on the Easter Offensive, David Elliott lists several possible reasons suggested by various foreign observers: (1) to influence the U.S. presidential elections, (2) to influence Hanoi's allies in Moscow and Peking, (3) to obtain a dramatic military victory and destroy pacification efforts, and (4) to seize a province or two in the South and influence negotiations.[41] A case can be made that all of these factors played a role in the final decision. Certainly the Party was not unaware of the effect that a successful offensive could have on the U.S. presidential elections and on attitudes toward the war in Moscow and Peking. But Elliott is probably correct in saying that the major objectives were to revise the military situation on the battlefield and to push the United States closer to negotiations. It is clear from the analysis above that the Party saw its primary hope for victory as stemming from a military defeat of the enemy's armed forces. A successful offensive could lead to the collapse or substantial weakening of the Saigon regime, forcing the United States to accept a negotiated withdrawal. Certainly the importance of a military success was foremost in the mind of the influential Party strategist Vo Nguyen Giap. In an article in December, he declared that the only way to defeat the U.S. policy of Vietnamization was to develop the combined guerrilla and regular forces and return to the strategy of a general offensive and uprising. A later article, published in *Nhan dan* only a few days before the launching of the offensive, declared that only large-scale attacks could bring about a "clear change" in the situation in the South. In Giap's view, the primary justification for a new offensive was to break the logjam on the battlefield through a decisive victory that could convincingly demonstrate to the Nixon administration that the situation in South Vietnam could not be stabilized without a major escalation in U.S. effort.[42]

The importance of the offensive for a diplomatic settlement was mentioned in another article published in April by the magazine *Tien Phong* [Vanguard], an organ of the PRP in South Vietnam. According to "N.C.," Party members "must be fully aware that victories on the battlefield constitute a decisive factor serving as a base for the attainment of a political settlement to end the war." The more decisive the military victory, it continued, the fewer the difficulties in the diplomatic phase: "When the head passes through the tail will go through."[43]

Hanoi's plan, apparently formally approved at the Twentieth Plenum in February, was to launch the offensive at the end of March, in the middle of the dry season. By that time, U.S. forces in South Vietnam would have been reduced to about 100,000 and the ARVN would be forced to bear the brunt of the fighting. The original plan called for a combination general offensive and uprising similar to the Tet Offensive four years before. Military attacks would be undertaken by main force units in several strategic areas. Then, at the appropriate moment, popular uprisings would be launched in key cities, several of which were scheduled for a possible takeover. Local PLAF units were to seize power in the outskirts and to prepare to welcome regular force troops as they approached. In contrast to 1968, however, Party planners did not envision an all-out urban insurrection in the cities, including assaults on government installations, simultaneous with the military attacks in rural areas. The Party's urban apparatus and PLAF forces in the outskirts were to move into an active phase only when main force units in the countryside had won substantial victories and had begun to move toward the urban fringe areas. In the meantime, they were to be prepared to take advantage of internal dissension and "sudden developments" while awaiting the sign to rise.

Captured documents provide some insight into the tactics that were to be used in the urban struggle. Students, organized in guerrilla or armed propaganda units, would be the motive force at the moment of uprising. Their mission was to establish initial control in areas where GVN authority was weak, such as in working-class residential districts. They would attempt to extend guerrilla warfare to other areas of the city and gradually to undermine governmental authority. In the meantime, Party cadres engaging in front work were to win the support of moderates for a new "leftist" alliance that would appeal for the overthrow of the Thieu regime and the formation of a coalition government.[44]

In at least one case, the Party apparently hoped that a popular uprising might be linked to the declaration of a cease-fire. One captured document showed that the local Party apparatus in Da Nang had been instructed to prepare for an uprising in the city following the signing of the prospective agreement but before it had come into effect. Official U.S. sources claimed that the capture of the document probably caused the plan to be abandoned.

The declining importance of the concept of the general uprising clearly reflects the sober realization, a clear consequence of Tet, that urban insurrections were not likely to succeed without substantial assistance from main force units in the immediate vicinity. But Hanoi was correspondingly more optimistic about the prospects for a decisive military victory in rural areas. One document pointed out that the situation was significantly different from that of 1968 because of the withdrawal of the bulk of U.S. forces and claimed that the new offensive might result in "important changes," either a total victory before the end of the year or a substantial weakening of the Saigon regime.[45] A "mature revolutionary situation" existed, it said, in which the revolutionary forces had made a great leap forward in all three strategic areas.

The Easter Offensive was launched in three successive phases. The first stage was to open on March 30 in the northern provinces, considered the most vulnerable region of South Vietnam. Here three PAVN divisions, armed with missiles, heavy artillery, and Russian T-54 tanks, struck in a three-pronged assault across the DMZ, eastward along Highway 9 from Laos, and through the A Shau valley to the south. The string of firebases just south of the DMZ was quickly seized, and within a week the Communists had occupied the entire ten-mile strip between the zone and the Cua Viet River.

The second phase of the offensive came in the Central Highlands and along the central coast. Beginning on the thirty-first, heavy attacks took place on the city of Kontum and in the lowland provinces of Binh Dinh and Phuoc Tuy, where a North Vietnamese division seized several coastal districts and revived the old threat to cut South Vietnam in two. Route 19, the key link between the coast and the highlands, was harassed and cut briefly in several places. The final phase took place in III Corps where, in early April, three North Vietnamese divisions attacked Binh Long Province along the Cambodian border, seized the city of Loc Ninh, and began to advance toward the provincial capital of An Loc. In the process they inflicted heavy casualties on the ARVN Fifth Division, which was forced to fall back to An Loc. That city was then put under siege.

Of these attacks, the strongest was in the north. The Saigon military command had expected trouble here and had reinforced the crack First Division with the new and inexperienced Third Division. The latter fell back under the ferocity of the first assault, retreating to Dong Ha where it attempted to hold while the PAVN units paused to regroup and await supplies. In the meantime, Nixon ordered the resumption of full-scale bombing of North Vietnam.

A few weeks later, the attacks in I Corps resumed. The Third Division abandoned Dong Ha and retreated in disorder toward the coast. On May 1 the Communists entered the provincial capital of Quang Tri and within a few days virtually the entire province was in their hands. Fleeing soldiers and civilians flooded Route 1. Thieu dismissed his corps commander and appointed General Ngo Quang Truong as his replacement. There was a sense of panic in Hué, but the North Vietnamese did not press on to the old imperial capital and gradually ARVN resistance stiffened. In June, Thieu sent his strategic reserves to the area and with the aid of heavy U.S. air strikes launched a counteroffensive. Finally, in September, South Vietnamese forces recaptured Quang Tri, the provincial capital that was virtually leveled.

Elsewhere, the Communists were somewhat less successful. In the highlands, North Vietnamese forces kept Kontum under siege and harassed Route 14, forcing the ARVN Twenty-second Division to fall back in disarray. The city was reinforced by air drops, however, and managed to hold. On the coast, ARVN units gradually cleared Communist units from three northern districts of Binh Dinh Province, but not before local pacification operations had been badly disrupted.[46] In III Corps, Thieu appealed to the Fifth Division to "hold An Loc at all costs" and transformed the city into a symbol. During mid-April, Communist forces were able to enter and hold parts of the city for several days but the defenders maintained their positions and eventually the Communists withdrew. Throughout the country, the ARVN had held, but it had been a near thing and two divisions had cracked under the pressure.

After-the-fact evaluations of the Easter Offensive varied widely and, as might be expected, tended to reflect the political persuasions of the particular observer. Gareth Porter, author of *A Peace Denied*, felt that Hanoi's primary objective had been to destabilize the Saigon regime and wear down ARVN units and claimed that in that sense it was "an unqualified success." General Ted Serong, an Australian military adviser with the Thieu regime, took the opposite view and described the offensive as a desperate and high-cost gamble that failed. Kissinger seemed to agree, calling it Hanoi's "last throw of the dice."[47] It is doubtful that either extreme view is correct, but Porter's is closer to the mark. The Party's strategy must be seen from the perspective of its long-range and flexible view of the course of the war. It is probable that, although the movement had suffered some setbacks in the South, the Party leadership was reasonably optimistic that, with the reduction in U.S. involvement, the offensive would lead either to a complete overthrow of the Saigon regime or to a breakthrough in the negotiations in Paris. At a minimum, it would result in a further disintegration of the ARVN, a disruption of pacification operations, and a rise in antiwar sentiment in the United States. It is hardly likely that it was viewed in Hanoi as a desperate gamble. With the departure of U.S. forces, the Party's long-term military prospects were reasonably bright. Failure to achieve the ambitious military objectives would set back Hanoi's schedule but, short of a disastrous defeat on the battlefield, would not reverse the course of the war.

As it turned out, the Party's hopes for a complete disintegration of the Saigon regime were premature. As in 1968, Hanoi had to be satisfied with its minimum goals. The ARVN had bent but, with some exceptions, had not broken. The Communists, plagued by logistical problems and a lack of experience in making effective use of artillery and armor, were unable to take full advantage of Saigon's weakness, even though they had committed most of their combat divisions in the attack. South Vietnamese casualties were high, but so were those of the PAVN. By some estimates, North Vietnamese losses were nearly 100,000 while the ARVN lost about 12,000.[48] The costs had been high and had not appreciably transformed the military balance in South Vietnam. On the other hand, the GVN had been weakened in crucial respects, thus laying the groundwork for a future Communist advance. The Easter Offensive forced the ARVN to transfer a number of its main force units from the delta to the northern provinces, thus opening up the populous Mekong delta to renewed low-level insurgency pressure and undermining the spurious sense of security of the previous year.

Peace Is at Hand

Did the Easter Offensive substantially affect the course of the peace talks in Paris? Hanoi clearly hoped that an ARVN defeat on the battlefield would compel Washington to negotiate. Henry Kissinger turned the issue around and contended that if the Easter Offensive could be defeated, Hanoi "would have no choice except to negotiate" as it had thrown everything into the effort. In the event, the results of the offensive were mixed and in Paris both parties moved in significant respects beyond their previous negotiating positions.

During the spring and early summer there was little movement at the conference table. Hanoi probably had little interest in a settlement until the results of the offensive came into clear focus. By late summer it had become obvious that the deadlock had not been broken on the battlefield and the Party leadership was prepared to make compromises in order to obtain a settlement. The decision to give diplomacy a chance was taken at a meeting of the Politburo in August. According to Gareth Porter, Hanoi saw three possible forms for a settlement: (1) a U.S. withdrawal with the war continuing, (2) a political settlement to replace the Thieu government with a coalition, and (3) a cease-fire, with Thieu staying, and formal recognition of the PRG.[49]

There was similar movement toward a settlement in Washington. For President Nixon, hopeful of having an agreement in his pocket before the November elections, virtually everything was negotiable—even the presence of North Vietnamese forces in the South—except Thieu himself. In April Kissinger had hinted to Brezhnev that the United States might not insist on a total withdrawal of the PAVN from the South if Hanoi would drop its demand for Thieu's removal. Hanoi had rejected the proposal and countered by offering to accept all members of the Saigon regime except Thieu. That, in turn, was rejected in Washington. For the moment, diplomacy was at a stalemate.

In September, a speech by Prime Minister Pham Van Dong failed to mention Nguyen Van Thieu in a speech discussing conditions for a settlement, thus hinting at a willingness to accept Thieu's retention in a future Saigon government. This assumption was confirmed in Moscow. The door was now open for serious negotiations, and Kissinger boasted that the deadlock had been broken "entirely by Hanoi."[50]

By October, discussion at the peace talks was centering on the nature of the political and administrative structure to follow a settlement in South Vietnam. Both sides agreed in principle on the formation of a National Council of Reconciliation and Concord (NCRC), composed of representatives from the GVN, the PRG, and the neutralist "third force." But Washington continued to resist any form of actual coalition government with Communist participation and refused to accept the NCRC formula as a "de facto" coalition. The major breakthrough came on October 8, when Le Duc Tho suggested that the NCRC could be considered simply as an "administrative structure" with the limited duties of implementing the agreements and organizing elections in South Vietnam. In the meantime, the Thieu regime would remain intact in Saigon.

From that point, a tentative agreement was quickly reached: a cease-fire in place, to take effect at the signing of an agreement; withdrawal of U.S. forces and release of prisoners of war within sixty days of the signing of the agreement; Hanoi's agreement to stop infiltrating troops from the North; continuation of limited U.S. military assistance to the GVN; and a promise by Washington to provide postwar assistance for the reconstruction of Vietnam. The agreement did not mention the GVN, the PRG, or the presence of North Vietnamese troops already in the South.

In a moment of optimism, Henry Kissinger now publicly announced that "peace is at hand." But the main obstacle to peace now came from Saigon. President Thieu was unhappy, not just with the details of the agreement, but with several of its main provisions, including the one calling for a U.S. withdrawal without a corresponding departure of North Vietnamese forces from South Vietnam. The details of the diplomatic exchanges that followed need not concern us here. Washington agreed to support some but not all of Thieu's objections. When Hanoi grew suspicious at the delay and appeared to draw back from some of its own commitments, Nixon decided in mid-December to resume the bombing of the D.R.V. to place pressure on the Party leadership. In the meantime, an intense struggle for control of territory—"the battle of the flags"—took place in South Vietnam as the two sides attempted to establish areas of control in advance of the anticipated cease-fire.

Talks were resumed on January 8, 1973. Le Duc Tho agreed to one of Saigon's major demands—prohibition of the movement of military units across the DMZ—and other issues were resolved without much difficulty. The White House then informed Saigon that it intended to sign the agreement, with or without the GVN. Reluctantly, Thieu gave his assent. On January 27, the peace treaty was signed in Paris.

Conclusions

As with virtually every other aspect of the Vietnamese conflict, the Paris Agreement is surrounded by controversy. In public, the D.R.V. described the settlement as a great victory for the Vietnamese revolution and a major step toward national reunification. Henry Kissinger labeled it a defeat for the Communists, "a pale shadow of their former demands for a coalition government," and "not much to show for a decade of heroic exertions and horrendous suffering."[51] Neither view is justified. The final settlement was a true compromise, involving substantial concessions on both sides. The Nixon administration conceded to the Communists an active political and military role in South Vietnam; Hanoi accepted the existence of the Thieu regime and continued U.S. aid to the GVN. On balance, however, Hanoi had the better of the deal, for the U.S. withdrawal was not matched by a similar pullback by the PAVN.

Why, after over a decade of bitter struggle, did the Party leadership decide to accept a settlement whose provisions represented a considerable retreat from its original demands? Hanoi's motives must, of course, be seen in the light of the existing situation, as well as the Party's long-term strategy. Since the escalation of the war in the early 1960s, the Party viewed the revolutionary struggle in the South as a two-stage process: a first stage, aimed at the withdrawal of the United States, presumably through negotiations; and a second stage, involving the complete takeover of the South through a combination of political and military struggle. The immediate objective was thus to maneuver the United States out of Vietnam on the most favorable terms possible. The most favorable circumstances, of course, would have been in the wake of a severe defeat of the enemy's armed forces along the lines of the battle of Dien Bien Phu in 1954, or a total collapse of the Saigon regime. Either or both would have created propitious conditions for the withdrawal of U.S. military forces and the formation of a coalition government with substantial participation by the NLF. Under such circumstances, negotiations would simply disguise the de facto triumph of the Communists.

The ambiguous results of the Easter Offensive made it clear to the Politburo that this scenario was not possible in 1972 or—because the revolutionary forces would need time to be reconstructed—for the forseeable future. And the Nixon administration appeared determined to resist the growing domestic pressure for a total U.S. withdrawal unless a satisfactory formula for peace could be found. Under such conditions, Hanoi in essence was faced with two alternatives: to insist on a coalition government without Nguyen Van Thieu that would be susceptible to manipulation and eventual domination by the Communists, or to struggle for a settlement that would result in the removal of U.S. troops from South Vietnam without a corresponding removal of North Vietnamese forces. The latter solution had been hinted at in April when Kissinger had suggested that the United States would not insist on the total removal of PAVN units if Thieu would be acceptable. From the standpoint of Hanoi, the removal of Thieu—who in any case had become in some respects a liability for the GVN—was probably less important than the presence of its military forces in the South. Although the Politburo had rejected this solution in April, it was willing to accept it in September. In that sense, Kissinger was correct in asserting that the limited success of the Easter Offensive had made Hanoi more responsive at the conference table.

What, then, was Hanoi's view of the postsettlement situation? Once U.S. forces had been removed and the political agreement signed, the conflict would return to its status before escalation in the mid-1960s. Although Thieu would remain in power, the Communists retained important political and military advantages in their competition with Saigon. A COSVN directive written in October 1972 provides some insight into Communist strategy for the period immediately following a political settlement and a cease-fire:

> During this period, we will have new advantages, new conditions, and new capabilities which never prevailed before, while the enemy contradictions and basic vulnerabilities will become more serious than ever before. This period will be a great opportunity for revolutionary violence, for gaining power in South Viet-Nam, for troop and enemy proselytizing, and for making great leaps in the balance of forces.[52]

Another directive took pains to show that the situation differed in essential respects from that of the previous cease-fire in 1954, implying that some Party members may have questioned whether the agreement would run into problems similar to those encountered with the Geneva settlement two decades earlier:

> Today, in South Viet-Nam we have large liberated areas, a people's administration, and strong people's liberation armed forces, especially the main forces; we have a political force, a complete system of leadership from high to low levels and a time-tested infrastructure; we have the National Front for the Liberation of South Viet-Nam and the Provisional Revolutionary Government of the Republic of South Viet-Nam which enjoy a great prestige on the international scene; and

we will occupy a position of equality in the administration of national concord.

Most important, perhaps, the Americans would have withdrawn:

> Since the enemy's main support, which is the U.S. massive military strength and
> the war which is his key measure, will be limited, we will be in an advantageous
> position over the enemy. Especially our political superiority, which is our basic
> strength, will have the condition to develop to the highest extent, opening new
> prospects.

The postsettlement period, then, was seen as a time of transition between two struggle phases of the Vietnamese revolution. Although Thieu remained in power, his strength had been decisively weakened, thus providing a great opportunity for "revolutionary violence" and "turbulent, abnormal developments." The period would involve a crucial race between the revolutionary forces and the GVN and an opportunity for the former to deal the latter decisive blows from which it could not recover.

The decision to accept the settlement was obviously based on the assumption that, once U.S. forces had been removed, victory over the Saigon government could be achieved in a relatively short time. The big risk was that U.S. power would be reintroduced in South Vietnam in the event that its client state was on the verge of collapse. There was no guarantee that this would not occur. As Kissinger put it in his memoirs, the Nixon administration made clear the implicit threat of U.S. retaliation should "massive violations" of the Paris Agreement take place. And, as he had demonstrated in the Christmas bombing in December, Nixon did not shrink from using his considerable powers to enforce the agreement. Hanoi gambled that the Nixon administration would not, could not, risk the political damage that would result from an effort to reimpose U.S. power in South Vietnam.

12
The Final Drama
(1973–1975)

The Paris Agreement was portrayed in the D.R.V. media as a great victory. Articles in *Hoc tap* demonstrated pride of achievement and labeled the Vietnamese revolution a "historic encounter" that would now stimulate a "great leap forward" in the world revolution against imperialism. A statement issued by the Central Committee on January 28, 1973, called it a new turning point in history and claimed that national liberation movements throughout the world would now develop strongly, for the victory of the Vietnamese revolution had set an example for other small nations attempting to become masters of their own destiny. There was no little self-gratification in the statement that "a number of people did not believe that we could fight the U.S."[1]

More sober analyses conceded that difficult obstacles remained before the final victory of the Vietnamese revolution could be consummated. An article by Hoang Tung in the March *Hoc tap* conceded that it was not a "complete victory" but was the best possible "considering the actual balance of forces." There may not, indeed, have been unanimous agreement within the Politburo on whether to accept the compromise settlement. And various sources indicated that there was a sense of disillusionment among some Party members over what they considered the failure to achieve the final objective of the revolution. For that reason, an article in the April issue of the same journal took considerable pains to explain that the situation in the South was different in essential respects from that of 1954: "The present situation in the South is different than the situation which existed in 1954 because in 1954 South Vietnam did not have two governments, two armies, two different zones, or fully equipped revolutionary armed forces occupying strategic areas."[2]

Clearly the Party did not anticipate a repetition of 1954 when the GVN had been able to retain its control over the South. How did it expect the situation to develop in the immediate postsettlement period? Evidently Party leaders were prepared to deal with a variety of eventualities. The article in the April *Hoc tap* cited above remarked that there were two possibilities for the future course of the Vietnamese revolution: victory through primarily political struggle or victory as the result of a resumption of war. The first alternative was

clearly preferable. For several reasons, the D.R.V. would benefit from implementation of the agreement. It would provide the Communists with a
legitimate political voice in South Vietnam; it would protect areas controlled
by the revolutionary forces; and it would relieve the Party leadership of the
necessity to prepare for a possible return to full-scale war or the reintroduction
of U.S. forces.

The immediate objective was thus to struggle for the faithful implementation
of the Paris Agreement and the eventual formation of a new government in
Saigon with active participation by the PRG. That did not mean that the Party
leadership was optimistic that total victory could be achieved through the legal
political process. It had always assumed that, since the Thieu regime would not
give up without a struggle, even a nonmilitary takeover would involve the
liberal use of the political violence of the masses. The goal would thus be to
work for the destabilization of the Saigon regime and then, at the appropriate
moment, to "proceed forward essentially through using the masses' violence
with the possibility to avoid an internal war."[3]

On the other hand, the possibility of a renewal of armed struggle could not
be ignored, for the Thieu government would do all in its power to repress the
revolutionary movement and crush the liberated areas. "We must make careful
preparations," said one report, "be ready to fight, and if necessary move quickly
to destroy the enemy." The military option, however, was not seen as an immediate possibility. According to U.S. intelligence specialist Frank Snepp, Van
Tien Dung toured South Vietnam in early 1973 and concluded that the revolutionary forces would not be in a position to launch another military offensive
for three to five years.[4]

Some observers suggest that there may have been controversy within the
Party leadership over the strategy to be followed in the post-agreement period.
Whether or not this was the case, the majority apparently agreed to prepare for
either peaceful struggle or a resumption of revolutionary war, while hoping for
the first. As always, it would be necessary to coordinate political and military
struggle, but the main emphasis would be placed on using the "political violence
of the masses" in order to move from a primarily political and legal struggle
toward a revolutionary high tide throughout the country. Armed struggle was
viewed as the last resort. This was seen most clearly in the Party's attitude
toward the struggle for territory. In order to avoid provoking the United States
or the Saigon government into military action, PLAF units were instructed to
respect the agreement and to resort to armed struggle only in self-defense.[5] In
some cases, revolutionary forces may have been withdrawn from areas seized
before the cease-fire in order to minimize the likelihood of conflict. Allan
Goodman, in *The Lost Peace*, quotes a captured document to this effect: "If we
attack our enemies, we will suffer politically . . . if we permit them to move into
our areas, then counterattack, our political image will remain intact."[6]

To compensate, the movement in the South was directed to take every opportunity to use political struggle to improve its situation and undermine that of the enemy. In contested areas, cadres were to urge the masses to push for freedom, democracy, and adherence to the agreement by the Saigon regime. South Vietnamese soldiers were to be encouraged to desert or to refuse to use force against the local population. In liberated areas, the main emphasis would be on recruitment and on raising food production in preparation for a possible resumption of armed conflict. And a special program was instituted to induce people in PRG-held areas to return to their native villages, where they were given incentives to return to the soil or were put to work improving the road network from Cambodia and North Vietnam.

Throughout the year, the two sides engaged in a low-level struggle over territory. The military text had made no mention of particular areas controlled by the Saigon government or the PRG in South Vietnam. That was to be left to the two parties to determine in military discussions to be held after the cease-fire. During 1973, the PRG abandoned several hundred hamlets it had seized earlier, presumably in an effort to consolidate its territory and encourage the GVN to disperse its forces. According to the testimony of one defector, Hanoi was especially concerned to build a "Third Vietnam" along the border with Cambodia and Laos as a base for political struggle. During the first year of peace this new base area was built from Quang Tri Province into the heart of the Central Highlands, with the aid of 30,000 cadres sent from the D.R.V.[7] A new highway was built from the DMZ to a camp north of Saigon, with spurs running eastward to the edge of the lowland plains. The old U.S. firebase at Khe Sanh was turned into a major Communist logistics base. More and more modern weapons, such as Russian rocket launchers and SAM missiles, were moved south. On the other hand, the North Vietnamese presence did not immediately increase and at the end of 1973 was estimated at 170,000 regular force troops, to supplement 60,000 Viet Cong regulars and guerrillas.[8]

According to Henry Kissinger, the Nixon administration was confident that the Saigon regime would be able to handle any low-level challenge from the Communists. U.S. involvement was now substantially limited by the agreement to the replacement of existing equipment. There was some unhappiness within the GVN over the quantity and quality of the military material provided by Washington. In particular, there was a sense of irritation among high-level military officers that the United States had trained the ARVN to fight an American-style war, with a liberal expenditure of firepower, and that now the ARVN would be forced to conserve its ammunition and equipment, thus cutting down seriously on its firepower and mobility. President Thieu, however, remained confident of U.S. support. In April he had received a promise from Richard Nixon that the United States would provide the necessary assistance and would respond vigorously to any major Communist violation of the agreement. Based on this reading of the situation in the United States, Thieu refused to compromise with the Communists and insisted on his program of "four no's":

(1) no abandonment of territory, (2) no coalition, (3) no negotiations, and (4) no Communist or neutralist activities in South Vietnam. During the summer, the GVN took advantage of the relative passivity of the revolutionary forces and launced pacification operations along the central coast and in the Mekong delta. As directed, the revolutionary leadership in the South limited its response to low-level harassment by guerrilla forces. According to COSVN estimates, the amount of land under PRG control was reduced to no more than 20 percent of the entire territory of the GVN, containing 12 percent of the population.

There is evidence that some of the militants in the Party, including Giap and Chief of Staff Van Tien Dung, wanted to respond and recommended a return to revolutionary violence.[9] The Politburo initially resisted the temptation to escalate, but by autumn it had become clear that Saigon's military offensive threatened to change the balance of forces in the government's favor, and in October the Twenty-first Plenum of the Central Committee met to consider a possible change of policy so that Communist forces would be instructed to respond if attacked by ARVN forces and in cases where the enemy was vulnerable. Chief of Staff Van Tien Dung, now a full member of the Politburo, was convinced that renewed warfare was inevitable. Others, fearful of U.S. intervention, were more cautious. Le Duan had just returned from a trip to Moscow and Peking, where he had attempted, apparently without success, to obtain the promise of heightened military assistance. There was some bitterness in Hanoi at Soviet "faintheartedness," but relations with China were particularly sour.[10] Peking was irritated at Hanoi's failure to heed Chinese advice to restrict the level of military violence in the South and at the D.R.V.'s continued dependence on the Soviet Union. Hanoi resented Peking's decision to improve relations with the United States and its failure to provide adequate aid and support to the Vietnamese revolution.

In the end, the committee approved a compromise. The PLAF was now permitted to respond if attacked, but only in areas where the GVN was considered vulnerable. Communist forces were permitted to undertake limited initiatives in mountainous areas but were instructed to adopt a defensive posture in the plains. According to the resolution issued at the close of the conference, followers were cautioned not to expect victory before 1979.

The first concrete indications of the new policy came in November, when a North Vietnamese division overran GVN border posts in the Central Highlands. In Washington, Congress had just passed the War Powers Act, which limited the president's authority to order military operations without congressional approval. When the Nixon administration did not react to the attacks, pressure for an escalation of the struggle mounted in Hanoi. The moderates in the Politburo were able to hold the line and at the Twenty-second Plenum they pushed through a strong commitment to domestic economic reconstruction. But the tide of events was running strongly in the militants' favor. In the South, Saigon's problems increased as the GVN attempted unsuccessfully to cope with the withdrawal of U.S. and other foreign troops. There was a pervasive sense of unease in South Vietnamese society, and concern about the government's ability to cope with the continuing presence of North Vietnamese forces in the South, now that the foreigners were gone.

The problem was not strictly military. A decade of the U.S. presence had radically transformed the Vietnamese economy and increased its dependence on outside assistance and on the purchases of Americans and other foreigners stationed in Vietnam. In the urban areas, a substantial proportion of the population depended for its livelihood on providing services for foreigners—taxi and cyclodrivers, clerks and secretaries in foreign establishments and offices, bar girls, and shoeshine boys. Despite a decade of modest efforts and substantial foreign aid, the GVN had not been able to stimulate the growth of a dynamic manufacturing and commercial sector and continued to be highly dependent upon imports for its consumer needs.[11] The departure of the foreigners and the removal of their substantial buying power created severe withdrawal symptoms in the Vietnamese economy.

The problem was exacerbated by the influx of refugees from the countryside. Military escalation had forced literally millions of Vietnamese to flee their native villages in an effort to find security in urban areas. In a moment of misplaced optimism, the American political scientist Samuel Huntington had viewed this process as an advantage for the GVN for, as he pointed out, the evacuation of the rural villages reduced the size of the manpower pool on which the PLAF must rely in order to find recruits for the revolutionary cause. That this was the case is indicated by the rising level of North Vietnamese involvement in the insurgency movement during the late 1960s and early 1970s. It had not been decisive, however, for Hanoi had been able to make up the deficiency by increased mobilization in the North.[12] But the long-run consequences were disastrous for the GVN. The flood of refugees, creating a pool of several millions of unemployed and often unemployable Vietnamese in the already burgeoning cities, created a time bomb that could ultimately explode in the face of the government and undermine all efforts to stabilize the situation in urban areas. The bill for a decade of emphasis on military issues and neglect of domestic problems was now about to come due.

Inevitably, such problems contributed to the social and political discontent seething beneath the surface of South Vietnamese society. Political opposition to the Thieu regime, long a factor in Saigon politics and only barely kept in control by the needs of the war, now began to surface. Militant Buddhists sniped at Thieu's refusal to share power and criticized his alleged pro-Catholic tendencies. Moderates criticized his rigidity toward the Communists and failure to make conciliatory gestures in favor of a compromise political settlement. On the right, a Catholic priest launched a movement against the endemic corruption in Vietnamese society, which, many felt, was tolerated and even encouraged by the government. In the delta, the sects were increasingly restive.

In Washington, the Nixon administration was being progressively weakened by the Watergate scandal and limited its efforts to proposing a demarcation of territory between the two sides in order to reduce the level of conflict. In March 1974, the D.R.V. Central Military Party Committee (a somewhat amorphous organization that apparently functions as a high-level planning body and a liaison between the Party leadership and the armed forces) met in Hanoi to discuss the resolution of the Twenty-first Plenum and to make plans for the 1974 campaign. In what may have been a reaction to the possibility of an agreement on territorial demarcation, the conference approved the launching of "strategic raids" on economic installations, roads, and airfields, to be followed in the summer months by an attempt to regain territory lost since the cease-fire. The liberated zones were to be expanded, and enemy forces were to be attacked and wiped out, not only in the mountains but also in the Mekong delta and along the Cambodian frontier. If this campaign proved successful, active consideration would be given to launching a large-scale offensive the following year. For this purpose the shipment of military supplies and equipment to the South was accelerated and thousands of South Vietnamese were mobilized to complete the road network, now extending more than 12,000 miles and wide enough for large trucks, and an oil pipeline from northern Quang Tri Province to Loc Ninh, northwest of Saigon.

The March conference concluded on a cautious but optimistic note:

> The Vietnamese revolution may have to pass through many transitional stages, and can only gain victory through revolutionary violence—carrying out popular uprisings, relying on our political and military forces, or in the event that large-scale war returns, carrying out revolutionary warfare to gain complete victory. The revolution in the South must hold firm to the concept of an offensive strategy . . . We must resolutely counterattack and attack, keep the initiative and develop it in all respects.[13]

Testing the Wind

During the early months of 1974, PLAF and North Vietnamese units expanded their attacks in vulnerable areas of South Vietnam in an effort to weaken Saigon's effort to consolidate its control in the countryside. The primary field of battle was in the Central Highlands, where ARVN forces were weak and military operations could be undertaken at relatively low risk, but a number of key engagements took place in provinces closer to Saigon, where PAVN regulars grappled with units of the ARVN Eighteenth Division near Ben Cat and inflicted heavy casualties, and in the Iron Triangle, where ARVN forces had been in a defensive position since early in the war. The Communists also began to move in force into the delta. For the first time main force units made their appearance there, although they continued to restrict their activities to the battalion or company level. Pacification operations were disrupted, and government outposts and even a few district capitals were attacked. When there was no direct response from the United States, such operations were increased. The ARVN tried to counter with its own initiatives and in a few provinces moved the local population into secure areas.

Hanoi's strategy during the spring and summer of 1974 continued to be based on an appreciation of the fluidity of the situation and the consequent need for flexibility. A captured COSVN directive, issued in August, reflected the Party's growing optimism that the tide was running strongly in favor of the revolution. Still, COSVN counseled caution and reiterated the belief that the situation offered two primary possibilities. The first was that the weak Saigon regime might be compelled to agree to a full implementation of the Paris Agreement and thus reopen negotiations with the PRG. Another possibility was an agreement on the demarcation of territory controlled by each side, and COSVN was instructed by the Politburo to prepare for hard last-minute fighting to increase the amount of land under revolutionary control.[14]

A second possibility was that a political settlement would be unobtainable, in which case it would be necessary to return to a "decisive revolutionary war" to win total victory. The directive, although it adhered to the current strategy in Hanoi—"We must take advantage of capability one and prepare for capability two"—implied strongly that the general situation was increasingly propitious for a military solution. In either case, it concluded, the Party should "grasp revolutionary violence to secure victory regardless of what development will happen. The road to success for the Revolution in the South is the road to violence based on political and military forces." In the background, of course, was the ever-present danger of U.S. intervention. The resignation of Richard Nixon in August was seen as reducing that likelihood, which, in the view of the COSVN directive cited above, was now considered slim. But it would be necessary to maintain watchfulness, and the directive called for "preventive measures and appropriate strategy so as not to leave room for a U.S. intervention."

By autumn, it was apparent that the 1974 campaign had been a success and that the situation in the South was even brighter than had been anticipated. One document captured in Binh Dinh Province remarked that the Party had been too conservative after the Paris Agreement and had overestimated the ability of the enemy to stabilize the situation.[15] In key areas, Saigon's position was weakening: in the Central Highlands, where North Vietnamese divisions were beginning to surround the provincial capitals of Pleiku and Kontum; in the populous coastal provinces, where guerrilla activities were making significant inroads into government-held areas; and in the delta, where revolutionary forces were approaching the key towns of Can Tho and My Tho and harassing Route 4, the key transportation link to Saigon. ARVN casualties were high—by one estimate, nearly 25,000 since the cease-fire—and the crucial divisions around Saigon were exhausted and undermanned. Shortages of ammunition and spare parts, a product of reduced U.S. assistance, were beginning to appear, leading Van Tien Dung to remark, gleefully no doubt, that Thieu was now being forced to fight "a poor man's war." Most ominous, Saigon's numerical advantage in military forces had all but disappeared. While the exact figures are in dispute, it seemed that main force units available to Hanoi had reached a point of virtual parity with ARVN.[16]

Across the border in Cambodia the situation was even more promising. The Communists were on the offensive throughout the country and were preparing to lay siege to the government capital of Phnom Penh. Signs of trouble within the movement were growing, of tension between radicals and followers of Prince Sihanouk and between pro-Hanoi and home-grown Communists within the Party. But such divisions did not appear to undermine Khmer Rouge military effectiveness, at least in comparison with the weak and poorly trained government troops of Lon Nol.

In October, the Politburo met again to hear a proposal by the general staff for a new military offensive to be launched during the coming year. In Van Tien Dung's account, the conference took an exuberant view of the general situation. The GVN was rapidly weakening, a revolutionary high wave was rapidly rising in the South, and political difficulties in the United States would make it difficult for the new Ford administration to intervene. The primary area of concern was the lingering possibility of a U.S. military reaction to Communist activities in the South. Le Duan apparently attempted to calm such fears, and the conference ultimately concluded that the U.S. would not intervene. Even if it did, asserted the resolution issued at the close of the meeting, it could no longer save the Saigon regime from total collapse.[17]

Nevertheless, the Politburo was cautious and finally approved a compromise. The proposal for a military offensive in 1975 was approved, but it would be initially limited in scope in order to test the U.S. reaction and the stamina of the GVN. The first phase of the attack would be directed along the Cambodian border, in the isolated and poorly defended province of Phuoc Long. If the operation there was successful, a second and larger assault would take place in the Central Highlands, which Hanoi's military strategists continued to view as the most vulnerable area of the GVN. Here Saigon had only two main force divisions to protect not only the highlands, but the coastal provinces from Binh Dinh to Binh Thuan as well. Also a factor was an agent's report that President Thieu was convinced that the Communists would not launch strong attacks in the highlands and had decided not to send reinforcements to the area.

The attack on Phuoc Long Province began in mid-December, when two divisions of North Vietnamese regulars launched assaults on district towns and gradually cut the roads leading to the provincial capital of Phuoc Binh. After a siege lasting nearly three weeks, Phuoc Binh fell on January 7. In nearby Tay Ninh, Communist units attacked and seized a vital ARVN outpost on Black Virgin Mountain, which overlooked the provincial capital, and began to shell the city. Thieu, though reportedly enraged at evidence that local militia had deserted during the battle, decided that it was "not worthwhile" to retake Phuoc Binh.[18]

The Politburo had been meeting in extended session throughout the battle, in order to permit the Party leadership to assess the rapidly changing situation, and the U.S. reaction to it, on a daily basis. When it became clear that Saigon's forces were unable or unwilling to mount an effective counterattack to seize Phuoc Binh and that the Ford administration—now evidently convinced that Hanoi did not intend to launch a major offensive in 1975—would not intervene, the Politburo approved the second stage of the military campaign, to begin in March. One factor that may have been involved in the decision was the promise of increased assistance from the Soviet Union. According to Frank Snepp, a high-level Soviet military official had attended the meeting and aid levels increased in the following weeks.

The plan called for heavy attacks in the Central Highlands, to be followed by an attempt to liberate the central coastal provinces from Binh Dinh northward. The final general offensive and uprising was to be launched the following year. But the meeting left open the possibility that final victory could be achieved in 1975. Le Duan concluded:

> Our conference has been exhilarating, with a high degree of agreement. This time we have had our comrades from Nam Bo and Zone 5 to come up to take part. The situation has become quite clear. We are resolved to complete our two-year plan. Two years is short, and yet long. The struggle in the South has, with the addition of the power of the North, the strength of the whole country. Now the Americans have withdrawn, we have our troops in the South, and the spirit of the masses is rising. This is what marks an opportune moment. We must seize it firmly and step up the struggle on all three fronts: military, political, and diplomatic.[19]

On January 9, the Standing Committee of the Central Military Party Committee met in Hanoi to make final plans for the attack on the highlands. According to General Van Tien Dung, who had been placed in charge of the campaign, prospects were good. Saigon still did not suspect the coming attack and had not reinforced its troops in the area. The airborne and marine divisions, which now constituted Saigon's de facto strategic reserve, were still in Da Nang. Hanoi had several combat-hardened divisions in the region, including the 10th and the 320th. Now the 316th was ordered in from across the Cambodian border, and the 341st, part of Hanoi's strategic reserve, was sent down from the North.

In its plan of attack, the Party counted on the element of surprise. Previous Communist attacks in the highlands had been directed at smaller targets, on special forces camps, district towns, or on the isolated provincial capitals of Pleiku and Kontum. Ban Me Thuot, the largest city in the region, with a population of more than 100,000, had heretofore been considered too large. At that moment, however, it was poorly defended, with only the understrength ARVN Twenty-third Division in the immediate vicinity. Two of the Twenty-third's three regiments were located at Kontum and at the corps headquarters in Pleiku, well to the north, where they were needed to protect Route 19, linking the entire region with the central coast.

The Communist plan was to isolate Ban Me Thuot by cutting all its links with the outside world and then launch a direct attack on the city. To preserve the element of surprise, the initial steps were to be taken without alerting the enemy to the final objective of the operation. For that purpose, in early March, assaults were launched on two ARVN outposts—on Route 19 west of Pleiku, and to the east near An Khe—to create the impression that the focus of the primary attack would be directed at Kontum and Pleiku to the north. Then, on March 5, North Vietnamese units cut Route 21 east of Ban Me Thuot, thus threatening to sever both major routes from the highlands to the coast. Pham Van Phu, the ARVN II Corps commander, still considered the major threat to be to the northern sector and dispatched two regiments of the Twenty-second Division in coastal Binh Dinh Province to clear Route 19 near An Khe and keep it open to Pleiku. On March 8, North Vietnamese forces hiding in the jungles and coffee plantations around Ban Me Thuot suddenly cut Route 14 and isolated the city from the north. Belatedly, Phu realized the implications of the attack and ordered an airlift of troops from Pleiku to Ban Me Thuot.

The ground was now prepared for an attack on the city. The method of attack, following a pattern used in previous battles, was called the "lotus flower approach," in which troops first assaulted the heart of the city in order to seize the enemy command post and vital installations and then branched out to complete the occupation of the suburban areas at leisure. In this case, armored and infantry units came right down the main highways into town and by midafternoon had seized most of the center of the city. Defending ARVN units were reduced to a perilous toehold at Twenty-third Division headquarters. General Phu, unable to bring reserve units down from Pleiku because of a lack of helicopters and the North Vietnamese hold on Route 14, decided to abandon the city.[20]

Not only the direction, but also the magnitude of the North Vietnamese attack came as a total surprise to the Saigon regime. In the conviction that the Communists were not strong enough to hold the larger cities, Thieu had expected smaller attacks on district capitals. The earlier attack in III Corps had apparently convinced him that Hanoi's major objective was to expand its control over the "Third Vietnam" along the border, in preparation for a larger offensive in the more distant future. The debacle in the highlands was thus a shock and threatened to throw Saigon into a panic. The capital area, protected by only three divisions and a few marine and airborne regiments, was now threatened by an estimated six PAVN divisions. Without consulting his subordinates, Thieu decided to abandon a number of exposed areas in the highlands and the northern provinces. His objective was to establish a defensible line at approximately the 13th parallel, anchored at Tay Ninh in the west and the port of Nha Trang along the coast. GVN authority in the north would be reduced to a few coastal enclaves around major cities, such as Hué and Da Nang, and the capitals of Quang Tin and Quang Ngai provinces.[21] From this stable position, Thieu would be able to defend against Communist attacks or to conduct negotiations on a further partition of South Vietnamese territory with the PRG.

Based on this strategy, Thieu ordered ARVN units still at Pleiku and Kontum to withdraw to the coast, where they were to regroup and prepare for a counterattack on Ban Me Thuot, which was to be the crucial hinge of the new defense line. In I Corps, General Ngo Quang Truong was directed to send the airborne division at Da Nang south to Saigon and to abandon unproductive rural areas by withdrawing to a more defensible position on the coast. Truong rushed to Saigon to protest but was only able to win Thieu's approval for a staggered withdrawal.

Attack in the North

While Nguyen Van Thieu desperately attempted to shore up GVN defenses, Communist military strategists were evaluating the first phase of their offensive. With the GVN in retreat throughout the region, there was a strong desire within Van Tien Dung's command in the South to maintain and even increase the pressure. Dung cabled Hanoi with a proposal that Communist units attempt to hold Ban Me Thuot, while extending their operations to complete the seizure of the entire highlands before the end of the dry season in May. After two days of discussion, the Central Military Party Committee in Hanoi approved. Under the new plan, revolutionary forces were to consolidate control of the area around Ban Me Thuot and then to strike northward to sever major highways and surround ARVN II Corps headquarters at Pleiku, while isolating Kontum in anticipation of a later seizure. They were then instructed to turn east in an effort to wipe out South Vietnamese units attempting to stabilize the government position along the coast.

Thieu's decision to abandon the bulk of the Central Highlands and fall back on the coast played into Communist hands. With Routes 14 and 19 interdicted, remnants of the ARVN Twenty-third Division still at Pleiku were directed to retreat to the coast along Route 7B, an old logging road that was poorly maintained and seldom used. Local militia forces, the bulk of which were composed of minority tribesmen, were to be left to fend for themselves. According to rumor, Thieu was enraged at the poor fighting discipline of minority troops and said that they could "return to the mountains."

The retreat became a fiasco. As troops began to withdraw from Pleiku, panic erupted among local civilians and militiamen, resulting in a disorderly flight along the mountain road, which under the weight of armored vehicles soon deteriorated into a sea of mud. At Communist headquarters, the evacuation took Van Tien Dung momentarily by surprise. He had been advised by a subordinate that Route 7B was unusable, and Communist units had not occupied the road. Now, realizing the vulnerability of the retreating column and the vital importance of preventing its safe arrival on the coast, Dung ordered General Kim Tuan, commander of the PAVN 320th Division, to intercept and wipe out the ARVN forces. Two of Tuan's regiments attacked South Vietnamese units on the road and seized Cheo Reo, inflicting heavy casualties and cutting the column in half. The retreat now disintegrated into a total rout. ARVN soldiers abandoned the road entirely, leaving artillery and armored vehicles on the road in disorder, and fled through the jungles toward the nearby district town of Son Hoa. Only a handful made it as far as Tuy Hoa, on the coast. For veteran observers, it was a vivid reminder of the disastrous French defeat in the area twenty-one years earlier.

The situation was equally perilous in the northern provinces. Thieu's order to dispatch the ARVN airborne division to III Corps left General Ngo Quang Truong with inadequate troops to defend both Da Nang and Hué from an expected Communist offensive. In Saigon, however, Thieu was still hoping to hold the major coastal enclaves while abandoning the remainder of the northern provinces to the enemy and ordered Truong to hold Hué with the ARVN First Division. To protect his communication routes, Truong dispatched units from Hué to defend Route 1 and the crucial Hai Van Pass (Pass of Clouds) on the mountain spur jutting out to the sea just north of Da Nang. A similar process of consolidation took place south of Da Nang when units of the ARVN Second Division pulled back from positions in rural areas to coastal enclaves around Chu Lai Air Base and the provincial capital of Quang Ngai.

The Politburo, continuously apprised of Thieu's strategy by agents, and anticipating an attempt by Ngo Quang Truong to withdraw the First Division from Hué to Da Nang, directed the North Vietnamese commander in the area to cut Route 1 between the two cities and then attempt to seize the imperial capital and destroy all ARVN units there. In the meantime, regional forces were to go on the offensive to the north and attempt to seize the provincial capital of Quang Tri. On March 21, PAVN units attacked Route 1 at several points south of Hué and effectively isolated the northern provinces from the rest of the South. Panic erupted along the highway, where thousands of refugees, in vehicles or on foot, had been retreating south to the deceptive safety of the major metropolis of Da Nang. In desperation, Ngo Quang Truong now requested and received Thieu's permission to abandon Hué. At first he hoped to evacuate by sea from the small seaport of Tan My, directly east of the city.

But the road from Hué soon became clogged with fleeing civilians, and he was compelled to withdraw his precious First Division toward the beaches in the hope of moving down the coast to link with ARVN forces on Route 1 at Hai Van Pass. But the coast east and south of Hué was punctuated by a number of inlets. Some could be crossed simply by walking through the surf, but at the Tu Hien estuary at the southern tip of the sandspit, a temporary bridge had to be created from the island to the mainland so that fleeing troops could return to Route 1 near Hai Van Pass.

The retreat degenerated into a rout and a tragic defeat for the GVN. Communist artillery harassed the soldiers as they fled along the beaches, while sappers mined the estuaries to prevent ships from entering to pick up beleaguered units. At the Tu Hien estuary, Communist guns shelled the naval units working on the temporary bridge and destroyed it before it could be completed. PAVN infantry units crossing from the mainland harassed the fleeing troops and completed the rout. On the twenty-fifth, Hué itself was attacked from all directions and fell almost without bloodshed.[22]

As reports on the situation in the South streamed in, the Politburo became increasingly convinced that total victory could be achieved before the monsoon season arrived in early May. At a meeting held on March 25, the Party leadership concluded:

> Our general strategic offensive began with the Tay Nguyen campaign. A new strategic opportunity has come, and conditions allow an early completion of our resolution to liberate the South. We resolve to rapidly concentrate our forces, technological weapons, and material *to liberate Saigon before the rainy season*. Seize the opportunity of the enemy's strategic withdrawal and the destruction and dispersal of Saigon's First Army Corps [I Corps] and the bulk of their Second Army Corps [II Corps] and do not allow them to withdraw and regroup around Saigon.[23]

At his headquarters near Ban Me Thuot, Van Tien Dung was informed of the Politburo's decision by telegram. He was instructed to concentrate three main force divisions, along with additional smaller units operating in the highlands, for an immediate advance toward the capital. The sense of urgency and opportunity was evident in the words of the telegram:

> Thus, we can still carry out the plan to liberate Saigon during the dry season, because there are nearly two months before the heavy rains, and once our forces have closed in on Saigon, even if we do run into the rainy season it will not be so great an obstacle. We must seek every means to overcome our difficulties. The situation is changing, and there must be new creative measures. . . . The situation now is developing very rapidly. This is a great leap. Saving time and grasping opportunities are decisive now.[24]

In his account of the campaign, Dung implied that the new directive was not entirely welcome. North Vietnamese units in the highlands were still advancing toward the central coast and had not yet finished mopping up ARVN resistance in the area. A precipitate advance toward Saigon, in these conditions, would be risky. As a compromise, he proposed that Communist forces be given a few extra days to complete the destruction of ARVN forces in the coastal provinces and only then turn south in time to meet the Party leadership's schedule for achieving total victory before the onset of the rainy season. When the Politburo signaled its approval, Dung directed Communist units to continue their advance into the lowlands to strike at the coastal cities of Qui Nhon, Tuy Hoa, and Nha Trang, as well as the vital seaport and staging area at Cam Ranh Bay. The attacks went off on schedule, forcing Pham Van Phu to abandon Nha Trang and withdraw his headquarters further to the south.

Meanwhile, Da Nang was in chaos. The road was now cut in several places to the south, as the ARVN Second Division had crumbled under successive North Vietnamese attacks, and the enclaves at Quang Ngai and Chu Lai were abandoned. With only 25,000 troops to counter a North Vietnamese force of more than two divisions—a total of more than 35,000 men—Ngo Quang Truong abandoned plans to defend the city and decided to order its evacuation. The final days, vividly portrayed in the news media, were marked by almost unparalleled chaos and the mass hysteria of the local population. While Communist infantry and armored units advanced toward the city from all directions, panic-stricken soldiers and civilians scrambled to board the last planes and ships departing for Saigon. On March 29, the Communists entered from the suburbs, while local guerrilla units seized bridges and key government installations inside the city. With the fall of Da Nang, the last GVN bastion in the north had been lost.

The Ho Chi Minh Campaign

The 1975 campaign had progressed with truly lightning speed, stunning the Saigon regime and even surpassing the expectations of the Party leadership in Hanoi. In three weeks, eight provinces had fallen to the Communists. Virtually all forces in Saigon's I and II Corps were wiped out. ARVN had lost almost half its main force units, and more than half its aircraft. The capital was in a state of evident panic, while Washington appeared impotent. On the final day of March, two days after the fall of Da Nang, the Politburo met again and concluded that the war had entered a stage of massive development. Van Tien Dung was instructed to prepare to launch a general offensive against Saigon with the objective of seizing total victory within four weeks: "Not only has the revolutionary war in the South entered a period of developing by leaps and bounds, but the time is ripe for carrying the general offensive and general uprising to the enemy's lair. From this moment, the final decisive battle of our army and people has begun; its aim is to complete the people's national democratic revolution in the South and bring peace and the reunification of the Fatherland."[25]

On April 2, Van Tien Dung ordered most North Vietnamese main force units to turn south. With seaports along the northern and central coast now open and ARVN prisoners pressed into service as truck drivers, war matériel began to flow south in vast quantities, while an air shuttle was set up from the D.R.V. to Kontum and Da Nang. Two more reserve divisions were sent south and a new military headquarters was set up near Saigon to replace COSVN. Van Tien Dung was named chairman, with Pham Hung as his chief political officer. Le Duc Tho was on hand to provide a direct link with the Politburo. After several days of intensive consultation, the new military command agreed on a basic strategy for the final assault, to be labelled the "Ho Chi Minh Campaign" because of Hanoi's intention to rename Saigon for the founder of the Party. According to Dung's account, the plan was to set up a strategic encirclement of the city by cutting Route 4 from the delta and Route 1 from Tay Ninh, while main force units marching down from the north would concentrate for a major thrust on the provincial capital of Xuan Loc, east of Saigon, where the crucial Eighteenth Division was located. As those main force units prepared for the final assault on Saigon, local forces would seize suburban areas, and the Party's suicide and guerrilla units in the city would prepare to surface to incite a general uprising.

In Saigon, hopes that the situation could be stabilized were rapidly evaporating. With the earlier plan to set up a defense line anchored at Tay Ninh and Nha Trang outdated by the swift pace of events, Thieu moved to set up a line from the city of Tay Ninh, still under siege, to Phan Rang on the coast, anchored at Xuan Loc, where the Eighteenth Division formed the last major bulwark against total collapse. Even this position might soon become untenable. With half of the ARVN gone, Saigon had only about six divisions plus a few brigades and ranger groups remaining, a total of less than 100,000 troops. Prospects for U.S. support appeared dim. The Ford administration was attempting to push through Congress a $1 billion aid package, but congressional resistance to any further aid to the Saigon regime had increased and approval appeared unlikely.

With military stabilization apparently out of the question, there was increasing talk of a compromise settlement. There had been hints from various diplomatic sources that Hanoi might accept a negotiated settlement. Hanoi's presumed price for peace was the departure of President Thieu and the immediate end of any further U.S. involvement in South Vietnam. Opposition politicians in Saigon clamored for the resignation of Nguyen Van Thieu and began to explore the possibility of a peace candidate such as the popular but enigmatic general Duong Van Minh. There had been some encouragement of this line from the PRG, when on April 2 Foreign Minister Nguyen Thi Binh had expressed a willingness to talk to Minh. Even top officials in the U.S.

Embassy were cautiously optimistic that a compromise agreement could be worked out.

It is doubtful, however, that Hanoi was interested in a political settlement. With military victory now within easy reach and little likelihood of a U.S. response, there seemed no persuasive reason to compromise. As intelligence reports showed, Party leaders had decided at the end of March to settle for nothing less than total victory. A diplomatic settlement was hinted at probably to increase divisiveness in Saigon.

By the third week of April, North Vietnamese divisions had occupied Phan Rang and were beginning to encircle Xuan Loc, moving in on the highway leading to Bien Hoa, site of a major GVN airbase and weapons arsenal. From the delta, Communist units were moving north toward Saigon. All of Tay Ninh Province had been occupied except the capital, which was still under siege. As the campaign neared its climax, Saigon's resistance briefly flared. At Xuan Loc, the Eighteenth Division dug in and proved tougher than expected, slowing down the Communist blitzkrieg and stimulating a brief flurry of optimism in Saigon that total defeat could yet be averted. But the odds were too great and, after a few days of stiff resistance, ARVN units began to withdraw southward toward Vung Tau, while Communist forces bypassed Xuan Loc and began to move directly on Bien Hoa and to shell its air base.

It was by now no secret that Hanoi intended to carry its offensive directly to the heart of enemy rule. The plan called for wearing down the five remaining ARVN divisions on the outskirts of the city and then launching a massive assault with main force and armored units directly into the city before government units in the suburbs could respond. The attack would be led by North Vietnamese mechanized forces, which would advance directly on the main highways into the heart of Saigon. There they would attempt to seize five major targets—the presidential palace, the headquarters of the Saigon city military command, the general police directorate, Tan Son Nhut Airport in the northwestern suburbs, and the nearby headquarters of the general staff. As described by Dung, the plan was

> to use whatever forces necessary from each direction to encircle enemy forces, isolating them and preventing them from pulling back to Saigon; to wipe out and disperse the enemy main-force infantry divisions in the outer defense perimeter right on the spot; and to save the greatest number of forces to thrust in quickly and capture key positions in the outskirts. This would open the way for mechanized and tightly organized assault units to advance rapidly along the main roads and strike directly at the five chosen objectives inside the city.[26]

The attacks in the suburbs went on schedule, as company or battalion-sized units in Go Vap, Nha Be, Binh Chanh, Hoc Mon, Thu Duc, and Cu Chi rose on April 27 and, with the aid of regular forces in the area, began to overrun military and government installations in the vicinity and to seize key bridges and guide the main force units into the city. Others were to eliminate traitors and call on ARVN soldiers to desert their units.

Meanwhile, within the city the Party's municipal apparatus activated its special action squads and sapper units and prepared to seize key government installations, while propaganda units prepared to distribute leaflets and set up loudspeakers at key points to arouse the populace to support the invading revolutionary forces. Special sapper units were organized at Nha Be and Long Tau to sabotage GVN shipping and to cut the river route to the sea. Others were active in Long Binh and Bien Hoa, while a few were infiltrated into the city to supplement the sixty special action cells and 300 armed civilians directed by the Party's municipal leadership. By the twenty-ninth, main force units were well established in key positions around the capital. In the east, routes to the south and west were cut and Bien Hoa Air Base and Vung Tau had been isolated. At command headquarters, Pham Hung and Le Duc Tho made preparations for forming a transitional revolutionary administration in the capital.

In Saigon, the situation raced to a climax. Phnom Penh had fallen to Communist forces on April 17. On the eighteenth the Ford administration, despite Ambassador Graham Martin's objections, ordered a gradual pullout of nonessential Americans. On the twenty-third President Ford announced that the war was finished as far as the United States was concerned. The South Vietnamese, he said, must confront whatever fate awaited them. Under considerable pressure, Thieu finally resigned on the twenty-first and was replaced by Tran Van Huong, a veteran Saigon politician who had achieved a moment of fame during a brief stint as prime minister in 1965. The change was futile, for the Communists refused to deal with him. Van Tien Dung described him as just a "very crafty civilian traitor" replacing a "savage military traitor." Huong resigned on the twenty-seventh and was replaced by Duong Van Minh. Minh quickly formed a new cabinet and ordered the United States to remove its personnel from the GVN in twenty-four hours. The demand had little significance, for current plans called for total evacuation by the twenty-ninth in any case. Nor had it any useful results, for the PRG contemptuously rejected negotiations with the new president.

The Divine Hammer

On April 26, as the first rains began in the delta, Van Tien Dung and his subordinates had moved by car to their advance campaign headquarters near Ben Cat. That afternoon the final campaign began with an artillery barrage on the outskirts of Saigon. From all directions, North Vietnamese forces advanced toward the city and relentlessly scattered resistance from the remaining ARVN forces on the outskirts of the capital. By the evening of the twenty-ninth,

Saigon was surrounded as by a vise and Hanoi's main force units, in the words of Van Tien Dung, were poised like a "divine hammer" held aloft, awaiting the word to launch the direct assault on the city of Saigon.

At 2:00 A.M. on April 30, as the last Americans were preparing to leave Vietnam from helicopter pads around the city, the PRG indicated its final refusal to the appeal for negotiations from the Saigon government. During the early morning, Hanoi's "deep strike units" began to move slowly down the major highways toward the city. Armored vehicles advanced in columns straight into the city, followed by infantry. As they entered without meeting resistance, special action squads occupied bridges while propaganda units passed out leaflets and revolutionary flags and called on the populace to welcome the revolutionary forces. There was some evidence of enthusiasm, particularly in working-class neighborhoods, but for the most part the advance was observed in silence.[27] The attacking troops were supposed to be guided by revolutionary squads, but in at least one case, a tank commander lost his way and had to ask directions from ARVN troops standing by the side of the road.

President Duong Van Minh had met with his ministers at Independence Palace in the heart of the city and at 10:00 A.M. issued an appeal for a cease-fire. The appeal was ignored. In an indirect response, the Politburo issued a directive to its troops advancing into Saigon: "Continue the attack on Saigon according to plan, advancing in the most powerful spirit, liberate and take over the whole city, disarm enemy troops, dissolve the enemy administration at all levels, and thoroughly smash all enemy resistance." Shortly before noon, the lead tank of the Second Army Corps rumbled up Thong Nhut Boulevard and rolled onto the green lawn of the Independence Palace. Troops arrested the government ministers inside the building and raised the revolutionary flag of the PRG over the palace. Two hours later, Duong Van Minh called on all ARVN forces to lay down their arms. The war, the long bitter struggle that had lasted in one form or another for an entire generation, was finally at an end.

Dénouement

The predominantly military character of the final campaign has led some observers to downgrade the political significance of the Communist victory and assert that the takeover of the South was a military conquest, pure and simple. A number of high Saigon civilian and military officials echo this contention by complaining that the war was lost primarily because of the failure of the Ford administration to provide adequate military assistance to the ARVN forces in the final months.[28] The charge is understandable. Although the 1975 campaign was described by Party spokesmen as a combined general offensive and uprising, an attack by revolutionary armed forces in rural areas coordinated with a popular uprising in the cities in the tradition of the Tet Offensive and the great August Revolution of 1945, the reality is somewhat different. The bulk of the fighting was undertaken by regular force units of the PAVN. Although the PLAF undoubtedly participated in attacks at the local level, the most damaging blows were inflicted by North Vietnamese troops. And what the Party lauded as a mass popular uprising in the cities consisted in the main of the mobilization of the Party's small municipal apparatus to welcome the North Vietnamese troops—the *bo doi*—as they entered the cities from the suburbs. While there was some organized jubilation in a few working-class areas, there was relatively little spontaneous enthusiasm among the general urban populace. It is not surprising that Hanoi would dress up the final stage of the conflict as a popular upsurge against an unpopular regime. In fact, however, the final triumph was achieved primarily by force of arms.

But the fact that the 1975 campaign was primarily a military offensive should not obscure the fundamental reality that the Party's success over a generation was attributable, above all, to nonmilitary factors. Hanoi's ability to organize and direct the insurgency and to exploit the chronic weaknesses of its adversary in Saigon were the cardinal factors in its success. Even at the end, the defeat of the GVN was probably caused less by a shortage of aircraft and ammunition than by a lack of nerve in Saigon and by the pervasive sense of malaise throughout South Vietnamese society, itself the legacy of a generation of failure by successive governments to build the foundations of a viable non-Communist society. Not least, the defeat was caused by serious deficiencies in the strategic planning of the Thieu regime. Thieu's hasty last-minute decision to abandon most of the northern provinces and the Central Highlands was ill-conceived and created a disastrous sense of confusion among top military officers as well as within the government. It contributed in no small measure to the completeness of the final collapse.

The U.S. failure to provide adequate military support in the final weeks, although not one of Washington's prouder moments, was not a decisive factor in the outcome of the war. For years the Communists had done better with less. Despite President John F. Kennedy's insistence that, in the last analysis, the war had to be waged and won by the Vietnamese, Washington's clients had come to depend heavily on U.S. largesse. It was a fatal flaw, for when the military shield represented by the power of the United States was withdrawn, the many weaknesses of the Saigon regime quickly surfaced and proved decisive.

13
At the Crossroads

All great revolutions are the product of multiple causes. They result from the convergence of several factors, some of them related directly to the overall political and cultural environment, others the consequence of individual human action. Marxist theory reflects this reality by locating the sources of revolution in both objective and subjective conditions. Objective conditions determine whether or not a mature revolutionary situation has arisen in a given society. Subjective conditions reflect the degree of preparedness and astute leadership provided by a revolutionary party. Revolution rarely succeeds unless both factors are present. The Marxist viewpoint is thus not simply a handy heuristic device, but a practical and often effective approach to the problem of waging revolution in human society.

But although all great revolutions share elements of both spontaneity and human will, the relative importance of these two factors has varied greatly over the years. Many of the classical revolutions in modern history—the French Revolution of 1789, the Russian Revolution of 1917, and, more recently, the revolution in Iran in the late 1970s—grew out of a relatively spontaneous eruption of popular discontent. Only after the initial stage of popular uprising did a revolutionary organization begin to manipulate these conditions to promote a final and total overthrow of existing authority.

The modern phenomenon of people's war has added a new dimension to the revolutionary process. Spontaneity has been replaced with calculation, the popular uprising with the concept of a protracted conflict. Although the presence of objective conditions favoring revolt is still considered to be ultimately essential, this factor is increasingly subordinated to the existence of a dedicated revolutionary organization whose duty it is to exacerbate the political and social tensions in societies undergoing the stress of change. The revolutionary party must serve as the catalyst to activate the latent revolutionary conditions in such societies and then take advantage of the resultant ferment to bring about a violent upheaval against the status quo and the formation of a revolutionary regime.

Although Lenin, because of his stress on the importance of individual human action in the revolutionary process, may claim partial credit for the liberation of the Marxist dialectic from the "iron laws" of history, it was Mao Tse-tung who carried Lenin's idea to its logical conclusion and, in the form of people's war, put it into practice. The Vietnamese carried on the Maoist tradition and set out deliberately to create revolutionary conditions that would topple the government and bring communism to power. Discontent against French colonial rule and later against the failures of the Saigon regime was undeniably a factor in creating the objective conditions underlying the Vietnamese revolution. But the Communist Party mobilized the inchoate frustration and anger of the mass of the Vietnamese population and fashioned it into a fierce and relentless weapon of revolutionary war.

Factors in Communist Success

Of all the great revolutions, then, the Vietnamese revolution was, above all, an act of human will. That does not mean that it took place in a vacuum. Even the Vietnamese Party leadership conceded that a revolutionary upsurge could not take place unless the proper opportunity—the semimystical *thoi co*—had arisen. Some of the conditions that are necessary are the classical symptoms that characterize the emergence of a prerevolutionary situation in any human society—widespread poverty, economic disorder, social inequality and unrest, an unpopular or incompetent government, and a "transfer of allegiance" on the part of the urban middle class. Such conditions, of course, do not necessarily lead to revolt. But without them, revolution is difficult, if not impossible.

At various times in its modern history, Vietnam has exhibited a number of these symptoms, and they were clearly a factor in the growth of the revolutionary movement. But it was characteristic of the situation in Vietnam that the Communists did not passively await the emergence of an economic and social crisis before launching their bid for power, but deliberately attempted to bring it about through exacerbating latent tensions in society and bringing the existing government to the point of collapse. Even in the late 1950s, when Diem's own actions had led to widespread discontent in South Vietnamese society, it was the Communists, above all, who set a match to the powder keg and thus inaugurated the revolutionary war.

In such conditions, the comparative political ability of revolutionaries and ruling elites becomes a crucial issue. And this was what was most extraordinary about the situation in Vietnam—the contrast between the chronic weakness and political ineptitude of the Saigon governing elite and the political genius of the Communist Party. The underlying reasons for the weakness of non-Communist nationalism have been the subject of scholarly analysis for decades, but satisfactory answers have been elusive. Was it merely an accident of history that could be rectified by time and effort? A generation of policymakers in Washington took this view, and based U.S. strategy on the assumption that with adequate military and economic assistance, a regime would eventually emerge that could establish an aura of political legitimacy and a popular base among the population at large. The Communists, of course, thought otherwise. They were convinced that Saigon's weaknesses were endemic and would eventually become the decisive factor in the war.

In retrospect, it appears that the Communists had a clearer view. A generation of U.S. technology and advice was unable to remedy the manifold deficiencies of the GVN. And although the mistakes of the United States may have contributed to the failure in Saigon, it seems probable that the key to the problem lay in Vietnam. The ineffectiveness of Vietnamese nationalism during the colonial period is a matter of record. It consistently failed to produce a challenge to French rule or to provide a nucleus for a mass movement of national proportions such as those formed in a number of other colonial or semicolonial societies in the region. It is surely significant that the first non-Communist government in Vietnam did not come to power as a result of its own efforts, but was imposed from above, by the French. The governments that arose in Saigon after the Geneva settlement bore the mark of that heritage. They were concerned over the need to overcome the chronic factionalism that had characterized nationalist behavior during the colonial period, but they failed to resolve the problem or to build a constituency among the mass of the population. To the end, the only real source of Saigon's authority was the U.S. military presence.

Why were the moderate forces in Vietnam less able than their counterparts elsewhere to emerge as the central force in the struggle for independence? Over the years, a number of hypotheses have been advanced. Some observers have suggested that the root cause lay in the stifling effects of French policy, that the brutal repression of the Vietnamese nationalist movement by the colonial regime left a vacuum that was filled by the Communists. This explanation may be emotionally satisfying to critics of French colonial policy, but it is not very persuasive. On the whole, moderate nationalist forces in Vietnam received little worse treatment than they did elsewhere in colonial Southeast Asia. Only those avowedly determined to root out French rule by force, such as the VNQDD, were exposed to systematic persecution. Although moderate political parties in Vietnam were seldom allowed to enjoy a legal existence, they were given tacit permission to operate during the late 1930s, with no visible effects on their capabilities. A few nationalist figures were arrested and condemned to terms in prison, but most, including such fervent critics of French rule as Nguyen An Ninh and Ta Thu Thau, were soon back on the streets as the result of periodic amnesties declared in Paris. In fact, a non-Communist nationalist movement based on quasi-legal action and mass support, such as the Indian Congress Party, failed to develop in Vietnam not solely because the French prevented it, but primarily because no one attempted to form one.

It can hardly be said, then, that French brutality repressed moderate nationalists, thus leaving the field, by elimination, to the Communists. To the contrary, released documents in the French archives show that the Sûreté had become concerned about the Communists as early as 1929 and throughout much of the following decade devoted the greater part of its efforts to relentlessly pursuing the Party and preventing it from spreading its roots throughout the country. If anything, it is likely that French harassment served to toughen the Communists for the generation of struggle that lay ahead.

Party historians have a different explanation for the weakness of their rivals. Predictably, they view the issue through the prism of Marxist class analysis, and explain it as a consequence of the belated development of the Vietnamese bourgeoisie under colonial rule and its resultant failure to assume an active role in the Vietnamese revolution.[1] By contrast, the Vietnamese working class developed early, in the mines, plantations, and factories run by French colonial interests, and was thus able to take the lead in the struggle for independence after the defeat of the VNQDD at Yen Bay in early 1930. This is an interesting hypothesis, but it lacks sufficient corroborative evidence based on a comparative analysis with other colonial societies in Southeast Asia, where similar conditions apparently existed without leading to a Communist victory. Moreover, it does not account for the fact that the Communist movement itself did not emerge directly from the Vietnamese proletariat but from among discontented members of the traditional ruling class, the sons and daughters of the patriotic scholar-gentry.

The question thus needs to be reformulated. The point is not that the Vietnamese middle class failed to assert its leadership over the nationalist movement, thereby leaving a vacuum to be filled by the proletariat. It is that such a high percentage of the most politically active elements within the educated elite chose to follow the Communists rather than their nationalist rivals, thus providing the Party with its early leadership and a significant advantage in the struggle to determine the course of the Vietnamese revolution. If such is the case, the cultural argument referred to earlier seems a more plausible hypothesis. Marxism exerted a peculiar attraction among the educated scholar-elite in Vietnam. Logical in its portrayal of the historical forces at work in the world, activist in its call for the formation of a disciplined revolutionary organization devoted to the struggle for change, ethical in its vision of a future utopia based on economic and social equality, it offered a persuasive alternative to the now discredited Confucian world view and provided patriotic Vietnamese with a basis on which to struggle for independence and build a new sense of national identity.

The fact that Marxism appealed particularly to the young generation of patriotic scholar-elites is crucial. This was the traditional ruling class in Vietnamese society. It had a heritage of educational leadership and service to society, and an equally strong awareness of the concept of Vietnamese nationhood. It was thus the logical class to lead the struggle against colonial rule. Many alienated members of this class were attracted to Marxism, giving the Party a momentum that it never relinquished. This must be recognized as one of the most significant facts in the history of modern Vietnam.

The weakness of their nationalist rivals was, of course, no guarantee that the Communists themselves would succeed. Economic and military support from Western powers provided non-Communist elites with a bulwark against social and political deterioration and a measure of protection against the spontaneous forces of popular discontent. The Communists could not wait for the proper conditions to arise. They must themselves bring them about by an act of will. Here, of course, was the challenge of people's war in South Vietnam—to hone the disparate sources of revolt into a well-oiled and highly disciplined instrument of revolutionary war. Only through the application of relentless pressure by the insurgency could the latent structural flaws in South Vietnamese society be magnified into yawning cracks that would eventually bring the entire structure to the ground. In Vietnam, there is little doubt that the Party met that challenge. If some revolutions are essentially a collapse of the old order, and others are the product of individual human action, the Vietnamese revolution is quintessentially an example of the latter.

The reasons for the Party's success have attracted considerable attention among scholars in recent years. Certainly one major factor was its comprehensive strategy of people's war.[2] The primary theme of this book is the gradual evolution of that strategy from the early years of the Communist movement down to the final triumph in 1975. The strategy began as a rather unquestioning application of Bolshevik doctrine, as passed on by the Comintern in Moscow. The Russian model had little relevance to Vietnam, however, and during World War II the Party replaced it with a new strategy designed to reflect local conditions. This new strategy owed a debt to the Chinese theory and practice of people's war, but above all it was a product of the fertile mind of Ho Chi Minh. Its major components were put into practice during the revolt that took place at the end of the Pacific War. The success of the August Revolution is adequate testimony to the genius of the concept.

The strategy used during the August uprising could not be applied successfully against a highly armed adversary, and during the Franco-Vietminh conflict the Party turned more explicitly to the Chinese model of three-stage war. The strategy was generally successful, but it had certain weaknesses, among which was the excessive reliance on military factors in the later stages of the war, thus matching the Party's major area of weakness (firepower) against the primary strength of its adversary. After Geneva, then, the Party leadership returned to the strategy used during the August Revolution. But with escalation in the early 1960s, the Party was forced once again to resort to the military option. Now, however, it appeared to recognize the limited relevance of the Maoist model and attempted to combine it with key elements from the Vietnamese approach. Specifically, it attempted to make greater use of the "political force of the masses" in an effort to achieve a better balance of political and

military struggle than had obtained during the previous conflict. It also returned to the August Revolution model by seeking to use the revolutionary
force of urban radicalism through the concept of a coordinated military offensive and general uprising. Finally, it now made deliberate use of diplomacy as a
means of achieving a psychological advantage over the United States and eventually maneuvering it out of the war.

There is, then, a coherent pattern in the development of Vietnamese revolutionary doctrine. Clearly, however, it would be foolhardy to suggest that it had
emerged full-blown from the minds of Party leaders in the mid-1940s. On the
contrary, Vietnamese revolutionary strategy, in its mature form, was the product of trial and error, of a series of pragmatic decisions taken over a period of
several decades and based on real contemporary situations. In the process, it
periodically ran into serious difficulties. On several occasions, Party leaders
miscalculated enemy intentions and capabilities. On others, they overestimated
(or underestimated) the force of the masses and their degree of support for the
revolutionary cause. Not surprisingly, problems were encountered in attempting to cope with the challenges of foreign involvement. In particular, U.S.
escalation in the mid-1960s presented Party strategists with a dilemma, and for
a while they appeared to grope almost in desperation for a solution.

It should also be kept in mind that under the carefully cultivated impression
of unity there was frequently dissension over policy within the Party leadership.
Virtually every major decision was accompanied by hesitation, vacillation, and
internal controversy over the strategy to be applied. There was disagreement
over timing, over the relationship between political and military struggle, and
over the relative priority to be assigned to revolutionary war in the South and
socialist construction in the North. It would be misleading to see in such dissent indications of serious factionalism within the Party leadership. It is
noteworthy that the Leninist tradition of democratic centralism was maintained throughout the struggle. But disagreement did exist. A clearer appreciation of the nature of such inner-Party tension, and the identity of the individuals involved, must await additional evidence.

Despite such problems, on the whole the strategy was effective. This must be
ascribed to several factors. In the first place Party leaders possessed a clear view
of the power relationships among and the security interests of the various forces
involved. They correctly assessed the chronic weakness of their rivals within
the nationalist camp; they correctly predicted that a significant proportion of
the population could be motivated to serve the revolutionary cause in a long
and difficult struggle; and they realized that France and the United States had
neither the patience nor national interests sufficient to justify a protracted conflict in Indochina. In such calculations, strategists in Hanoi proved to be more
clear-sighted than their counterparts in Paris and Washington.

A key factor in the Party's ability to mobilize support within Vietnam was the
success of its effort to link the force of nationalism with that of social reform.

The essentials of that strategy had been drawn up in 1941 with the formation of the Vietminh Front. As this study has attempted to show, this linkage was not easily achieved. Radical programs of benefit to the poor undermined the effort to win the support of moderate nationalists. But a neglect of the issue of land reform left poor peasants indifferent and difficult to mobilize for the war effort. In the late 1940s, Party strategy had placed heavier emphasis on the anti-imperialist than on the antifeudal cause. This was rectified in the early 1950s, and during the war against the United States Hanoi attempted to place relatively equal weight on both factors—the national liberation struggle and the land revolution.

How successful was the Party's effort to "walk on two legs," to construct a strategy on the dual issues of patriotism and social revolution? A definitive judgment must await further study, but available information suggests that the policy was reasonably successful. At some stages (the early years of the Party and during the first stages of the Franco-Vietminh conflict) the national issue predominated; at other times (the Nghe-Tinh revolt, the August Revolution, just prior to the 1954 settlement, and during the late 1950s) economic issues played a crucial role. During the struggle in the South, both issues contributed to support for the revolutionary cause. Interviews with prisoners and defectors show that those who joined the NLF did so for a variety of reasons. The majority were poor peasants or members of the rural proletariat, but urban volunteers were by no means rare. Most cited patriotism or personal motives as their reasons for joining, although social pressure undoubtedly played a role and there is evidence of compulsion in some instances. Members who joined before 1954 frequently mentioned patriotism as the primary reason. Those who joined after Geneva seemed to offer a wider variety of motives—a desire for adventure or for land, hopes for career advancement, a desire to avoid government conscription or to escape from personal problems.[3] In his study of the movement in Long An Province, Jeffrey Race alluded to the importance of the NLF's ability to provide an alternate road to personal identity and upward mobility for those discontented with life under the GVN.

It is worthy to note that idealism—resentment against government corruption and injustice, or a wish to evict the U.S. imperialists—was often cited as a major factor in recruitment. Virtually all mentioned the idea of the "just cause," the "righteous war" against foreign control and the reactionary government in Saigon. It is particularly significant that patriotic motives played a part in recruitment in rural areas, a sign that nationalism had taken root among the village population. This concept of the "just war" was not just a passing enthusiasm, or one that would be easily undermined as a result of sacrifice and hardship. A surprising number of deserters gave personal reasons for leaving the movement and continued to believe that the revolutionary cause was a righteous one.

In general, then, the Party's propaganda had a fairly broad appeal within the population, and in both urban and rural areas. Still, Party leaders must have been somewhat disappointed by their failure to operate more effectively in the cities. Active support in urban areas never reached the levels apparently expected by the party. This failure was generally ascribed in internal documents to organizational weaknesses, or to the influence of the "noxious weeds" of bourgeois attitudes in the cities of South Vietnam. Whatever the reason, the failure to build a more dynamic movement in Saigon, Da Nang, and Hué was undoubtedly a factor in compelling the Party to turn to a more military approach. That in turn led to increasing reliance on troops from the North, thus diluting somewhat the issue of nationalism. Whatever the case, the concept of the popular uprising steadily lost force in Hanoi's strategy and at the end had become more the ritualistic perpetuation of a myth than a building block of victory. In the final analysis, the Communist takeover did not differ substantially from the Maoist dictum of surrounding the cities from the countryside. This was not a crucial weakness, in China or in Vietnam. In both instances Communist policy was aided by errors committed by the enemy and was thus able to prevent the urban population from committing itself wholeheartedly to the government's cause. That, in itself, was a solid achievement, and an important factor in revolutionary success.

It has been observed that the Party's achievement was a triumph of organization rather than spirit.[4] Certainly organization, indoctrination, and the application of pressure and the threat or use of force played a major role in realizing and maintaining commitment to the revolutionary cause. The nature of the Party's organizational genius has been competently explored in previous studies, and need not detain us here.[5] Suffice it to say that the Communists had striking success in mobilizing all available human and material resources in a total and concentrated effort to seize power. Women, children, and even the aged were put to use so that young males could be released for combat. But the effectiveness of the Party's organizational efforts should not lead us to underestimate the emotional appeal of the cause. In fact, as one American researcher reported, as late as 1964 nearly 90 percent of all members of the PLAF were volunteers.

One final factor remains to be explored. A paramount feature in almost all modern revolutions has been the existence of dynamic and charismatic leadership. It is difficult to imagine the revolts in Russia, China, or Cuba, for example, without reference to the roles played by Lenin, Mao Tse-tung, and Fidel Castro. Curiously, this factor is frequently overlooked in Vietnam. Because Ho Chi Minh lacked theoretical inclinations, his role in shaping revolutionary strategy has often been ignored; because his style of leadership was quiet rather than forceful, conciliatory rather than aggressive, his influence in the decision-making process has frequently seemed ambiguous; and because his part in directing Party strategy probably diminished in the final years of his life, the importance of his influence in the latter stages of the war is difficult to substantiate. Still, over the course of the Vietnamese revolution as a whole, his influence towers. He is best known, of course, as the living symbol of the Vietnamese revolution. For more than a generation his personality, embodying the qualities of virtue, integrity, dedication, and revolutionary asceticism, transcended issues of party and ideology and came to represent, in an Eriksonian sense, the struggle for the independence and self-realization of the Vietnamese nation. Nikita Khrushchev alluded to this trait in his memoirs, when he referred to the Vietnamese leader as a "holy apostle" of the revolution, a man whose sincerity, conviction, and incorruptibility could win anyone over to belief in his cause.[6]

But if Ho Chi Minh is best remembered as the spiritual leader of the Vietnamese revolution, his practical contributions should not be ignored. The key building blocks in the Party's revolutionary strategy bear the stamp of his genius. His fine hand can be seen in the careful attention to organization and detail, in the concern for unity (both internal and within the socialist camp as a whole), and in the delicate structure of the united front. It is perhaps most obvious in the Party's astute handling of the international situation and in its use of diplomacy as a cardinal feature of its revolutionary strategy.[7] In an age when many of the leaders of newly independent nations in Asia lacked the administrative and organizational abilities to match their personal charisma (Sukarno and U Nu come immediately to mind), Ho Chi Minh was an unusual composite of moral leader and organizational genius, half Gandhi, half Lenin. It was a dynamic combination. It is not too much to say that, without Ho Chi Minh, there might not have been a Vietnamese revolution, at least in the form we know.

Vietnam as Model

For two decades, U. S. presidents justified their policies in Vietnam on the grounds that if the insurgency movement there was not contained, it would set a precedent for similar movements around the globe. In recent years Party spokesmen in Hanoi have appeared to adopt the same view and have occasionally declared that the Vietnamese struggle for national liberation could provide a model for aspiring insurgency movements in other countries throughout the Third World. Vietnam, they have said, is where the three great currents of the world revolution—democracy, nationalism, and socialism—have converged. The victory in Saigon conclusively demonstrated that a national liberation movement led by a Communist party can triumph over the aggressive forces of world imperialism led by the United States and thus open a new stage in the world revolution, a stage that will conclude with the final victory of the forces of peace, democracy, and socialism throughout the globe.

Can the Vietnamese revolution serve as a model for national liberation struggles elsewhere in Asia, Africa, and Latin America? Will there be, as some have suggested, "one, two, many Vietnams" in our future? Or is it better viewed as a unique expression of the Vietnamese revolutionary art? The Party is tantalizingly vague on this point. It contends that a number of the key components of Vietnamese revolutionary doctrine—the united front under Party leadership, the flexible use of town and country and of urban and rural struggle, the revolutionary army directed by the Party—can be applied with profit elsewhere. On the other hand it also concedes, with no little pride, that the seeds of the Communist victory must be sought primarily in the native soil of Vietnam, in the unique characteristics of its history and geography, in the perseverance and stalwart patriotism of its people, and in the Party's firm and astute leadership.

What the Party appears to be saying is that the broad framework of Vietnamese revolutionary doctrine can be transplanted effectively to a different cultural environment, although the specific details have relevance only to Vietnam. Generally speaking this hypothesis appears to be true. There are indeed a number of useful lessons that other insurgency movements can learn from the Vietnamese experience—the careful crafting of the united front to reflect the specific political and social conditions in a given society; the flexible use of political, military, and diplomatic techniques to further the revolutionary cause; and the need for discipline, patience, and a willingness to sacrifice within the movement itself. On the other hand, the Party is certainly correct that a number of the most important ingredients in its victory were unique to Vietnam. The character of its people, the favorable topography, the quality of its leadership, and the contiguity with China were all factors not easily reproduced elsewhere. Those who view the Vietnamese revolution as a pattern for similar upheavals throughout the Third World are guilty of historical simplification similar to that of U.S. policymakers who applied the lessons of Munich to the complex realities of Southeast Asia.

This does not mean that the victory of communism in Vietnam did not give a significant impetus to the cause of revolution in the Third World. In an inspirational sense, it provided evidence that a national liberation movement led by a Communist party could come to power even in the face of the concerted opposition of the United States. Equally important, perhaps, the war exerted a strongly corrosive effect on the U.S. policy of containment and gave rise to a new mood of caution and limited commitment in world affairs. Some feel that recent revolts in Africa, Latin America, and the Middle East might not have occurred had the United States not been chastened by its experience in Vietnam and thus been hesitant to undertake actions that might lead to a repeat performance. The long-term effects of this "Vietnam syndrome," however, are more difficult to predict. At this writing, there are clear signs that the shock waves created by the tragedy in Vietnam have already begun to decrease in their intensity. The reaction in the United States to the Iranian crisis and to the Soviet military occupation of Afghanistan suggests that fear of another Vietnam is rapidly being replaced by concern over Soviet expansion in the Middle East. Critics have cited such indications as disquieting evidence that U.S. foreign policy has now come full circle and is about to reembark on the road to a new Cold War, with the Carter Doctrine replacing SEATO and the Persian Gulf primed to play the role of Indochina a generation ago.

Looking Forward

For the Party, the revolution did not conclude with the initial triumph over the Saigon regime. The period that followed has been one of severe challenge. Politically, power had to be consolidated and the lingering forces of the previous regime destroyed. Society had to be transformed from a wartime to a peacetime footing, and the population persuaded to accept the new revolutionary leadership and its program for the future. With the U.S. presence removed, South Vietnam had to learn to wean itself from chronic reliance on foreign aid and the provision of services for foreigners. Refugees had to be persuaded to return to the countryside, and jobs found for the millions of unemployed in the cities.

Beyond such immediate concerns lay more complex long-range problems of ideological remolding and unification with the North. South Vietnam had to be transformed from a capitalist economic structure to a socialist one. The industrial and commercial sectors had to be nationalized, and the rural economy placed under collective ownership. The poisonous weeds of decadent Western bourgeois ideology had to be rooted out, and the seeds of a new socialist culture planted. A revolutionary administration had to be constructed to replace the Saigon regime and a schedule drawn up for the eventual assimilation of the South into the D.R.V., so that together the two regions could advance toward communism.

The details of this process are beyond the scope of this study, but a few brief comments to indicate the general course of events since the Communist takeover might be appropriate. Some parts of the program were accomplished with relative ease, but others have remained problems beyond immediate resolution. Indeed, portents soon appeared that the building of a prosperous and peaceful socialist Vietnam would be as complicated as and present perhaps even more intractable problems than the struggle to seize power.

Few difficulties were encountered in the consolidation of power. Active opposition to the new order in the South was limited. A few members of the old government, most of whom were apparently officers or enlisted men of the Saigon army, fled to remote areas to continue their resistance, but most South Vietnamese seemed willing to tolerate their new rulers. For this the Party could claim partial credit, for it appeared to go out of its way to avoid any semblance of a revolutionary "reign of terror." There was no "bloodbath" for the enemies of the revolution, as had been widely predicted. Instead, the Party relied primarily on incarceration and indoctrination. By the end of 1975, several hundred thousand South Vietnamese suspected of loyalty to the old regime had been rounded up and dispatched to reeducation camps, some for only a few weeks, others for an indefinite period of time. In order to avoid antagonizing the local population, revolutionary cadres were instructed to avoid enforcing the revolutionary ethic too strenuously among the relatively easygoing and decadent Saigonese. When zealots harassed prostitutes or attempted to cut the long hair of Westernized southern youth, they were severely reprimanded by the authorities. The policy paid off. After a few months, the Party felt sufficiently confident to dismantle the Military Management Committee that had been established immediately after the fall of Saigon and turn power over to the Provisional Revolutionary Government.

For a time, the Party gave serious consideration to maintaining a separate governmental administration in the South for the foreseeable future, but by the late summer it had decided to move rapidly toward reunification of the country under a single government in order to facilitate social and economic reforms. In early 1976, elections were held for the National Assembly for the entire country and in July the unification of the two zones was realized with the formal establishment of a new Socialist Republic of Vietnam (S.R.V.) with its capital in Hanoi. For the first time in more than a century, Vietnam was united, from the Friendship Gate along the Chinese border to the southern tip of the Ca Mau peninsula.

The second major objective of the Party leadership was to restore the economy in the South to a peacetime footing and to prepare for the gradual imposition of governmental controls. Here the Party immediately ran into difficulties. To prevent rampant inflation and increased unemployment, the local authorities announced that normal economic activities should continue and assured businessmen that their profits would be respected. In the economic sector, a few major industries and utilities were taken over by the government, and the property of wealthy businessmen (many of whom were Overseas Chinese classified as members of the reactionary "comprador bourgeoisie") was confiscated. A few show trials of flagrant offenders (called "barbed wire kings" or "pharmaceutical kings") were held to discourage speculation and manipulation of the market. The Saigon middle class as a whole was not attacked, however. Indeed, it was encouraged to take part in the campaign against the wealthy in order to demonstrate loyalty to the new order. To minimize disruption of productive activities, technological experts were instructed to remain at their jobs and, if there were no indications of potential disloyalty to the new regime, were frequently released from the obligation of attending indoctrination programs.

The major problem in the South, from a social as well as economic point of view, was unemployment. In 1975 there were nearly 3 million without jobs in urban areas. Some were refugees from the countryside, living in squalid camps along the fringes of the burgeoning cities. Others had lost their jobs with the departure of the Americans and the fall of the Saigon regime. The Party's long-term solution was to encourage those who were not considered suitable for gainful employment in the cities to return to the countryside through the creation of so-called New Economic Areas (NEAs), resettlement zones established on uncultivated land in underpopulated rural provinces. Plans called for the eventual resettlement of several million Vietnamese (some to be transplanted from densely populated provinces in the North) in these new areas, which were scheduled to become the focus for a system of centers of agricultural and industrial development at the district level. Before the end of the first year of Communist rule, several hundred thousand refugees and other urban residents had been resettled in the new zones. In theory, the centers had been prepared in advance by government cadres and settlers were to receive seeds, tools, and farm equipment. In reality, conditions in the new camps were frequently frightful and life there was harsh and unrewarding. In theory, participation was voluntary. In practice there were complaints that many were compelled to go against their will and that selection was made on a racial basis (many were Overseas Chinese from Cholon) or on the basis of suspected disloyalty to the new regime. Before long, there were reports of residents leaving the zones and returning secretly to the cities.

The New Economic Areas provided one potential long-term solution for the high rate of unemployment in the South. But the government soon began to discover that the problems of economic reconstruction were immense and seemed largely resistant to solutions, despite the Party's efforts to apply the techniques used during the war. Years of neglect had left the economic sector ill-prepared to cope with the demands of technological modernization. Investment capital was lacking, as were skilled workers. Within the population, there was a perceptible tendency to relax after the long years of war and a growing resistance to the familiar appeals by the Party and government for personal sacrifice in the struggle to achieve the new peacetime goals. Foreign assistance was solicited, but with limited success. The main source of aid was the Soviet Union, but even Moscow was unwilling to meet Hanoi's massive economic needs, despite a growing willingness by the latter to tailor its own foreign policy to Soviet requirements.

One major aspect of the problem lay in the countryside. Food output was totally inadequate, forcing the government to import grain from the Soviet Union, thus placing a heavy burden on the already adverse balance of payments. The Party hoped that the South would eventually recover its prewar role as the major supplier of food for the nation, but the effects of the war had left thousands of acres of land uncultivated in the region. In order to encourage production increases, the government attempted to avoid frightening the southern peasants by moving too rapidly toward collectivization. For the time being, it declared, land would remain in private hands. Land reform, which had caused severe strains in the D.R.V. during the mid-1950s, was not initiated, on the grounds that previous programs launched by the PRG and the GVN had substantially eliminated the landlord class in the southern provinces. Even private trade in rice was permitted. But in order to eliminate speculation and hoarding by rice merchants, the government moved gradually into the rice market. Rice merchants were permitted to continue their activities only if they registered with the state and conformed to its price regulations. The results were mixed. Prices continued to fluctuate, while peasants, unhappy at the official price of rice and the lack of consumer goods, grew only what they needed, thus creating shortages. The problem was soon compounded by bad weather. By 1977, with the rice crop damaged by floods, droughts, and cold weather in the North, the food situation was growing desperate.

The general economic deterioration compelled the Party to reevaluate its position. Plans mapped out at the Party's Fourth National Congress in December 1976 had called for the gradual transformation of the southern economy to socialized forms, with industry and commerce nationalized by the end of the decade and collectivization in the countryside scheduled to begin in the early 1980s. With the Five-year Plan launched in 1976 in serious trouble, the leadership decided to accelerate the pace of socialization in the South as a means of gaining control over the urban economy and increasing grain production on the farms. The first move came virtually without warning in March 1978, with the announcement that all private trade in South Vietnam was abolished. Merchants were directed to shift to productive activities or to join collectively owned or joint private-state enterprises. All goods held by private merchants were to be purchased by the state. Youth assault squads were mobilized the night before the announcement to confiscate goods before they could be dispersed (as had happened during the previous campaign against the comprador bourgeoisie in 1975). The government promised to provide compensation to the owner, but only if proof of ownership could be furnished. Because the bulk of the goods had been obtained through the black market, many businessmen were wiped out.

In one respect, the new policy was effective. By the end of the year, 30,000 private firms had been abolished and government control over the urban economy in South Vietnam had been established. The social effects were profound. Most of the shopkeepers affected by the move were ethnic Chinese. According to reports, similar restrictions were imposed on Chinese small merchants resident in the North. In late spring, they began to leave Vietnam by the thousands. Those in North Vietnam often left overland for China; those in the South attempted to depart by ship. Many of the refugees indicated that the exodus was tolerated and perhaps even encouraged by government authorities.

Those wishing to depart by sea were charged a fee of $2,000 in gold for each adult. One-half went to the government, while the remainder was used to pay the intermediaries and to defray the cost of the journey.

The government vehemently denied that it was making a profit on the refugee outflow, but it conceded that some corrupt officials were accepting bribes to permit refugee departures. It attempted to justify the exodus by saying that after every major revolution there are people who do not wish to live under the new order. There were many in South Vietnam, Hanoi admitted, who were unwilling to bear the hardships that would be required to build a socialist society. Permitting them to leave, it implied, was a more humane policy than compelling them to adhere to the stringent regulations of the new revolutionary regime.

While the government was moving swiftly to tighten its control over the urban economy, there were signs that it was beginning to prepare for collectivization in the countryside. In the period immediately following the seizure of the South, there had been few indications of impending change in rural areas. In late 1976, landholdings in excess of family requirements were nationalized. In selected areas, a few experimental cooperatives were formed and labor exchange teams, a work-sharing program traditionally used as the first step toward socialism in the countryside, were formed. As an inducement to peasants to join, the government allocated extra rations of fuel and fertilizer to members.

Sometime in 1977, the Party began to move toward the next stage. In preparation for collectivization, each province in the South was directed to set up pilot cooperatives at the district level by early 1978. The objective, in the words of the Five-year Plan approved in 1976, was to "basically achieve the establishment of socialist production relations in the southern countryside during the first years of the 1980s." To direct the process, the Department for the Transformation of Southern Agriculture was established under the Central Committee in Hanoi. More than a thousand specialists were sent to the South to set up schools to train southern cadres to handle the transformation. By late summer of 1978, according to one government report, there were 132 agricultural cooperatives in South Vietnam.

As the decade came to an end, however, there appeared to be little relief from Vietnam's severe economic problems. Food shortages provided a dismal counterpoint to the lack of consumer goods and the continuation of high unemployment in the cities. The Party put up a brave front and appeared publicly confident that rich resources, human ingenuity, and its social-engineering approach would pave the way to a brighter future. By the final years of the decade, the prospects that such a view could become a reality appeared increasingly problematical, and in 1979 a Party plenum called for a slowdown in the pace of socialization and the encouragement of material incentives to increase production.

Foreign Policy

One reason for the Party's inability to resolve domestic problems was the sad fact that the end of the war did not bring lasting peace to Vietnam. Great revolutions often emit shock waves that bring long-term instability to neighboring areas. The Vietnamese revolution has been no exception. Less than half a decade after the fall of Saigon, Hanoi was again involved in full-scale war on two fronts, with China to the north and with Cambodia to the west. Ironically, both had been allies of the Vietnamese during the long struggle for power against the United States.

Troubles with the new revolutionary government of Democratic Kampuchea, of course, had appeared before the end of the war. The mutual suspicion between Hanoi and the Pol Pot leadership of the KCP had reached serious proportions in the early 1970s and led to a purge of pro-Hanoi elements in the Cambodian party. Vietnamese Party leaders allegedly gave serious consideration to a proposal to overthrow Pol Pot and replace him with a leader more sympathetic to Hanoi. As soon as the Vietnam War ended, the dispute broke into the open. The first signs took the form of armed conflict along the Vietnam-Cambodia border. In the spring of 1975, Cambodian forces attacked several offshore islands held by the Vietnamese. The latter counterattacked and briefly seized Wai Island, from which some of the attacks had been launched. Attempts to achieve a negotiated settlement foundered. While the two sides appeared willing to agree on the land border as established by the French (Sihanouk had earlier expressed Cambodia's willingness to abandon its historic claim to the lands lost to the Vietnamese two centuries earlier in return for Hanoi's recognition of the current frontier), conflicting claims on the territorial seabed in the Gulf of Thailand, stimulated by global interest in offshore oil and undersea resources, proved harder to resolve.

A more fundamental cause of conflict, however, lay in the long-term relations between the two countries. Hanoi, while publicly disavowing its earlier proposal for the formation of an "Indochinese Federation" linking Vietnam, Laos, and Cambodia, continued to press for the realization of a "special relationship" between the three countries because of their shared experience of opposition to imperialism. The new Pol Pot government in Cambodia, fed by a tradition of hostility and distrust of Vietnamese intentions, viewed the concept as a prescription for Vietnamese domination of its smaller neighbors and resisted Hanoi's proposal for intimate relations. As Hanoi drew closer to Moscow, Phnom Penh approached Peking, which now viewed the Pol Pot government as a bulwark against Vietnamese expansion in Southeast Asia. By mid-1978, with border conflicts continuing, Hanoi lost patience and began to prepare for the overthrow of the Pol Pot regime. Guerrilla forces were recruited from among Cambodian refugees who had fled to Vietnam to escape the brutal policies of the Pol Pot leadership. In December a new united front—the Kampuchean National United Front for National Salvation (KNUFNS)—was established with the avowed aim of toppling Pol Pot and installing a new government in Phnom Penh. Shortly afterwards, Vietnamese regular units with the support of Cambodian guerrillas launched a massive invasion of eastern Cambodia and in a series of lightning assaults occupied the Cambodian capital on January 7, 1979. As the Pol Pot regime fled to the hills to continue its resistance, pro-Hanoi elements within the KCP under Heng Samrin set up a new Democratic People's Republic of Kampuchea. Within weeks, the new regime had signed the Treaty of Friendship and Cooperation with Vietnam. Having initialed a similar pact with Laos the previous year, Hanoi had now achieved its "special relationship" with its western neighbors.[8]

On the debit side, the Vietnamese invasion of Cambodia had serious repercussions on Vietnamese foreign policy objectives beyond Indochina. On a global scale, the action was condemned by a majority vote in the United Nations General Assembly, and a number of Western nations canceled planned aid projects with the S.R.V. Sporadic efforts to normalize relations with the United States and thus permit the establishment of trade ties were broken off *sine die*. More than ever, the Vietnamese were economically dependent upon their ally in Moscow. The implications of this situation had already been realized and acted upon. In mid-1978 Vietnam officially joined the Soviet-directed Council for Mutual Economic Assistance (CEMA) and began to integrate its economic planning with that of Moscow and its socialist allies.

Within Southeast Asia, the invasion derailed delicate negotiations between Hanoi and the five members of the Association for the Southeast Asian Nations (ASEAN). To the ASEAN nations, the invasion of Cambodia offered incontrovertible evidence that Vietnam still harbored expansionist objectives in the area and they retreated from tentative steps to improve relations with Hanoi. ASEAN took the lead in proposing a resolution in the United Nations requesting Vietnam to withdraw its troops from Cambodia, and some promised military assistance to fellow member Thailand should it be attacked by Vietnamese troops along the border. As the decade came to an end, continued resistance by Pol Pot forces inside Cambodia and signs of disaffection from the Heng Samrin government in Phnom Penh lent substance to the supposition that the Cambodian conflict had not yet reached a final resolution.

A more serious consequence of the Vietnamese invasion of Cambodia, perhaps, was the exacerbation of Vietnamese relations with China. Ties between Hanoi and Peking had become increasingly strained during the final years of the Vietnam War. The Vietnamese had resented China's limited support for their struggle in South Vietnam, as well as Peking's decision in the early 1970s to seek a rapprochement with the United States. In turn, China had disapproved of Vietnamese willingness to strengthen its ties with Moscow.

At war's end, relations were correct but cool. China refused to increase economic assistance for peacetime reconstruction and simply continued to provide aid as called for by previous agreements. The first sign of increasing tension took the form of territorial disagreements. Peking and Hanoi registered conflicting claims over ownership of the Paracel and Spratly islands in the South China Sea. Soon clashes began to take place along the land frontier, and by 1978 complaints had begun to appear in the Chinese press that the Vietnamese were unilaterally moving border markers and harassing and even shooting Chinese citizens.

The refugee issue and the Cambodian crisis provided additional causes for Chinese anger. As the exodus of ethnic Chinese rose to a flood during the spring of 1978, Peking charged that Hanoi was mistreating its residents of Chinese descent and reneging on a 1955 agreement that the assimilation of Overseas Chinese would be gradual and voluntary. Hanoi retorted that the outflow of refugees had been provoked by rumors deliberately spread by Chinese Embassy officials in Hanoi and added that Vietnam was only doing what all Communist societies, including that of China, had done previously: taking measures to abolish the private trade sector. In mid-1978, China canceled all remaining aid projects in Vietnam, withdrew its advisers and technicians, and continued to complain of provocative Vietnamese activities along the frontier. It was also drawn increasingly to provide support to the government of Democratic Kampuchea, despite an apparent distaste for the radical policies of the Pol Pot regime.

If Peking's actions were motivated by a desire to persuade Hanoi to change the course of its foreign policy, the gambit failed. During 1978, Vietnam moved closer to confrontation with Phnom Penh and an open military alliance with the Soviet Union. Soviet ships made limited but regular use of Vietnamese naval facilities at Da Nang and the old U.S. base at Cam Ranh Bay, leading to Chinese charges that Vietnam was being turned into a cat's-paw of Soviet aggression in Southeast Asia. Then in November, Hanoi and Moscow signed a treaty of friendship and cooperation. Although the pact did not call for automatic military assistance in case of war, it did provide for mutual consultations, and there were unsubstantiated rumors of a secret military protocol. An increase in the Soviet military presence in Vietnam during the months following the signing of the treaty lent credence to such reports.

The tension increased when Vietnamese troops entered Cambodia, and Peking warned Vietnam that its actions would not go unpunished. Early in 1979, Chinese military forces advanced into Vietnam at several points along the frontier. In a series of short but sometimes bitter battles, the Chinese seized a number of provincial capitals along the border, including Lao Cai and Lang Son, and destroyed Vietnamese installations and frontier defenses. The Vietnamese began to shift their regular forces toward the Viet Bac, but Peking announced that it had no intention of attempting to advance into the Red

River delta or to seize the capital of Hanoi, and in early March its forces withdrew into Chinese territory. Negotiations began in April, but Peking's primary demands for a settlement—Vietnamese withdrawal from Cambodia, recognition of Chinese territorial claims, and Hanoi's disentanglement from its alliance with Moscow—were obviously unacceptable to Hanoi.

A number of observers have contended that the recent conflicts in Southeast Asia are a product of the Sino-Soviet dispute. Presidential adviser Zbigniew Brzezinski claimed that the clash between Vietnam and Cambodia was actually a "proxy war" between Moscow and Peking. There is undoubtedly a great deal of truth in this. The Chinese attack on Vietnam in early 1979 was motivated in part by Peking's fear that Hanoi was acting as a stalking-horse for Soviet influence in Southeast Asia. In turn, growing Soviet ties with Hanoi are presumably viewed in Moscow as a means of further isolating China from other countries in the area. But the heightened tension in the area should also be seen as representing the resumption of a historical process that had been temporarily submerged during the colonial period and the Vietnam War. In the precolonial era, the thrust of Vietnamese expansion to the south and west was one of the most dynamic political forces in Southeast Asia. This advance had been held in abeyance under French rule, but with the reunification of Vietnam in 1975 it resumed, now generated by the strong energetic impetus of the Vietnamese revolution. Whether it will ultimately engulf the remainder of mainland Southeast Asia remains to be seen. Inescapably, it affects the general political situation in the region today.

With U.S. power now substantially absent from the area, the strongest potential counterbalance to the force of Vietnamese expansionism is provided by the resurgence of China as a major influence in the affairs of Southeast Asia. Strictly speaking, China's interest in the area does not appear to be one of territorial aggrandizement. A more realistic objective would be the establishment of a system of friendly states resistant to domination by a major external power potentially inimical to Chinese interests. Such a relationship has sometimes been portrayed as a resuscitation of the traditional tributary relationship in modern dress. But it is not really necessary to search for historical antecedents to Chinese foreign policy interests in Southeast Asia. China's behavior reflects the same desire for secure borders and friendly neighbors shared by all the great powers.

Therein lies the problem. Ambitious and deeply distrustful of Peking's long-term objectives in Southeast Asia, the present leadership in Hanoi appears to view China as a potential rival and has grasped at the link with Moscow as the most reliable counterpoise to fend off Chinese dominance of the area. In the short run, the policy seems to be effective. With Moscow playing the role of Hanoi's silent partner, Peking's options for controlling Vietnamese behavior are limited. As a long-term solution for Vietnam's foreign policy interests, however, the treaty with Moscow may not be a formula to inspire confidence.

By turning to Moscow, Hanoi pours fuel on the fires of Peking's hostility and distrust and makes conflict between the two more likely. The result could be tragic for both, but particularly for Vietnam.

The strain of dealing with such issues has clearly begun to appear within the Party leadership. For the first time in half a century, the carefully preserved unity within the Central Committee shows signs of unraveling. At the Fourth Party Congress in December 1976, members suspected of sympathy with China were removed from positions of authority in the Party. The decision to move rapidly toward socialism in the South evidently caused controversy within the leadership, leading to a somewhat defensive outburst in the Party press in August 1978 against the weak and traitorous elements. The conflicts with Cambodia and China have intensified the problem. Several military officers of minority extraction, including resistance leaders Chu Van Tan and Le Quang Ba, have been deprived of their posts, apparently out of concern that they might be lured to support a Chinese-sponsored anti-Vietnamese united front among the ethnic minorities in the border area. In July, the first major defection in the history of the Party occurred when Hoang Van Hoan, one-time ambassador to Peking and a leading exponent of friendship with China, defected and blasted Le Duan for betraying the sacred heritage of Ho Chi Minh. Further shake-ups occurred in 1980 as the Le Duan leadership apparently attempted to tighten its control over the security apparatus and set up a new generation of Party and government leaders loyal to current policies. The issues and the protagonists involved are not clearly defined to the outside observer, but it is clear that a struggle for control of the revolution has been taking place.

At the moment of writing, five years after the fall of Saigon, many of the fears expressed by U.S. policymakers to justify involvement in the Vietnam conflict appear to be coming true. The end of the war did not bring peace and stability, but continued tension and suffering. Within Indochina it has brought untold hardship to millions. Abroad, it has resulted in the revival of ancient rivalries and an expansion of Soviet influence in the area, thus bringing Southeast Asia once again into the vortex of the Cold War. For nearly 50 million Vietnamese, the immediate future hardly looks bright. As with so many of the great revolutions of modern times, the aftershocks are frequently as severe as the initial explosion.

Perhaps, however, we should reserve our final judgment on the Vietnamese revolution. Revolutions generate a force that transcends facile moral generalizations and, although their destructive power is evident to the most casual observer, their fruits are often not visible to the naked eye until decades have passed. The civil war in China, which concluded with the victory of the Communists in 1949, is a case in point. The establishment of the P.R.C. emitted shock waves that destabilized the entire Pacific area for a generation. Within China, it unleashed a struggle for control and definition of the revolution which may not yet have concluded. Yet, a contemporary view might place the long-term consequences of the Chinese revolution in somewhat more benign terms. Internally, the P.R.C. now appears to be entering a period of political stability marked by a relatively pragmatic concern for the improvement of the welfare of its citizens. In foreign affairs, it has emerged in recent years as a reasonably moderate force interested in promoting the stability of the Pacific region. In the process, the likelihood of East Asia becoming the focal point of a new world crisis, although hardly eliminated, has been somewhat reduced. China is no longer the "sick man of Asia," enticing great-power rivalry to the area, but a legitimate force in East Asian politics. The consequences, of course, are not entirely on the side of stability and moderation. The current conflict between Hanoi and Peking is convincing evidence that the expansionistic forces generated by the revolutions in both China and Vietnam have not yet been slaked. But at least for the moment, China seems better prepared to play a mature role in world affairs than at any time in the last century.

It is too early to predict whether the Vietnamese revolution will undergo a similar process. At the moment, in its effort to realize the manifest destiny of the Vietnamese nation, it projects a primordial force that has created instability throughout the region. In a natural fear of its northern neighbor Hanoi has turned to Moscow for protection and thus once again focused Cold War antagonisms in the area. Yet it is also clear that political weakness and internal decisions were major factors in making Southeast Asia into a snakepit of great power rivalries. It is doubtful that the region can transform itself from victim to active participant in Asian politics until the nations in the area can begin to exert sufficient influence to fill the political vacuum that has historically been the source of their servitude. The emergence of ASEAN is one promising sign that this transition may be taking place. The revolution in Vietnam, in the long run, may be another. A united and healthy Vietnam, willing and able to play a mature role in the affairs of the region, is a prerequisite for the emergence of a strong and independent Southeast Asia. Although its current manifestations are to many observers harsh and forbidding, the Vietnamese revolution may be the first step in a process by which a talented, courageous, and industrious people can begin to play a formative and vital role in the affairs of humanity.

Notes

ABBREVIATIONS

AOM   Archives Nationales de France, Section Outre-Mer
DDRS   *Declassified Documents Reference Service*
JPRS   Joint Publications Research Service
NCLS   *Nghien cuu lich su* [Historical research]
SLOTFOM   Service de Liaison avec les Originaires de Territoires de la France d'Outre-Mer
TLTK   *Tai lieu tham khau lich su cach mang can dai Viet Nam* [Historical research materials
           concerning the modern revolution in Vietnam]
VDRN   *Vietnam Documents and Research Notes*

Chapter 1: Introduction

1. Three of the best recent studies on various aspects of the Communist movement are Douglas Pike, *Viet Cong* (Cambridge, Mass., 1966); Jeffrey Race, *War Comes to Long An* (Berkeley and Los Angeles, Calif., 1972); and Alexander Woodside, *Community and Revolution in Modern Vietnam* (Boston, 1976).

2. Within the last two years two important new histories, one of the Party and the other of the armed forces, have been published in Hanoi. At the moment of writing, the early volumes of *Nhung su kien lich su dang* [Incidents in the history of the Party] and *Lich su quan doi nhan dan Viet Nam* [A history of the People's Army of Vietnam], dealing with the period up to 1954, have been published. Unfortunately I have been unable to obtain copies. They will presumably require revisions of some of the facts and conclusions in this study.

3. A similar view has been expressed by Douglas Pike, *History of Vietnamese Communism, 1925-1976* (Stanford, Calif., 1978), p. xiv.

Chapter 2: The Rise of the Revolutionary Movement

1. "Ho Chu tich noi ve chu nghia Le-nin va cach mang Viet Nam" [Chairman Ho discusses Leninism and the Vietnamese revolution], *Hoc tap*, March 1970, p. 2.

2. This section is necessarily brief. I have covered the subject in more detail in William J. Duiker, *The Rise of Nationalism in Vietnam, 1900–1941* (Ithaca, N.Y., 1976).

3. In the interest of brevity I have resorted to generalization. In reality, French educational policies, like colonial policy as a whole, reflected considerable confusion in terms of long-range objectives.

4. The comparison with the Chinese case is instructive. For an examination of the

Chinese radical movement at a similar stage of development, see Mary B. Rankin, *Early Chinese Revolutionaries* (Cambridge, Mass.: Harvard University Press, 1971).

5. For one analysis, see Ralph B. Smith, "Some Vietnamese Elites in Cochin China, 1943," *Modern Asian Studies*, Vol. 6, part 4 (October 1972).

6. Unfortunately, statistical evidence to support this point is scanty. This generalization is based on scattered but fairly persuasive evidence.

7. The economic and social effects of such conditions have been explored in the context of another colonial society by Clifford Geertz in his ground-breaking *Agricultural Involution* (Berkeley: University of California Press, 1963).

8. The standard work on the origins of the Vietnamese working class is Tran Van Giau, *Giai cap cong nhan Viet Nam* [The working class of Vietnam] (Hanoi, 1961).

9. There are a number of sources for information on rural conditions in the colonial period. Three recent studies are Joseph Buttinger, *Vietnam: A Dragon Embattled*, 2 vols. (New York, 1967); Robert L. Sansom, *The Economics of Insurgency in the Mekong Delta of Vietnam* (Cambridge, Mass., 1970); and Ngo Vinh Long, *Before the Revolution* (Cambridge, Mass., 1973).

10. It is interesting that the Constitutionalists, like similar reformist movements in Burma and the Dutch East Indies, originally focused their attention on the alleged domination of the economic sector by foreign Asians, e.g., Overseas Chinese and Indians.

11. The standard biography of Li is Maurice Meisner, *Li Ta-chao and the Origins of Chinese Marxism* (Cambridge, Mass.: Harvard University Press, 1967). Li, of course, inspired many young Chinese radicals to join the Marxist movement and was one of the first to point to the need to "go to the village" to seek peasant support.

12. Apter's comments can be found in David Apter (ed.), *Ideology and Discontent* (Glencoe, Ill. and New York: Free Press, 1964), pp. 20–24. I have gone into this issue in more detail in my book cited in note 2, Chapter 2 (above), but the issue deserves more study, in light of the similarities between China and Vietnam.

13. The endemic weaknesses of urban-based nationalist movements in Asia have been explored in a number of recent studies. For an interesting treatment in a comparative framework, see Harry J. Benda, "Non-Western Intelligentsias as Political Elites," in *Continuity and Change in Southeast Asia: Collected Journal Articles of Harry J. Benda* (New Haven, Conn: Yale Southeast Asian Studies, 1972).

14. There are a number of biographies of Ho Chi Minh, but none is truly definitive. The fault is partly Ho's; he was unusually secretive about his life and activities. Because of much misinformation in existing biographies, I have included the brief sketch in the text.

15. The possibilities for comparison with Mao Tse-tung are fascinating. Both probably faced emotional difficulties during adolescence as a result of attending school with students more sophisticated than themselves. But whereas Mao was descended from a non-scholar-gentry family, thus inclining him to a lifelong resentment against the traditional order, Ho Chi Minh's father had considerable prestige in his native area. Ho never projected the "populist" qualities so characteristic of Mao and, unlike the latter, subconsciously identified with the traditional elite.

16. The best source, of course, is Lenin's "Theses on the National and Colonial Questions."

17. Ho Chi Minh, "Some Considerations on the Colonial Question," in *l'Humanité*, May 25, 1922; cited in Bernard Fall, *Ho Chi Minh: On Revolution* (New York, 1967), p. 9.

18. Interestingly, most members of this inner core were fellow provincials from Nghe An Province. Most were members of a radical group, the *Tam Tam Xa* [Association of like minds], which had been formed from remnants of Phan Boi Chau's organization in South China. Activist in temperament, they scorned ideology as irrelevant to the immediate needs of the revolution—a Vietnamese equivalent of Auguste Blanqui's insurrectionists in nineteenth-century France and of many terrorist groups today. Ho Chi Minh evidently persuaded them of the need for organization and a strategy.

19. I have seen no complete version of this pamphlet, although excerpts have appeared in several Hanoi publications. Curiously, although a complete text appears to exist in Hanoi, it is not included in Ho Chi Minh's selected writings. The essentials of the pamphlet are sufficiently clear from the available excerpts to justify analysis. See Thep Moi, "Uncle Ho in Canton," *Vietnam Courier*, No. 48 (May 1976); Joint Publications Research Service (hereafter JPRS) 50,557, Translations on North Vietnam No. 725, "Historic documents of the ICP," p. 51; Nguyen An, "Understanding the History of Our Army: From the Initial Military Viewpoints of the Party to the Initial Organizations of the Revolutionary Armed Forces," in *Tap chi Quan doi Nhan dan* [Journal of the People's Army] No. 2 (February 1974), pp. 52–57, in JPRS 62,057, Translations on North Vietnam 1551; Vu Tho, "From 'the Road to Revolution' to the 'Political Program' of the Indochinese Communist Party," *Nghien cuu lich su* [Historical research, hereafter NCLS], No. 72 (March 1965); *Ho Chi Minh: notre camarade* (Paris: Editions Sociales, 1970), pp. 42–43.

20. There is a French-language version of the speech in the French archives in Paris. See Archives Nationales de France, Section Outre-Mer, Service de liaison avec les originaires de territoires de la France d'outre-mer (SLOTFOM), Series III, Carton 103, November 23, report on activities of Nguyen Ai Quoc. A more available indication of his views is his article in *La Vie Ouvrière* (January 4, 1924) entitled "Annamese Peasant Conditions," in Fall, *Ho Chi Minh*, pp. 24–26.

21. Fall, *Ho Chi Minh*, p. 67.

22. Italics in the original. For this article, one of the few expositions of his views on Party doctrine, see A. Neuberg [pseud.] (ed.), *Armed Insurrection* (London: NLB, 1970), pp. 255–271.

23. Ibid., p. 259.

24. Hanoi appears to agree and has made little effort to publicize the pamphlet. Party historians do not appear to be aware of the more sophisticated exposition of his ideas in ibid.

25. Gareth Porter, "Proletariat and Peasantry in Early Vietnamese Communism," *Asian Thought and Society* Vol. 1, no. 3 (December 1976).

26. Robert C. North and Xenia J. Eudin, *Soviet Russia and the East, 1920–1927* (Stanford, Calif.: Stanford University Press, 1927), pp. 326–328.

27. A flagrant example of this can be found in Archives Nationales de France, section outre-mer (hereafter AOM) Carton 335, Dossier 2690, "Déclarations dernières de Nguyen Dinh Tu, dit provisoirement Phan Van Cam . . . sur sa vie depuis Juin 1925 jusqu'à son arrestation en date du 5 Août 1929 à Ha Tinh." This source also contains one of the few references to revolutionary strategy in the literature of the time. According to the prisoner Nguyen Dinh Tu, he was taught at the institute in Canton that there would be three phases in the revolution to overthrow the French: (1) a secret phase; (2) a semi-secret phase, involving strikes and mass agitations, with the Party operating in the open and proclaiming its moderation; and (3) a final phase of violent revolution, when the Party had the strength and the mass base to launch the final insurrection.

28. This point is easily verified through an examination of the Sûreté's files, now open to scholars in Paris.

29. Tran Van Giau, *Giai cap cong nhan Viet Nam*, p. 395. AOM, Carton 325, Dossier 2634, "Observations du Résident Supérieur en Annam concernant les jugements rendus en 1929 par les tribunaux mandarins contre les membres du Viet Nam Cach Mang Thanh Hoi."

30. On the background of early members of the CCP and the Kuomintang, see C. Martin Wilbur, "The Influence of the Past: How the Early Years Helped to Shape the Future of the Chinese Communist Party," in John Wilson Lewis (ed.), *Party Leadership and Revolutionary Power in China* (Cambridge: Cambridge University Press, 1970).

31. This point has often been made with respect to China. For a similar statement by a Vietnamese, see Nguyen Khac Vien, "Confucianism and Marxism in Vietnam," in Nguyen Khac Vien (ed.), *Tradition and Revolution in Vietnam* (Berkeley, Calif. and Washington, D.C., 1974), pp. 15–74.

32. An interesting if brief discussion of this issue in an Asian context is given in Lucian Pye, *Politics, Personality, and Nation-Building* (New Haven, Conn.: Yale University Press, 1962), pp. 52–53.

33. I am fully aware that Ho Chi Minh does not meet all the criteria for the Confucian "superior man" in his traditional guise. A more detailed analysis of the question would be of interest.

34. For the list, see Thep Moi, "Uncle Ho in Canton," p. 27.

35. John T. McAlister, *Viet-Nam: The Origins of Revolution* (New York, 1969), pp. 326–327.

36. For a recent discussion of this period, see Porter, "Proletariat and Peasantry in Early Vietnamese Communism."

37. For a discussion, see William J. Duiker, "The Revolutionary Youth League: Cradle of Communism in Vietnam," *China Quarterly*, No. 51 (July-September 1972). Also see Tran Van Cung's memoirs in *Buoc ngoat vi dai cua lich su cach mang Viet Nam* [A great step forward in the history of the Vietnamese revolution] (Hanoi: n.d.).

38. A French-language version of this statement is located in Gouvernement Générale de l'Indochine (Direction des Affaires Politiques et de la Sûreté Générale), 5 vols., Vol. 1, annex 2.

39. For the memoirs of one of the participants, see Nguyen Nghia, "Cong cuoc hop nhat cac to chuc cong san dau tien o Viet Nam va vai tro cua dong chi Nguyen Ai Quoc" [The unification of the first Communist organizations in Vietnam and the role of Comrade Nguyen Ai Quoc], *NCLS*, No. 59 (February 1964).

40. Ibid.

41. An English-language version of the appeal is in Fall, *Ho Chi Minh*, pp. 127–129.

42. There are several useful studies of the revolt and its causes. See, in particular, James C. Scott, *The Moral Economy of the Peasant: Rebellion and Subsistence in Southeast Asia* (New Haven, Conn.: Yale University Press, 1976); Samuel L. Popkin, *The Rational Peasant: The Political Economy of Rural Society in Vietnam* (Berkeley: University of California Press, 1979); Milton Osborne, "Continuity and Motivation in the Vietnamese Revolution: New Light from the 1930s," *Pacific Affairs* Vol. 47, no. 1 (1974); and William J. Duiker, "The Red Soviets of Nghe-Tinh: An Early Communist Rebellion in Vietnam," *Journal of Southeast Asian Studies*, No. 4 (September 1973).

43. There is disagreement over whether *per capita* income in the villages was rising or

falling under French colonial rule. For a perceptive analysis, see Robert L. Sansom, *The Economics of Insurgency in the Mekong Delta of Vietnam* (Cambridge, Mass., 1970).

44. Two contrasting views are located in Scott, *Moral Economy of the Peasant*, and Popkin, *Rational Peasant*.

45. SLOTFOM, Series III, Carton 48, *Note périodique* (December 1929), pp. 4–5.

46. For a brief discussion of this issue, see Kermit E. McKenzie, *Comintern and World Revolution, 1928–1943* (New York: Columbia University Press, 1964), pp. 135–139.

47. AOM Carton 333, Dossier 2686, Billet report of June 27, 1931. This source contains an interesting interview with a prisoner who was apparently a member of the Communist Party. Explaining that he had become a Communist because of his hatred of the French and his desire for independence, Thai Van Giai, a teacher and a graduate of the National Academy at Hué, said that the local Communist apparatus prepared the movement during early 1930: "It founded cells, spread tracts and organized conferences. It was able to act freely in the villages with no interference. The notables were too fearful to say anything, while the mandarins paid no attention to us and the French administration was totally ignorant of what was taking place." The riots were organized by beating a drum at the communal house and then persuading the villagers to act after they arrived. Those who were reluctant could be converted by intimidation. A few assassinations of class enemies took place, but they were to be conducted secretly to avoid frightening the masses.

48. Details of the Phu Rieng strike can be found in AOM Carton 322, Dossier 2614, telegrams of February–April 1930.

49. AOM Carton 333, Dossier 2687, report of July 8, 1931.

50. Duiker, *Rise of Nationalism in Vietnam*, p. 222.

51. The French archives contain the translation of a circular allegedly issued by the Nghe An Provincial Committee on October 9 calling for the distribution of landlord land to the poor. It conceded that the policy might be only temporary but contended that it would provide "moral comfort" to the masses. All such proposals, however, were to be submitted to the Provincial Committee for approval. See AOM Carton 326, Dossier 2637. The issue of land redistribution caused controversy within the Party. Articles written in Comintern journals at the time encouraged it. Ho Chi Minh had advocated a radical land program in his 1927 article written in Moscow. A few years later Tran Van Giau, one of the party's rising young leaders, who had been at the Stalin School in Moscow at the time of the revolt, contended that all landlord land should have been confiscated. See Ho Nam (pseud.), *Ky nien Nghe An bao dong* [Memoirs of the Nghe An revolt] (no publisher, 1932). In later years, however, Party historians were critical of the radicalism of the land revolution under the soviets, claiming that it alienated potentially sympathetic moderate elements.

52. Trung Chinh, "Tinh chat tu phat cua xo viet Nghe Tinh" [The spontaneous character of the Nghe Tinh soviets], *NCLS*, No. 32 (November 1961), p. 5

53. Ibid. Italics in the original. I have not been able to ascertain whether this directive was dispatched before or after the full meeting of the Central Committee held the same month. It seems probable that the former is the case.

54. The bureau consisted of Tran Phu, Nguyen Trong Nga (a worker), and Ngo Duc Tri. See "Cac co so bi mat cua co quan lanh dao Dang Cong San Dong Duong" [The secret basis of the leading organs of the Indochinese Communist Party], *NCLS*, No. 37 (April 1962), p. 22. Others on the Central Committee were Nguyen Phong Sac, Tran

Van Lan, and Cat (another worker). All but the latter were arrested and died in French prisons soon after. SLOTFOM, Séries III, Carton 48, Note périodique (March–April 1931).

55. SLOTFOM, Séries III, Carton 49, Note périodique (May 1931).

56. Ho Chi Minh, "The Party's Military Work among the Peasants," in A. Neuberg, *Armed Insurrection*, has his comments. Ho's precise views on the revolt have never been made clear, even in available letters written at this time. He may well have been skeptical of success, however. Earlier in the year he had labeled the VNQDD revolt at Yen Bay adventuristic and premature.

Chapter 3: The Stalinist Years

1. For a discussion of the school and its students, see SLOTFOM, Séries III, Carton 44, dossier entitled "Les élèves annamites à l'école Staline et le Pacte Franco-Soviétique." This comment is located in SLOTFOM, Séries III, Note périodique (third trimester 1934).

2. AOM Carton 323, Dossier 2625, Secret annex to the Note périodique (third trimester 1934).

3. Moscow's policy of granting preference to workers for admission to the Stalin School did not work out very well. Most of those recruited apparently lacked either talent or motivation. See SLOTFOM, Séries III, Carton 44, September 11, 1934. Meanwhile, in Vietnam the size of the working class continued to drop throughout the early 1930s, from 54,000 in 1929 to 34,800 in 1934. See Cao Van Bien, "Su phat trien cua doi ngu cong nhan truoc Cach mang Thang tam" [The development of the working class before the August Revolution], *NCLS*, No. 2 (March-April 1972), pp. 57–67.

4. For an ICP directive on peasant activities, see SLOTFOM, Séries III, Carton 30, Note périodique (third trimester 1934), annex.

5. SLOTFOM, Séries III, Carton 30, Note périodique (first trimester 1934), annex, translation of "La question du mouvement ouvrier," *Tap chi Cong san*.

6. SLOTFOM, Séries III, Carton 30, Note périodique (fourth trimester 1934), annex.

7. Ibid. Party historians today are critical of this narrow approach and contend that a greater effort should have been made to recruit among the middle class. See Van Tao, "Tim hieu qua trinh hinh thanh va phat trien cua mat tran dan toc thong nhat Viet Nam" [Exploring the process of formation and development of the Vietnamese national united front], *NCLS*, No. 1 (March 1959).

8. Daniel Hémery, *Révolutionnaires vietnamiens et pouvoir colonial en Indochine* (Paris, 1975), pp. 53–54.

9. There is a copy of the report in the Paris archives. See SLOTFOM, Séries III, Carton 62, Orgwald note.

10. The two best-known delegates from the ICP were Le Hong Phong and his wife Nguyen Thi Minh Khai. Ho Chi Minh attended, but not as a representative of the Vietnamese Party. He spoke to the congress under the name of Chajan (Ha jen).

11. SLOTFOM, Séries III, Carton 45, Note périodique (October 1936), annex, confidential letter of the Central Committee. According to French sources, the letter was probably written by either Ho Chi Minh or Le Hong Phong.

12. SLOTFOM, Séries III, Carton 59, Note périodique (February 1937), p. 53.

13. There has been considerable partisan controversy over the degree of ICP activity in

the rural villages during the popular front period. There is no doubt that, as recent Party historians contend, activists began to operate in the provinces of the Mekong delta with increasing frequency in the late 1930s. And a short analysis of the rural question by Vo Nguyen Giap and Truong Chinh, *The Peasant Question*, translated by Christine Pelzer White (Ithaca, N.Y., 1974), suggests that Party leaders were aware of the significance of the issue. The authors of this brief pamphlet contended that poor peasants could be mobilized "and with leadership can be an invincible force" in the Vietnamese revolution, suggesting that the Maoist revolution in China had begun to exert an impact on the ICP. But it is difficult to take seriously the contention that a Maoist "rural strategy" was already under consideration.

14. SLOTFOM, Séries III, Carton 59, Note périodique (August-September 1936), annex 1.

15. SLOTFOM, Séries III, Carton 59, Note périodique (August-September 1937), annex 2.

16. Ibid. This letter is also printed in *La Lutte*, August 29, 1937.

17. SLOTFOM, Séries III, Carton 59, Notes périodiques for August-September 1937, December 1937, and February 1939 all have French estimates of Party strength. The Party today views the Popular Front period as the Vietnamese equivalent of the May Fourth Movement in China. Recently, Party Secretary General Le Duan commented that the period from 1936 to 1939 provided a "political education" to millions of Vietnamese.

Chapter 4: Prelude to Revolt

1. *Dan chung* (October 29, 1938), cited in Tran Van Giau, *Giai cap cong nhan Viet Nam*, Vol. 2 (1936–1939), pp. 383–384.

2. Tran Van Giau, *Giai cap cong nhan Viet Nam*, Vol. 3 (1939–1945), pp. 24–25.

3. There is a brief biographical sketch of Nguyen Van Cu in *NCLS*, No. 145 (July-August 1972), pp. 7–18.

4. The meeting also discussed how best to defend Stalin's treaty with Nazi Germany. In Party histories this is referred to as a question of how to "demonstrate the correctness of the Soviet Union's revolutionary stratagem of being temporarily moderate toward Germany in order to expose the true colors of the French and English imperialists who, since Munich, were plotting to surrender to Germany in order to push it to annihilate the Soviet Union." See Trung Chinh, "Hoi nghi trung uong lan thu sau va hai cuoc khoi nghia dau tien do dang ta lanh dao" [The Sixth Plenum and the first two uprisings led by our Party], *NCLS*, No. 146 (September-October 1972).

5. Ibid. This area had been a revolutionary base for the Party since the early 1930s.

6. Ibid.

7. Tran Van Giau, *Giai cap cong nhan Viet Nam*, Vol. 3, p. 37.

8. Tranh Dau Bai, "Boc Son khoi ngia" [The Bac Son Uprising], *Nhan Dan*, September 27, 1970.

9. Tran Huy Lieu, *Tai lieu tham khao lich su cach mang can dai Viet Nam* [Historical research materials concerning the modern revolution in Vietnam, hereafter *TLTK*] (Hanoi, 1958), Vol. 10, pp. 20–21. Also see *Saigon: From the Beginnings to 1945*, Vietnamese Studies 45 (Hanoi: 1977), p. 81.

10. A meeting in March had resulted in an agreement to train troops, obtain weapons, and undertake propaganda among the enemy. See Trung Chinh, "The Sixth Plenum."

11. *Histoire de la Révolution d'Août* (Hanoi, 1972), p. 20. Hereafter *Histoire*.

12. *TLTK*, Vol. 10, pp. 216–217.

13. Most were executed. One of the few to survive was a promising young Party member by the name of Le Duan. See *Saigon*, p. 82.

14. According to *Saigon*, pp. 80–82, the heart of the attack was to take place in Saigon, a major staging area for sending Cochin Chinese troops to the Thai border. An insurrection committee had been set up, and more than thirty guerrilla units of three to nine members each were formed among workers and students. Quick French action aborted the revolt. For an account, see *Vietnam's Fight Against Fascism* (D.R.V. Delegation in France, 1948).

15. Most of the information on Ho Chi Minh's activities in China comes from King C. Chen, *Vietnam and China, 1938–1954* (Princeton, N.J., 1969), and Chiang Yung-ching, *Hu Chih-ming tsai Chung-kuo* [Ho Chi Minh in China] (Taipei: Chuan-chi wen-hsueh, 1972). Party biographies have little to say about Ho's activities during this period.

16. Giap's memoirs on the period are in *Tu nhan dan ma ra* [From the people] (Hanoi, 1964). See pp. 10–16.

17. According to King Chen, he had sent an emissary to Yenan in August to conclude a secret agreement calling for military cooperation and the coordination of the wartime activities of the two parties. (*Vietnam and China*, p. 41).

18. *Souvenirs sur Ho Chi Minh* (Hanoi: Foreign Languages Press, 1962), pp. 161–162.

19. A brief biographical sketch of Truong Chinh is in the introduction by Bernard Fall to Truong Chinh's *Primer for Revolt* (New York, 1963), introduction by Bernard Fall.

20. Quang Vinh, "The Initial Feat of Arms," *Tap chi quan doi nhan dan*, No. 1 (January 1974), in JPRS 62,057, Translations on North Vietnam 1551.

21. *Souvenirs*, p. 165.

22. Tran Van Giau, "Trong giai doan chien tranh the gioi lan thu 2 va cach mang thang tam" [In the stage of the Second World War and the August Revolution], *Hoc tap*, No. 5 (1959), p. 42. Also see Vo Nguyen Giap, *Nhung kinh nghiem lon cua Dang ta ve lanh dao dau tranh vu trang va xang dung luc luong vu trang cach mang* [The Party's experiences in leading the armed struggle and building the armed strength of the revolution] (Hanoi: Su That, 1961), pp. 10–12.

23. Tran Huy Lieu, *Lich su tam muoi Nam chong Phap* [A history of eighty years of resistance against the French], 2 vols. (Hanoi: Van Su Dia, 1958), Vol. 2, p. 70.

24. Vo Nguyen Giap, *Nhung kinh nghiem*, p. 12.

25. Tran Huy Lieu, *Lich su*, p. 71.

26. Le Quoc Su, "Kheo ket hop cach hinh thuc dau tranh chinh tri va vu trang trong cach mang thang tam" [Searching for the forms of political and military struggle in the August Revolution], *NCLS*, No. 50 (May 1963), p. 16.

27. Truong Chinh's *The Resistance Will Win*, published in 1947, would establish his reputation as an advocate of Maoism in Vietnam.

28. For one example, see Ho Chi Minh, "Kinh nghiem du kich Tau" [Chinese guerrilla experience], in his *Ve dau tranh vu trang va luc luong vu trang nhan dan* [On armed struggle and the armed strength of the people] (Hanoi: Quan Doi Nhan Dan, 1970), pp. 137–151.

29. *Histoire*, p. 21.

30. Vo Nguyen Giap, *Nhung kinh nghiem*, p. 17.

31. Fall, *Ho Chi Minh*, pp. 132–134.

32. The importance of the minority nationalities in this phase of the revolution is emphasized in McAlister, *Viet-Nam: The Origins of Revolution*. In a limited sense, McAlister is quite correct. The border areas and the population living there were of crucial importance in the Party's effort to build up a liberated zone under the eyes of the French and the Japanese. The peoples themselves, however, were less important than the rugged terrain in the Vietnamese revolution. This was to be a persistent factor in Communist strategy until the final victory in 1975.

33. *Histoire*, pp. 37–38.

34. Ibid., p. 46.

35. *Nhung nguoi cong san Viet Nam* [Some Vietnamese Communists] (Hanoi, 1957), Vol. 1, pp. 7–37, has a brief biography.

36. Chen, *Vietnam and China*, pp. 56–57.

37. Chang's memoirs are currently being chronicled in the Oral History Project at Columbia University. Perhaps they will clear up this matter.

38. Chen, *Vietnam and China*, pp. 68–71.

39. Ibid., p. 78.

40. Vo Nguyen Giap, *The Military Art of People's War* (New York: Monthly Review Press, 1970), p. 66.

41. *Souvenirs*, p. 200.

42. *Histoire*, p. 68.

43. *Souvenirs*, p. 204.

44. Jean Sainteny, *Histoire d'une paix manquée* (Paris, 1953), p. 57.

45. *Histoire*, pp. 91–96, has an extended discussion.

46. Phillipe Devillers, *Histoire du Vietnam, 1940–1952* (Paris, 1952), p. 111.

47. English-language excerpts are located in JPRS 50,557, Translations on North Vietnam 725, document no. 5.

48. Jean Lacouture, *Ho Chi Minh: A Political Biography* (New York, 1968), p. 92.

49. John R. McLane, "Archaic Movements and Revolution in Southern Vietnam," in Norman Miller and Roderick Aya (eds.), *National Liberation: Revolution in the Third World* (New York: Free Press, 1971), pp. 68–101.

50. Pham Ngoc Thach's memoirs are located in *Nhung ngay Thang tam* [The days of August] (Hanoi: Van Hoc, 1961), pp. 237–246.

51. Originally the congress was scheduled for July, according to a Communist source, but it was postponed, perhaps because of the coming Japanese surrender. See Huynh Kim Khanh, "The Vietnamese Revolution Reinterpreted," *Journal of Asian Studies*, Vol. 30, no. 4 (August 1971), p. 777.

52. The issue of rural versus urban strategy is briefly discussed in Ho Hai, "Mot vai y kien ve moi quan he giua nong thon va thanh thi nuoc ta trong thoi ky 1939–1945" [A few opinions of the relationship between the villages and the cities during the period 1939–1945], NCLS, No. 52 (July 1963).

53. Lacouture, *Ho Chi Minh*, p. 54.

Chapter 5: The Days of August

1. Truong Chinh, *Primer for Revolt*, p. 24.

2. Tran Huy Lieu, *Lich su thu do Ha Noi* [A history of the city of Hanoi] (Hanoi, 1960), has a discussion. Party historians later admitted that there was little effort to encourage troops to desert during the August uprising.

3. Ibid., pp. 213–215.

4. *Nhung ngay thang tam*, p. 131.

5. For a detailed account of the uprising in the provinces, see Tran Van Giau, *Giai cap cong nhan Viet Nam*, Vol. 3, pp. 238–243.

6. Tran Huy Lieu, *Lich su*, pp. 215–216.

7. See the account of the Ba To uprising in *Vietnam Courier*, No. 35 (April 1975).

8. This is one of the reasons why there were occasional disagreements between the Central Committee and the leadership in the South over strategy. See Tran Van Giau, *Giai cap cong nhan Viet Nam*, Vol. 3, p. 147.

9. Nguyen Van Kinh (ed.), *Saigon: thanh pho Ho Chi Minh* [Saigon: the city of Ho Chi Minh] (Saigon, 1971), p. 34.

10. George Johnson and Fred Feldman, "On the Nature of the VCP," *International Socialist Review* (July-August 1973), p. 69.

11. Tran Huy Lieu, later to become a prominent historian in the D.R.V., joined the Party in the late 1920s after beginning with the VNQDD.

12. Undoubtedly the costume was chosen carefully for its effect.

13. Vo Nguyen Giap, *Unforgettable Days* (Hanoi, 1975), p. 31.

14. For a discussion of this issue, see John T. McAlister and Paul Mus, *The Vietnamese and Their Revolution* (New York, 1970).

15. McAlister, *Viet-Nam: The Origins of Revolution*, has an interesting discussion of the effect of the Japanese occupation on Vietnamese nationalism. See Chapter 13.

16. Vo Nguyen Giap, *The Military Art of People's War*, p. 168.

17. Tran Van Giau, *Giai Cap cong nhan Viet Nam*, Vol. 3, pp. 221–228, has statistics on the extent of the famine.

18. Alexander B. Woodside, *Community and Revolution in Modern Vietnam*, p. 230.

Chapter 6: The Uneasy Peace

1. Nguyen Kien Giang, *Viet Nam nam dau tien sau Cach mang Thang tam* [Vietnam in the years immediately following the August Revolution] (Hanoi, 1961), pp. 140–141.

2. Ibid., p. 63.

3. Ibid., p. 77

4. Ibid., pp. 146–147.

5. Vo Nguyen Giap, *Unforgettable Days*, p. 46.

6. See Nguyen Cong Binh, "Ban ve tinh chat cuoc Cach mang Thang tam" [Discussing the nature of the August Revolution], *NCLS*, No. 17 (August 1960), especially pp. 7–8.

7. Jean-Raoul Clementin, "Le comportement politique des institutions catholiques au Vietnam," in Jean Chesneaux (ed.), *Tradition et révolution au Vietnam* (Paris, 1971), p. 121. There was, however, some local harassment of Catholics. See Devillers, *Histoire du Vietnam*, p. 187.

8. Chen, *Vietnam and China*, p. 122.

9. Ibid., p. 121.

10. There is an extended discussion of Ho's tactics in Vo Nguyen Giap, *Unforgettable Days*, pp. 96–103.

11. McAlister, *Viet-Nam: The Origins of Revolution*, p. 217.

12. Devillers, *Histoire du Vietnam*, p. 200, has a discussion.

13. Nguyen Van Kinh, *Saigon*, p. 58.

14. For a Trotskyite view, see Johnson and Feldman, "On the Nature of the VCP."

15. Nguyen Kien Giang, *Viet Nam*, pp. 108–109, has a few statistics on Party strength in Cochin China. One of the areas most sympathetic to the revolution was along the Cambodian border where rubber workers took power in the rubber plantation region after the surrender of Japan and briefly set up a people's administration.

16. Harold Isaacs, *No Peace for Asia* (New York: Macmillan, 1947), p. 173.

17. Nguyen Kien Giang, *Viet Nam*, pp. 105–106.

18. Nguyen Khac Huyen, *Vision Accomplished?* (New York, 1971), p. 125.

19. Vo Nguyen Giap, *Unforgettable Days*, p. 143.

20. Devillers, *Histoire du Vietnam*, p. 247.

21. There was, indeed, considerable nervousness that the arrival of French troops in Hanoi would result in military clashes and all-out conflict.

22. Devillers, *Histoire du Vietnam*, p. 216.

23. The issue became a primarily semantic one: how to translate the Vietnamese term *"doc lap,"* used in the D.R.V. Declaration of Independence of September 2. Should it be translated as "freedom" or "independence"? The original Chinese term *(tu-li)* means "to stand alone" and is usually translated as "independent."

24. Nguyen Kien Giang, *Viet Nam*, pp. 168–169.

25. Ibid., pp. 170–171.

26. Sainteny, *Histoire d'une paix manquée*, p. 65. Reaction was particularly negative in the South where the major sacrifice was expected of Vietminh supporters.

27. For an account of the speech, see Devillers, *Histoire du Vietnam*, p. 230.

28. General Valluy, *Indochine: octobre 45-mars 47* (Paris: Revue des Deux Mondes, 1967), p. 39.

29. There was considerable speculation on why he took the long route home. Did he fear assassination? Or did he fear a negative response from Party leaders to the modus vivendi? It is likely that he wanted to let time pass and passions cool. Vo Nguyen Giap, in *Unforgettable Days* (p. 338), claims that the French held up the ship.

30. The nationalists had made a tactical error in opposing the French, a misstep that the Vietminh quickly took advantage of. Ibid., p. 281.

31. Ibid., p. 394.

32. Ibid., p. 331.

33. Devillers, *Histoire du Vietnam*, p. 318.

34. Vo Nguyen Giap, *Unforgettable Days*, p. 354.

35. Charles B. McLane, *Soviet Strategies in Southeast Asia* (Princeton, N.J.: Princeton University Press, 1966), p. 271.

36. Vo Nguyen Giap, *Unforgettable Days*, p. 396.

37. Devillers, *Histoire du Vietnam*, pp. 349–350.

Chapter 7: The Franco-Vietminh War

1. For statistics on weapons, see McAlister, *Viet-Nam: the Origins of Revolution*, pp. 232–234. McAlister also says that, in early 1947, the Vietminh had 100,000 men under arms, not including 35,000 self-defense militia. Of their main force troops, 40,000 were in

Tonkin. There were 20,000 guerrillas in the South and 15,000 in the Center.

2. Ellen J. Hammer, *The Struggle for Indochina, 1940–1955* (Stanford, Calif., 1965), p. 207.

3. JPRS 50,557, Translations on North Vietnam, 725, "Historic Documents of the ICP."

4. Truong Chinh, *The Resistance Will Win*, is translated into English in *Primer for Revolt*.

5. Ibid., p. 188. Mao later retracted this view. See *Selected Writings of Mao Tse-tung* (Peking: Foreign Languages Press, 1972), p. 186n.

6. Ibid., p. 155.

7. Tran Huy Lieu, *Lich su*, pp. 234–235.

8. Devillers, *Histoire du Vietnam*, p. 414.

9. Chen, *Vietnam and China*, p. 174.

10. Ngo Tien Chat, "Notes on the Tradition of Heroic Struggle of Nationalities in the Northwest from the August Revolution to the Present Resistance Against America," *NCLS*, No. 95, February 1967, in JPRS 9609, Translations on North Vietnam No. 151, p. 6. Also see *Outline History of the Vietnam Workers' Party* (Hanoi: Foreign Languages Press, 1972), p. 56. There has been some disagreement over the date of the beginning of the second stage. Vo Nguyen Giap once commented to a Cuban journalist that it was difficult to pinpoint, as there was no firm demarcation between the two stages. For the view of a historian in Hanoi, see Bui Dinh Thanh, "Nghien cuu cac giai doan cua cuoc Khang chien" [Studying the stages in the War of Resistance], *NCLS*, No. 45 (December 1962).

11. Vo Nguyen Giap, *People's War, People's Army* (New York, 1962), p. 92. For the directive on activating guerrilla warfare, see Gareth Porter (ed.), *Vietnam: The Definitive Documentation of Human Decisions* (Stanfordville, N.Y., 1979), Vol. 1, pp. 169–171.

12. See discussion in Bui Dinh Thanh, "Nghien cuu," pp. 13–14.

13. Many scholars have viewed the Calcutta Youth Congress in 1948 as the moment when Moscow's change of strategy was passed on to Asian Communist parties. Nothing in the Vietnamese literature substantiates this.

14. U.S. Department of State, *Working Paper on North Viet-Nam's Role in the War in South Viet-Nam* (Washington, D.C., 1968), Appendix Item No. 1. For a similar estimate, see Bernard Fall, *Le Vietminh* (Paris, 1960), p. 151. Of the total, nearly two-thirds were located in North Vietnam.

15. According to this observer, the Vietminh controlled three-quarters of Cochin China outside the main urban centers. See Devillers, *Histoire du Vietnam*, p. 318.

16. Fall, *Vietminh*, p. 79.

17. Van Tao, "Vai net ve qua trinh xay dung va phat trien cua nha nuoc cach mang Viet Nam 20 nam qua" [A few features of the process of building and developing the Vietnamese revolution over the last twenty years], *NCLS*, No. 77 (August 1965), p. 23. For an extended discussion of Vietminh land policy, see Truong Chinh, *Ban ve cach mang Viet Nam* [On the Vietnamese revolution] (Hanoi, 1956), a speech given at the National Congress in February 1951. This pamphlet is available from the Library of Congress on microfilm in *Communist Vietnamese Publications*, Reel 2, Document 60.

18. Van Tao, "Vai net," p. 20.

19. U.S. Department of State, *Working Paper*, Appendix Item No. 211. The cause of Nguyen Binh's death is a matter of dispute. Party sources assert that he was killed in a

French attack. It has been alleged, however, that he was assassinated by order of the Party leadership. For this charge, see Tran Kim Truc, *Toi giet Nguyen Binh* [I killed Nguyen Binh] (Saigon: Dong Nai, 1972).

20. For this issue, see "May net long ve phong trao cong nhan Saigon tu 1945 den 1954" [A few major features of the workers' movement in Saigon from 1945 to 1954], *NCLS*, No. 2 (February 1967). In the August Revolution, there were 120,000 enrolled in the Party's labor organizations in Saigon.

21. Chen, *Vietnam and China*, p. 162. According to Hoang Van Hoan, one-time D.R.V. ambassador to Peking who defected to China in 1979, the P.R.C. in 1950 sent Vice-minister of Defense Ch'en Keng to Vietnam to train cadres and prepare for a military offensive in the border region. At the same time, a Chinese military advisory group under Wei Kuo-ch'in was sent to Vietnam at the request of Ho Chi Minh to plan future campaigns. See Hoan's interview in *Beijing Review*, November 23, 1979.

22. For similar conclusions, see Jay Taylor, *China and Southeast Asia: Peking's Relations with Revolutionary Movements* (New York: Praeger Publishers, 1974), p. 6. A Vietnamese comment is in Hammer, *Struggle for Indochina*, p. 253.

23. For a discussion and references, see Chen, *Vietnam and China*, p. 226. According to Hoang Van Hoan, Chinese political experience was passed on to the Vietnamese by a political advisory group under the chairmanship of Lo Kwei-po, soon to become Peking's ambassador to the D.R.V. *Beijing Review*, November 23, 1979.

24. Chen, *Vietnam and China*, p. 231. The comment about possible neutrality is in Devillers, *Histoire du Vietnam*, p. 453. For an English translation of a speech by Truong Chinh signalling the new approach, see Porter, *Vietnam*, Vol. 1, pp. 242–243.

25. Politburo members included Ho Chi Minh, Truong Chinh, Le Duan, Pham Van Dong, Vo Nguyen Giap, Nguyen Chi Thanh, and Hoang Quoc Viet. Le Van Luong was an alternate.

26. Truong Chinh, *Ban ve*, p. 6.

27. U.S. Department of State, *Working Paper*, Appendix Item No. 1, p. 2-2.

28. Vo Nguyen Giap, *Nhiem vu quan su truoc mat chuyen sang tong phan cong* (Hanoi, 1950).

29. Lucien Bodard, *The Quicksand War* (Boston, 1967), has a dramatic reconstruction of the battle.

30. For a discussion of the background of this decision, with reference documents, see *The Pentagon Papers* (Senator Gravel Edition) (Boston, 1971), Vol. 1, pp. 34–41.

31. Henri Navarre, *Agonie de l'Indochine* (Paris, 1956), p. 20. A U.S. estimate undertaken in late 1950 placed total Vietminh strength at 225,000 (including 93,000 regulars) against 147,000 French main force troops throughout Indochina. According to this source, without a significant strengthening of the French armed forces, the war would be lost in six to nine months. See NIE-5 dated December 29, 1950, cited in Porter, *Vietnam*, Vol. 1, pp. 309–312.

32. George Tanham, *Communist Revolutionary Warfare* (New York, 1967), p. 13, quotes Hoang Van Thai as saying that "partial offensives" would precede the general offensive.

33. Vo Nguyen Giap, *Nhiem vu*, p. 28. Also see *Bao gio ta tong phan cong* [When we will launch the counteroffensive] (Hanoi, 1950), a collection of study materials on the issue. Both are in *Communist Vietnamese Publications*, Reel 1, Documents 11 and 40.

34. Vo Nguyen Giap, *People's War, People's Army*, p. 88.

35. Vo Nguyen Giap, *Nhiem vu*, p. 33.

36. Truong Chinh, "Hoan thanh nhiem vu chuan bi chuyen manh sang tong phan cong" [Complete the task of preparation, switch strongly to the general counteroffensive] in Porter, *Vietnam*, Vol. 1, pp. 268–272.

37. See Ho Chi Minh's Political Report at the Second National Congress, February 1951, in Ho Chi Minh, *Selected Writings*, p. 115.

38. For this and later stages of the offensive, see Fall's classic study, *Street Without Joy* (Harrisburg, Pa., 1961). French casualties were also high. See the telegram from Heath to Acheson dated January 21, 1951, cited in Porter, *Vietnam*, Vol. 1, p. 322. According to this source Party leaders were disappointed at their failure to puncture the French defenses. Reputedly Giap had bragged that Ho Chi Minh "would be in Hanoi for Tet."

39. Chen, *Vietnam and China*, p. 267. Ironically the Chinese ambassador to the D.R.V. allegedly recommended the offensive to Vietminh leaders. See Hoang Van Chi, *From Colonialism to Communism* (New York, 1961), pp. 63–64.

40. The *Outline History* (p. 74) says that there are two main points of view: (1) that it began in 1950 during the fall campaign, and (2) that it began with the attacks in 1951 and remained at that level until 1954 with a series of partial offensives.

41. Chen, *Vietnam and China*, p. 267.

42. Bui Dinh Thanh, "Nghien cuu," p. 14.

43. Devillers, *Histoire du Vietnam*, p. 457.

44. Navarre, *Agonie de l'Indochine*, p. 23.

45. "May net lon ve," p. 12.

46. Tran Huy Lieu, *Lich su*, has a brief discussion. For an internal Party document discussing the weakness of the Hanoi municipal apparatus, see U.S. Department of State, *Working Paper*, Appendix Item No. 1.

47. See *Van de cai cach ruong dat* [The problem of land reform] (Hanoi, 1950), Vol. 2; *Communist Vietnamese Publications*, Reel 1, Document 4; and Truong Chinh's *Ban ve*, Reel 2, Document 60.

48. Truong Chinh, *Ban ve*, p. 46.

49. *Economic Policy and National Liberation War* (Hanoi, 1976), Vietnamese Studies, No. 45, pp. 73–79.

50. The statistics cited here are from "Tang lop phu nong trong cach mang Viet Nam" [The rich peasant class in the Vietnamese revolution], *NCLS*, No. 11 (February 1960). Other evidence, however, suggests that the program was less comprehensive and may have resulted in the transfer of less than 2 percent of landlord land. I am indebted to Edwin Moise for this information.

51. Joseph Starobin, *Eyewitness in Indochina* (New York, 1954), p. 90. According to Edwin Moise, the decision to exempt the rich peasants was reversed, possibly in July 1954.

52. Navarre, *Agonie de l'Indochine*, p. 46. They were divided into 125,000 main force troops, 75,000 regional guerrillas, and 150,000 local militia.

53. Ibid., p. 72.

54. Arthur J. Dommen, "Vague Policy Gets the Blame for Dien Bien Phu," *Washington Post*, January 26, 1969. Dommen cites a commission report undertaken in the fall of 1955 that, although critical of some aspects of Navarre's strategy, substantially exonerated him from responsibility for the failure of French strategy.

55. See the map in Navarre, *Agonie de l'Indochine*, p. 44.

56. For a map of the Vietminh plan, see ibid., p. 159.

57. See the comments in *Outline History*, pp. 70–71.

58. Dommen, "Vague Policy."

59. Navarre, *Agonie de l'Indochine*, pp. 193–194. Some French military figures were critical of Navarre's conviction that the occupation of Dien Bien Phu could interdict Vietminh movement into Laos and told him so at the time.

60. Ta Xuan Linh, "The Fifth Interzone during the Dien Bien Phu Campaign," *Vietnam Courier*, No. 25 (June 1974), pp. 9–13.

61. For details, see Chen, *Vietnam and China*, pp. 282–283.

62. Vo Nguyen Giap, *People's War, People's Army*, p. 148.

63. There are some discrepancies in the French figures. See Navarre, *Agonie de l'Indochine*, p. 181; Bernard Fall, *Hell in a Very Small Place* (Philadelphia, 1966), p. vii; and Vo Nguyen Giap, *People's War, People's Army*, p. 179.

64. Taylor, *China and Southeast Asia*, pp. 13–14.

65. Vo Nguyen Giap, *People's War, People's Army*, p. 153.

66. Devillers and Lacouture, *End of a War*, p. 149.

67. Arthur J. Dommen, "Vague Policy."

68. On contemporary complaints by Vietnamese delegates at Geneva, see the article by Tillman Durdin in the *New York Times*, July 25, 1954. The recent complaints about Chinese interference at Geneva are in Hanoi's White Paper, *The Truth About Viet Nam–China Relations Over the Last Thirty Years* (Hanoi: Ministry of Foreign Affairs, 1979), pp. 12–15. Hanoi also claims that at Geneva Chou En-lai enforced the partition of Indochina into three separate countries in order to facilitate Chinese domination of the area. The Chinese vigorously deny such charges. On the one hand they claim that Pham Van Dong himself admitted that the Vietminh could not have achieved total victory in 1954. As for the Vietnamese allegation of lack of Chinese support, the Chinese further contend that the real hero of Dien Bien Phu is not Vo Nguyen Giap, but General Yeh Chien-ying, later P.R.C. minister of defense. See "Blaming in on the Hans," *Far Eastern Economic Review*, March 2, 1979, pp. 10–11; and *Beijing Review*, November 30, 1979, p. 13. China insists that all decisions at Geneva were taken unanimously by the governments of China, the D.R.V., and the Soviet Union.

69. Ho Chi Minh, *Selected Writings*, p. 180.

70. This document, presumably issued by the Central Committee in Hanoi, makes it clear that the Party was seriously concerned about possible U.S. intervention and was determined to prevent it. It also implies a similar concern in Peking. See U.S. Department of State, *Working Paper*, Appendix Item No. 200, p. 17.

71. Devillers and Lacouture, *End of a War*, p. 369, cite a French official to the effect that the 13th parallel would have been more appropriate than the 17th. For a recent Vietnamese discussion of Hanoi's views on the question, see *The Truth About Viet Nam–China Relations*, p. 13.

72. Geertz, *Agricultural Involution*. See especially Chapter VI.

73. Tanham, *Communist Revolutionary Warfare*, p. 57.

74. J. Bowyer Bell, *The Myth of the Guerrilla* (New York: Knopf, 1971), p. 59.

Chapter 8: Peace and Division

1. According to a Chinese publication, after Geneva the Soviet Union advised the

D.R.V. to seek reunification by peaceful means. China, on the other hand, felt that unification elections would not be held and advised the Vietnamese to prepare for protracted war. See *Beijing Review*, November 23, 1979.

2. One student of modern Vietnam has suggested that the D.R.V. moved slowly toward socialism in North Vietnam in the hope of early unification with the South. See David W. P. Elliott, "North Vietnam Since Ho," *Problems of Communism*, Vol. 24, no. 4 (July-August 1975), p. 35.

3. U.S. Department of State, *Working Paper*, Appendix Item No. 200, has a policy document that may be a directive from the Central Committee to the southern leadership after the July conference. According to the directive, the Party had decided to resolve the Indochina question peacefully but said, "Peace is not unconditional."

4. For the quote, see Robert F. Turner, *Vietnamese Communism: Its Origins and Development* (Stanford, Calif., 1975), p. 105.

5. U.S. Department of State, *Working Paper*, Appendix Item No. 20, p. 3.

6. Captured documents make it clear that although the Party hoped that reunification could take place by peaceful means, it was determined to prepare for a possible resumption of armed struggle if necessary. See Ibid., Appendix Item No. 29.

7. Tran Van Giau, *Mien Nam giu vung thanh dong* [The South on the road to victory] (Hanoi, 1964), pp. 86–88. Tho had first become involved in Saigon demonstrations in 1950 and later spent three years in prison.

8. U.S. Department of State, *Working Paper*, Appendix Item No. 210. This source includes a fairly detailed description of the Party organization at the upper level in the South. The original COSVN set up in 1951 is described in Appendix Item No. 211.

9. Ta Xuan Linh, "How Armed Struggle Began in South Vietnam," *Vietnam Courier*, No. 22 (March 1974), p. 19. Also see "A Party Account of the Situation in the Nam Bo Region of South Vietnam from 1954–1960" (hereafter "Situation in the South"), pp. 8–9. This undated document was captured by U.S. forces in Phuoc Long Province in April 1969. It was probably written by a member of the Regional Committee of the South.

10. A detailed account of such issues is located in Race, *War Comes to Long An*, pp. 26–27 and 37–39. Also see Joseph J. Zasloff, "Political Motivation of the Viet Cong: the Viet Minh Regroupees," Rand Report RM 4703-2 ISA/ARPA (Santa Monica, Calif.: Rand Corporation, May 1966). The quote is from "Situation in the South," p. 19.

11. See the communiqué in Vietnam News Agency (hereafter VNA), August 22, 1955, or in *Nhan dan*, August 22, 1955.

12. Carlyle A. Thayer, "Southern Vietnamese Revolutionary Organizations and the Vietnamese Workers' Party: Continuity and Change, 1954–1974," in Joseph J. Zasloff and MacAlister Brown (eds.), p. 35. "Situation in the South" (p. 39) says that the cautious attitude of the southern leadership was a product of inadequate indoctrination after Geneva and an overly cautious attitude on the internal situation under the GVN.

13. Ta Xuan Linh, "Armed Struggle," pp. 19–24; "Situation in the South," pp. 5–6. U.S. Department of State, *Working Paper*, Appendix Item No. 205, has a brief discussion of the conference. Ba Cut evidently assisted Party units in infiltrating the U Minh forest after arriving in Cambodia.

14. These issues are discussed in U.S. Department of State, *Working Paper*, Appendix Item Nos. 19, 21, and 22. According to Item 19, Le Duan contended that the struggle had reached the stage where military force should be used. According to Appendix Item No. 204, Le Duan commented that the Party's political struggle in the South "will

sometimes have to be backed up with military action in order to show the strength of the forces which won at Dien Bien Phu."

15. VNA, April 30, 1956. The reference to Mikoyan's speech can be found in VNA, April 7, 1956.

16. VNA, April 27, 1956.

17. *Nhan dan* editorial, July 22, 1956. A Party history appearing in successive issues of *Nhan dan* in February 1980 cites a Politburo resolution dated June 1956 to the effect that although existing policy was to stress political struggle, that did not mean that armed struggle of a self-defense nature could not be used under certain circumstances. This history appears in English translation in JPRS 75,579, Translations on North Vietnam No. 2185.

18. Giap's comment is located in Porter, *Vietnam*, Vol. 2, pp. 23–24.

19. Race Documents, No. 1002. An English-language version is located in Porter, *Vietnam*, Vol. 2, pp. 24–30.

20. *Nhan dan*, December 30, 1956.

21. "Situation in the South," pp. 46–48. According to this source, advocates of a peaceful policy contended that the world balance of forces had now changed decisively in favor of the socialist camp. The author retorted that it was mistaken to apply a worldwide trend (peaceful coexistence) to the conditions in a particular society (Vietnam). The fact that the Diem regime had become a new type of colonialism (i.e., tied to the United States) meant that the struggle would be fierce and would involve violence (p. 41).

22. For an internal reference to the policy of selected terrorism, see the letter from the Regional Committee of the South dated March 28, 1960 in Race Documents, No. 1044.

23. See Vo Nguyen Giap's speech, "Strengthening National Defense and Building up the People's Armed Forces," in *Vietnam Documents and Research Notes*, Document 98, p. 45. (Hereafter this source, issued by the U.S. Mission in Saigon, will be cited as *VDRN*.)

24. Jean Lacouture, *Vietnam: Between Two Truces* (New York, 1966), p. 246.

25. Race, *War Comes to Long An*, pp. 92–97. Also see U.S. Department of State, *Working Paper*, Appendix Item No. 200, p. 17.

26. This quote is in *United States–Vietnam Relations, 1945–1967* (Washington, D.C.: Government Printing Office, 1971), Vol. 2, p. 48.

27. Ibid., Vol. 2, p. 50.

28. For a comment by Truong Chinh on the situation, see his "Let Us Be Grateful to Karl Marx and Follow the Path Traced by Him," *VDRN*, Document 51, p. 16.

29. Tran Van Giau, "Great Strategic Effect of the Guerrilla War in South Vietnam Through Ten Years of Armed Struggle," in *NCLS* (July 1969), pp. 19–32, in JPRS 49,387, Translations on North Vietnam No. 639; Ta Xuan Linh, "Armed Struggle," p. 23. "Situation in the South" provides a fairly detailed statistical estimate of Party losses during the period. In many base areas, government forces destroyed up to 90 percent of the Party's armed forces. The party apparatus in the Saigon suburbs, in Go Vap, Gia Dinh, and Tan Binh was virtually eliminated. See pp. 11, 26, and 36–37.

30. Tran Van Giau, "Great Strategic Effect."

31. Ta Xuan Linh, "Armed Uprisings by Ethnic Minorities Along the Truong Son," Part 1, *Vietnam Courier*, No. 28 (September 1974), p. 19.

32. Ibid., Part 2, *Vietnam Courier*, No. 29 (October 1974), p. 19.

33. Ibid. See the account of Pham Thanh Bien entitled "The 1959 Autumn Tra Bong

and Western Quang Ngai Uprisings," in *NCLS*, No. 146 (February 1972), in JPRS 58,128, Translations on North Vietnam No. 1326, for an extended discussion.

34. "Situation and Tasks for '59," in Race Documents, No. 1025. One interesting reference to the Party's delayed decision to resort to armed struggle comes from Hoang Van Hoan, the Politburo member who defected to China in 1979. According to Hoan, because of suggestions within the Party that it return to armed struggle in the South, the Chinese were asked for advice. They advised against such a proposal on the grounds that it would be premature. Later, said Hoan, the Chinese admitted that they had erred. See Hoang Van Hoan, "Distortion of Facts About Militant Friendship Between Viet Nam and China is Impermissible," in *Beijing Review*, December 7, 1979, p. 15. In its White Paper published the same year, Hanoi contended that the P.R.C. exerted pressure on the Vietnamese to prevent them from resuming armed struggle. See *The Truth About Viet Nam-China Relations*, pp. 17–19.

35. The date of the Fifteenth Plenum has caused some confusion among scholars. Some Party sources refer to a meeting in January, others in May. Either there were two sessions (not an impossibility given the urgency of the decision) or the delayed issue of the communiqué in May gave rise to confusion over the date of the meeting itself. The communiqué was broadcast by VNA on May 13, 1959.

36. *Outline History*, p. 87.

37. JPRS 75,579, Translations on North Vietnam No. 2185. A captured notebook, seized by ARVN forces during Operation CRIMP in 1966, remarked that the Fifteenth Plenum had ended "rightist thoughts which were based on vague and incorrect appraisals of the enemy and overconfidence in the legalism of the Geneva Agreement, began to seek new measures to implement the revolutionary struggle and oppose the revisionist thoughts of simplistic and peaceful political legalism." See U.S. Department of State, *Working Paper*, Appendix Item No. 301, p. 84. (Hereafter this source will be cited as CRIMP Document.)

38. *Outline History*, p. 108.

39. "Situation in the South," p. 18.

40. CRIMP Document, p. 5.

41. Ibid., p. 21.

42. A special group, called Group 559 (an apparent reference to the May 1959 founding date), was set up at the direction of the Central Committee to assist in the infiltration process. See U.S. Department of State, *Working Paper*, Appendix Item No. 72. This source includes several other items with further details on the infiltration effort. See also Zasloff, "Political Motivation," pp. 76, 79. Zasloff reported that some South Vietnamese resented the "autumn combatants" from the North who received special treatment and tended to be haughty (see pp. 81–83).

43. Tran Van Giau, "Great Strategic Effect."

44. For a description, see Joseph J. Zasloff, *Rural Resettlement in Vietnam: An Agroville in Development* (East Lansing: Michigan State University, Vietnam Advisory Group, n.d.). If "Situation in the South" can be believed, the Party leadership was quite concerned that the agrovilles might succeed.

45. Ta Xuan Linh, "Ben Tre: Land of Concerted Uprising," in *Vietnam Courier*, No. 27 (August 1974), p. 5.

46. Ibid., p. 6.

47. Nguyen Thi Dinh, *No Other Road to Take* (Ithaca, N.Y., 1976), p. 64.

48. Pham Thanh Bien, "The 1959 Uprisings." There were nineteen in Tra Bong District, ten in Son Tay, eight in Song Ha, four in Minh Long, and eight in Ba To.

49. See the letter by the Committee of the South dated March 28, 1960, in Race Documents, No. 1044. This source gives a useful summation of the period of struggle since the inauguration of the new policy by the Fifteenth Plenum.

50. Telegram from Durbrow to Secretary of State, March 7, 1960, in *United States-Vietnam Relations*, Book 10, pp. 1254-1257.

51. Le Duan, Political Report of September 5, 1960, in *Third National Congress of the Vietnam Workers' Party*, 3 vols. (Hanoi: Foreign Languages Press, 1960), Vol. 1, p. 62.

52. Speech by Vo Nguyen Giap, in *Third National Congress*, Vol. 3, p. 54.

53. *United States-Vietnam Relations*, Vol. 2, p. 68. Moscow and Peking would frequently clash in later years over the level of their support for the Vietnamese revolution, but it is probable that neither was particularly enthusiastic over Hanoi's decision to resort to revolutionary war. China's view, stressing the need for an "area of peace," was contained in an address by Chou En-lai, dated September 2, 1960, at the Fifteenth Anniversary of the founding of the D.R.V. See Porter, *Vietnam*, Vol. 2, p. 72.

54. *United States-Vietnam Relations*, Vol. 2, p. 68.

55. JPRS 75,579, Translations on Vietnam 2185. The reference to "initial hesitation" above is from the CRIMP Document, p. 4.

56. Ta Xuan Linh, "Armed Struggle," p. 22.

57. Speech by Ton Duc Thang, in *Third National Congress*, Vol. 3, pp. 24-26.

58. For a discussion by a Hanoi observer, see Bui Dinh Thanh, NCLS, No. 119 (November 1968), in JPRS 47,563, Translations on North Vietnam 513.

59. The most detailed exposition of the NLF and its program is Pike, *Viet Cong*.

Chapter 9: The Dialectics of Escalation

1. The U.S. Embassy in Saigon agreed. See AmEmbassy Telegram of October 2, 1961, in *Declassified Documents Reference System* (hereafter *DDRS*), Retrospective Collection, item 789b.

2. The full statement has apparently not been published. See CRIMP document, p. 5, for a reference to its importance.

3. "Situation and Tasks," Document No. 241 in Douglas Pike, Documents of the National Liberation Front of South Vietnam, at the Center for International Studies, Massachusetts Institute of Technology. The first document, entitled "Muc tieu phan dau cua toan Dang va toan dan ta hien nay" [The struggle objectives of the entire Party and the entire people at the present time], is located in Race Documents, No. 1038. An English-language version is in Porter, *Vietnam*, Vol. 2, pp. 53-56.

4. An English translation of this resolution is in Porter, *Vietnam*, Vol. 2, pp. 119-123. The resolution made it clear that further escalation of military conflict could take place either because of new U.S. schemes or because Party policy "strayed from the path leading to the general uprising in its leadership." An interesting reference to the October resolution and its reception at lower echelons is in "Situation of the Revolution in South Vietnam," in Pike, Documents of the National Liberation Front, Document No. 257. Unfortunately the translation is confusing and the grammar is garbled (perhaps a reflection of the original) so it is difficult to make a precise analysis.

5. "Situation of the Revolution."

6. "Notes by a VC," in Pike, Documents of the National Liberation Front, Document No. 1.

7. "Situation of the Revolution," p. 9. Italics in the original.

8. Memo from Chin Nam (COSVN) to lower echelons, explaining the policies of the Party leadership in the new situation. This is document No. 855 in Douglas Pike, Catalog of Viet Cong Documents, Series 20. It was captured in Tuyen Duc Province in November 1962. Like the document cited above, it is not clearly written and the meaning is often elusive. On page 43 it declares that the October plenum had foreseen that the war might climax in a general offensive, while a similar meeting the following April had predicted a protracted conflict involving political struggle.

9. Gareth Porter, A Peace Denied (Bloomington, Ind., 1975), p. 17. Donald Zagoria remarks that a member of the Polish delegation to the International Control Commission (ICC) mentioned to him that Hanoi was briefly convinced that the United States would agree to a settlement of the Vietnam conflict on the Laotian model. See Donald Zagoria, Vietnam Triangle (New York, 1967), p. 108.

10. Memo from Chin Nam, in Pike, Catalog of Viet Cong Documents, Document No. 855, p. 39. For a public statement of Hanoi's views on a possible coalition government, see the article by Truong Chinh in the April 1961 issue of Hoc tap.

11. Allan Goodman, The Lost Peace (Stanford, Calif., 1978), pp. 13–14.

12. For the Nhan dan editorial, see Porter, Vietnam, Vol. 2, pp. 160–161.

13. CRIMP document, pp. 14–17.

14. Ibid., pp. 38–39.

15. Tran Van Giau, "Great Strategic Effect."

16. Chief, Military Assistance Advisory Group (MAAG), telegram No. 1570 to Commander in Chief, Pacific Theater (CINCPAC), in DDRS, Retrospective Collection, item 74c.

17. Pike, Viet Cong, pp. 233–234; M. Anderson, M. Arnsten, and H. Averch, "Insurgent Organization and Operations; A Case Study of the Viet Cong in the Delta, 1964–1966," in Rand Report RM 5239-1-ISA/ARPA (Santa Monica, Calif.: Rand Corporation, August 1967).

18. Marvin E. Gettleman (ed.), Viet Nam: History, Documents, and Opinions on a Major World Crisis (New York, 1965), p. 287.

19. These programs are dealt with in Pentagon Papers, Vol. 2, Chapter 7.

20. For a study document on how the Communists attempted to deal with the strategic hamlets, see Pike, Documents of the National Liberation Front, Document No. 35, "Experiences in the Anti-Strategic Hamlet Program." The document is dated October-November 1962.

21. Fall, Vietnam Witness, pp. 197–198. An evaluation of some of the basic weaknesses in the program can be found in Pentagon Papers, Vol. 2, p. 131.

22. Tran Van Giau, "Great Strategic Effect"; William C. Westmoreland, Report on the War in Vietnam (Commander in Chief, Pacific Commander U.S. Military Assistance Command, Vietnam), Section 2, pp. 81–82. For a Western account, see Roger Hilsman, To Move a Nation (New York: 1969), p. 444.

23. Nguyen Hoai, "From the NLF to the PRG of the RSV," NCLS, No. 153 (November-December 1973), in JPRS 62,136, Translations on North Vietnam 15,555.

24. For a discussion, see W. P. Davison, "Some Observations on Viet Cong Operations

in the Villages," Rand report RM 5267/2-ISA/ARPA (Santa Monica, Calif.: Rand Corporation, May 1968), pp. 94–101. For a brief analysis, see Race, *War Comes to Long An*, pp. 125–128.

25. Nguyen Hoai, "The Direct Rear of the Battlefield of South Vietnam," NCLS, No. 129 (December 1969), pp. 42–58, in JPRS 50,553, Translations on North Vietnam 724.

26. R. Michael Pearce, "The Insurgent Environment," RAND report RM 5533-1-ARPA (Santa Monica, Calif.: Rand Corporation, May 1969), p. 46.

27. Vo Nguyen, *Phong trao cong nhan Mien Nam* [The workers' movement in the south] (Hanoi, 1961) (in Communist Vietnamese Publications, Reel 2, Document 77), has a discussion of the history of the movement. According to this source, there were nearly 300,000 members of the proletariat in South Vietnam in 1961, including 55,000 workers on rubber plantations. Le Quang Dao, *Cach mang mien Nam nhat dinh thang loi nhung phuc tap* [The revolution in the South will definitely overcome all obstacles] (Hanoi: Su That, 1963) (in Communist Vietnamese Publications, Reel 3, Document 86), puts the figure at 316,000 (p. 103).

28. Vo Nguyen, *Phong trao cong nhan*, p. 51, has a Communist estimate of the total number of participants.

29. Pike, *Viet Cong*, p. 180.

30. "Situation of the Revolution," Document No. 257 in Pike, *Documents of the National Liberation Front*.

31. Ibid.

32. Pike, *Viet Cong*, pp. 203–204.

33. For an account, see David Halberstam, "The Buddhist Crisis in Vietnam," in Gettleman, *Viet Nam*, pp. 262–270.

34. Washington's gradual disenchantment with Diem is chronicled in *Pentagon Papers*, Vol. 2, Chapter 4. Among other things, the U.S. Embassy did not believe that Tri Quang and his fellow Buddhist leaders were Communists. See DDRS, Retrospective Collection, item 863D, Saigon telegram dated January 31, 1964.

35. Halberstam, "The Coup in South Vietnam," in Gettleman, *Viet Nam*, pp. 272–280.

36. Memo, Secretary of Defense to President, dated December 21, 1963, in DDRS, Retrospective Collection, item 88E.

37. Pike, *Viet Cong*, p. 116; William Andrews, *The Village War: Vietnamese Communist Revolutionary Activities in Dinh Tuong Province, 1960–1964* (Columbia: University of Missouri Press, 1973), p. 127.

38. Resolution of Ninth Plenum, in VDRN, Document 96, p. 15. Italics in the original.

39. Zagoria, *Vietnam Triangle*, p. 43. For a discussion, see John C. Donnell and Melvin Gurtov, "North Vietnam: Left of Moscow, Right of Peking," Rand report P-3794 (Santa Monica, Calif.: Rand Corporation, February 1968), p. 22.

40. Zagoria, *Vietnam Triangle*, p. 109, citing *Hoc tap* article of July 1963.

41. This statement is Document 98 in VDRN. It was issued in September 1971.

42. VNA, April 18, 1964.

43. "The World Situation," VDRN, Document 98, pp. 49 and 57.

44. *The Truth About Viet Nam–China Relations*, p. 20.

45. This article is in Russell Stetler (ed.), *The Military Art of People's War* (New York: Monthly Review Press, 1970), pp. 185–225. Italics in the original.

46. Cited in Pike, *War, Peace, and the Viet Cong*, pp. 150–151.

47. A Communist claim is in Nguyen Hoai, "The Direct Rear"; official American

estimates are located in COMUSMACV telegram MACJ 23 2062 to JCS, March 18, 1964, in *DDRS*, Retrospective Collection, item 89D, and CIA report of February 18, 1964, *DDRS*, Retrospective Collection, item 246D.

48. The most detailed exposition of the U.S. point of view is in U.S. Department of State, "Aggression from the North," in Gettleman, *Viet Nam*, pp. 284–316. Acording to U.S. sources, total infiltration in 1964 was more than 10,000. See telegram 1502 to U.S. Embassy, Saigon, dated January 26, 1965, in *DDRS*, Retrospective Collection, item 860E.

49. CIA report of February 18, 1964, in *DDRS*, Retrospective Collection, item 246D; memo from William Colby, February 10, 1964, *DDRS* Retrospective Collection, item 39E.

50. This program is discussed in *Pentagon Papers*, Vol. 2, pp. 521–526.

51. For a Communist discussion of how to conduct terrorist activities, see Document No. 1087, in Pike, *Catalog*. Also see Document No. 882, "We bomb the Kinh Do theater." The reference to the "battle of the cities" is in Pierre Rousset, *Le parti communiste vietnamien* (Paris: Maspero, 1975), p. 225.

52. Lacouture, *Vietnam: Between Two Truces*, p. 221.

53. *VDRN*, Document 102, Vol. 1, pp. 49–51.

54. Robert Gallucci, *Neither Peace nor Honor: The Politics of American Military Policy in Vietnam* (Baltimore, Md.: Johns Hopkins Press, 1975), p. 43.

55. Fall, *Vietnam Witness*, p. 314. According to Allan Goodman, Hanoi later denied that it was willing to talk. See Goodman, *Lost Peace*, p. 19.

56. *VDRN*, Document 67 (September 1969) p. 7. The reference to Moscow's support for a general offensive is from Porter, *A Peace Denied*, p. 23.

57. Westmoreland, *Report*, p. 90.

58. For the Communist estimate of the situation in early 1965, see the Directive from Headquarters Command, People's Liberation Armed Forces, dated January 1965, in Captured Documents Evaluation Center (CDEC), Log No. 01-0520-70. The estimate is generally optimistic about the overall situation in the South, but it openly concedes that the revolutionary forces did not yet possess adequate military strength to defeat the enemy. It also suggested growing concern among Party leaders over the possibility of U.S. intervention, but called for a continuation of the present strategy of moving gradually toward a high-level confrontation with the enemy. I am grateful to Bill Turley for providing me with a copy of this document. The captured letter, dated early 1966, is in U.S. Department of State, *Working Paper*, Document 302. See p. 5.

Chapter 10: War of Attrition

1. William C. Westmoreland, *A Soldier Reports* (New York, 1976), p. 114.

2. For a reference, see Townsend Hoopes, *The Limits of Intervention* (New York: David McKay Co., 1969), pp. 7–10.

3. The ratio of superiority required for a government to repress an insurgency movement has been a matter of considerable controversy. For one comment, see Robert Thompson, *No Exit from Vietnam* (New York, 1969), p. 53.

4. Westmoreland, *A Soldier Reports*, p. 114.

5. Hilsman (*To Move a Nation*, p. 531) has a discussion.

6. Westmoreland, *Report*, Section II, p. 98; also his *A Soldier Reports*, p. 122.

7. This plan is described in Westmoreland's message to Admiral U.S.G. Sharp, dated June 14, 1965, in Porter, *Vietnam*, Vol. 2, pp. 378–379.

8. Westmoreland, *A Soldier Reports*, p. 135.

9. The Communist view of the battle was that it demonstrated the capacity of the revolutionary forces to hold their own against the better-armed Americans and thus symbolically represented a decisive stage in the history of the war. See Hoang Tung, "Historic Encounter," *Hoc tap* (March 1973), in JPRS 59,055, Translations on North Vietnam 1384. One called it a "Stalingrad" for the Americans. See Pike, Catalog of Viet Cong Documents, Series 2, Document No. 1076.

10. Westmoreland, *Report*, Section II, p. 110.

11. According to Robert Shaplen, *The Road from War* (New York: Harper & Row, 1970), p. 24, the Communists had 80,000 hard-core troops in the South to supplement 120,000 guerrillas and locals.

12. Hoang Tung ("Historic Encounter") remarked that if Hanoi did not respond, it would have to return to guerrilla war and wait indefinitely for a second opportunity.

13. Zagoria, *Vietnam Triangle*, p. 48.

14. Fall, *Vietnam Witness*, p. 134.

15. *Outline History*, p. 123.

16. The letter from "Anh Sau" to "Anh Tam" is in Pike, Documents of the National Liberation Front, Series 2, Document No. 1076. Thanh is occasionally referred to by the pseudonym of "Sau Di" in internal Party documents.

17. The article appeared in English in the September 3, 1965 issue of *Peking Review*.

18. Duan's speech, broadcast by Radio Hanoi in July, appears in excerpted form in Zagoria, *Vietnam Triangle*, p. 84.

19. An abridged version of Giap's article is in Stetler, *Military Art of People's War*, pp. 252–274. For Vinh's contribution, see Zagoria, *Vietnam Triangle*, Appendix, pp. 246–265.

20. Westmoreland, *A Soldier Reports*, pp. 159–160.

21. For a brief account, see *Pentagon Papers*, Vol. 2, pp. 278–282.

22. Ibid., 533–536.

23. A detailed exposition of this problem can be found in Jon Van Dyke, *Hanoi's Strategy for Survival* (Palo Alto, Calif.: Pacific Books, 1972).

24. Patrick J. McGarvey, *Visions of Victory: Selected Vietnamese Communist Military Writings, 1964–1968* (Stanford, Calif., 1969), Document No. 1, p. 65.

25. Ibid., Document No. 6, pp. 119–149.

26. Ibid., Document No. 9, pp. 199–251.

27. Ibid., Document No. 4, pp. 101–113. A discussion of the poor coordination between mobile and guerrilla forces is located in VDRN, Document 2 (October 1967).

28. VDRN, Document 102, Vol. 1, p. 33.

29. Ibid. It has been speculated that "Ba" was Le Duan. From the context, it appears more likely that it was a high-ranking member of the southern hierarchy, perhaps Pham Hung or Nguyen Van Linh.

30. Excerpts from the letter are reproduced in VDRN, Document 8.

31. Ibid. General Vinh was not specific about the timing of negotiations. He did suggest at one point that Hanoi's plan was to achieve a decisive victory in about four years' time.

32. On the other hand, Hoang Van Hoan contends that Hanoi was still seeking

China's advice on war strategy. According to him, Ho Chi Minh advised Le Duan to seek China's advice on whether to request Soviet assistance as a mediator with the United States. In the fall of 1966 Nguyen Chi Thanh visited Peking and was advised by Chou En-lai that negotiations would not be successful unless victory had been achieved on the battlefield. That, according to Hoan, was Ho's feeling also. See "On Hanoi's White Book," in *Beijing Review*, November 23, 1979, pp. 18–19. China claims that between 1965 and 1968 it dispatched 320,000 Chinese support troops to Vietnam to help build bridges, railroads, and an air defense system. All were withdrawn by the summer of 1970.

33. McGarvey, *Visions of Victory*, Document No. 6, p. 127.

34. Westmoreland, *A Soldier Reports*, p. 193.

35. Shaplen, *Road from War*, pp. 101–105.

36. Denis Warner, *Not With Guns Alone* (London, 1977), pp. 137–150, has a description.

37. Westmoreland, *A Soldier Reports*, p. 204. According to Denis Warner (*Not With Guns Alone*, p. 137), Hanoi's objectives were to cause high casualties, absorb allied units in defensive operations, and draw government units to the perimeter in order to permit guerrilla operations in highly populated areas, as in 1953.

38. Two accounts of the operations, from different points of view, are Bernard Rogers, *Cedar Falls–Junction City: A Turning Point* (Washington, D.C., 1974), and Jonathan Schell, *Village of Ben Suc* (New York: Alfred A. Knopf, 1967).

39. Guenter Lewy, *America in Vietnam* (New York: Oxford University Press, 1978), p. 70, citing Military Assistance Command, Civil Operations and Rural Development Support (MACCORDS), "Evaluation report: Task Force Oregon Operations," September 13, 1967, p. 8, U.S. Forces and Pacification, 1961–1968 File, Office of the Chief of Military History (OCMH), Washington, D.C.

40. For a discussion of this issue, see *DDRS* (1977), item 178E, CIA, Office of Economic Research, Memo of March 1, 1968.

41. Westmoreland, *Report*, Section 2, p. 36.

42. Vo Nguyen Giap, article in *Nhan dan*, September 14, 1967.

43. For one analysis, see Melvin Gurtov, "The War in the Delta: Views from Three Vietcong Battalions," Rand report RM-5353-1-ISA/ARPA (Santa Monica, Calif.: Rand Corporation, September 1967), pp. 9–10.

44. *VDRN*, Document 2 (October 1967), pp. 3–5; also see *VDRN*, Document 12 (January 1968), p. 3.

45. *VDRN*, Document 39 (July 1968), p. 5.

46. Vo Nguyen Giap, "Great Victory, Great Task," in Stetler, *Military Art of People's War*, p. 301.

47. Pike, *War, Peace,. and the Viet Cong*, pp. 124–125.

48. Robert F. Rogers, "Policy Differences Within the Hanoi Leadership," *Studies in Comparative Communism*, Vol. 9, nos. 1-2 (Spring-Summer 1976), p. 120.

49. *VDRN*, Document 45 (October 1968), "The Process of Revolution and the General Uprising." This document, of unknown authorship, is an interesting analysis of the revolutionary process in Vietnam.

50. *VDRN*, Document 29 (April 1968), "Two directives for Tet," p. 11.

51. *VDRN*, Document 45, p. 14. Italics in the original.

52. Pike, *War, Peace, and the Viet Cong*, p. 127, claims that phase one cost the

Viet Cong 5,000 killed and wounded.

53. *VDRN*, Document 38 (July 1968), "The Sixth Resolution, Central Office of South Viet-Nam," pp. 3–4.

54. Westmoreland, *A Soldier Reports*, p. 324.

55. Lewy (*America in Vietnam*, p. 122) said that air strikes killed more than 500 civilians and wounded 1,200. See MACCORDS provincial report, Dinh Tuong and Kien Hoa provinces, January-February 1968 (OCMH).

56. Lewy, *America in Vietnam*, p. 274. There have been several analyses of the alleged massacre from varying political perspectives. Douglas Pike (*The Viet Cong Strategy of Terror* [Saigon: U.S. Mission in Vietnam, 1970], p. 23) gave a figure of 5,800 persons killed or missing. Although the statistics are a matter of controversy, there seems no doubt that mass executions did occur, whether deliberately or in the course of the battle.

57. Westmoreland, *A Soldier Reports*, p. 330.

58. *VDRN*, Document 45, p. 12.

59. Shaplen (*Road from War*, p. 198) and Donald Oberdorfer (*Tet!* [New York, 1971]) have good descriptions.

60. Westmoreland, *Report*, Section 2, p. 161. A CIA report lists enemy losses at 38,000 See *DDRS* (1977), item 178E, Joint Office of Current Intelligence and Office of Economic Research Memo, dated March 1, 1968, p. 15.

61. Warner, *Not With Guns Alone*, p. 154.

62. *VDRN*, Document 30 (April 1968), "After Tet: Three VC Assessments," p. 5. For a U.S. viewpoint, see Joint Chiefs of Staff report dated February 27, 1968, in Porter, *Vietnam*, Vol. 2, p. 507.

Chapter 11: Fighting and Negotiating

1. *VDRN*, Document 38 (July 1968), "The Sixth Resolution, Central Office of South Viet-Nam." Italics in the original.

2. Shaplen, *Road from War*, p. 211.

3. In *A Soldier Reports* (p. 337), General Westmoreland remarked that at one staff meeting the command historian presented a gloomy view of the situation at Khe Sanh. Westmoreland emphatically disagreed and strode angrily from the room.

4. Pike, *War, Peace, and the Viet Cong*, p. 128.

5. Goodman, *Lost Peace*, p. 69.

6. Kamil Tangri, "Is the Viet Cong Finished?", in *Bonn Vorwärts*, August 29, 1968. See JPRS 46,590, Translations on North Vietnam No. 447. According to a joint CIA-Defense Intelligence Agency (DIA) report dated March 30, 1968, and entitled "The Attrition of Vietnamese Communist Forces, 1968–1969," local recruitment in the South was running at about 85,000 per year. With annual losses in the war running at about 300,000 per year, the remainder would have to be made up by increased mobilization in the D.R.V. With 120,000 young people reaching draft age each year, the Party would have to dip into its labor pool to compensate for the difference. The report concluded that this was a "worst case" hypothesis and that in all likelihood manpower would not be a major factor in limiting Hanoi's ability to continue with the war. See *DDRS* (1977), item 38C.

7. See Shaplen, *Road from War*, p. 234, for a brief discussion of the Phoenix Program.

8. *VDRN*, Document 67 (September 1969), "An Elaboration of the Eighth Resolution

(of the) Central Office of South Viet-Nam," p.18

9. Shaplen, *Road from War*, p. 265. Truong Chinh's speech is cited on p. 240.

10. *VDRN*, Document 64 (July 1969), "Summer 1969: A Viet Cong Study of the Situation and Prospects," p. 8.

11. Ibid.

12. *VDRN*, Document 82 (August 1970), "COSVN's Preliminary Report on the 1969 Autumn Campaign," p. 6.

13. To outside observers, Ho's death appeared to have little effect on Hanoi's war strategy. More recently, however, it has become clear that under the leadership of Le Duan, Ho Chi Minh's policy of balancing Moscow and Peking was increasingly replaced by a pro-Soviet stance. Hoang Van Hoan, whose defection to Peking in 1979 suggests that his views should be evaluated with caution, claims that Le Duan took over gradually after Ho Chi Minh's health began to deteriorate in 1965. In later years, Le Duan abandoned the principle of collective leadership that had flourished under Ho and assumed a dictatorial stance through his control of the security apparatus and a system of spies throughout the Party leadership. Then, at the Fourth Party Congress in 1976, says Hoan, Le Duan moved against pro-Chinese elements in the Party and removed many of them from the Central Committee. "Distortion of Facts About Militant Friendship Between Viet Nam and China is Impermissible," *Beijing Review*, December 7, 1979, p. 11. Ironically Nikita Khrushchev observed in his memoirs that he feared that the death of Ho Chi Minh would lead to a takeover of the VWP by an anti-Soviet faction in the Party. See Nikita Khrushchev, *Khrushchev Remembers* (Boston: Little, Brown, and Co., 1970), p. 483.

14. *VDRN*, Document 70 (January 1970), p. 90.

15. Ibid., p. 61. Italics in the original.

16. *VDRN*, Document 71 (January 1970), "Under the Party's Banner, Viet-Nam's Military Art Has Constantly Developed and Triumphed," p. 15. Italics in the original.

17. *VDRN*, Document 72 (January 1970), article by Song Hao, "Party Leadership is the Cause of the Growth and Victories of our Army."

18. For a discussion, see David W. P. Elliott, "North Vietnam Since Ho," *Problems of Communism*, Vol. 24, no. 4 (July-August 1975), p. 40.

19. Hanoi's strategy to string out the negotiations is discussed in *VDRN*, Document 61 (June 1969), "Decisive Victory: Step by Step, Bit by Bit," p. 5.

20. *VDRN*, Document 20 (March 1968), "The New Situation and Mission: A Training Document," p. 4.

21. Article in *Nhan dan*, June 11, 1969, in JPRS 48,699, Translations on North Vietnam No. 589.

22. *New York Times*, May 9, 1969, p. 1.

23. *VDRN*, Document 88 (January 1971), "The Viet Cong's March-April 1970 Plans for Expanding Control in Cambodia." Information on the early years of the KCP is located in "The Bloody Border," *Far Eastern Economic Review*, April 21, 1978, pp. 18–20. For a highly partisan Cambodian acount, see the famous *Black Paper: Facts and Evidences of the Acts of Aggression and Annexation of Vietnam Against Kampuchea* (Department of Press and Information of the Ministry of Foreign Affairs of Democratic Kampuchea, September 1978), pp. 17–26. I am grateful to King C. Chen for providing me with a copy of this document.

24. *Time*, October 8, 1979, p. 34. Kissinger claimed that secrecy was necessary to avoid

embarrassing Sihanouk, who tolerated the air raids. Sihanouk later admitted to a journalist that he had told Chester Bowles "en passant" in 1968 that Washington could bomb the sanctuaries but claimed that he had not been informed of the use of the massive B-52s.

25. *Far Eastern Economic Review*, April 21, 1978. For two recent scholarly accounts, see Justus Van der Kroef, "Cambodia: From 'Democratic Kampuchea' to 'People's Republic,'" *Asian Survey*, Vol. 19, no. 8 (August 1979), and J.A.S. Girling, "The Resistance in Cambodia," *Asian Survey*, Vol. 12, no. 7 (July 1972).

26. The official record of the conference is located in *VDRN*, Document 80 (June 1970), "The Indochinese People's Summit Conference" (April 24-25, 1970)." Hanoi now claims that Peking forced the Indochinese parties to meet in South China in order to establish its control over them. See *The Truth About Viet Nam–China Relations*, p. 33.

27. William Shawcross, *Sideshow: Kissinger, Nixon, and the Destruction of Cambodia* (New York, 1979), p. 171. Hanoi's role in persuading the KCP and the Chinese to accept Sihanouk is recounted on pp. 32-33.

28. Goodman, *Lost Peace*, pp. 105–106.

29. *Time*, October 8, 1979, pp. 36–37; Henry Kissinger, *The White House Years* (Boston, 1979), p. 486n.

30. The above comments can be found in *VDRN*, Document 88 (January 1971).

31. Ibid., p. 58.

32. *VDRN*, Document 91 (March 1971), "The Nineteenth Plenary Session of the Central Committee of the Viet-Nam Workers Party and Its Reference Documents," p. 10.

33. *VDRN*, Document 99 (September 1971), "The Study of COSVN Resolution 10."

34. Cited in David W. P. Elliott, *NLF-DRV Strategy and the 1972 Spring Offensive* (Ithaca, N.Y., 1974), p. 16. The official was John Paul Vann. For statistics on Pacification, see J. M. Silverman, "South Vietnam and the Elusive Peace," *Asian Survey*, Vol. 13, no. 1 (January 1973), p. 27.

35. For such complaints, see *VDRN*, Document 102, Vol. 3, p. 1, and Shaplen, *Lost Revolution*, p. 335.

36. For several articles dealing with the issue, see *Asian Survey* Vol. 10, no. 8 (August 1970).

37. FitzGerald, *Fire in the Lake*, pp. 554–555.

38. Van Tien Dung, *Our Great Spring Victory* (New York, 1977), p. 124.

39. Goodman, *Lost Peace*, p. 115; *Time*, October 8, 1979, p. 39.

40. Robert F. Rogers, "Policy Differences Within the Hanoi Leadership," in *Studies in Comparative Communism*, Vol. 9, nos. 1-2 (Spring-Summer 1976), p. 124; Goodman, *Lost Peace*, p. 117; Lewy, *America in Vietnam*, p. 196.

41. Elliott, *NLF-DRV Strategy*, p. 25.

42. *VDRN*, Document 106, Vol. 3 (October 1972), *Nhan dan* article entitled "Arm the Revolutionary Masses and Build the People's Army."

43. *VDRN*, Document 109 (December 1972), "The Communists' Aborted Plans for the Seizure of Da Nang," p. 17.

44. Ibid., pp. 18–24.

45. Ibid., pp. 15–16.

46. See the account in the *New York Times*, April 29, 1972, p. 1.

47. Kissinger, *White House Years*, p. 1098; Porter, *A Peace Denied*, p. 106; and Ted Serong, "The 1972 Easter Offensive," *Southeast Asian Perspectives*, no. 10 (Summer 1974).

48. Lewy, *America in Vietnam*, p. 198; Elliott, *NLF-DRV Strategy*, p. 23.

49. Porter, *A Peace Denied*, p. 116, citing *Washington Post*, November 12, 1972.

50. *Time*, October 8, 1979, p. 44.

51. Ibid.

52. This and the following directives are located in *VDRN*, Document 108 (November 1972), "PRP Abandons Plans for a Revolution in Saigon."

Chapter 12: The Final Drama

1. Hoang Tung, "Historic Encounter," *Hoc tap* (March 1973), in JPRS 59,055, Translations on North Vietnam 1384. The author was the editor of *Nhan dan*.

2. Hoang Tung, "Our Very Great Victory and Our New Task," *Hoc tap* (April 1973), in JPRS 59,150, Translations on North Vietnam 1391.

3. *VDRN*, Document 109 (December 1972), "The Communists' Aborted Plans for the Seizure of Da Nang," p. 47.

4. Frank Snepp, *A Decent Interval* (New York, 1977), pp. 49–50.

5. *VDRN*, Document 113, cited in Gareth Porter, "The Paris Agreement and Revolutionary Strategy in South Vietnam," in Zasloff and Brown, *Communism in Indochina*, p. 62.

6. Goodman, *Lost Peace*, p. 169.

7. Snepp, *Decent Interval*, p. 53.

8. Paul Kattenberg, "DRV External Relations in the New Revolutionary Phase," in Zasloff and Brown, *Communism in Indochina*, p. 117.

9. Snepp, *Decent Interval*, pp. 91–92.

10. Kattenberg, "DRV External Relations," p. 122.

11. See *Asian Survey*, Vol. 9, no. 4 (April 1971), for a symposium on postwar economic development in South Vietnam. The writers assume the continued existence of the Saigon regime.

12. *DDRS* (1977), item 38C. Samuel P. Huntington, "The Bases of Accommodation," *Foreign Affairs* 46, 4 (July 1968), p. 652, has a comment.

13. Van Tien Dung, *Our Great Spring Victory*, p. 10.

14. Goodman, *Lost Peace*, Appendix 0, Directive NR 08/CT 74.

15. Goodman, *Lost Peace*, Appendix L, "Advancing the Revolution by means of Peace or War, Violence or Negotiations."

16. Snepp, *Decent Interval*, p. 159; Van Tien Dung, *Our Great Spring Victory*, p. 37; Stephen T. Hosmer, Konrad Kellen, and Brian M. Jenkins, "The Fall of South Vietnam: Statements by Vietnamese Military and Civilian Leaders," Rand report, R-2208-OSD (HIST) (Santa Monica, Calif.: Rand Corporation, December 1978), pp. 61–62.

17. Van Tien Dung, *Our Great Spring Victory*, p. 20.

18. Ibid., p. 22.

19. Ibid., p. 23.

20. This account is based on Van Tien Dung, *Our Great Spring Victory*, and Snepp, *Decent Interval*.

21. According to Denis Warner (*Not With Guns Alone*, p. 13), Thieu's adviser Ted Serong had been a major influence in the decision.

22. Van Tien Dung, *Our Great Spring Victory*, pp. 100–106; Snepp, *Decent Interval*, pp. 206–208.

23. Van Tien Dung, *Our Great Spring Victory*, p. 120. Italics in the original.

24. Ibid., p. 121.

25. Ibid., p. 132.

26. Ibid., p. 187.

27. Tiziano Terzani, *Giai Phong! The Fall and Liberation of Saigon* (New York, 1976), p. 88.

28. Hosmer, Kellen, and Jenkins, "The Fall of South Vietnam."

Chapter 13: At the Crossroads

1. For one general discussion of the issue of class leadership of the Vietnamese Revolution, see Tran Van Giau, *Giai cap cong nhan Viet Nam*, pp. 443–444.

2. This argument is presented in Race, *War Comes to Long An*, p. 141.

3. This information is available in Rand reports cited above. See, for example, John C. Donnell, Guy J. Pauker, and Joseph J. Zasloff, "Viet Cong Motivation and Morale in 1964: A Preliminary Report." Rand report, RM-4507/3-ISA (Santa Monica, Calif.: Rand Corporation, March 1965).

4. Pike argued that if the essence of the Vietminh movement was "spirit," the essence of the NLF was "organization." See Pike, *Viet Cong*, preface, p. ix.

5. The most complete analysis to date is Pike, *Viet Cong*.

6. Khrushchev, *Khrushchev Remembers*, pp. 480–481.

7. It is interesting to note, however, that Ho Chi Minh may have credited Mao Tse-tung with the concept of "fighting while negotiating." According to Hoang Van Hoan, Ho suggested that Vietnamese Party figures consult with the Chinese leader on how best to undertake negotiations with the Americans because of the latter's experience with the strategy. Given the Vietnamese Party's own long experience, it seems unlikely that it had much to learn from the Chinese. Perhaps this is an example of Ho's lifelong habit of flattering those who might be of use to him.

8. There are some indications of the existence of a pro-Chinese (or an anti-Vietnamese) faction within the Lao People's Revolutionary Party. As of 1980, the pro-Hanoi elements appear to be in full control.

Selected Bibliography

A complete listing of all the books, articles, and documents consulted in the course of this study is too extensive to be included in its entirety in this bibliography. To assist the reader interested in further investigation of topics dealt with in this book, I have listed below some of the major sources for the study of Vietnamese communism and the Vietnamese revolution. Readers requiring detailed information on sources may refer to the notes.

PRIMARY SOURCES

Archives Nationales de France, Section Outre-Mer (AOM), located at the Ministry of Overseas France, Paris.

Communist Vietnamese Publications. Microfilm series of selected documents issued by the Library of Congress, Washington, D.C.

Declassified Documents Reference System (DDRS). Washington, D.C.: Carrollton Press, 1976.

Fall, Bernard (ed.). *Ho Chi Minh: On Revolution.* New York: Praeger Publishers, 1967.

Ho Chi Minh. *Selected Writings.* Hanoi: Foreign Languages Press, 1977.

———. Ve dau tranh vu trang va luc luong vu trang nhan dan [On armed struggle and the armed strength of the people]. Hanoi: Quan Do Nhan Dan, 1970.

McGarvey, Patrick, ed. *Visions of Victory: Selected Vietnamese Communist Military Writings, 1964–1968.* Stanford, Calif.: Hoover Institution Press, 1969.

A Party Account of the Situation in the Nam Bo Region of South Vietnam from 1954–1960. Captured document, no date.

The Pentagon Papers (Senator Gravel edition). 4 vols. Boston: Beacon Press, 1971.

Pike, Douglas. Catalog of Viet Cong Documents. Series 2. Collection of documents deposited at Cornell University Library, Ithaca, N.Y., February 1969.

———. Documents of the National Liberation Front of South Vietnam. Microfilm collection deposited at the Center for International Studies, Massachusetts Institute of Technology, Cambridge, Mass., 1967.

Porter, Gareth. *Vietnam: The Definitive Documentation of Human Decisions.* 2 vols. Stanfordville, N.Y.: Earl M. Coleman Publishers, 1979.

Race Documents. A collection of materials deposited by Jeffrey Race with the Center for Research Libraries, Chicago, Ill.

Service de Liaison avec les Originaires de Territoires de la France d'Outre-Mer

(SLOTFOM), located at the Ministry of Overseas France, Paris.

Third National Congress of the Vietnam Workers' Party. 3 vols. Hanoi: Foreign Languages Press, 1960.

Vietnam Documents and Research Notes (VDRN). A series of translations of captured Communist documents published by the U.S. mission in Saigon.

_____ . *Working Paper on North Viet-Nam's Role in the War in South Viet-Nam.* Washington, D.C., 1968.

SECONDARY SOURCES

General Studies of the Vietnamese Communist Movement

Buttinger, Joseph. *Vietnam: A Dragon Embattled.* 2 vols. New York: Praeger Publishers, 1967.

Lacouture, Jean. *Ho Chi Minh: A Political Biography.* New York: Random House, 1968.

Nguyen Khac Huyen. *Vision Accomplished?* New York: Collier, 1971.

An Outline History of the Vietnam Workers' Party. Hanoi: Foreign Languages Press, 1970.

Pike, Douglas. *A History of Vietnamese Communism, 1925–1976.* Stanford, Calif.: Hoover Institution Press, 1978.

Rousset, Pierre. *Le parti communiste vietnamien.* Paris: Maspero, 1975.

Turner, Robert F. *Vietnamese Communism: Its Origins and Development.* Stanford: Hoover Institution Press, 1975.

Woodside, Alexander B. *Community and Revolution in Vietnam.* Boston: Houghton Mifflin Co., 1976.

The Period up to 1945

Buoc Ngoat Vi Dai cua Lich Su Cach Mang Viet Nam [A great step forward in the history of the Vietnamese revolution]. Hanoi, n.d.

Chesneaux, Jean (ed.). *Tradition et révolution au Vietnam.* Paris: Anthropos, 1971.

Duiker, William J. *The Comintern and Vietnamese Communism.* Athens: Ohio University Southeast Asia Program, 1975.

_____ . *The Rise of Nationalism in Vietnam, 1900–1941.* Ithaca, N.Y.: Cornell University Press, 1976.

Hémery, Daniel. *Révolutionnaires vietnamiens et pouvoir colonial en Indochine.* Paris: Maspero, 1975.

Histoire de la Révolution d'Août. Hanoi: Foreign Languages Press, 1972.

Marr, David F. *Vietnamese Anti-Colonialism, 1885–1925.* Berkeley and Los Angeles: University of California Press, 1971.

Ngo Vinh Long. *Before the Revolution.* Cambridge, Mass.: M.I.T. Press, 1973.

Nhung ngay thang tam [The days of August]. Hanoi: Van Hoc, 1961.

McAlister, John T. *Viet-Nam: The Origins of Revolution.* New York: Alfred A. Knopf, 1969.

McAlister, John T. and Paul Mus. *The Vietnamese and Their Revolution.* New York: Harper & Row, 1970.

Popkin, Samuel. *The Rational Peasant.* Berkeley: University of California Press, 1979.

Sacks, I. Milton. "Marxism in Vietnam," in Frank Trager (ed.), *Marxism in Southeast Asia*. Stanford, Calif.: Stanford University Press, 1960.

Sainteny, Jean. *Histoire d'une paix manquée*. Paris: Dumont, 1953.

Tran Huy Lieu. *Lich su thu do Ha Noi* [A history of the city of Hanoi]. Hanoi: Su Hoc, 1960.

_____ . *Tai lieu tham khao lich su cach mang can dai Viet Nam* (TLTK) [Historical research materials concerning the modern revolution in Vietnam]. Hanoi: Van Su Dia, 1958.

Tran Van Giau. *Giai cap cong nhan Viet Nam* [The working class of Vietnam]. Hanoi: Su That, 1961. Deals with the period up to 1930.

_____ . *Giai cap cong nhan Viet Nam*. Hanoi: Su That, 1961–1963. Vol. 1 (1961) deals with the 1930–1935 period, Vol. 2 (1962) with the 1936–1939 period, and Vol. 3 (1963) with the 1939–1945 period.

Vo Nguyen Giap. *Unforgettable Days*. Hanoi: Foreign Languages Press, 1975.

Vo Nguyen Giap and Truong Chinh. *The Peasant Question*. Translated by Christine Pelzer White. Ithaca, N.Y.: Southeast Asia Program, Data Paper No. 94, 1974.

The Period of the Franco-Vietminh War

Bodard, Lucien. *The Quicksand War*. Boston: Little, Brown and Co., 1967.

Chen, King C. *Vietnam and China, 1938–1954*. Princeton, N.J.: Princeton University Press, 1969.

Devillers, Phillipe. *Histoire du Vietnam, 1940–1952*. Paris: Editions du Seuil, 1952.

Devillers, Phillipe and Jean Lacouture. *End of a War*. New York: Praeger Publishers, 1969.

Fall, Bernard. *Hell in a Very Small Place*. Philadelphia: J.B. Lippincott Co., 1966.

_____ . *Le Vietminh*. Paris: Armand Colin, 1960.

_____ . *Street Without Joy*. Harrisburg, Pa.: Stackpole Press, 1961.

Gurtov, Melvin. *The First Vietnam Crisis*. New York: Columbia University Press, 1967.

Hammer, Ellen J. *The Struggle for Indochina, 1940–1955*. Stanford, Calif.: Stanford University Press, 1965.

Navarre, Henri. *Agonie de l'Indochine*. Paris: Plon, 1956.

Nguyen Kien Giang. *Viet Nam nam dau tien sau Cach Mang Thang Tam* [Vietnam in the years immediately following the August Revolution]. Hanoi: Su That, 1961.

Starobin, Joseph. *Eyewitness in Indochina*. New York: Cameron and Kahn, 1954.

Truong Chinh. *Ban ve Cach Mang Viet Nam* [On the Vietnamese revolution]. Hanoi: Ban Chap Han Truong Uong, 1956.

Truong Chinh. *Primer for Revolt*. New York: Praeger Publishers, 1963.

Vo Nguyen Giap. *Nhiem vu quan su truoc mat chuyen sang tong phan cong* [The military responsibility for preparing the counteroffensive]. Hanoi, 1950.

_____ . *People's War, People's Army*. New York: Praeger Publishers, 1962.

_____ . *Tu nhan dan ma ra* [From the people]. Hanoi: Quan Doi Nhan Dan, 1964.

The Period of American Involvement

Cooper, Chester L. *The Lost Crusade: America in Vietnam*. Greenwich, Conn.: Fawcett, 1972.

Elliott, David. *NLF-DRV Strategy and the 1972 Spring Offensive*. Ithaca, N.Y. : Cornell University, International Relations of East Asia (IREA) project, 1974.

Fall, Bernard. *The Two Vietnams*. New York: Praeger Publishers, 1961.

———— . *Vietnam Witness, 1953–1966*. New York: Praeger Publishers, 1966.

Fishel, Wesley (ed.). *Vietnam: Anatomy of a Conflict*. Itasca, Ill.: Peacock, 1968.

FitzGerald, Frances. *Fire in the Lake*. New York: Vintage, 1972.

Gettleman, Marvin E. (ed.). *Viet Nam: History, Documents, and Opinions on a Major World Crisis*. New York: Fawcett, 1965.

Goodman, Allan. *The Lost Peace*. Stanford, Calif.: Hoover Institution Press, 1978.

Hilsman, Roger. *To Move a Nation*. New York: Doubleday & Co., 1969.

Hoang Van Chi. *From Colonialism to Communism*. New York: Praeger Publishers, 1971.

Hoopes, Townsend. *The Limits of Intervention*. New York: David McKay Co., 1969.

Kahin, George McT. and John W. Lewis. *The United States in Vietnam*. New York: Delta Books, 1967.

Kissinger, Henry. *The White House Years*. Boston: Little, Brown and Co., 1979.

Lacouture, Jean. *Vietnam: Between Two Truces*. New York: Random House, 1966.

Lewy, Guenther. *America in Vietnam*. New York: Oxford University Press, 1978.

Nguyen Khac Vien (ed.). *Tradition and Revolution in Vietnam*. Berkeley, Calif., and Washington: Indochina Resource Center, 1974.

Nguyen Thi Dinh. *No Other Road to Take*. Ithaca, N.Y.: Southeast Asia Program, 1976.

Oberderfor, Donald. *Tet!* New York: Doubleday & Co., 1971.

Pike, Douglas. *Viet Cong*. Cambridge, Mass.: M.I.T. Press, 1966.

———— . *War, Peace, and the Viet Cong*. Cambridge, Mass.: M.I.T. Press, 1969.

Porter, Gareth. *A Peace Denied*. Bloomington: Indiana University Press, 1975.

Race, Jeffrey. *War Comes to Long An*. Berkeley and Los Angeles: University of California Press, 1972.

Sansom, Robert L. *The Economics of Insurgency in the Mekong Delta of Vietnam*. Cambridge, Mass.: M.I.T. Press, 1970.

Scigliano, Robert. *South Vietnam: Nation Under Stress*. Boston: Houghton Mifflin Co., 1963.

Shaplen, Robert. *The Lost Revolution*. New York: Harper & Row, 1966.

Shawcross, William. *Sideshow: Kissinger, Nixon, and the Destruction of Cambodia*. New York: Simon & Schuster, 1979.

Snepp, Frank. *A Decent Interval*. New York: Random House, 1977.

Stettler, Russell (ed.). *The Military Art of People's War*. New York: Monthly Review Press, 1970.

Tanham, George. *Communist Revolutionary Warfare*. New York: Praeger Publishers, 1967.

Terzani, Tiziano. *Giai Phong! The Fall and Liberation of Saigon*. New York: St. Martin's Press, 1976.

Thompson, Robert. *No Exit from Vietnam*. New York: David McKay Co., 1969.

Tran Van Giau. *Mien Nam giu vung thanh dong* [The South on the road to victory]. Hanoi: Khoa Hoc, 1964.

Van Tien Dung. *Our Great Spring Victory*. New York: Monthly Review Press, 1977.

Vo Nguyen. *Phong trao cong Nhan Mien Nam* [The workers' movement in the South]. Hanoi: Su That, 1961.

Warner, Denis. *Not With Guns Alone*. London: Hutchinson, 1977.

Westmoreland, William C. *A Soldier Reports*. New York: Doubleday & Co., 1976.

Zagoria, Donald. *Vietnam Triangle*. New York: Pegasus, 1967.

Zasloff, Joseph J. and MacAlister Brown (eds.). *Communism in Indochina: New Perspectives*. Lexington, Mass.: D.C. Heath & Co., 1975.

COMMUNIST NEWSPAPERS AND PERIODICALS

Hoc tap [Study]. Hanoi.

La lutte. Saigon.

Nghien cuu lich su [Historical research]. Hanoi.

Nhan dan. [The people]. Hanoi.

Quan doi nhan dan [People's Army]. Hanoi.

Vietnam Courier. Hanoi.

Vietnam Studies. Hanoi.

Index

A Shau valley, 258, 267, 275, 293
Abrams, Creighton, 283–284
ACP. See Annam Communist Party
Agrovilles, 191, 203
Alliance of National Democratic and
    Peace Forces (ANDPF) (Lien Mien
    Dan Toc Dan Chu va Hoa Binh),
    269, 281
Along Bay, 120
An Khe, 238–239
An Lao valley, 247, 259
An Loc, 293–294
An Quang Buddhist Association,
    218–219
ANDPF. See Alliance of National
    Democratic and Peace Forces
Anh Sau (pseudonym), 243–244
Annam. See Central Vietnam
Annam Communist Party (ACP)
    (Annam Cong San Dang), 31–32
Anti-Imperialist National United Front,
    59
Ap Bac, battle of, 215
Apter, David, 13
Armed propaganda units, 80, 211
Army of the Republic of Vietnam
    (ARVN), 204, 215, 228, 249–250,
    252–254, 266, 273–275, 285, 294–295
  corps structure, 238
  in Franco-Vietminh War, 155
  origins of, 146
  in Vietnam War, 184, 189, 190–191,
    214–215, 221, 232, 236–237, 244,
    246–247, 257–258, 261, 270, 290,
    292, 303–305, 310–318
  First Division, 246, 267, 293, 313
  Second Division, 314

  Third Division, 294
  Fifth Division, 293–294
  Eighteenth Division, 306, 315–316
  Twenty-second Division, 294
  Twenty-third Division, 310–311
ASEAN. See Association for the
    Southeast Asian Nations
Associated State of Vietnam, 137, 140,
    169
Association for the Southeast Asian
    Nations (ASEAN), 337, 341
August Revolution, 28, 72, 122, 143,
    173, 179, 204, 209, 211, 222–223,
    253, 264, 325–327
  in Central Vietnam, 95–96
  in Hanoi, 92–93
  nature of, 9
  in North Vietnam, 91–92
  in Saigon, 96–98
  in South Vietnam, 96–98
August uprising. See August Revolution
Australia
  forces in South Vietnam, 247

Ba (pseudonym), 252–253
Ba Cut, 176
Ba To uprising, 85, 95–96, 184, 187
Bac Can, 74, 86, 131
Bac Giang Province, 85
Bac Lieu, 64
Bac Ninh Province, 76, 84
Bac Son, 74, 76
Bac Son rebellion, 61–63, 67–68, 70, 72,
    74, 77
Ban Me Thuot, 228, 267, 309–311, 313
Bandung Conference, 170

Bao Dai, 82–83, 98–99, 118, 120, 133,
    171
Bao Dai formula, 133–134, 137–139, 160
Bao Dai government, 82, 87, 139,
    163–165, 169–170, 218
Batagnan peninsula, 238
Battle of the Flags, 297
Bay of Pigs invasion, 201
Ben Cat, 122, 306, 317
Ben Thuy, 36–37
Ben Tre (Kien Hoa) Province, 115, 191
Ben Tre uprising, 191–192, 196
Berlin crisis, 206
Bien Hoa, 122
Bien Hoa Air Base, 238, 316–317
Binh Dinh Province, 159, 239, 246,
    293–294, 307–309
Binh Duong Province, 214
Binh Gia, 61
Binh Gia, battle of, 232
Binh Long Province, 293
Binh Thuan Province, 308
Binh Xuyen, 170, 176
Black Virgin Mountain, 309
Blum, Léon, 52, 125, 128
Bolovens Plateau, 159
Bolshevik Revolution, 101–102, 108,
    164, 231, 253–254, 264–265, 321,
    325
Bong Son valley, 247, 259
Border offensive (1950), 145, 147
Borodin, Michael, 17
Bourgeoisie
    and communism, 25, 29, 39, 52, 59–60,
        69, 102–104, 212, 216–218, 252
    early development of, 9
Brest-Litovsk, Treaty of, 120
Brevie, Jules, 57
Brezhnev, Leonid, 296
Brzezinski, Zbigniew, 339
Buddhism, 13, 69, 133, 170, 218–220,
    229, 247, 252, 305
    An Quang Buddhist Association,
        218–219
    Committee for the Safeguarding of
        Buddhism, 219
    in Communist strategy, 230, 252

Buddhist force, 252
Bui Chow Province, 150
Bui Quang Chieu, 11, 115
Bundy, McGeorge, 236
Burma, 223

Ca Mau peninsula, 115, 176, 184, 332
Cam Lo, 258
Cam Ranh Bay, 338
Cambodia, 62, 122, 142–143, 157, 171,
    176, 184, 232, 243–244, 246–247,
    259–260, 265, 273, 278, 283–288,
    302–303, 308
    invasion of, 283–288
    Lon Nol coup, 284
    relations with Vietnam, 283–284,
        336–339
Cambodian People's Revolutionary
    Party (Pracheachon), 283
Camp Carroll, 258
Can Tho, 64, 98, 115, 307
Canton, 17, 19, 24–25, 65–66, 133
Cao-Bac-Lang liberated area, 86–87
Cao Bang Province, 76, 80, 84, 86, 132,
    144–145
Cao Dai, 77, 85, 97–98, 115, 134, 137
    and Diem regime, 171, 176
    rivalry with Vietminh, 121–122, 132,
        176
CAPs. *See* Combined Action Platoons
Carpentier, General, 147
Carter Doctrine, 331
Castro, Fidel, 328
Catholic National Salvation
    Association, 110
Catholics, 137, 170, 185, 229, 232, 252,
    305
    in D.R.V., 110, 133
Catroux, Georges, 57–58, 60
Cédile, Jean, 114
CEMA. *See* Council for Mutual
    Economic Assistance
Central Committee. *See* Vietnamese
    Workers' Party, Central Committee
Central Highlands, 158, 160, 184–185,
    191, 210, 227–228, 236, 238–239,
    247, 250, 265–267, 273, 293,

303–304, 306–311, 319

Central Highlands Autonomy
  Movement (Uy Ban Dan Toc Tu Tri
  Tay Nguyen), 216

Central Intelligence Agency (CIA), 228,
  277

Central Military Party Committee. *See*
  Vietnamese Workers' Party, Central
  Military Party Committee

Central Minority School, 185

Central Office for South Vietnam
  (COSVN), 174, 195–196, 205–207,
  212–213, 223, 232, 259, 266, 274,
  278–279, 285–286, 298, 307
  abolished, 175
  Current Affairs Section, 262
  founded, 138
  reestablished, 195–196

Central Vietnam (Annam), 7–8, 11–12,
  25, 30, 33–35, 38–41, 52, 66, 125,
  150, 155, 159
  Regional Committee in, 38, 40–41, 186

Chang Fa-k'uei, 67, 77–78, 80–81

Chen, King, 160

Chi Né forest, 121

Chiang Kai-shek, 49, 60, 64, 71, 101, 135

Chieu Hoi program, 248

China, 160, 194
  assistance to D.R.V., 139, 156, 161,
    164–165, 224, 242, 256, 304
  founding of P.R.C., 139
  at Geneva Conference, 162–163
  influence over Vietnam, 8, 49, 67, 69,
    71–72, 78, 128–131, 139–144, 150
  occupation forces in Vietnam,
    110–112
  relations with Cambodia, 285
  relations with D.R.V., 170, 226, 245,
    256, 337–341
  use of, in Vietnamese Communist
    strategy, 74, 79, 139–144

Chinese Civil War, 101–103

Chinese Communist Party (CCP),
  24–25, 29–30, 49, 64, 73, 101, 103,
  130, 135, 153, 179, 235
  relations with Vietnamese
    Communists, 49, 66, 139,

142, 226, 337

Chinese Nationalist Party (KMT)
  (Kuomintang), 12, 22, 24–25, 29–30,
  49, 74, 101

Chinese revolution, 21–22, 35, 101, 153,
  164, 224, 322

Chingsi, 67, 74, 77

Cholon, 220, 269, 333

Chu Lai, 238, 312, 314

Chu Pong Mountain, 239

Chu Van Tan, 74–76, 84, 340

Chung King, 76

CIA. *See* Central Intelligence Agency

CIDG. *See* Civilian Irregular Defense
  Groups

CINCPAC. *See* Commander in Chief,
  Pacific

Civic Action Program, 180

Civil Operations and Rural
  Development Support (CORDS),
  248

Civilian Irregular Defense Groups
  (CIDG), 228, 239

Clifford, Clark, 270

Coastal plains region, 10, 211

Cochin China, 52
  communism in, 46–47, 52–55, 58–59,
    62 64, 73, 113–117
  economic conditions, 10, 33–34, 36,
    39, 62, 83, 85
  French conquest of, 7–8
  nationalism, 12, 52
  1940 uprising in, 62–63
  political situation in, 7, 11–12, 52–53
  Regional Committee in, 62–63, 114

Colby, William, 228

Cold War, 168, 170, 331, 340

Collectivization, 109, 334–335

Colonial Commission, 52, 54

Combined Action Platoons (CAPs), 247

Comintern, 12, 66, 68
  Far Eastern Bureau, 40
  ideological direction, 17, 22, 24–25,
    30–32, 34–35, 41–43, 47–48, 50–54,
    69
  relations with ICP, 32–33, 35, 38,
    41–43, 45–48, 50–54

relations with Revolutionary Youth
League, 17–18, 30–32
training programs in Moscow, 16–17,
32, 43, 45–46
Second National Congress (1920), 7,
30, 35
Fifth National Congress (1924), 16, 21,
30
Sixth National Congress (1928), 30
Seventh National Congress (1935), 51,
68
Commander in Chief, Pacific
(CINCPAC), 239
Committee for the Safeguarding of
Buddhism, 218
Committee of Resistance and
Administration (CRA), 136
Committee of the South, 97, 113–115
Communist Party of the Soviet Union
(CPSU), 28, 45, 71
Twentieth National Congress (1956),
176–178
Con Thien, 265–266
Conference of Communist and Workers'
Parties in Socialist Countries, 182,
194
Confucianism, 100
and communism, 25, 27
decline of, in Vietnam, 8, 13
ethical system, 25, 27–29
Constitutionalist Party, 11–12, 24,
54–55, 58, 60, 79, 137
CORDS. See Civil Operations and Rural
Development Support
COSVN. See Central Office for South
Vietnam
Council for Mutual Economic
Assistance (CEMA), 337
CRA. See Committee of Resistance and
Administration
CRIMP document, 208, 210–212, 222
Cuba, 224, 243, 328
Cuban missile crisis, 224
Cuong De, Prince, 61
Cuu Long (pseudonym), 250
Cuu quoc hoi. See National salvation
associations

Da Nang, 11, 131, 156, 184, 211, 228,
238, 252, 254, 267, 293, 309,
311–315, 328, 338
Dak To, 265
Dalat, 120
Dalat conference (1946), 120
Dan Chung (The people), 58
d'Argenlieu, Admiral Thierry, 120, 133
de Lattre de Tassigny, General, 146–147,
150
de Lattre line, 147, 151
Declaration of Independence, 99–100
Decoux, Jean, 60–61, 84
DeGaulle, Charles, 80–82
Demilitarized Zone (DMZ), 210, 236,
246, 257–259, 261, 266, 276, 293,
297, 303
Democratic People's Republic of
Kampuchea (DPRK), 337
Democratic Republic of Vietnam
(D.R.V.)
bombing by U.S. Air Force, 236, 249
Declaration of Independence, 99–100
economic policy, 105–110
effect of war on, 249
election of 1946, 117
at Geneva Conference, 162–165
negotiations with United States,
206–208, 230–231, 254–256, 273,
280–283, 291, 295–297, 316
political system, 109, 112–113
religious policies, 110
tax policies, 109
"Denounce the Communists" (To Cong)
campaign, 174, 181, 183, 190
Deo Van Long, 132
Dien Bien Phu, battle of, 158, 160–162,
275, 297
Dinh Tuong Province, 260
DMZ. See Demilitarized Zone
Dong Ha, 258, 294
Dong Hoi, 236, 240
Dong Khe, 144–145
Dong Minh Hoi. See Vietnamese
Revolutionary League
Dong Xoai, 238
DPRK. See Democratic People's Republic

of Kampuchea
Duong Bac Mai, 113
Duong Van Minh, 220, 315, 317–318
Durbrow, Eldridge, 193
Dutch East Indies, 30, 166

Easter Offensive, 291–295, 297
Education
  under D.R.V., 109
  under French, 8
Eisenhower, Dwight D., 170–171, 173,
  201–202
Elliott, David, 291
Erikson, Erik, 27
External Direction Bureau (Ban Chi
  Huy Hai Ngoai), 46, 48, 53

Fall, Bernard, 215, 246
"False negotiations," 130
Famine, 82, 102–103, 108, 136
Farm Credit Bureau, 109
Fatherland Front (Mat Tran To Quoc),
  175, 196
FCP. *See* French Communist Party
FEF. *See* France, French Expeditionary
  Forces
Fishhook, 285
Fontainebleau conference, 120–121
"Four no's," 303–304
Four points (NLF), 208, 241, 276
France
  colonial system in Indochina, 7–8,
    42–43, 52, 76
  conquest of Vietnam, 7
  defense of Indochinese Union, 57
  economic policies in Vietnam, 10
  French Expeditionary Forces, 146,
    155, 158, 164
  military mission in South China,
    80–81
  negotiations with D.R.V., 117–121,
    124–125, 127–128, 160–162
  strategy in Franco-Vietminh War,
    131–132, 144–147, 151, 154–160
  suppression of Communists, 40–41,
    46, 58–60, 63–64, 75, 82, 114–117,
    138, 323–324

Treaty of 1884, 82
Vichy government, 60, 75
French Communist Party (FCP), 16, 52,
  54, 58, 97, 116, 120
French Union, 118, 128, 160
FUNK. *See* National United Front of
  Kampuchea

Gandhi, Mahatma, 13, 27, 329
Geertz, Clifford, 166
General offensive, 129–130, 143–152,
  221–224, 263–264, 292–293
General uprising, 76, 101, 222–223, 274
  in August Revolution, 91–97, 204
  conditions for, 73
  origins of conception, 59–60, 62–63, 72
  preparations for, 76, 79–80, 83–89,
    252–254, 263–264, 292–293
Geneva Conference
  in 1954, 160–165, 169–170, 172, 209,
    217, 227, 231, 261, 325
  in 1962, 206–207
Germany, 57, 59, 76, 120, 249
Gia Dinh Province, 59
Go Cong, 115
Goodman, Allan, 207, 302
Government of Resistance and National
  Reconstruction, 118
Government of Vietnam (GVN), 171,
  198, 201–203, 223, 228–229, 238,
  242, 295–297
  Civic Action Program, 181
  collapse of, 314–318
  economic policies, 181, 305
  formation of, 169
  political system, 172, 181, 261
  U.S. support for, 170
  weakness of, 233, 237, 261, 264,
    270–271, 294–295, 305, 318–320,
    322–326
Gracey, General Douglas, 114
Great Britain, 76, 87, 119, 144, 148
  at Geneva Conference, 162
  occupation troops in Vietnam, 87,
    107, 113–115
Groupes Mobiles, 151, 155, 157, 159
Guerrilla war, 35, 72, 79

in Ho Chi Minh's strategy, 22–23, 71–72
in South Vietnam, 191, 204–205, 209, 212, 228, 245, 279–280, 289
in Vietminh strategy, 61–62, 68, 70–71, 73–74, 79, 116, 121, 129–131, 135, 138
GVN. *See* Government of Vietnam

Ha Dong Province, 95, 119, 125, 156
Ha Giang Province, 86
Ha Tinh Province, 35, 37, 191
Hai Duong Province, 156
Hai Van Pass, 312–313
Haiphong, 57, 61, 121, 123, 149, 161, 165
Haiphong incident (1946), 123–124
Hanoi, 9, 25, 31, 39, 57, 61–62, 74, 77, 82–84, 86, 91–96, 115, 120, 122, 124–125, 131–132, 149, 152, 161, 164–165, 190, 193, 217, 240, 339
  Party Municipal Committee, 93, 98–99, 111, 152
Hanyang, 65
Harkins, Paul, 206
Harriman, Averell, 201, 207
Heng Samrin, 337
Herter, Christian, 193
Hiep Hoa, 85
Hitler, Adolf, 50, 58
Ho Chi Minh, 29, 38, 49, 68, 87–88, 98–100, 102–103, 108–109, 116–118, 121–125, 127, 132, 140–141, 149, 154, 163–164, 167, 182–183, 195, 227, 340
  activities in China, 17–19, 23–24, 27, 29, 32–33, 40–41, 64–68, 77–84
  activities in France, 16
  activities in the Soviet Union, 16–17, 21, 29, 45, 64
  death of, 279, 289
  early life, 15–16
  influence on Vietnamese revolution, 4, 27, 32–33, 41, 48, 71–72, 75, 79–80, 122–123, 325–326
  intellectual growth, 7, 20–29, 43, 48,

65–66, 70–73
  president of D.R.V., 99, 109–112, 118
  The Road to Revolution (Duong Cach Menh), 19–21, 27–28
Ho Chi Minh Campaign, 314–318
Ho Chi Minh trail, 228, 250, 290, 302
Ho Ngoc Lam, 67
Ho-Sainteny Agreement, 117–121, 128, 160
Hoa Binh, battle of, 151
Hoa Binh Province, 121, 150
Hoa Hao, 85, 97–98, 115, 134, 137
  and Diem regime, 171, 176
  rivalry with Vietminh, 121–122, 132, 176
Hoang Dinh Giam, 128, 133
Hoang Dinh Giong, 75
Hoang Hoa Tham, 74
Hoang Quoc Viet, 67–68, 97, 116
Hoang Tung, 301
Hoang Van Hoan, 355(n21, 23), 360(n34), 368(n11)
Hoang Van Thu, 68, 71, 75, 77
Hoc Mon, 59, 316
Hoc Tap (Study), 179, 224–225, 231, 249–250, 301
Hong Bang dynasty, 73
Hong Kong, 32, 34, 38, 40–41, 49, 65, 133
Honolulu conference, 248
"Hope of Youth" (Thanh Nien Cao Vong) Party, 12
Hsiao Wen, General, 80, 111
Hué, 7, 15, 83, 95–96, 99, 131, 169, 218–219, 247, 252, 267–268, 275, 312–313, 328
Hung Yen Province, 152
Huynh Phu So, 132

I Corps, 238, 247, 252, 257, 269, 273–275
Ia Drang valley, battle of, 239, 246
ICC. *See* International Control Commission
ICP. *See* Indochinese Communist Party
India, 223
Indochinese Communist League (Dong Duong Cong San Lien Doan), 31–32
Indochinese Communist Party (ICP)

(Dang Cong San Dong Duong)
abolition of, in 1945, 112
Central Committee, 38–41, 45–46,
  51, 59, 62–63, 65–67, 76, 86, 97, 110,
  116, 120, 122, 125, 138
defense of Indochina, 57–59
External Direction Bureau, 46, 48, 53
factionalism in, 53
formation of, 31–33
founding meeting, 32–33
membership, 35, 41, 45–47, 58–59
name, 38–39, 142–143
permanent bureau, 40
Political Program, 74–75
relations with the bourgeoisie, 32
relations with the Comintern, 34–35,
  39–43, 45–49, 54
relations with the FCP, 54
relations with the nationalist parties,
  46, 48, 51–55, 59–60, 66–67, 69–71,
  77, 121–123
relations with the peasantry, 32, 35,
  52–53
relations with the proletariat, 32, 35,
  52–53
reorganized as VWP, 141–143
Standing Committee, 84, 91–92, 95,
  118–119, 134
Second Plenum (1931), 4
1937 Plenum, 53
Sixth Plenum (1939), 59–62, 153
Seventh Plenum (1940), 62–63, 70
Eighth Plenum (1941), 67–71, 73
Ninth Plenum (1945), 87–89, 109
Indochinese congress, 52, 54
Indochinese Federation, 143, 336
Indonesia, 223
Infiltration, 190–191, 228, 236, 239, 250,
  258, 275, 303
Institute for the Study of National and
  Colonial Questions, 64
Intercolonial Union, 16
International Control Commission
  (ICC), 230
Interzone V, 156, 158, 184
Iran, 321
Iron Triangle, 259, 306
Isaacs, Harold, 116

Japan
  expansion into Southeast Asia, 50, 57,
    60–61, 76
  influence on Vietnamese nationalism,
    8, 15, 61, 77
  policies in Indochina, 76–77, 82–83,
    92, 95
  surrender of, in 1945, 92, 95, 113
Johnson, Lyndon B., 221, 230, 235,
  238, 247

Kampuchean National United Front for
  National Salvation (KNUFNS), 337
K'ang Yu-wei, 8
KCP. *See* Khmer Communist Party
Kennedy, John F., 201, 221, 319
Kent State massacre, 219
Khe Sanh, 257–261, 266, 303
  battle of, 274–276
Khmer Communist Party (KCP), 163,
  283–285, 288
  origins of, 142–143, 163
  relations with Vietnamese
    Communists, 283–285, 336–337
Khmer Rouge (Red Khmer), 162, 308
Khrushchev, Nikita, 177, 195, 201, 224,
  231–232, 256, 329
Kiangsi Province, 49, 64–65
Kim Tuan, 312
Kissinger, Henry, 286–287, 291,
  294–296, 298–299, 303
KMT. *See* Chinese Nationalist Party
KNUFNS. *See* Kampuchean National
  United Front for National
  Salvation
Kontum Province, 159, 193, 214, 267,
  293–294, 307, 310–311, 315
Korea, 223, 226, 243
  forces in South Vietnam, 247
Kosygin, Alexei, 232, 240–241
Krestintern. *See* Peasant International
Kunming, 80–81
Kuomintang. *See* Chinese Nationalist
  Party
Kwangsi Province, 65–66, 78
Kweichow Province, 81
Kweilin, 65

Kweiyang, 67

La lutte (The struggle), 53–54
Lai Chau, 152, 158
Land reform
    in Communist strategy, 69–70, 102,
        136, 153, 154
    in GVN, 181–182, 215–216, 289–290
"Land-to-the-tiller" program, 289–290,
    332
Lang Coc, 76
Lang Son, 61–62, 74, 84, 86, 132,
    144–145, 161, 338
Lang Ve, 275
Laniel, Joseph, 160
Lao Cai, 144–145, 338
Lao tu tap chi (The prison review), 46
Laos, 142–143, 152, 157–159, 161–162,
    170, 188, 201, 206, 223, 243–244,
    250, 257–258, 260, 278, 293, 303,
    333–337
    Geneva settlement of (1962), 206, 223,
        226, 230
    invasion of, in 1971, 290–291
Laotian People's Revolutionary Party,
    142–143
Laotian solution, 230
Le Duan, 116, 138, 176, 182, 187, 194,
    221, 225–227, 231–232, 243, 245,
    254–255, 278, 279, 304, 308–309, 340
    The Path of Revolution in the South,
        178–180, 185
    secretary general, 182–183, 193
Le Duc Tho, 177, 194, 225, 227, 286,
    291, 297, 315
Le Hong Phong, 46, 51, 63
Le Quang Ba, 75, 340
Le Quang Liem, 58
League for the Independence of
    Vietnam. *See* Vietminh
Lenin, Vladimir I., 7, 10, 16, 21, 22, 28,
    43, 69, 72, 98, 165, 179, 224–225,
    265, 321–322
    "Theses on the National and Colonial
        Questions," 7, 16, 35
Lewy, Guenter, 267
Li Ta-Chao, 12–13

Liang Ch'i-ch'ao, 8
Lien Viet Front, 143
Limited war, 242
Lin Piao, Marshall, 245
Liuchow, 81
Loc Ninh, 265, 293, 306
Lon Nol, 284, 287
Long An Province, 327
Long Binh, 317
Lu Han, General, 111
Luang Prabang, 152, 158
Lungchow, 65
Luong Van Chi, 74–75

Macao, 51
MACV. *See* Military Assistance
    Command, Vietnam
Manchuria, 57
Mansfield, Michael, 239
Manuilsky, Dmitri, 24, 50
Mao Khe, 149
Mao Tse-tung, 49, 64, 73, 142, 225,
    344(n15)
    Maoist strategy, 49, 64–66, 69, 71,
        128–131, 150, 179, 184, 188,
        225–226, 240, 255, 322
    Mao's "three treasures," 140
Marxism
    appeal in Vietnam, 25–27, 324–326
    in D.R.V., 141–142
    early appearance in Vietnam, 14–18
    in Revolutionary Youth League, 17–18
Mass associations
    origins of, 53
    in South Vietnam, 173, 196, 217
    and Vietminh, 69, 75, 93
McAlister, John T., 28
McNamara, Robert, 221, 238, 261
Meiji Restoration, 8, 35
Mekong river delta, 10, 12, 64, 86, 108,
    137–138, 171, 184, 191, 211, 238,
    266–267, 274, 289–290, 295, 306–307
Mendès-France, Pierre, 145
Mikoyan, Anastas, 177
Military Assistance Command, Vietnam
    (MACV), 229, 236–237, 247–248,
    250, 260, 283–284

Military Management Committee, 332
Military Revolutionary Council, 220, 229
Militia, 75, 122, 131, 186, 212, 291
Mini-Tet, 275
Mo Cay District, 192
Mo Nhai, 61
Mong Cay, 144–145
Moutet, Marius, 121
Munich Conference, 4, 120, 330
Mus, Paul, 100, 128, 159, 166
My Tho, 62, 115, 215, 260, 307

Na Ngan, 80
Na Sam, 152
Nam Dinh, 36, 67, 156
National Assembly, 109, 112, 123, 154
National Council of Reconciliation and Concord (NCRC), 296
National Front for the Liberation of South Vietnam (NLF) (Mat Tran Dan Toc Giai Phong Mien Nam Viet Nam), 3, 213, 221, 228, 232, 235, 242, 269, 281, 298
  First National Congress, 215
  founding of, 195–197
  organization, 197
National Liberation Committee, 88
National minorities, 132
  Communist policies toward, 74–75, 184–186
  in Vietnam War, 216, 228
National Salvation Army (Cuu Quoc Quan), 67, 74–76, 84
National salvation associations (*Cuu quoc hoi*), 69, 75, 93
National United Front, 64, 96, 133
National United Front of Kampuchea (FUNK), 285
National United Front of Vietnam (Hoi lien hiep quoc dan Viet Nam), 121
Nationalism
  in Comintern strategy, 48, 52
  in Communist strategy, 67–70, 323
  early stages, 7–14
  and peasantry, 10–11
  reformists, 11

rivalry with Communists, 24–26, 48, 54–55, 121–123
  urban, 9–14
  weakness of, 13–14, 322, 324
Nationalist Party of Vietnam. *See* Vietnamese Nationalist Party
Navarre, General Henri, 146, 154–159, 162
Navarre Plan, 154–157
Nazi-Soviet pact, 58
Nazism, 50, 59
Nechaev, Sergei, 28
New Economic Areas (NEAs), 332–333
New life hamlets, 248
New Revolutionary Party. *See* Tan Viet (New Revolutionary Party)
Nghe An Province, 15, 29–30, 35–37, 116, 191, 345(n18)
Nghe Tinh revolt, 47, 50, 51, 68, 72, 77, 327
  causes, 33–35
  French response to, 40–43
  and ICP, 35–43
  results, 40–41, 43, 45
  Soviets, 37, 40
Nghia Lo, 152
Ngo Dinh Diem, 169–172, 174–175, 180–181, 187, 189, 218–219, 221
  "Denounce the Communists" campaign, 174–175, 181, 183–184, 188, 190–192
  fall of, 219–221
  policies, 171, 214
  on unification elections, 172–173, 180
  weakness of, 204
Ngo Dinh Nhu, 219
Ngo Duc Tri, 40
Ngo Quang Truong, 311
Nguyen Ai Quoc. *See* Ho Chi Minh
Nguyen An Ninh, 12, 14, 323
Nguyen Binh, 117, 122, 132, 137–139
Nguyen Cao Ky, 248, 261
Nguyen Chanh Thi, 247, 252
Nguyen Chi Thanh, 194, 196, 224, 248–249, 254, 256–257, 261, 263, 280
Nguyen Dinh Tu, 345(n27)
Nguyen dynasty, 7, 99

Nguyen Hai Than, 77, 112, 133
Nguyen Huu Tho, 172, 197
Nguyen Khang, 92
Nguyen Phan Long, 137–138
Nguyen Phong Sac, 40
Nguyen Tat Thanh. *See* Ho Chi Minh
Nguyen Thi Binh, 315
Nguyen Thi Dinh, 192, 197
Nguyen Thi Minh Khai, 63
Nguyen Tuong Tam, 133
Nguyen Van Cu, 59, 63
Nguyen Van Sam, 115
Nguyen Van Tam, 138
Nguyen Van Tao, 97–98
Nguyen Van Thieu, 248, 252, 261, 266,
    291, 295–297, 303, 305–306, 311
Nguyen Van Vinh, 245, 255–256
Nha Be, 317
Nha Trang, 117, 211, 267, 311, 315
Nhan dan (The people), 177, 187, 208,
    245, 258, 263, 292
Ninh Binh, 149, 157
Ninh Giang, 156
Nishihara, General, 61
Nixon, Richard, 282, 285, 295–296, 299,
    303, 307
NLF. *See* National Front for the
    Liberation of South Vietnam
North Vietnam, 7, 10, 12, 67, 87
    communism in, 25, 29–30, 41–43, 47,
        52, 54–55, 61–62, 79, 103–105
    economic conditions in, 34, 82–83, 85
    Military Revolutionary Committee in,
        85
    nationalism in, 12, 52
    political system, 7–8, 52
Northern expedition, 64
Northwest, 132, 155, 157
Nuclear Test Ban Treaty, 224
Nung minority, 68

October resolution, 205
Office of Strategic Services (OSS), 81
Opération Atlante, 159
Operation Cedar Falls, 259
Operation Fairfax, 259
Operation Hop Tac, 229, 232

Operation Junction City, 259
Operation Rolling Thunder, 236, 255
Orgwald. *See* Manuilsky, Dmitri
OSS. *See* Office of Strategic Services
Overseas Chinese, 11, 69, 332–333, 338

Pacific War, 75–76, 88, 92, 101, 325
Pac Bo, 67–71, 76, 79
Pac Bo Plenum. *See* Indochinese
    Communist Party, Eighth Plenum
Pacification, 248, 259–260, 262, 277,
    289–290
Paise, 81
Paracel Islands, 338
Paris Agreement (1973), 295–299,
    301–302
Parrot's Beak, 176, 285
Pathet Lao, 163, 201
Peasant associations, 136
Peasant International (Krestintern), 17,
    21
Peasantry
    in Annam, 41–42
    in Cochin China, 10, 33–34, 41–42,
        47, 54–55, 62, 86
    in Comintern strategy, 30, 41–43,
        47–49, 50, 182
    and communism, 17–23, 35–36, 52–55,
        69–71, 77, 86, 102–104, 136,
        153–154, 252
    conditions under colonialism, 10–11,
        33–34, 76–77, 82, 102–103
    revolts, 11, 33–35, 41–43
    in Tonkin, 34, 41–42, 85
Pentagon Papers, 2–3
People's Army of Vietnam (PAVN), 110,
    112, 115, 121, 245
    in August Revolution, 91
    founding of, 80, 85
    in Franco-Vietminh War, 127
    moderation of, 180, 280
    origins of, 37
    in South Vietnam, 228, 236, 239, 241,
        250, 259, 266–268, 274–275,
        292–298, 309–318
People's Liberation Armed Forces
    (PLAF), 1, 196, 212–215, 222,

227–228, 232, 237, 244, 246–250,
257, 266–268, 274, 278–279,
288–290, 302
organization, 212–213
origins, 176, 184, 193
relations with Cambodians, 287–288
sources of appeal, 327–329
strains of war on, 261–263, 276–277,
289–290
People's Liberation Army (PLA). *See*
People's Army of Vietnam
People's Republic of China. *See* China
People's Revolutionary Party (PRP)
(Dang Nhan Dan Cach Mang
Viet Nam), 213
People's Self-Defense Force Program, 290
Personalism, 174
Phai Cat, 80
Pham Cong Tac, 132
Pham Hong Thai, 19
Pham Hung, 194, 263, 315
Pham Ngoc Thach, 86
Pham Quynh, 115
Pham Van Dong, 66–67, 77–78, 120,
133, 172, 230, 241, 296
Pham Van Phu, 340
Phan Boi Chau, 8, 14, 61, 66, 77
Phan Dang Luu, 62–64
Phan Dinh Phung, 7, 59
Phan Ke Toai, 87, 133
Phan Rang, 315
Phan Thiet, 15
Phat Diem Province, 150, 156
Philippines, the, 76
Pho Lu, 145
Phoenix Program, 248, 277
Phoumi Nousavan, 201
Phu Ly, 149
Phu My, 259
Phu Rieng rubber plantation, 35
Phu Yen Province, 159, 239, 262
Phuc Quoc Party, 66, 78
Phuc Yen Province, 95
Phung Chi Kien, 66–68, 74–75
Phuoc Binh, 308–309
Phuoc Long Province, 238, 308
Phuoc Tuy Province, 293

Pike, Douglas, 279
Plain of Jars, 158
Plain of Reeds, 64, 115, 122, 135, 138,
176, 190, 211
Plei Me, 239
Pleiku, 159, 239, 307, 310–311
Pleiku incident, 236
Pol Pot, 283, 336–337
Popular Front
in France, 52
origins of, 51–52
results, 54–55, 58
in Vietnam, 52–54
Porter, Gareth, 294–295
Potsdam Conference, 87
Pracheachon. *See* Cambodian People's
Revolutionary Party
P.R.C. *See* China
Proletariat
in Comintern strategy, 30, 47–50
and communism, 19–21, 30, 35–36,
52–55, 69, 77, 138–139, 211–212,
217–218, 252
conditions in Vietnam, 33–34, 76–77,
108
early development, 9–10
in Tonkin, 77, 85
Provisional Resistance Committee, 122
Provisional Revolutionary Government
of South Vietnam (PRG), 192,
281–282, 289, 295–296, 298,
303–304, 307, 315, 317–318

Quang Nam Province, 11, 116, 159, 193
Quang Ngai Province, 85, 95, 110, 116,
159, 184–185, 191–192, 247, 260,
277, 311
Quang Tin Province, 311–312, 314
Quang Tri Province, 116, 257, 267, 294,
303, 306
Qui Nhon, 236, 259, 267
Quoc ngu (national language), 8, 37, 87

Race, Jeffrey, 327
Radical Socialist Party (Dang Xa Hoi
Cap Tien), 197
RAND Corporation, 216

Red River delta, 7–8, 10, 14, 34, 61,
    74–75, 79, 91, 95, 103, 123, 131,
    146–147, 149–150, 156–157, 165,
    250, 338–339
Refugees, 251–252, 260, 305, 333, 338
Regional Committee for the South (Xu
    Uy Nam Bo), 174–176, 178, 181,
    193
Revolutionary Youth League (Viet Nam
    Thanh Nien Cach Mang Dong Chi
    Hoi), 66, 130
  dissolution, 29–33
  First Congress, 31
  formation of, 17–18
  leadership, 29, 31–32
  membership, 18–19, 23–25, 28–30, 45
  policies, 19, 23–25, 33, 48, 55, 72
  relations with nationalists, 24–26, 30,
    48
Rockpile, the, 258
Roth, Andrew, 140, 241
Royal National United Government of
    Kampuchea (GRUNK), 285
Rural development centers, 185
Rusk, Dean, 235

Saigon, 9, 12–13, 15, 29, 39, 42, 53–54,
    59, 64, 85–86, 96–98, 110, 113–116,
    120, 136–139, 171, 175–176, 191,
    201, 203, 209–210, 214, 217,
    219–221, 229–231, 235, 238–239,
    246, 254, 257, 264, 266, 268–269,
    306, 310–312, 319, 328
  Party Municipal Committee, 96, 114
Saigon-Cholon Peace Movement,
    173–174, 196
Saigon Municipal Council, 53, 58
Saigon Uprising Committee, 269
Sainteny, Jean, 81–82, 117–118
SAM. *See* Surface-to-air missiles
Sam Neua, 152, 158
Scholar-gentry, 8
Scorched earth tactics, 116
Serong, Ted, 294
Shansi Province, 64
Shaplen, Robert, 277
Sharp, Admiral Grant, 239

Shawcross, William, 286
Siam, Gulf of, 98, 283, 336
Sian, 64
Sihanouk, Norodom, 283–285, 287, 308,
    336
Singapore, 41
Snepp, Frank, 302
Soc Trang, 64
Socialist Republic of Vietnam (SRV)
  founded, 332
  policies, 332–341
Son Hoa, 312
Son Ngoc Minh, 283
Son Tay Province, 156
Song Be, 238, 265
Soong Ch'ing-ling (Madame Sun Yat
    Sen), 49
South Vietnam Democratic Party (Dang
    Dan Chu Mien Nam), 197
Southeast Asian Treaty Organization
    (SEATO), 170, 331
Souvanna Phouma, 201
Soviet Union, 49, 57, 64, 88, 119–120,
    130, 201
  assistance to D.R.V., 161, 164, 182,
    194–195, 224–225, 231–232,
    241–242, 256, 304, 333, 338–341
  at Geneva, 162
  relations with D.R.V., 116, 127, 135,
    170, 177, 182–183, 224–225, 240,
    337–341
"Special war," 204–205, 223, 242
Spratly Islands, 338
Stalin, Joseph, 30, 38, 51, 58, 59, 64–65,
    135, 142, 170
Stalin School, 16, 32, 35, 43, 45–47, 50,
    117, 123
Strategic hamlets, 203, 208, 214–215,
    228
Sukarno, 223, 329
Sun Yat-sen, 8, 12, 17, 24–25, 112
Sûreté, 14, 17, 45–47, 346(n28)
Surface-to-air missiles (SAM), 241, 303
Szechwan Province, 65

Ta Thu Thau, 323
T'ai Federation, 132, 157

Tam Dao Mountains, 149
Tam Tam Xa (Association of like minds), 345(n18)
Tan An, 64, 97
Tan My, 312
Tan Son Nhut Airport, 268, 275, 316
Tan Trao, 84–85, 87, 91, 124
Tan Trao Conference. *See* Indochinese Communist Party, Ninth Plenum
Tan Viet (New Revolutionary Party), 12, 24, 30–31, 48, 66
Tap chi Cong san (*Communist Review*), 47–49, 148
Tay Ninh Province, 115, 135, 259, 286, 309, 311, 315–316
Taylor, Maxwell, 203, 235–236, 238
Teng Hsiao-p'ing, 226
Tet Offensive, 263–274, 280–281, 292–293, 319
Thai Binh Province, 156–157
Thai Nguyen, 74, 76, 84
Thai Nguyen Province, 84, 86, 91
Thailand (Siam), 32, 57, 62
Thakhek, 159
Thanh Nien (Youth), 19
Third Vietnam, 303, 310
Thompson, Robert K., 203, 215
Thu Dao Mot, 122, 136
Tien Phong (Vanguard), 292
To Huu, 75, 225
Ton Duc Thang, 10, 29, 133, 196
Ton That Dinh, 252
Tonkin. *See* North Vietnam
Tonkin, Gulf of, 57, 230–231, 257
Tonkin Gulf Resolution, 230, 256
Tra Bong District, 186
Tra Bong uprising, 191–193
Tran Huy Lieu, 99
Tran Nam Trung, 196
Tran Phu, 32, 35, 40–41, 46
Tran Trong Kim, 82, 87, 92–93, 98
Tran Van Cung, 30–31
Tran Van Giau, 46, 63, 96–97, 114–115, 117, 132, 184, 213, 347(n51)
Tran Van Hung, 317
Tran Van Tra, 137

Tri Quang, 218–219, 229, 252
Tribune Indochinoise, 58
Trotsky, Leon, 94, 165
Trotskyites, 53–54, 58, 101, 113, 115
Truman, Harry S, 146
Truong Boi Cong, 78
Truong Chinh, 67–68, 71–72, 74, 84, 88, 91, 129, 136, 148, 152–154, 168, 177, 277–278
  The Resistance Will Win, 129–131
  secretary general of VWP, 141, 183, 189
Truong Son (pseudonym), 257
Tu Hieu estuary, 313
Tuy Hoa, 247, 312
Tuyen Quang Province, 84, 86, 91, 121, 131–132, 141

U Minh forest, 115, 122, 135, 184, 211
U Nu, 223, 329
U Thant, 230
United Nations, 182, 230–231, 337
United States, 190, 194–195, 243, 337–340
  counterinsurgency program, 203, 223
  early involvement in Vietnam, 81, 116, 119
  entrance into Pacific War, 75–76
  and Franco-Vietminh War, 127, 137, 142, 144, 148–149, 160, 163, 165, 168
  and GVN, 169–171, 187, 201–203, 205–206, 214, 218, 220–221, 229–230, 235–240, 269–271, 295–299, 315–318
  invasion of Cambodia, 285–287, 305
  Joint Chiefs of Staff, 230
  negotiations, 207–208, 230–231, 241, 254–256, 280–283, 291, 295–297
  strategy in South Vietnam, 236–238, 246–248, 259–261
  War Powers Act, 304
  wartime activities in South China, 81
  withdrawal from Vietnam, 315–318
U.S. Air Force
  bombing of the north, 232, 236–237, 240, 256, 296–297, 299

U.S. Army, 244, 249, 264, 266–271, 292
  Civil Operations and Rural
    Development Support
    (CORDS), 248
  First Cavalry (Airmobile) Division,
    238–239, 246–247, 259
  First Infantry Division, 246–257
  Fourth Infantry Division, 246, 260
  introduction of, into South Vietnam,
    236–240, 246
  origins of role in South Vietnam,
    296–299
  Vietnamization, 292
  withdrawal from South Vietnam,
    296–299
U.S. Marines, 238–239, 246–247,
    257–258
  Combined Action Platoons (CAPs),
    247

Van Tien Dung, 176, 280, 290, 302, 304,
    308–309, 311–318
Van Tuong, battle of, 239
Vanguard Youth (Thanh Nien Tien
    Phong), 86, 96–97, 113
Vasilyeva, Madame, 123
Versailles Peace Conference, 16
Vichy government, 60, 75
Viet Bac, 63, 67, 74–76, 79, 80, 85–86,
    88, 131–132, 134–135, 143, 145, 150,
    155, 158–159, 338
Viet Cong. *See* People's Liberation
    Armed Forces
Viet Nam Cach Menh Dong Minh Hoi.
    See Vietnamese Revolutionary
    League
Viet Nam Doc Lap Dong Minh. *See*
    Vietminh
Viet Nam Giai Phong Dong Minh Hoi.
    See Vietnamese Liberation League
Vietminh (Viet Nam Doc Lap Dong
    Minh, or League for the
    Independence of Vietnam)
  abolished, 143
  attack French in Hanoi, 124–125, 128
  foundation of, 68
  name, 68

National Congress (1945), 87–88, 91
  negotiations with French, 117–121,
    124–125, 127–128, 159–160
  organization, 75, 136, 138, 197
  origins of, 67–68
  policy in Cochin China, 113–117
  relations with United States, 76, 83
  strategy, 69–72, 75, 77–78, 84–89,
    102–103, 129–136, 141, 143–152,
    157–162, 166–167
Vietnam-Khmer-Laotian Federation,
    143
"Vietnam syndrome," 4, 330–331
Vietnamese Communist Party (VCP)
    (Viet Nam Cong San Dang), 32
Vietnamese Democratic Party (Dan Chu
    Dang), 104, 124, 133
  in South Vietnam, 197
Vietnamese Liberation League (Viet
    Nam Giai Phong Dong Minh Hoi),
    67, 77
Vietnamese National Liberation Front
    (Mat Tran Quoc Gia Giai Phong
    Viet Nam), 176
Vietnamese Nationalist Party (VNQDD)
    (Viet Nam Quoc Dan Dang), 12, 14,
    24, 39, 42, 48, 51–52, 54–55, 111,
    117, 119, 323–324
  activities in South China, 66, 77–79,
    81
  rivalry with ICP, 107, 111–113, 121
Vietnamese Revolutionary League (Viet
    Nam Cach Menh Dong Minh Hoi,
    or Dong Minh Hoi), 111
  activities of, 79, 81, 87
  founding of, 78
  rivalry with ICP, 107, 112–113
Vietnamese Revolutionary Youth
    League. *See* Revolutionary Youth
    League
Vietnamese Workers' Party (VWP)
    (Dong Lao Dong Viet Nam)
  Central Committee, 141, 143, 148,
    152–153, 163, 174–180, 187, 189,
    193, 195, 204, 213, 221, 227, 242
  Central Military Party Committee,
    157, 195, 300, 306, 309, 311

Department for the Transformation of Southern Agriculture, 335
factionalism in, 177–179, 194, 225–226, 244–245, 276–278, 302, 326–327, 340
founded, 141–143
name, 142
Politburo, 141, 157, 194, 221, 251, 265, 279, 304, 307–309, 313, 314
Reunification Department, 245
strategy in South Vietnam, 176–180, 182–183, 193–195, 204–206, 210–212, 223–225, 240–245, 248–254, 258–261, 263–266, 273–280, 288–292, 301–302, 307–308, 326–328
Second Party Congress (1951), 141–142, 149, 153
Sixth Plenum (1954), 163, 172
Ninth Plenum (1956), 176–177, 183
Tenth Plenum (1956), 178–179
Eleventh Plenum (1956), 178–180
Twelfth Plenum (1957), 180
Fifteenth Plenum (1959), 187–190, 204
Third National Congress (1960), 193–195, 197, 240
Third Plenum (1961), 195
Ninth Plenum (1963), 221–224, 264
Twelfth Plenum (1965), 242–245, 248, 251
Thirteenth Plenum (1966), 255, 263
Fourteenth Plenum (1967), 263
Nineteenth Plenum (1971), 288
Twentieth Plenum (1972), 292
Twenty-first Plenum (1973), 304, 306
Twenty-second Plenum (1974), 304
Fourth Party Congress (1976), 334, 340
Vinh, 9, 15, 34, 36–37, 40
Vinh Long, 64, 115
Vinh Yen Province, 95, 149
VNQDD. *See* Vietnamese Nationalist Party
Vo Chi Cong, 185
Vo Nguyen Giap, 66–67, 71–72, 77, 79–80, 84–85, 100–102, 110, 116–117, 120, 123–125, 133, 135, 139, 143–144, 147–148, 150–152, 161–162, 178, 194, 222, 223, 226–227, 245, 250, 258–259, 261–263, 279–280, 292
People's War, People's Army, 148, 227
Vo Van Mong, 176
"Voice of Nam Bo," 137
Vong La, 76
Vu Anh, 66–68
Vu Hong Khanh, 119–120
Vu Nhai, 74
Vung Tau, 316–317

Wai Island, 336
Walt, Lewis, 257
War Powers Act, 304
Westmoreland, William C., 229, 232, 236–239, 246–248, 257, 261, 266, 269–270
Whampoa Academy, 66
Women
in Communist strategy, 69, 75, 252–253
role in Vietnamese revolution, 192
Workers' Liberation Association of Vietnam (Hoi Lao Dong Giai Phong Viet Nam), 217

Xa Mat, 286
Xuan Loc, 315–316
Xuan Mai Training School, 190

Y Bih Aleo, 197
Yeh Chien-ying, 65, 163
Yen Bay revolt, 14, 42, 51, 348(n56)
Yenan, 64–67, 130
Yunnan Province, 65–66, 77–78, 81
Yunnan railway, 60, 65

Zhdanov, Andrei, 135
Zone C, 214, 246–247, 259
Zone D, 184, 196, 214, 237–238, 246, 259